THE MESSIANIC WRITINGS

TRANSLATED AND ANNOTATED BY

Daniel Gruber

ISBN 978-0-9669253-6-4

ELIJAH PUBLISHING
PO Box 776
Hanover, NH 03755
www.Elijahnet.net

Designed by Sandy Kent

TABLE *of* CONTENTS

ADDITIONAL NOTES

Introduction to
The Messianic Writings

These are Jewish writings about Hebrew Biblical concepts, employing corresponding ways of thinking and reasoning. They present themselves as completely dependent upon and flowing from Tanakh — the standard Hebrew acronym for the Law (*Torah*), the Prophets (*Nevi'im*), and the Writings (*Ketuvim*). Tanakh was the authorized, accepted revelation from the God of Israel. All subsequent revelations were to be judged by it.

In Tanakh, God laid out His purposes for humanity, for Israel, and for "Messiah". The Messianic Writings present Yeshua as the prophesied Messiah of Israel, the way those being trained by him (i.e. his disciples) should live, and how this age will end. This translation is an attempt to give a faithful rendering of these first century Jewish-Greek writings in their own context.

These texts — like the Septuagint, the writings of Josephus, Philo, and others — are written in a kind of Greek that had its own peculiarities. As Jewish-Greek writings, they were written in a way that reflected concepts and definitions which could only be found, in their wholeness, in the Hebrew Biblical world. Without reference to that world, both the concepts and the definitions remain obscure. The concepts and definitions remained Hebrew even though the translated appearance of the language was Greek.

Isidore of Pelasium commented in the 5th century that, "The Greeks... despise the divine Scripture as barbarous language, and composed of foreign-sounding words, abandoning necessary conjunctions, and confusing the mind with the addition of extraordinary words." (4Epistle 4. 28, in Migne, Patrologia Graeca, cited in Semitic Interference in Marcan Syntax, Elliott C. Maloney, Scholars Press, Chico, CA, 1981, P. 5) That was because the Scriptures use Greek words in ways that the Greeks did not, and also use words which the Greeks did not know.

> These texts are written in a kind of Greek that had its own peculiarities. As Jewish-Greek writings, they were written in a way that reflected concepts and definitions which could only be found, in their wholeness, in the Hebrew Biblical world

Consequently, the Septuagint Greek translation of Tanakh, begun in about 250 B.C.E. is an indispensable bridge for understanding the ways in which words are used in the Messianic Writings. These were the Greek Scriptures referred to more often than any others by the authors of the Messianic Writings. The authors of the classic Bauer/Arndt-Gingrich Greek-English Lexicon of the New Testament and Other Early Christian Literature [sic] noted that, "As for the influence of the Septuagint, every page of this lexicon shows that it outweighs all other influences in our literature." (Second Edition, 1979, P. xxi)

Though the Septuagint — signified by "LXX" — often diverges from the Hebrew text, and sometimes quite significantly, it still generally enables us to locate the way in which original

Hebrew concepts and definitions were put into a particular Greek form. (See the ADDITIONAL NOTE on "The Septuagint".) It is that same peculiar Greek — which is neither "classical" nor "common" — that appears in the Messianic Writings. Because of this, the Septuagint Greek text of Tanakh can be used to indicate how a particular word, phrase, or text should be translated.

These Messianic Writings are universally, erroneously called "The New Testament". This is an error of immense magnitude, leading to serious theological distortions, some of which have had disastrous historical consequences. There is no "testament" spoken of in these texts. There are references to the "old covenant," i.e. the one God made with Israel at Sinai, and the "new covenant," i.e. the one God promised to Israel in Jer. 31:31-34, and confirmed in Yeshua. These, however, are covenants, not testaments or books of the Bible.

"Christianity" and the "Church" have been built upon "Christian" interpretations of "Christian" translations of these Jewish documents. Though often a great amount of good scholarship has gone into those translations, they are marred by traditional, theological renderings which cannot be supported from the text. They create the image of a world, a religious world, that is not presented in the text. Additionally, they foster the illusion that God's purpose for humanity has departed from Israel and from the earth itself. The Messianic Writings do not mention Christianity, Christians, or the Church.

The Jewish translators of the Septuagint used *christos* to represent *mashiakh*, i.e. the Anointed One. For Greeks, the word only meant rubbed or smeared with oil or ointment; it did not refer to a person. The Greeks had no concept of God's Anointed One, the Messiah, and so the LXX translators used *christos* as a linguistic marker to point to *mashiakh*. Christian translations speak of "Christ" only because the translators choose not to translate *christos*.

Notes on Translation

MANUSCRIPTS: We do not have any of the original manuscripts. We have numerous copies of copies. Some of these copies show "family" resemblances to one another. Within the different manuscript families, however, there are still numerous differences in text. Among all these manuscript copies, there are thousands of different readings — sometimes a single letter, sometimes a word, sometimes much more.

The Scriptures present themselves as being inspired by God and, therefore, without error. They do not make any such claim for the people who made copies or for those who combined and compiled a full Greek text from the fragments of various copies. Nor do they make any such claims for any translation, including this one. Every reader should know and understand that scribes, textual critics, linguists, and translators are all fallible human beings, and therefore subject to making mistakes. All claims for the infallibility of particular human efforts do a disservice to both man and God.

Modern translations do not follow the order of the books that is found in the Greek manuscripts. They follow instead the order that appears in the Latin Vulgate translation, a translation which was begun by Jerome in the fifth century. I have chosen to follow the order that appears in the Greek manuscripts, an order which was essentially followed in the Peshitta Aramaic. The Peshitta differs in placing Hebrews right before Hazon/Revelation, and in not including some of the shorter letters. Some non-English translations follow this manuscript order. Russian translations, for example, use the order presented in this translation, except they follow the Peshitta in the placement of Hebrews.

Here is the order used in these Messianic Writings:

- Matthias, Mark, Luke, Yoḥanan, and Acts/*Ma'asei haShliḥim*
- Jacob, First and Second Kefa, First, Second, and Third Yoḥanan, and Judah
- Romans, First and Second Corinthians, Galatians, Ephesians, Philippians, Colossians, First and Second Thessalonikans, Hebrews, First and Second Timothy, Titus, and Philemon
- Hazon/Revelation

Starting from the public domain American Standard Version, a fairly literal translation, I worked through both major compilations of the Greek text, the Textus Receptus and the UBS. I considered the evidence and reasonings for the differences between the two. In all choices, my desire was to be faithful to the Jewish-Greek expression of Hebrew Biblical concepts.

APPROACH: There are two basic approaches to translation. One is to bring the text into the world of the reader. The other is to bring the reader into the world of the text. To some extent, both are necessary and neither is possible. Any translation is an approximation of meaning. My emphasis has been to try to bring the reader to the world of the text, believing that the meaning of the text is most accurately found in the world in which it was given; but recognizing that it is impossible for us to truly enter into that world. We are far removed from the time, culture, and mindset in which the texts were written. We do not think as the people of those times thought; nor do we know as they knew.

Additionally, Greek and Hebrew grammar do not correspond exactly to each other; nor does either correspond exactly to English grammar. Consequently, the exact literal sense of a particular text can be both awkward and difficult to understand in English. Sometimes a word-for-word literal translation does not communicate what the text actually says. Words have a range of meaning, and there may not be one word in the target language that includes all the range of the word to be translated. Often the word order itself carries a meaning or emphasis that cannot be translated.

Given a divinely inspired original, the translator wants to translate each word, even if every word does not convey meaning in the secondary language. For example, *hineh* in Hebrew and *idou* in Greek call out to the reader or audience to pay close attention to what follows. But "behold" does not always do that in English. It is too old a word. Most often I have used "look," "listen," or something similar to try to convey a sense of expectation. Occasionally I have used "behold," and occasionally I have omitted the word altogether, or placed an exclamation mark at the end of the sentence.

Another difficulty is that a long sentence or thought in the text may extend over four, five, or more verses — let's say from verse 8 to verse 12. But the most understandable translation of the text into English may not follow the verse numbers or divisions, which are not part of the text itself. The most faithful and true translation into English may put verse 10 after verse 8, and verse 9 between verses 11 and 12. I have kept the traditional verse numbering, but have occasionally presented the words in a different order.

> My emphasis has been to try to bring the reader to the world of the text, believing that the meaning of the text is most accurately found in the world in which it was given; but recognizing that it is impossible for us to truly enter into that world.

ADDITIONAL CHOICES: Because of the violent, tragic events and teachings of many centuries, some English words that have been traditionally used in translating these Scriptures now actually

obscure the meaning of the original text. I have not used these traditional words. Instead, I have tried to use more faithful English terms or, occasionally, equivalent Hebrew transliterations. The Hebrew terms are not numerous, and should present no more than initial difficulty for those unfamiliar with them.

The text says that Yeshua was put to death on a *stauros*, *tzelav* in Hebrew. The classical Greek lexicon of Liddell & Scott says that *stauros* meant "upright pale or stake... [also used of] piles driven in to serve as a foundation". Josephus, in referring to Esther 7:9, uses *stauros* for the Hebrew *etz*. (Antiquities of the Jews, 11:267) The Hebrew of Esther 7:9 has, "'See the *etz* [i.e., tree/stake/gallows] which Haman prepared for Mordechai...' Then the king said, "Hang him on it!" The LXX has, "'See the *xulon*/tree/stake which Haman prepared for Mordechai...' Then the king said, "Hang him on it/ *staurotheto!*" (Mid. Esther 3.15 says *nitzalav Haman*, i.e. they hung him on a stake.) In translating *stauros*, I have used "stake," "deathstake," and "tree of death." depending upon whether the context emphasizes the physical or the metaphorical aspect.

I have tended to use the Hebrew form of names rather than the English transliteration of their Greek transliterations, but in some cases I have retained the traditional English transliteration of familiar names in Tanakh: Yosef rather than Joseph, but Abraham, Isaac, and Jacob. Otherwise, names and place names are (usually) transliterated from the Hebrew originals and not from the Greek transliterations. This introduces a measure of subjective "feel," rather than the automatic application of a strict rule, but "feel" is an indispensable part of literary translation. I have usually rendered the guttural "h" sound as "h", rather than as "ch", e.g. "Beit Lehem," but occasionally I have used "kh" where it seemed to be helpful, e.g. Pesakh.

Other commonly used transliterations of Greek words have been replaced by translation. Transliteration creates a new word without meaning, unless the meaning is already known. I have avoided it as much as possible.

We do not know exactly how to translate the tetragrammaton, the four letter Hebrew Name of the God of the Bible. It is often rendered in English as "LORD," following the choice of the LXX translators to use *kurios*. [The current Hebrew substitution of *Adonai* expresses the same.] However, the thousands of times that the Name appears in the Scriptures indicate that it is related to God's eternal nature and His covenant relationship with Israel. It is clear that people pronounced this Name of God from the earliest times, as, for example, Havah did in Gen. 4:1.

However, a transliteration of the Name, even if it were correct, would not carry the meaning of the Name. Most translations say that God told Moses, "I am who I am." (Ex. 3:14) It would be just as correct to translate it as, "I will be who I will be." The LXX has "I am THE BEING." This meaning, not the sound, is what is important in the tetragrammaton. God does not change, all existence depends upon Him, and Israel's security is found in Him. (cf. Mal. 3:6)

Calvin and other French translators used "l'Eternel" (the Eternal) to give the sense of God's presence in all of time. The Rabbis sometimes used *haMakom*, i.e. "the place," to give the sense of God's presence in every place. (e.g. Tal. Abot 5.4) In an attempt to give a sense of these different aspects of the Name, I have used "the Everpresent Lord" in the appropriate places where it appears. He is "the ever-living God" (e.g. 1Sam. 17:26, Ps. 42:3H, Jer. 10:10, Dan.6:21H, Mt. 16:16), who is everywhere. (cf. Ps. 139:7-12)

The Hebrew *goyim*, Greek *ethnoi*, is somewhat problematic. Because the Gentiles/nations/people-

groups existed before Israel did, it would be anachronistic and distorted to call them "non-Jews". They are the peoples who came into existence through God's division at the Tower of Babel. Their existence and identity was not, and is not, dependent upon Israel, though the fulfillment of their identity and purpose is. Israel was created out of the nations to be a special nation and a community of nations. (e.g. Gen. 28:3, 48:4) *Goyim* expresses both the commonality of and difference between the nations/Gentiles and the holy nation/Israel. It also sometimes expresses the sense of the different groups and sometimes the multitude of individuals within those groups. Since we do not have one English word that does the same, I have used "nations" in some places and "Gentiles" in others.

In modern English, "you" and "your" can be either singular or plural. Hebrew, Greek, and many other languages distinguish between the singular and plural pronoun. Sometimes the correct understanding of a verse depends upon this distinction. In the text, I have added a plus sign (+) to signify the plural — "you+" and "your+".

Where quotations from Tanakh appear in the Messianic Writings, or where particular passages from Tanakh are relevant, they are cited in [brackets] following the phrase or sentence. In these citations, I have used the standard English abbreviations. In the common Jewish usage of the times, such quotations were given either to indicate the fulfillment of a specific prophecy, or to apply it in a particular way. Occasionally, references from the Apocrypha or other contemporary Jewish writings are also cited. Though these writings are not part of the Biblical text, they were well-known in the first century, and were sometimes used by the Biblical writers for illustration or example. Since verse numbering sometimes varies from language to language, in the citations, "1:1H" refers to the Hebrew text, "1:1E" to the English, "1:1LXX" to the Septuagint.

I have included some notes in which, in addition to explanatory comments, I have tried to give some relevant material from the Talmud, Midrash, and traditional liturgy, as well as from the Dead Sea Scrolls (DSS) of Qumran, and other sources. These are by no means either comprehensive or systematic. Nor do they indicate approval or disapproval, but rather an attempt to help illustrate the context. It should not, however, be assumed that the Rabbinic material is contemporary with the Messianic Writings. Usually it is later. Nor should it be assumed that the material presents the only rabbinic view. "Tal." indicates a Talmudic tractate, "Mid." the Midrash Rabbah.

Following the text of the Messianic Writings, there are some longer, explanatory notes, usually on selected problematic issues.

Despite the current grammatical rule that all punctuation added to a quotation belongs within the quotation marks, I have not followed the rule with hard punctuation — question marks, exclamation marks, and periods — that changes the sense of the original.

I have greatly profited from: 1) other translations, especially Robert Young's *A Literal Translation*, André Chouraqui's *La Bible*, and David Stern's *Jewish New Testament and Commentary*; 2) the Soncino Publishers translation of the *Talmud* and *Midrash Rabbah*, Jacob Neusner's translation of the *Tosefta*, and William Braude's *Midrash on Psalms* — though in all these cases, I have given my own slightly more literal renderings; 3) the proof-reading and critical comments of Jeff Green and David Stern; 4) the design and layout work of Sandy Kent and Rachel Wolf; and 5) the invaluable support of my family. All mistakes belong solely to me.

The Report of Matthias

[1] ¹The record of the lineage of Yeshua the Messiah, the Son of David, the son of Abraham. ²Abraham fathered Isaac. Isaac fathered Jacob. Jacob fathered Judah and his brothers. ³Judah fathered Peretz and Zerah by Tamar. Peretz fathered Hetzron. Hetzron fathered Rahm.

⁴Rahm fathered Amminadav. Amminadav fathered Nahshon. Nahshon fathered Salmon. ⁵Salmon fathered Boaz by Rahav. Boaz fathered Oved by Ruth. Oved fathered Yishai. ⁶Yishai fathered David the king. David fathered Solomon by the wife of Uriyah. ⁷Solomon fathered Rehav'am.

Rehav'am fathered Aviyah. Aviyah fathered Asa. ⁸Asa fathered Yehoshafat. Yehoshafat fathered Yoram. Yoram fathered Uzziyahu. ⁹Uzziyahu fathered Yotam. Yotam fathered Ahaz. Ahaz fathered Hizkiyahu. ¹⁰Hizkiyahu fathered Menasheh. Menasheh fathered Amon. Amon fathered Yoshiyahu. ¹¹Yoshiyahu fathered Yehonyahu and his brothers, at the time of the exile to Babel. [1Chr. 1-3]

Matthias, a short form of Mattathias, bears the same name as the faithful Jewish priest who sparked the Maccabean revolt. (1Mac. 2:1ff) The name appears in the Hebrew of Tanakh as Mattityahu. (1Ch. 9:31, 15:21) Early sources tell us that Matthias wrote his report in Hebrew. We have Greek translations of what he wrote, but no Hebrew copies. To demonstrate that Yeshua is the Messiah, Matthias often points out the fulfillment of Messianic references from Tanakh, or makes particular application of familiar scriptures.

1:1 "The record of the lineage/origin" The Greek phrase appears in LXX in Gen. 2:4, referring to the creation of heaven and earth, and in Gen. 5:1, referring to Adam and his descendants.

"the Son of David" is an explicit designation of the Messiah in the Scriptures (e.g. 2Sam. 7:12-16; Is. 9:6-7) and in the rabbinic writings (e.g. Tal. Sanhedrin 97a). Matthias begins with a genealogy because to understand who Yeshua is and what he comes to do, it is first necessary to know that he is "the son of Abraham," the Father of the Jewish people, and "the son of David," the King of Israel.

"the Messiah" In commenting on Lev. 26:11, Rashi says, "They used to anoint/moshkhin a leather shield with cooked fat to cause the blow of an arrow or spear to slip off from it and not pierce the leather." (cf. 2Sam. 1:21, Is. 21:5) The Greek word christos, used to translate the Hebrew mashiakh, meant rubbed with an oil, but it did not contain any of the Biblical meaning of being set apart by God for a specific function; christos referred to the physical action only.

1:2 The Biblical genealogies of Israel are patrilineal, tracing the male line. Rashi notes concerning "by their fathers' houses" in Num. 26:2 that, "They are to trace according to the tribe of the father and not after the mother." He cites Tal. Baba Bathra 109, which refers to the precedence of a son in inheritance. "The only ones who are called family are those from the side of the father." (Rashi on Num. 27:11)

1:3 Because of the variant spelling of the Hebrew toldot, i.e. "generations" or "origin," certain rabbis said that what Adam lost through his sin will be restored through Messiah, "the son of Peretz". (Mid. Genesis 12.6, cf. Ruth 4:12)

1:3,5,6,16 Though Biblical genealogies are generally patrilineal Matthias includes several women in this genealogy,: Tamar (v. 3), Rahav (v. 5), Ruth (v. 5), "the wife of Uriyah" (v. 6), and Miriam (v. 16).

[12]After the exile to Babel, Ye<u>h</u>onyahu fathered Shealtiel. Shealtiel fathered Zerubbabel. [13]Zerubbabel fathered Avi<u>h</u>ud. Avi<u>h</u>ud fathered Elyakim. Elyakim fathered Azur. [14]Azur fathered Tzadok. Tzadok fathered Ya<u>h</u>in. Ya<u>h</u>in fathered Eliud. [15]Eliud fathered Eleazar. Eleazar fathered Mattan. Mattan fathered Jacob. [16]Jacob fathered Yosef, the husband of Miryam, from whom was born Yeshua, who is called Messiah.

[17]So all the generations from Abraham to David are fourteen generations; from David to the exile to Babel fourteen generations; and from the carrying away to Babel to the Messiah, fourteen generations.

[18]Now the birth of Yeshua, the Messiah, was like this. After his mother, Miryam, was engaged to Yosef, before they became one [Gen. 2:24], she was found to be pregnant from the Ruakh Kodesh. [19]Yosef, her husband, being a righteous man and not wanting to publicly disgrace her, intended to divorce her secretly. [20]But as he thought about these things, an angel of the Everpresent Lord appeared to him in a dream and said, "Yosef, son of David, do not be afraid to take Miryam, your wife, because what is conceived in her from the Spirit is holy. [21]She will bring forth a son. You are to name him Yeshua, for it is he who will save his people from their sins."

[22]Now all this happened that what was spoken by the Everpresent Lord through the prophet might be accomplished: [23]"Behold, the virgin will be pregnant, and will bring forth a son. They will call his name Emmanuel," [Is. 7:14] which when translated is "God with us."

[24]Having been awakened from his sleep, Yosef did as the angel of the Everpresent Lord commanded him, and received his wife. [25]And he did not know her sexually until she had brought forth her son, the firstborn. And he named him Yeshua.

1:16 The genealogy concludes with "Jacob fathered Yosef, the husband of Miryam, from whom was born Yeshua, who is called Messiah." The text presents the genealogy of Yosef, but does not present Yosef as the father of Yeshua. He is presented as the husband of Miryam, the mother of Yeshua. Verses 18 & 20 record that Yeshua was conceived from the Ruakh Kodesh. Yosef is his "adoptive" father.

1:18 The Hebrew word *ruakh*, as well as the Greek *pneuma*, is translated into English as "spirit," "wind," and "breath". The context is usually sufficient for determining which English word is most appropriate. Sometimes I have retained it untranslated.

1:21 The angel tells Yosef to call the child "Yeshua," meaning "savior," because he "will save his people from their sins" — a necessary task. Yeshua bin Nun, i.e. "Joshua," led Israel into their inheritance. Yeshua, the Kohen Gadol in the time of Zekhariah, symbolizes Messiah, "the Branch," and the removal of Israel's sin and iniquity. [Zekh. 3] Messiah is to build the Temple of the Everpresent, and rule as a priest upon His throne. [Zekh. 6]

1:23 See "The Virgin will be Pregnant," in the ADDITIONAL NOTES. No one ever "calls" Yeshua by the name of Emmanuel. It is not a name in the sense of a sound that labels a particular person, it is a "name" in the sense of who he is, what he is to be known for, i.e. "God with us". (In Hebrew, "is" is understood, i.e., "God is with us.")

1:25 "the firstborn" appears in the Textus Receptus, but not in the UBS.

MATTHIAS 2

2 [1] Now when Yeshua was born in Beit Le<u>h</u>em of Judea in the days of Herod the king, magi from the east came to Yerushala'im, saying, [2] "Where is the one who has been born King of the Jews? For we saw his star in the east, and have come to bow down to him."

[3] When Herod the king heard it, he was troubled, and all Yerushala'im with him. [4] Gathering together all the chief Kohanim and Torah scholars of the people, he asked them where the Messiah would be born. [5] They said to him, "In Beit Le<u>h</u>em of Judea, for that is what is written by the prophet, [6] 'You Beit Le<u>h</u>em, land of Judea, are in no way least among the rulers of Judea. For out of you will come forth a ruler, who will shepherd My people, Israel.'" [Mic. 5:1H; 2Sam. 5:2; Ps. 78:70-71]

[7] Then Herod secretly called the magi, and learned from them exactly what time the star appeared. [8] He sent them to Beit Le<u>h</u>em, and said, "Go and search diligently for the young child. When you[+] have found him, bring me word, so that I also may come and bow down to him."

[9] Having listened to the king, they went their way. And the star which they had seen in the east went before them, until it came and stood over where the young child was! [10] When they saw the star, they were filled with great joy. [11] They came into the house, saw the young child with Miryam his mother, and they fell down and bowed down before him. Opening their treasures, they presented presents to him: gold, frankincense, and myrrh. [1Kgs. 4:21; Sir. 24:15] [12] Being warned in a dream that they should not return to Herod, they went back to their own country another way.

[13] Now when they had departed, an angel of the Everpresent Lord appeared to Yosef in a dream! He said, "Arise and take the young child and his mother, and flee into Egypt. And stay there until I tell you, because Herod will seek the young child to destroy him."

[14] So he arose at night and took the young child and his mother, and departed into Egypt. [15] He was there until the death of Herod, so that there might be fullness to what was spoken by the Everpresent Lord through the prophet, "Out of Egypt I called My son." [Hos. 11:1]

[16] Then when Herod saw that he was deceived by the magi, he was furious. He then sent out and slaughtered all the male children who were in Beit Le<u>h</u>em and in all the surrounding countryside, from two years old and under, according to the exact time which he had learned from the magi. [17] Then what was spoken by Jeremiah the prophet was given fullness, [18] "A voice was heard in Ramah, lamentation, weeping, and great mourning — Rachel weeping for her children. She would not be comforted, because they are no more." [Jer. 31:15]

[19] But when Herod was dead, an angel of the Everpresent Lord appeared in a dream to Yosef in Egypt! He said, [20] "Arise and take the young child and his mother, and go into the land of Israel, for those who sought the young child's life are dead." [Ex. 4:19]

[21] He arose and took the young child and his mother, and came into the land of Israel. [22] But when

2:2-4,16 Bowing down to a king is a recognition of his sovereignty. Herod, and everyone else, understood that. Because the magi were looking for the one who was "born" King of the Jews — as distinct from one who was appointed — Herod knew that they were speaking of Messiah. That is why he asked the chief priests and Torah scholars where the Messiah was to be born. Herod had been appointed King of Judea by Rome. In killing the boy babies of Beit Le<u>h</u>em, he was seeking to protect his position. [*Kohen* means "priest," *kohanim* is the plural.]

2:19 In <u>Antiquities</u> 17:168ff, Josephus describes the death of Herod.

>>

he heard that Archelaus was reigning over Judea in the place of his father Herod, he was afraid to go there. Being warned in a dream, he withdrew into the region of the Galil, [23]and came and lived in a city called Natzrat. In that way, there was fullness to what was spoken through the prophets: "He will be called a *netzer*." [Is. 11:1, 60:21; Jer. 23:5, 33:15; Zech. 3:8, 6:12]

3 [1]In those days, Yoḥanan the Immerser came into the wilderness of Judea and proclaimed, [2]"Change your[+] ways, because Heaven's kingdom has come near." (Dan. 2:44) [3]For this is the one who was spoken of by Isaiah the prophet: "The voice of one crying in the wilderness, 'Make ready the way of the Everpresent Lord. Make His paths straight.'" [Is. 40:3]

[4]Now Yoḥanan himself wore clothing made of camel's hair, with a leather belt around his waist. His food was locusts and wild honey. [5]Then people from Yerushala'im, all of Judea, and all the region around the Yarden went out to him. [6]Confessing their sins, they were immersed by him in the Yarden. [7]But when he saw many of the Perushim and Tzadukim coming to be immersed by him, he said to them, "Offspring of vipers, who warned you[+] to flee from the wrath to come? [8]Therefore bring forth

---

Commenting on Jer. 23:7-8 Tos. Berakhot 1:12 says, "And surely we remember the going out from Egypt in the days of the Messiah.... It is not that the going out from Egypt will be removed from its place, but rather to say that the going out from Egypt will be additional to the the reign of the King, but the reign of the King will be the principal thing, and the going out from Egypt secondary."

2:23 "Natzrat... Netzer." From the Greek text that we have, it is not possible to know with certainty the linguistic connection which was made in Matthias's original Hebrew text. The most likely reference seems to be to Is. 11:1b, "A *netzer* [branch, offshoot] from his roots will bear fruit." In that case, Matthias's prophetic application would be similar to that in Jer. 1:11-12, where God shows Jeremiah an almond/*sha'ked* to signify that "I will watch/*sho'ked* over My word to do it." It would be connected in meaning to passages like Zech. 3:8, where God speaks of Messiah as "My Servant the Branch [*tzemakh*]".

The likelihood of this being Matthias's original is supported by a related usage in Tal. Sanhedrin 43a: "Our Rabbis taught: Yeshu the Notzri had five disciples, Matthai, Nakai, Netzer... When Netzer was brought in [before the Sanhedrin], he said; 'Will Netzer be killed? Is it not written, *And a Netzer from his roots will bear fruit.*' 'Not so,' they said, 'Netzer will be killed, because it is written, *But you are cast out of your grave like an abhorred Netzer*' [Is. 14:19]..."

3:2 "The Kingdom of God" and "the Kingdom of Heaven" were synonymous terms used to indicate the time when God would dwell upon, and rule over the earth. (See the discussion following Tal. Berachot II. 1) The ancient Rabbis understood that, "the goal of Creation is that the Kingdom of God... shall be established on earth, as it is in heaven." (Tal. Pesakhim 54a, Soncino n. 31)

Mid. Song of Songs Rabba 2:33: "The time of the song is come: the time has come for Israel to be delivered; the time has come for uncircumcision to be cut off; the time has come for the kingdom of the Cutheans to end; the time has come for the kingdom of heaven to be revealed, as it says, 'And the Everpresent Lord will be king over all the earth' (Zech. 14:9). And the voice of the turtledove is heard in our land.' [Song of Songs 2:12] Who is this? This is the voice of the Messiah proclaiming, 'How beautiful upon the mountains are the feet of the messenger of good news' (Is. 53:7)."

3:4 There is a discussion in Tal. Menachot 39b about what kind of garments require tzitzit. A teacher from the school of R. Ishmael exempted garments made of camel's hair, goat's hair, etc.

fruit worthy of repentance. [9]Do not think to say to yourselves, 'We have Abraham for our father,' for I tell you[+] that God is able to raise up children to Abraham from these stones.

[10]"Even now the axe lies at the root of the trees. So every tree that does not bring forth good fruit is cut down, and cast into the fire. [11]I indeed immerse you[+] in water unto repentance, but the one who comes after me is mightier than I, whose sandals I am not worthy to carry. He will immerse you[+] in the Ruakh Kodesh. [12]His winnowing fork is in his hand, and he will thoroughly cleanse his threshing floor. He will gather his wheat into the barn, but he will burn up the chaff with unquenchable fire."

[13]Then Yeshua came from the Galil to the Yarden to Yohanan to be immersed by him. [14]But Yohanan sought to dissuade him, saying, "I need to be immersed by you, and yet you come to me?"

[15]But Yeshua responded and said to him, "Permit it now, for this is the appropriate way for us to confirm all righteousness." Then he let him.

[16]When Yeshua was immersed, as soon as he came up from the water, the heavens were opened to him! He saw the Spirit of God descending as a dove, and coming upon him. [17]A voice out of the heavens said, "This is my beloved Son, in whom I delight." [Is. 42:1]

3:11 "R. Joshua b. Levi said, 'All work which a slave does for his master a disciple does for his master, except that of taking off his shoe.'" (Tal. Ketubot 96a)

3:16 The text does not tell us why the Spirit descended "as a dove," but perhaps it is because the dove on the ark [Gen. 8:8-12 signalled the end of the judgment of the flood and a new beginning for humanity.

Ben Zoma said, "'It is said, *And the spirit of God hovered over the surface of the waters* — as a dove hovers over her children but does not touch [them].' Then R. Joshua said to his disciples, 'Ben Zoma is still outside [i.e. excommunicated].'" (Tal. Hagigah 15a) The Talmud says that Ben Zoma was one of only four men to enter the Garden of Eden. (Tal. Hagigah 14b) In some way he departed from rabbinically acceptable belief, perhaps by becoming a disciple of Yeshua.

But Mid. Gen. 2:4 says, "'And the Spirit of God hovered...' This is the spirit of Messiah the King." (cf. Mid. Gen. Alt. 97.1 and the reference to Messiah and the Spirit in Is. 11:2)

3:17 (cf. Mk. 1:11; Lk. 3:17) When Yeshua is immersed, the voice from heaven says (in the Greek text), "This is My Son/*huios*, whom I love; with him I am well pleased." This seems to be a reference to Is. 42:1: "Here is My Servant/*ebed*, whom I uphold, My chosen one in whom My soul delights; I will put My Spirit on him and he will bring justice to the nations." The Hebrew word *ebed* means "servant," and the Greek word *huios* means "son." The LXX, however, sometimes translates *ebed* into Greek as *pais*, which means either "servant" or "child". (e.g. Gen. 24:28; Prov. 29:1) As Israel's King, Messiah represents the people of Israel — God's "firstborn son," cf. Ex. 4:22. He represents them before God, even as Yeshua the High Priest does in Zech. 3.

"The Holy One, blessed be He, spoke to Moses saying, 'Even as I made Jacob a firstborn, for it says, *Israel is My son, My firstborn* [Ex. 4:22], so I will also make King Messiah My firstborn, as it is written, *I will make him My firstborn.*' [Ps. 89:28H]" (Mid. Ex. 19:7)

A voice from heaven, called a *bat kol*, appears often in apocalyptic and rabbinic literature. In the Talmud, a *bat kol* tells Solomon which woman is truly the mother of the child (Tal. Makkot 23b); a *bat kol* rebukes Nebuchadnezzar (Tal. Pesahim 93a); and a *bat kol* signals the shift in authority from Beth Shammai to Beth Hillel (Tal. Eruvin 13b). For more detail, see the chapter "It is not in Heaven" in my book, Rabbi Akiba's Messiah: The Origins of Rabbinic Authority.

4 [1]Then Yeshua was brought by the Spirit into the wilderness to be tempted by the Enemy. [2]He fasted forty days and forty nights. Afterwards he was hungry, [3]and the Tempter came and said to him, "If you are the Son of God, command that these stones become bread."

[4]But he answered, "It is written, 'A person is not to live by bread alone, but by every word that proceeds out of the mouth of God.'" [Dt. 8:3]

[5]Then the Enemy took him into the holy city. He set him on the pinnacle of the Temple, [6]and said to him, "If you are the Son of God, throw yourself down, for it is written, 'He will give His angels charge concerning you,' and 'on their hands they will bear you up, so that you do not strike your foot against a stone.'" [Ps. 91:11,12]

[7]Yeshua said to him, "Again, it is written, 'You are not to test the Everpresent Lord, your God.'" [Dt. 6:16]

[8]Again the Enemy took him to an exceedingly high mountain, and showed him all the kingdoms of the world and their glory. [9]He said to him, "I will give you all of these things, if you will fall down and bow down to me."

[10]Then Yeshua said to him, "Accuser, get back, because it is written, 'You are to bow down to the Everpresent Lord, your God and you will serve Him only.'" [Dt. 6:13]

[11]Then the Enemy left him, and angels came and ministered to him! [12]Now when Yeshua heard that Yoḥanan was arrested, he withdrew into the Galil. [13]Leaving Natzrat, he came and lived in Kfar Naḥum, which is by the lake in the region of Zevulun and Naftali. [14]In that way, what was spoken through Isaiah the prophet came to be fulfilled: [15]"The land of Zevulun and the land of Naftali, toward the lake, beyond the Yarden, Galil of the Gentiles — [16]the people who sat in darkness have seen a great light. To those who sat in the region and shadow of death, a light has dawned." [Is. 8:23-9:1H]

[17]From that time, Yeshua began to proclaim, "Change your[+] ways, because Heaven's kingdom has come near."

[18]Walking by the lake of the Galil, he saw two brothers, Shimon, who is called Kefa, and Andreas, his brother. They were casting a net into the lake, because they were fishermen. [19]He said to them, "Come after me, and I will make you[+] fishers of men." [Prov. 11:30, Dan. 12:3, Jer. 16:16] [20]They immediately left their nets and followed him.

[21]Going on from there, he saw two other brothers, Jacob the son of Zevadyah and Yoḥanan his brother, in the boat with Zevadyah their father. They were mending their nets. He called them. [22]They immediately left the boat and their father, and followed him. [1Ki. 19:19-21]

[23]Yeshua went around in all of the Galil, teaching in their meetingplaces, proclaiming the good

---

4:23 In these texts, the Greek *sunagoge* is often translated as "synagogue". I have not done that because it is not what the word meant at that time. It meant only a gathering or collection of something. It did not mean anything religious or something particularly Jewish. Plato used it to mean "a bringing together or uniting," or "forming an army in a column." Thucydides used the word in the sense of mustering an army for war. Polybius used *sunagoge* for "a gathering in of harvest." Aristotle used it for "a collection of writings." (An Intermediate Greek-English Lexicon, Liddell and Scott, Oxford Univ. Press, Clarendon, 1999, P. 766)

When *sunagoge* is translated as "synagogue," it significantly distorts the meaning of numerous verses. See the chapter "A Good Church is Hard to Find," in my Copernicus and the Jews.

news of the kingdom, and healing every disease and every sickness among the people. [24]The report about him went out into all Syria. They brought to him all who were sick, afflicted with various diseases and torments. And they brought to him those afflicted by demons, those not in their right minds, and those who were paralyzed. And he healed them. [25]Large crowds from the Galil, the Ten Towns, Yerushala'im, Judea and from beyond the Yarden followed him.

5 [1]Seeing the multitudes, he went up onto the mountain. When he had sat down, his disciples came to him. [2]He opened his mouth and taught them:

[3]"There is good for the poor in spirit [Ps. 1:1-3; Is. 11:4,61:1], because Heaven's kingdom is theirs.

[4]"There is good for those who mourn [Is. 61:3], because they will be comforted.

[5]"There is good for the humble, because they will inherit the land. [Ps. 37:9,11]

[6]"There is good for those who hunger and thirst after justice, because they will be filled. [Dt. 16:20]

[7]"There is good for the merciful, because they will obtain mercy.

[8]"There is good for the pure in heart, because they will see God. [Prov. 28:14]

[9]"There is good for the peacemakers, because they will be called children of God.

[10]"There is good for those who have been persecuted on account of justice, because Heaven's kingdom is theirs.

[11]"When people insult you[+], persecute you[+], and say all kinds of evil against you[+] falsely for my sake, there is good for you[+]. [12]Rejoice and be exceedingly glad, because your[+] reward in heaven is great, for that is how they persecuted the prophets who were before you[+].

[13]"You[+] are the salt of the earth, but if the salt has lost its flavor, with what will it be salted? It is then good for nothing except to be cast out and trampled under the feet of men. [14]You[+] are the light of the world. A city situated on a hill cannot be hidden. [15]Nor do they light a lamp, and put it under a

---

5:1-11 It is not easy to clearly define the concept represented by *ashrei/makarios* which begins each of these statements. It seems to carry the sense of well-being as a result of being in God's purpose and care. Some passages that may help are Ps. 1:1-3, 32:1-2, 40:4, 94:12-13, and Prov. 28:14.

5:3 To a people suffering under Roman domination, Yeshua proclaims the good news that there is a kingdom coming, God's kingdom. He later sends out his disciples as heralds and ambassadors, i.e. *shlihim*, of that kingdom.

5:8 "'For man will not see Me and live' (Ex. 33:20). In their lives they do not see, but they will see in the hour of their deaths; because it says, All who go down to the dust will kneel before Him, and cannot keep their soul alive' (Ps. 22:30)." (Mid. Numbers Rabbah 14:22)

5:9 "These are the things of which a man eats their fruits in this age while the strength remains for him in the age to come: honoring father and mother, the practice of lovingkindness, and to bring peace between a man and his friend; but the study of the Torah is equal to all of them." (Tal. Pe'ah I.1)

5:13 In Tal. Bechorot 8b, there is a fanciful story where the question is asked, "When salt becomes unsavory, with what can it be salted?" The final answer given is that salt cannot become unsavory. I.e., it is only a hypothetical question.

5:14 Tal. Baba Bathra 4a: Herod said: "'If I had known how enlightened the Rabbis were, I would not have killed them. Now show me, how I can repair this.' He [Baba b. Buta] said, 'As you caused the light of the world

>

basket, but on a stand; and it gives light to all who are in the house. ¹⁶In the same way, let your⁺ light shine before men, so that they may see your⁺ good deeds, and glorify your⁺ Father who is in heaven.

¹⁷"Do not think that I came to bring an end to the Torah or the prophets. I did not come to bring an end, but to bring fullness. ¹⁸For I assure you⁺ that until heaven and earth pass away, not even one of the smallest letters or one tiny stroke will ever pass away from the Torah, until all things have come. ¹⁹So whoever relaxes one of the least of these commandments and teaches others to do so will be called least in Heaven's kingdom. But whoever does and teaches them, this is the one who will be called great in Heaven's kingdom. ²⁰For I tell you⁺ that unless your⁺ righteousness exceeds that of the Torah scholars and Perushim, there is no way you⁺ will enter into Heaven's kingdom.

²¹"You⁺ have heard that it was said to the ancient ones, 'You⁺ are not to murder,' [Ex. 20:13, Dt. 5:17] and 'Whoever murders will be guilty in the judgment.' ²²But I tell you⁺ that everyone who is angry with his brother without a cause will be guilty in the judgment. And whoever calls his brother, 'Brainless!' will be in danger of the Council. And whoever says, 'Stupid fool!' will be in danger of the fire of Gehinnom.

to go — as it is written, *For the commandment is a candle and Torah is light* [Prov. 6:23] — go and do your business in the light of the world, as it is written, 'And all the nations stream to it.' [Is. 2:2]"

Mid. Gen. Rabbah 59:5: "Yerushala'im is the light of the world, as it says, 'And nations will walk to your light. [Is. 60:3]' And who is He who is the light of Yerushala'im? The Holy One, blessed be He, as it is written, 'But the Everpresent will be an everlasting light to you.' [Is. 60:19]"

5:17 "to bring fullness" This expression corresponds to Hebrew *lemalay* and Jewish-Greek *plêroô*. In several places in Tanakh, these verbs describe the coming into being of something that was promised, the confirmation of an earlier statement, or the bringing to fruition of something already begun. (E.g., 1Kgs.1:14, 2:27, 8:15, 8:24; 2Chr. 6:4, 6:15; Psa. 20:5-6H/19:5-6LXX/20:4-5E.) See "God's Law and the New Covenant" in the ADDITIONAL NOTES.

5:21-22 Rashi comments on Dt. 19:11, "But if any man hates his neighbor": "Through hating him he comes to 'lie in wait for him.' Hence (our Rabbis) said: 'If one transgresses a commandment of minor importance, eventually he will transgress a commandment of major importance. Because he transgressed against "You shall not hate," (Lev. 19:17), he will eventually come to shed blood." (The Pentateuch and Rashi's Commentary: Deuteronomy, Abraham ben Isaiah & Benjamin Sharfman, S.S.&R. Publishing Co. Inc., Brooklyn, 1950)

5:22 *Rayka* is the word I have translated as "Brainless!" In 2 Sam. 6:20, Michal despises David and compares him to one of the *raykim* (the plural of *rayka*) who uncover themselves in public. [cf. usage in the beginning of Tal. Taanit 20b] The commandment of Lev. 19:16 — "You are not to go as a tale-bearer among your people. Do not stand by the blood of your neighbor. I am the Everpresent." — is taken to be a prohibition against denigrating another.

"The one who calls his neighbour 'slave', let him be under the ban; 'mamzer,' ...he is beaten with forty [lashes]; 'wicked,' he may go after his life." (Tal. Kiddushin 28a)

"R. Joshua b. Levi said: Whoever relates stories about the disciples of the wise after their death falls into Gehinnom." (Tal. Berachot 19a)

[23]"Therefore if you are offering your gift at the altar, and remember there that your brother has something against you, [24]leave your gift there before the altar, and go your way. First be reconciled to your brother, and then come and offer your gift. [25]Agree with your opponent quickly, while you are with him in the way, so that the opponent does not deliver you to the judge, and the judge deliver you to the officer, and you be cast into prison. [26]I tell you faithfully that you will never get out of there until you have paid the last cent.

[27]"You[+] have heard that it was said, 'You are not to commit adultery.' [Ex. 20:14, Dt. 5:18] [28]But I tell you[+] that everyone who gazes at a woman to desire her has committed adultery with her already in his heart. [Pr. 6:25-26] [29]If your right eye causes you to stumble, pluck it out and throw it away from you. For it is more profitable for you that one of your members should be destroyed, than for your whole body to be thrown into Gehinnom. [30]If your right hand causes you to stumble, cut it off, and throw it away from you, because it is more profitable for you that one of your members should be destroyed, and your whole body not go away into Gehinnom.

[31]"It was also said, 'Whoever sends away his wife, let him give her divorce papers.' [Dt. 24:1] [32]But I tell you[+] that whoever sends away his wife, except on account of sexual immorality, causes her to commit adultery. And whoever marries her when she is put away commits adultery.

[33]"Again you[+] have heard that it was said to those of long ago, 'You shall not make false vows, but shall perform your vows to the Everpresent Lord.' [Lev. 19:12, Num. 30:2, Dt. 23:21-23/22-24H] [34]But I tell you[+]: do not swear at all, not by heaven, for it is the throne of God; [35]nor by the earth, for it is the footstool of His feet [Is. 66:1], nor by Yerushala'im, for it is the city of the great King. [Ps. 48:2] [36]Nor should you swear by your head, for you cannot make one hair white or black. [37]Rather let your[+] word be 'Yes, yes.' 'No, no.' Whatever is more than these is from what is evil. [Sirach 23:9-11]

[38]"You[+] have heard that it was said, 'An eye for an eye, and a tooth for a tooth.' [Ex. 21:24, Lev. 24:20, Deut 19:21] [39]But I tell you[+]: do not be the opponent of the evil person; instead, whoever strikes you

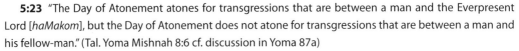

5:23 "The Day of Atonement atones for transgressions that are between a man and the Everpresent Lord [*haMakom*], but the Day of Atonement does not atone for transgressions that are between a man and his fellow-man." (Tal. Yoma Mishnah 8:6 cf. discussion in Yoma 87a)

5:27-30 "A man who counts money from his hand into the hand of a woman so as to gaze at her, even if there is Torah in his hand and good deeds as Moses our teacher, he will not be innocent of the sentence of Gehinnom." (Tal. Berachot 61a cf. Tal. Sotah 4b)

Tal. Niddah 13a-b speak of certain types of immorality as deserving having the hand cut off. That was not an actual punishment, it was just a way of expressing the importance of not committing such sin.

5:31-32 Among the Perushim, the school of Shammai maintained that only sexual infidelity constituted grounds for divorce. The school of Hillel said that any unpleasant characteristic provided sufficient grounds for divorce. See note to Mt. 19:3.

5:33-37 The Rabbis made provisions for annulling vows, but recognized that they were not scriptural. "The setting aside of vows flies in the air and there is nothing that supports it." (Tal. Hagigah 1.5 [10a])

"'It is better not to vow than to vow and not complete it.' [Eccl. 5:5] Better than both of these is that you not vow." (Tal. Nedarim 9a)

on your right cheek, turn to him the other also. [40]If anyone wants to bring you to judgment to take away your shirt, let him have your coat also. [41]Whoever compels you to go one mile, go with him two. [42]Give to the one who asks of you, and do not turn away the one who desires to borrow from you. [Dt. 23:20-21]

[43]"You[+] have heard that it was said, 'You are to love your neighbor [Lev. 19:18], and hate your enemy.' [44]But I tell you[+]: love your[+] enemies; bless those who curse you[+]. Do good to those who hate you[+], and pray for those who mistreat and persecute you[+]. [45]Then you[+] become children of your[+] Father who is in heaven. For He makes His sun to rise on the evil and the good, and sends rain on the just and the unjust. [46]For if you[+] love those who love you[+], what reward do you[+] have? Do not even the tax collectors do the same? [47]If you[+] only greet those close to you[+], what do you[+] do more than others? Do not even the Gentiles do the same? [48]Therefore be blameless even as your[+] Father in heaven is blameless. [Dt. 18:13]

5:38-42 There are three passages in Torah where the phrase appears. Ex. 21:22-24 prescribes "eye for eye, tooth for tooth..." for harm done to a pregnant woman. Lev. 24:19-20 prescribes the same for a person who disfigures another. Dt. 19:16-21 prescribes the same for the punishment that a false witness, seeking to use the law to injure the innocent, would have brought on the one falsely accused.

In the Scriptures, this is not a general legal principle or formula, but a standard to be applied for these specific cases which involve a callous disregard of someone else's humanity. It appears that during the time of Yeshua, as today, some people used the expression to justify a legal disregard of the humanity of the offender.

Yeshua does not address these specific legal specifications. Instead, he seems to be addressing an attitude of demanding an exact retribution for every offense committed against "me," an attitude which includes both an unwillingness to accept any less than is required and also an unwillingness to give any more than is required. He seems to be saying that, for the sake of the other, I should be willing to go beyond both the exact enumeration of my rights and also the exact limits of my obligations. From what Yeshua says next, he seems to be implying that I will do this if I am committed to obey the law to love my neighbor.

The purpose of "an eye for an eye, a tooth for a tooth" in the three passages in the Torah is to remind us of that our injured neighbor, in these cases innocent, is made in the image and likeness of God. The purpose of Yeshua's remarks is to remind us that our neighbor, even when not innocent, is also made in the image and likeness of God.

The normative rabbinic view is that, where the Torah prescribes "an eye for and eye," monetary compensation is to be given. "R. Shimon ben Yohai says, '*An eye for an eye* means money [*mammon*].' ...R. Zebid said in the name of Raba, 'Scripture says, *wound for wound*. This means to give compensation in the place of punishment.' ...R. Ashi said, 'It is written here *eye for eye* [Ex. 21:24], even as it is written there *he is to fully recompense ox for ox* [21:36].'" (Tal. Baba Kama 84a)

5:39-44 Some say that this is not traditional Jewish teaching, but there are corresponding incidents in Tanakh. It can be compared to David's response to Saul in 1Sam. 24:1-15 and 1Sam. 26:7-12. Or it can be compared to Elisha's treatment of the Syrian army in 2Kings 6:11-23.

5:44 "bless those who curse you[+]. Do good to those who hate you[+]," follows the Textus Receptus

5:47 "those close to you[+]," literally "your[+] brothers"

6 [1]"Be careful that you[+] do not do your[+] deeds of compassion before the children of Adam in order to be seen by them, or else you[+] have no reward from your[+] Father who is in heaven. [2]Therefore when you do deeds of compassion, do not sound a shofar before yourself as the pretenders do in the meetingplaces and in the streets, so that they may get glory from people. I assure you[+] they have received their reward. [3]But when you do deeds of compassion, do not let your left hand know what your right hand is doing, [4]so that your deeds of compassion may be in secret. Then your Father who sees in secret will reward you.

[5]"When you[+] pray, don't be like the pretenders, for they love to stand and pray in the meetingplaces and on the streetcorners, so that they may be seen by the children of Adam. I assure you[+] they have received their reward. [6]But you, when you pray, go into your room, shut your door, and pray to your Father who is in secret. And your Father who sees in secret will reward you.

[7]"But in praying, do not babble as the Gentiles do, for they think that they will be heard because of their many words. [8]Therefore do not be like them, for your[+] Father knows what things you[+] need before you[+] ask him.

[9]"Pray like this: 'Our Father in heaven, may Your Name be kept holy. [10]May Your kingdom come, Your will be done on earth as it is in heaven. [11]Give us today our daily bread. (Ex. 16:4-5) [12]Forgive us our debts, as we also forgive those indebted to us. [Sir. 28:2-5] [13]Do not bring us into temptation, but deliver us from what is evil. For the kingdom, the power, and the glory are Yours forever. Amen.' [1Chr. 29:11]

6:1-4 The Greek is *anthropoi*, i.e. "people". The Hebrew would be *bnay adam*, i.e. children of Adam".
Yeshua speaks about praying for the purpose of being seen by men.

"R. Yannai saw a man give a silver coin to a poor person publicly, so he said to him, 'It would have been better if you had not given to him than that you have given to him publicly." (Tal. Chagigah 5a)

6:7 "...Study is not the principle thing, but doing, and everyone who multiplies words brings sin." (Tal. Pirke Avot 1:17; cf. Prov. 10:19)

6:9-10 The third person imperative form, translated here as "may," functions as an affirmation of the goal. "R. Judah b. Tema said, 'Be strong as the leopard and swift as the eagle, fleet as the deer and courageous as a lion to do the will of your Father in heaven.'" (Tal. Pesachim 112a)

6:10 The Sephardic half-Kaddish and Kaddish al-Yisrael say: "...May His Kingdom reign, *and may He cause His redemption to sprout, and may He bring near His Messiah* — in your lifetime and in your days..." The Ashkenazic does not have the part in italics.

"Do His will as your own will, so that He will do your will as if it were His; let your will cease before His will, so that the will of others will cease before yours." (Tal. Pirke Avot 2:4)

6:11 R. Simeon ben Yohai said, "I will tell a parable to you. This thing is similar to a king of flesh and blood who had one son, and apportioned to him provisions once a year. And he did not receive his father but once a year. He considered and apportioned [to him] his provisions every day. And so he received his father every day. So it is with Israel." (Tal. Yoma 76a)

6:12 "Cause us to be forgiving even as we ask to be forgiven." Opening Prayer, Kol Nidre

6:13 In the morning blessings, we read: "Do not bring me into the power of sin, or the power of iniquity, or the power of temptation, or the power of contempt. And keep me far from the evil inclination... and from the destroying Adversary, ...and make me cling to the good inclination."

¹⁴"For if you⁺ forgive the children of Adam their transgressions, your⁺ heavenly Father will also forgive you⁺. ¹⁵But if you⁺ do not forgive the children of Adam their transgressions, neither will your⁺ Father forgive your⁺ transgressions.

¹⁶"Moreover, when you⁺ fast, do not be like the pretenders with despondent faces. For they distort their faces so that people see them to be fasting. I assure you⁺ they have received their reward. ¹⁷But you, when you fast, anoint your head and wash your face, ¹⁸so that you are not noticed to be fasting by people, but by your Father who is in secret. And your Father, who sees in secret, will reward you.

¹⁹"Do not lay up treasures for yourselves on the earth, where moth and rust consume, and where thieves break in and steal. ²⁰Instead, lay up treasures for yourselves in heaven, where neither moth nor rust will spoil them, and where thieves do not break in and steal. ²¹For where your treasure is, there your heart will be also.

²²"The lamp of the body is the eye. If therefore your eye is generous, your whole body will be full of light. ²³But if your eye is covetous, your whole body will be full of darkness. If therefore the light that is in you is darkness, how great is the darkness. [Gen. 1:2-3, Is. 60:1-3]

²⁴"No one can serve two masters, for either he will hate the one and love the other, or else he will be devoted to one and despise the other. You⁺ cannot serve both God and Mammon. ²⁵Therefore I tell you⁺, do not be anxious about your⁺ life — what you⁺ will eat, or what you⁺ will drink; nor for your⁺ body — what you⁺ will wear. Isn't life more than food, and the body more than clothing? ²⁶See and consider the birds of the heaven, that they do not sow, nor do they reap or gather into barns. Your⁺ heavenly Father feeds them. Aren't you⁺ of much more value than they?

²⁷"Which of you⁺, by being anxious, can add one cubit to the measure of his life? ²⁸Then why are you⁺ anxious about clothing? Consider the lilies of the field, how they grow. They do not toil, nor do they spin yarn. ²⁹Yet I tell you⁺ that not even Solomon in all his glory was dressed like one of these. ³⁰But if in this way God clothes the grass of the field, which exists today and is thrown into the fire tomorrow, won't He take more care to clothe you⁺, you⁺ of little faith?

³¹"So don't be anxious, saying, 'What will we eat?' 'What will we drink?' or, 'With what will we be clothed?' ³²For the Gentiles pursue all these things. Indeed, your⁺ heavenly Father knows that you⁺

6:22-23 Literally, "If your eye is healthy... if your eye is evil". This is a Hebrew idiom. (cf. Mt. 20:15)

"Any one who has common sense will remember that the bewilderments of the eyes are of two kinds, and arise from two causes, either from coming out of the light or from going into the light, which is true of the mind's eye, quite as much as of the bodily eye; and he who remembers this when he sees any one whose vision is perplexed and weak, will not be too ready to laugh; he will first ask whether that soul of man has come out of the brighter life, and is unable to see because unaccustomed to the dark, or having turned from darkness to the day is dazzled by excess of light. And he will count the one happy in his condition and state of being, and he will pity the other; or, if he have a mind to laugh at the soul which comes from below into the light, there will be more reason in this than in the laugh which greets him who returns from above out of the light into the den." ("Republic," BK. VII, The Dialogues of Plato, trans. B. Jowett, Vol. 3 Oxford, Clarendon, 1892, P. 218)

6:30 "Everone who has a piece of bread in his basket and says, 'What will I eat tomorrow?' these are only those who are small in faith." (Tal. Sotah 48b)

need all these things, [33]but first seek God's kingdom and His justice, and all these things will be given to you[+] as well. [Dt. 16:20; Mic. 6:8] [34]So don't be anxious about tomorrow, because tomorrow will be anxious for itself. Each day has enough trouble of its own. [Prov. 27:1]

7 [1]"Do not judge, so that you[+] are not judged. [2]For with whatever judgment you[+] judge, you[+] will be judged. And with whatever measure you[+] measure, it will be measured to you[+].

[3]"Why do you see the speck that is in your brother's eye, but do not consider the beam that is in your own eye? [4]Or how will you tell your brother, 'Let me remove the speck from your eye' — but look, the beam is in your own eye. [5]You pretender! First remove the beam out of your own eye, and then you will see clearly to remove the speck out of your brother's eye.

[6]"Do not give what is holy to the dogs, nor throw your[+] pearls before the pigs, or they might trample them under their feet, turn, and attack you[+].

[7]"Ask, and it will be given to you[+]. Seek, and you[+] will find. Knock, and it will be opened for you[+]. [8]For everyone who asks receives; the one who seeks finds; and to the one who knocks, it will be opened. [9]Or who is there among you[+] that, if his son asks him for bread, will give him a stone? [10]Or if he asks for a fish, who will give him a serpent? [11]So if you[+], being evil, know to give good gifts to your[+] children, how much more will your[+] Father who is in heaven give good things to those who ask Him. [12]Therefore whatever you[+] would want that men do to you[+], so you[+] also do to them; because this is the Torah and the prophets.

[13]"Enter in by the narrow gate, because the gate is wide and the way is broad that leads to destruction, and many are those who enter in by it. [14]How narrow is the gate, and harassed is the way that leads to life! Few are those who find it.

[15]"Beware of false prophets who come to you[+] in sheep's clothing, but inwardly are voracious wolves. [16]You[+] will know them by their fruits. Do men gather grapes from thorns, or figs from

---

6:34 In Tal. Sanhedrin 100b, there is a discussion of fruitless anxiety. In part, it says, "'Do not let anxiety enter your heart, because anxiety has surely detroyed many.' Solomon said so [Prov. 12:25], 'Anxiety in the heart of man makes it stoop....' Do not be anxious over tomorrow, because you do not know to what a day may give birth, and perhaps tomorrow he is no more. He will have found anxiety over a world that is not his."

7:3 "R. Tarfon said, 'I wonder if there is one in this generation who receives a rebuke. If one says to him: *Remove the speck from between your eyes*, he answers back to him: *Remove the beam from between your eyes!*'" (Tal. Arachin 16b, cf. Tal. Baba Bathra 15b) R. Tarfon, active after the Great Revolt, treats the response as a rejection of authority.

7:12 Some people prefer the negative "Silver" rule as expressed by Hillel: "What is hateful to you, do not do to your neighbor." (Tal. Shabbat 31a) It is found in Tobit 4:15 as "Do not do to anyone what you hate..." It is encompassed in Rom. 13:10: "Love does not work evil to a neighbor. Therefore love is the fulness of the Law." While the rule itself is good, it does not fulfill the positive command of Lev. 19:18: "You are to love your neighbor as yourself."

7:13-14 After Adam's sin, "Then were the entrances of this world made narrow, full of sorrow and travail: they are but few and evil, full of perils, and very painful." (2Esdr. 7:12)

7:14 A related phrase in Dt. 28:53 is "siege and affliction," *matzor/stenochoria* and *matzok/thlipsei*. The related phrase in Mt. 7:14 is *tzar/stene* and *mootzak/tethlimmene*.

thistles? ¹⁷Even so, every good tree produces beautiful fruit, but the rotten tree produces evil fruit. ¹⁸A good tree cannot produce evil fruit, nor can a rotten tree produce beautiful fruit. ¹⁹Every tree that does not produce beautiful fruit is cut down, and thrown into the fire. ²⁰Therefore you⁺ will know them by their fruits. ²¹Not everyone who says to me, 'Lord, Lord,' will enter into Heaven's kingdom, but the one who does the will of my Father who is in heaven. ²²Many will tell me in that day, 'Lord, Lord, didn't we prophesy in your name, cast out demons in your name, and do many mighty works in your name?' ²³Then I will tell them, 'I never knew you⁺. Depart from me, you⁺ who labor at what is contrary to the Law.' [Ps. 6:8; 13:4LXX; 52:5LXX; 91:7,9LXX; 93:4LXX]

²⁴"Therefore everyone who hears these words of mine and does them will be like a wise man who built his house on a rock. ²⁵The rain came down, the rivers came up, and the winds blew and beat on that house. Yet it did not fall, because it was founded on the rock. ²⁶Everyone who hears these words of mine and does not do them will be like a foolish man who built his house on the sand. ²⁷The rain came down, the rivers came up, and the winds blew and beat on that house. So it fell, and great was its fall."

²⁸When Yeshua had finished saying these things, the multitudes were astonished at his teaching, ²⁹because he taught them as one having authority, and not as the Torah scholars.

8 ¹When he came down from the mountain, a large crowd followed him. ²A leper came, bowed down to him, and said, "Lord, if you want to, you can make me clean."

³Yeshua stretched out his hand and touched him, saying, "I want to. Be made clean." Immediately his leprosy was cleansed. ⁴Yeshua said to him, "See that you tell no one, but go, show yourself to the Kohen, and offer the gift that Moses commanded, as a testimony to them." [Lev. 14]

⁵When he came into Kfar Nahum, a centurion came to implore him, ⁶"Lord, my servant is lying in the house paralyzed, extremely afflicted."

⁷Yeshua said to him, "I will come and heal him."

⁸The centurion answered, "Lord, I am not worthy for you to come under my roof. Just say the word, and my servant will be healed. ⁹For I also am a man under authority, having soldiers under me. I tell this one, 'Go,' and he goes. And I tell another, 'Come,' and he comes. And I tell my servant, 'Do this,' and he does it."

¹⁰When Yeshua heard it, he marveled and said to those who followed, "I assure you⁺, not even in Israel have I found so great a faith. ¹¹I tell you⁺ that many will come from the east and the west, and will sit down with Abraham, Isaac, and Jacob in Heaven's kingdom, ¹²but there will be children of the kingdom thrown out into the outer darkness. There will be weeping and gnashing of teeth."

¹³Yeshua said to the centurion, "Go your way. Let it be done for you as you have believed." His servant was healed in that hour.

The observation of Rebbe Nachman of Breslov, in the beginning of the 1800s, is interesting: "All the world is a very narrow bridge, and the principle thing is to not be afraid." [Kol ha'olam kulo gesher tzar meod, ve'ha'ikkar lo lefached.]

7:23 "you⁺ who labor at what is contrary to Torah" (ergazemenoi ten anomian) The original phrase in Hebrew, poalei aven, is often translated as "workers of iniquity," i.e. those who do what is contrary to God's Law.

[14]When Yeshua came into Kefa's house, he saw his mother-in-law lying sick with a fever. [15]He touched her hand, and the fever left her. She got up and served him. [16]When evening came, they brought to him many afflicted by demons. He cast out the spirits with a word, and healed all who were sick. [17]In this way, what was spoken through Isaiah the prophet was fulfilled: "He took our infirmities, and bore our diseases." [Is. 53:4] [18]Now when Yeshua saw a large crowd around him, he gave a command to depart to the other side.

[19]A Torah scholar came, and said to him, "Rabbi, I will follow you wherever you go."

[20]Yeshua said to him, "The foxes have holes, and the birds of the heaven have nests, but the Son of Adam has nowhere to lay his head."

[21]Another of his disciples said to him, "Lord, allow me first to go and bury my father."

[22]But Yeshua said to him, "Follow me, and leave the dead to bury their own dead." [Num. 6:5-8]

[23]When he got into a boat, his disciples followed him. [24]A big storm arose in the lake, so much that the boat was covered with the waves! Yet he was asleep. [25]They came to him and woke him up, saying, "Save us, Lord! We are lost!"

[26]He said to them, "Why are you+ fearful and of little faith?" Then he got up, rebuked the wind and the lake, and there was a great calm.

[27]The men were amazed, saying, "What kind of man is this, that even the wind and the lake obey him?"

[28]When he came to the other side into the country of the Gadarenes, two people afflicted by demons met him there. They would come out from the graveyard with great violence, so that nobody could pass by that way. [29]They cried out, "What do we have to do with you, Yeshua, Son of God? Have you come here to torment us before the time?" [30]Now there was a herd of many pigs feeding at a distance from them. [31]The demons begged him, "If you cast us out, let us go away into the herd of pigs."

8:15 "Rabbi [Judah the Prince] had suffered from a toothache for thirteen years. The prophet Elijah came to him in the form of R. Hiyya the Elder. He said to him, 'How are you, sir?' He answered him, 'A tooth bothers me.' The other said, 'Show me.' When he showed him, he put his finger on the tooth and it was cured." (Jer. Tal. Ketubot 12,35a, cited in Samuel Tobias Lachs, A Rabbinic Commentary on the New Testament, Ktav Publishing, NY, 1987, P. 250)

8:17 "The Rabbis said, 'His [Messiah's] name is 'the sufferer rabbi,' as it is written, 'Surely he has carried our griefs, and was loaded down with our sorrows: yet we thought him to be a leper, stricken by God, and afflicted.' [Is. 53:4]" (Tal. Sanhedrin 98b)

8:19 Yhn. 1:38 tells us that "Rabbi" is translated as *didaskalos*/"Teacher". "He who has talmidim, they call him 'Rabbi'. If his talmidim are praised, they call him 'Rabban'. If these and those [talmidim of his talmidim] are praised, they call him by his name." (Tos. Eduyot 3:4)

8:28-32 In philosophy, there is a logical fallacy called The Gadarene Swine Fallacy, which "is the fallacy of supposing that because a group is in the right formation, it is necessarily on the right course; and conversely, of supposing that because an individual has strayed from the group and isn't in formation, that he is off course. The individual may seem lost to the group but not off course to an ideal observer." www.philosophicalsociety.com/Archives/TheGadareneSwineFallacy.htm

[32]He said to them, "Go." They came out and went into the herd of pigs. Then the whole herd of pigs rushed down the cliff into the lake, and drowned in the water!

[33]Those who herded them fled, went away into the city, and told everything, including what happened to those who were afflicted by the demons. [34]All the city came out to meet Yeshua. When they saw him, they begged that he would depart from their area.

9 [1]He entered into a boat, crossed over, and came into his own city. [2]They brought to him a man who was paralyzed, lying on a bed! Seeing their faith, Yeshua said to the paralytic, "Son, be encouraged. Your sins are forgiven you."

[3]Some of the Torah scholars said to themselves, "This man is blaspheming."

[4]Knowing their thoughts, Yeshua said, "Why do you[+] think evil in your[+] hearts? [5]For which is easier, to say: 'Your sins are forgiven;' or to say, 'Get up, and walk'? [6]But so that you[+] may know that the Son of Adam has authority on earth to forgive sins" — then he said to the paralytic — "Get up, take up your mat, and go home." [7]He arose and departed to his house. [8]Now when the crowd saw it, they were astonished and glorified God, who had given such authority to the children of Adam.

[9]As Yeshua passed by from there, he saw a man called Matthias sitting at the tax collection office. He said to him, "Follow me." He got up and followed him. [10]Now as Yeshua sat in the house, many tax collectors and sinners came and sat down with him and his disciples.

[11]When the Perushim saw it, they said to his disciples, "Why does your[+] teacher eat with tax collectors and sinners?"

[12]When Yeshua heard it, he said to them, "Those who are healthy have no need for a physician, but those who are sick do. [13]Now go and learn what this means: 'I desire mercy, and not sacrifice.' [Hos. 6:6] For I did not come to call the righteous, but sinners."

[14]Then Yohanan's disciples came to him, saying, "Why do we and the Perushim fast often, but your disciples do not fast?"

[15]Yeshua said to them, "Can the friends of the bridegroom mourn as long as the bridegroom is with them? Nevertheless, the days will come when the bridegroom will be taken away from them, and then they will fast. [16]No one puts a piece of unshrunk cloth on an old garment, because the patch tears away from the garment, and a worse hole is made. [17]Nor do people put new wine into old wineskins, or else the skins would burst, the wine be spilled, and the skins ruined. No, they put new wine into fresh wineskins, and both are preserved."

[18]While he told them these things, a ruler came, bowed down before him, and said, "My daughter has just died, but come and lay your hand on her, and she will live."

9:12-13 In the liturgy in Taḥanun, we pray to "the One who opens a hand to receive repentant transgressors and sinners."

9:14-17 Yeshua is responding to the question about fasting. The parables illustrate that some things are appropriate at one time or in one circumstance, but not in another. His disciples will fast later, when it is appropriate.

9:17 "Rabbi said, 'Don't focus on this flask but on what is in it; there can be a new flask filled with old [wine] and an old flask in which there is not even new [wine].'" (Tal. Avot 4:20)

[19]Yeshua got up and followed him, as did his disciples. [20]A woman who had a discharge of blood for twelve years came behind him, and touched the tzitzit of his garment. [21]For she thought to herself, "If I just touch his garment, I will be made well."

[22]Now turning around and seeing her, Yeshua said, "Daughter, be encouraged. Your faith has made you well." And the woman was made well from that hour.

[23]When Yeshua came into the ruler's house and saw the flute players and the crowd making a commotion, [24]he said to them, "Step back, because the girl is not dead, but sleeping." And they ridiculed him. [25]But when the crowd was put out, he entered in, took her by the hand, and the girl arose. [26]The news of this went out into that whole region.

[27]As Yeshua passed by from there, two blind men followed him, calling out, "Have mercy on us, Son of David!" [28]When he had come into the house, the blind men came to him. Yeshua said to them, "Do you[+] believe that I am able to do this?"

They told him, "Yes, Lord."

[29]Then he touched their eyes, saying, "As your[+] faith is, be it done unto you[+]." [30]Their eyes were opened. Yeshua strongly warned them, "See that no one knows about this." [31]But they went out and spread abroad his fame in that whole region.

[32]As they went out, a mute man who was afflicted by a demon was brought to him. [33]When the demon was cast out, the mute man spoke. The crowds were amazed, saying, "Nothing like this has ever been seen in Israel!"

[34]But the Perushim said, "He casts out demons by the prince of the demons."

[35]Yeshua went about all the cities and the villages, teaching in their meetingplaces, proclaiming the good news of the kingdom, and healing every disease and sickness among the people. [36]Now when he saw the crowds, he was moved with compassion for them, because they were troubled and abandoned, like sheep without a shepherd. [Num. 27:17, 1K. 22:17, Zech. 10:2] [37]Then he said to his disciples, "The harvest indeed is plentiful, but the laborers are few. [38]Pray therefore that the Lord of the harvest will send out laborers into his harvest."

10 [1]He called his twelve disciples to himself, and gave them authority over unclean spirits, to cast them out, and to heal every disease and every sickness. [2]Now the names of the twelve ambassadors are these: the first, Shimon, who is called Kefa, Andreas his brother, Jacob the son of Zevadyah, Yohanan his brother, [3]Philip, Bar Talmai, Toma, Matthias the tax collector, Jacob the son of Halfai, and Taddi, [4]Shimon the zealot, and Judah from K'riyot, who also delivered him up.

9:20 God commanded Israel to wear fringes/tzitzit with a blue cord on the corners of their (four-cornered, covering) garments so "that you may look upon it and remember all the commandments of the Everpresent and do them." (Num. 15:38-40, Dt.22:12) Yeshua faithfully remembered and observed all the commandments of the Everpresent. By touching Yeshua's tzitzit, the woman was making her appeal to God on the basis of Yeshua's righteousness.

10:1-4 "The ambassador/shaliakh of a man is as the man." (Tal. Berachot 34b)

10:4 "Shimon the zealot" The Greek kananaios is understood to be a transliteration of the Aramaic kan'anaya, meaning "zealot". It may be a personality characterization, or an indication that he belonged to the political Zealots. In Acts 1:13, he is called Shimon ho zelotes. (cf. Lk. 6:15)

⁵Yeshua sent these twelve out, and instructed them, "Do not go among the Gentiles, and do not enter into any city of the Samaritans. ⁶Go instead to the lost sheep of the house of Israel. [Jer. 50:6] ⁷As you⁺ go, proclaim, 'Heaven's kingdom has come near.' ⁸Heal the sick, cleanse the lepers, and cast out demons. You⁺ received freely, so give freely. ⁹Do not take any gold, or silver, or bronze in your⁺ money belts. ¹⁰Take no bag for the journey, nor two coats, nor sandals, nor a staff, because the workman is worthy of his livelihood. ¹¹Into whatever city or village you⁺ enter, find out who in it is worthy, and stay there until you⁺ go on. ¹²As you⁺ enter into the household, greet it with peace. ¹³If the household is worthy, let your⁺ peace come upon it, but if it is not worthy, let your⁺ peace return to you⁺. ¹⁴Whoever does not receive you⁺ or hear your⁺ words, shake off the dust from your⁺ feet as you⁺ depart from that house or that city. ¹⁵I assure you⁺ that it will be more tolerable for the land of Sedom and Amorah in the day of judgment than for that city.

¹⁶"Know that I am sending you⁺ out as sheep in the midst of wolves. Therefore be wise as serpents, and harmless as doves. ¹⁷But beware of men, for they will deliver you⁺ up to councils, and they will scourge you⁺ in their assemblies. ¹⁸Yes, and you⁺ will be brought before governors and kings for my sake, for a testimony to them and to the Gentiles. ¹⁹But when they deliver you⁺ up, do not be anxious about how or what you⁺ will say, because what you⁺ will say will be given to you⁺ in that hour. ²⁰For it is not you⁺ who speak, but the Spirit of your⁺ Father who speaks in you⁺.

²¹"Brother will deliver up brother to death, and the father his child. Children will rise up against parents, and cause them to be put to death. ²²You⁺ will be hated by all men for my name's sake, but the one who endures to the end will be saved. ²³Now when they persecute you⁺ in this city, flee into the next, for I assure you⁺ that you⁺ will not have gone throughout the cities of Israel before the Son of Adam has come.

²⁴"A disciple is not above his teacher, nor a servant above his lord. ²⁵It is enough for the disciple that he be like his teacher, and the servant like his lord. If they have called the master of the house Baal Zevul, how much more those of his household! [2Kgs. 1:2] ²⁶Therefore do not be afraid of them, because there is nothing covered that will not be revealed, nor hidden that will not be known. ²⁷What

10:8 In Tal. Bekorot 29a, Prov. 23:23 — "Buy the truth and do not sell it" — is used as support for Rab Judah's statement, "Just as I teach without charge, so you should teach without charge."

10:9-10 "Let a man not be disrespectful to the Eastern Gate because it is straight across from the Holy of Holies. A man should not enter the Temple Mount with his staff or in his shoes or with his pouch or with dust on his feet." (Tal. Berachot IX:1)

10:16 "Caesar said [about Israel] to R. Yehoshua, 'Great is the sheep that stands among seventy wolves.' He responded to him, 'Great is the Shepherd who delivers it and breaks them publicly. As it is written [Is.54:17] *Any weapon formed against you will not succeed.*'" (Mid. Esther 10.11)

"R. Judah said in the name of R. Simon: 'The Holy One, blessed be He, said about Israel, *With Me they are innocent like doves, but with the peoples of the world they are cunning like serpents.*'" (Mid. Song of Songs Rabba II:34)

10:25 Some texts have *Baal Zevul*, which means "lord of dung or garbage". Other texts have *Baal Zevuv*, which means "lord of flies" (a Canaanite god).

I tell you[+] in the darkness, speak in the light. And what you[+] hear whispered in the ear, proclaim on the housetops. [28]Do not be afraid of those who kill the body, but are not able to kill the soul. Rather fear the One who is able to destroy both soul and body in Gehinnom.

[29]"Are not two sparrows sold for a copper coin? Not one of them falls to the ground apart from your[+] Father, [30]and the very hairs of your[+] head are all numbered. [31]So do not be afraid, you[+] are of more value than many sparrows.

[32]"Therefore everyone who confesses me before men, I also will confess him before my Father who is in heaven. [33]But whoever denies me before men, I also will deny him before my Father who is in heaven.

[34]"Do not think that I came to send peace on the earth. I did not come to send peace, but a sword. [35]For I came to turn a man against his father, a daughter against her mother, and a daughter-in-law against her mother-in-law. [36]A man's foes will be those of his own household. [Mic. 7:5-6] [37]The one who loves father or mother more than me is not worthy of me. And the one who loves son or daughter more than me is not worthy of me. [38]The one who does not accept his tree of death, and follow after me, is not worthy of me. [39]The one who finds his life will lose it, and the one who loses his life for my sake will find it. [40]The one who receives you[+] receives me, and the one who receives me receives the One who sent me. [41]The one who receives a prophet in the name of a prophet will receive a prophet's reward. And the one who receives a just man in the name of a just man will receive a just man's reward. [42]Whoever gives one of these little ones merely a cup of cold water to drink in the name of a disciple, I assure you[+] that he will certainly not lose his reward."

11 [1]When Yeshua had finished instructing his twelve disciples, he departed from there to teach and proclaim in their cities. [2]Now when Yoḥanan in prison heard the works of the Messiah, he sent two of his disciples [3]and said to him, "Are you the One who is coming, or should we look for another?"

10:28 "When Rabban Johanan ben Zakkai was sick, his disciples came in to visit him. When he saw them he began to weep. His disciples said to him: 'Candle of Israel, pillar of the right hand, hammer of strength! In front of what are you weeping?' He said to them: 'If I were being taken before a king of flesh and blood who is here today and tomorrow in the grave, if he is angry with me, his anger is not an everlasting anger. And if he imprisons me, his imprisonment is not an everlasting imprisonment. And if he puts to death, his putting to death is not an everlasting death — and I can persuade with words and bribe with money — even so I would weep. Now I am being taken before the King of kings of kings, the Holy One, blessed be He, who lives and endures for ever and ever and ever. And if He is angry with me, His anger is an everlasting anger. And if He imprisons, His imprisonment is an everlasting imprisonment. And if He puts me to death, He puts me to death for ever, and I cannot persuade Him with words or bribe Him with money. And even more, there are two ways before me, one of the Garden of Eden and one of Gehinnom, and I do not know by which I will be taken. Should I not weep?'" (Tal. Berachot 28b)

10:34-37 Tal. Sotah 49b: "In the footsteps of the Messiah, harshness will increase and honor decrease... A son will despise his father, a daughter will rise against her mother, a daughter-in-law against her mother-in-law, and a man's enemies will be the men of his household." (cf. Tal. Sanhedrin 97a)

[4]Yeshua answered them, "Go and tell Yoḥanan the things which you[+] hear and see — [5]the blind receive their sight [Is. 35:5], the lame walk, the lepers are cleansed, the deaf hear, the dead are raised up, and the poor have the good news proclaimed to them. [Is. 61:1] [6]There is good for the one who is not offended by me."

[7]As these went their way, Yeshua began to say to the crowd concerning Yoḥanan, "What did you[+] go out into the wilderness to see? A reed shaken by the wind? [8]But what did you[+] go out to see? A man in soft clothing? Look, those who wear soft clothing are in the houses of kings.

[9]"But why did you[+] go out? To see a prophet? Yes, I tell you[+], and much more than a prophet. [10]For this is the one about whom it is written, 'Behold, I send My messenger before your face, who will prepare your way before you.' [Mal. 3:1] [11]I assure you[+] that among those who are born of women there has not arisen anyone greater than Yoḥanan the Immerser. Yet the one who is least in Heaven's kingdom is greater than he. [12]From the days of Yoḥanan the Immerser until now, Heaven's kingdom is subjected to violence, and the violent plunder it. [13]For all the prophets and the Torah prophesied unto Yoḥanan. [14]If you[+] are willing to receive it, this is Eliyahu, who is to come. [Mal. 3:23-24H] [15]He who has ears to hear, let him hear. [Dt. 29:4, Ezek. 3:27]

[16]"But to what shall I compare this generation? It is like children sitting in the marketplaces, who call to their companions [17]and say, 'We played the flute for you[+], and you[+] did not dance. We lamented for you[+], and you[+] did not mourn.' [18]For Yoḥanan came neither eating nor drinking, and they say, 'He has a demon.' [19]The Son of Adam came eating and drinking, and they say, 'Look, a gluttonous man and a drunkard, a friend of tax collectors and sinners.' Yet wisdom is shown to be righteous by her children." [Prov. 8:1-9:6]

11:4-5 In the traditional prayer Nishmat, we bless the Everpresent Lord, who "resurrects the dead and heals the sick, gives sight to the blind, causes those who are bent over to stand upright, and gives speech to the mute." The Birkat haShaḥar uses similar language.

11:10 The Hebrew *malakh*, and the Greek *aggelos*, can be translated as either "messenger" or "angel". "'Behold, I send an angel.' Wherever the angel appeared, the Shekhinah appeared, as it says, 'And the angel of the Everpresent Lord appeared to him in a flame of fire' (Ex. 3:2), and immediately, 'God called to him' (v. 4). Even more, in the hour Israel calls out before Him, salvation comes to them... In the Age to Come, likewise, when He will reveal himself, redemption will come to Israel, as it says, 'Behold, I send My messenger, and he will turn the way before Me.'" (Mid. Exodus Rabba 32:9)

11:11 No matter how great one "born of woman" is, he must be born of the Spirit to enter the kingdom of God. No matter how "small" one is in the kingdom, he is greater than all those outside it.

11:12 "Eliyahu does not come to say 'unclean' or 'clean,' to put far off or bring near, but only to put far off those who were brought near by an arm [of force] and to bring near those who were put far off by an arm [of force]." (Tal. Eduyot 8.7)

11:14; 17:12 "he is the Eliyahu who was to come" can be compared to the statement "Pinḥas is Eliyahu." [e.g. Yalkut Shim'oni, chapter 771] The Rabbis equated the two because of the zeal for righteousness of Pinchas. (cf. Luke 1:17) They understood that Eliyahu would be sent before the coming of Messiah. (e.g. Tal. Shabbat 118a, Tal. Eruvin 43b)

²⁰Then he began to denounce the cities in which most of his mighty works had been done, because they did not change their ways. ²¹"Woe to you, Korazin! Woe to you, Beit Tzaidah! For if the mighty works which were done in you⁺ had been done in Tzor and Tzidon, they would have returned long ago in sackcloth and ashes. ²²But I tell you⁺ that it will be more tolerable for Tzor and Tzidon on the day of judgment than for you⁺. ²³You, Kfar Na<u>h</u>um, will not be lifted up to Heaven; you will go down to Sheol! For if the mighty works which were done in you had been done in Sedom, it would have remained until this day. ²⁴But I tell you⁺ that it will be more tolerable for the land of Sedom on the day of judgment than for you."

²⁵At that time, Yeshua answered, "I thank you Father, Lord of heaven and earth, that You have hidden these things from the wise and understanding, and have revealed them to little children. ²⁶Yes, Father, for doing this was very pleasing to You. ²⁷All things have been delivered to me by my Father. No one knows the Son, except the Father. Nor does anyone know the Father except the Son, and the one to whom the Son desires to reveal Him.

²⁸"Come to me, all you⁺ who labor and are heavily burdened, and I will give you⁺ rest. ²⁹Take my yoke upon you⁺, and learn from me, for I am gentle and humble in heart. Then you⁺ will find rest for your⁺ souls [Jer. 6:16], ³⁰because my yoke is easy, and my burden is light."

12 ¹At that time, Yeshua went through the grain fields on Shabbat. His disciples were hungry and began to pluck heads of grain and eat. ²But when the Perushim saw it, they said to him, "Look, your disciples do what is not permitted to do on Shabbat."

³But he said to them, "Have you⁺ not read what David did, when he and those who were with him were hungry? ⁴He entered into the house of God, and ate the bread of the Presence, which was not permitted to him to eat, nor for those who were with him, but only for the Kohanim.

⁵Or have you⁺ not read in the Torah that on Shabbat the Kohanim in the Temple profane Shabbat, and are guiltless? ⁶Now I tell you⁺ that one greater than the Temple is here. ⁷But if you⁺ had known what this means, 'I desire mercy, and not sacrifice,' [Hos. 6:6] you⁺ would not have condemned the guiltless. ⁸For the Son of Adam is Lord of Shabbat."

11:23 Sheol is the realm of the dead.

11:29-30 "One should begin by receiving upon himself the yoke of the Kingdom of Heaven and after that receive upon himself the yoke of the commandments." (Tal. Berachot Mishnah II. 1 The discussion continues through Berachot 13a-14b.)

In the Talmud, there is praise for the later generations which "make the yoke of the Torah heavy upon themselves, and are therefore worthy to have a miracle done for them." (Tal. Sanhedrin 94b)

12:5 "Slaughter [of sacrifices] overrides Shabbat and uncleanness." (Tos. Mena<u>h</u>ot 1:3)

The Rabbis recognized that their own regulations concerning Shabbat did not come from the Scriptures. "Halakhot [i.e. rabbinic decrees] for Shabbat, offerings for the festivals, and unfaithful actions, they are as mountains which are hanging from a hair, because there is little scripture, but multiplied halakhot." (Tal. <u>H</u>agigah 10a)

12:8 God created Shabbat and commanded Israel to observe it forever. [Ex. 31:13-17] Yeshua is claiming to have authority over Shabbat as to what is permitted and what is prohibited.

[9]He departed there, and went into their meetingplace, [10]and there was a man with a withered hand. In order to accuse him, they asked him, "Is it permitted to heal on Shabbat?"

[11]He said to them, "What man is there among you[+], who if he has one sheep and this one falls into a pit on Shabbat, won't he take hold of it and lift it out? [12]So how much more valuable is a man than a sheep? Therefore it is permitted to do good on Shabbat." [13]Then he told the man, "Stretch out your hand." He stretched it out, and it was restored whole, just like the other. [14]But the Perushim went out and conspired against him, as to how they might destroy him. [15]Perceiving this, Yeshua withdrew from there.

Large crowds followed him, and he healed them all, [16]And he instructed them that they should not make him known, [17]so that what was spoken through Isaiah the prophet might be given fullness: [18]"Behold, My servant whom I have chosen, My beloved in whom My soul is well pleased. I will put My Spirit on him. He will proclaim justice to the Gentiles. [19]He will not strive or shout, nor will anyone hear his voice in the streets. [20]He will not break a bruised reed, and he will not quench smoking flax, until he leads justice to victory. [21]In his name, the Gentiles will hope." [Is. 42:1-4LXX]

[22]Then a man afflicted by a demon was brought to him, blind and mute. And he healed him so that the blind and mute man both spoke and saw. [23]All in the crowd were amazed, and said, "Can this be the Son of David?"

[24]But when the Perushim heard it, they said, "This man does not cast out demons, except by Baal Zevul, the prince of the demons."

[25]Knowing their thoughts, Yeshua said to them, "Every kingdom divided against itself is brought to desolation, and every city or house divided against itself will not stand. [26]If the Accuser casts out the Accuser, he is divided against himself. How then will his kingdom stand? [27]If I cast out demons by Baal Zevul, by whom do your[+] children cast them out? Therefore they will be your[+] judges. [28]But if I cast out demons by the Spirit of God, then God's kingdom has come upon you[+]. [29]Or how can one enter into the house of the strong man and plunder his goods, unless he first binds the strong man? Then he will plunder his house. [Is. 49:24-25]

12:10 Beit Shammai did not allow praying for the sick on Shabbat. Beit Hillel permitted it. (Tos.Shab. 17:14, c.f. Shab. 12a) The word translated as "hand" may also mean "arm".

12:10-14 The prevailing view in the Talmud is different from that of these Perushim. "R. Eleazar said: 'One may determine humanitarian justice to the poor on Shabbat.' Again, R. Jacob b. Idi said in R. Johanan's name: 'One may attend to the saving of a life or saving many on Shabbat, and one may go to the meetingplaces to attend to affairs of the community on Shabbat.' The School of Manasseh taught: 'One may make arrangements on Shabbat for the betrothal of young girls and to educate a child and to teach him a trade.' Scripture says, [refrain] 'from finding your own desires or speaking your own words.' [Is. 58:13] 'Your desires' are forbidden, the desires of Heaven are permitted." (Tal. Shab. 150a)

12:23 See note to Mt.1:1 for the Messianic characterization of "the Son of David".

12:24 Josephus says that God taught Solomon how to cast out demons, and that method was still in use in Josephus' time. (Antiq. 8:45-49 [8.2.5.45-49])

³⁰"The one who is not with me is against me, and the one who does not gather with me scatters. ³¹Therefore I tell you⁺ that every sin and blasphemy will be forgiven the children of Adam, but the blasphemy against the Spirit will not be forgiven the children of Adam. ³²Whoever speaks a word against the Son of Adam, it will be forgiven him. But whoever speaks against the Ruakh Kodesh, it will not be forgiven him, neither in this age, nor in that which is to come.

³³"Either make the tree beautiful and its fruit beautiful, or make the tree rotten and its fruit rotten, because the tree is known by its fruit. ³⁴Offspring of vipers, how can you⁺, being evil, speak good things? For the mouth speaks from what flows out of the heart. ³⁵The good man brings good things out of his good treasure, and the evil man brings evil things out of his evil treasure. ³⁶I tell you⁺ that every idle word that men speak — they will give an account of it in the day of judgment. ³⁷For from your words you will be acquitted, and from your words you will be condemned."

³⁸Then certain of the Torah scholars and Perushim responded, "Rabbi, we want to see a sign from you."

³⁹But he answered them, "An evil and adulterous generation seeks after a sign, but no sign will be given to them except the sign of Yonah the prophet. ⁴⁰For as Yonah was three days and three nights in the belly of the great fish [Yon. 2:1H; Est. 4:16-5:1], so will the Son of Adam be three days and three nights in the heart of the earth. ⁴¹The men of Nineveh will stand up in the judgment with this generation, and will condemn it, because they repented at the proclamation of Yonah. And look, more than Yonah is here! ⁴²The Queen of the South will rise up in the judgment with this generation, and will condemn it, because she came from the ends of the earth to hear the wisdom of Solomon. [1Kings 10:1-10] And look, more than Solomon is here!

⁴³"But when an unclean spirit is gone out of the man, it passes through waterless places seeking rest, and does not find it. ⁴⁴Then it says, 'I will return into my house from which I came out.' And when it has come back, it finds it empty, swept, and put in order. ⁴⁵Then it goes, and takes with itself seven other spirits more evil than itself, and they enter in and dwell there. The last state of that man becomes worse than the first. Even so will it also be to this evil generation."

⁴⁶While he was still speaking to the crowds, his mother and his brothers stood outside, seeking to speak to him. ⁴⁷Someone said to him, "Look, your mother and your brothers stand outside, seeking to speak to you."

⁴⁸But he answered the one who spoke to him, "Who is my mother and who are my brothers?" ⁴⁹He stretched out his hand towards his disciples and said, "Look, my mother and my brothers. ⁵⁰For whoever does the will of my Father who is in heaven, he is my brother, and sister, and mother."

13 ¹On that day Yeshua went out of the house, and sat by the lake. ²Large crowds gathered to him, so he entered into a boat and sat, while all the crowd stood on the shore. ³He told them many things in parables. He said, "Listen, a sower went out to sow. ⁴As he sowed, some seeds fell by the roadside, and the birds came and devoured them. ⁵Others fell on rocky ground where they did not have much soil. And because they had no depth of soil, they sprang up immediately. ⁶When the sun had risen, they were scorched. Because they had no root, they withered away. ⁷Others fell among

---

12:40 Esther told Mordechai to fast for "three days, night and day" (Est. 4:16), but she then went to the king on the third day. (Est. 5:1)

thorns, and the thorns grew up and choked them. ⁸And others fell on good soil, and yielded fruit — some one hundred times as much, some sixty, and some thirty. [Gen. 26:12] ⁹He who has ears to hear, let him hear." [Dt. 29:4, Ezek. 3:27]

¹⁰The disciples came and said to him, "Why do you speak to them in parables?"

¹¹He answered them, "To you⁺ it is given to know the mysteries of Heaven's kingdom, but it is not given to them. ¹²For whoever has, to him will be given and he will have abundance. But whoever does not have, even what he does have will be taken away from him. ¹³Therefore I speak to them in parables, because seeing they do not see, and hearing they do not hear, nor do they understand. ¹⁴The prophecy of Isaiah is fulfilled in them, which says, 'In hearing you⁺ will hear, and will not at all understand. Seeing you⁺ will see, and will not at all perceive. ¹⁵For the heart of this people has grown callous, their ears are dull of hearing. They have shut their eyes. Otherwise they might perceive with their eyes, hear with their ears, understand with their heart, and return. Then I would heal them.' [Is. 6:9, 10, Ps. 119:70, Zech. 7:11]

¹⁶"But your⁺ eyes are blessed, because they see, and your⁺ ears, because they hear. ¹⁷For I assure you⁺ that many prophets and righteous men desired to see the things which you⁺ see, and did not see them; and to hear the things which you⁺ hear, and did not hear them.

¹⁸"Listen then to the parable of the sower. ¹⁹When anyone hears the message of the kingdom and does not understand it, the Evil One comes and snatches away what has been sown in his heart. This is what was sown by the roadside. ²⁰What was sown on the rocky places, this is the one who hears the message and immediately receives it with joy. ²¹Yet he has no root in himself, but endures for a while. When affliction or persecution arises because of the message, he immediately stumbles. ²²What was sown among the thorns, this is the one who hears the message, but the cares of this world and the deceitfulness of riches choke the message, and he becomes unfruitful. ²³What was sown on the good ground, this is the one who hears the message and understands it. He then brings forth and produces fruit — some one hundred times as much [Gen.26:12], some sixty, and some thirty."

²⁴He set another parable before them, saying, "Heaven's kingdom is like a man who sowed good seed in his field, ²⁵but while people slept, his enemy came and sowed over with poisonous weeds also among the wheat, and went away. ²⁶But when the blade sprang up and brought forth fruit, then the poisonous weeds appeared also. ²⁷The servants of the master of the house came and said to him, 'Sir, didn't you sow good seed in your field? Where did these poisonous weeds come from?'

²⁸"He said to them, 'An enemy has done this.'

13:24-30; 36-43 This weed is said to have a similar appearance to wheat, but bears a poisonous seed. The Hebrew word would be *zunin*, which is similar to the word *zonot*, i.e. "harlots," as is the Greek *zizania*. The Rabbis said, "Wheat and *zunin* are not a prohibited mixture..." (Tal. Kilayin 1:1; cf. Mid. Genesis Rabba 28:8) If they were a prohibited mixture, then any field of wheat that had *zunin* growing in it would be forbidden for human use.

In speaking about the generation of the flood when "the earth was corrupt before God," R. Luliani bar Tavrin said, "Even the earth committed immorality. They would sow wheat in it, and it would put out *zunin*." (Mid. Genesis 28.8)

"The servants asked him, 'Do you want us to go and gather them up?'

²⁹"But he said, 'No, because while you⁺ gather up the poisonous weeds, you⁺ might root up the wheat with them. ³⁰Let both grow together until the harvest, and in the harvest time I will tell the harvesters, First gather up the poisonous weeds, and bind them in bundles to burn them. Then gather the wheat into my barn.'"

³¹He set another parable before them, saying, "Heaven's kingdom is like a grain of mustard seed which a man took and sowed in his field. ³²It indeed is smaller than all seeds, but when it is grown, it is bigger than the herbs, and becomes a bush, so that the birds of the air come and lodge in its branches." [Ezek. 17:23, 31:6]

³³He spoke another parable to them. "Heaven's kingdom is like leaven which a woman took and mixed into three measures of meal until it all was leavened."

³⁴Yeshua spoke all these things to the crowds in parables, and did not speak to them without a parable. ³⁵In this way, what was spoken through the prophet was fulfilled: "I will open my mouth in parables. I will utter things hidden from the foundation of the world." [Ps. 78:2]

³⁶Then Yeshua sent the crowds away, and went into the house. His disciples came to him, saying, "Explain to us the parable of the poisonous weeds of the field."

³⁷He answered them, "The one who sows the good seed is the Son of Adam. ³⁸The field is the world. The good seed, these are the children of the kingdom, and the poisonous weeds are the children of the evil one. ³⁹The enemy who sowed them is the Accuser. The harvest is the culmination of the age, and the harvesters are angels. ⁴⁰Therefore, as the poisonous weeds are gathered up and burned with fire, so it will be at the end of this age. ⁴¹The Son of Adam will send out his angels, and they will gather out of his kingdom everything that causes stumbling, and those who do what is contrary to the Law, ⁴²Then he will cast them into the furnace of fire. There will be weeping and the gnashing of teeth. ⁴³Then the righteous will shine forth like the sun in the kingdom of their Father. [Dan. 12:3] He who has ears to hear, let him hear. [Dt. 29:4, Ezek. 3:27]

⁴⁴"Again, Heaven's kingdom is like a hidden treasure in the field, which a man found and hid. In his joy, he goes and sells all that he has, and buys that field.

⁴⁵"Again, Heaven's kingdom is like a man who is a merchant seeking fine pearls. ⁴⁶Having found one pearl of great price, he went and sold all that he had, and bought it.

13:28-30 "R. Joshua answered: 'Let the owner of the vineyard [God] come and weed out the thorns.'" (Tal. Baba Metzia 83b)

13:44 The rabbinic views about finding unidentified valuables is presented in Tal. Baba Metzia 25a-29b.

13:45-48 Rashi says something similar in his commentary on Gen. 37:1. "And so like this with the ten generations from Noah to Abraham, it is short with them, but when it reaches Abraham it is long with him. It may be compared to a pearl which fell into the sand; a man searches in the sand and sifts it in a sieve until he finds the pearl; and from the time he finds it he throws away the pebbles from his hand and keeps the pearl."

Also Tal. Berachot 33b: "Rab and Samuel instituted for us a precious pearl in Babylon: 'And You, O Everpresent Lord, our God, made us know Your righteous judgments and taught us to do the statutes that You willed, and made us inherit times of gladness and pilgrimages of freewill-offering, and did give us the ≫

[47]"Again, Heaven's kingdom is like a dragnet that was cast into the sea, and gathered some fish of every kind. [48]When it was filled, they drew it up on the beach. They sat down, and gathered the good into containers, but the bad they threw away. [49]It will be like this in the culmination of the age. The angels will come forth and separate the wicked from among the just, [50]and will cast them into the furnace of fire. There will be weeping and the gnashing of teeth." [51]Yeshua said to them, "Have you[+] understood all these things?"

They answered him, "Yes, Lord."

[52]He said to them, "Therefore every Torah scholar who has been made a disciple in Heaven's kingdom is like a man who is master of a house, who brings new and old things out of his treasure."

[53]When Yeshua had finished these parables, he departed from there. [54]Coming into his own region, he taught them in their meetingplace, so that they were amazed and said, "Where did this man get this wisdom, and these mighty works? [55]Isn't this the son of the craftsman? Isn't his mother called Miryam, and his brothers, Jacob, Yosef, Shimon, and Judah? [56]Aren't all of his sisters with us? Where then did this man get all of these things?" [57]And they were offended by him.

But Yeshua said to them, "A prophet is not without honor, except in his own region and in his own house." [58]And because of their disbelief, he did not do many mighty works there.

14 [1]At that time, Herod, the ruler of a fourth of the province, heard the report concerning Yeshua [2]and said to his servants, "This is Yohanan the Immerser. He has been raised from the dead. That is why these powers work in him." [3]For Herod had seized Yohanan, bound him, and put him in prison because of Herodias, the wife of his brother Philip. [4]For Yohanan had said to him, "It is not permitted for you to have her." [Lev. 18:16] [5]Though he wanted to kill him, he feared the multitude, because they esteemed him as a prophet. [6]But when the anniversary of Herod's accession came, the daughter of Herodias danced before them and pleased Herod. [7]Consequently he promised with an

---

holiness of Shabbat and the glory of the appointed season and the celebration of the pilgrimage festival. You have divided between the holiness of Shabbat and the holiness of the festival, and have made the seventh day holy above the six work days: You have set apart and sanctified Your people Israel with Your holiness. And You have given us...' etc."

In Tal. Makkot 21b, R. Yannai said to R. Yohanan, "Had I not picked up the broken pot for you, you would have forgotten the pearl beneath it." I.e., 'If I hadn't removed the rubble covering it, you would not have found this great understanding.'

14:1 Herod Antipas was the ruler (tetrarch) of Galilee and Perea, which formed a portion of the greater Roman province of Iudaea.

14:3-12 Josephus gives some background and a different perspective in Antiquities 18:111-119/18.5.1-2.

14:4 "There are in the Torah thirty-six transgressions punishable with being cut off: When one has intercourse with... his brother's wife." (Tal. K'ritot 1:1) The one exception to this ban was levirate marriage after a childless brother's death. (Dt. 25:5-10, Gen. 38)

14:6 The Greek word genesia ordinarily means "birthday," but its Jewish usage also encompasses the day a king ascends the throne. "What is the day of genosia of their kings? Rab Yehudah said, 'The day on which they cause him to stand [as king].'" (Tal. Avodah Zara 10a, Edersheim, The Life and Times of Jesus the Messiah, Vol. 1, P.672n, points this out.)

oath to give her whatever she might ask. [8]Being persuaded by her mother, she said, "Give me the head of Yohanan the Immerser, here on a platter."

[9]The king was grieved, but because of his oaths, and because of those who sat at the table with him, he commanded it to be given. [10]Then he sent and beheaded Yohanan in the prison. [11]His head was brought on a platter, and given to the girl. Then she brought it to her mother.

[12]His disciples came, took the body, buried it, and went and told Yeshua. [13]Now when Yeshua heard this, he withdrew from there in a boat to a private, deserted place. When the multitudes heard it, they followed him on foot from the cities.

[14]Yeshua went out, and he saw a large crowd. He had compassion on them, and healed their sick. [15]When evening had come, his disciples came to him saying, "This place is deserted, and the hour is already late. Send the crowds away, so that they may go into the villages, and buy food for themselves."

[16]But Yeshua said to them, "They do not need to go away. You[+] give them something to eat."

[17]They told him, "We have nothing here but five loaves and two fish."

[18]He said, "Bring them here to me." [19]He commanded the crowds to sit down on the grass. He took the five loaves and the two fish, and he looked up to heaven and said a blessing. Having broken the loaves, he then gave them to the disciples, and the disciples gave them to the multitudes. [20]They all ate, and were filled. [Dt. 8:20] They took up twelve baskets full of what was left over of the broken pieces. [21]Those who ate were about five thousand men, besides women and children.

[22]Yeshua immediately made the disciples get into the boat to go ahead of him to the other side, while he sent the multitudes away. [23]After he had sent the multitudes away, he went up onto the mountain by himself to pray. When evening had come, he was there alone.

[24]But the boat was now in the middle of the lake, battered by the waves, because the wind was against it. [25]In the fourth watch of the night, Yeshua came to them, walking on the lake. [26]When the disciples saw him walking on the lake [Job 9:8], they were troubled, saying, "It's a ghost!" and they cried out for fear. [27]But immediately Yeshua said to them, "Be encouraged. It is I. Do not be afraid."

[28]Kefa answered him and said, "Lord, if it is you, command me to come to you on the water."

[29]He said, "Come."

Kefa stepped down from the boat, and walked on the waters to come to Yeshua. [30]But when he saw that the wind was strong, he was afraid and, beginning to sink, he cried out, "Lord, save me!"

[31]Immediately Yeshua stretched out his hand, took hold of him, and said to him, "You of little faith, why did you waver?" [32]When they got into the boat, the wind ceased. [33]Those who were in the boat came and bowed down before him, saying, "You are truly the Son of God!"

[34]When they had crossed over, they came to the land of Kinneret. [35]When the men of that place recognized him, they sent into all that surrounding region, and brought to him all who were sick. [36]Then they begged him that they might just touch the tzitzit of his garment. As many as touched it were made whole.

14:34 It seems likely that the Greek *Gennessaret* is the Hebrew Kinneret, which has variant spellings in Num. 34:11, Dt. 3:17, Josh.13:27, and Josh. 19:35.

14:36 See note on 9:20.

15 [1]Then Perushim and Torah scholars came to Yeshua from Yerushala'im. They said, [2]"Why do your disciples disobey the tradition of the Elders? For they do not wash their hands when they eat bread."

[3]He answered them, "And why do you[+] disobey the commandment of God for the sake of your[+] tradition? [4]For God commanded, 'Honor your father and your mother.' [Ex. 20;12, Dt. 5:16] And, 'He who speaks evil of father or mother, let him be put to death.' [Ex. 21:17, Lev. 20:9] [5]But you[+] are saying, 'Whoever has told his father or his mother, Whatever help you might otherwise have gotten from me is a gift devoted to God, he [6]is not required to honor his father or his mother.' You[+] are voiding the commandment of God through your[+] tradition. [7]Pretenders! Isaiah prophesied correctly about you[+], [8]"These people draw near to Me with their mouth, and honor Me with their lips, but their heart is far from Me. [9]And they worship Me in vain, teaching teachings that are commandments of men."' [Is. 29:13]

[10]He summoned the multitude, and said to them, "Listen and understand. [11]What comes into the mouth does not defile the man, but what comes out of the mouth, this defiles the man."

[12]Then the disciples came, and said to him, "Do you know that the Perushim were offended when they heard this saying?"

[13]But he answered, "Every plant which my heavenly Father did not plant will be uprooted. [14]Leave them alone. They are blind guides of the blind. If the blind guide the blind, both will fall into a pit."

[15]Kefa responded to him, "Explain the parable to us."

15:1-9 It is clear in Talmud that the Rabbis thought their own authority was sufficient to overrule God. The classic example is the *tanoor akhnai* incident, where R. Eliezer is excommunicated for disagreeing with the majority of Rabbis, even though God attests that R. Eliezer is correct. (Tal. Baba Metzia 59b) There is the interesting story in Tal. Baba Metzia 86a about a disagreement in the heavenly academy over whether a certain skin appearance means that a person has leprosy or is clean. God says the person is clean but all the other members of the heavenly academy say he is unclean. So the issue remained unresolved until Rabba b. Nahmani, who was considered THE authority on leprosy, died and then cast the deciding vote.

15:2 Beit Hillel and Beit Shammai strongly disagreed with each other over whether the hands were to be washed before the filling the cup or after. (Tal. Berakhot 51b-52b)

15:2-20 The issue is whether or not a lack of ceremonial washing of the hands makes clean food (i.e., what is permissible to eat) unclean (i.e., impermissible to eat). Eating impermissable food would profane the one who eats. The prayer Netilat Yadaim marks the significance of hand washing. The Talmud connects unwashed hands with the first step in defilement.

"When R. Dimi came, he said: 'First [no] water, then the eating of pig's flesh, and afterwards the wife separates from her husband.' When Rabin came, he said: 'The first things, then the eating of *nebelah* [i.e. an animal that died of itself], and the last things killed the soul.'" (Tal. Chullin 106a)

15:4 "Our Rabbis taught: There are three who come together in a person, the Holy One, blessed be He, the person's father, and his mother. In the time when a person honors his father and his mother, the Holy One, blessed be He, says: 'In this, I consider it for them as if I had lived among them and they had honored Me.'" (Tal. Kid. 30b)

[16]So Yeshua said, "Are you⁺ also still without understanding? [17]Don't you⁺ understand that whatever goes into the mouth passes into the belly, and then out of the body? [18]But the things which come out of the mouth come out of the heart, and they defile the man. [19]For out of the heart come forth evil thoughts, murders, adulteries, sexual sins, thefts, perjury, and blasphemies. [20]These are the things which defile the man. But to eat with unwashed hands does not defile the man."

[21]Yeshua went out from there, and withdrew into the region of Tzor and Tzidon. [22]A Canaanite woman came out from those borders, and cried out, "Have mercy on me lord, Son of David! My daughter is severely afflicted by a demon!"

[23]But he did not respond a word to her. His disciples came and urged him, "Send her away, because she is crying out after us."

[24]But he answered, "I was not sent to anyone but the lost sheep of the house of Israel." [Jer. 50:6, Ezek. 34:12]

[25]But she came and bowed down before him, saying, "Lord, help me."

[26]But he answered, "It's not good to take the children's bread and throw it to the little dogs."

[27]But she said, "Yes, Lord, but even the little dogs eat the crumbs which fall from their masters' table."

[28]Then Yeshua answered her, "Woman, your faith is great. Let it be done to you even as you desire." And her daughter was healed from that hour.

[29]Yeshua left there, and came near to the lake of the Galil. And he went up onto the mountain, and sat down there. [30]Large crowds of people came to him, having with them the lame, blind, mute, maimed, and many others. And they put them down at his feet. He healed them, [31]so that the multitude of people were amazed when they saw the mute speaking, the crippled made whole, the lame walking, and the blind seeing. Then they glorified the God of Israel.

[32]Yeshua summoned his disciples and said, "I have compassion on the multitude, because they have continued with me now three days and have nothing to eat. I do not want to send them away fasting, otherwise they might faint on the way."

[33]The disciples said to him, "In a deserted place, where could we get enough loaves to satisfy so large a crowd?"

[34]Yeshua said to them, "How many loaves do you⁺ have?"

They said, "Seven, and a few small fish."

[35]He commanded the multitude to sit down on the ground. [36]Then he took the seven loaves and the fish. He gave thanks, broke them, and gave them to the disciples; and the disciples to the multitudes. [37]They all ate, and were filled. They took up seven baskets full of the broken pieces that were left over. [38]Those who ate were four thousand men, besides women and children. [39]Then he sent away the multitudes, got into the boat, and came into the borders of Magdala.

15:22-28 The woman first recognizes Yeshua as the Son of David, i.e. the Messiah, but he does not respond. She appeals to his mercy, but he still does not help her. After she affirms that the children of Israel are the rightful members of the household, then he heals her daughter.

15:24 "God, please save us because we have wandered like a lost sheep." (Sukkot Hoshanot)

16

¹The Perushim and Tzadukim came and tested him, asking him to show them a sign from Heaven. ²But he answered them, "When it is evening, you⁺ say, 'It will be fair weather, for the sky is red.' ³In the morning, 'It will be foul weather today, for the sky is red and threatening.' You⁺ know how to discern the appearance of the sky, but you⁺ cannot discern the signs of the times. ⁴An evil and adulterous generation seeks after a sign, and there will be no sign given to them, except the sign of the prophet Yonah."

He left them and departed. ⁵The disciples came to the other side, having forgotten to take bread. ⁶Yeshua said to them, "Take heed and beware of the leaven of the Perushim and Tzadukim."

⁷They said to each other, "It is because we brought no bread."

⁸Knowing that, Yeshua said, "You⁺ of little faith, why are you⁺ discussing with each other that you⁺ have brought no bread? ⁹Do you⁺ not yet perceive or remember the five loaves for the five thousand, and how many baskets you⁺ took up? ¹⁰Nor the seven loaves for the four thousand, and how many baskets you⁺ took up? ¹¹How is it that you⁺ do not perceive that I did not speak to you⁺ concerning bread, but to beware of the leaven of the Perushim and Tzadukim?"

¹²Then they understood that he did not tell them to beware of the leaven of bread, but of the teaching of the Perushim and Tzadukim. ¹³Now when Yeshua came into the region of Kaesarea Philippi, he questioned his disciples, "Who do men say that the Son of Adam is?"

¹⁴They said, "Some say, 'Yohanan the Immerser.' Some, 'Eliyahu.' And others, 'Jeremiah, or one of the prophets.'"

¹⁵He said to them, "But who do you⁺ say that I am?"

¹⁶Shimon Kefa answered, "You are the Messiah, the Son of the living God."

¹⁷Yeshua responded to him, "There is good for you, Shimon son of Yonah, because flesh and blood has not revealed this to you, but my Father who is in heaven. [Is. 28:16] ¹⁸I also tell you that you

16:13 In Hebrew (and Greek), the soft C of Caesar becomes a hard K.

16:16 Cf. Ps. 2:2-7, "...against the Everpresent Lord and against His Anointed/Messiah... The Everpresent Lord has said to me, 'You are My Son, today I have begotten You.'"

16:17 Yeshua calls Shimon "son of Yonah/Jonah," whereas in Yhn. 1:42 he calls him "the son of Yohanan/John". It is possible that there is a scribal error in the copying of one of these Greek texts, but it seems more likely that both texts are correct, and that in the incident recorded in Matthias, Yeshua is characterizing Shimon. Yonah was called to proclaim God's message to the Gentiles. In a few years, Shimon will be called to do the same. Additionally, Yonah went to Yaffa to escape God's call to go to Nineveh. [Jon. 1:3] Shimon Kefa was in Yaffa when God called him to go to Cornelius. [Acts 10:5; Mt. 12:39-41] In the same sense that a man who does the deeds of Abraham is a son of Abraham, so one who does the deeds of Yonah is a son of Yonah.

The Greek text transliterates the Aramaic *bar yonah*, and does not have a definite article; whereas the text in Yohanan — "son of Yohannes" — contains a definite article, but no Aramaic. So our text has "a son of Yonah," seemingly tied by the Aramaic to the Yonah who went to Nineveh. The text in Yohanan, on the other hand, seems to speak definitely of physical descent, "<u>the</u> son of Yohanan".

16:18 "you are Kefa [a rock]. And on this bedrock [*kef*]" The Greek translation of Matthias's text has *petros* for the Aramaic *kefa*. As Yohanan 1:42 explains, "Yeshua looked at him, and said, 'You are Shimon the >>

are Kefa. And on this bedrock I will build my community, and the powers of Sheol will not prevail against it. [Gen. 24:60] ¹⁹I will give to you the keys of Heaven's kingdom, and whatever you bind on earth will be bound in heaven; and whatever you release on earth will be released in heaven." ²⁰Then Yeshua commanded the disciples that they tell no one that he is the Messiah. ²¹From that time, Yeshua began to show his disciples that he must go to Yerushala'im and suffer many things from the Elders, chief Kohanim, and Torah scholars; and be killed, and raised up the third day.

²²Kefa took him aside, and began to rebuke him, "Far be it from you, Lord! This will never be done to you."

²³But he turned, and said to Kefa, "Get out of my way, adversary. You are an offense to me, for you are not setting your mind on the things of God, but on the things of men." ²⁴Then Yeshua said to his disciples, "If anyone wants to come after me, let him deny himself, take up his tree of death, and follow me. ²⁵For whoever desires to save his life will lose it, and whoever will lose his life for my sake will find it. ²⁶For what will it profit a man if he gains the whole world, and destroys his soul? Or what will a man give in exchange for his soul? ²⁷For the Son of Adam will come in the glory of his Father with His angels, and then he will give to each one according to his deeds. [Ps. 62:12, Prov. 24:12; Is. 62:11] ²⁸I assure you⁺ that there are some standing here who will certainly not taste of death, until they see the Son of Adam come in his kingdom."

17 ¹After six days, Yeshua took with him Kefa, Jacob, and Yoḥanan his brother, and brought them up by themselves into a high mountain. ²His appearance was changed before them. His face shone like the sun, and his garments became as white as the light. ³Moses and Eliyahu were visible to them, talking with him!

son of Yoḥanan. You will be called Kefa,' (which is translated as *Petros*)." Yeshua announces that he intends to build his community/*kahal/ekklesia*, which is that of the Everpresent Lord. The Scriptures explicitly proclaim that to be *kahal Yisrael*. (E.g. Dt. 23:2-9H/LXX)

According to Liddell and Scott, *petros* means "a stone"; *petra*, which is used to refer to Yeshua, means "a rocky peak or ridge, fixed rock," i.e. bedrock. The Peshitta Aramaic uses Kefa rather than Petros in every instance, except Acts 1:13, 1Kefa 1:1, and 2Kefa 1:1. Judges 6:19-20 is an interesting passage where the phrase "on this rock/*petra*" also appears.

Sheol is the realm of the dead.

16:21 Other ancient Jewish sources speak of "The Death of Messiah". See the ADDITIONAL NOTES.

16:23 In Mid. Genesis Rabba 56:4, the Adversary tries to dissuade Abraham from sacrificing Isaac. When that fails, he tries to dissuade Isaac from being a willing sacrifice.

16:24 "'And Abraham took the wood of the burnt offering' [Gen. 22:6] like one who carries his stake [*tzelav*] on his shoulder." (Mid. Genesis 56:3)

16:28 See "Your Children Saw Your Kingdom" in the ADDITIONAL NOTES.

17:3-13 "The Holy One, blessed be He, said 'Moses, by your life, as you have given your life to them in this world, so too in the Age to Come when I bring Eliyahu the prophet to them, the two of you will come as one.'" (Mid. D'varim Rabbah 3:17)

[4]Kefa responded, and said to Yeshua, "Lord, it is good for us to be here. If you are willing, let us make three shelters here — one for you, one for Moses, and one for Eliyahu."

[5]While he was still speaking, a bright cloud suddenly overshadowed them. A voice came out from the cloud saying, "This is My beloved Son, in whom I delight [Gen. 22:2]. Listen to him."

[6]When the disciples heard it, they fell on their faces and were very afraid. [7]Yeshua came, touched them, and said, "Get up, and do not be afraid." [8]Lifting up their eyes, they saw no one except Yeshua alone. [9]As they were coming down from the mountain, Yeshua commanded them, "Do not tell anyone what you[+] saw, until the Son of Adam has risen from the dead."

[10]His disciples asked him, "Then why do the Torah scholars say that Eliyahu must come first?" [Mal. 4:5]

[11]Yeshua answered them, "Eliyahu indeed is coming first, and will restore all things. [12]Nevertheless I tell you[+] that Eliyahu has come already, and they did not recognize him, but did to him whatever they wanted. In the same way, the Son of Adam will also soon suffer under them." [13]Then his disciples understood that he spoke to them of Yohanan the Immerser.

[14]When they came to the multitude, a man came to him, kneeling down to him, saying, [15]"Lord, have mercy on my son, because he is sometimes not in his right mind, and suffers severely, often falling into the fire, and often into the water. [16]So I brought him to your disciples, and they could not heal him."

[17]Yeshua answered, "Unfaithful and obstinate generation! How long will I be with you[+]? How long will I bear with you[+]? Bring him here to me."

[18]Yeshua rebuked the demon, and it went out of him, and the boy was healed from that hour.

[19]Then the disciples came to Yeshua privately and said, "Why weren't we able to cast it out?"

[20]He said to them, "Because of your[+] lack of faith. For I assure you[+] that if you[+] have faith as a grain of mustard seed, you[+] will tell this mountain, 'Move from here to there,' and it will move. And nothing will be impossible for you[+]." [21]

[22]While they were staying in the Galil, Yeshua said to them, "The Son of Adam is about to be delivered up into the hands of men, [23]and they will kill him. Then he will be raised up the third day." They were extremely distressed.

[24]When they had come to Kfar Nahum, those who collected the two drachma tax came to Kefa,

17:5 The Greek text says, "This is my beloved son [*ho huios mou ho agapetos en hoi eudokesa*] ..." In the LXX of Gen. 22:2, God says to Abraham about Isaac, "Take your beloved son whom you have loved [*ton huion sou ton agapeton hon egapesas*] ..."

17:11 In the Morning Service, we pray, "Give us joy, our Everpresent Lord, in Your servant Eliyahu the prophet, in the kingdom of the house of David, your Anointed..."

17:12 "Eliyahu has come already" can be compared to the statement "Pinchas is Eliyahu." [e.g. Yalkut Shim'oni, chapter 771] The Rabbis equated the two because of the zeal for righteousness of Pinchas.

17:20 In Tal. Berakhot 64a, Rabba, a great rabbi, was called "an uprooter of mountains".

17:24-27 "He [Caesar] also laid a tribute upon the Jews wheresoever they were and enjoined every one of them to bring two drachmae every year into the Capitol, as they used to pay the same to the Temple at Jerusalem. And this was the state of the Jewish affairs at this time." (Josephus, The Jewish War, 7.6.6.218)

and said, "Doesn't your⁺ teacher pay the two drachma tax?" ²⁵He said, "Yes." When he came into the house, Yeshua anticipated Kefa and said, "What do you think, Shimon? From whom do the kings of the earth collect tribute or tax? From their children, or from strangers?"

²⁶Kefa said to him, "From strangers."

Yeshua said to him, "Therefore the children are exempt. ²⁷But so that we do not offend them, go to the lake, cast a hook, and take up the first fish that comes up. When you have opened its mouth, you will find a four drachma coin. Take that, and give it to them for me and you."

18 ¹At that time the disciples came to Yeshua, saying, "Who then is greater in Heaven's kingdom?" ²And calling a little child to himself, Yeshua set him in the middle of them. ³Then he said, "I assure you⁺ that unless you⁺ return and become as little children, you⁺ will certainly not enter into Heaven's kingdom. ⁴Whoever therefore humbles himself as this little child, that is the one who is greater in Heaven's kingdom. ⁵Whoever receives one such little child in my name receives me. ⁶But whoever causes one of these little ones who believe in me to stumble, it would be better for him that a heavy millstone were hung around his neck, and that he were sunk in the depths of the sea.

⁷"Woe to the world because of stumbling-blocks! For the coming of stumbling-blocks is unavoidable, but woe to that person through whom they come! ⁸If your hand or your foot causes you to stumble, cut it off, and cast it from you. It is better for you to enter into Life maimed or crippled, rather than to be cast into the eternal fire having two hands or two feet. ⁹If your eye causes you to stumble, pluck it out, and cast it from you. It is better for you to enter into Life with one eye, rather than to be cast into the Gehinnom of fire having two eyes.

¹⁰See that you⁺ do not despise one of these little ones, for I tell you⁺ that in heaven their angels always behold the face of my Father who is in heaven. ¹¹For the Son of Adam has come to save what was lost.

17:27 In Mid. Genesis Rabba 11.4, the story is told of a Jewish tailor in Rome who, in honor of the coming fast of Yom Kippur, pays a large sum for a fish. In turn, God honored the tailor, because there was a valuable pearl inside the fish. The tailor sold it and lived off the amount for the rest of his life. (The Soncino translation does not include the last part of the story.)

18:6-7 Rashi comments on Dt. 23:4-9, referring to the Midrash. He compares the Edomites and the Egyptians, who can enter the community/kahal/ekklesia of the Everpresent Lord after three generations, to the Ammonites and Moabites who cannot even enter through the tenth generation. "Other nations, however, are permitted immediately. So you learn that one who causes a person to sin, it is harder for him than for one who kills him; because the one who kills him kills him in this world, but the one who causes him to sin, he takes him out of this world and from the age to come. Consequently the Edomites who attacked them with the sword, were not abhorred; and similarly the Egyptians who drowned them; but those who caused them to sin, were abhorred (Siphre)." The commentary in the Midrash, BaMidbar 21:4, is on Num. 25:17. See also Mid. Vayikra 34:8.

18:8-9 Tal. Niddah 13a-b speak of certain types of immorality as deserving having the hand cut off. That was not an actual punishment, it was just a way of expressing the importance of not committing such sin.

[12]"What do you[+] think? If a man has one hundred sheep, and one of them goes astray, doesn't he leave the ninety-nine, go to the mountains and seek the one which has gone astray? [13]If it happens that he finds it, I assure you[+] that he rejoices over it more than over the ninety-nine which have not gone astray. [14]Even so it is not the will of your[+] Father who is in heaven that one of these little ones should perish.

[15]"If your brother sins against you, go and show him his fault between you and him alone. If he listens to you, you have gained back your brother. [Lev. 19:17] [16]But if he does not listen, take one or two more with you, so that every word may be established at the mouth of two or three witnesses. [Dt. 19:15] [17]If he refuses to listen to them, tell it to the community. If he also refuses to hear the community, let him be to you as a Gentile or a tax collector. [18]I assure you[+] that whatever things you[+] will bind on earth will be bound in heaven, and whatever things you[+] will loose on earth will be loosed in heaven. [19]Again, I assure you[+] that if two of you[+] will agree on earth concerning anything that they will ask, it will be done for them by my Father who is in heaven. [20]For where two or three are gathered together in my name, there I am among them."

[21]Then Kefa came and said to him, "Lord, how often may my brother sin against me and I forgive him? Up to seven times?"

[22]Yeshua said to him, "I'm not telling you up to seven times, but up to seventy times seven! [23]Therefore Heaven's kingdom is like a certain king, who wanted to settle accounts with his servants. [24]When he had begun to settle them, one was brought to him who owed him ten thousand talents. [25]But because he could not pay, his lord commanded him to be sold with his wife, his children, and all that he had, and payment to be made. [26]The servant therefore fell down and knelt before him, saying, 'Lord, have patience with me, and I will repay you everything.' [27]Being moved with compassion, the lord of that servant released him, and forgave him the debt.

[28]"But having gone out, that servant found one of his fellow servants who owed him one hundred denarii. He grabbed him, and took him by the throat, saying, 'Pay me what you owe!'

[29]"So his fellow servant fell down at his feet and begged him, 'Have patience with me, and I will repay you.' [30]Yet he was not willing, but went and threw him into prison until he should pay back what was owed. [31]So when his fellow servants saw what had happened, they were very upset, and came and told their lord all that had taken place. [32]Then his lord called him in, and said to him, 'You

18:15-17 "No man is to bring a charge against his fellow before the general membership unless he has previously rebuked that man before witnesses. By these rules they are to govern themselves wherever they dwell, in accordance with each legal finding that bears upon communal life..." (DSS 1QS 6:1-2)

18:17 "A Gentile or a tax collector" would be outside the community of Israel, until they turn to the Everpresent Lord. One would, therefore, not have table fellowship with them.

18:19-20 "R. Hananiah b. Teradion said, '...when two sit together and there are words of Torah between them, the Shekhinah abides among them.'" (Tal. Avot 3:2)

18:21-22 "R. Yosi bar Yehudah said, 'A man who transgresses [against another man] the first time, it is forgiven him; the second time it is forgiven him; the third time it is forgiven him; the fourth time it is not forgiven him.'" (Tal. Yoma 86b)

wicked servant! I forgave you all that debt, because you begged me. [33]Shouldn't you also have had mercy on your fellow servant, even as I had mercy on you?' [34]His lord was angry, and delivered him to the torturers, until he should pay all that was due to him. [35]So my heavenly Father will also do to you[+], if you[+] do not each forgive your[+] brother from your[+] hearts for his offenses."

19 [1]When Yeshua had finished these words, he departed from the Galil, and came into the borders of Judea across the Yarden. [2]Large crowds followed him, and he healed them there. [3]Perushim came to him, testing him, "Is it permitted for a man to divorce his wife for any reason at all?"

[4]He answered, "Haven't you[+] read that from the beginning, He who made them made them male and female? [Gen. 1:27, 5:2] [5]He also said, 'For this cause a man will leave his father and mother, and will be joined to his wife. And the two will become one flesh.' [Gen. 2:24] [6]Consequently they are no longer two, but one flesh. What therefore God has joined together, do not let man tear apart."

[7]They asked him, "Why then did Moses command us to give her a written divorce and send her away?" [Dt. 24:1-4]

[8]He said to them, "Because of the hardness of your[+] hearts, Moses allowed you[+] to divorce your[+] wives, but from the beginning it has not been so. [9]I tell you[+] that whoever divorces his wife, except for sexual immorality, and marries another commits adultery. And he who marries the one who is divorced commits adultery."

[10]His disciples said to him, "If this is the case of the man with his wife, it is better not to marry!"

[11]But he said to them, "Not all men can receive this saying, but those to whom it is given. [12]For there are eunuchs who were born that way from their mother's womb, and there are eunuchs who were made eunuchs by men. There are also eunuchs who made themselves eunuchs for the sake of Heaven's kingdom. He who is able to receive it, let him receive it." [Jer. 16:2]

[13]Then little children were brought to him so that he would lay his hands on them and pray, but the disciples rebuked them. [14]However Yeshua said, "Allow the little children to come to me, and do not forbid them, because Heaven's kingdom belongs to such as these." [15]He laid his hands on them, and departed from there.

19:3 "Mishnah. Beit Shammai says, 'A man should not divorce his wife unless he has truly found in her shameful nakedness, as it says, *Because he has found an act of shameful nakedness in her.*' [Dt. 24:1] But Beit Hillel says, 'Even if she has spoiled his meal...' R. Akiba says, 'Even if he finds another woman more pleasant than she is, as it says, *if it happens that she finds no grace in his eyes.*' [Dt. 24:1]... R. Eleazar said, 'Everyone who divorces his first wife, even the altar sheds tears over it.'" (Tal. Gittin 90a-b)

19:8 "because of the hardness of your hearts" Dt. 19:11 speaks of a man desiring to make an attractive captive woman his wife. Rashi says, "The Torah would not speak this except in opposition to the evil inclination, because if the Holy One, blessed be He, does not make her permitted, he will marry her though forbidden. But if he does marry her, his end will be to hate her..." See "Regulating the Actions of Hard Hearts" in the ADDITIONAL NOTES.

19:10-12 "A man has no right to live without a wife, and [a woman] has no right to live without a husband." (Tos. Yebamot 8:2)

¹⁶One came to him and said, "Rabbi, what good thing should I do that I may lay hold of eternal life?"

¹⁷He said to him, "Why do you ask me about what is good? There is One who is good. Now if you want to enter into Life, keep the commandments."

¹⁸He said to him, "Which ones?"

Yeshua said, "'You are not to murder.' 'You are not to commit adultery.' 'You are not to steal.' 'You are not to commit perjury.' ¹⁹'Honor your father and mother.' [Ex. 20:12-16; Dt. 5:16-20] And, 'You are to love your neighbor as yourself.'" [Lev. 19:8]

²⁰The young man said to him, "All these things I have observed from my youth. What do I still lack?"

²¹Yeshua said to him, "If you want to be complete, go sell what you have and give to the poor, and you will have treasure in heaven. Then come, follow me." ²²But when the young man heard what was said, he went away grieved, for he was one who had great possessions. ²³Yeshua said to his disciples, "I assure you⁺ that it is with difficulty that a rich man will enter into Heaven's kingdom. ²⁴Again I tell you⁺ that it is easier for a camel to go through the eye of a needle, than for a rich man to enter into God's kingdom."

²⁵When the disciples heard it, they were extremely astonished and said, "Who then can be saved?"

²⁶Looking at them, Yeshua said, "With men this is impossible, but with God all things are possible."

²⁷Then Kefa answered, "Look, we have left everything and followed you. What then will we have?"

²⁸Yeshua said to them, "I assure you⁺ that in the time of restoration, when the Son of Adam will sit on the throne of his glory [Dan. 7:9-10], you⁺ who have followed me, you⁺ also will sit on twelve thrones, judging the twelve tribes of Israel. ²⁹Everyone who has left houses, or brothers, or sisters, or father, or mother, or wife, or children, or lands, for the sake of my name, will receive one hundred times as much, and will inherit eternal life. ³⁰But many who are first will be last, and many who are last, first.

20 ¹"For Heaven's kingdom is like a man, the master of a household, who went out early in the morning to hire laborers for his vineyard. ²When he had agreed with the laborers for a denarius for the day, he sent them into his vineyard. ³He went out about the third hour, and saw others standing idle in the marketplace. ⁴To them he said, 'You⁺ also go into the vineyard, and I will

---

19:17 "There is no good except Torah." (Tal. Berakhot 5a)

19:18 The young man asks a very revealing question, "Which ones?" The question implies that there are some less important ones that he can break and still have eternal life.

19:21 "Monobaz the king spent all his treasure in years of hardship. His brothers said to him, 'Your fathers stored up treasure and added to that of their fathers. But you have continued to spend all your treasures, yours and your fathers.' He said to them, 'My fathers stored up treasures below, and I have stored up treasures above.... My fathers stored up treasures of Mammon, but I have stored up treasures of souls.... My fathers stored up treasures in this age, but I have stored up for the age to come." (Tos. Peah 4:18)

19:24 "A man is not shown [in a dream] a date palm of gold nor an elephant going through the eye of a needle." (Tal. Berakhot 55b)

give you⁺ whatever is right.' So they went their way. ⁵Again he went out about the sixth and the ninth hour and did likewise. ⁶About the eleventh hour he went out and found others standing idle. He said to them, 'Why do you⁺ stand here idle all day?'

⁷"They said to him, 'Because no one has hired us.'

"He said to them, 'You⁺ also go into the vineyard, and you⁺ will receive whatever is right.' ⁸When evening had come, the lord of the vineyard said to his manager, 'Call the laborers and pay them their wages, beginning from the last to the first.'

⁹"When those who were hired at about the eleventh hour came, they each received a denarius. ¹⁰When the first came, they thought that they would receive more, but they likewise each received a denarius. ¹¹When they received it, they complained against the ruler of the household, ¹²'These last ones have worked one hour, and you have made them equal to us, who have carried the weight of the day and the scorching heat.'

¹³"But he answered one of them, 'Friend, I am doing you no wrong. Didn't you agree with me for a denarius? ¹⁴Take what is yours, and go your way. It is my desire to give to this last one the same as to you. ¹⁵Am I not allowed to do what I want to with what I own? Or is your eye covetous, because I am good?' ¹⁶In this way the last will be first, and the first last. For many are called, but few are chosen." ⟨,

¹⁷As Yeshua was going up to Yerushala'im, he took the twelve disciples aside, and on the way he said to them, ¹⁸"Listen, we are going up to Yerushala'im, and the Son of Adam will be delivered to the chief Kohanim and Torah scholars. And they will condemn him to death. ¹⁹They will hand him over to the Gentiles to mock, to scourge, and to put to death on the tree. And the third day he will be raised up."

²⁰Then the mother of the sons of Zevadyah came to him with her sons, kneeling and asking something of him. ²¹He said to her, "What do you want?"

She said to him, "Say that these two sons of mine may sit in your kingdom one on your right hand, and one on your left hand."

²²But Yeshua answered, "You⁺ do not know what you⁺ are asking. Are you⁺ able to drink the cup that I am about to drink?"

They said to him, "We are able."

²³He said to them, "You⁺ will indeed drink my cup, but to sit on my right hand and on my left hand is not mine to give. It is instead for those for whom it has been prepared by my Father."

²⁴When the ten heard it, they were indignant with the two brothers. ²⁵But Yeshua summoned them and said, "You⁺ know that the rulers of the Gentiles lord it over them, and their great ones exercise authority over them. ²⁶It is not to be so among you⁺, but whoever desires to become great among you⁺

20:19 Here, and throughout, I have translated the Greek *stauros* as in LXX Esther 7:9; 17:16. As the Talmud says about Haman, "They hung him and his sons on the tree." (Tal. Megilah 19a)

20:25-28 "Our Rabbis taught: Every day, the Holy One, blessed be He, weeps over these three: over the one for whom it is possible to occupy himself with Torah and does not; and over the one for whom it is not possible to occupy himself with Torah but he does; and over a leader who lifts himself above the community." (Tal. Chagigah 5b)

>>

is to be your⁺ servant. ²⁷Whoever desires to be first among you⁺ is to be your⁺ bondservant, ²⁸even as the Son of Adam did not come to be served, but to serve, and to give his life as a ransom for many."

²⁹As they went out from Yeriho, a large crowd followed him. ³⁰Two blind men were sitting by the road. When they heard that Yeshua was passing by, they cried out, "Lord, Son of David, have mercy on us!" ³¹The crowd rebuked them, telling them that they should be quiet, but they cried out even more, "Lord, Son of David, have mercy on us!"

³²Yeshua stood still, called them, and asked, "What do you⁺ want me to do for you⁺?"

³³They told him, "Lord, that our eyes may be opened."

³⁴Moved with compassion, Yeshua touched their eyes. Immediately they received their sight, and they followed him.

21 ¹When they drew near to Yerushala'im and came to Beit Pagei, to the Mount of Olives, Yeshua then sent two disciples, ²saying to them, "Go into the village that is opposite you⁺, and immediately you⁺ will find a donkey tethered there, and a colt with her. Untie them, and bring them to me. ³If anyone says anything to you⁺, you⁺ are to say, 'The Lord needs them,' and right away he will send them."

⁴All this was done so that what was spoken through the prophet might be fulfilled: ⁵"Tell the daughter of Zion, Behold, your King comes to you, humble and riding on a donkey, on a colt, the foal of a donkey." [Is. 62:11, Zech. 9:9]

Socrates said that those who want to rule are the least fit to do so. "[T]he truth is surely this: that city in which those who are going to rule are least eager to rule is necessarily governed in the way that is best and freest from faction, while the one that gets the opposite kind of rulers is governed in the opposite way. ...The good aren't willing to rule for the sake of money or honor.... For it is likely that if a city of good men came to be, there would be a fight over not ruling, just as there is now over ruling; and there it would become manifest that a true ruler really does not naturally consider his own advantage but rather that of the one who is ruled." (Plato, The Republic, Section 520d & Section 347b-d)

21:5 "R. Joshua b. Levi brought two verses that are written, 'And behold, one like the son of man coming with the clouds of heaven,' [Dan. 7:13] but it is written, 'humble, and riding upon a donkey! [Zech. 9:9]'— If they are worthy, 'with the clouds of heaven'; if they are not worthy, 'humble and riding on a donkey'. King Shavur said to Samuel, 'You say the Messiah will come on a donkey: I will send him instead my white horse.' He answered him, 'Do you have one of a hundred colors?'" (Tal. Sanhedrin 98a) "R. Joseph said: Let him come, and may I be worthy to sit in the shadow of his donkey's saddle." (Tal. Sanhedrin 98b)

"The one who sees a donkey in a dream will look for salvation, because it says (Zech. 9:9), 'Look, your king is coming to you; he is righteous, victorious, and humble, and is riding on a donkey.'" (Tal. Berachot 56b) In "The Epistle to Yemen [to Jacob al-Fayyumi]," Maimonides refers Zech. 9:9 to Messiah." (Crisis and Leadership: Epistles of Maimonidies, trans. by Abraham Halkin, JPS, Philadelphia, 1985, P.121)

If one sees in a dream "a choice vine, he is to look for Messiah, because it says (Gen. 49:11), 'He binds his donkey to a vine and its foal to a choice vine.'" (Tal. Berachot 57a) Rashi says Targum Onkelos connects the prophecy about Judah in Gen. 49:11 — "binding a foal to the vine, and the colt of a donkey to the choice vine" — to King Messiah, the "choice vine" being Israel.

⁶The disciples went, did just as Yeshua commanded them, brought the donkey and the colt, and laid their garments on them. Then he sat on the garments. ⁸A very large crowd spread their garments on the road. Others cut branches from the trees, and spread them on the road. ⁹The crowds who went before him and who followed kept shouting, "Please deliver us by the Son of David! Blessed is he who comes in the Name of the Everpresent Lord! [Ps. 118:26] Please deliver us by the Most High!"

¹⁰When he had come into Yerushala'im, all the city was stirred up, saying, "Who is this?" ¹¹The multitudes said, "This is the prophet Yeshua, from Natzrat of the Galil."

¹²Yeshua entered into the Temple of God, drove out all of those who bought and sold in the Temple, and overthrew the tables of the money-changers and the seats of those who sold the doves. ¹³He said to them, "It is written, 'My house will be called a house of prayer,' [Is. 56:7] but you⁺ have made it a den of bandits." [Jer. 7:11]

¹⁴The blind and the lame came to him in the Temple, and he healed them. ¹⁵But the chief Kohanim and the Torah scholars were indignant when they saw the amazing things that he did and the children who were crying out in the Temple, "Please deliver us by the Son of David!"

¹⁶They said to him, "Do you hear what these are saying?"

Yeshua said to them, "Yes. Did you⁺ never read, 'Out of the mouth of infants and nursing babies You have established praise'?" [Ps. 8:2] ¹⁷He left them, and went out of the city to Beit Anya, and spent the night there.

¹⁸Now as he returned to the city in the morning, he was hungry. ¹⁹Seeing a fig tree by the road, he came to it, and found nothing but leaves on it. He said to it, "Let there be no fruit from you forever."

Immediately the fig tree withered away. ²⁰When the disciples saw it, they were amazed and said, "How did the fig tree immediately wither away?"

21:8-9,15 The waving branches and shouts of "Hoshanna!" — i.e. "Deliver us!" — are a normal part of the observance of Sukkot, which anticipates the coming of God's kingdom. It is, apparently, in that anticipation that the crowd has responded to Yeshua.

21:12-13 "This (Temple) market was what in Rabbinic writings is styled 'the bazaars of the sons of Annas' (*Chanuyoth beney Chanan*), the sons of that High-Priest Annas, who is so infamous in New Testament history... From the unrighteousness of the traffic carried on in these Bazaars, and the greed of the owners, the 'Temple-market' was at the time most unpopular. This appears, not only from the conduct and words of the patriarch Simeon [the grandson of Hillel, cf. Ker. i. 7] and of Baba ben Buta... [Jerus. Chag. 78a], but from the fact that popular indignation, three years before the destruction of Jerusalem, swept away the Bazaars of the family of Annas, and this, as expressly stated, on account of the sinful greed which characterized their dealings." (Alfred Edersheim, The Life and Times of Jesus the Messiah, Anson D.F. Randolph and Company, New York, 1883, Vol. I, Pp. 371-372)

21:18-22 (Mk. 11:12-14, 20-24) Yeshua cursed a fig tree which did not have any fruit when he looked for it. Since it was not the season for figs, why did he do this?

It is similar to the confrontation in Num. 17 over who is to be the High Priest, the Kohen Gadol. A rod to represent each tribe was put in the Tabernacle overnight. Aaron's name was written on the rod of the ››

²¹Yeshua answered them, "I assure you⁺ that if you⁺ have faith and do not doubt, you⁺ will not only do what is done to the fig tree, but even if you⁺ told this mountain, 'Be taken up and cast into the sea,' it would be done. ²²Whatever you⁺ ask in prayer believing, all this you⁺ will receive."

²³When he had come into the Temple, the chief Kohanim and the Elders of the people came to him as he was teaching, and said, "By what authority do you do these things? Who gave you this authority?"

²⁴Yeshua answered them, "I also will ask you⁺ one question, which if you⁺ tell me, I likewise will tell you⁺ by what authority I do these things. ²⁵The immersion of Yoḥanan, where was it from? From heaven or from men?"

They reasoned with each other, "If we say, 'From heaven,' he will ask us, 'Why then did you⁺ not believe him?' ²⁶But if we say, 'From men,' we fear the multitude, because everyone thinks of Yoḥanan as a prophet." ²⁷They answered Yeshua, and said, "We do not know."

He also said to them, "Neither will I tell you⁺ by what authority I do these things. ²⁸But what do you⁺ think? A man had two sons, and he came to the first, and said, 'Son, go work today in my vineyard.' ²⁹He answered, 'I will not,' but afterward he changed his mind, and went. ³⁰He came to the second, and said the same thing. He answered, 'I am going, sir,' but he did not go. ³¹Which of the two did the will of his father?"

They said to him, "The first."

Yeshua said to them, "I assure you⁺ that the tax collectors and the prostitutes are entering before you⁺ into God's kingdom. ³²For Yoḥanan came to you⁺ in the way of righteousness, and you⁺ did not believe him, but the tax collectors and the prostitutes believed him. Nevertheless, having seen it, you⁺ did not afterwards repent and believe him.

³³"Hear another parable. There was a man who was a ruler of a household, who planted a vineyard, set a hedge about it, dug a winepress in it, and built a tower. [Is. 5:1-2] He leased it out to farmers, and went into another country. ³⁴When the season for the fruit drew near, he sent his servants to

tribe of Levi. God said that the rod which blossomed overnight would indicate whom He had chosen to be the High Priest. In the natural order of things, none could be expected to blossom. All the rods were dead.

The next day it was seen that the rod of Aaron had supernaturally budded, blossomed, and borne fruit. The rods which represented the other tribes did not. The purpose of this sign was to demonstrate that God had chosen Aaron to be Kohen Gadol. What was natural was not sufficient. It was necessary to show by a supernatural demonstration who it was that God had chosen to exercise His authority.

The cursing of the fig tree may also serve to indicate that there are times when what is natural is simply not sufficient. As Sha'ul writes in 2Tim. 4:2, "Be ready in season and out of season."

The blood of the sin offering was sprinkled on the altar seven times (Lev.4:6); Naaman immersed himself in the Yarden River seven times (2Ki. 5:14); the righteous falls seven times and rises again (Prov. 24:16).

21:33-46 "What did the officers of Israel say to Pharaoh? (Ex. 5:16) *'Straw is not given to your servants... but it is your people's sin.* This means you have sinned against your people and you have sinned against your nation. And because of what you have done to yourself, the kingdom will be taken from you and given to another people.'" (Mid. Song of Songs 2:20)

≫≫

the farmers to receive his fruit. [35]The farmers took his servants, beat one, killed another, and stoned another. [36]Again he sent other servants, more than the first, and they treated them the same way. [37]But afterward he sent his son to them, saying, 'They will respect my son.' [38]But the farmers, when they saw the son, said among themselves, 'This is the heir. Come, let's kill him, and seize his inheritance.' [39]So they took him, and threw him out of the vineyard, and killed him. [40]So when the lord of the vineyard comes, what will he do to those farmers?"

[41]They told him, "He will destroy those evil men completely, and will lease out the vineyard to other farmers who will give him the fruit in its season."

[42]Yeshua said to them, "Did you[+] never read in the Scriptures, 'The stone which the builders rejected, it was made the head of the corner. This was from the Everpresent Lord. It is marvelous in our eyes'? [Ps. 118:22-23]

[43]"So I tell you[+] that God's kingdom will be taken away from you[+], and will be given to a people who will produce its fruits. [44]The one who falls on this stone will be broken, but on whomever it falls, it will scatter him as dust."

[45]When the chief Kohanim and the Perushim heard his parables, they understood that he spoke about them. [46]Though they were trying to arrest him, they feared the multitudes, because the multitudes considered him to be a prophet.

22 [1]Yeshua responded and spoke to them again in parables, saying, [2]"Heaven's kingdom is like a certain king who made a marriage feast for his son. [3]He sent out his servants to call those who were invited to the marriage feast, but they would not come. [4]Again he sent out other servants,

---

The text says explicitly that the parable was spoken against "the chief Kohanim and Elders... and Perushim". (vv. 23,45) They understood that Yeshua was saying that the kingdom would be taken away from them. They were unwilling to change their ways, but they could not act openly against him because they feared the people, who gladly received his teachings. This is what is spoken of in Ezek. 34:1-16.

Leaders are to be servants of those they lead. Their task is to enable the people to fulfill their identity and purpose. The reality of servant-leadership is not readily found in the political or religious governments of this world. (cf. Mt. 20:25, Eph. 4:11-12)

"For the house of Israel is the vineyard of the Everpresent Commander of forces, and the men of Judah are the plant of His delight. He expected justice/*mishpat*, but behold, oppression/*mishpakh*! righteousness/*tz'daka*, but behold, a cry/*tz'aka* [for help]!" (Is. 5:7)

In the Midrash on Psalms (2:17), there is an interesting parable: "[In another comment the verse is read *Do homage to the son*] (Ps. 2:12). What parable fits here? That of a king who became angry at the inhabitants of a certain city and the inhabitants of the city went and pleaded with the king's son to mollify the king. So he went and mollified his father. After the king was mollified by his son, the inhabitants of the city were about to sing a song of homage to the king. But the king said to them: "Is it to me that ye would sing a song of homage? Go and sing the song of homage to my son: had it not been for him, I would long ago have destroyed the inhabitants of this city.'" (The Midrash on Psalms, Vol. 1, trans. by William G. Braude, Yale U. Press, New Haven, 1959, P. 47)

22:1-5 "And even Solomon said in his wisdom, "Let your garments always be white; and do not let your head lack oil.' R. Johanan b. Zakkai said: 'This may be compared to a king who invited his servants to a >>

saying, 'Tell those who are invited, Look, I have prepared my dinner. My oxen and my fatlings are killed, and everything is ready. Come to the marriage feast.' ⁵But they paid no attention, and went their ways, one to his own farm, another to his merchandise. ⁶And the rest grabbed his servants, treated them disgracefully, and killed them. ⁷When the king heard that, he was angry. And he sent his armies, destroyed those murderers, and burned their city.

⁸"Then he said to his servants, 'The wedding is ready, but those who were invited were not worthy. ⁹So go to the intersections of the main roads, and invite to the marriage feast as many as you⁺ find.' ¹⁰Those servants went out to the roads, and gathered together as many as they found, both good and bad. The wedding was filled with guests. ¹¹But when the king came in to see the guests, he saw a man there who was not wearing appropriate clothes for the marriage feast. ¹²And he said to him, 'Friend, how did you come in here not wearing appropriate clothes for the marriage feast?' He was speechless. ¹³Then the king said to the servants, 'Bind him hand and foot, take him away, and throw him into the outer darkness where there will be weeping and gnashing of teeth.' ¹⁴For many are called, but few chosen."

¹⁵Then the Perushim went and thought about how they might trap him in what he said. ¹⁶They sent their disciples to him along with the Herodians, saying, "Rabbi, we know that you are true, and teach the way of God in truth. And you are not anxious concerning anyone because you do not see the appearance of men. [1Sam. 16:7] ¹⁷Tell us therefore, what do you think? Is it permitted to pay taxes to Caesar, or not?"

¹⁸But Yeshua perceived their malice, and said, "Pretenders, why do you⁺ test me? ¹⁹Show me the tax money."

They brought a denarius to him.

banquet, but did not appoint a time for them. The wise ones of them prepared themselves and sat at the door of the king's palace. They said, "Nothing is lacking in a king's palace." The foolish ones of them went about their work. They said, "There can be no banquet without preparation." Suddenly the king requested his servants [to come]. The wise of them entered before him because they were prepared. The foolish entered before him but were unpresentable. The king was happy to greet the wise, but angry to greet the foolish ones. He said, "Those who prepared themselves for the banquet, let them sit, eat, and drink. But those who did not prepare themselves for the banquet, let them stand and watch."" (Tal. Shab. 153a)

The Midrash on Ruth (Prologue II) says: "Israel was too preoccupied to show kindness to Joshua when he died. The land of Israel was divided, and the division took too much of their attention. All Israel was occupied in their regular work. One was occupied with his field, another was occupied with his vineyard, and another with his olive trees, and another with quarrying stones... They therefore did not show kindness to Joshua after his death, and the Holy One, blessed be He, sought to bring an earthquake upon all the inhabitants of the world."

22:8-10 "To take out a corpse [from the Temple] is a commandment for the priests. If there are no priests, Levites enter. If there are no Levites, any man of Israel enters. It is a commandment for the clean. If there are no clean ones, unclean people enter. It is a commandment for unblemished people. If there are no unblemished ones, blemished people enter." (Tos. Keilim 1:9)

²⁰He asked them, "Whose image and inscription is this?"

²¹They said to him, "Caesar's."

Then he said to them, "Then give back to Caesar the things that are Caesar's, and to God the things that are God's."

²²When they heard it, they were amazed. They left him, and went away.

²³On that day some Tzadukim — who say there is no resurrection — came to him and asked, ²⁴"Rabbi, Moses said, 'If a man dies having no children, his brother is to marry his wife, and raise up descendants for his brother.' [Dt. 25:5] ²⁵Now there were seven brothers with us. The first married and died. And having no descendants, he left his wife to his brother. ²⁶In like manner the second also, and the third, to the seventh. ²⁷After them all, the woman died. ²⁸So in the resurrection, whose wife of the seven will she be? For they all had her."

²⁹But Yeshua answered them, "You⁺ are mistaken, not knowing the Scriptures nor the power of God. ³⁰For in the resurrection they neither marry, nor are given in marriage, but are like the angels

---

22:23-32 Some modern scholars follow the Tzadukim in saying that resurrection is not taught in Tanakh, at least not until the book of Daniel. This is simply not true. Resurrection is taught throughout the Torah, Prophets, and Writings, as Yeshua's response indicates.

For example, in Torah, in response to Yosef's dream, Jacob says, "Shall your mother and I and your brothers indeed come to bow down to the earth before you?" (Gen. 37:10) But Rachel, Yosef's mother, was dead. Only after the resurrection could she bow down to him.

In the Writings, we are told that David believed, "I will live in the house of the Everpresent Lord forever [lit. "for a length of days]." (Ps. 23:6) But the house of the Everpresent Lord was not built on the earth until after David's death.

Or, as an example in the Prophets, the 37th chapter of Ezekiel: "Thus says the Everpresent Lord God: 'Look, My people, I will open your graves, cause you to come up from your graves, and bring you into the land of Israel. Then you will know that I am the Everpresent Lord, because I have opened your graves, O My people, and caused you to come up from your graves." vv. 12-13

Someone might say, 'But that is just a metaphor.' Yes it is, but what is the metaphor? ¿that God brought decaying corpses up from their graves and put them on the surface of the land? No, rather that God restored the dead to wholeness and to life. As He promises in Is. 26:19, "Your dead will live — My dead body — they will arise. Awake and sing, you+ who dwell in the dust; for your dew is as the dew of herbs, and the earth will cast out the departed spirits."

There is also the explicit statement of Hannah in her prayer: "The Everpresent Lord kills and makes alive; He brings down to the grave and brings up." (1 Sam. 2:6)

"When all the blessings in the Temple were completed, they would say, 'for ever.' When the Tzadukim erred and said there is only one age, it was established that they would say, 'from everlasting to everlasting.'" (Tal. Berachot Mishnah IX.1 , 54a) "All Israel have a portion [in the age to come] except... he who maintains there is no resurrection of the dead [taught] from the Torah, and there is no Torah from Heaven..." (Tal. Sanhedrin Mishnah 11:1) In Sanhedrin 91b, the Rabbis point to a variety of verses to prove that resurrection is taught in Torah.

of God in heaven. [31]But concerning the resurrection of the dead, haven't you[+] read what was spoken to you[+] by God, [32]'I am the God of Abraham, and the God of Isaac, and the God of Jacob?' [Ex. 3:6] God is not the God of the dead, but of the living."

[33]When the multitudes heard it, they were astonished at his teaching. [34]But when the Perushim heard that he had put the Tzadukim to silence, they gathered themselves together. [35]One of them, a Torah scholar, asked him a question, testing him. [36]"Rabbi, which is the greatest commandment in the Torah?"

[37]Yeshua said to him, "'You are to love the Everpresent Lord, your God, with all your heart, and with all your soul, and with all your mind.' [Dt. 6:5] [38]This is the first and great commandment. [39]And a second is like it: 'You are to love your neighbor as yourself.' [Lev. 19:18] [40]The entire Torah and the prophets are hung upon these two commandments."

[41]Now while the Perushim were gathered together, Yeshua asked them a question, [42]"What do you[+] think of the Messiah, whose son is he?"

They said to him, "David's."

[43]He said to them, "How then does David, by the Spirit, call him 'Lord,' saying, [44]'The Everpresent Lord said to my Lord, Sit on My right hand, until I make your enemies a footstool for your feet?' [Ps. 110:1] [45]If David calls him 'Lord,' then how is he his son?"

[46]No one was able to answer him a word, nor did anyone dare from that day on to ask him any more questions.

23 [1]Then Yeshua said to the crowds and to his disciples, [2]"The Torah scholars and the Perushim have been sitting on the seat of Moses. [3]So do and observe all things that they tell you[+], but do not do according to their deeds, because they say, and do not do. [4]For they tie up heavy burdens that are hard to bear, and lay them upon men's shoulders, but they themselves will not lift a finger to help them. [Is. 58:6] [5]And they do all their works to be seen by men. They make their tefillin broad, and enlarge the tzitzit of their garments. [6]They love the place of honor at feasts, the best seats in the

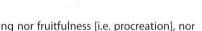

22:30 "In the Age to Come, there is neither eating nor drinking nor fruitfulness [i.e. procreation], nor increase [i.e. business], nor burden nor giving, nor jealousy nor hatred nor rivalry..." Tal Berachot 17a)

22:40 The Midrash Sifra, Kedoshim, says that "all the congregation" (Lev. 19:1) teaches that "the multitude of the body of Torah is hung upon it," i.e. upon the core of the chapter.

23:2-3 See "The Seat of Moses" in the ADDITIONAL NOTES. Some manuscripts of the medieval Hebrew translation of Shem Tov ibn Shafrut have: "The Perushim and the Sages are seated on the seat of Moses. And now, all that he says to you, observe and do; but do not do according to their reforms and their deeds, since they are ones who say, but they are not ones who do." (The original text is not in bold.)

23:6-7 "Everyone who gives his daughter to a disciple of the wise, or does business for the disciples of the wise, or makes it pleasant for the disciples of the wise from his riches is regarded by Scripture as if he had clung to the Shekhinah." (Tal. Ketubot 111b, cf. Tal.Sanhedrin 99a) According to the Rabbis, there is greater reward for one who feeds and supports one of their disciples than for one who houses the ark of the Tabernacle. (cf. Tal. Berachot 63b) "R. Johanan said: Whoever throws his posssessions into the pockets of the disciples of the wise will merit to sit in the Heavenly Yeshiva." (Tal. Pesaḥim 53b)

>>

meetingplaces, [7]the greetings in the marketplaces, and to be called 'Rabbi' by men. [8]But don't you[+] be called 'Rabbi,' because one is your[+] teacher, the Messiah, and all of you[+] are brothers. [9]Call no man on the earth your[+] 'Father,' because one is your[+] Father — He who is in heaven. [10]Neither be called 'Masters,' for one is your[+] Master, the Messiah. [11]But the greatest among you[+] will be your[+] servant. [12]Whoever exalts himself will be humbled, and whoever humbles himself will be exalted.

[13]"Woe to you[+] Torah scholars and Perushim, pretenders! For you[+] shut up Heaven's kingdom in front of the people! But you[+] do not enter in, and you[+] do not permit those who are entering to enter! [14]

[15]"Woe to you[+] Torah scholars and Perushim, pretenders! For you[+] travel around by sea and land to make one proselyte, and when he becomes one, you[+] make him twice as much a son of Gehinnom as yourselves!

[16]"Woe to you[+] blind guides who say, 'Whoever swears by the Temple, it is nothing; but whoever swears by the gold of the Temple, he is obligated.' [17]Blind fools! For which is greater, the gold or the Temple that sanctifies the gold? [18]And 'Whoever swears by the altar, it is nothing; but whoever swears by the gift that is on it, he is obligated.' [19]You[+] are blind! For which is greater, the gift or the altar that sanctifies the gift? [20]Therefore the one who swears by the altar swears by it, and by everything on it. [21]The one who swears by the Temple swears by it, and by Him who inhabits it. [22]The one who swears by heaven swears by the throne of God, and by Him who sits on it.

"Everyone who is not generous to the disciples of the wise in this age, his eyes will be filled with smoke in the age to come." (Tal. Baba Bathra 75a)

23:7-8 At the time, "Rabbi" was an honorific title, not a job description. Rabban Yohanan ben Zakkai, after the destruction of the Second Temple, is the first individual to be called by this title in the Talmud. But the Talmud does project the title back into earlier times, as in Tal. Makkot 24a: "He honors those who fear the Everpresent Lord.' [Ps. 15:4] This was Yehoshaphat, king of Judah, who, whenever he saw a disciple of the Sages, stood from his throne and hugged him and kissed him, and called him 'Father, Father,' and 'Rabbi, Rabbi,' and 'Lord, Lord.'"

23:13-36 A passage in Tal. Sotah 22b speaks of seven types of Perushim, including those who do the right thing for the wrong motive, those who show false humility, those who are eager to do some commandments but blind to others, those who think they have obeyed all the commandments, and those who seek to please God from love of Him. The discussion concludes: "King Yannai said to his wife, 'Do not be afraid of the Perushim nor of those who are not Perushim, but the ones of multiple appearances, who seem like the Perushim, and though their deeds are those of Zimri yet they seek a reward like Pinchas.'" [Num. 25:11-13]

"There are ten portions of pretension in the world, nine in Jerusalem and one in all [the rest of] the world." (Mid. Esther 1.17)

23:14 The UBS does not include this verse: [14]"Woe to you[+] Torah scholars and Perushim, pretenders! Because you[+] devour widows' houses, and as a pretense you[+] make long prayers. Therefore you[+] will receive greater condemnation!

²³"Woe to you⁺ Torah scholars and Perushim, pretenders! For you⁺ give the tenth of mint, dill, and cummin, yet have left undone the weightier matters of the Torah: justice, mercy, and faith! But it is necessary to do these things, and not to have left the other undone. [Mi. 6:8] ²⁴Blind guides who strain out a gnat, and swallow a camel!

²⁵"Woe to you⁺ Torah scholars and Perushim, pretenders! For you⁺ clean the outside of the cup and of the platter, but within they are full of extortion and self-indulgence! ²⁶Blind Parush! First clean the inside of the cup and of the platter, so that the outside of it may become clean also.

²⁷"Woe to you⁺ Torah scholars and Perushim, pretenders! For you⁺ are like whitened tombs which outwardly appear beautiful, but inwardly are full of dead men's bones and all uncleanness. ²⁸Even so you⁺ also outwardly appear righteous to men, but inwardly you⁺ are full of pretense and opposition to the Torah.

²⁹"Woe to you⁺ Torah scholars and Perushim, pretenders! For you⁺ build the tombs of the prophets, decorate the tombs of the righteous, ³⁰and say, 'If we had lived in the days of our fathers, we would not have been partakers with them in the blood of the prophets.' ³¹By this you⁺ testify of yourselves that you⁺ are children of those who killed the prophets. ³²And you⁺ fill up the measure of your⁺ fathers. ³³Serpents, offspring of vipers, how will you⁺ escape the judgment of Gehinnom?

³⁴"Therefore I am sending prophets, wise men, and Torah scholars to you⁺! Some of them you⁺ will kill and hang on the stake; and some of them you will scourge in your⁺ meetingplaces and persecute from city to city. ³⁵In this way, all the righteous blood shed on the earth will come upon you⁺, from the blood of the righteous Hevel [Gen. 4:10] to the blood of Zeharyah son of Berekhyah, whom you⁺ killed between the sanctuary and the altar. [2Ch. 24:20-21] ³⁶I assure you⁺ that all these things will come upon this generation.

³⁷"Yerushala'im, Yerushala'im, who kills the prophets, and stones those who are sent to her. How often I wanted to gather your children together, even as a bird gathers her young under her wings,

23:23 Yeshua provides this key: the function of God's Law is judgment, mercy, and faith.

23:25-26 "Beth Hillel says, 'The outside of the cup is always unclean.'" (Tos. Berakhot 5:26)

23:35 "R. Yudan asked R. Aha, 'Where did they kill Zeharyah, in the Court of Israel or the Court of Women?' He replied, 'Not in the Court of Israel or in the Court of Women, but in the Court of the Priests. ...Israel committed seven transgressions on that day: they killed a priest, a prophet, and a judge, and shed innocent blood, they profaned the Divine Name, they defiled the Temple Court, and it was on sabbath and the Day of Atonement.'" (Mid. Ekah Rabbah 4:16)

"Berekhyah" means "the Everpresent Lord blesses". It may be a characterization rather than a name, referring to the faithful priest of 2 Chr. 22-24. His son Zeharyah was stoned at the command of King Joash. (2 Chr. 24:20-21)

Josephus, The Jewish War 4:335-344, refers to the murder of Zeharyah ben Baruch by the zealots in the Temple.

23:37-39 In the Musaf Shabbat service, for Rosh Hodesh, we say, "Because we sinned against You, we and our fathers, our city is destroyed, and our holy House is desolate, our precious things are exiled, and the glory of the House of our life is lifted. Therefore we are not able to do our duty in Your chosen House, >>

and you[+] did not want it. [Ruth 2:12; Ps. 17:8; 61:4; 91:4] [38]Listen, your[+] house is left to you[+] desolate. [Jer. 26:9] [39]For I tell you[+] that you[+] will no longer see me, until you[+] say, 'Blessed is he who comes in the Name of the Everpresent Lord.'" [Ps. 118:26; Hos. 5:15-6:3]

24 [1]Yeshua went out from the Temple, and was going on his way. His disciples came to him to draw his attention to the buildings of the Temple. [2]But he answered them, "You[+] see all of these things, don't you[+]? I assure you[+] that there will not be left here one stone on another, that will not be thrown down."

[3]As he sat on the Mount of Olives, the disciples came to him privately, saying, "Tell us, when will these things be? What is the sign of your coming, and of the culmination of the age?"

[4]Yeshua answered them, "Be careful that no one leads you[+] astray, [5]because many will come in my

---

in the great and holy house on which Your Name is called, because of the hand that was sent out against Your holy Sanctuary."

"Its destruction brings atonement. The Shekhinah does not return until it has been made a mountain [without the Temple]." (Tos. Berakhot 1:16)

"The 70 bulls [offered during Sukkot] represent the 70 nations... When the Temple stood, the altar atoned for them, but now who will atone for them?" (Tal. Sukkah 55b) "And everyone who mourns for her [Yerushala'im] in this age will rejoice with her in the age to come." (Tosefta Sotah 15:15, cf. Ps. 137:5-6)

23:39 The Amidah contains the prayer: "Return in compassion to Your city Yerushala'im and live in it as You have spoken. And build it soon in our days, an eternal building. And quickly establish in it the throne of David.... Quckly cause the Branch of David Your servant to sprout, and exalt his strength in Your salvation.... May our eyes envision Your return to Zion with compassion. Blessed are You, Everpresent Lord, who returns His divine presence to Zion." Ps. 118:26 is part of the morning service Hallel for the major holy days and the beginning of the month.

"As the gazelle appears and then returns and is hidden, so the first redeemer [Moses] appeared and then was hidden.... Like the first redeemer, so will the final redeemer [Messiah] be." (Mid. Num. 11:2, cf. Mid. Ruth 5:6) "And everyone who mourns for her [Yerushala'im] in this age will rejoice with her in the age to come." (Tosefta Sotah 15:15, cf. Ps. 137:5-6)

24:1-3 "The one who has not seen Herod's building has not seen a beautiful building. Of what did he build it? Rabbah said: 'Of stones of yellow and white. Some say stones of blue, yellow and white.'" (Tal. Baba Bathra 4a)

"Caesar gave orders that they should now demolish the entire city and Temple. ...it was so thoroughly laid even with the ground by those that dug it up to the foundation, that there was left nothing to make those who came there believe it had ever been inhabited." (Josephus, The Jewish War, 7.1.1.1-3)

"Woe to the children on account of whose iniquities I destroyed My House and burned My Temple and exiled them among the peoples of the world." (Tal. Berachot 3a)

In Mid. Ekah Rabbah 1:51, we read: "It happened that a certain man was standing and plowing, and his ox lowed before him. A certain Arab was passing and said, 'What are you?' 'I am a Jew.' He [the Arab] said to him, 'Loose your ox and loose thy plow, because the temple of the Jews has been made desolate.' ...The ox lowed again, and he [the Arab] said to him [the Jew], 'Bind your ox, and bind your plow, because the deliverer of the Jews is born.'"

name, saying, 'I am the Messiah,' and will lead many astray. [6]You[+] will hear of wars and war reports. See that you[+] are not troubled, because all this must happen, but it is not yet the end. [7]For peoples will rise against each other, and kingdoms against each other; and there will be famines, plagues, and earthquakes in various places. [2Esd. 8:3-4] [8]But all these things are the beginning of birth pains. [9]Then they will deliver you[+] up to affliction, and will kill you[+]. You[+] will be hated by all the nations for my name's sake. [10]Then many will stumble, and will deliver up one another, and will hate one another. [11]Many false prophets will arise, and will lead many astray. [12]The love of many will grow cold because of the spread of unlawful behavior. [13]But the one who endures to the end, that one will be saved. [14]This good news of the kingdom will be proclaimed in the whole world for a testimony to all the nations, and then the end will come.

[15]"So when you[+] see the abomination of desolation which was spoken of through Daniel the prophet standing in the holy place (let the reader understand) [Dan. 9:27,11:31,12:11; 1Macc. 1:54,6:7], [16]then let those who are in Judea flee to the mountains. [17]Let the one who is on the housetop not go down to take out things that are in his house. [18]Let the one who is in the field not return to get his clothes. [19]But woe to those who are with child and to nursing mothers in those days! [20]Pray that your[+] flight will not be in the winter, nor on Shabbat, [21]for then there will be great affliction such as has not been from the beginning of the world until now; no, nor ever will be. [Dan. 12:1] [22]Unless those days had been shortened, no flesh would have been saved. But for the sake of those who are chosen, those days will be shortened.

[23]"If any man then tells you[+], 'Look, here is the Messiah,' or, 'There,' do not believe it. [24]For there will arise false messiahs, and false prophets, and they will show great signs and wonders, so as to lead astray, if possible, even those who are chosen.

[25]"Listen, I have told you[+] beforehand. [26]So if they tell you[+], 'Look, he is in the wilderness,' do not go out; 'Look, he is in the inner rooms,' do not believe it. [27]For as the lightning comes forth from the east and is seen even to the west, so the appearing of the Son of Adam will be. [28]Where there is a carcass, there the vultures will be gathered together. [Job 39:27-30]

[subject switch]

[apostate church unburied]

24:7 "When you see the kingdoms terrorizing one another, be on the lookout for the feet [i.e. the coming] of Messiah." (Mid. Genesis 42.4)

24:13 "At the end of days He will send His Messiah to redeem those who wait for the end of His salvation." (Yigdal 12)

24:21-22 "R. Johanan said, 'When you see a generation with many troubles come upon it as a river, wait for him, as it is said, *When the enemy will come like a forceful river, the Spirit of the Everpresent Lord will lift up a standard against him*; which is followed by, *And a redeemer will come to Zion.*' [Is.59:19-20]... R. Yohanan said the same, 'Let him come, but let me not see him.' ... because it is written, Ask now, and see whether a male travails in childbirth? Why do I see every man with his hands on his loins as a woman in childbirth, and all faces have turned pale? [Jer.30:6] " (Tal. Sanhedrin 98a-b)

Maimonides said, "He will be sent by God at a time of great catastrophe and dire misfortune for Israel... A later prophet too was alluding to the Messianic tribulations when he declared 'But who can endure the day of his coming?' (Malachi 3:2)." (Iggeret Teman 15, trans. by Boaz Cohen, http://en.wikisource.org/wiki/Epistle_to_Yemen/XV)

²⁹"But immediately after the affliction of those days, the sun will be darkened, the moon will not give its light, the stars will fall from heaven [Is. 13:10, 24:23, Ezek. 32:7, Joel 2:10, 31, 3:15, Amos 5:20, Zeph. 1:15], and the powers of the heavens will be shaken. ³⁰And then the sign of the Son of Adam will appear in the heavens. Then all the tribes of the land will mourn, and they will see the Son of Adam coming on the clouds of heaven with power and great glory. [Zech. 12:10] ³¹He will send out his angels with a great sound of a shofar [Zech. 9:14], and they will gather together his chosen from the four winds, from one end of the heavens to the other.

³²"Now learn this parable from the fig tree. When its branch has already become tender, and it puts forth its leaves, you⁺ know that the summer is near. ³³Even so you⁺ also, when you⁺ see all these things, know that it is near, even at the doors. ³⁴I assure you⁺ that this people will not pass away even with the coming of all these things. [Jer. 31:35-36] ³⁵Heaven and earth will pass away, but my words will not pass away. ³⁶But no one knows of that day and hour, not even the angels of heaven, but my Father only.

³⁷"As the days of Noah were, so will the coming of the Son of Adam be. ³⁸For they were eating and drinking, marrying and giving in marriage in those days which were before the flood, until the day that Noah entered into the ark. ³⁹And they did not know until the flood came and took them all away. So the coming of the Son of Adam will also be. ⁴⁰Then two men will be in the field; one will be taken and one will be left. ⁴¹Two women will be grinding at the mill; one will be taken and one will be left. ⁴²Therefore, be alert! because you⁺ do not know in what day your⁺ Lord comes. ⁴³But know this, that if the master of the house had known in what watch of the night the thief was coming, he would have been alert, and would not have allowed his house to be broken into. ⁴⁴Therefore you⁺ also be ready, because the Son of Adam will come in an hour that you⁺ do not anticipate.

⁴⁵"Who then is the faithful and wise servant whom his lord has set over his household to give them their food in due season? ⁴⁶There is good for that servant whom his lord finds doing this when he comes. ⁴⁷I assure you⁺ that he will set him over all that he has. ⁴⁸But if that evil servant should say in

---

24:29 "The Rabbis taught: 'In the time of an eclipse, it is a bad sign for all the entire world.'" (Tal. Sukkah 29a)

24:32-34 In "The Revelation of Peter," which was considered canonical in the second century, Yeshua says explicitly, "Don't you understand that the fig-tree is the house of Israel? ...Haven't you understood that the fig-tree is the house of Israel? I faithfully say to you, when the twigs of it have sprouted forth in the last days, then shall feigned Messiahs come and awake expectation saying: 'I am the Messiah, who is now come into the world.' ...Then the twigs of the fig-tree, that is, the house of Israel, will shoot forth."

"There is no greater sign for you of redemption than this: 'And you mountains of Israel, you will send out your branches and give your fruit to My people Israel, for they are about to come.' (Ezek. 36:8)" (Tal. Sanhedrin 98a)

24:34 In the Scriptures, *genea* is usually translated as "generation". In this verse, it would refer to the generation that sees the things Yeshua has just described. I have translated it here in accordance with what Liddell and Scott give as its first meaning: "persons in a family". For *genea* as "people" or "kindred," see God's promise to Jacob in LXX Gen. 31:3.

his heart, 'My lord is delaying his coming,' [49]and begin to beat his fellow-servants, and eat and drink with the drunkards, [50]the lord of that servant will come on a day when he does not expect it, and in an hour which he does not know. [51]And he will cut him in pieces, and his portion will be with the pretenders. There will be weeping and gnashing of teeth there.

25 [1]"Heaven's kingdom will then be like ten virgins who took their lamps and went out to meet the bridegroom. [2]Five of them were foolish, and five were wise. [3]Those who were foolish, took no oil with them when they took their lamps. [4]But the wise took oil in their containers with their lamps. [5]Now while the bridegroom delayed, they all became drowsy and slept. [6]But at midnight there was a cry, 'Look, the bridegroom is coming! Come out to meet him!' [7]Then all those virgins arose, and trimmed their lamps. [8]The foolish said to the wise, 'Give us some of your[+] oil, because our lamps are going out.' [9]But the wise answered, 'No, or there might not be enough for us and for you[+]. Go instead to those who sell, and buy for yourselves.' [10]While they went away to buy, the bridegroom came, and those who were ready went in with him to the marriage feast, and the door was shut. [11]Afterward the other virgins also came, saying, 'Lord, lord, open to us.' [12]But he answered, 'I assure you[+] that I do not know you[+].' [13]Therefore, be alert! for you[+] do not know the day or the hour.

[14]"For it is like a man going into another country who called his own servants and entrusted his goods to them. [15]He gave five silver talents to one, two to another, one to another — to each according to his own ability. Then he went on his journey. [16]Immediately the one who received the five silver talents went and traded with them, and made another five silver talents. [17]In the same way the one who got the two also gained another two. [18]But the one who received the one went away and dug in the earth, and hid his lord's money.

[19]"Now after a long time the lord of those servants came, and settled accounts with them. [20]The one who received the five silver talents came and brought another five silver talents, saying, 'Lord, you delivered to me five silver talents. Look, I have gained another five silver talents besides them.'

[21]"His lord said to him, 'Well done, good and faithful servant. You have been faithful over a few things, I will set you over many things. Enter into the joy of your lord.'

[22]"And the one who had received the two silver talents came and said, 'Lord, you delivered to me two silver talents. Look, I have gained another two silver talents besides them.'

[23]"His lord said to him, 'Well done, good and faithful servant. You have been faithful over a few things, I will set you over many things. Enter into the joy of your lord.'

[24]"And the one who had received the one silver talent came and said, 'Lord, I knew you, that you are a hard man, reaping where you did not sow, and gathering where you did not scatter. [25]I was afraid, and went away and hid your silver talent in the earth. Look, you have what is yours.'

[26]"But his lord answered him, 'You wicked and lazy servant. Did you know that I reap where I did not sow, and gather where I did not scatter? [27]Then you ought to have deposited my money with the

25:15 "to each according to his own ability" Karl Marx changed this to "From each according to his ability, to each according to his needs." Marx, Lenin, and Stalin were all familiar with the Scriptures. Stalin studied at the Georgian Orthodox seminary in Tiflis/Tbilisi. They rejected God, but modified and adopted some of His principles.

moneylenders. Then, at my coming, I would have received back my own with interest. [28]So take away the silver talent from him, and give it to the one who has the ten silver talents. [29]For to everyone who has will be given, and he will have abundance. But from the one who does not have, even what he has will be taken away. [30]Throw out the unprofitable servant into the outer darkness, where there will be weeping and gnashing of teeth.'

[31]"But when the Son of Adam comes in his glory, and all the holy angels with him, then he will sit on the throne of his glory. [32]All the Gentiles will be gathered before him, and he will separate them one from another, as a shepherd separates the sheep from the goats. [33]He will set the sheep on his right hand, but the goats on the left. [34]Then the King will tell those on his right hand, 'Come, blessed of my Father, inherit the kingdom prepared for you[+] from the foundation of the world. [35]For I was hungry, and you[+] gave me food to eat. I was thirsty, and you[+] gave me drink. I was a stranger, and you[+] took me in; [36]naked, and you[+] clothed me. I was sick, and you[+] visited me. I was in prison, and you[+] came to me.'

[37]"Then the righteous will answer him, 'Lord, when did we see you hungry, and feed you; or thirsty, and give you a drink? [38]When did we see you as a stranger, and take you in? or naked, and clothe you? [39]When did we see you sick, or in prison, and come to you?'

[40]"The King will answer them, 'I assure you[+] that inasmuch as you[+] did it to one of the least of these brothers of mine, you[+] did it to me.' [41]Then he will also say to those on the left hand, 'Depart from me, you[+] who are cursed, into the eternal fire which is prepared for the Enemy and his angels. [42]For I was hungry, and you[+] did not give me food to eat. I was thirsty, and you[+] gave me no drink. [43]I was a stranger, and you[+] did not take me in; naked, and you[+] did not clothe me. I was sick, and in prison, and you[+] did not visit me.'

25:31-46 When the Son of Adam returns to redeem Israel and establish his kingdom, he will judge the Gentiles according to God's promise to Abraham, Jacob, and all Israel: "I will bless those who bless you, and curse those who curse you." (Gen. 12:3, 27:29, Num. 24:9) The acts of mercy which Yeshua mentions should be done for anyone, but there have been times in Jewish history when those who showed such mercy to Jews did so at the risk of their lives and the lives of their families.

"R. Hama son of R. Hanina said: 'What is the meaning of the text: You are to walk after the Everpresent your God? [Dt. 13:5] ... to walk after the attributes of the Holy One, blessed be He. As He clothes the naked, for it is written: And the Everpresent Lord made for Adam and for his wife coats of skin, and clothed them. Even so, you are to clothe the naked. The Holy One, blessed be He, visits the sick, for it is written: And the Everpresent Lord appeared unto him by the oaks of Mamre. Even so you are to visit the sick. The Holy One, blessed be He, comforts mourners, for it is written: And it came to pass after the death of Abraham, that God blessed Isaac his son. Even so, you are to comfort mourners. The Holy one, blessed be He, buries the dead, for it is written: And He buried him in the valley. Even so you are to bury the dead.'" (Tal. Sotah 14a)

"'Open to me the gates of righteousness' [Ps. 118:19]. In the age to come, they will ask a man, 'What was your work?' When he answers: 'I fed the hungry,' then they will say to him, 'This is the gate of the Everpresent Lord (v.20). You who fed the hungry, enter into it.'" (Mid. Psalms 118.17) This is repeated for "I gave drink to the thirty," "I clothed the naked," and for "the one who brought up the fatherless, and to those who gave humanitarian aid and also those who did deeds of lovingkindness."

⁴⁴"Then they will also answer, 'Lord, when did we see you hungry, or thirsty, or a stranger, or naked, or sick, or in prison, and did not help you?' ⁴⁵"Then he will answer them, 'I assure you⁺ that inasmuch as you⁺ did not do it to one of the least of these, you⁺ did not do it to me.' ⁴⁶These will go away into eternal punishment, but the righteous into eternal life." [Gen. 12:3, 27:29; Num. 24:9, Dan. 12:1-2]

26 ¹When Yeshua had finished all these words, he said to his disciples, ²"You⁺ know that after two days Pesakh is coming; then the Son of Adam will be delivered up to be put to death on the tree."

³Then the chief Kohanim and the Elders of the people were gathered together in the court of the Kohen Gadol, who was called Kayafa. ⁴They took counsel together so that they might take Yeshua by deceit, and kill him. ⁵But they said, "Not during the feast, so a riot doesn't occur among the people."

⁶Now when Yeshua was in Beit Anya, in the house of Shimon the leper, a woman came to him, having an alabaster jar of very expensive ointment. And she poured it on his head as he sat at the table. ⁸But when his disciples saw this, they were indignant, saying, "Why this waste? ⁹For this ointment might have been sold for a large sum, and given to the poor."

¹⁰But knowing this, Yeshua said to them, "Why do you⁺ trouble the woman? For she has done a good work for me. ¹¹You⁺ always have the poor with you⁺ [Dt. 15:11], but you⁺ do not always have me. ¹²For in putting this ointment on my body, she did it to prepare me for burial. ¹³I assure you⁺ that wherever this good news is proclaimed in the whole world, what this woman has done will also be spoken of as a memorial to her."

¹⁴Then one of the twelve, who was called Judah from K'riyot, went to the chief Kohanim ¹⁵and said, "What are you⁺ willing to give me so that I deliver him to you⁺?" They weighed out for him thirty pieces of silver. ¹⁶From that time he sought an opportunity to deliver him up.

¹⁷Now on the first day of Matzot [Ex.12:14-17], the disciples came to Yeshua, saying to him, "Where do you want us to prepare for you to eat the Pesakh?"

¹⁸He said, "Go into the city to a certain man, and tell him, 'The Teacher says, *My time is near. I will keep Pesakh at your house with my disciples.*'"

¹⁹The disciples did as Yeshua commanded them, and they prepared the Pesakh. ²⁰Now when evening had come, he was reclining at the table with the twelve disciples. ²¹As they were eating, he said, "I assure you⁺ that one of you⁺ will deliver me up."

²²They were extremely grieved, and each began to say to him, "Surely not I, Lord!"

26:3-5 The Talmud speaks of how these High Priests robbed the common priests of their due, and disregarded all appeals to restrain themselves. (e.g. Tal. Pesachim 57a) Josephus speaks of them as violent men, greedy for money and power. (Antiquities of the Jews, XX, 9, 2-4)

26:5 The consistent testimony of the Scriptures is that the people were very supportive of Yeshua. Here we are told that the leaders were afraid that if they arrested him, the people would riot. See "The People Came to Him," in my The Separation of Church and Faith: Copernicus and the Jews.

26:18 It seems that Yeshua specified a particular person, but the name was not included in the recorded text.

[23]He responded, "The one who dipped his hand with me in the dish, the same will deliver me up. [24]The Son of Adam goes away, even as it is written of him, but woe to that man through whom the Son of Adam is delivered up. It would be better for that man if he had not been born."

[25]Judah, who was delivering him up, said, "Surely not I, Rabbi!"

He said to him, "You have said it."

[26]As they were eating, Yeshua took bread, said a blessing, and broke it. He gave to the disciples, and said, "Take, eat. This is my body."

[27]He took a cup, gave thanks, and gave to them, saying, "All of you[+] drink it, [28]for this is my blood of the new covenant, which is poured out for many for the forgiveness of sins. [29]But I tell you[+] that I will not drink of this fruit of the vine from now on, until that day when I drink it anew with you[+] in my Father's kingdom." [30]When they had sung praises, they went out to the Mount of Olives.

[31]Then Yeshua said to them, "Tonight, all of you[+] will be caused to stumble because of me, for it is written, 'I will strike the shepherd, and the sheep of the flock will be scattered.' [Zech. 13:7] [32]But after I am raised up, I will go before you[+] into the Galil."

[33]But Kefa answered him, "Even if all are caused to stumble because of you, I will never be made to stumble."

[34]Yeshua said to him, "I tell you faithfully that this very night, before the rooster calls out, you will completely deny me three times."

[35]Kefa said to him, "Even if I must die with you, I will never deny you." All of the disciples also said the same.

[36]Then Yeshua came with them to a place called Gat Shemanim, and said to his disciples, "Sit here, while I go there and pray." [37]He took with him Kefa and the two sons of Zevadyah, and began to be sorrowful and severely troubled. [38]Then he said to them, "My soul is extremely sorrowful, even to death. Stay here and keep watch with me."

[39]He went forward a little, went down on his face, and prayed, "My Father, if it is possible, let this cup pass away from me; nevertheless, not as I desire, but as You desire."

26:24 "Everyone who does not seek refuge in the honor of the One to whom he belongs, it would be better for him if he had not come into the world." (Tal. Hagigah 16a)

26:28 The New Covenant of the Scriptures, Jer. 31:31-34/Heb. 8:8-12, is an affirmation of God's faithfulness to Israel.

26:30 As Pesakh is traditionally observed, the "Hallel," or "Praise," consisting of several psalms, is sung just before the close of the seder.

26:34 The Hebrew word *gever* can mean either "rooster" or "man". There was a man in the Temple who cried out in the morning to begin the service of the Temple. "What does *keri'ath ha-geber* mean? Rab said, 'The call of a man,' R. Shila said, 'The call of the rooster.' ...There is a teaching in accord with Rab: What does Gebini the Temple crier say? 'You priests, stand for your service, Levites to your platform, Israel to your post!' And his voice was audible for three parasangs. ...From Yerushala'im to Yeriho is ten parasangs..." (Tal. Yoma 20b:)

[40]He came to the disciples, and found them sleeping. Then he said to Kefa, "Even so, could you not keep watch with me for one hour? [41]Keep watch and pray that you⁺ do not enter into temptation. The spirit indeed is willing, but the flesh is weak."

[42]Again, he went away a second time and prayed, "My Father, if this cup cannot pass away from me unless I drink it, Your desire be done." [43]He came again and found them sleeping, because their eyes were heavy. [44]He left them again, went away, and prayed a third time, saying the same words. [45]Then he came to his disciples, and said to them, "Sleep on now, and take your⁺ rest. The hour has come near, and the Son of Adam is delivered into the hands of sinners! [46]Arise, let us be going. Look, the one who delivers me up has come near."

[47]While he was still speaking, Judah came, one of the twelve, and with him a large multitude from the Kohen Gadol and Elders of the people, with swords and clubs! [48]Now the one who delivered him up had given them a sign, saying, "Whomever I kiss, he is the one. Seize him."

[49]Immediately he came to Yeshua, saying, "Greetings, Rabbi," and kissed him.

[50]Yeshua said to him, "Friend, why are you here?" Then they came and laid hands on Yeshua, and took him. [51]One of those with Yeshua stretched out his hand, drew his sword and struck the servant of the Kohen Gadol, taking off his ear! [52]Then Yeshua said to him, "Put your sword back into its place, because all those who take up the sword will be destroyed by the sword. [53]Or do you think that I am unable to ask my Father now, and He would send me more than twelve legions of angels? [54]How then would the Scriptures be fulfilled that it must happen this way?"

[55]In that hour Yeshua said to the crowd, "Have you⁺ come out with swords and clubs, as against a bandit, to arrest me? I sat daily in the Temple teaching, and you⁺ did not arrest me. [56]But all this has happened so that the writings of the prophets might be given fullness."

Then all the disciples left him, and fled. [57]Those who had taken Yeshua led him away to Kayafa the Kohen Gadol, where the Torah scholars and the Elders were gathered together. [58]But Kefa followed him from a distance to the court of the Kohen Gadol, entered in, and sat with the officers to see the outcome. [59]Now the chief Kohanim, the Elders, and the whole Council sought false testimony against Yeshua that they might put him to death; [60]but they found none. Many false witnesses came forward, but at last two came forward [61]and said, "This man said, 'I am able to destroy the Temple of God, and build it in three days.'"

[62]The Kohen Gadol stood up and said to him, "Have you no answer? What is this that these testify against you?" [63]But Yeshua held his peace. The Kohen Gadol said to him, "By the living God, I put you under oath that you tell us whether you are the Messiah, the Son of God."

[64]Yeshua said to him, "You have said it. Yet I tell you⁺ that after this you⁺ will see the Son of Adam sitting at the right hand of the Power [Ps. 110:1] and coming on the clouds of the heavens." [Dan. 7:13]

[65]Then the Kohen Gadol tore his clothing, saying, "He has spoken blasphemy! Why do we need any more witnesses? Look, now you⁺ have heard his blasphemy. [66]What do you⁺ think?"

26:60-61 See "Destroy This Temple" in the ADDITIONAL NOTES.

26:65 Tal. Moed Katan 26a says that the High Priest is to tear his clothes on hearing blasphemy.

They answered, "He is worthy of death!" [67]Then they spit in his face and beat him with their fists. And some slapped him, [68]saying, "Prophesy to us, you Messiah! Who hit you?"

[69]Now Kefa was sitting outside in the court, and a servant girl came to him, saying, "You also were with Yeshua from the Galil."

[70]But he denied it before them all, saying, "I do not know what you are talking about."

[71]When he had gone out onto the porch, someone else saw him, and said to those who were there, "This man was with Yeshua of Natzrat."

[72]Again he denied it with an oath, "I do not know the man."

[73]After a little while those who stood by came and said to Kefa, "Surely you are also one of them, for even your speech makes you known."

[74]Then he began to bind himself under a curse and swear, "I do not know the man!"

Immediately a rooster called out. [75]Kefa remembered the word which Yeshua had said to him, "Before the rooster calls out, you will completely deny me three times." He went out and wept bitterly.

27 [1]Now when morning had come, all the chief Kohanim and the Elders of the people took counsel against Yeshua to put him to death. [2]They bound him, led him away, and delivered him up to Pilate, the governor. [3]Then Judah, who delivered him up, when he saw that Yeshua was condemned, felt remorse, and brought back the thirty pieces of silver to the chief Kohanim and Elders, [4]saying, "I have sinned in that I delivered up innocent blood." [Ex. 23:1,7]

But they said, "What is that to us? You see to it."

[5]He threw down the pieces of silver in the sanctuary, and departed. He went away and hung himself. [6]The chief Kohanim took the pieces of silver, and said, "It is not permitted to put them into the treasury, since it is the price of blood." [7]They took counsel, and bought the Potter's Field with them, to bury strangers in. [8]Therefore, that field has been called "The Field of Blood" to this day. [9]Then what was spoken through Jeremiah the prophet was fulfilled: "They took the thirty pieces of silver — the payment for the one on whom some from the children of Israel set a price — [10]and they gave them for the potter's field, as the Everpresent Lord commanded me." [Zech. 11:12, 13]

27:1 The Council — those who were present — spent the night of Pesakh judging Yeshua, in violation of accepted procedure. "Judgments over materia things [Mammon] are tried by day, and concluded at night. But capital charges must be tried by day and concluded by day.... There are no trials held on the evening of Shabbat or a festival." (Tal. Sanhedrin 32a ff., Mishnah 4:1)

27:9 The quotation is from Zeḥaryah, not Jeremiah. Why then does Matthias say "Jeremiah"? Tal. Baba Bathra 14b explains the practice of placing Jeremiah before Isaiah as the first of the prophets. The reference to Jeremiah would then function as a designation for all the prophets, even as "the Psalms" in Lk. 24:44 serves as a designation for all the Writings. John Lightfoot, A Commentary on the New Testament from the Talmud and Hebraica, mentions this. Later tradition sometimes did the same thing with Isaiah, using his name as a designation for the prophets generally. (Cf. Bruce Metzger, A Textual Commentary on the Greek New Testament, Pp. 8, 27, 44, 55, 62. See also the note to Mk. 1:2.)

The text, **apo huion Israel**, indicates that those who sold him were from the children of Israel.

[11]Now Yeshua stood before the governor, and the governor questioned him, "Are you the King of the Jews?"

Yeshua said to him, "You say so."

[12]When he was accused by the chief Kohanim and Elders, he answered nothing. [Is. 53:7] [13]Then Pilate said to him, "Don't you hear how many things they testify against you?"

[14]He gave him no answer, not even one word, so that the governor was greatly amazed. [15]Now at the feast the governor was accustomed to release to the crowd one prisoner whom they desired. [16]They had then a well-known prisoner, called Bar Abba. [17]Therefore when they were gathered together, Pilate said to them, "Whom do you[+] want me to release to you[+], Bar Abba or Yeshua, who is called Messiah?" [18]For he knew that they had delivered him up because of envy.

[19]While he was sitting on the judgment seat, his wife sent to him, saying, "Have nothing to do with that righteous man, for I have suffered many things this day in a dream because of him." [20]Now the chief Kohanim and the Elders persuaded the crowds that they should ask for Bar Abba, and should destroy Yeshua. [21]And the governor responded to them, "Which of the two do you[+] want me to release to you[+]?"

They said, "Bar Abba!"

[22]Pilate said to them, "What then shall I do to Yeshua, who is called Messiah?"

They all said to him, "Put him to death on the stake!"

[23]Then he said, "Why? What evil has he done?"

But they cried out the more, "Put him to death on the stake!"

[24]So when Pilate saw that nothing was being gained, but rather that a disturbance was starting, he took water, and washed his hands before the crowd, saying, "I am innocent of the blood of this man. You[+] see to it."

[25]All the people answered, "May his blood be on us, and on our children!" [Ezek. 3:17-21; 33:2-9]

[26]Then he released Bar Abba to them, but he whipped Yeshua and delivered him to be put to death on the stake. [27]Then the governor's soldiers took Yeshua into the Praetorium, and gathered the whole garrison together against him. [28]They stripped him, and put a scarlet robe on him. [29]They braided a crown of thorns and put it on his head, and put a reed in his right hand. Kneeling before him, they ridiculed him, saying, "Hail, King of the Jews!" [30]They spat on him, and took the reed and struck him on the head. [31]While they mocked him, they took the robe off of him, put his clothes on him, and led him away to be put to death on the stake.

[32]As they came out, they found a man of Kyrene, Shimon by name, and they compelled him to go with them, so that he might carry his stake. [33]They came to a place called "Gulgolta," that is to say, "place of a skull." [34]They gave him wine mixed with a bitter substance to drink. When he had tasted it, he did not want to drink. [35]When they had hung him on the stake, they divided his clothing among

---

27:25 This is similar to the language that God uses in Ezek. 3:17-21 and 33:2-9. Those in the crowd who said this were declaring their willingness to take responsibility for the death of this man.

27:33 *goolgolet* is the Hebrew for skull.

them, casting lots [Ps. 22:19H], ³⁶and they sat and watched him there. ³⁷They set up over his head the accusation written against him, " THIS IS YESHUA, KING OF THE JEWS."

³⁸And there were two bandits hung on stakes with him, one on the right hand and one on the left. ³⁹Those who passed by maligned him, wagging their heads ⁴⁰and saying, "You who destroy the Temple and build it in three days, save yourself! If you are the Son of God, come down from the stake!"

⁴¹Likewise the chief Kohanim, with the Torah scholars and the Elders, also mocked, saying, ⁴²"He saved others, but he's not able to save himself. Is he the King of Israel? Let him come down from the stake now, and we will believe in him. ⁴³He trusts in God; let God deliver him now, if He desires him [Ps. 22:9H], for he said, 'I am the Son of God.'" ⁴⁴The bandits who were hung on stakes with him also mocked him in the same way.

⁴⁵Now from the sixth hour there was darkness over all the land until the ninth hour. ⁴⁶About the ninth hour Yeshua cried with a loud voice, "*Eli, Eli, lama azavtani?*" That is, "My God, my God, why have You forsaken me?" [Ps. 22:2H]

⁴⁷When they heard it, some of those who stood there said, "This man is calling Eliyahu."

⁴⁸Immediately one of them ran, took a sponge, filled it with wine vinegar, put it on a reed, and gave it to him to drink. ⁴⁹The rest said, "Let him be. Let's see whether Eliyahu comes to save him."

⁵⁰Yeshua cried again with a loud voice, and yielded up his spirit. ⁵¹And the veil of the Temple was torn in two from the top to the bottom! The earth quaked and the bedrock was split. ⁵²And tombs were opened, and many bodies of holy people who had fallen asleep were raised. ⁵³Coming out of the tombs after his resurrection, they entered into the holy city and appeared to many. ⁵⁴Now the centurion and those who were with him keeping a watch on Yeshua, when they saw the earthquake and the things that were done, were extremely afraid. They said, "Truly this was a son of God."

⁵⁵Many women who had followed Yeshua from the Galil, serving him, were there watching from afar. ⁵⁶Among them were Miryam from Magdala, Miryam the mother of Jacob and Yosef, and the mother of the sons of Zevadyah. ⁵⁷When evening had come, a rich man named Yosef from Ramatayim came. He himself was also a disciple of Yeshua. ⁵⁸This man went to Pilate, and asked for Yeshua's body. [Dt. 21:23] Then Pilate commanded the body to be given up. ⁵⁹Yosef took the body and wrapped it in a clean linen cloth. ⁶⁰Then he laid it in his own new tomb, which he had hewn out in the bedrock. And he rolled a large stone to the opening of the tomb, and departed. ⁶¹Miryam from Magdala was there, and the other Miryam, sitting opposite the tomb.

⁶²Now on the following morning, which is in the midst of the Preparation, the chief Kohanim and the Perushim were gathered together to Pilate. ⁶³They said, "Lord, we remember what that deceiver

27:37 "King of the Jews," the Son of David, was the announcement of the prophets and the archangel, as well as the beginning and ending of Matthias's report. It is also the warning of Messiah's identification in his return. (cf. Rev./Hazon 22:16)

27:46 The Codex Bezae has *zafthani* for the Hebrew *azavtani* of Ps.22:2H. (See Metzger, <u>A Textual Commentary on the Greek New Testament</u>, Pp. 70, 119.)

27:52-53 Tal. Moed Katan 25b tells of miraculous occurrences at the death of certain rabbis.

27:62 "in the midst of the Preparation" (*meta ten paraskeuen*) The Biblical day begins at sundown. Herodotus uses *meth hemeran* as "in the course of the day". Liddell and Scott, P. 501

said while he was still alive: 'After three days I will rise again.' [64]Therefore command that the tomb be made secure until the third day, otherwise his disciples may come, steal him away, and tell the people, 'He has been raised from the dead.' The last deception would then be worse than the first."

[65]Pilate said to them, "You[+] have a guard. Go make it as secure as you[+] can." [66]So they went with the guard and made the tomb secure, sealing the stone.

28 [1]Now after the Sabbaths, as it began to dawn on the first of the week, Miryam from Magdala and the other Miryam came to see the tomb. [2]There was a big earthquake, for an angel of the Everpresent Lord descended from heaven, came and rolled away the stone from the opening, and sat upon it! [3]His appearance was like lightning, and his clothing white as snow. [4]The guards trembled from fear of him, and became like dead men.

[5]The angel responded to the women, "Do not be afraid, for I know that you[+] are seeking Yeshua, who was put to death on the stake. [6]He is not here, because he has been raised, just as he said. Come, see the place where he was lying. [7]Go quickly and tell his disciples that he has been raised from the dead. Know that he goes before you[+] into the Galil. There you[+] will see him. Listen, I have told you[+]."

[8]They departed quickly from the tomb with fear and great joy, and ran to bring word to his disciples. [9]As they went to tell his disciples, Yeshua met them, saying, "Rejoice!" They came and took hold of his feet, and bowed down before him.

[10]Then Yeshua said to them, "Don't be afraid. Go tell my brethren that they should go into the Galil, and there they will see me."

[11]Now while they were going, some of the guards came into the city, and told the chief Kohanim all the things that had happened! [12]When they were assembled with the Elders and had taken counsel, they gave a large amount of silver to the soldiers, [13]saying, "Say, 'His disciples came by night, and stole him away while we slept.' [14]If this comes to the governor's ears, we will persuade him and make you[+] secure." [15]So they took the money and did as they were told. This saying was spread abroad among the Jewish people, and continues until this day.

[16]But the eleven disciples went into the Galil, to the mountain where Yeshua had sent them. [17]When they saw him, they bowed down to him, but some were hesitant. [18]Yeshua came to them and said to them, "All authority has been given to me in heaven and on earth. [19]Go make disciples of all the Gentiles, immersing them in the Name of the Father and the Son and the Ruakh Kodesh [Dt. 6:7; 1Chr. 16:8,23-24], [20]teaching them to observe all things which I have commanded you[+]. [Dt. 6:6-7] Know that I am with you[+] always, even to the culmination of the age."

28:1 "after the Sabbaths" God prescribes the weekly sabbath, and He also prescribes other sabbaths for the holy days. Here the plural likely indicates the first sabbath of the feast of Matzot together with the regular weekly sabbath. See, e.g., Lev. 23:5-8.

28:18 "...For the heav]vens and the earth shall listen to His Messiah." (DSS 4Q521)

28:19 "If there are no little ones, there are no disciples. If there are no disciples, there are no sages. If there are no sages, there are no elders. If there are no elders, there are no prophets. If there are no prophets, there is none for the Holy One, blessed be He, to cause His Shekhinah to remain upon." (Mid. Genesis 42:3)

The Report of Mark

1 [1]The beginning of the good news of Yeshua the Messiah, the Son of God. [2]As it is written in Isaiah the prophet, "Behold, I send My messenger before you, who will prepare your way before you. [Mal. 3:1] [3]The voice of one crying out in the wilderness, 'Make ready the way of the Everpresent Lord! Make His paths straight!'" [Is. 40:3]

[4]Yoḥanan the Immerser came in the wilderness, proclaiming the immersion of repentance for forgiveness of sins. [5]All the land of Judea and the whole of Yerushala'im went out to him. They were immersed by him in the Yarden River, confessing their sins.

[6]Now Yoḥanan was clothed with camel's hair and a leather belt around his waist. He ate locusts and wild honey. [7]He announced, "After me comes one who is mightier than I. I am not worthy to stoop down and loosen the strap of his sandals. [8]I have immersed you[+] in water, but he will immerse you[+] in the Ruakh Kodesh."

[9]In those days, Yeshua came from Natzrat of the Galil, and was immersed in the Yarden by Yoḥanan. [10]As soon as Yeshua came up from the water, he saw the heavens parting, and the Spirit descending upon him like a dove. [11]A voice came out of the heavens, "You are My beloved Son, in whom I delight." [Gen. 22:2]

[12]The Spirit immediately drove him out into the wilderness. [13]And he was in the wilderness forty days, tempted by the Accuser. He was with the wild animals, and the angels were serving him.

[14]Now after Yoḥanan was imprisoned, Yeshua came into the Galil, proclaiming the good news of God's kingdom. [15]He said, "The time is completed, and God's kingdom has come near! Change your ways, and believe in the good news."

1:2 The Textus Receptus has "in the prophets," but the original is most likely, as in the UBS, "in Isaiah the prophet," "a reading found in the earliest representative witnesses of the Alexandrian, the Western, and the Caesarean types of text". (Metzger, A Textual Commentary, P.73) This would be an example of the practice of designating The Prophets by the name of the first prophet, even as The Writings are designated by "Psalms," the first writing. See the note to Mt. 27:9)

1:6 There is a discussion in Tal. Menachot 39b about what kind of garments require tzitzit. A teacher from the school of R. Ishmael exempted garments made of camel's hair, goat's hair, et alia.

1:7 "R.Joshua b. Levi ruled: 'All work which a slave does for his master a disciple does for his teacher, except that of taking off his shoe.'" (Tal. Ketubot 96a)

1:10 The text does not tell us why the Spirit descended "as a dove," but perhaps it is because the dove on the ark [Gen. 8:8-12] signalled the end of the judgment of the flood and a new beginning for humanity.

Ben Zoma said, "'It is said, And the spirit of God hovered over the surface of the waters — as a dove which hovers over her children but does not touch [them].' Then R. Joshua said to his disciples, 'Ben Zoma is still outside [i.e. excommunicated].'" (Tal. Hagigah 15a)

But Mid. Gen. 2:4 says, "'And the Spirit of God hovered...' This is the spirit of Messiah the King." (cf. Mid. Gen. Alt. 97.1 and the reference to Messiah and the Spirit in Is. 11:2)

[16]Passing along by the lake of the Galil, he saw Shimon and Andreas, the brother of Shimon, casting a net in the lake, for they were fishermen.

[17]Yeshua said to them, "Come after me, and I will make you[+] fishers of men." [Prov. 11:30, Dan. 12:3, Jer. 16:16]

[18]They immediately left their nets, and followed him. [1Ki. 19:19-21] [19]Going on a little from there, he saw Jacob the son of Zevadyah, and his brother Yoḥanan, who were also in the boat preparing the nets. [20]As soon as he called them, they left their father Zevadyah in the boat with the hired servants, and went after him.

[21]They went into Kfar Naḥum, and when it was Shabbat he entered into the meetingplace and taught. [22]They were astonished at his teaching, because he taught them as one having authority and not as the Torah scholars. [23]In their meetingplace there was a man with an unclean spirit, and he cried out, [24]"Ah! What do we have to do with you, Yeshua of Natzrat? Have you come to destroy us? I know who you are, you are the Holy One of God!"

[25]Yeshua rebuked him, saying, "Be quiet, and come out of him!"

[26]The unclean spirit came out of him, convulsing him and crying out with a loud voice. [27]They were all so amazed that they asked each other, "What is this? A new teaching? For with authority he commands even the unclean spirits, and they listen to him!" [28]His fame immediately went out everywhere throughout the region of the Galil and its surrounding area.

[29]As soon as they had come out of the meetingplace, they came into the house of Shimon and Andreas, with Jacob and Yoḥanan. [30]Now Shimon's mother-in-law lay sick with a fever, and they immediately told him about her. [31]He came, took her by the hand, and raised her up. The fever left her, and she began serving them.

[32]At evening, when the sun had set, they brought to him all who were sick, and those who were afflicted by demons. [33]All the city was gathered together at the door. [34]He healed many who were sick with various diseases, and cast out many demons. He did not allow the demons to speak, because they recognized him.

[35]Early in the night, he rose up, went out, departed into a deserted place, and prayed there. [36]Shimon and those who were with him followed after him. [37]Then they found him, and told him, "Everyone is looking for you."

[38]He said to them, "Let's go into the neighboring towns, that I may speak there also, because this is the reason I came out." [39]He came proclaiming a message in their meetingplaces throughout all the Galil, and casting out demons.

[40]A leper came to him, begging him, kneeling down and saying to him, "If you want to, you can make me clean."

[41]Being moved with compassion, he stretched out his hand, touched him, and said to him, "I want to. Be cleansed." [42]When he had said this, the leprosy immediately departed from the man, and he was made clean. [43]Having strictly warned him, he immediately sent him out, [44]saying to him, "See that you say nothing to anyone, but go show yourself to the Kohen, and offer for your cleansing the things which Moses commanded, for a testimony to them." [Lev. 14]

1:40-42 "And he [the leper] is to cry, 'Unclean, unclean': it is necessary to make his affliction known to many, so that the many may seek mercy for him." (Tal. Shabbat 67a)

[45]But he went out, and began to proclaim it freely, and to spread the report widely, so that Yeshua could no longer openly enter into a city, but was in outlying, wilderness places. Yet they came to him from everywhere.

2 [1]When he entered again into Kfar Nahum some days later, it was heard that he was in the house. [2]Right away many were gathered together, so that there was no more room, not even around the door. Then he spoke the word to them.

[3]Four people came carrying a paralytic to him. [4]When they could not come near him because of the crowd, they removed the roof where he was. When they had opened it up, they let down the mat on which the paralytic was lying. [5]Seeing their faith, Yeshua said to the paralytic, "Son, your sins are forgiven you."

[6]But there were some of the Torah scholars sitting there, and thinking in their hearts, [7]"Why does this man speak blasphemies in this way? Who can forgive sins but God alone?"

[8]Perceiving at once in his spirit that they were thinking this way within themselves, Yeshua said to them, "Why do you[+] think like this in your[+] hearts? [9]Which is easier, to tell the paralytic, 'Your sins are forgiven,' or to say, 'Arise, and take up your bed, and walk'? [10]But in order for you[+] to know that the Son of Adam has authority on earth to forgive sins" — he then said to the paralytic, [11]"Arise, I tell you, take up your mat, and go to your home."

[12]He arose, immediately took up the mat, and went out in front of them all. They were all amazed by this, and glorified God, saying, "We never saw anything like this!"

[13]He went out again by the shore. All the multitude came to him, and he taught them. [14]As he passed by, he saw Levi, the son of Halfai, sitting at the tax office, and he said to him, "Follow me." And he arose and followed him. [15]As he was reclining at the table in his house, many tax collectors and sinners sat down with Yeshua and his disciples, because there were many, and they were following after him.

[16]When the Torah scholars and the Perushim saw that he was eating with the sinners and tax collectors, they said to his disciples, "Why does he eat and drink with tax collectors and sinners?"

[17]When Yeshua heard it, he said to them, "Those who are healthy have no need of a physician, but those who are sick do. I did not come to call the righteous, but sinners."

[18]Yohanan's disciples and the Perushim were fasting, and they came and asked him, "Why do Yohanan's disciples and the disciples of the Perushim fast, but your disciples do not fast?"

[19]Yeshua said to them, "Can the friends of the bridegroom fast while the bridegroom is with them? As long as they have the bridegroom with them, they cannot fast. [20]But the days will come when the bridegroom will be taken away from them, and then they will fast in that day. [21]No one sews a piece of unshrunk cloth on an old garment, or else the patch shrinks and the new tears away from the old,

---

2:4 Tal. Moed Katan 25a says of the funeral of R. Huna: "The casket could not be brought through the doorway, and they intended to lower it by way of the roof."

2:17 In the liturgy in Tahanun, we pray to "the One who opens a hand to receive repentant transgressors and sinners."

2:22 "R. Meir said, 'Do not regard this flask but what is in it; there can be a new flask filled with old wine and an old flask in which there is not even new wine.'" (Tal. Avot 4:27)

and a worse hole is made. ²²No one puts new wine into old wineskins, or else the new wine will burst the skins, the wine pours out, and the skins will be destroyed. They put new wine into fresh wineskins instead."

²³He was going through the grain fields on Shabbat, and his disciples began to pluck the ears of grain as they went. ²⁴The Perushim said to him, "Look, why do they do what is not lawful on Shabbat?"

²⁵He said to them, "Have you⁺ never read what David did, when he had need and was hungry — he and those who were with him? ²⁶How he entered into the house of God in the time of Evyatar, the Kohen Gadol, and ate the consecrated bread, and gave also to those who were with him? It is not lawful for any to eat it except the Kohanim." ²⁷Yeshua said to them, "Shabbat was made for Adam, not Adam for Shabbat. ²⁸For this reason, the Son of Adam is lord even of Shabbat."

3 ¹He entered again into the meetingplace, and there was a man there who had a withered hand. ²They watched Yeshua to see if he would heal him on Shabbat, so that they might accuse him. ³He said to the man who had a withered hand, "Stand up."

⁴He said to them, "Is it lawful on Shabbat to do good, or to do harm? To save a life, or to kill?" But they were silent. ⁵Being grieved at the hardening of their hearts, when he had looked around at them angrily, he said to the man, "Stretch out your hand." He stretched it out, and his hand was restored as healthy as the other. ⁶The Perushim went out, and immediately conspired with the Herodians against him, how they might destroy him.

⁷Yeshua withdrew to the lake with his disciples, and a large crowd followed him from the Galil, from Judea, ⁸from Yerushala'im, from Idumaea, from beyond the Yarden, and those from around Tzor and Tzidon. Hearing what great things he was doing, a large crowd came to him.

⁹He told his disciples that a small boat should stay near him because of the crowd, so that they would not crush him. ¹⁰Because he had healed many, all those who had diseases pushed towards him so that they might touch him. ¹¹The unclean spirits, whenever they saw him, fell down before him and cried, "You are the Son of God!" ¹²He sternly warned them that they should not make him known.

¹³He went up onto the mountain, and called to himself those whom he wanted. And they came to him. ¹⁴He appointed twelve so that they might be with him, and that he might send them out to make public proclamation ¹⁵and have authority to heal sicknesses and cast out demons: ¹⁶Shimon,

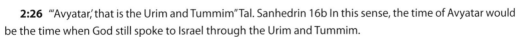

2:26 "'Avyatar,' that is the Urim and Tummim" Tal. Sanhedrin 16b In this sense, the time of Avyatar would be the time when God still spoke to Israel through the Urim and Tummim.

2:27-28 "From where do we know that saving a life sets aside Shabbat?… If circumcision, which applies to one of the two hundred and forty-eight members of the human body, sets aside Shabbat, how much more [kal v'chomer] does what applies to [the saving of] the whole body set aside Shabbat! …R. Jonathan b. Joseph said: 'For it is holy to you [Ex. 31:14] — it [Shabbat] is delivered into your hand; but you are not delivered to its hand.'" (Tal. Yoma 85a-b)

3:3 UBS has "Stand up in the middle."

3:5 Or it may have been his "arm".

to whom he gave the name Kefa, [17]Jacob the son of Zevadyah, Yoḥanan, the brother of Jacob (and he nicknamed them *Bnei Rogez*, which means "Sons of Thunder") [18]Andreas, Philip, Bar Talmai, Matthias, Toma, Jacob the son of Ḥalfai, Taddi, Shimon the zealot, [19]and Judah from K'riyot (who also delivered him up).

He came into a house, [20]and the crowd came together again, so that they could not so much as eat bread. [21]When his own family heard it, they went out to take custody of him, because they said, "He is confused." [22]The Torah scholars who came down from Yerushala'im said, "He has Baal Zevul," and, "By the Prince of the demons he casts out the demons."

[23]He called them to himself, and spoke to them in parables, "How can the Accuser cast out himself? [24]If a kingdom is divided against itself, that kingdom cannot stand. [25]If a house is divided against itself, that house cannot stand. [26]If the Accuser has risen up against himself and is divided, he cannot stand, but has an end. [27]But no one can enter into the house of the strong man to plunder his things, unless he first binds the strong man. And then he will plunder his house. [28]I assure you[+] that all of the sins of the children of men will be forgiven them, including their blasphemies with which they might blaspheme. [29]However, whoever blasphemes against the Ruakh Kodesh never has forgiveness, but is guilty of an eternal sin"— [30]because they said, "He has an unclean spirit."

[31]His mother and his brothers came and, standing outside, they sent and called him. [32]A crowd was sitting around him, and they told him, "Your mother, your brothers, and your sisters are outside asking for you!"

[33]He answered them, "Who are my mother and my brothers?" [34]Looking around at those who sat around him, he said, "Behold, my mother and my brothers. [35]For whoever does the will of God, the same is my brother, or my sister, or mother."

4 [1]He began to teach again by the shore. A large crowd was gathered to him, so he entered into a boat on the lake, and sat down. All the crowd was on the land by the lake. [2]He taught them many things in parables, and said to them in his teaching, [3]"Listen, the sower went out to sow, [4]and as he sowed, some seed fell by the road, and the birds came and devoured it. [5]Other seed fell on the rocky ground, where it had little soil, and it sprang up right away, because it had no depth of soil. [6]When the sun had risen, it was scorched. And because it had no root, it withered away. [7]Other seed fell among the thorns, and the thorns grew up and suffocated it, and it yielded no fruit. [Ps. 1]

[8]Others fell into the good ground, and yielded fruit, growing up and increasing. Some brought forth thirty times, some sixty times, and some one hundred times as much." [9]He said, "Whoever has ears to hear, let him hear." [Dt. 29:4, Ezek. 3:27]

[10]When he was alone, those who were around him with the twelve asked him about the parables. [11]He said to them, "The mystery of God's kingdom is given to you[+], but to those who are outside,

3:17 "*Rigzu*/tremble and do not sin." (Ps. 4:5H)

3:18 "Shimon the zealot" The Greek *kananaios* is understood to be a transliteration of the Aramaic *kan'anaya*, meaning "zealot". It may be a personality characterization, or an indication that he belonged to the political Zealots. In Acts 1:13, he is called Shimon *ho zelotes*. (cf. Lk. 6:15)

3:22 Some texts have *Baal Zevul*, which means "lord of dung or garbage". Other texts have *Baal Zevuv*, which means "lord of flies" (a Canaanite god).

all things become parables, ¹²so that 'seeing they see and do not perceive; and hearing they hear and do not understand; otherwise they would turn and it would be forgiven them." [Is. 6:9-10, 43: 8; Jer 4:21; Ezek. 12:2]

¹³He said to them, "Don't you⁺ understand this parable? How will you⁺ understand all of the parables? ¹⁴The sower sows the word. ¹⁵These are the ones by the road where the word is sown: when they have heard, the Accuser comes immediately, and takes away the word which has been sown in them. ¹⁶Similarly, these are those which are sown on the rocky places: when they have heard the word, they immediately receive it with joy. ¹⁷They have no root in themselves, but are only for a season. When affliction or persecution arises because of the word, they immediately stumble. ¹⁸Others are those which are sown among the thorns: these are those who have heard the word, ¹⁹yet the cares of this age, the deceit of riches, and the desires for other things enter in and choke the word, and it becomes unfruitful. ²⁰These are those which were sown on the good ground: such as hear the word, and accept it, and bear fruit, some thirty, some sixty, and some one hundredfold." [Gen. 26:12, Is. 55:10-11]

²¹He said to them, "Is the lamp brought to be put under a basket or under a bed? Isn't it put on a lampstand? ²²For there is nothing hidden which will not be made known. Nor has anything secret taken place, but that it will come to light. [Eccl. 12:14] ²³If any man has ears to hear, let him hear." [Dt. 29:4, Ezek. 3:27]

²⁴He said to them, "Pay attention to what you⁺ hear. With whatever measure you⁺ measure, it will be measured to you⁺, and more will be given to you⁺ who hear. ²⁵For whoever has, to him more will be given. And he who does not have, even what he does have will be taken away from him."

²⁶He said, "God's kingdom is as if a man were to cast seed on the earth, ²⁷sleep and rise night and day, while the seed springs up and grows, but he does not know how. ²⁸For the earth bears fruit — first the blade, then the ear, then the full grain in the ear. ²⁹But when the fruit is ripe, he sends out the sickle right away, because the harvest has come."

³⁰He said, "To what shall we compare God's kingdom? Or with what parable can we illustrate it? ³¹It is like a grain of mustard seed, which, when it is sown in the earth, is smaller than all the seeds that are on the earth. ³²Yet when it is sown, it grows up and becomes larger than all the garden herbs, and puts out large branches so that the birds of the heaven can nest under its shade." [Ezek. 17:23, 31:6, Ps. 104:12, Dan. 4:12]

³³He spoke the message to them with many parables like this, as they were able to hear. ³⁴He did not speak to them without a parable, but privately he explained all things to his own disciples.

³⁵On that day, when evening had come, he said to them, "Let's go over to the other side." ³⁶Since he was in the boat, they left the multitude, and set out with him. Other small boats were also with him. ³⁷There arose a large windstorm, and the waves beat into the boat, so much that the boat was already filled. ³⁸He himself was in the stern, asleep on the cushion, but they woke him up, and said to him, "Rabbi, don't you care that we are about to die?"

4:12 See the ADDITIONAL NOTE on "Pharaoh's Heart".

4:32 "'the birds of the heaven dwell' (Ps. 104:12) — these are the nations of the world, that they will gather against Israel and work on them, to go far from the Holy One, blessed be He." (Mid. Psalms 104.10)

4:38 Yhn. 1:38 tells us that "Rabbi" is translated as didaskalos/"Teacher".

³⁹He awoke, rebuked the wind, and said to the lake, "Peace! Be still!" The wind ceased, and there was a great calm. ⁴⁰He said to them, "Why are you⁺ so afraid? How is it that you⁺ have no faith?"

⁴¹They were extremely afraid, and said to one another, "Who then is this, that even the wind and the lake obey him?"

5 ¹They came to the other side of the lake, into the region of the Gadarenes. ²As soon as he had come out of the boat, a man met him from the tombs. ³He had an unclean spirit, and had his dwelling in the tombs. Nobody could bind him any more, not even with chains, ⁴because he had often been bound with shackles and chains, and he had torn apart the chains and broken the shackles in pieces. Nobody had the strength to subdue him. ⁵Continually, night and day, in the tombs and in the mountains, he was crying out and cutting himself with stones.

⁶When he saw Yeshua from afar, he ran and bowed down to him. ⁷Crying out with a loud voice, he said, "What have I to do with you, Yeshua, Son of God Most High? I implore you by God, do not torment me!" ⁸For he was saying to him, "Come out of the man, you unclean spirit!"

⁹He asked him, "What is your name?"

He said to him, "My name is Legion, for we are many." ¹⁰He fervently begged him that he would not send them away out of the country. ¹¹Now on the mountainside there was a large herd of pigs feeding. ¹²All the demons begged him, "Send us into the pigs, that we may enter into them."

¹³Yeshua gave them permission. The unclean spirits came out and entered into the pigs. The herd of about two thousand rushed down the steep bank into the lake, and they were drowned in the lake. ¹⁴Those who tended them fled, and told it in the city and in the country.

The people came to see what it was that had happened. ¹⁵They came to Yeshua, and saw the one who had been afflicted by demons — the one who had the legion — sitting, clothed, and in his right mind. And they were afraid. ¹⁶Those who saw it related to them what had happened to the one who was afflicted by demons, and about the pigs. ¹⁷They began to beg him to depart from their region.

¹⁸As he was entering into the boat, the one who had been possessed by demons begged him that he might be with him. ¹⁹He did not let him, but said to him, "Go to your house, to your friends, and tell them what great things the Everpresent Lord has done for you, and how He had mercy on you." ²⁰He went his way, and began to proclaim in the Ten Towns how Yeshua had done great things for him, and everyone was astonished.

²¹When Yeshua had crossed back over in the boat to the other side, a large multitude was gathered to him, as he was by the lake. ²²Seeing him, one of the rulers of the assembly, Yair by name, came and fell at his feet. ²³He was fervently begging him, "My little daughter is at the point of death! Please come and lay your hands on her, that she may be made healthy, and live."

²⁴He went with him, and a large crowd followed him, pressing upon him. ²⁵There was a woman who had had a discharge of blood for twelve years. ²⁶She had suffered extensively under many physicians and had spent all that she had. Yet she was no better, but grew worse instead. ²⁷Having

5:9 "Our Rabbis taught: A legion which passes from place to place and enters a house, the house is unclean, for every legion that comes to you, there is no legion that does not have some scalps." (Tal. Chullin 123a)

5:11-13 See note to Mt. 8:28-32.

heard the things concerning Yeshua, she came up behind him in the crowd, and touched his clothing [Lev. 15:2-12], ²⁸for she said, "If I just touch his clothing, I will be made well." ²⁹The flow of her blood was immediately dried up, and she felt in her body that she was healed of her affliction.

³⁰Perceiving in himself that the power had gone out from him, Yeshua turned around at once in the crowd, and asked, "Who touched my clothes?"

³¹His disciples said to him, "You see the crowd pressing against you, yet you say, 'Who touched me?'"

³²He looked around to see who had done this. ³³Now the woman, fearing and trembling, knowing what had happened to her, came and fell down before him. Then she told him the whole truth. ³⁴He said to her, "Daughter, your faith has made you well. Go in peace, and be healed of your disease."

³⁵While he was still speaking, some came from the house of the ruler of the assembly saying, "Your daughter is dead. Why bother the Rabbi any more?"

³⁶But having heard what was said, Yeshua immediately said to the ruler of the assembly, "Do not be afraid, only believe." ³⁷He allowed no one to follow him, except Kefa, Jacob, and Yoḥanan the brother of Jacob. ³⁸He came to the house of the ruler of the assembly and saw a commotion — weeping and great wailing. ³⁹When he had entered in, he said to them, "Why do you⁺ make a commotion and weep? The child is not dead, but asleep."

⁴⁰They ridiculed him, but he, having put them all out, took the father of the child and her mother and those who were with him, and went in where the child was lying. ⁴¹Taking the child by the hand, he said to her, "*Talita, kumi*," which is translated as, "Little girl, I tell you, arise." ⁴²Immediately the girl rose up and walked around. She was twelve years old. They were overcome with great amazement. ⁴³He strictly ordered them that no one should know this, and said that something should be given to her to eat.

6 ¹He went out from there and came into his own country, and his disciples followed him. ²When Shabbat had come, he began to teach in the meetingplace. And many who heard him were astonished, saying, "Where did this man get these teachings? And what is this wisdom that is given to this man that such mighty works take place by his hands? ³Isn't this the craftsman, the son of Miryam, and brother of Jacob, Yosi, Judah, and Shimon? Aren't his sisters here with us?" They were shocked by him.

⁴Yeshua said to them, "A prophet is not without honor, except in his own country, among his own relatives, and in his own house." ⁵He could do no mighty work there, except that he put his hands on a few sick people, and healed them. ⁶He was amazed at their disbelief, but he went around the villages teaching.

⁷He called the twelve to himself, and began to send them out two by two. And he gave them authority over the unclean spirits. ⁸He commanded them that they should take nothing for their journey except a staff only — no bread, no wallet, no money in their bag, ⁹but to wear sandals, and not put on two tunics. ¹⁰He said to them, "Wherever you⁺ enter into a house, stay there until you⁺ leave that place. ¹¹Whoever will not receive you⁺ nor hear you⁺, shake off the dust under your⁺ feet as a testimony to them."

¹²They went out and proclaimed that people should change their ways. ¹³They cast out many demons, anointed with oil many who were sick, and healed them. ¹⁴King Herod heard this, because Yeshua's name had become known, and he said, "Yoḥanan the Immerser has been raised from the

dead, and therefore these powers are at work in him." [15]But others said, "It is Eliyahu." Others said, "It is the Prophet [Dt. 18:15], or someone like one of the prophets."

[16]But when he heard this, Herod said, "This is Yoḥanan, whom I beheaded. He has been raised from the dead." [17-18]Herod had married Herodias, the wife of his brother Philip. Yoḥanan had said to Herod, "It is not lawful for you to have your brother's wife." [Lev. 18:16] Therefore Herod himself had sent and arrested Yoḥanan, and bound him in prison. [19]Herodias held it against Yoḥanan, and wanted to kill him. She was unable, however, [20]because Herod feared Yoḥanan, knowing that he was a righteous and holy man, and kept him safe. When he heard him, he was very perplexed, but heard him gladly.

[21]When the appropriate day came, on the anniversary of his accession, Herod made a supper for his nobles, the high officers, and the chief men of the Galil. [22]When the daughter of Herodias herself came in and danced, she pleased Herod and those sitting with him. The king said to the girl, "Ask me whatever you want, and I will give it to you." [23]He swore to her, "Whatever you will ask of me, I will give to you, up to half of my kingdom."

[24]She went out and said to her mother, "What should I ask?"

She said, "The head of Yoḥanan the Immerser."

[25]Immediately she hurriedly came in to the king, and asked, "I want you to give me the head of Yoḥanan the Immerser on a platter right now."

[26]The king was deeply grieved, but on account of his oaths and his dinner guests, he did not wish to refuse her. [27]The king immediately sent out a soldier of his guard, and ordered his head to be brought. Then he went and beheaded him in the prison. [28]He brought his head on a platter, and gave it to the girl. And the girl gave it to her mother. [29]When his disciples heard this, they came and took up his corpse, and laid it in a tomb.

[30]The ambassadors gathered themselves together to Yeshua, and told him everything, both what they had done, and what they had taught. [31]He said to them, "Come aside into a deserted place, and rest awhile." For there were many coming and going, and they had no opportunity even to eat. [32]They went away in the boat to a wilderness place by themselves. [33]The multitudes saw them going, and many recognized him and ran there on foot from all the cities. These arrived before them.

[34]Yeshua came out, saw a large multitude, and had compassion on them, because they were like sheep without a shepherd. [Num. 27:17, 1K. 22:17, Zech. 10:2] Then he began to teach them many things. [35]When it was late in the day, his disciples came to him, and said, "This place is deserted, and it is late in the day. [36]Send them away so that they may go into the surrounding countryside and villages, and buy themselves bread, because they have nothing to eat." [2Ki. 4:42-44]

6:17-29 Josephus gives some background and a different perspective in Antiquities 18:111-119 [18.5.1-2].

6:18 Tal. K'ritot 1:1 says, "In the Torah there are thirty-six [transgressions punished by] being cut off: When one has intercourse with… his brother's wife."

6:21 The Greek word *genesia* ordinarily means "birthday," but its Jewish usage also encompasses the day a king ascends the throne. "What is the day of *genosia* of their kings? Rab Yehudah said, 'The day on which they cause him to stand [as king].'" (Tal. Avodah Zara 10a, Edersheim, The Life and Times of Jesus the Messiah, Vol. 1, P. 672n, points this out.)

[37]But he answered them, "You[+] give them something to eat."

They asked him, "Are we to go and buy two hundred denarii worth of bread, and give them something to eat?"

[38]He said to them, "How many loaves do you[+] have? Go see."

When they found out, they said, "Five, and two fish."

[39]He commanded them to have everyone sit down in groups on the green grass. [40]They sat down in orderly groups of hundreds and fifties.

[41]He took the five loaves and the two fish, and looking up to heaven, he said a blessing, then he broke the loaves and gave to his disciples to set before them. Then he divided the two fish among them all. [42]They all ate, and were filled. [43]They took up twelve baskets full of broken pieces and also of the fish. [44]There were five thousand men of those who ate the loaves.

[45]Right away he made his disciples get into the boat and go ahead to the other side, to Beit Tzaidah, while he himself sent the multitude away. [46]After he had taken leave of them, he went away to the mountain to pray.

[47]When evening had come, the boat was in the middle of the lake, and he was alone on the land. [48]Seeing them rowing with great difficulty because the wind was contrary to them, he came to them about the fourth watch of the night, walking on the lake [Job 9:8], and intending to pass by them. [49]But when they saw him walking on the lake, they thought it was a ghost, and cried out, [50]for they all saw him, and were troubled. But he immediately spoke with them, and said to them, "Be strong. It is I. Do not be afraid." [51]He got into the boat with them, and the wind ceased. And they were quite astonished among themselves, [52]because they had not understood about the loaves, but their hearts were hardened instead.

[53]When they had crossed over, they came to land at Kinneret, and came near to the shore. [54]When they had come out of the boat, the people recognized him right away. [55]Then they ran throughout that whole region, and began to bring those who were sick, on their mats, to where they heard he was. [56]Wherever he entered into villages, or into cities, or into the country, they laid the sick in the marketplaces, and begged him that they might touch just the tzitzit of his garment. And as many as touched him were healed.

7 [1]Then the Perushim and some of the Torah scholars, who had come from Yerushala'im, gathered together to him. [2]And they saw some of his disciples eating bread with common (that is, unwashed) hands. [3](For the Perushim and all the sectarian Jews do not eat without washing their hands, holding to the tradition of the Elders. [4]They do not eat when they come from the marketplace unless they wash themselves. And there are many other traditions which they have received and keep: washings of cups, pitchers, bronze vessels, and beds.) [5]The Perushim and the Torah scholars

6:53 It seems likely that the Greek *Gennessaret* is the Hebrew Kinneret, which has variant spellings in Num. 34:11, Dt. 3:17, Josh.13:27, and Josh. 19:35.

7:1-7 A passage in Tal. Eiruvin 21b teaches that R. Akiba was given only a little water while in prison after the Bar Kokhba revolt. Rather than drink the water to sustain his life, he wanted to wash his hands and fulfill the tradition. In Sotah 4b, R. Avira taught, "Everyone who eats bread without washing his hands is as if he had intercourse with a prostitute."

asked him, "Why don't your disciples walk according to the tradition of the Elders, but instead eat their bread with unwashed hands?"

[6]He answered them, "Isaiah prophesied well of you[+] pretenders, as it is written, 'This people honors Me with their lips, but their heart is far from Me. [7]And they worship Me in vain, teaching teachings that are commandments of men.' [Is. 29:13] [8]"Neglecting the commandment of God, you[+] hold tightly to the tradition of men."

[9]He said to them, "Is it right to despise the commandment of God in order to uphold your[+] tradition? [10]For Moses said, 'Honor your father and your mother,' [Ex. 20:12, Dt. 5:16] and, 'He who speaks evil of father or mother, let him be put to death.' [Ex. 21:17, Lev. 20:9] [11]But you[+] say, if a man were to tell his father or his mother, 'Whatever profit you might have received from me is korban' — that is to say, *given to God* — [12]then you[+] would permit him to no longer do anything for his father or his mother. [13]You[+] nullify the word of God by your[+] tradition which you[+] have handed down! You[+] do many things like this."

[14]He called all the multitude to himself, and said to them, "Listen to me, all of you[+], and understand. [15]There is nothing from outside of the man that can defile him by going into him, but the things which proceed out of the man are those that defile the man. [16]If anyone has ears to hear, let him hear." [Dt. 29:4, Ezek. 3:27]

[17]When he had entered into a house away from the multitude, his disciples asked him about the parable. [18]He said to them, "Are you[+] likewise without understanding? Don't you[+] perceive that whatever goes into the man from outside cannot defile him, [19]because it does not go into his heart, but into his stomach, then into the latrine, cleansing all the food in this way?" [20]And he said, "What proceeds out of the man, that defiles the man. [21]For from within, out of the hearts of men, proceed evil thoughts, adulteries, sexual sins, murders, thefts, [22]covetings, wickedness, deceit, lustful desires, an evil eye, blasphemy, pride, and foolishness. [23]All these evil things come from within, and defile the man."

[24]He arose from there and went away into the borders of Tzor and Tzidon. He entered into a house and did not want anyone to know it, but he could not escape notice. [25]Instead, a woman, having heard of him, immediately came and fell down at his feet. Her little daughter had an unclean spirit. [26]Now

7:1-13 It is clear in Talmud that the Rabbis thought their own authority was sufficient to overrule God. The classic example it the *tanoor akhnai* incident, where R. Eliezer is excommunicated for disagreeing with the majority of Rabbis, even though God attests that R. Eliezer is correct. (Tal. Baba Metzia 59b) There is the interesting story in Tal. Baba Metzia 86a about a disagreement in the heavenly academy over whether a certain appearance means that a person has leprosy or is clean. God says he is clean but all the other members of the heavenly academy say he is not. The issue cannot be resolved until Rabba b. Nahmani dies and then casts the deciding vote.

7:4 The Talmudic tractate Kelim deals with the cleanness of vessels.

7:6-9 "Everyone who studies halakhot every day, it is promised to him that he is a son of the age to come." (Tal. Megila 28b)

7:18-19 See the note to Mt. 15:2-20, and "Cleansing the Food" in the ADDITIONAL NOTES.

7:25-29 See the note to Mt. 15:22-28.

the woman was a Greek, of the Syrophoenician people. She begged him that he would cast the demon out of her daughter. [27]But Yeshua said to her, "Let the children be filled first, for it is not good to take the children's bread and throw it to the little dogs."

[28]But she answered him, "Yes, Lord, yet even the little dogs under the table eat the children's crumbs."

[29]He said to her, "Because of what you have said, go your way. The demon has gone out of your daughter." [30]She went away to her house, and found the child thrown on the bed, with the demon gone out.

[31]Again he departed from the borders of Tzor, and came through Tzidon to the lake of the Galil, through the middle of the region of the Ten Towns. [32]They brought to him one who was deaf and had a speech impediment. They begged him to lay his hand on him. [33]He took him aside privately from the multitude, and put his fingers into his ears. Then he spat, and touched his tongue. [34]Looking up to heaven, he sighed deeply, and said to him, "*Ippatah*," that is, "Be opened." [35]Immediately his ears were opened, the impediment of his tongue was released, and he spoke clearly. [36]Yeshua commanded them that they should tell no one, but the more he commanded them, so much the more widely they proclaimed it. [37]They were overwhelmed with astonishment, saying, "He has done all things well. He even makes the deaf hear, and the mute speak!"

8 [1]In those days, when there was a very large crowd and they had nothing to eat, Yeshua called his disciples to himself and said to them, [2]"I have compassion on the crowd, because they have stayed with me now three days, and have nothing to eat. [3]If I send them away to their home fasting, they will faint on the way, for some of them have come a long way."

[4]His disciples answered him, "From where could one satisfy these people with bread here in a deserted place?"

[5]He asked them, "How many loaves do you+ have?"

They said, "Seven."

[6]He commanded the crowd to sit down on the ground, and he took the seven loaves. Having given thanks, he broke them, and gave them to his disciples to serve. Then they served the crowd. [7]They had a few small fish. Having given a blessing, he wanted these served also. [8]They ate and were filled. They took up seven baskets of broken pieces that were left over. [9]Those who had eaten were about four thousand. Then he sent them away.

[10]He entered into the boat right away with his disciples, and came into the region of Dalmanuta. [11]The Perushim came out and began to question him, seeking from him a sign from Heaven, and testing him. [12]He sighed deeply in his spirit, and said, "Why does this generation seek a sign? I assure you+ that no sign will be given to this generation."

7:33 "A tradition: the spit of a firstborn of a father is healing, but the spit of a firstborn of a mother is not healing." (Tal. Baba Bathra 126b) "There is a portion in the age to come for all Israel... These are those who have no portion in the age to come... one who whispers over a wound... R. Johanan said, 'But only if he spits in doing this, because the Name of Heaven may not be remembered with spitting.'" (Tal. Sanhedrin 11.1 [90a])

8:4 Their question is natural, but strange. Every day for forty years, God provided bread in the wilderness for our ancestors He brought out of Egypt.

[13]He left them, and entering into the boat again, he departed to the other side. [14]They forgot to take bread, and did not have any in the boat with them, except one loaf. [15]He admonished them, "Listen, beware of the leaven of the Perushim and the leaven of Herod."

[16]They spoke with one another, saying, "It's because we have no bread."

[17]Perceiving it, Yeshua said to them, "Why do you+ think that it's because you+ have no bread? Do you+ still not perceive or understand? Is your+ heart still hardened? [18]Having eyes, do you+ not see? Having ears, do you+ not hear? [Jer. 5:21, Ezek. 12:2] Do you+ not remember? [19]When I broke the five loaves among the five thousand, how many baskets full of broken pieces did you+ take up?"

They told him, "Twelve."

[20]"When the seven loaves fed the four thousand, how many baskets full of broken pieces did you+ take up?"

They told him, "Seven."

[21]He asked them, "Do you+ still not understand?"

[22]He came to Beit Tzaidah. They brought a blind man to him, and begged him to touch him. [23]He took hold of the blind man by the hand, and brought him out of the village. When he had spit on his eyes, and laid his hands on him, he asked him if he saw anything.

[24]He looked up and said, "I see men, in that I see them as trees walking around."

[25]He then laid his hands on his eyes again, and made him look up. He was restored, and saw everything clearly. [26]He sent him away to his house, saying, "Do not enter into the village."

[27]Yeshua went out with his disciples into the villages of Caesarea Philippi. On the way he asked his disciples, "Who do men say that I am?"

[28]They told him, "Yoḥanan the Immerser. And others say Eliyahu, but others, one of the prophets."

[29]He said to them, "But you+, who do you+ say that I am?"

Kefa answered, "You are the Messiah."

[30]He charged them that they should tell no one about him. [31]He began to teach them that the Son of Adam must suffer many things, and be rejected by the Elders, the chief Kohanim, and the Torah scholars, and be killed, and rise again after three days. [32]He spoke to them openly. Kefa took him and began to rebuke him. [33]But turning around and seeing his disciples, he rebuked Kefa, and said, "Get behind me, adversary. For your thoughts are not on the things of God, but on the things of men."

[34]He called the multitude to himself with his disciples, and said to them, "Whoever wants to come after me, let him say no to himself, take up his tree of death, and follow me. [35]For whoever wants to save his life will lose it, and whoever will lose his life for my sake and for the good news will save it. [36]For what does it profit a man to gain the whole world and forfeit his soul? [37]For what will a man give in exchange for his soul? [38]For whoever will be ashamed of me and of my words in this adulterous and sinful generation, the Son of Adam also will be ashamed of him, when he comes in the glory of his Father with the holy angels."

9 [1]He said to them, "I assure you+ there are some standing here who will certainly not taste death until they see God's kingdom come with power."

8:23 See note to 7:33.

9:1 See "Your Children Saw Your Kingdom" in the ADDITIONAL NOTES.

²After six days Yeshua took with him Kefa, Jacob, and Yoḥanan, and brought them up onto a high mountain privately by themselves. And his appearance was changed before them. ³His clothing became radiant, shining like bright, white snow, such as no launderer on earth can whiten them. ⁴Eliyahu and Moses appeared to them, and they were talking with Yeshua.

⁵Kefa said to Yeshua, "Rabbi, it is good for us to be here. Let us make three temporary shelters — one for you, one for Moses, and one for Eliyahu." ⁶For he did not know what to say, because they were very afraid.

⁷A cloud came, overshadowing them, and a voice came out of the cloud, "This is My beloved Son. Listen to him." ⁸Looking around, they suddenly no longer saw anyone with them, except Yeshua only.

⁹As they were coming down from the mountain, he commanded them that they should tell no one what things they had seen, until after the Son of Adam had risen from the dead. ¹⁰They focused on this saying among themselves, arguing about what the rising from the dead is.

¹¹They asked him, "Why do the Torah scholars say that Eliyahu must come first?"

¹²He said to them, "Indeed, Eliyahu does come first and restores all things. Yet why is it written about the Son of Adam that he must suffer many things and be treated with contempt? ¹³However, I tell you⁺ that Eliyahu has also come, and they have done to him whatever they wanted to, even as it is written about him."

¹⁴Coming to the disciples, he saw a large crowd around them, and Torah scholars questioning them. ¹⁵When they saw him, all the crowd was immediately filled with awe, and ran to him to greet him. ¹⁶He asked, "What are you⁺ discussing with them?"

¹⁷One from the crowd responded, "Rabbi, I brought to you my son, who has a mute spirit. ¹⁸And wherever it seizes him, it throws him down, and he foams at the mouth, grinds his teeth, and becomes rigid. I asked your disciples to cast it out, and they could not."

¹⁹He answered him, "Unbelieving generation, how long shall I be with you⁺? How long shall I bear with you⁺? Bring him to me."

²⁰They brought him to him. And when he saw him, the spirit immediately convulsed him, and he fell on the ground, rolling and foaming at the mouth.

²¹Yeshua asked his father, "How long a time has this been happening to him?"

He said, "From childhood. ²²Often it has cast him both into the fire and into the water, to destroy him. But if you can do anything, have compassion on us, and help us."

²³Yeshua said to him, "If you can believe, all things are possible to him who believes."

²⁴The father of the child immediately cried out, "I believe. Help me with the unbelief!"

²⁵When Yeshua saw that a crowd was running together, he rebuked the unclean spirit, saying to it, "You mute and deaf spirit, I command you, come out of him, and never enter him again!"

9:3-13 "The Holy One, blessed be He, said: 'Moses, by your life, as you gave your life to them in this age, so too in the age to come when I bring Eliyahu the prophet to them, you two will come together.'" (Mid. D'varim Rabbah 3:17)

9:13 "Eliyahu has come." can be compared to the statement "Pinchas is Eliyahu." [e.g. Yalkut Shim'oni, chapter 771] The rabbis equated the two because of the zeal for righteousness of Pinchas. (cf. Luke 1:17)

[26]Having cried out and thrown him into great convulsions, it came out of him. The boy became as if dead, so that many said that he was dead. [27]But Yeshua took him by the hand and raised him up, and he arose.

[28]When he had come into the house, his disciples asked him privately, "Why couldn't we cast it out?" [29]He said to them, "This kind will go out by nothing except prayer."

[30]They went out from there, and passed through the Galil. He did not want anyone to know it, [31]because he was teaching his disciples. And he said to them, "The Son of Adam is being delivered into the hands of men, and they will kill him. And when he is killed, he will rise again on the third day." [32]But they did not understand what he said, and were afraid to ask him.

[33]He came to Kfar Naḥum, and when he was in the house he asked them, "What were you[+] discussing among yourselves on the way?" [34]But they were silent, because on the way they had been arguing with one another about who was the greatest.

[35]He sat down, called the twelve, and said to them, "If any man wants to be first, he will be last of all and servant of all." [36]He took a little child, and set him in the middle of them. Taking him in his arms, he said to them, [37]"Whoever receives one such little child in my name, receives me. And whoever receives me, does not receive me, but the One who sent me."

[38]Yoḥanan said to him, "Rabbi, we saw someone who does not follow us casting out demons in your name. And we stopped him, because he does not follow us."

[39]But Yeshua said, "Do not stop him, for there is no one who will do a mighty work in my name, and be able quickly to speak evil of me. [40]For whoever is not against us is on our side. [41]For whoever will give you[+] a cup of water to drink in my name because you[+] are Messiah's, I assure you[+] he will surely not lose his reward. [42]Whoever causes one of these little ones who believe in me to stumble, it would be better for him if he were thrown into the sea with a millstone hung around his neck. [43]If your hand causes you to stumble, cut it off. It is better for you to enter into Life maimed, rather than to go into Gehinnom having two hands, into the unquenchable fire. [44]

9:41 Mid. Ruth 5:6: "In the past when a man did a good deed, the prophet recorded it; but now when a man does a good deed, who records it? Eliyahu records it, then Messiah the king and the Holy One, blessed be He, seal it with their hands. This is the meaning of the verse (Mal. 3:16), 'Then those who feared the Everpresent Lord spoke with one another; and the Everpresent Lord paid attention, and heard, and a book of remembrance was written before Him.'"

9:42 "The one who causes his friend to stumble takes his place for all punishment." (Rashi on Num. 30:16, citing Sifre) Rashi also comments on Dt. 23:4-9, referring to the Midrash Bemidbar 21:4 on Num. 25:17. He compares the Edomites and the Egyptians, who can enter the community/*kahal/ekklesia* of the Everpresent Lord after three generations, to the Ammonites and Moabites who cannot even enter through the tenth generation. "The rest of the peoples are permitted immediately. This teaches that one who causes a person to sin, it is harder for him than the one who kills him; because the one who kills him kills him in this age, but the one who causes him to sin takes him out of this age and from the age to come. Because of this, Edom, who met them with the sword, were not abhorred; and in the same way, Egypt, who drowned them. But those who caused them to sin were abhorred (Siphre)."

⁴⁵"If your foot causes you to stumble, cut it off. It is better for you to enter into Life lame, rather than having your two feet to be cast into Gehinnom, into the fire that will never be quenched. ^{46 47}If your eye causes you to stumble, cast it out. It is better for you to enter into God's kingdom with one eye, rather than to be cast into the Gehinnom of fire having two eyes, ⁴⁸where their worm does not die, and the fire is not quenched.' [Is. 66:24] ⁴⁹For everyone will be salted with fire, and every sacrifice will be seasoned with salt. [Lev. 2:13] ⁵⁰Salt is good, but if the salt has lost its saltiness, with what will you⁺ season it? Have salt in yourselves, and be at peace with one another."

10 ¹He arose from there and came into the borders of Judea and by the other side of the Yarden. Multitudes came together to him again. As he usually did, he was teaching them. ²Some Perushim came to him, testing him, and asked him, "Is it lawful for a man to divorce his wife?"

³He answered, "What did Moses command you⁺?"

⁴They said, "Moses allowed a certificate of divorce to be written, and to have her depart." [Deut 24:1,3]

⁵But Yeshua said to them, "Because of your⁺ hardness of heart, he wrote this commandment for you⁺. ⁶But from the beginning of the creation, 'God made them male and female. [Gen 1:27, 5:2] ⁷For this cause a man will leave his father and mother, and will be joined to his wife. ⁸And the two will become one flesh,' [Gen. 2:24] so that they are no longer two, but one flesh. ⁹So let no man separate what God has joined together."

¹⁰In the house, his disciples asked him again about the same matter. ¹¹He said to them, "Whoever divorces his wife and marries another commits adultery against her. ¹²If a woman herself divorces her husband, and marries another, she commits adultery."

¹³They were bringing little children to him so that he might touch them, but the disciples rebuked those who were bringing them. ¹⁴But when Yeshua saw it, he was angry, and said to them, "Allow the

9:44, 46 "where their worm does not die, and the fire is not quenched" is not repeated in the important early texts in these verses, but is in v. 48.

9:48 Tal. Sanhedrin 100b also refers to Is. 66:24. It says, "Concerning the measure of punishment it is written, 'And they will go forth, and see the corpses of the men who have transgressed against Me, for their worm will not die, and their fire will not be quenched: and they will be an abhorring unto all flesh.'"

9:49 "They then cleanse the bodies, and divide them into parts, and salt them with salt, and lay them upon the altar, while the pieces of wood are piled one upon another, and the fire is burning; they next cleanse the feet of the sacrifices and the inwards in an accurate manner, and so lay them to the rest to be purged by the fire, while the priests received the hides. This is the way of offering a burnt offering." (Josephus, *Antiq.* 3:227 [3.9.1.227])

"Even as it is impossible to offer sacrifices without a priesthood, even so it is impossible to offer sacrifices without salt!" (Tal. Menachot 20a in a lengthy discussion of sacrifices and salt.)

10:2 "Mishnah. Beth Shammai says: A man should not divorce his wife unless he has found indecent behavior in her.... But Beth Hillel says, 'even if she has burned his food... R. Akiba says, 'even if he finds another more pleasing than she is...'" (Tal. Gittin 90a)

"Everyone who divorces his first wife, even the altar sheds tears over it." (Tal. Gittin 90b)

10:5 See "Regulating the Actions of Hard Hearts" in the ADDITIONAL NOTES.

little children to come to me. Do not forbid them, because God's kingdom belongs to such as these. ¹⁵I assure you⁺ that whoever does not receive God's kingdom as a little child will never enter into it." ¹⁶He gathered them in his arms, laid his hands on them, and blessed them.

¹⁷As he was going out on the road, someone ran to him, knelt before him, and asked him, "Good Teacher, what shall I do that I may inherit eternal life?"

¹⁸Yeshua said to him, "Why do you call me good? No one is good except one — God. ¹⁹You know the commandments: Do not murder. Do not commit adultery. Do not steal. Do not give false testimony. Do not defraud. Honor your father and mother." [Ex. 20:12-16, Dt. 5:16-20; Mal. 3:5; Sirach 34:21-22]

²⁰He said to him, "Teacher, I have observed all these things from my youth."

²¹Looking at him, Yeshua loved him and said to him, "You lack one thing. Go, sell all that you have, give to the poor, and you will have treasure in heaven. Then come, follow me."

²²But this word made him sorrowful, and he went away grieved, because he was one who had great possessions. ²³Yeshua looked around, and said to his disciples, "How difficult it is for those who have riches to enter into God's kingdom."

²⁴The disciples were overwhelmed at his words. But Yeshua responded again, "Children, how hard it is for those who trust in riches to enter into God's kingdom. ²⁵It is easier for a camel to go through the eye of a needle than for a rich man to enter into God's kingdom."

²⁶They were all the more astonished, saying to him, "Then who can be saved?"

²⁷Looking at them, Yeshua said, "With men it is impossible, but not with God, for all things are possible with God."

²⁸Kefa began to say to him, "Look, we have left all, and have followed you."

²⁹Yeshua said, "I assure you⁺ there is no one who has left house, or brothers, or sisters, or father, or mother, or wife, or children, or land, for my sake and for the good news, ³⁰who will not receive one hundred times more of these now in this time — houses, brothers, sisters, mothers, children, and land — accompanied by persecutions, and eternal life in the age that is coming. ³¹But many who are first will be last, and the last first."

10:17-23 The response of Yeshua to the rich young man — "You know the commandments" — is interesting. Yeshua states some of the Ten Commandments and adds one commandment that is expressed elsewhere — "Do not defraud." This commandment primarily refers to giving the hired laborer all that is due to him. The young man, who had many possessions, claimed to have always done this.

When Yeshua told him to give his many possessions to the poor and then come follow him, the young man turned and walked away. He valued the riches of earth more than the riches of the kingdom. "How difficult it is for those who have riches to enter into God's kingdom."

10:21 "Monobaz the king spent all his treasure in years of hardship. His brothers said to him, 'Your fathers stored up treasure and added to that of their fathers. But you have continued to spend all your treasures, yours and your fathers.' He said to them, 'My fathers stored up treasures below, and I have stored up treasures above…. My fathers stored up treasures of Mammon, but I have stored up treasures of souls…. My fathers stored up treasures in this age, but I have stored up for the age to come.'" (Tos. Peah 4:18)

[32]They were on the road, going up to Yerushala'im, and Yeshua was going in front of them. They were overwhelmed, and those who followed were fearful. He again took the twelve, and began to tell them the things that were going to happen to him. [33]"Listen, we are going up to Yerushala'im. The Son of Adam will be delivered to the chief Kohanim and the Torah scholars. They will condemn him to death, and will deliver him to the Gentiles. [34]They will mock him, spit on him, scourge him, and kill him. Then after three days he will rise again."

[35]Jacob and Yohanan, the sons of Zevadyah, came near to him, saying, "Rabbi, we want you to do for us whatever we ask."

[36]He said to them, "What do you+ want me to do for you+?"

[37]They said to him, "Grant to us that in your glory we may sit, one at your right hand, and one at your left hand."

[38]But Yeshua said to them, "You+ do not know what you are asking. Are you+ able to drink the cup that I drink, and to be immersed with the same immersion with which I am immersed?"

[39]They said to him, "We are able."

Yeshua said to them, "You+ will indeed drink the cup that I drink, and you+ will be immersed with the same immersion with which I am immersed. [40]However, to sit at my right hand and at my left hand is not mine to give, but it is for those for whom it has been prepared."

[41]When the ten heard it, they began to be indignant towards Jacob and Yohanan. [42]Yeshua called them, and said to them, "You+ know that those who are recognized as rulers over the Gentiles lord it over them, and their great ones exercise authority over them. [43]However, it is not like this with you+, but whoever wants to become great among you+ is to be your+ servant. [44]Whoever of you+ wants to become first among you+ is to be bondservant of all. [45]For the Son of Adam also came not to be served, but to serve, and to give his life as a ransom for many."

[46]They came to Yeriho. As he went out from Yeriho with his disciples and a large crowd, Bar Timai (the son of Timai), a blind beggar, was sitting by the road. [47]When he heard that it was Yeshua the Natzri, he began to cry out and say, "Yeshua, Son of David, have mercy on me!" [48]Many rebuked him, so that he would be quiet, but he cried out all the more, "Son of David, have mercy on me!"

[49]Yeshua stood still, and said, "Call him."

They called the blind man, saying to him, "Be encouraged. Get up. He is calling you." [50]Throwing aside his cloak, he sprang up and came to Yeshua.

[51]Yeshua asked him, "What do you want me to do for you?"

The blind man said to him, "My rabbi, that I may see again."

[52]Yeshua said to him, "Go your way. Your faith has made you well." He received his sight at once, and followed Yeshua on the road.

11 [1]When they drew near to Yerushala'im, to Beit Pagei and Beit Anyah, at the Mount of Olives, he sent two of his disciples [2]and said to them, "Go your+ way into the village that is opposite you+. As soon as you+ enter it, you+ will find a young donkey tethered, on which no one has sat. Untie it, and bring it. [3]And if someone asks you+, 'Why are you+ doing this?' say, 'The Lord has need of it.' And he will send it here right away."

[4]They went away, and found a young donkey tethered at the door outside in the open street, and they untied him. [5]Some of those who stood there asked them, "What are you+ doing, untying the young donkey?" [6]They spoke to them just as Yeshua had commanded, and they let them go.

[7]They brought the young donkey to Yeshua and threw their garments on it, and Yeshua sat on it. [8]Many spread their garments on the road, and others leafy branches which they had cut from the fields. [9]Those who went in front and those who followed cried out, "Please deliver us! Blessed is he who comes in the Name of the Everpresent Lord! [Ps. 118:26] [10]Blessed is the kingdom of our father David that comes in the Name of the Everpresent Lord! Please deliver us by the Most High!"

[11]Yeshua entered into the Temple in Yerushala'im. When he had looked around at everything, it being now evening, he went out to Beit Anyah with the twelve.

[12]The next day, when they had come out from Beit Anyah, he was hungry. [13]Seeing far off a fig tree with leaves, he came to see if perhaps he might find anything on it. When he came to it, he found nothing but leaves, for it was not the season for figs. [14]Yeshua said to it, "May no one ever eat fruit from you again," and his disciples heard it.

[15]They came to Yerushala'im, and Yeshua entered into the Temple. He began to throw out those who sold and those who bought in the Temple, and overthrew the tables of the money-changers and the seats of those who sold the doves. [16]He would not allow anyone to carry a container through the Temple. [17]Then he taught, saying to them, "Has it not been written, 'My house will be called a house of prayer for all the nations'? [Is. 56:7] But you[+] have made it a den of bandits!" [Jer. 7:11] [18]The chief Kohanim and the Torah scholars heard it, and tried to find a way they might destroy him, for they feared him, because all the multitude were astonished at his teaching.

[19]When evening came, he went out of the city. [20]As they passed by in the morning, they saw the fig tree withered away from the roots. [21]Remembering, Kefa said to him, "Rabbi, look. The fig tree which you cursed has withered away." [Is. 24:4-6; Jer. 23:10-11; Jon. 4:7; Num. 17:16-26H/1-11]

[22]Yeshua answered and said to them, "Have faith in God. [23]For I assure you[+] that whoever will say to this mountain, 'Be taken up and cast into the sea,' and does not doubt in his heart, but believes that what he says will happen — he will have whatever he says. [24]Therefore I tell you[+] that whatsoever things you[+] ask for in prayer, believe that you[+] receive, and you[+] will have them. [25]Whenever you[+] stand praying, forgive if you[+] have anything against anyone; so that your[+] Father, who is in heaven, may also forgive you[+] your[+] transgressions." [26]

11:8-10 The waving branches and shouts of "Hoshanna!" — i.e. "Deliver us!" — are a normal part of the observance of Sukkot, which anticipates the coming of God's kingdom. It is, apparently, in that anticipation that the crowd has responded to Yeshua.

11:15-18 "This (Temple) market was what in Rabbinic writings is styled 'the bazaars of the sons of Annas' (*Chanuyoth beney Chanan*), the sons of that High-Priest Annas, who is so infamous in New Testament history... From the unrighteousness of the traffic carried on in these Bazaars, and the greed of the owners, the 'Temple-market' was at the time most unpopular. This appears, not only from the conduct and words of the patriarch Simeon [the grandson of Hillel, cf. Ker. i. 7] and of Baba ben Buta... [Jerus. Chag. 78a], but from the fact that popular indignation, three years before the destruction of Jerusalem, swept away the Bazaars of the family of Annas, and this, as expressly stated, on account of the sinful greed which characterized their dealings." (Alfred Edersheim, <u>The Life and Times of Jesus the Messiah</u>, Anson D.F. Randolph and Company, New York, 1883, Vol. I, Pp. 371-2)

²⁷They came again to Yerushala'im, and as he was walking in the Temple, the chief Kohanim, and the Torah scholars, and the Elders came to him. ²⁸Now they began saying to him, "By what kind of authority do you do these things? Or who gave you this authority to do these things?" ²⁹Yeshua said to them, "I will ask you⁺ one question. Answer me, and I will tell you⁺ by what authority I do these things. ³⁰The immersion of Yoḥanan — was it from Heaven, or from men? Answer me."

³¹They reasoned with each other, "If we say, 'From Heaven,' he will say, 'Why then did you⁺ not believe him?' ³²If we say, 'From men'"— they feared the people, for all held Yoḥanan to truly be a prophet. ³³They answered Yeshua, "We do not know."

Yeshua said to them, "Neither will I tell you⁺ by what authority I do these things."

12 ¹He began to speak to them in parables. "A man planted a vineyard, put a hedge around it, dug a pit for the winepress, and built a tower. [Is. 5:1,2] He rented it out to farmers, and left the country. ²And in season, he sent a servant to the farmers to get from the farmers his share of the fruit of the vineyard. ³They took him, beat him, and sent him away empty-handed. ⁴Again he sent another servant to them, and they threw stones at him, wounded him in the head, and sent him away shamefully treated. ⁵Again he sent another and they killed him. And he sent many others. Some they beat. Some they killed. ⁶So still having his one son whom he loved, he sent him last to them, saying, 'They will respect my son.' ⁷But those farmers said to each other, 'This is the heir. Come, let's kill him, and the inheritance will be ours.' ⁸They took him, killed him, and threw him outside the vineyard. ⁹What therefore will the lord of the vineyard do? He will come and destroy the farmers, and will give the vineyard to others. ¹⁰Have you⁺ not even read this scripture: 'The stone which the builders rejected, the same was made the head of the corner. ¹¹This was from the Everpresent Lord, and it is marvelous in our eyes.'" [Ps. 118:22, 23]

¹²They tried to seize him, but they feared the multitude, because they knew that he spoke the parable against them. They left him, and went away. ¹³They sent certain Perushim and Herodians to him, in order to trap him in words. ¹⁴When they had come, they asked him, "Rabbi, we know that you are truthful, and do not defer to anyone; for you are not partial to anyone, but teach in truth the way of God. Is it lawful to give tribute to Caesar, or not? ¹⁵Should we give, or should we not give?"

But he, knowing their pretension, said to them, "Why do you⁺ test me? Bring me a denarius, that I may see it."

¹⁶They brought it. He said to them, "Whose image and inscription is this?"

They said to him, "Caesar's."

¹⁷Yeshua answered them, "Give back to Caesar the things that are Caesar's, and to God the things that are God's." They were astonished at him.

¹⁸Some Tzadukim, who say there is no resurrection, came to him. They questioned him, ¹⁹"Rabbi, Moses wrote to us, 'If a man's brother dies, and leaves a wife behind him, but leaves no children, his

12:1-12 The text says explicitly that the parable was spoken against "the chief Kohanim and Elders". vv. 11:27; 12:12 The kingdom would be taken away from them. They understood what Yeshua said, but they couldn't act openly against him because they feared the people, who gladly received his teachings. God's purpose for leaders is that they enable the people to be fruitful. See the note to Mt. 21:33-46.

12:8 "The vineyard of the Everpresent Commander of forces is the house of Israel..." (Is. 5:7)

brother should take his wife, and raise up children for his brother.' [20]There were seven brothers. The first took a wife, and died, leaving no children. [21]The second took her, and died, leaving no children behind him. The third likewise. [22]And the seven took her and left no children. Last of all the woman also died. [23]Therefore, when they rise in the resurrection, whose wife will she be? For all seven had her as a wife."

[24]Yeshua answered and said to them, "Isn't it because of this that you[+] are in error? — that you[+] do not know the Scriptures nor the power of God. [25]For when they rise from the dead, they neither marry nor are given in marriage, but are like angels in heaven. [26]But about the dead, that they are raised, have you[+] not read in the writing of Moses how God said to him at the bush, 'I am the God of Abraham, the God of Isaac, and the God of Jacob?' [27]He is not the God of the dead, but of the living. Therefore you[+] are in great error."

[28]One of the Torah scholars came, and heard them reasoning together. Knowing that he had answered them well, he asked him, "Which commandment is the greatest of all?"

[29]Yeshua answered, "The greatest is, 'Hear, O Israel, the Everpresent Lord, our God, the Everpresent Lord is one. [30]And you are to love the Everpresent Lord, your God, with all your heart, with all your soul, with all your mind, and with all your strength.' [Dt. 6:4,5] This is the first commandment. [31]And this is the second: 'You are to love your neighbor as yourself.' [Lev. 19:18] There is no other commandment greater than these."

[32]The Torah scholar said to him, "Well said, Rabbi. You have spoken the truth in saying that God is one, and there is none other besides Him. [Dt. 4:35] [33]And to love Him with all the heart, with all the understanding, with all the soul, and with all the strength [Dt. 6:5], and to love one's neighbor as oneself [Lev. 19: 18] is more than all whole burnt offerings and sacrifices."

[34]When Yeshua saw that he answered wisely, he said to him, "You are not far from God's kingdom." No one dared to question him any more.

[35]Yeshua responded as he taught in the Temple: "How is it that the Torah scholars say that the Messiah is the Son of David? [36]For David himself said by the Ruakh Kodesh, 'the Everpresent Lord said to my Lord, *Sit at my right hand, until I make your enemies the footstool of your feet.*' [Ps. 110:1] [37]Therefore David himself calls him 'Lord,' so how can he be his son?"

And the large crowd enjoyed listening to him. [38]In his teaching he said to them, "Beware of the Torah scholars who like to walk about in long robes, and to receive greetings in the marketplaces,

---

12:25 "In the Age to Come, there is neither eating nor drinking nor fruitfulness [i.e. procreation], nor increase [i.e. business], nor burden nor giving, nor jealousy nor hatred nor rivalry..." (Tal Berachot 17a)

12:26-27 "The Holy One, blessed by He, said to Moses, 'I request of you what I requested concerning Sodom: present Me with ten righteous men among them and I will not destroy them.' He replied, 'Lord of the Universe, I will present them to You. Here they are: myself, Aaron, Eleazar, Itamar, Pinchas, Joshua, and Caleb.' God said to him, 'These are seven.' Moses did not know what to do. He said, 'Lord of the Universe! Are the dead alive?' He said to him: 'Yes.' He said: 'If the dead are alive, remember Abraham, Isaac, and Israel, and there will be ten for You.'" (Mid. Ex. Rabbah 44:7)

12:28-30 "Hear O Israel, the Everpresent Lord, our God..." This identifies the God who is to be loved with all one's being, i.e. the God of Israel.

³⁹the best seats in the meetingplaces, and the best places at feasts. ⁴⁰These who devour the houses of widows and make long prayers for a pretense, these will receive greater condemnation."

⁴¹Yeshua sat down opposite the treasury, and saw how the multitude cast money into the treasury. Many who were rich were casting in much. ⁴²A poor widow came, and she cast in two small bronze coins, which equal a small fraction of a day's wage. ⁴³He called his disciples to himself, and said to them, "I assure you⁺ that this poor widow gave more than all those who were giving into the treasury, ⁴⁴for they all gave out of their abundance, but she, out of her poverty, gave all that she had to live on."

13 ¹As he went out of the Temple, one of his disciples said to him, "Rabbi, look at these stones, and these buildings!"

²Yeshua said to him, "Do you see these great buildings? There will not be left here one stone on another which will not be thrown down."

³As he sat on the Mount of Olives opposite the Temple, Kefa, Jacob, Yoḥanan, and Andreas asked him privately, ⁴"Tell us, when will these things be? What is the sign that these things are all about to be accomplished?"

⁵Yeshua began to tell them, "Be careful that no one leads you⁺ astray. ⁶For many will come in my name, saying, 'I am he!' and will lead many astray. ⁷When you⁺ hear of wars and war reports, do not be troubled, because it must happen. But that is not yet the end. ⁸For nation will rise against nation, and kingdom against kingdom. There will be earthquakes in various places. There will be famines and troubles. These things are the beginning of birth pains. ⁹But watch yourselves, because they will deliver you⁺ up to councils. You⁺ will be beaten in assemblies. You⁺ will stand before rulers and kings for my sake, for a testimony to them. ¹⁰The good news must first be proclaimed to all the nations. ¹¹When they lead you⁺ away and deliver you⁺ up, do not be anxious beforehand, or premeditate what you⁺ will say, but say whatever is given you⁺ in that hour. For it is not you⁺ who speak, but the Ruakh Kodesh.

¹²"Brother will deliver up brother to death, and the father his child. Children will rise up against parents, and cause them to be put to death. ¹³You⁺ will be hated by all men for my name's sake, but the one who endures to the end will be saved.

12:43 "One offers much and one offers little, [it is the same] so long as he directs his heart to heaven." (Tal. Menachot 110a)

13:1-2 "Whoever has not seen the buiding of Herod has never seen a beautiful building. Of what did he build it? Rabbah said: 'Of yellow and white marble. Some say, of blue, yellow and white marble.'" (Tal. Baba Bathra 4a)

"Caesar gave orders that they should now demolish the entire city and Temple. ...it was so thoroughly laid even with the ground by those that dug it up to the foundation, that there was left nothing to make those who came there believe it had ever been inhabited." (Josephus, The Jewish War, 7.1.1.1-3)

"Woe to the children on account of whose iniquities I destroyed My House and burned My Temple and exiled them among the peoples of the world." (Tal. Berachot 3a)

13:8 "When you see the kingdoms terrorizing one another, be on the lookout for the feet [i.e. the coming] of Messiah." (Mid. Genesis 42.4)

13:13 "At the end of days He will send His Messiah to redeem those who wait for the end of His salvation." (Yigdal 12)

[14]"Now when you[+] see the abomination of the desolation which was spoken of by Daniel the prophet [Dan. 9:27, 11:31, 12:11] standing where it should not be — (let the reader understand) — then let those who are in Judea flee to the mountains. [15]And let the one who is on the housetop not go down or enter in to take anything out of his house. [16]Let the one who is in the field not go back to take his cloak. [17]But woe to those who are with child and to those who nurse babies in those days.

[18]"Pray that your[+] flight will not be in the winter, [19]because in those days there will be affliction, such as there has not been from the beginning of the creation which God created until now, and never will be. [20]Unless the Everpresent Lord had shortened the days, no flesh would be saved. But for the sake of those chosen, whom He chose, He shortened the days.

[21]"At that time, if anyone tells you[+], 'Look, here is the Messiah!' or, 'Look, there!' do not believe it. [22]False messiahs and false prophets will arise and show signs and wonders, so that they may lead astray, if possible, even those chosen. [23]But be alert. Listen, I have told you[+] all things beforehand.

[24]"But in those days, after that affliction, the sun will be darkened, and the moon will not give its light. [Is. 13:10, Ezek. 32:7, Joel 2:10,31, 3:15] [25]The stars of the heavens will be falling [Is. 34:4], and the powers that are in the heavens will be shaken. [26]Then they will see the Son of Adam coming in clouds [Dan. 7:13] with great power and glory. [27]Then he will send out his angels, and will gather together his chosen ones from the four winds, from the ends of the earth to the ends of the heavens.

[28]"Now learn this parable from the fig tree. When its branch has already become tender, and puts forth its leaves, you[+] know that the summer is near. [29]So you[+] also, when you[+] see these things coming to pass, know that it is near, at the door. [30]I assure you[+] that this people will not pass away until all these things have taken place. [Jer. 31:35-36] [31]Heaven and earth will pass away, but my words will not pass away. [32]But of that day or that hour no one knows, not even the angels in heaven, nor the Son, but only the Father. [33]Be alert, watch and pray, because you[+] do not know when the time is.

[34]"It is like a man going out of the country, leaving his house and giving authority to his servants, to each one his work, and also commanding the doorkeeper to keep watch. [35]Watch therefore, because you[+] do not know when the lord of the house is coming — whether at evening, at midnight, when the rooster calls out, or in the morning. [36]Otherwise, coming suddenly, he will find you[+] sleeping. [37]What I say to you[+], I say to all: Be alert."

13:28-30 Some translate as "this generation," i.e. the generation that sees the things Yeshua has just described. Liddell and Scott give the first meaning of *genea* as "persons in a family". For *genea* as "people," see God's promise to Jacob in LXX Gen. 31:3.

In "The Revelation of Peter", which was considered canonical in the second century, Yeshua says explicitly, "Do you not understand that the fig-tree is the house of Israel? ...Have you not understood that the fig-tree is the house of Israel? I faithfully say to you, when the twigs of it have sprouted forth in the last days, then shall feigned Messiahs come and awake expectation saying: 'I am the Messiah, who is now come into the world.' ...Then the twigs of the fig-tree, that is, the house of Israel, will shoot forth."

"There is no greater sign for you of redemption than this: 'And you mountains of Israel, you will send out your branches and give your fruit to My people Israel, for they are about to come.' (Ezek. 36:8)" (Tal. Sanhedrin 98a)

14 ¹It was now two days before the feast of Pesakh and Matzot, and the chief Kohanim and the Torah scholars sought a way they might deceitfully seize him and kill him. ²For they said, "Not during the feast, otherwise there might be a riot of the people."

³While he was at Beit Anyah, as he sat at the table in the house of Shimon the leper, a woman came with an alabaster jar of ointment of very expensive pure nard. She broke the jar, and poured it over his head. ⁴But there were some among them who were indignant, saying, "What was the point of wasting this ointment? ⁵For this might have been sold for more than three hundred denarii, and given to the poor." And they were angry with her.

⁶But Yeshua said, "Leave her alone. Why do you⁺ trouble her? She has done a good deed to me. ⁷For you⁺ always have the poor with you⁺ [Dt. 15:11], and whenever you⁺ want to, you⁺ can do good to them, but you⁺ will not always have me. ⁸She has done what she could; she has anointed my body beforehand for the burial. ⁹I assure you⁺ that wherever this good news is proclaimed throughout the whole world, what this woman has done will also be spoken of for a memorial of her."

¹⁰Judah from K'riyot, who was one of the twelve, went away to the chief Kohanim, so that he might deliver him to them. ¹¹When they heard it, they were glad, and promised to give him money. He searched for a way he might conveniently deliver him up.

¹²On the first day of Matzot, when they sacrificed the Pesakh, his disciples asked him, "Where do you want us to go and prepare so that you can eat the Pesakh?"

¹³He sent two of his disciples, and said to them, "Go into the city, and there you⁺ will meet a man carrying a pitcher of water. Follow him, ¹⁴and wherever he enters, tell the master of the house, 'The Rabbi says, "Where is the guest room where I can eat the Pesakh with my disciples?"' ¹⁵He himself will show you⁺ a large upper room, furnished and ready. Prepare for us there."

¹⁶His disciples went out, and came into the city. And they found things as he had said to them, and they prepared the Pesakh.

¹⁷When it was evening he came with the twelve. ¹⁸As they were reclining and eating, Yeshua said, "I assure you⁺ that one of you⁺ who is eating with me will deliver me up."

¹⁹They began to be grieved, and to ask him one by one, "Surely not I?" And another said, "Surely not I?"

²⁰He answered them, "It is one of the twelve who dips with me in the dish. ²¹For the Son of Adam goes, even as it is written about him, but woe to that man by whom the Son of Adam is delivered up. It would be better for that man if he had not been born."

²²As they were eating, Yeshua took bread, and when he had given a blessing, he broke it, gave it to them, and said, "Take, eat. This is my body."

²³He took the cup, and when he had given thanks, he gave it to them. They all drank of it. ²⁴He said to them, "This is my blood of the new covenant, which is poured out for many. ²⁵I assure you⁺ I will not again drink of the fruit of the vine, until that day when I drink it anew in God's kingdom." ²⁶When they had sung praises, they went out to the Mount of Olives.

14:25 "I will not again drink of the fruit of the vine." The cup symbolizes Yeshua's blood, but it is "the fruit of the vine".

[27]Yeshua said to them, "All of you⁺ will be made to stumble tonight because of me, for it is written, 'I will strike the shepherd, and the sheep will be scattered.' [Zech. 13:7] [28]However, after I am raised up, I will go before you⁺ into the Galil."

[29]But Kefa said to him, "Although everyone may stumble, yet I will not."

[30]Yeshua said to him, "I assure you that today, even this night before the rooster calls out twice, you will deny me three times."

[31]But he vehemently said all the more, "If I must die with you, I will never deny you." They all said the same thing.

[32]They came to a place which was named Gat Shemanim. He said to his disciples, "Sit here, while I pray." [33]He took with him Kefa, Jacob, and Yohanan, and began to be extremely troubled and distressed. [34]He said to them, "My soul is very sorrowful, even unto death. Stay here and keep watch."

[35]He went forward a little, fell on the ground, and prayed that if it were possible the hour might pass by him. [36]He said, "Abba (Father), to You all things are possible. Please remove this cup from me. However, not what I desire, but what You desire."

[37]He came and found them sleeping. Then he said to Kefa, "Shimon, are you sleeping? Could you not keep watch one hour? [38]Be alert and pray so that you⁺ will not enter into temptation. The spirit indeed is willing, but the flesh is weak."

[39]Again he went away and prayed, saying the same thing. [40]Again he returned and found them sleeping, for their eyes were very heavy. And they did not know what to answer him. [41]He came the third time and said to them, "Are you⁺ still sleeping and resting? That is not for now. The hour has come. Listen, the Son of Adam is delivered up into the hands of sinners. [42]Arise, let us go. Look, the one who delivers me up has come near."

[43]At that moment, while he was still speaking, Judah — one of the twelve — came, and with him a multitude with swords and clubs from the chief Kohanim, the Torah scholars, and the Elders. [44]Now the one who was delivering him up had given them a sign, saying, "Whomever I kiss, that is he. Grab him, and lead him away securely." [45]When he had come, he came to him right away and said, "Rabbi, Rabbi!" and kissed him.

[46]They laid their hands on him, and seized him. [47]But a certain one of those who stood by drew his sword, struck the servant of the Kohen Gadol, and cut off his ear.

[48]Yeshua responded to them, "Have you⁺ come out as against a bandit, with swords and clubs to seize me? [49]I was with you⁺ daily teaching in the Temple, and you⁺ did not arrest me. But this is so the Scriptures might be fulfilled."

[50]They all left him and fled. [51]A certain young man followed him, having a linen cloth thrown around himself, over his naked body. The young men grabbed him, [52]but he left the linen cloth, and fled naked. [53]They led Yeshua away to the Kohen Gadol. All the chief Kohanim, the Elders, and the Torah scholars came together with him.

14:47 In Tos. Parah 3:5, Yohanan b. Zakkai tears the ear of a particular man to make him unfit to be the High Priest.

14:58 See "Destroy this temple" in the ADDITIONAL NOTES.

14:63-64 Tal. Moed Katan 26a says that the High Priest is to tear his clothes on hearing blasphemy.

[54]Kefa had followed him from a distance until he came into the court of the Kohen Gadol. He was sitting with the officers, and warming himself in the light of the fire. [55]Now the chief Kohanim and the whole Council sought witnesses against Yeshua to put him to death, but they found none. [56]For many gave false testimony against him, but their testimony did not agree. [Ex. 20:16] [57]Some stood up and gave false testimony against him, saying, [58]"We heard him say, 'I will destroy this Temple that is made with hands, and in three days I will build another made without hands.'" [59]Even so, their testimony did not agree.

[60]The Kohen Gadol stood up in the middle, and asked Yeshua, "Have you nothing to answer? What is it these testify against you?" [61]But he was silent, and answered nothing. Again the Kohen Gadol asked him, "Are you the Messiah, the Son of the blessed One?"

[62]Yeshua said, "I am, and you[+] will see the Son of Adam sitting at the right hand of Power [Ps. 110:1], and coming with the clouds of the heavens." [Dan. 7:13]

[63]The Kohen Gadol tore his clothes, and said, "What further need do we have of witnesses? [64]You[+] have heard the blasphemy! What do you[+] think?" They all condemned him to be worthy of death. [65]Some began to spit on him, to blindfold him, and to beat him. Then they said to him, "Prophesy!" The officers slapped him with the palms of their hands.

[66]As Kefa was in the courtyard below, one of the servant girls of the Kohen Gadol came. [67]Seeing Kefa warming himself, she looked at him and said, "You were also with the Natzri, Yeshua!"

[68]But he denied it, saying, "I do not know nor even understand what you are saying." He went out on the porch, and the rooster called out.

[69]The servant girl saw him, and began again to tell those who stood by, "This is one of them." [70]But he again denied it. After a little while, again those who stood by said to Kefa, "You truly are one of them, for you are from the Galil, and your speech shows it." [71]But he began to take an oath and swear, "I do not know this man you[+] are talking about!" [72]The rooster called out the second time. Kefa remembered the word that Yeshua said to him, "Before the rooster crows twice, you will deny me three times." Thinking on this, he wept.

15 [1]As soon as it was morning, the chief Kohanim, with the Elders, Torah scholars, and the whole Council consulted with each other. They bound Yeshua, took him away, and delivered him up to Pilate. [2]Pilate asked him, "Are you the King of the Jews?"

He answered, "As you say."

[3]The chief Kohanim accused him of many things. [4]Pilate again asked him, "Have you no answer? See how many things they testify against you!" [5]But Yeshua made no further reply, so that Pilate was amazed.

[6]Now at the feast he used to release to them one prisoner, whomever they asked of him. [7]There was one called Bar Abba, chained with his companions in the uprising, men who had committed murder in the revolt. [8]The crowd rose up, beginning to demand what he always did for them. [9]Pilate answered them, "Do you[+] want me to release to you[+] the King of the Jews?" [10]For he knew that the chief Kohanim had delivered him up because of jealousy. [11]But the chief Kohanim stirred up the crowd so that he would release Bar Abba to them instead. [12]Pilate again asked them, "What then should I do to him whom you[+] call the King of the Jews?"

[13]They cried out again, "Put him to death on the stake!"

[14]Pilate said to them, "Why, what evil has he done?"

But they cried out all the more, "Put him to death on the stake!"

[15]Wanting to satisfy the crowd, Pilate released Bar Abba to them. And when he had flogged Yeshua, he handed him over to be put to death on the stake. [16]The soldiers led him away inside the court, which is the Praetorium; and they called together the whole garrison. [17]They clothed him with purple cloth, and wove a crown of thorns, which they put on him. [18]They began to salute him, "Hail, King of the Jews!" [19]They struck his head with a rod of reed, and spat on him. Bending their knees, they bowed down before him. [20]When they had mocked him, they took the purple cloth off of him, and put his own garments on him.

They led him out to put him to death on the stake. [21]They compelled a passerby who was coming from the country, Shimon of Kyrene, the father of Alexander and Rufus, to go with them, so that he might carry his stake. [22]They brought him to the place called Gulgolta, which is translated as, "The place of a skull." [23]They offered him wine mixed with myrrh to drink, but he did not take it.

[24]Having hung him on the stake, they divided his garments among them, casting lots for what each should take of them. [25]It was the third hour when they hung him on the stake. [26]The inscription of his accusation was written over him, "THE KING OF THE JEWS." [27]They hung two bandits by him on stakes, one on his right hand, and one on his left. [28]The scripture was fulfilled which says, "He was numbered with transgressors." [Is. 53:12]

[29]Those who passed by maligned him, wagging their heads and saying, "Ha! You who destroy the Temple and build it in three days, [30]save yourself and come down from the stake!"

[31]In the same way, the chief Kohanim with the Torah scholars were also mocking him among themselves. They said, "He saved others. He cannot save himself. [32]The Messiah! The King of Israel! Let him come down now from the stake, that we may see and believe." Those hung on stakes with him mocked him.

[33]When the sixth hour had come, there was darkness over the whole land until the ninth hour. [34]At the ninth hour Yeshua cried with a loud voice, "Eli, Eli, lama azavtani?" which is translated as, "My God, my God, why have You forsaken me?" [Ps. 22:1]

[35]When they heard it, some of those who stood by said, "Listen, he is calling Eliyahu."

[36]One ran and filled a sponge full of wine vinegar, put it on a rod of reed, and gave it to him to drink, saying, "Let him be. Let's see whether Eliyahu comes to take him down."

[37]Yeshua cried out with a loud voice, and breathed his last. [38]The veil of the Temple was torn in two from the top to the bottom. [39]When the centurion who stood facing him saw that he cried out like this and breathed his last, he said, "Truly this man was a son of God."

[40]There were also women watching from afar, among whom were both Miryam from Magdala, and Miryam the mother of the younger Jacob, Yosi, and Sh'lomit, and many other women who came

15:15 Tal. Ketubot 37a forbids flogging a person who is to be executed.

15:26 27:37 "King of the Jews," the Son of David, was the announcement of the prophets and the archangel, as well as the beginning and ending of Matthias's report. It is also the warning of Messiah's identification in his return. [Rev./Hazon 22:16]

15:34 The Codex Bezae has *zafthani* for the Hebrew *azavtani* of Ps.22:2H. (See Metzger, A Textual Commentary on the Greek New Testament, Pp. 70, 119.)

up with him to Yerushala'im. [41]When he was in the Galil, they followed him and served him.

[42]When evening had now come, because it was the Preparation that is before Shabbat, [43]Yosef of Ramatayim, an honorable member of the Council, came. He himself was also waiting for God's kingdom. He boldly went in to Pilate, and asked for Yeshua's body. [44]Pilate wondered whether he was already dead. Summoning the centurion, he asked him whether he had been dead long. [45]When he found out from the centurion, he granted the body to Yosef.

[46]He bought a linen cloth, took him down, wrapped him in the linen cloth, and laid him in a tomb which had been cut out of a rock. He rolled a stone against the door of the tomb. [47]Miryam from Magdala and Miryam the mother of Yosi saw where he was laid.

16 [1]When Shabbat was past, Miryam from Magdala, and Miryam the mother of Jacob, and Sh'lomit bought fragrant ointments, so that they might come and anoint him. [2]Very early on the first day of the week, they came to the tomb when the sun had risen. [3]They were saying to each other, "Who will roll away the stone from the door of the tomb for us?" — [4]because it was very large. Looking up, they saw that the stone was rolled back.

[5]Entering into the tomb, they saw a young man sitting on the right side, dressed in a white robe, and they were astonished. [6]He said to them, "Do not be astonished. You[+] seek Yeshua the Natzri, who was put to death on the stake. He has been raised, he is not here. Look, the place where they laid him. [7]Now go, tell his disciples and Kefa that he goes before you[+] into the Galil. There you[+] will see him, as he told you[+]." [8]They went out and fled from the tomb, because they were trembling and in shock. They said nothing to anyone, because they were afraid.

{[9]Now when he had been raised early on the first of the week, he appeared first to Miryam the Magdalene, from whom he had cast out seven demons. [10]She went and told those who had been with him, as they mourned and wept. [11]When they heard that he was alive and had been seen by her, they did not believe. [12]After these things he appeared in another form to two of them, as they walked on their way into the countryside. [13]They went away and told it to the others. They did not believe them either.

[14]Afterward he appeared to the eleven themselves as they sat at the table. And he rebuked them for their disbelief and hardness of heart, because they did not believe those who had seen him after he had been raised. [15]He said to them, "As you[+] go into all the world, proclaim the good news to all creation. [16]The one who believes and is immersed will be saved, but the one who will not believe will be condemned. [17]These signs will accompany those who believe: they will cast out demons in my name and they will speak with new languages. [18]They will take up serpents, and if they drink any deadly thing, it will not harm them in any way. They will lay hands on the sick, and they will recover."

[19]So then, after he had spoken to them, the Lord was received up into heaven, and sat at the right hand of God. [20]They went out and proclaimed everywhere, the Lord working with them and confirming the word by the signs that followed. Amen.}

16:9-20 does not appear in many manuscripts.

The Report of Luke

1 [1-2]Those who were eyewitnesses from the beginning and servants of the Word delivered to us those matters which have been fully believed among us. Even as many have attempted to organize a narrative concerning these things, [3]so it seemed good to me also, having traced the course of all things accurately from the first, to write them in sequence to you, Most Excellent Theophilus, [4]so that you might know the certainty concerning the things in which you were verbally informed.

[5]In the days of Herod, the king of Judea, there was a certain Kohen named Zeḥaryaḥ, of the priestly division of Aviyah. He had a wife of the daughters of Aaron, and her name was Elisheva. [6]They were both righteous before God, walking blamelessly in all the commandments and statutes of the Everpresent Lord. [7]But they were childless, because Elisheva was barren, and they both were well advanced in years. [8]Now while he was fulfilling the service of a Kohen before God in the order of his division, [9]his lot, according to the custom of the service of the Kohanim, was to enter into the Temple of the Everpresent Lord and burn incense. [10]The whole multitude of the people were praying outside at the hour of incense.

[11]An angel of the Everpresent Lord appeared to him, standing on the right side of the altar of incense. [12]Zeḥaryah was troubled when he saw him, and fear fell upon him. [13]But the angel said to him, "Do not be afraid, Zeḥaryah, because your request has been heard. Your wife Elisheva will bear you a son, and you are to call his name Yoḥanan. [14]You will have joy and gladness; and many will rejoice at his birth, [15]because he will be great in the sight of the Everpresent Lord. And he will drink no wine or strong drink. He will be filled with the Ruakh Kodesh, even from his mother's womb. [16]He will turn many of the children of Israel to the Everpresent Lord, their God. [17]He will go before Him in the spirit and power of Eliyahu, 'to turn the hearts of the fathers to the children,' [Mal. 4:6] and the disobedient to the wisdom of the just; to make ready a people prepared for the Everpresent Lord."

[18]Zeḥaryah said to the angel, "How can I be sure of this? For I am an old man, and my wife is well advanced in years."

[19]The angel answered him, "I am Gavriel, who stands in the presence of God. I was sent to speak to you, and to bring you this good news. [20]You will be silent and not able to speak until the day that these things happen, because you did not believe my words, which will be fulfilled in their proper time."

1:3 Theophilus, like the governors Felix (Acts 23:26; 24:3) and Festus (Acts 26:25), bears the title, "Most Excellent".

1:9 According to Tal. Tamid 3.1, the priests cast lots for each of the different tasks of their service.

1:25 The rabbis considered the inability to bear children as grounds for divorce. (Tal. Gittin 46b)

1:19, 26 Mid. Ex. Rabba 18:5 gives examples of God using Mikhael and Gabriel as guardians of Israel, "as it says, 'O Jerusalem, I have appointed guardians over your walls.' [Is. 62:6]"

²¹The people were waiting for Zeḥaryah, and they were surprised that he took so long in the Temple. ²²When he came out, he could not speak to them, but they understood that he had seen a vision in the Temple. He continued making signs to them, and remained mute. ²³When the days of his service were completed, he departed to his house. ²⁴After these days, his wife Elisheva conceived, and she hid herself five months, saying that, ²⁵"The Everpresent Lord has done this for me in the days in which He looked upon me to take away my reproach among men."

²⁶Now in the sixth month, the angel Gavriel was sent from God to a city of the Galil named Natzrat, ²⁷to a virgin pledged to be married to a man whose name was Yosef, of the house of David. The virgin's name was Miryam. ²⁸Having come in, the angel said to her, "Rejoice, you who have received grace. The Everpresent Lord is with you. You are blessed among women."

²⁹But when she saw him, she was extremely troubled at what he said, and wondered what kind of greeting this could be. ³⁰The angel said to her, "Do not be afraid, Miryam, for you have found grace with God. [Gen. 6:8] ³¹Know that you will conceive in your womb, and bring forth a son, and will call his name 'Yeshua'. ³²He will be great, and will be called the Son of the Most High. God, the Everpresent Lord, will give him the throne of his father David. ³³And he will reign over the house of Jacob forever. There will be no end to his kingdom." [Is. 9:6-7]

³⁴Miryam said to the angel, "How can this be, since I am a virgin?"

³⁵The angel answered her, "The Ruakh Kodesh will come on you, and the power of the Most High will overshadow you. Therefore also the holy one who is born from you will be called the Son of God. ³⁶Your relative Elisheva also has conceived a son in her old age! And this is the sixth month for her who was called barren, ³⁷because nothing God has spoken will be impossible." [Gen. 18:13-14]

³⁸Miryam said, "Here is the handmaid of the Everpresent Lord; let it be to me as you have said." The angel departed from her.

³⁹Miryam arose in those days and went with haste into a city of Judea in the hill country. ⁴⁰Then she entered into the house of Zeḥaryah and greeted Elisheva. ⁴¹When Elisheva heard Miryam's greeting, the baby leaped in her womb, and Elisheva was filled with the Ruakh Kodesh. ⁴²She called out with a loud voice and said, "You are blessed among women, and the fruit of your womb is blessed. ⁴³How does it happen to me that the mother of my Lord should come to me? ⁴⁴For when the voice of your greeting came into my ears, the baby leaped for joy in my womb! ⁴⁵Blessed is she who believed, for there will be a fulfillment of the things which have been spoken to her from the Everpresent Lord."

⁴⁶Miryam said, "My soul magnifies the Everpresent Lord. ⁴⁷My spirit has rejoiced in God my Savior, ⁴⁸because He has looked upon the humble state of His handmaid. For from now on, all generations will call me blessed, ⁴⁹because the Mighty One has done great things for me. Holy is His name. ⁵⁰"His mercy is to generations of generations of those who fear Him. [Ex. 34:7; Ps. 103:17] ⁵¹He has shown strength with His arm. He has scattered the proud in the imagination of their heart. ⁵²He has put down princes from their thrones, and has exalted the lowly. ⁵³He has filled the hungry with good things. [Ps. 107:9] He has sent the rich away empty. ⁵⁴He has given help to Israel, His servant, to remember mercy, ⁵⁵as He spoke to our fathers, to Abraham and his seed forever."

1:27 See "The Virgin will be Pregnant" in the ADDITIONAL NOTES.
1:31, 2:21 "Yeshua" means "savior".

[56]Miryam stayed with her about three months, and then returned to her house. [57]Now the time was fulfilled for Elisheva to give birth, and she brought forth a son. [58]Her neighbors and her relatives heard that the Everpresent Lord had shown great mercy towards her, and they rejoiced with her. [59]On the eighth day they came to circumcise the child; and they were calling him Zeḥaryah, after the name of the father. [60]His mother responded, "No, but he will be called Yoḥanan."

[61]They said to her, "There is no one among your relatives who is called by this name." [62]They made signs to his father as to what he wanted him to be called.

[63]He asked for a writing tablet, and wrote, "His name is Yoḥanan." They were all amazed. [64]His mouth was opened immediately, and his tongue freed, and he spoke, blessing God. [65]Fear came on all who lived around them, and all these happenings were talked about throughout all the hill country of Judea. [66]All who heard them laid them up in their heart, saying, "What then will this child be?" For the hand of the Everpresent Lord was with him.

[67]His father, Zeḥaryah, was filled with the Ruakh Kodesh, and prophesied, [68]"Blessed be the Everpresent Lord, the God of Israel, for He has visited and brought about redemption for His people. [69]He has raised up a horn of salvation for us in the house of His servant David, [70]as He spoke by the mouth of His holy prophets long ago, [71]salvation from our enemies and from the hand of all who hate us. [Ps. 106:10] [72]It is to show the promised mercy towards our fathers, to remember His holy covenant, [73]the oath which He spoke to Abraham, our father; [74]to grant to us that we, being delivered out of the hand of our enemies, should serve Him without fear, [75]in holiness and righteousness before Him all the days of our life.

[76]"And you, child, will be called a prophet of the Most High, because you will go before the presence of the Lord to prepare His ways [Mal. 3:1], [77]to give knowledge of salvation to His people by the forgiveness of their sins; [78]because of the tender mercy of our God, whereby the dawn from on high will visit us; [79]to shine on those who sit in darkness and the shadow of death; [Is. 9:2] to guide our feet into the way of peace."

[80]The child grew, and was strengthened in spirit, and was in the wilderness until the day of his public appearance to Israel.

2 [1]Now in those days, a decree went out from Caesar Augustus that all the world should be registered. [2]This became "the first census" when Kyrenius was governor of Syria. [3]Everyone went to be registered, each to his own city. [4]Because he was of the house and family of David, Yosef also went up from the Galil, out of the city of Natzrat into Judea. He went to the city of David, which is called Beit Leḥem, [5]to register himself with Miryam, who was betrothed as his wife, and was pregnant.

[6]While they were there, the day came for her to give birth. [7]She brought forth her firstborn son. Then she wrapped him in bands of cloth, and laid him in a feeding trough, because there was no room for them in the inn.

[8]There were shepherds in the same region staying out at night, and keeping guard over their flock. [9]An angel of the Everpresent Lord stood by them, and the glory of the Everpresent Lord shone

2:9 "The Sages said, "In the hour when Moses was born, the whole house was filled with light." (Tal. Sotah 12a)

around them, and they were terrified![10]The angel said to them, "Do not be afraid, because I bring you[+] good news of great joy which will be to all the people! [11]For this day in the city of David, there is born to you[+] a savior, who is Messiah the Lord. (Is. 9:5H) [12]This is the sign to you[+]: you[+] will find a baby wrapped in bands of cloth, lying in a feeding trough." [13]Suddenly there was with the angel a multitude of the forces of heaven praising God and saying, [14]"Glory to God Most High, and peace on the earth, good will to men."

[15]When the angels went away from them into heaven, the shepherds said to each other, "Let's go to Beit Lehem now, and see this thing that has happened, which the Everpresent Lord has made known to us." [16]They came quickly, and found Miryam and Yosef, and the baby was lying in the feeding trough.

[17]When they had seen this, they made what was spoken to them about this child widely known. [18]All who heard it wondered at the things which the shepherds told them. [19]But Miryam kept all these sayings in mind, pondering them in her heart. [20]The shepherds returned, glorifying and praising God for all the things that they had heard and seen, just as it was told them.

[21]When eight days were fulfilled for the circumcision of the child, they called his name "Yeshua" — what he was called by the angel before he was conceived in the womb. [22]When the days of their purification according to the Torah of Moses were fulfilled, they brought him up to Yerushala'im, to present him to the Everpresent Lord. [23]As it is written in the Torah of the Everpresent Lord, "Every male who opens the womb shall be called holy to the Everpresent Lord." [Ex. 13:2, Num. 3:13, 8:17] [24]And they offered a sacrifice according to what is said in the Torah of the Everpresent Lord, "a pair of turtledoves, or two young pigeons." [Lev. 5:11, 12: 8]

[25]There was a man in Yerushala'im whose name was Shimon. This man was righteous and devout, looking for the comfort of Israel [Is. 40:1-11], and the Ruakh Kodesh was upon him. [26]It had been revealed to him by the Ruakh Kodesh that he would not see death before he had seen the Messiah of the Everpresent Lord. [27]When the parents brought in the child Yeshua so that they might do for him what was according to the custom of the Torah, he came, by the Spirit, into the Temple. [28]Then he received him into his arms, blessed God, and said, [29]"Now Master, let Your servant go in peace, according to Your word, [30]because my eyes have seen Your salvation, [31]which You have prepared before the face of all peoples — [32]a light for revelation to the Gentiles [Is. 9:2, 42:6, 49:6, 9, 51:4, 60:1-3], and glory to Your people Israel."

[33]His mother and Yosef were filled with wonder at the things which were spoken concerning him. [34]Then Shimon blessed them, and said to Miryam, his mother, "Listen, this child is set in place for the falling and the rising of many in Israel, and for a sign to be spoken against — [35]yes, a sword will pierce through your own soul — so that the thoughts of many hearts may be revealed."

[36]There was one Hannah, a prophetess, the daughter of Penuel, of the tribe of Asher. She was quite old. Having lived with a husband seven years from her virginity, [37]she was a widow eighty-four years old. She did not depart from the Temple, serving night and day with fastings and prayers. [38]Coming up at that very hour, she gave thanks to the Everpresent Lord, and spoke of him to all those waiting for the redemption of Yerushala'im.

2:24 The particular offering presented by Yosef and Miryam shows that they were poor. It was for cleansing her from her uncleanness.

[39]When they had completed all things according to the Torah of the Everpresent Lord, they returned to the Galil, to their own city, Natzrat. [40]The child grew, and became strong in spirit, being filled with wisdom; and the grace of God was upon him.

[41]Every year his parents went to Yerushala'im at the feast of Pesakh. [42]When he was twelve years old, they went up to Yerushala'im according to the custom of the feast. [43]Then when they had completed the days, as they were returning, the boy Yeshua stayed behind in Yerushala'im. His mother and Yosef did not know it, [44]but supposing him to be in the caravan of travelers, they went a day's journey. Then they looked for him among their relatives and acquaintances. [45]When they did not find him, they returned to Yerushala'im, looking for him. [46]It was after three days they found him in the Temple, sitting in the middle of the teachers, both listening to them, and asking them questions. [47]All who heard him were amazed at his perceptive responses. [48]When they saw him, they were astonished, and his mother said to him, "Son, why have you treated us this way? Your father and I were anxiously looking for you!"

[49]He said to them, "Why were you+ looking for me? Didn't you+ know it was necessary for me to be with what belongs to my Father?" [50]They did not understand the reply which he spoke to them.

[51]And he went down with them, and came to Natzrat. He was obedient to them, and his mother kept all these sayings in her heart. [52]And Yeshua increased in wisdom and stature, and in favor with God and men.

3 [1]Now in the fifteenth year of the rule of Tiberius Caesar, Pontius Pilate was governor of Judea, Herod was ruler of the Galil — a fourth of the province — and his brother Philip was ruler of the region of Ituraea and Trachonitis — a fourth of the province. Lysanias was ruler of Abilene — a fourth of the province, [2]and Hanan and Kayafa were the Kohanim Gedolim. Then the word of God came to Yohanan the son of Zeharyah, in the wilderness. [3]He came into all the region around the

---

3:2 It was not unusual for there to be more than one high priest. (cf. Tal. Pes. 57a, Tal. Yoma 18a, Tal. Makkot 11b)

3:19-20 Josephus gives some background and a different perspective in <u>Ant</u>. 18:111-119/18. 5.1-2.

3:22 The text does not tell us why the Spirit descended "as a dove," but perhaps it is because the dove on the ark [Gen. 8:8-12 signalled the end of the judgment of the flood and a new beginning for humanity.

Ben Zoma said, "'It is said, *And the spirit of God hovered over the face of the waters* — as a dove hovers over her children but does not touch [them].' Then R. Joshua said to his disciples, 'Ben Zoma is still outside [i.e. excommunicated].'" (Tal. Hagigah 15a)

But Mid. Gen. 2:4 says, "'And the Spirit of God hovered...' This is the spirit of Messiah the King." (cf. Mid. Gen. Alt. 97.1 and the reference to Messiah and the Spirit in Is. 11:2)

3:23 Num. 27:1-11 gives God's response to the appeal of the daughters of Tzelofehad. The name and possessions of a man who had daughters but no sons, was to be preserved by those who married the daughters. The son-in-law was to be considered a son of Tzelofehad. And we read in Ezra 2:61/Neh. 7:63 "And from among the priests: the descendants of... Barzillai (a man who had married a daughter of Barzillai the Gileadite and was called by that name)." And when Obed was born to Ruth, the women said, "A son has been born to Naomi," though the child was not physically descended from Naomi.

3:25-26 *Mattityahu* is the Hebrew name from which the Greek form of *Matthias/Mattathias* comes.

Yarden, proclaiming the immersion of repentance for forgiveness of sins. [4]As it is written in the scroll of the words of Isaiah the prophet, "The voice of one crying in the wilderness, 'Make ready the way of the Everpresent Lord. Make His paths straight. [5]Every valley will be filled. Every mountain and hill will be brought low. The crooked will become straight, and the rough ways smooth. [6]All flesh will see the salvation of God.'" [Is. 40:3-5]

[7]So he said to the multitudes who went out to be immersed by him, "Offspring of vipers, who warned you+ to flee from the coming wrath? [8]Bring forth therefore fruits worthy of repentance. And do not begin to say to yourselves, 'We have Abraham for our father,' because I tell you+ that God is able to raise up children to Abraham from these stones. [9]And even now the ax is laid to the root of the trees. Therefore every tree that does not bring forth good fruit will be cut down, and thrown into the fire."

[10]The multitudes asked him, "What then must we do?"

[11]He answered them, "The one who has two coats, let him give to the one who has none. The one who has food, let him do likewise."

[12]Tax collectors also came to be immersed, and they said to him, "Teacher, what must we do?"

[13]He said to them, "Collect no more than what is appointed to you+."

[14]Soldiers also asked him, "What about us? What must we do?" He said to them, "Do not oppress anyone, nor accuse anyone wrongfully. Be content with your+ wages."

[15]Now the people were waiting, and all of them wondered in their hearts concerning Yohanan, whether or not he was the Messiah. [16]Yohanan responded to them all, "I indeed immerse you+ in water, but one comes who is mightier than I; I am not worthy to loosen the strap of his sandals. He will immerse you+ in the Ruakh Kodesh and fire. [17]His fan is in his hand, and he will thoroughly cleanse his threshing floor, and will gather the wheat into his barn. But he will burn up the chaff with unquenchable fire." [18]Then with many other exhortations he proclaimed the good news to the people.

[19]He rebuked Herod the tetrarch concerning Herodias, his brother's wife, and concerning all the evil things which he had done. [20]Herod, however, imprisoned Yohanan, adding this also to them all.

[21]Now when all the people were immersed, Yeshua also was immersed, and was praying. Heaven was opened, [22]and the Ruakh Kodesh descended in the bodily appearance of a dove upon him. Then a voice came out of heaven saying "You are My beloved Son. I am truly pleased with you."

[23]Yeshua himself was about thirty years old when he began to teach. He was considered as the son of Yosef, of Eli, [24]of Matthat, of Levi, of Malki, of Yannai, of Yosef, [25]of Mattityahu, of Amos, of Nahum, of Hesli, of Naggai, [26]of Machat, of Mattityahu, of Shimei, of Yosef, of Judah, [27]of Yohanan, of Rhesa, of Zerubbabel, of Shealtiel, of Neri, [28]of Malki, of Addi, of Kosam, of Elmadan, of Er, [29]of Yeshua, of Eliezer, of Yoram, of Matthat, of Levi, [30]of Shimon, of Judah, of Yosef, of Yonam, of Elyakim, [31]of Mal'ah, of Manah, of Mattatah, of Natan, of David, [32]of Yishai, of Oved, of Boaz, of Salmon, of Nahshon, [33]of Amminadav, of Aram, of Yoram, of Hetzron, of Peretz, of Judah, [34]of Jacob, of Isaac, of Abraham, of Terah, of Nahor, [35]of Serug, of Re'u, of Peleg, of Ever, of Shelah [36]of Kenan, of Arpahshad, of Shem, of Noah, of Lameh, [37]of Metushelah, of Hanokh, of Yered, of Mahalal'el, of Kenan, [38]of Enosh, of Shet, of Adam, of God.

4 [1]Full of the Ruakh Kodesh, Yeshua returned from the Yarden. He was led by the Spirit into the wilderness. [2]Being tempted by the Enemy for forty days, he ate nothing in those days. Afterward, when the days were finished, he was hungry. [3]The Enemy said to him, "If you are the Son of God, command this stone to become bread."

[4]Yeshua answered him, "It is written, 'A person is not to live by bread alone, but by every word of God.'" [Dt. 8:3]

[5]Leading him up onto a high mountain, the Enemy showed him all the kingdoms of the world in a moment of time. [6]The Enemy said to him, "I will give you all this authority and their glory, because it has been delivered to me, and I give it to whomever I want. [7]So if you will bow down before me, it will all be yours."

[8]Yeshua answered him, "It is written, 'You are to bow down to the Everpresent Lord, your God, and you are to serve Him only.'" [Dt. 6: 13, 10:20]

[9]He led him to Yerushala'im, set him on the pinnacle of the Temple, and said to him, "If you are the Son of God, cast yourself down from here, [10]for it is written, 'He will give His angels charge concerning you, to guard you. [11]And on their hands they will bear you up, so that you do not strike your foot against a stone.'" [Ps. 91:11,12]

[12]Yeshua said to him in response, "It has been said, 'You are not to test the Everpresent Lord, your God.'" [Dt. 6:16] [13]When the Enemy had completed every temptation, he departed from him until another time.

[14]Yeshua returned in the power of the Spirit into the Galil, and news about him spread through all the surrounding area. [15]He taught in their meetingplaces, being praised by all.

[16]He came to Natzrat, where he had been brought up. As was his custom, he entered into the meetingplace on Shabbat, and stood up to read. [17]The scroll of the prophet Isaiah was handed to him. He unrolled the scroll, and found the place where it was written, [18]"The Spirit of the Everpresent Lord is upon me, because He has anointed me to proclaim the good news to the poor. He has sent me to heal the brokenhearted, to proclaim release to the captives, recovering of sight to the blind, to deliver those who are pressed down, [19]and to proclaim the acceptable year of the Everpresent Lord." [Is. 61:1-2; Lev. 25:10]

[20]He closed the scroll, gave it back to the attendant, and sat down. The eyes of all in the meetingplace were fastened on him. [21]He began by saying to them, "Today, in your[+] hearing, this scripture has been given fullness."

4:4 The Hebrew in Dt. 8:3 is *ha'Adam* — i.e. the being God made, the one who is the father of all humanity — "shall not live by bread alone".

4:16 The Writings [*Ketuvim*] could be read either standing or sitting, but the one reading the Torah was to stand. (cf. Tal. Megila 21a)

4:17-21 In the contemporary cycle of haftarah readings, we read Is. 60, 62, and 63. We also read Is. 61:10-63:9. For some reason, the passage which Yeshua read is skipped. Likewise, we currently read Is. 51:12-52:12 and Is. 54, but do not read Is. 52:13-53:12. Is. 54 is read on three different occasions.

4:18 "Messiah [is indicated], as it is written (Is.11:2):'And upon him will rest the Spirit of the Everpresent Lord, Spirit of wisdom and understanding, Spirit of counsel and power, Spirit of knowledge and fear of the Everpresent Lord.'" (Tal. Sanhedrin 93b)

4:18-19 "to proclaim release" *D'ror*, the Hebrew word in the text of Isaiah which Yeshua read, is the same word which is used in Lev. 25:10 for the year of Jubilee — "to proclaim liberty throughout all the land". It also appears in Jer. 34:8,15,17.

[22]Everyone was speaking in affirmation of him, and they were amazed at the gracious words which proceeded out of his mouth. They said, "Isn't this the son of Yosef?" [1Sam. 17:58]

[23]He said to them, "Doubtless you+ will tell me this parable, 'Physician, heal yourself.' Whatever we have heard done at Kfar Nahum, do here also in your hometown." [24]He said, "I assure you+ that no prophet is accepted in his hometown. [25]In faithfulness, I tell you+ there were many widows in Israel in the days of Eliyahu, when the sky was shut up three years and six months, when a severe famine came over all the land. [26]Eliyahu was sent to none of them, except to Tzarafat, in the land of Tzidon, to a woman who was a widow. [1Kgs. 17:9-24] [27]There were many lepers in Israel in the time of Elisha the prophet, yet not one of them was cleansed, except Naaman the Syrian." [2Kgs. 5:1-19]

[28]All in the meetingplace were filled with anger as they heard these things. [29]They rose up, forced him out of the city, and led him to the brow of the hill on which their city was built, to throw him off the cliff. [30]But passing through the midst of them, he went his way.

[31]He came down to Kfar Nahum, a city of the Galil. He was teaching them on Shabbat, [32]and they were astonished at his teaching, because there was authority in his word. [33]In the meetingplace there was a man who had a spirit of an unclean demon, and he cried out with a loud voice, [34]"Ah, what have we to do with you, Yeshua of Natzrat? Have you come to destroy us? I know you, who you are, the Holy One of God!"

[35]Yeshua rebuked him, "Be silent, and come out of him!" When the demon had thrown him down in their midst, he came out of him, having done him no harm.

[36]Amazement came upon all, and they spoke together, one with another, saying, "What message is this? For with authority and power he commands the unclean spirits, and they come out!" [37]News about him went out into every place of the surrounding region.

[38]He rose up from the meetingplace, and entered into Shimon's house. Shimon's mother-in-law was afflicted with a high fever, and they appealed to him for her. [39]He stood over her and rebuked the fever, and it left her. Immediately she rose up and served them.

[40]As the sun was setting, all those who had any sick with various diseases brought them to him. He laid his hands on every one of them, and healed them. [41]Demons also came out from many, crying out and saying, "You are the Messiah, the Son of God!" Rebuking them, he did not allow them to speak, because they knew that he was the Messiah.

[42]When it was day, he departed and went into an uninhabited place. Then the multitudes looked for him, came to him, and were keeping him so that he would not go away from them. [43]But he said to them, "I must proclaim the good news of God's kingdom to the other cities also. I have been sent for this reason." [44]He was speaking out in the meetingplaces of the Galil.

5 [1]Now as he was standing by the lake of Kinneret, the crowd pressed upon him to hear the word of God. [2]He saw two boats standing by the lake, but the fishermen had gone out of them, and were cleaning their nets. [3]He entered into one of the boats, which was Shimon's, and asked him to put out a little from the land. He sat down and taught the multitudes from the boat. [4]When he had finished speaking, he said to Shimon, "Return to the deep, and let down your+ nets for a catch."

5:1 It seems likely that the Greek *Gennessaret* is the Hebrew Kinneret, which has variant spellings in Num. 34:11, Dt. 3:17, Josh.13:27, and Josh. 19:35.

[5]Shimon answered him, "Master, we worked all night and caught nothing. But at your word I will let down the net." [6]When they had done this, they caught a large number of fish, and their net was breaking. [7]They beckoned to their partners in the other boat to come and help them. They came and filled both boats, so that they began to sink. [8]But when Shimon Kefa saw it, he fell down at Yeshua's knees, saying, "Depart from me Lord, for I am a sinful man." [9]For he was astonished at the catch of fish which they had caught, and so were all who were with him, [10]including Jacob and Yoḥanan, sons of Zevadyah, who were partners with Shimon. Yeshua said to Shimon, "Do not be afraid. From now on you will be catching men." [11]When they had brought their boats to land, they left everything and followed him.

[12]While he was in one of the cities, there was a man full of leprosy! When he saw Yeshua, he fell on his face, and begged him, "Lord, if you want to, you can make me clean." [13]He stretched out his hand and touched him, saying, "I want to. Be made clean." Immediately the leprosy left him. [14]He directed him, "Tell no one, but go your way, show yourself to the Kohen. Offer for your cleansing what Moses commanded, as a testimony to them." [Lev. 14] [15]But the report concerning him spread much more, and large crowds came together to hear and to be healed by him of their infirmities. [16]He, however, withdrew into the wilderness, and prayed.

[17]He was teaching on one of those days, and there were Perushim and teachers of the Torah sitting nearby who had come out of every village of the Galil, Judea, and Yerushala'im. The power of the Everpresent Lord was with him to heal them. [18]Men brought a paralyzed man on a pallet, and they asked about bringing him in to lay him before Yeshua! [19]Not finding a way to bring him in because of the crowd, they went up to the housetop, and let him down with his pallet through the tiles into the middle before Yeshua. [20]Seeing their faith, he said to him, "Man, your sins are forgiven you."

[21]The Torah scholars and the Perushim began to reason, "Who is this that speaks blasphemies? Who can forgive sins, but God alone?"

[22]But perceiving their thoughts, Yeshua answered them, "Why are you[+] reasoning this way in your[+] hearts? [23]Which is easier to say, 'Your sins are forgiven you,' or to say, 'Arise and walk'? [24]But so that you[+] may know that the Son of Adam has authority on earth to forgive sins" — he then said to the paralyzed man — "I tell you, get up, take up your pallet, and go home."

[25]Immediately he rose up before them, took up what he was lying on, and departed to his house, glorifying God. [26]Astonishment took hold of them all, and they glorified God. They were filled with fear, saying, "We have seen incredible things today."

[27]After these things he went out, saw a tax collector named Levi sitting at the tax office, and said to him, "Follow me." [28]He left everything, rose up, and followed him.

[29]Levi made a great feast for him in his house. There was a large crowd of tax collectors and others who were reclining with them. [30]Their Torah scholars and the Perushim murmured against his disciples, saying, "Why do you[+] eat and drink with the tax collectors and sinners?"

[31]Yeshua answered them, "Those who are healthy have no need for a physician, but those who are sick do. [32]I have not come to call the righteous, but sinners to change their ways."

5:31-32 In the liturgy in Taḥanun, we pray to "the One who opens a hand to receive repentant transgressors and sinners."

³³They said to him, "The disciples of Yoḥanan often fast and pray, likewise also the disciples of the Perushim, but yours eat and drink."

³⁴He said to them, "Can you⁺ make the friends of the bridegroom fast, while the bridegroom is with them? ³⁵But the days will come when the bridegroom will be taken away from them. Then they will fast in those days." ³⁶He also told a parable to them. "No one puts a piece from a new garment on an old garment, or else he will tear the new, and also the piece from the new will not match the old. ³⁷No one puts new wine into old wineskins, or else the new wine will burst the skins, and it will be spilled, and the skins will be destroyed. ³⁸But new wine must be put into fresh wineskins, and both are preserved. ³⁹No man who has drunk old wine immediately desires new, for he says, 'The old is better.'"

6 ¹Now he was going through the grain fields on Shabbat. His disciples plucked the heads of grain, rubbed them in their hands, and ate. [Dt. 23:25] ²But some of the Perushim said to them, "Why are you⁺ doing what is not permitted on Shabbat?"

³Answering them, Yeshua said, "Haven't you⁺ read what David did when he was hungry, he and those who were with him? ⁴how he entered into the house of God, and took and ate the bread of the Presence, and gave some also to those who were with him? It is not permitted for anyone to eat it except the Kohanim alone." ⁵He said to them, "The Son of Adam is lord of Shabbat."

⁶On another Shabbat, it also happened that he entered into the meetingplace and taught. There was a man there whose right hand was withered. ⁷The Torah scholars and the Perushim watched him, to see whether he would heal on Shabbat, so that they might find an accusation against him. ⁸But he knew their thoughts, and he said to the man who had the withered hand, "Rise up, and stand apart." He arose and stood.

⁹Then Yeshua said to them, "I will ask you⁺ something. Is it permitted on Shabbat to do good, or to do harm? To save a life, or to kill?"

5:33-39 Yeshua responds that his disciples were not fasting at that time, because it was not appropriate for them to fast. He says that they will fast when he is no longer with them, because it will then be appropriate for them. The two parables illustrate his answer.

It is inappropriate to put a new patch on an old garment, because the new patch will stretch and shrink at a different rate than the old garment, creating a bigger tear. A new patch is fine for a new garment, but an old garment requires an old patch.

It is inappropriate to put new wine into old skins because the fermentation of the new wine produces enough pressure to break the old skins. New skins can withstand the pressure, because they have more strength and elasticity. Old skins are appropriate for old wine, which, as everyone knows, is better than new.

Traditional theological interpretations of the parables do not fit the text or context.

5:37-38 "Rabbi said, 'Don't focus on this flask but on what is in it; there can be a new flask filled with old [wine] and an old flask in which there is not even new [wine].'" (Tal. Avot 4:20)

6:1 "One who husks barley may husk one by one and eat, but if he husked and put them in his hand, he is obligated [to tithe]. He who rubs dried ears of wheat may blow from hand to hand and eat, but if he blows and puts the grain in his lap, he is obligated." (Tal. Ma'aserot 4:5)

6:9 1Mac. 2:32-41 records how those faithful to the Everpresent Lord and His commandments were attacked and slaughtered on Shabbat. "Therefore they decided then, saying, 'If anyone comes to war ≫

[10]He looked around at them all, and said to the man, "Stretch out your hand." He did, and his hand was restored as healthy as the other. [11]But they were filled with rage, and deliberated with one another about what they should do to Yeshua.

[12]It was in these days that he went out to the mountain to pray, and he continued all night in prayer to God. [13]When it was day, he called his disciples, and from them he chose twelve, whom he also named ambassadors: [14]Shimon, whom he also named Kefa, his brother Andreas, Jacob, Yohanan, Philip, Bar Talmai, [15] Matthias, Toma, Jacob, the son of Halfai, Shimon, who was called the zealot, [16]Judah the son of Jacob, and Judah from K'riyot, who also became a traitor. [17]He came down with them, and stood on a level place with a large group of his disciples, and a large crowd of the common people from all Judea, Yerushala'im, and the sea coast of Tzor and Tzidon. They came to hear him and to be healed of their diseases. [18]There were also those who were troubled by unclean spirits, and they were being healed. [19]All the multitude sought to touch him, for power came out from him and healed them all.

[20]He lifted up his eyes upon his disciples, and said, "There is good for the poor, because God's kingdom is yours[+]. [21]There is good for you[+] who hunger now, because you[+] will be filled. There is good for you[+] who weep now, because you[+] will laugh.

[22]"When men will hate you[+], and when they will exclude and ridicule you[+], and spurn your[+] name as evil on account of the Son of Adam, there is good for you[+]. [23]Rejoice in that day, and leap for joy, because your[+] reward is great in heaven! For their fathers did the same thing to the prophets.

[24]"But woe to you[+] who are rich, because you[+] have received your[+] comfort. [25]Woe to you[+] who are full now, because you[+] will be hungry. Woe to you[+] who laugh now, because you[+] will mourn and weep. [26]Woe when all men speak well of you[+], because their fathers did the same to the false prophets.

[27]"But I say to you[+] who hear, love your[+] enemies, do good to those who hate you[+]. [28]Bless those who curse you[+], and pray for those who mistreat you[+]. [29]To the one who strikes you on the cheek, offer the other also. And from the one who takes away your cloak, do not withhold your coat either. [30]Give to everyone who asks you, and do not ask him who takes away your goods to give them back again. [Dt. 23:20-21]

[31]"As you[+] would want people to do to you[+], do the same to them. [32]If you[+] love those who love you[+], what praise do you[+] deserve? For even sinners love those who love them. [33]If you[+] do good to those who do good to you[+], what praise do you[+] deserve? For even sinners do the same. [34]If you[+] lend to those from whom you[+] hope to receive, what praise do you[+] deserve? Even sinners lend to sinners, to receive back as much. [35]But love your[+] enemies, and do good. Lend, expecting nothing back. Your[+] reward will be great, and you[+] will be children of the Most High, because He is kind to ungrateful and evil men. [36]So be compassionate, even as your[+] Father is also compassionate.

---

against us on the sabbath day, we will fight against him, so that we all not die, as our brothers who died in the hiding places." (1 Mac. 2:41)

6:14-16 The use of nicknames was common, as can be seen in 1 Mac. 2:2-5.

6:37 "As Raba said, 'Every one who passes over what is due him, all his transgressions will be passed over. As it is said [Micah 7:18] *Who takes iniquity and passes over transgression.* Whose iniquity is taken? The one who passes over transgression.'" (Tal. Meg. 28a)

[37]"Do not pass judgment, and they will not pass judgment on you[+]. Do not condemn, and you[+] will not be condemned. Set others free, and you[+] will be set free. [38]Give, and it will be given to you[+] — good measure, pressed down, shaken together, and running over. For with the same measure you[+] measure, it will be measured back to you[+]."

[39]He spoke a parable to them. "Can the blind guide the blind? Won't they both fall into a pit? [40]A student is not above his teacher, but everyone when he is fully trained will be like his teacher. [41]Why do you see the particle that is in your brother's eye, but do not perceive the beam that is in your own eye? [42]Or how can you tell your brother, 'Brother, let me remove the particle that is in your eye,' when you yourself do not see the beam that is in your own eye? Pretender. First remove the beam from your own eye, and then you can see clearly to remove the particle that is in your brother's eye.

[43]"For there is no good tree that brings forth rotten fruit, nor again a rotten tree that brings forth good fruit, [44]because each tree is recognized by its own fruit. For people do not gather figs from thorns, nor do they gather grapes from a bush. [45]The good man brings out what is good from the good treasure of his heart, and the evil man brings out what is evil from the evil treasure of his heart, because his mouth speaks from what flows out of the heart.

[46]"Why do you[+] call me, 'Lord, Lord,' and do not do the things which I say? [47]Everyone who comes to me, hears my words, and does them, I will show you[+] who he is like. [48]He is like a man building a house, who dug and went deep, and laid a foundation on the rock. When a flood arose, the stream broke against that house, and could not shake it, because it had been well-built. [49]But the one who hears and does not do is like a man who built a house on the earth without a foundation. The stream broke against it, and immediately it fell, and the ruin of that house was great."

7 [1]After he had finished speaking in the hearing of the people, he entered into Kfar Na<u>h</u>um. [2]A certain centurion had a beloved servant who was sick, close to death. [3]When he heard about Yeshua, he sent elders of the Jews to him, asking him to come and save his servant. [4]When they came to Yeshua, they begged him earnestly, "He is worthy for you to do this for him, [5]because he loves our nation, and he built our meetingplace for us."

[6]Yeshua went with them. By the time he was not far from the house, the centurion sent friends to him, saying to him, "Lord, do not trouble yourself, for I am not worthy for you to come under my roof. [7]So I did not even think myself worthy to come to you, but say the word, and my servant will be healed. [8]For I also am a man appointed under authority, having soldiers under me. I tell this one, 'Go,' and he goes; and to another, 'Come,' and he comes; and to my servant, 'Do this,' and he does it."

[9]When Yeshua heard these things, he was amazed at him, and turned and said to the crowd who followed him, "I tell you[+], not even in Israel have I found such great faith." [10]On returning to the house, those who were sent found that the servant who had been sick was well.

6:39 "they were guilty men, and had been like the blind and like those groping for the way..." (DSS 2Q32/ CD 1:9)

7:2-10 "He is worthy for you to do this for him, [5]because he loves our nation, and he built our meetingplace for us." Yeshua does not respond that no one is worthy. He immediately goes to heal the man's servant. This would seem to be in fulfillment of God's promise to Abraham and Israel: "I will bless those who bless you..." (Gen. 12:3, cf. Num. 24:9)

[11]Soon afterwards Yeshua went to a city called Naim. Many of his disciples went with him, along with a large crowd. [12]Now when he drew near to the gate of the city, a dead man was carried out — his mother's only son, and she was a widow! Many people of the city were with her. [13]When the Lord saw her, he had compassion on her, and said to her, "Do not weep." [14]He came near and touched the coffin, and the bearers stood still. He said, "Young man, I tell you, arise." [15]The one who was dead sat up and began to speak. Then he gave him to his mother.

[16]Fear took hold of everyone, and they glorified God, saying, "A great prophet has been raised up among us!" and, "God has visited His people!" [17]This report about him went out into the whole of Judea, and in all the surrounding region.

[18]Yohanan's disciples told him about all these things. [19]Calling to himself two of his disciples, Yohanan sent them to Yeshua, saying, "Are you the One who is coming, or should we look for another?" [20]When the men had come to him, they said, "Yohanan the Immerser has sent us to you, saying, 'Are you the One who is coming, or should we look for another?'"

[21]In that hour he healed many people of sicknesses, infectious diseases, and evil spirits. And he gave sight to many who were blind. [22]Yeshua responded to them, "Go and tell Yohanan the things which you+ have seen and heard: that the blind receive their sight, the lame walk, the lepers are cleansed, the deaf hear, the dead are raised up, and the poor have the good news proclaimed to them. [23]There is good for the one who is not scandalized by me."

[24]When Yohanan's messengers had departed, he began to speak to the multitudes about Yohanan. "What did you+ go out into the wilderness to see? A reed shaken by the wind? [25]No. What did you+ go out to see? A man dressed in delicate clothing? Listen, those who are impressively dressed and live delicately are in the courts of kings. [26]No, what did you+ go out to see? A prophet? Yes, I tell you+, and much more than a prophet. [27]This is the one of whom it is written, 'Look, I send My messenger before your face, who will prepare your way before you.' [Mal. 3:1] [28]"For I tell you+ that among those who are born of women there is not a greater prophet than Yohanan the Immerser. Yet the one who is least in God's kingdom is greater than he."

[29]When all the people and the tax collectors heard this, they affirmed the righteousness of God, having received the immersion of Yohanan. [30]But the Perushim and the Torah scholars rebelled against the purpose of God for themselves, not receiving immersion from him.

[31]"To what then shall I liken the people of this generation? What are they like? [32]They are like children who sit in the marketplace, and call to each other, saying, 'We played the flute for you+, and you+ did not dance. We mourned, and you+ did not weep.' [33]For Yohanan the Immerser came neither eating bread nor drinking wine, and you+ say, 'He has a demon.' [34]The Son of Adam has come eating and drinking, and you+ say, 'Look, a gluttonous man and a drunkard, a friend of tax collectors and sinners.' [35]Yet wisdom is shown to be righteous by all her children."

7:28 No matter how great one "born of woman" is, he must be born of the Spirit to enter the kingdom of God. No matter how "small" one is in the kingdom, he is greater than all those outside it.

7:30 "But the Perushim and the Torah scholars rebelled against/*hethetesan* the purpose of God..." God had a different purpose for them than what they chose. I.e., they freely chose something other than God's purpose for them. For this usage of *hethetesan*, see LXX 2K. 8:20.

³⁶One of the Perushim invited him to eat with him. He entered into the house of the Parush, and sat at the table. ³⁷A sinful woman in the city, when she knew that he was reclining in the house of the Parush, brought an alabaster jar of ointment! ³⁸Standing behind at his feet weeping, she began to wet his feet with her tears, and she wiped them with the hair of her head, kissed his feet, and anointed them with the ointment. ³⁹Now when the Parush who had invited him saw it, he said to himself, "If he were a prophet, this man would have perceived who and what kind of woman this is who touches him, that she is a sinner."

⁴⁰Yeshua responded to him, "Shimon, I have something to tell you."

He said, "Teacher, say it."

⁴¹"A certain lender had two debtors. The one owed five hundred denarii, and the other fifty. ⁴²When they could not pay, he forgave them both. Which of them therefore will love him most?"

⁴³Shimon answered, "I suppose the one to whom he forgave the most."

He said to him, "You have judged correctly." ⁴⁴Turning to the woman, he said to Shimon, "Do you see this woman? I entered into your house, and you gave me no water for my feet, but she has wet my feet with her tears, and wiped them with the hair of her head. ⁴⁵You gave me no kiss, but she, since the time I came in, has not ceased to kiss my feet. ⁴⁶You did not anoint my head with oil, but she has anointed my feet with ointment. ⁴⁷So I tell you that her sins, which are many, are forgiven, because she loved much. But to whom little is forgiven, that one loves little." ⁴⁸He said to her, "Your sins are forgiven."

⁴⁹Those who sat at the table with him began to say to themselves, "Who is this who even forgives sins?"

⁵⁰He said to the woman, "Your faith has saved you. Go in peace."

8 ¹Soon afterwards he went about through cities and villages, announcing and proclaiming the good news of the kingdom of God. With him were the twelve, ²and certain women who had been healed of evil spirits and infirmities. There was Miryam who was called Magdala, from whom seven demons had gone out, ³and Yoḥanna (the wife of Kusa, Herod's manager), Shoshanna, and many others, who served them from what they owned.

⁴When a large crowd came together, and people from every city were coming to him, he spoke in a parable: ⁵"The sower went out to sow his seed. As he sowed, some fell along the road, and it was trampled under foot, and the birds of the heaven devoured it. ⁶Other seed fell on the rock, and as soon as it grew, it withered away, because it had no moisture. ⁷Other fell in the middle of thorns, and the thorns grew with it, and choked it. ⁸Other fell into the good ground, and grew, and brought forth fruit one hundredfold. [Gen.26:12]" As he said these things, he called out, "He who has ears to hear, let him hear." [Dt. 29:4, Ezek. 3:27]

⁹Then his disciples asked him, "What does this parable mean?"

¹⁰He said, "To you⁺ it is given to know the mysteries of the kingdom of God, but to the others in parables, so that 'seeing they may not see, and hearing they may not understand.' [Is. 6:9] ¹¹Now the parable is this: the seed is the word of God. ¹²Those along the road are those who hear, then the Enemy comes and takes away the word from their heart so that they do not believe and are not saved. ¹³Those on the rock are the ones who receive the word with joy when they hear, and they believe for a while. But these have no root, and then fall away in time of testing. ¹⁴What fell among the thorns, these are those who have heard, but as they go on their way they are choked with the cares, riches, and

pleasures of life, and they bring no fruit to maturity. ¹⁵That which is in the good ground, these are such as, having heard the word, hold it tightly in an upright and good heart, and endure to bring forth fruit.

¹⁶"No one, when he has lit a lamp, covers it with a container, or puts it under a bed, but puts it on a stand, so that those who enter in may see the light. ¹⁷For nothing is hidden that will not be revealed, nor anything secret that will not be known and come to light. ¹⁸So be careful how you⁺ hear. For whoever has, to him will be given; and whoever does not have, even what he thinks he has will be taken away from him."

¹⁹His mother and brothers came to him, and they could not come close to him because of the crowd. ²⁰Some told him, "Your mother and your brothers stand outside, wanting to see you."

²¹But he answered them, "My mother and my brothers are these who hear the word of God, and do it."

²²Now on one of those days, he himself and his disciples entered into a boat, and he said to them, "Let's go over to the other side of the lake." So they launched out. ²³But as they sailed, he fell asleep. A windstorm came down upon the lake, and they were taking on dangerous amounts of water. ²⁴They came to him and awoke him, saying, "Master, master, we are going to die!" He awoke, and rebuked the wind and the raging of the water. Then they subsided, and it was calm. ²⁵He said to them, "Where is your⁺ faith?"

They were afraid and in awe. They said to each other, "Who is this, then, that he commands even the winds and the water, and they obey him?"

²⁶They arrived at the country of the Gerasenes, which is opposite the Galil. ²⁷When Yeshua stepped ashore, a certain man from that city met him. He had had demons for a long time, wore no clothes, and did not live in a house, but in the tombs. ²⁸When he saw Yeshua, he cried out, and fell down before him. He said with a loud voice, "What do I have to do with you, Yeshua, Son of the Most High God? I beg you, do not torment me!" ²⁹For Yeshua was commanding the unclean spirit to come out of the man. Because the unclean spirit had often seized the man, he was kept under guard, and bound with chains and shackles. Breaking the restraints apart, he was driven by the demon into the wilderness.

³⁰Yeshua asked him, "What is your name?"

He said, "Legion," for many demons had entered into him. ³¹They begged him that he would not command them to go into the abyss. ³²Now there was a herd of many pigs feeding there on the mountain, and they begged him that he would let them enter into these. He permitted them to. ³³The demons came out from the man, entered into the pigs, and the herd rushed down the steep bank into the lake, and were drowned. ³⁴When the herders saw what had happened, they fled, and told it in the city and in the countryside.

³⁵People went out to see what had happened. They came to Yeshua, and found the man from

---

8:26,37 In Mt. 8:28 and Mk. 5:1, we read "the country of the Gadarenes". Gadara and Gerasa, both part of the Decapolis/Ten Cities, were about 12 miles apart. Josephus mentions Gadara 30 times and Gerasa five times; Gadara probably being the larger of the two. (e.g. <u>Wars</u> 2. 18. 1. 458-9; 5. 478-80),

8:31-33 See note to Mt. 8:28-32.

whom the demons had gone out. He was sitting at Yeshua's feet, clothed and in his right mind, and they were afraid. ³⁶Those who saw it told them how the one who had been possessed by demons was healed. ³⁷All the people of the surrounding country of the Gerasenes asked him to depart from them, for they were very much afraid. He entered into the boat, and went back.

³⁸But the man from whom the demons had gone out begged him that he might go with him. Yeshua, however, sent him away, saying, ³⁹"Return to your home, and declare what great things God has done for you." He went his way, proclaiming throughout the whole city what great things Yeshua had done for him.

⁴⁰When Yeshua returned, the multitude welcomed him, for they were all waiting for him. ⁴¹There came a man named Yair, who was a ruler of the assembly. He fell down at Yeshua's feet, and begged him to come into his house, ⁴²because he had an only daughter, about twelve years of age, and she was dying. Now as Yeshua went, the multitudes pressed against him. ⁴³A woman who had a flow of blood for twelve years, who had spent all her living on physicians and could not be healed by any, ⁴⁴came behind him and touched the tzitzit of his garment. Immediately the flow of her blood stopped. ⁴⁵Yeshua said, "Who touched me?"

When all denied it, Kefa and those with him said, "Master, the multitudes press and crowd around you, and you say, 'Who touched me?'"

⁴⁶But Yeshua said, "Someone did touch me, for I know that power went out from me." ⁴⁷When the woman saw that she could not hide, she came trembling. Then falling down before him, she declared to him in the presence of all the people the reason why she had touched him, and how she was immediately healed. ⁴⁸He said to her, "Daughter, be encouraged. Your faith has made you well. Go in peace."

⁴⁹While he still spoke, someone from the house of the ruler of the assembly came, saying to him, "Your daughter is dead. Do not trouble the Teacher."

⁵⁰But hearing it, Yeshua answered him, "Do not be afraid. Only believe and she will be healed." ⁵¹When he came to the house, he did not allow anyone to enter in, except Kefa, Yohanan, Jacob, the father of the child, and her mother.

⁵²All were weeping and bewailing her, but he said, "Do not weep. She is not dead, but sleeping." ⁵³They ridiculed him, knowing that she was dead, ⁵⁴but he put them all outside. Taking her by the hand, he called, "Child, arise." ⁵⁵Her spirit returned, and she immediately rose up. He commanded that something be given to her to eat. ⁵⁶Her parents were amazed, but he directed them to tell no one what had been done.

9 ¹He called the twelve together, and gave them power and authority over all demons and to cure diseases. ²He sent them forth to proclaim God's kingdom, and to heal the sick. ³He said to them, "Take nothing for your⁺ journey — neither staff, nor wallet, nor bread, nor money, and do not have two coats apiece. ⁴Into whatever house you⁺ enter, stay there, and go out from there. ⁵As many as do not receive you⁺, when you⁺ depart from that city, shake off even the dust from your⁺ feet for a testimony against them." ⁶They departed and went throughout the villages, proclaiming the good news, and healing everywhere.

⁷Now Herod, the ruler of a fourth of the province, heard of all that was done by him, and he was very perplexed, because it was said by some that Yohanan had been raised from the dead, ⁸and by some that Eliyahu had appeared, and by others that one of the ancient prophets had risen again.

⁹Herod said, "I beheaded Yo<u>h</u>anan, but who is this about whom I hear such things?" He was seeking to see him.

¹⁰When the ambassadors had returned, they told Yeshua what things they had done. He took them and withdrew apart privately by a city called Beit Tzaida. ¹¹But the multitudes, finding out, followed him. He welcomed them, spoke to them of God's kingdom, and healed those who needed healing. ¹²The day began to fade, and the twelve came and said to him, "Send the multitude away, so that they may go into the surrounding villages and farms, rest, and get provisions, because we are here in a deserted place."

¹³But he said to them, "You⁺ give them something to eat."

They said, "We have no more than five loaves and two fish, unless we were to go and buy food for all these people." ¹⁴For there were about five thousand men.

He said to his disciples, "Have them sit down in groups of about fifty each." ¹⁵They did that and had them all sit down. ¹⁶He took the five loaves and the two fish, and looking up to heaven, he said a blessing, broke them, and gave them to the disciples to set before the multitude. ¹⁷They ate and were all filled. They gathered up twelve baskets of broken pieces that were left over.

¹⁸As he alone was praying, the disciples were with him, and he asked them, "Who do the multitudes say that I am?"

¹⁹They answered, "'Yo<u>h</u>anan the Immerser,' but others say, 'Eliyahu,' and others say, 'One of the ancient prophets is risen again.'"

²⁰He said to them, "But who do you⁺ say that I am?"

Kefa answered, "The Messiah of God."

²¹But he cautioned them and commanded them to tell this to no one. ²²He said, "The Son of Adam must suffer many things, and be rejected by the Elders, chief Kohanim, and Torah scholars; then be killed, and the third day be raised up."

²³He said to all, "If anyone desires to come after me, let him completely deny himself, take up his tree of death, and follow me. ²⁴For whoever desires to save his life will lose it, but whoever will lose his life on account of me, that one will save it. ²⁵For what does it profit a man if he gains the whole world, and destroys or loses his own soul? ²⁶For whoever is ashamed of me and my words, the Son of Adam will be ashamed of him when he comes in his glory, the glory of the Father, and of the holy angels. ²⁷But I tell you⁺ the truth, there are some of those who stand here who will certainly not taste of death until they see God's kingdom."

²⁸About eight days after he said these things, he took Kefa, Yo<u>h</u>anan, and Jacob with him, and went up onto the mountain to pray. ²⁹As he was praying, the appearance of his face was changed, and his clothing became white and dazzling. [Ex,34:29-35] ³⁰Two men were talking with him, Moses

9:27 See "Your Children Saw Your Kingdom" in the ADDITIONAL NOTES.

9:30-33 "He [God] added: 'Moses, by your life, as you gave your life to their service in this age, so too in the time to come when I bring Eliyahu the prophet to them, the two of you will come together.'" (Mid. D'varim Rabbah 3.17)

9:31 The Greek word translated as "departure" is *exodus*.

and Eliyahu! ³¹They appeared in glory, and spoke of his departure, which he was about to fulfill in Yerushala'im.

³²Now Kefa and those who were with him had been heavy with sleep, but when they were fully awake, they saw his glory and the two men who stood with him. ³³As they were parting from him, Kefa said to Yeshua, "Master, it is good for us to be here. Let us make three shelters — one for you, one for Moses, and one for Eliyahu," not knowing what he said.

³⁴While he said these things, a cloud came and overshadowed them, and they were fearful as they entered into the cloud. ³⁵A voice came out of the cloud, saying, "This is My beloved Son. Listen to him." ³⁶When the voice stopped, Yeshua alone remained. They were silent, and told no one in those days any of the things which they had seen.

³⁷On the next day, when they had come down from the mountain, a large crowd met him. ³⁸A man from the crowd called out, "Teacher, I beg you to look at my son, for he is my only child. ³⁹A spirit takes him, he suddenly cries out, and it convulses him so that he foams. And it painfully leaves him, bruising him severely! ⁴⁰I begged your disciples to cast it out, and they could not."

⁴¹Yeshua responded, "A faithless generation which has distorted the way, how long will I be with you⁺ and bear with you⁺? Bring your son here." ⁴²While he was still coming, the demon threw him down and convulsed him violently. But Yeshua rebuked the unclean spirit, healed the boy, and gave him back to his father. ⁴³They were all astonished at the majesty of God.

But while all were amazed at all the things which Yeshua did, he said to his disciples, ⁴⁴"Let these words sink into your⁺ ears, for the Son of Adam will be delivered up into the hands of men." ⁴⁵But they did not understand what he said. It was concealed from them, so that they could not perceive it, and they were afraid to ask him about what he said.

⁴⁶There arose an argument among them about which of them was the greatest. ⁴⁷Knowing the thoughts of their hearts, Yeshua took a little child, and set him by his side. ⁴⁸Then he said to them, "Whoever receives this little child in my name receives me. Whoever receives me receives Him who sent me. For whoever is least among all of you⁺ — this one will be great."

⁴⁹Yohanan responded, "Master, we saw someone casting out demons in your name, and we stopped him, because he does not follow with us."

⁵⁰Yeshua said to him, "Do not stop him, for the one who is not against us is for us."

⁵¹When the days were near that he should be taken up, he intently set his face to go to Yerushala'im ⁵²and sent messengers before him. In order to prepare for him, they went and entered into a village of the Samaritans. ⁵³Because he was traveling with his face set towards Yerushala'im, they did not receive him. ⁵⁴When his disciples Jacob and Yohanan saw this, they said, "Lord, do you want us to command fire to come down from heaven and destroy them, just as Eliyahu did?"

⁵⁵But he turned and rebuked them, "You⁺ do not know what spirit you⁺ are from. ⁵⁶For the Son of Adam did not come to destroy men's lives, but to save them."

They went to another village. ⁵⁷As they went on the way, a certain man said to him, "Lord, I want to follow you wherever you go."

⁵⁸Yeshua said to him, "The foxes have holes, and the birds of the heaven have nests, but the Son of Adam has no place to lay his head."

⁵⁹He said to another, "Follow me."

But he said, "Lord, allow me first to go and bury my father."

⁶⁰But Yeshua said to him, "Leave the dead to bury their own dead, but you go and proclaim God's kingdom."

⁶¹Another also said, "Lord, I want to follow you, but first allow me to say goodbye to those who are at my house."

⁶²But Yeshua said to him, "No one who puts his hand to the plow and looks back is fit for God's kingdom." [1K. 19:19-21]

10 ¹Now after these things, the Lord also designated seventy others, and sent them two by two ahead of him into every city and place where he was about to come. [Num. 11:16] ²Then he said to them, "The harvest is indeed great, but the laborers are few. So ask the Lord of the harvest that He send out laborers into His harvest.

³"Go. I send you⁺ out as lambs among wolves! ⁴Carry no bag, nor wallet, nor sandals. Do not greet anyone on the way. ⁵Into whatever house you⁺ enter, first say, 'Peace be to this house.' ⁶If a son of peace is there, your⁺ peace will rest on him; but if not, it will return to you⁺. ⁷Remain in that same house, eating and drinking the things they give, for the laborer is worthy of his wages. Do not go from house to house. ⁸Into whatever city you⁺ enter and they receive you⁺, eat the things that are set before you⁺. ⁹Heal the sick who are there, and tell them, 'God's kingdom has come near to you⁺.' ¹⁰But into whatever city you⁺ enter and they do not receive you⁺, go out into its open square and say, ¹¹'Even the dust that clings to us from your⁺ city, we wipe off against you⁺. Nevertheless know this, that God's kingdom has come near.' ¹²I tell you⁺ that it will be more tolerable in that day for Sedom than for that city.

¹³"Woe to you, Korazin. Woe to you, Beit Tzaidah. For if the mighty works which were done in you⁺ had been done in Tzor and Tzidon, they would have turned to God long ago, sitting in sackcloth and ashes. ¹⁴But it will be more tolerable for Tzor and Tzidon in the judgment than for you⁺. ¹⁵Kfar Na<u>h</u>um, will you not be exalted to Heaven? You will be brought down to Sheol.

¹⁶"Whoever listens to you⁺ listens to me, and whoever rejects you⁺ rejects me. Whoever rejects me rejects the One who sent me."

¹⁷The seventy returned with joy, saying, "Lord, even the demons are subject to us in your name!"

¹⁸He said to them, "I saw the Accuser fallen out of heaven like lightning. [Is. 14:12-15, Exek. 28:16,17] ¹⁹I give you⁺ authority to tread on serpents and scorpions, and over all the power of the enemy! Nothing will in any way hurt you⁺. ²⁰Nevertheless, do not rejoice in this, that the spirits are subject to you⁺, but rejoice that your⁺ names are written in heaven."

²¹In that same hour Yeshua rejoiced in the Ruakh Kodesh, and said, "I thank you, Father, Lord of heaven and earth, that You have hidden these things from the wise and understanding, and revealed them to little children. Yes, Father, for so it was well-pleasing in Your sight."

²²Turning to the disciples, he said, "All things have been delivered to me by my Father. No one knows who the Son is, except the Father, and who the Father is, except the Son, and whomever the Son desires to reveal Him to."

²³Turning to the disciples, he said privately, "There is good for the eyes which see the things that

10:15 Sheol is the realm of the dead.
10:18 See the ADDITIONAL NOTE on "War in Heaven".

you⁺ see, ²⁴because I tell you⁺ that many prophets and kings desired to see the things which you⁺ see, and did not see them, and to hear the things which you⁺ hear, and did not hear them."

²⁵A certain Torah scholar stood up and tested him, "Teacher, what am I to do to inherit eternal life?"

²⁶He said to him, "What is written in the Torah? How do you read it?"

²⁷He answered, "You are to love the Everpresent Lord, your God, with all your heart, with all your soul, with all your strength, and with all your mind, and your neighbor as yourself." [Dt. 6:5, Lev. 19:8]

²⁸He said to him, "You have answered correctly. Do this, and you will live."

²⁹But desiring to declare himself righteous, he asked Yeshua, "Who is my neighbor?"

³⁰Yeshua answered, "A certain man was going down from Yerushala'im to Yeriḥo, and he fell among bandits who both stripped and beat him, then departed, leaving him half-dead. ³¹Coincidentally, a certain Kohen was going down that way. When he saw him, he passed by on the other side. ³²In the same way a Levite also, when he came to the place and saw him, passed by on the other side. ³³But as a certain Samaritan traveled, he came where he was. When he saw him, he was moved with compassion. ³⁴He came to him and bound up his wounds, pouring on oil and wine. He set him on his own animal, brought him to an inn, and took care of him. ³⁵On the next day, when he departed, he took out two denarii, gave them to the innkeeper, and said to him, 'Take care of him. Whatever you spend beyond that, I will repay you when I return.' ³⁶Now which of these three seems to you to have been a neighbor to the one who fell among the bandits?"

³⁷He said, "The one who showed mercy to him."

Then Yeshua said to him, "Go and do likewise."

³⁸As they went on their way, he entered into a particular village, and a certain woman named Marta received him into her house. ³⁹She had a sister called Miryam, who seated herself at Yeshua's feet and listened to what he said. ⁴⁰But Marta was worried about a lot of serving, and she came up to him and said, "Lord, don't you care that my sister left me to serve alone? So ask her to help me."

⁴¹Yeshua answered her, "Marta, Marta, you are anxious and troubled about many things, ⁴²but one thing is needed, and Miryam has chosen the good part, which will not be taken away from her."

11 ¹When he finished praying in a certain place, one of his disciples said to him, "Lord, teach us to pray, just as Yoḥanan also taught his disciples."

²He said to them, "When you⁺ pray, say, 'Our Father in heaven, may Your Name be kept holy. may Your kingdom come, Your will be done on earth as in heaven. ³Give us each day our needed bread.

10:30-37 Dt. 22:1-4 lays out responsibilities towards a brother's possessions, e.g. his livestock or garments, if they are lost or in need. "You may not hide yourself from them." How much more are we responsible towards our brother himself.

11:2 The Sephardic half-Kaddish and Kaddish al-Yisrael say: "...May His Kingdom reign, *and may He cause His redemption to sprout, and may He bring near His Messiah* — in your lifetime and in your days..." The Ashkenazic does not have the part in italics.

"Do His will as your own will, so that He will do your will as if it were His; let your will cease before His will, so that the will of others will cease before yours." (Tal. Pirke Avot 2:4)

(Ex. 16:4-5) ⁴Forgive us our sins, because we ourselves also forgive everyone who is indebted to us. Do not bring us into temptation, but deliver us from what is evil.'"

⁵He said to them, "Which of you⁺ has a friend like this? You go to him at midnight and tell him, 'Friend, lend me three loaves of bread, ⁶because a friend of mine has come to me from a journey, and I have nothing to set before him.' ⁷And the friend will answer from inside and say, 'Do not bother me. The door is now shut, and my children are with me in bed. I cannot get up and give it to you.' ⁸I tell you⁺ that although he will not rise and give it to him because he is his friend, yet because of his persistence, he will get up and give him as much as he needs.

⁹"I tell you⁺ to keep asking, and it will be given to you⁺. Keep seeking, and you⁺ will find. Keep knocking, and it will be opened to you⁺. ¹⁰For everyone who asks receives. The one who seeks finds. To the one who knocks it will be opened.

¹¹"Which of the fathers among you⁺, if the son asks for bread, will give him a stone? Or if he asks for a fish, he will not give him a snake instead of a fish, will he? ¹²Or if he asks for an egg, he will not give him a scorpion, will he? ¹³If you⁺ then, being evil, know how to give good gifts to your⁺ children, how much more will your heavenly Father give the Ruakh Kodesh to those who ask him."

¹⁴He was casting out a demon from a mute man. When the demon had gone out, the mute man spoke, and the multitudes were amazed. ¹⁵But some of them said, "He casts out demons by Baal Zevuv, the prince of the demons." ¹⁶Others, testing him, sought from him a sign from Heaven. ¹⁷But knowing their thoughts, he said to them, "Every kingdom divided against itself is brought to desolation. A house divided against itself falls. ¹⁸Likewise if the Accuser is divided against himself — because you⁺ say that I cast out demons by Baal Zevuv — how will his kingdom stand? ¹⁹But if I cast out demons by Baal Zevuv, by whom do your⁺ children cast them out? Therefore they will be your⁺ judges. ²⁰But if I cast out demons by the finger of God, then God's kingdom has come to you⁺.

²¹"When the strong man, fully armed, guards his own courtyard, his goods are safe. ²²But when someone stronger attacks him and overcomes him, he takes up his whole armor in which he trusted, and divides his spoils.

²³"Whoever is not with me is against me. Whoever does not gather with me scatters.

²⁴"When the unclean spirit has gone out of the man, it passes through dry places seeking rest. Finding none, it then says, 'I will return to my house from which I came out.' ²⁵When it returns, it finds it swept and put in order. ²⁶Then it goes and takes seven other spirits more evil than itself, and they enter in and dwell there. The last state of that man becomes worse than the first."

²⁷As he said these things, a certain woman out of the crowd lifted up her voice and said to him, "The womb that bore you and the breasts which nursed you are blessed!"

²⁸But he said, "On the contrary, those who hear the word of God and keep it are blessed."

²⁹When the multitudes were gathering together to him, he began to say, "This is an evil generation. It seeks after a sign. No sign will be given to it but the sign of Yonah, the prophet. ³⁰For even as Yonah became a sign to the Ninevites, so also will the Son of Adam be to this generation. ³¹The Queen of

11:4 "Cause us to be forgiving even as we ask to be forgiven." (Opening Prayer, Kol Nidre)

11:18-19 Some texts have *Baal Zevul*, which means "lord of dung or garbage". Other texts have *Baal Zevuv*, which means "lord of flies" (a Canaanite god).

the South will rise up in the judgment with the men of this generation, and will condemn them, because she came from the ends of the earth to hear the wisdom of Solomon, but look, one greater than Solomon is here. [32]The men of Nineveh will stand up in the judgment with this generation, and will condemn it, because they turned to God at the proclamation of Yonah, but look, one greater than Yonah is here.

[33]"No man, when he has lit a lamp, hides it in secret or under a basket, but on a stand, so that those who enter in may see the light. [34]The lamp of the body is the eye. So when your eye is completely whole, your entire body is also full of light. But when it is evil, your body also is full of darkness. [35]So be careful that the light that is in you is not darkness. [36]If your whole body is then full of light, without any part dark, it will be wholly full of light, as when the lamp gives you light with its radiance."

[37]Now as he spoke, a certain Parush asked him to have lunch with him. He went in, and sat at the table. [38]When the Parush saw it, he was astonished that he had not first washed before dinner. [39]The Lord said to him, "Now you[+] Perushim cleanse the outside of the cup and of the platter, but your[+] inside is full of extortion and wickedness. [40]You[+] are without understanding. Did not the One who made the outside also make the inside? [41]But give gifts of compassion from what is within, and see, all things will be clean to you[+].

[42]"But woe to you[+] Perushim! For you[+] tithe mint and rue and every herb, but pass by justice and the love of God. Now it is necessary to have done these things and yet not neglected the other. [43]Woe to you[+] Perushim! For you[+] love the best seats in the meetingplaces, and the greetings in the marketplaces. [44]Woe to you[+]! For you are like hidden tombs, and the men who walk over them do not know it."

[45]One of the Torah scholars responded to him, "Rabbi, in saying this, you insult us also."

11:34-36 "Any one who has common sense will remember that the bewilderments of the eyes are of two kinds, and arise from two causes, either from coming out of the light or from going into the light, which is true of the mind's eye, quite as much as of the bodily eye; and he who remembers this when he sees any one whose vision is perplexed and weak, will not be too ready to laugh; he will first ask whether that soul of man has come out of the brighter life, and is unable to see because unaccustomed to the dark, or having turned from darkness to the day is dazzled by excess of light. And he will count the one happy in his condition and state of being, and he will pity the other; or, if he have a mind to laugh at the soul which comes from below into the light, there will be more reason in this than in the laugh which greets him who returns from above out of the light into the den." ("Republic," BK. VII, The Dialogues of Plato, trans. B. Jowett, Vol. 3, Oxford, Clarendon, 1892, P. 218)

11:36 "R. Ḥanin said [about the priests], 'By the merit of causing a lamp to continually go up [Lev. 24:2], you[+] are worthy to welcome the lamp of King Messiah.'" (Mid. Lev. 31.11)

11:38 The Perushim observed a ritual washing before eating.

11:39 "All items which have an outside and an inside, such as cushions, feather-beds, coverings and sacks, if its inside is defiled, its outside is defiled; if its outside is defiled, its inside is not defiled. R. Judah said: Where are these things said? Where they are defiled by a liquid; but if they are defiled by a swarming creature, if its inside is defiled its outside is defiled; if its outside is defiled its inside is defiled." (Tal. Pes. 17b)

11:45; 12:13; 19:39; 20:21,39; 21:7 Yhn. 1:38 tells us that "Rabbi" is translated into Greek as *didaskalos/* teacher.

⁴⁶He said, "Woe to you⁺ Torah scholars also! because you⁺ load men with burdens that are difficult to carry, and you⁺ yourselves will not even lift one finger to help carry those burdens. ⁴⁷Woe to you⁺! because you⁺ build the tombs of the prophets, and your⁺ fathers killed them. ⁴⁸So you⁺ testify and consent to the works of your⁺ fathers, because they killed them, and you⁺ build their tombs. ⁴⁹Therefore also the Wisdom of God [Prov. 8] said, 'I will send to them prophets and ambassadors. And some of them they will kill and persecute, ⁵⁰in order that the blood of all the prophets, which has been poured out since the foundation of the world, may be required of this generation — ⁵¹from the blood of Hevel to the blood of Zeharyah, who perished between the altar and the sanctuary.' Yes, I tell you⁺, it will be required of this generation. ⁵²Woe to you⁺ Torah scholars! because you⁺ took away the key of knowledge. You⁺ did not enter in yourselves, and you⁺ hindered those who were entering in."

⁵³As he said these things to them, the Torah scholars and the Perushim began to insistently press him, and challenge him about many things. ⁵⁴They were lying in wait for him, seeking to catch him in something he might say, so that they might accuse him.

12 ¹Meanwhile, when a crowd of many thousands had gathered together, so much so that they pressed against each other, he began to tell his disciples first of all, "Beware of the leaven of the Perushim, which is pretense. ²But there is nothing covered up that will not be revealed, nor hidden that will not be known. ³So whatever you⁺ have said in the darkness will be heard in the light. What you⁺ have spoken in the ear in the inner chambers will be proclaimed on the housetops.

⁴"I tell you⁺, my friends, do not be afraid of those who kill the body and after that have no more that they can do. ⁵But I will warn you⁺ whom you⁺ should fear. Fear the One who after He has killed has power and authority to cast into Gehinnom. Yes, I tell you⁺, fear Him.

⁶"Are not five sparrows sold for two copper coins, and not one of them is forgotten by God? ⁷But

---

11:51 "R. Yudan asked R. Aha: Where did Israel kill Zeharyah, in the Court of Israel or the Court of Women? He replied: 'Not in the Court of Women and not in the Court of Israel, but it was in the Court of the Priests.' …Israel committed seven transgressions on that day: they killed a priest, a prophet, and a judge, they shed innocent blood, they profaned the Name, they defiled the Court, and it was on the sabbath which was the Day of Atonements." (Mid. Ekah Rabbah 1:23)

12:5 "When Rabban Johanan ben Zakkai was sick, his disciples came in to visit him. When he saw them he began to weep. His disciples said to him: 'Candle of Israel, pillar of the right hand, hammer of strength! In front of what are you weeping?' He said to them: 'If I were being taken before a king of flesh and blood who is here today and tomorrow in the grave, if he is angry with me, his anger is not an everlasting anger. And if he imprisons me, his imprisonment is not an everlasting imprisonment. And if he puts to death, his putting to death is not an everlasting death. And I can persuade with words and bribe with money — even so I would weep. Now I am being taken before the King of kings of kings, the Holy One, blessed be He, who lives and endures for ever and ever and ever. And if He is angry with me, His anger is an everlasting anger. And if He imprisons, His imprisonment is an everlasting imprisonment. And if He puts me to death, He puts me to death for ever, and I cannot persuade Him with words or bribe Him with money. And even more, there are two ways before me, one of the Garden of Eden and one of Gehinnom, and I do not know by which I will be taken. Should I not weep?'" (Tal. Berachot 28b)

the very hairs of your head are all numbered. So do not be afraid, you⁺ are of more value than many sparrows.

⁸"I tell you⁺ that everyone who acknowledges me before men, the Son of Adam will also acknowledge him before the angels of God. ⁹But the one who denies me in the presence of men will be denied in the presence of the angels of God. ¹⁰Everyone who speaks a word against the Son of Adam will be forgiven, but those who blaspheme against the Ruakh Kodesh will not be forgiven. ¹¹When they bring you⁺ before the assemblies, the rulers, and the authorities, do not be anxious about how or what you⁺ will answer, or what you⁺ will say. ¹²For the Ruakh Kodesh will teach you⁺ in that same hour what you⁺ must say."

¹³One in the crowd said to him, "Rabbi, tell my brother to divide the inheritance with me."

¹⁴But he said to him, "Man, who made me a judge or an arbitrator over you?" [Ex. 2:14] ¹⁵He said to them, "Beware. Keep yourselves from covetousness, for a man's life does not consist of the abundance of the things which he possesses."

¹⁶He told them a parable: "The ground of a certain rich man brought forth abundantly. ¹⁷He reasoned within himself, 'What shall I do, since I do not have room to store my crops?' ¹⁸He said, 'This is what I will do. I will pull down my barns, and build bigger ones, and there I will store all my grain and my goods. ¹⁹I will tell my soul, "Soul, you have many goods laid up for many years. Take your ease, eat, drink, be merry."'

²⁰"But God said to him, 'You fool, tonight your soul is required of you. The things which you have prepared — whose will they be?' ²¹So is the one who lays up treasure for himself, and is not rich toward God."

²²He said to his disciples, "I tell you⁺, therefore, do not be anxious for your⁺ life, what you⁺ will eat, nor yet for your⁺ body, what you⁺ will wear. ²³Life is more than food, and the body is more than clothing. ²⁴Consider the ravens. They do not sow, they do not reap. They have no warehouse or barn, yet God feeds them. How much more valuable you⁺ are than the birds. ²⁵Which of you⁺ by being anxious can add a cubit to his height? ²⁶If you⁺ then are not able to do even the least things, why are you⁺ anxious about the rest? ²⁷Think about the lilies, how they grow. They do not weary themselves, nor do they spin yarn. Yet I tell you⁺ that even Solomon in all his glory was not arrayed like one of these. ²⁸But if this is how God clothes the grass in the field, which exists today, but is thrown into the oven tomorrow, how much more will He clothe you⁺, O you⁺ of little faith? ²⁹Do not search after what you⁺ will eat or what you⁺ will drink — do not be anxious either. ³⁰For all the nations of the world search after these things, and your⁺ Father knows that you⁺ need these things. ³¹Seek God's kingdom instead, and all these things will be added to you⁺. ³²Do not be afraid, little flock, for it is your⁺ Father's good pleasure to give you⁺ the kingdom. ³³Sell your⁺ possessions, and give to those in need. Keep your⁺ wealth where it will stay available, a treasure in the heavens that does not fail, where no thief approaches, and no moth destroys. ³⁴For where your⁺ treasure is, there your⁺ heart will be also.

³⁵"Let your⁺ waist be girded and your⁺ lamps burning. ³⁶Be like men watching for their master when he returns from the marriage feast, so that when he comes and knocks, they may immediately open to him. ³⁷There is good for those servants whom the master will find watching when he comes. I assure you⁺ he will prepare himself, have them recline, and will come and serve them. ³⁸If he comes in the second watch or in the third watch and finds them ready, there is good for those servants. ³⁹But know this, that if the master of the house had known in what hour the thief was coming, he

would have watched, and would not have allowed his house to be broken into. [40]Therefore you[+] also be ready, for the Son of Adam is coming in an hour you[+] do not expect him."

[41]Kefa said to him, "Lord, are you telling this parable to us, or to everybody?"

[42]The Lord said, "Who then is the faithful and wise manager, whom his master will set over his household to give them their allotment of food at the appropriate times? [43]There is good for that servant whom his master will find doing this when he comes. [44]I assure you[+] that he will set him over all that he has.

[45]"But if that servant says in his heart, 'My master delays his coming,' and begins to beat the menservants and the maidservants, and to eat and drink, and get drunk, [46]then the master of that servant will come in a day when he is not expecting him, and in an hour that he does not know. And he will cut him in two, and place his portion with the unfaithful. [47]That servant who knew his master's will and did not prepare, nor do what his master wanted, will be beaten with many stripes. [48]But the one who did not know, and did things worthy of lashes, will be beaten with few lashes. Much will be required from the one to whom much is given, and more will be asked from the one to whom much was entrusted.

[49]"I have come to cast fire upon the earth, and how I wish it were already kindled. [50]But I have an immersion in which to be immersed, and how I am driven until it is accomplished. [51]Do you[+] think that I have come to give peace in the earth? I tell you[+] no, but rather division. [52]For from now on, there will be five in one house divided three against two, and two against three. [53]They will be divided father against son, and son against father; mother against daughter, and daughter against her mother; mother-in-law against her daughter-in-law, and daughter-in-law against her mother-in-law." [Mic. 7:5-6]

[54]He said to the multitudes also, "When you[+] see a cloud rising from the west, immediately you[+] say, 'A rainstorm is coming,' and so it happens. [55]When a south wind blows, you[+] say, 'There will be a scorching heat,' and it happens. [56]Pretenders. You[+] know how to discern the appearance of the earth and the sky, but how is it that you[+] do not know how to discern this time? [57]Why do you[+] not judge for yourselves what is right? [58]For as you are going with your adversary before a magistrate, try diligently on the way to be released from him, so that he does not drag you to the judge, and the judge deliver you to the officer, and the officer throw you into prison. [59]I tell you that you will not get out of there by any means until you have paid the very last bronze coin."

13 [1]Now at that same time there were some present who told him about the Galileans whose blood Pilate had mixed with their sacrifices. [2]Yeshua responded to them, "Do you[+] think that these Galileans suffered such things because they were worse sinners than all the other Galileans? [3]I tell you[+], 'No, but unless you[+] change your[+] ways, you[+] will all perish in the same way.' [4]Or those

---

13:1 King Agrippa wrote to the Emperor, complaining that Pilate "was a man of very inflexible disposition, and very merciless as well as very obstinate..." ("On the Embassy to Gaius," The Works of Philo, Translated by C.D. Yonge, Hendrickson Publishers, 2002, P.784, [Chapter XXXVIII, 301]) Agrippa also accused Pilate "in respect of his corruption, and his acts of insolence, and his rapine, and his habit of insulting people, and his cruelty, and his continual murders of people untried and uncondemned, and his never ending, and gratuitous, and most grievous inhumanity." (Ibid., 302)

eighteen, on whom the tower in Shiloah fell and killed them — do you⁺ think that they were worse offenders than all the other men who dwell in Yerushala'im? ⁵I tell you⁺, 'No, but unless you⁺ change your⁺ ways, you⁺ will all perish in the same way.'"

⁶He told this parable. "A certain man had a fig tree planted in his vineyard, and he came seeking fruit on it, but found none. ⁷He said to the vinedresser, 'Look, I have come these three years looking for fruit on this fig tree, but found none. Cut it down. Why does it use up the ground?' ⁸He answered, 'Lord, leave it alone this year also, until I dig around it and fertilize it. ⁹If it bears fruit, fine. But if not, after that you can cut it down.'"

¹⁰He was teaching in one of the meetingplaces on Shabbat. ¹¹There was a woman who had a spirit of weakness for eighteen years, and she was bent over and unable to straighten herself up! ¹²When Yeshua saw her, he called her, and said to her, "Woman, you are freed from your weakness." ¹³He laid his hands on her, and immediately she stood up straight, and glorified God.

¹⁴The ruler of the assembly, being indignant because Yeshua had healed on Shabbat, said to the multitude, "There are six days made for work. Therefore come on those days and be healed, but not on Shabbat!"

¹⁵Therefore the Lord answered him, "Pretenders. Doesn't each one of you⁺ free his ox or his donkey from the stall on Shabbat, and lead him away to water? ¹⁶Should not this woman, being a daughter of Abraham whom the Accuser has bound eighteen long years, be set free from this bondage on Shabbat?"

¹⁷As he said these things, all his opponents were put to shame, and all the multitude rejoiced because of all the glorious things that were being done by him.

¹⁸He said, "What is God's kingdom like? To what shall I compare it? ¹⁹It is like a grain of mustard seed, which a man took and put in his own garden. It grew and became a tree, and the birds of the heaven lodged in its branches." [Ezek. 17:23; Dan. 4:10-12]

²⁰Again he said, "To what shall I compare God's kingdom? ²¹It is like leaven which a woman took and hid in three measures of flour until it was all leavened."

²²He went on his way teaching through cities and villages, and traveling on to Yerushala'im. ²³A certain man said to him, "Lord, are there few who are being saved?"

He said to them, ²⁴"Strive to enter in by the narrow door, for I tell you⁺ that many will seek to enter in and will not be able. ²⁵When once the master of the house has risen up and shut the door, and you⁺ begin to stand outside and knock at the door, saying, 'Lord, Lord, open to us!' then he will answer and tell you⁺, 'I do not know you⁺ or where you⁺ are from.' ²⁶Then you⁺ will begin to say, 'We ate and drank in your presence, and you taught in our streets.' ²⁷He will say, 'I tell you⁺, I do not know where you⁺ are from. Depart from me, all you⁺ workers of injustice.' [Ps. 6:9H/8] ²⁸There will be weeping

13:15-16 This is in accordance with the principle enunciated in Is. 58:6: "to loosen the bonds of wickedness, to undo the heavy burdens, to let the oppressed go free, and that you break every yoke." It is in accordance with the calling of Messiah: "to proclaim good news to the poor, to heal the brokenhearted, to proclaim liberty to the captives, and the opening of the prison to those who are bound." (Is. 61:1)

13:23-24 "As with their entering into the land [of Israel], there were two [i.e. Joshua and Caleb] from six hundred thousand... it will be so in the days of the Messiah." (Tal. Sanhedrin 11a)

and gnashing of teeth when you[+] see Abraham, Isaac, Jacob, and all the prophets in God's kingdom, but yourselves being thrown outside. [29]They will come from the east, west, north, and south, and will sit down in God's kingdom. [30]Listen, there are some who are last who will be first, and there are some who are first who will be last."

[31]On that same day, some Perushim came, saying to him, "Get out of here and go away, because Herod wants to kill you."

[32]He said to them, "Go and tell that fox, 'Look, I cast out demons and perform healings today and tomorrow, and the third day I accomplish my goal. [33]Nevertheless I must keep going today, tomorrow, and the next day, for it can scarcely be that a prophet should perish outside of Yerushala'im.'

[34]"Yerushala'im, Yerushala'im, who kills the prophets, and stones those who are sent to her. How often I wanted to gather your children together, like a hen gathers her own brood under her wings, and you[+] did not want it. [Ruth 2:12; Ps. 17:8; 61:4; 91:4] [35]Look, your[+] house is left to you[+] desolate. I tell you[+] that you[+] will surely not see me, until you[+] say, 'Blessed is the one who comes in the Name of the Everpresent Lord.'" [Ps. 118:26]

14 [1]When he went on Shabbat into the house of one of the rulers of the Perushim to eat bread, they were watching him. [2]A certain man who was swollen from dropsy was in front of him! [3]Yeshua said to the Torah scholars and Perushim, "Is it permitted to heal on Shabbat?" [4]But they were silent.

He took him, healed him, and released him. [5]He responded to them, "Which of you[+], if a son or an ox fell into a well, would not immediately pull him out on Shabbat?" [6]They could not answer him regarding these things.

[7]When he noticed how those who were invited chose the best seats, he told a parable and said to them, [8]"When you are invited by someone to a marriage feast, do not sit in the best seat, because perhaps someone more esteemed than you may have been invited by him. [9]Then the one who invited you both might come and tell you, 'Make room for this person.' And with shame you would begin to take the lowest place. [10]But when you are invited, go and sit in the lowest place, so that when the one who invited you comes, he may say to you, 'Friend, move up higher.' Then you will be honored in the presence of all who sit at the table with you. [Prov. 25:6-7] [11]For everyone who exalts himself will be humbled, and whoever humbles himself will be exalted."

[12]He also said to the one who had invited him, "When you give a dinner or a supper, do not call

14:2 Dropsy is an excessive internal accumulation of fluid.

14:5 "[N]o one should help an animal give birth on the Sabbath; and if it falls into a well [(CD 11:14) or a pit, he may not lift it out on the Sab]bath. No one should rest in a place near (CD 11:15) to Gentiles on the Sabbath. [No one should profane the Sabbat]h for wealth or spoil on the Sabbath. (CD 11:16) Any living human who falls [into a body of water or a cister]n (CD 11:17) shall not be helped out with ladder, rope, or instrument." (DSS 4Q271 f5i:8-11)

14:7-11 Tal. Berakhot 46b describes the order in which honored guests recline at a meal.

14:13-14 "Let your house be open to the street, and let the poor be children of your house." (Tal. Avot 1:5)

your friends, or your brothers, or your kinsmen, or rich neighbors; otherwise they also might invite you in return, and pay you back. [13]But when you give a feast, ask the poor, the maimed, the lame, or the blind. [14]Then there is good for you, because they are not able to repay you. For you will be repaid in the resurrection of the righteous."

[15]When one of those who sat at the table with him heard these things, he said to him, "Blessed is the one who will eat bread in God's kingdom!"

[16]But he said to him, "A certain man gave a great supper, and he invited many people. [17]He sent out his servant at supper time to tell those who were invited, 'Come, because everything is ready now.' [18]They all as one began to make excuses. The first said to him, 'I have bought a field, and I must go and see it. Please have me excused.' [19]Another said, 'I have bought five yoke of oxen, and I must go test and approve them. Please have me excused.' [20]"Another said, 'I have married a wife, and so I cannot come.' [21]That servant came, and told his lord these things. Then the head of the house was angry and said to his servant, 'Go out quickly into the streets and lanes of the city, and bring in the poor, maimed, blind, and lame.' [22]The servant said, 'Lord, it is done as you commanded, and there is still room.'

[23]"The lord said to the servant, 'Go out into the main roads and hedges, and compel them to come in, so that my house may be filled. [24]For I tell you[+] that none of those men who were invited will taste of my supper.'"

[25]Now large crowds were going with him. He turned and said to them, [26]"If anyone comes to me and does not hate his own father, mother, wife, children, brothers, and sisters, yes, and his own life also, he cannot be my disciple. [27]Whoever does not carry his own tree of death, and come after me, cannot be my disciple. [28]For which of you[+], desiring to build a tower, does not first sit down and count the cost to see if he has enough to complete it? [29]Or otherwise, when he has laid a foundation and is not able to finish, everyone who sees begins to mock him, [30]saying, 'This man began to build, and was not able to finish.' [31]Or what king, as he goes to encounter another king in war, will not sit down first and consider whether he is able with ten thousand to meet the one who comes against him with twenty thousand? [32]Or else, while the other is still a long way off, he sends an envoy, and asks for terms of peace. [33]In the same way, anyone of you[+] who does not renounce all that he has cannot be my disciple. [34]Salt is good, but if the salt becomes flat and tasteless, with what will it be seasoned? [35]It is fit neither for the soil nor for the manure heap. It is thrown out. He who has ears to hear, let him hear." [Dt. 29:4, Ezek. 3:27]

14:25-26 This is comparative. Yeshua is placing the importance of home and family in perspective. These relationships are very important, but less important than seeking and doing the will of God. We find the same prioritization in God's call to Abram in Gen. 12:1 and in Dt. 13:6-11, where God places family ties below faithfulness to Him. We find the same prioritization in Num. 6:7, where God says of the Nazirite, "He is not to make himself unclean even for his father or his mother, for his brother or his sister, when they die, because his separation to God is on his head." We find the same prioritization for the priesthood — consider Aaron at the time of the death of his sons. (c.f. Lev. 10) See also the notes to Rom.9:12 and 1Co. 9:9.

14:34-35 In Tal. Bechorot 8b, there is a fanciful story where the question is asked, "When salt becomes unsavory, with what can it be salted?" The final answer given is that salt cannot become unsavory. I.e., it is only a hypothetical question.

15 [1]Now all the tax collectors and sinners drew near to him to hear him. [2]The Perushim and the Torah scholars grumbled, saying, "This man welcomes sinners, and eats with them."

[3]He told them this parable. [4]"Which of you[+], if you had one hundred sheep and lost one of them, would not leave the ninety-nine in the wilderness, and go after the one that was lost until he found it? [5]When he has found it, he carries it on his shoulders, rejoicing. [6]When he comes home, he calls together his friends and his neighbors and says to them, 'Rejoice with me, for I have found my sheep which was lost!' [7]I tell you[+] that even so there will be more joy in heaven over one sinner who turns to God, than over ninety-nine righteous people who do not need to.

[8]"Or what woman having ten drachma coins, if she should lose one, would not light a lamp, sweep the house, and seek diligently until she found it? [9]When she has found it, she calls together her friends and neighbors and says, 'Rejoice with me, for I have found the drachma which I had lost.' [10]Even so, I tell you[+] that there is joy in the presence of the angels of God over one sinner turning to God."

[11]He said, "A certain man had two sons. [12]The younger of them said to his father, 'Father, give me my share of your resources.' He divided his income between them.

[13]"Not many days afterwards, the younger son gathered everything and traveled into a far country. There he wasted his resources with reckless living. [14]When he had spent all of it, there arose a severe famine in that country, and he began to be in need. [15]He went and joined himself to one of the citizens of that country, who sent him into his fields to feed pigs. [16]He wanted to fill his belly with the husks that the pigs ate, but no one gave him any. [17]Now when he came to his senses he said, 'How many of my father's hired servants have more than enough bread, and I'm dying with hunger! [18]I will get up and go to my father, and I will tell him, "Father, I have sinned against Heaven, and in your sight. [19]I am no longer worthy to be called your son. Make me as one of your hired servants."'

[20]"He arose, and came to his father. But while he was still far off, his father saw him, was moved with tenderness, and ran, fell upon his neck, and kissed him. [21]The son said to him, 'Father, I have sinned against Heaven, and in your sight. I am no longer worthy to be called your son.'

[22]"But the father said to his servants, 'Bring out the best robe, and put it on him. Put a ring on his hand, and shoes on his feet. [23]Bring the fattened calf, and kill it. Then let us eat and celebrate, [24]because this son of mine was dead, and is alive again. He was lost, and is found.' They began to celebrate.

15:3-7 When Moses said [Ex. 5:22], "'Since I came to Pharaoh to speak in Your Name, he has done evil to this people.' The Holy One, blessed be He, said to him, 'Mourn for those who are lost and are not found.'" (Tal. Sanhedrin 111a)

15:8 "R. Pinchas b. Yair opened his teaching with, 'If you seek her as silver, etc.' (Prov. 2:4). If you search for words of Torah as after hidden treasures, the Holy One, blessed be He, will not withhold your reward. It is like a man who loses a coin worth four denarii or a small coin inside his house, he lights some candles, some wicks, until he finds it. Now if it is so with these things of this age which last a short time, how much more will a man light so many candles and wicks until he finds them, the words of Torah, which are life for this age and for the age to come — isn't it necessary for you to search after them as for hidden treasures?" (Mid. Song Rabbah 1:9)

²⁵"Now his elder son was in the field. As he came near to the house, he heard music and dancing. ²⁶He called one of the servants to him, and asked what was happening. ²⁷He said to him, 'Your brother has come, and your father has killed the fattened calf, because he has received him back safe and healthy.' ²⁸He was angry, however, and would not go in. So his father came out and entreated him. ²⁹But he answered his father, 'These many years I have served you, and I never disobeyed your command. But you never gave me a goat so that I could celebrate with my friends! ³⁰But when this son of yours came, who has devoured your living with prostitutes, you killed the fattened calf for him.'

³¹"He said to him, 'Son, you are always with me, and all that is mine is yours. ³²But it was appropriate to celebrate and be glad, for this brother of yours was dead, and is alive again. He was lost, and is found.'"

16 ¹He also said to his disciples, "There was a certain rich man who had a manager. An accusation was made to him that this man was wasting his possessions. ²He called him, and said to him, 'What is this that I hear about you? Give an accounting of your management, for you can no longer be manager.'

³"The manager said to himself, 'What will I do, since my lord is taking away the management position from me? I don't have strength to dig; I am ashamed to beg. ⁴I know what I will do so that when I am removed from being manager, they will receive me into their houses.' ⁵Calling each one of his lord's debtors to him, he said to the first, 'How much do you owe to my lord?' ⁶He said, 'A hundred measures of oil.' He said to him, 'Take your bill, and sit down quickly and write fifty.' ⁷Then he said to another, 'How much do you owe?' He said, 'A hundred measures of wheat.' He said to him, 'Take your bill, and write eighty.'

⁸"His lord commended the dishonest manager because he had acted shrewdly. For the children of this age are wiser towards their own people than the children of the light are. ⁹I tell you⁺, make friends for yourselves by means of the riches of unrighteousness, so that when it fails, they will receive you⁺ into the eternal dwellings.

¹⁰"The one who is faithful with a very little is faithful also with much. The one who is dishonest with a very little is also dishonest with much. ¹¹So if you⁺ have not been faithful with the riches of unrighteousness, who will commit the true riches to your⁺ trust?

¹²If you⁺ have not been faithful with what is another's, who will give you⁺ what is your⁺ own? ¹³No servant can serve two masters, for either he will hate the one and love the other, or else he will hold to one and despise the other. You⁺ cannot serve God and riches."

16:1-12 In this parable, the manager knows that the time in which he controls his master's possessions is coming to an end. So while he still has control over those possessions, he uses that control to make friends who will receive him into their homes after his stewardship comes to an end. Yeshua presents this manager — his understanding and subsequent action — as an example for the children of light. I.e., 'You see what he did to gain a temporal dwelling. How much more should you use the things of this world to gain an eternal dwelling?'

It might also be that the manager had been overcharging the debtors. See note to Lk. 19:2-8.

16:9-13 "Mammonas" was the Syrian god of riches. "Mammon," therefore, was a term designating the riches of this world.

[14]Hearing all these things, those Perushim who were lovers of money scoffed at him. [15]He said to them, "You[+] are those who in the sight of men declare yourselves righteous, but God knows your[+] hearts. For what is exalted among men is an abomination in the sight of God.

[16]"The Torah and the prophets lead to Yoḥanan; God's kingdom is proclaimed from that time, and all are assaulting it. [17]But it is easier for heaven and earth to pass away, than for the least stroke in the Torah to fall. [18]Everyone who divorces his wife and marries another commits adultery. He who marries one who is divorced from a husband commits adultery.

[19]"Now there was a certain rich man who was clothed in purple and fine linen, living in luxury every day. [20]A certain beggar named Eleazar was laid at his gate, full of sores. [21]And he longed to be satisfied with the crumbs that fell from the rich man's table. Even the dogs came and licked his sores. [22]The beggar died, and he was carried away by the angels to Abraham's bosom. The rich man also died, and was buried. [23]In Sheol, being in torment, he lifted up his eyes and saw Abraham far off, and Eleazar at his bosom. [24]He cried and said, 'Father Abraham, have mercy on me, and send Eleazar, so that he may dip the tip of his finger in water, and cool my tongue! For I am in agony in this flame.'

[25]"But Abraham said, 'Child, remember that in your lifetime you received your good things, and Eleazar, in like manner, bad things. But now he is comforted here and you are in anguish. [26]Besides all this, there is a large gulf fixed between us and you[+], so that those who want to pass from here to you[+] are not able, and so that none may cross over from there to us.'

[27]"He said, 'I ask you therefore, father, that you would send him to my father's house — [28]for I have five brothers — so that he may testify to them, so that they will not also come into this place of torment.'

[29]"But Abraham said to him, 'They have Moses and the prophets. Let them listen to them.'

[30]"He said, 'No, father Abraham, but if one goes to them from the dead, they will change their ways.'

[31]"He said to him, 'If they do not listen to Moses and the prophets, they will not be persuaded even if one rises from the dead.'"

17 [1]He said to the disciples, "It is inevitable that there be stumbling blocks, but woe to the one through whom they come. [2]It would be better for him if a millstone were hung around his neck, and he were thrown into the sea, rather than that he should cause one of these little ones to stumble. [3]Watch yourselves, and if your brother sins against you, rebuke him. [Lev. 19:17] If he repents, forgive him. [4]If he sins against you seven times in the day, and returns seven times saying, 'I repent,' forgive him."

[5]The ambassadors said to the Lord, "Give us more faith."

[6]The Lord said, "If you[+] had faith like a grain of mustard seed, you[+] would tell this sycamore tree, 'Be uprooted, and planted in the sea,' and it would listen to you[+]. [7]But who is there among you[+], having a servant plowing or keeping sheep, that would say this when he comes in from the field? — 'Come immediately and sit down at the table.' [8]Would he not tell him this instead? — 'Prepare my

---

16:23 Sheol is the realm of the dead.

17:4 The blood of the sin offering was sprinkled on the altar seven times (Lev.4:6); Naaman immersed himself in the Yarden River seven times (2Ki. 5:14); the righteous falls seven times and rises again (Prov. 24:16).

supper, clothe yourself properly, and serve me while I eat and drink. Afterward you are to eat and drink.' ⁹Does he thank that servant because he did the things that were commanded? I don't think so. ¹⁰Even so, you⁺ also, when you⁺ have done all the things that are commanded you⁺, say, 'We are unworthy servants. We have done what we were obligated to do.'"

¹¹As he was on his way to Yerushala'im, he was passing along the borders of Shomron and the Galil. ¹²As he entered into a certain village, ten men who were lepers met him. They stood afar off. ¹³They lifted up their voices and said, "Yeshua, Master, have mercy on us!"

¹⁴When he saw them, he said to them, "Go and show yourselves to the Kohanim." Now as they went, they were cleansed.

¹⁵One of them, when he saw that he was healed, turned back, glorifying God with a loud voice. ¹⁶He fell on his face at Yeshua's feet, giving thanks to him. He was a man of Shomron. ¹⁷Yeshua responded, "Were there not ten cleansed? But where are the nine? ¹⁸Were there none found who returned to give glory to God, except this foreigner?" ¹⁹Then he said to him, "Get up and go your way. Your faith has healed you."

²⁰Being asked by the Perushim when God's kingdom would come, he answered them, "God's kingdom does not come with careful observation. ²¹Nor will they say, 'Look, here!' or, 'Look, there!' because, listen, God's kingdom is before you⁺."

²²He said to the disciples, "The days will come when you⁺ will desire to see one of the days of the Son of Adam, and you⁺ will not see it. ²³They will tell you⁺, 'Look, here!' or 'Look, there!' Do not go out or follow. ²⁴For as the lightning which flashes under part of the the sky shines to other parts under the sky, so will the Son of Adam be in his day. ²⁵But he must first suffer many things and be rejected by this generation.

²⁶"As it happened in the days of Noaḥ, even so will it be also in the days of the Son of Adam. ²⁷They were eating, they were drinking, they were marrying, they were given in marriage, until the day that Noaḥ entered into the ark, and the flood came, and destroyed them all. ²⁸Likewise, even as it happened in the days of Lot, they were eating, they were drinking. They were buying, they were selling, they were planting, they were building. ²⁹But in the day that Lot went out from Sedom, it rained fire and brimstone from heaven, and destroyed them all. ³⁰That is the way it will be in the day that the Son of Adam is revealed. ³¹In that day, if someone is on the housetop, but his goods are in the house, let him not go down to take them away. Let the one who is in the field likewise not turn back. ³²Remember Lot's wife. ³³Whoever seeks to save his life will lose it, but whoever loses his life will preserve it. ³⁴I tell

---

17:10 "R. Tarfon said, 'The day is short; the work is extensive; the workmen are lazy; the reward is much, and the master of the house is insistent." (Tal. Avot 2:15)

In Tal. Niddah 30b, there is a discussion about every child in the womb being taught Torah, instructed as to how to live in the world, and made to take an oath before being born. "Be righteous and do not be wicked. And even if all the entire world says to you, 'You are righteous,' be in your own eyes as one who is wicked...."

17:20 See LXX Mi. 3:11 as an illustration of *meta* meaning "in response to".

17:33 "Alexander of Makedon asked ten questions of the elders of the Negev.... He said to them: 'Who is called wise?' They replied: 'This one is wise, the one who sees what will come.' He said to them: 'Who is called >>

you⁺ that in that night there will be two people in one bed. One will be taken, and the other will be left. ³⁵There will be two grinding grain together. One will be taken, and the other will be left."

³⁷They responded, asking him, "Where, Lord?"

He said to them, "Where the body is, there also the vultures will be gathered together."

18 ¹He also spoke a parable to them that they should always pray, and not give up. ²He said, "There was a judge in a certain city who did not fear God, and did not respect man. ³There was a widow in that city who often came to him saying, 'Give me justice against my opponent!' ⁴For some time he would not, but afterward he said to himself, 'Though I neither fear God nor respect man, ⁵yet because this widow bothers me, I will give her justice, so that she doesn't wear me out by her continual coming.'"

⁶The Lord said, "Listen to what the unrighteous judge said. ⁷Will not God execute justice for His chosen who are crying out to Him day and night while He is longsuffering beside them? ⁸I tell you⁺ that He will execute justice for them speedily. Nevertheless, when the Son of Adam comes, will he find faith on the earth?"

⁹He also told this parable to certain people who were convinced of their own righteousness, and who despised all others: ¹⁰"Two men went up into the Temple to pray. One was a Parush, and the other was a tax collector. ¹¹The Parush stood and was praying to himself like this: 'God, I thank you that I am not like the rest of men — thieves, unjust, adulterers — or even like this tax collector. ¹²I fast twice a week. I give tithes of all that I get.' ¹³But the tax collector, standing far away, would not even lift up his eyes to heaven, but beat his breast, saying, 'God, be merciful to me, a sinner!' ¹⁴I tell you⁺ that this man went down to his house justified rather than the other, because everyone who exalts himself will be humbled, but the one who humbles himself will be exalted."

---

a mighty man?' They replied: 'This one is mighty, the one who subdues his desire.' He said to them: 'Who is called a rich man?' They replied: 'This one is rich, the one who is happy with his portion.' He said to them: 'What shall a man do and live?' They replied: 'Put himself to death.' 'What should a man do and die?' They replied: 'Keep himself alive.'" (Tal. Tamid 31b-32a)

18:9-11 R. Simeon ben Yoḥai said, "The world could not endure with fewer than thirty men as righteous as Abraham our father... And if there are ten, I and my son are among them. And if there are five, I and my son are among them. And if there are two, I and my son are they. And if there is one, I am he." (Mid. Genesis 35.2)

18:11-12 "On his leaving [a house of Torah study] what does a man say? 'I give thanks before You, O Everpresent Lord, my God, that You have set my portion with those who sit in the house of study, and You have not set my portion with those who sit on corners, for I wake up and they wake up, but I wake up to words of Torah, but they wake up to words that do not last; I labor and they labor. I labor and receive a reward but they labor and do not receive a reward; I run and they run, but I run to the life of the age to come and they run to the pit of destruction.'" (Tal. Berachot 28b)

Rashi comments on the inclusion of galbanum in the making of the holy anointing oil: "A spice whose smell is bad... And the Scripture includes it among the spices of the incense to teach us that it should not be insignificant in our eyes to put the transgressors of Israel in the refining fire with us in our associations and our fastings and our prayers, that they will be numbered with us. (Commentary on Ex. 30:34)

[15]They were also bringing their little children to him so that he might touch them. But when the disciples saw it, they rebuked them. [16]Yeshua summoned them, saying, "Let the little children come to me, and do not hinder them, for God's kingdom belongs to such as these. [17]I assure you[+] that whoever does not receive God's kingdom as a little child will never enter into it."

[18]A certain ruler asked him, "Good Teacher, what should I do to inherit eternal life?"

[19]Yeshua asked him, "Why do you call me good? No one is good, except One — God. [20]You know the commandments: Do not commit adultery. Do not murder. Do not steal. Do not give false testimony. Honor your father and your mother." [Ex. 20:12-16, Dt. 5:16-20]

[21]He said, "I have observed all these things from my youth."

[22]When Yeshua heard these things, he said to him, "You still lack one thing. Sell all that you have, distribute it to the poor, and you will have treasure in heaven. Then come, follow me."

[23]But when he heard these things, he became very sorrowful, since he was very rich. [24]Seeing that he became very sorrowful, Yeshua said, "How hard it is for those who have riches to enter into God's kingdom. [25]For it is easier for a camel to enter in through the eye of a needle than for a rich man to enter into God's kingdom."

[26]Those who heard it said, "Then who can be saved?"

[27]But he said, "The things which are impossible with men are possible with God."

[28]Kefa said, "Look, we left all and followed you."

[29]He said to them, "I assure you[+] there is no one who has left house, or wife, or brothers, or parents, or children, for the sake of God's kingdom, [30]who will not receive many times more in this time, and eternal life in the age to come."

[31]He took the twelve aside, and said to them, "Listen, we are going up to Yerushala'im, and all the things that are written by the prophets concerning the Son of Adam will be fulfilled. [32]For he will be delivered up to the Gentiles, will be mocked, insulted, and spit on. [33]They will scourge and kill him. On the third day, he will rise again." [34]They understood nothing of these things, and what he said was hidden from them. They did not understand the things that were said.

[35]As he came near Yeriho, a certain blind man sat begging by the road. [36]Hearing a crowd going by, he asked, "What is this?" [37]They told him that Yeshua of Natzrat was passing by. [38]He cried out, "Yeshua, Son of David, have mercy on me!" [39]Those who led the way rebuked him so that he would be quiet, but he cried out all the more, "Son of David, have mercy on me!"

[40]Then Yeshua stood still and commanded him to be brought to him. When he had come near, he asked him, [41]"What do you want me to do for you?"

He said, "Lord, that I may see again."

[42]Yeshua said to him, "Receive your sight again. Your faith has healed you."

[43]Immediately he received back his sight, and followed him, glorifying God. When all the people saw it, they praised God.

18:22 "Monobaz the king spent all his treasure in years of hardship. His brothers said to him, 'Your fathers stored up treasure and added to that of their fathers. But you have continued to spend all your treasures, yours and your fathers.' He said to them, 'My fathers stored up treasures below, and I have stored up treasures above.... My fathers stored up treasures of Mammon, but I have stored up treasures of souls.... My fathers stored up treasures in this age, but I have stored up for the age to come." (Tos. Peah 4:18)

19

¹He came into Yeriḥo and was passing through it. ²There was a man named Zakkai, who was a chief tax collector, and he was rich. ³He was trying to see who Yeshua was, and, since he was short, could not because of the crowd. ⁴He ran on ahead and climbed up into a sycamore tree to see him, because he was about to pass that way. ⁵When Yeshua came to the place, he looked up, saw him, and said to him, "Zakkai, hurry and come down, because it's necessary that I stay at your house today." ⁶He hurried, came down, and received him joyfully. ⁷When they saw it, they all murmured, saying, "He has gone in to stay with a man who is a sinner."

⁸Zakkai stood and said to the Lord, "Listen Lord, half of my goods I give to the poor. If I have wrongfully exacted anything from anyone, I restore four times as much."

⁹Yeshua said to him, "Today, salvation has come to this house, because he also is a son of Abraham. ¹⁰For the Son of Adam came to seek and to save what was lost."

¹¹As they listened to these things, he went on and told a parable, because he was near Yerushala'im, and they thought that God's kingdom would be revealed immediately. ¹²He said therefore, "A certain nobleman was going into a far country to receive for himself a kingdom, and return. ¹³He called ten servants of his, gave them each a gold piece, and told them, 'Conduct business until I come.' ¹⁴But his citizens hated him, and sent an envoy after he went, saying, 'We do not want this man to reign over us.'

¹⁵"When he had come back again, having received the kingdom, he commanded the servants to whom he had given the money to be called to him, so that he might know what they had gained by conducting business. ¹⁶The first came before him, saying, 'Lord, your gold piece has made ten more.' ¹⁷He said to him, 'Well done, you good servant. Because you were faithful with a very little, you will have authority over ten cities.'

¹⁸"The second came saying, 'Lord, your gold piece has made five gold pieces.' ¹⁹So he said to him, 'Then you are to be over five cities.'

²⁰"Another came, saying, 'Lord, here is your gold piece, which I kept laid away in a handkerchief ²¹because I feared you, since you are a demanding man. You take up what you did not lay down, and reap what you did not sow.' ²²He said to him, 'Out of your own mouth I will judge you, you wicked servant. You knew that I am a demanding man, taking up what I did not lay down, and reaping what I did not sow. ²³Then why didn't you give my money to the moneylenders, and at my coming, I would have received interest on it?'

²⁴"He said to those who stood by, 'Take the gold piece away from him, and give it to the one who has the ten gold pieces.' ²⁵They said to him, 'Lord, he has ten gold pieces!'

²⁶"'I tell you⁺ that to everyone who has, more will be given, but from the one who does not have, even what he has will be taken away from him. ²⁷But bring here those enemies of mine who did not want me to reign over them, and kill them in my presence.'"

19:2-8 "It happened that a certain man sought to make restitution. His wife said to him, '*Rayka*, if you make restitution, even your belt is not yours.' So he refrained and did not make restitution.... For shepherds, tax collectors and publicans it is difficult for them to make restitution, yet they must make restitution to those they know [they have exploited]." (Tal. Baba Kama 94b)

19:17 "Be just as concerned about a light commandment as about a heavy commandment, because you do not know the gift of reward for commandments." (Tal. Pirke Avot 2:1)

²⁸Having said these things, he went on ahead, going up to Yerushala'im. ²⁹When he drew near to Beit Pagei and Beit Anya, at the mountain that is called the Mount of Olives, he sent two of his disciples, ³⁰saying, "Go into the village on the other side. As you⁺ enter it, you⁺ will find in it a colt tied, on which no one has ever yet sat. Untie it, and bring it. ³¹If anyone asks you⁺, 'Why are you⁺ untying it?' say to him: 'The Lord needs it.'"

³²Those who were sent went off, and they found things just as he had told them. ³³As they were untying the colt, the owners of it said to them, "Why are you⁺ untying the colt?"

³⁴They said, "The Lord needs it." ³⁵They brought it to Yeshua. They threw their cloaks on the colt, and set Yeshua on them. ³⁶As he went, they spread their cloaks in the way. ³⁷As he was now getting near the descent of the Mount of Olives, the whole company of the disciples began to rejoice and praise God with a loud voice for all the mighty works which they had seen. ³⁸They were saying, "Blessed is the King coming in the Name of the Everpresent Lord! [Ps. 118:26] Peace in heaven, and glory in the highest!"

³⁹From the crowd, some of the Perushim said to him, "Rabbi, rebuke your disciples!"

⁴⁰He answered them, "I tell you⁺ that if these were silent, the stones would cry out."

⁴¹When he drew near, he saw the city and wept over it. ⁴²He said, "If you had known — in this, your day — the things which belong to your peace, but now, they are hidden from your eyes. ⁴³For the days will come upon you when your enemies will throw up a barricade against you, surround you, shut you in on every side, ⁴⁴and will level you and your children within you to the ground. Since you did not know the time of your visitation, instead they will not leave in you one stone upon another,."

⁴⁵He entered into the Temple, and began to drive out those who bought and sold in it. ⁴⁶He was saying to them, "It is written, 'My house is a house of prayer,' but you⁺ have made it a den of bandits." [Is. 56:7, Jer. 7:11]

⁴⁷He was teaching daily in the Temple, but the chief Kohanim, the Torah scholars, and the leading men among the people sought to destroy him. ⁴⁸They could not find a way to do it, because all the people hung onto every word that he said.

20 ¹On one of those days, as he was teaching the people in the Temple and proclaiming the good news, the Kohanim and Torah scholars came to him with the Elders. ²They asked him, "Tell us by what kind of authority you are doing these things? Or who gives you this authority?"

³He answered them, "I also will ask you⁺ one question. Tell me, ⁴the immersion of Yohanan, was it from Heaven, or from men?"

19:40 "But maybe a man will say, 'Who will witness against me?' The stones of the house of the man and the walls of the house of the man will witness against him." (Tal. Ta'anit 11a) "The stones and walls of a mans house witness against him, for it is said, 'A stone from a wall will cry out and a beam of wood will answer it.' [Hab. 2:11]" (Tal. Chagigah 16a)

19:44 "Caesar gave orders that they should now demolish the entire city and Temple. ...it was so thoroughly laid even with the ground by those that dug it up to the foundation, that there was left nothing to make those who came there believe it had ever been inhabited." (Josephus, The Jewish War, 7.1.1.1-3)

"Woe to the children on account of whose iniquities I destroyed My House and burned My Temple and exiled them among the peoples of the world." (Tal. Berachot 3a)

⁵They reasoned with each other, "If we say, 'From Heaven,' he will say, 'Why didn't you⁺ believe him?' ⁶But if we say, 'From men,' all the people will stone us, because they are persuaded that Yoḥanan was a prophet." ⁷They answered that they did not know where it was from.

⁸Yeshua said to them, "Neither will I tell you⁺ by what authority I do these things."

⁹He began to tell the people this parable. "A man planted a vineyard, rented it out to some farmers, and went away on a journey for a long time. ¹⁰At the appropriate season, he sent a servant to the farmers to collect his share of the fruit of the vineyard. But the farmers beat him, and sent him away emptyhanded. ¹¹He again sent another servant, and they also beat him, treated him shamefully, and sent him away emptyhanded. ¹²He sent yet a third, and they also wounded him, and threw him out. ¹³The lord of the vineyard said, 'What shall I do? I will send my beloved son. It may be that seeing him, they will respect him.'

¹⁴"But when the farmers saw him, they reasoned with each other, 'This is the heir. Come, let's kill him, so that the inheritance may be ours.' ¹⁵They threw him out of the vineyard, and killed him. What therefore will the lord of the vineyard do to them? ¹⁶He will come and destroy these farmers, and will give the vineyard to others."

When they heard it, they said, "May it never be!"

¹⁷But he looked at them and said, "Then what is this that is written? 'The stone which the builders rejected, the same was made the chief cornerstone.' [Ps. 118:22] ¹⁸"Everyone who falls on that stone will be broken, but it will scatter as dust anyone on whom it falls." [Dan. 2:44]

¹⁹The chief Kohanim and the Torah scholars sought to lay hands on him that very hour, but they feared the people, because they knew he had spoken this parable against them. ²⁰They watched him, and sent out spies who pretended to be righteous, so that they might trap him in something he said, in order to deliver him up to the rule and authority of the governor. ²¹They asked him, "Rabbi, we know that you say and teach what is right, and are not partial to anyone, but truly teach the way of God. ²²Is it lawful for us to pay taxes to Caesar, or not?"

²³But he perceived their scheming and said to them, "Why do you⁺ test me? ²⁴Show me a denarius. Whose image and inscription are on it?"

They answered, "Caesar's."

²⁵He said to them, "Then give back to Caesar the things that are Caesar's, and to God the things that are God's." ²⁶They were not able to trap him in his words before the people. They were astonished at his answer, and were silent.

²⁷Some of the Tzadukim came to him, those who deny that there is a resurrection. ²⁸They asked him, "Rabbi, Moses wrote to us that if a man's married brother dies and he is childless, his brother should take the wife, and raise up children for his brother. [Dt. 26:6] ²⁹Now there were seven brothers. The first took a wife, and died childless. ³⁰The second took her as wife, and he died childless. ³¹The third took her, and likewise the seven, who all died and left no children. ³²Afterward the woman also died. ³³So in the resurrection, whose wife will she be? For the seven had her as a wife."

³⁴Yeshua said to them, "The children of this age marry, and are given in marriage. ³⁵But those who

20:9-19 See the note to Mt. 21:33-46.

20:16 The expression, _halilah_ in Hebrew, has the sense of 'Such a thing is blasphemy.'

are considered worthy to attain to that age and the resurrection from the dead neither marry, nor are given in marriage. [36]For they cannot die any more, because they are like the angels and are children of God, being children of the resurrection. [37]But that the dead are raised, even Moses showed at the bush, when he called the Everpresent Lord 'the God of Abraham, the God of Isaac, and the God of Jacob.' [Ex. 3:6] [38]Now He is not the God of the dead, but of the living, for all are alive to Him."

[39]Some of the Torah scholars responded, "Rabbi, you have spoken well." [40]They did not dare to ask him any more questions.

[41]He said to them, "Why do they say that the Messiah is David's son? [42]David himself says in the scroll of Psalms, 'the Everpresent Lord said to my lord, Sit at my right hand, [43]until I make your enemies the footstool of your feet.' [Ps. 110:1] [44]David therefore calls him 'lord,' so how is he his son?"

[45]In the hearing of all the people, he said to his disciples, [46]"Beware of the Torah scholars who like to walk in long robes, and love greetings in the marketplaces, the best seats in the meetingplaces, and the best places at feasts. [47]They devour widows' houses, and pray at great length as a pretense. These will receive greater condemnation."

21 [1]He looked up and saw the rich people who were putting their gifts into the treasury. [2]He saw a certain poor widow putting in two small bronze coins. [3]He said, "I assure you[+] that this poor widow put in more than all of them, [4]because all these put in gifts for God from what they had in abundance, but she, out of her poverty, put in all that she had to live on."

[5]As some were talking about the Temple and how it was decorated with beautiful stones and gifts, he said, [6]"As for these things which you[+] see, the days will come in which there will not be left here one stone upon another that will not be thrown down."

[7]They asked him, "Rabbi, when then will these things be? What is the sign that these things are about to happen?"

[8]He said, "Be careful that you[+] do not get led astray, because many will come in my name saying, 'I am he,' and, 'The time has come near.' So do not follow them. [9]When you[+] hear of wars and uprisings, do not be terrified, because these things must happen first, but the end will not come right away."

[10]Then he said to them, "Nation will rise against nation, and kingdom against kingdom. [11]In various

20:35 "In the Age to Come, there is neither eating nor drinking nor fruitfulness [i.e. procreation], nor increase [i.e. business], nor burden nor giving, nor jealousy nor hatred nor rivalry..." (Tal. Berachot 17a)

20:37-38 "The Holy One, blessed by He, said to Moses: 'I request of you what I requested concerning Sedom, present Me with ten righteous men among them and I will not destroy them.' He replied, 'Lord of the Universe, I will present them to You. Here they are: myself, Aaron, Eleazar, Itamar, Pinchas, Joshua, and Caleb.' God said to him, 'These are seven.' Moses did not know what to do. He said, 'Lord of the Universe! Are the dead alive?' He said to him, 'Yes.' He said: 'If the dead are alive, remember Abraham, Isaac, and Israel, and there will be ten for You.'" (Mid. Ex. Rabbah 44:7)

21:3 "it is the same whether a man offers much or little, so long as he directs his heart to heaven." (Tal. Menachot 110a)

21:6 See note to Lk. 19:44.

21:10 "When you see the kingdoms terrorizing one another, be on the lookout for the feet [i.e. the coming] of Messiah." (Mid. Genesis 42.4)

places there will be big earthquakes, famines, and plagues. There will be things to fear and great signs from heaven. [12]But before all these things, they will lay their hands on you[+] and will persecute you[+], delivering you[+] up to assemblies and prisons, bringing you[+] before kings and governors for my name's sake. [13]It will turn out as an opportunity for you[+] to testify. [14]So purpose in your[+] hearts not to prepare ahead of time to defend yourself, [15]for I will give you[+] words and wisdom which all your[+] adversaries will be unable to withstand or to contradict. [16]You[+] will be handed over even by parents, brothers, relatives, and friends. They will cause some of you[+] to be put to death. [17]You[+] will be hated by all men for my name's sake. [18]Not a hair of your head will perish. [19]You[+] will preserve your[+] souls by your[+] endurance.

[20]"But when you[+] see Yerushala'im surrounded by armies, then know that its desolation has come near. [21]Let those who are in Judea then flee to the mountains. Let those who are in her midst depart. Let those who are in the country not go in. [22]For these are days of avenging, that all things which are written may be fulfilled. [23]Woe to those who are pregnant and to those who nurse infants in those days. For there will be great distress in the land, and wrath against this people. [24]They will fall by the edge of the sword, and will be led captive into all the nations.

"Yerushala'im will be trampled down by the Gentiles, until the times of the Gentiles are fulfilled. [25]There will be signs in the sun, moon, and stars, roaring of the sea and surging waves. And on the earth there will be distress of nations in perplexity, [26]There will be men fainting for fear in anticipation of the things which are coming on the world, because the powers of the heavens will be shaken. [27]Then they will see the Son of Adam coming in a cloud with power and great glory. [28]But when these things begin to happen, look up, and lift up your[+] heads, because your[+] redemption is near."

[29]He told them a parable. "See the fig tree, and all the trees. [30]When they are already budding, you[+] yourselves see and know that the summer is already near. [31]Even so you[+] also, when you[+] see these things happening, know that God's kingdom is near. [32]I assure you[+] this people will not pass away until all has taken place. [Jer. 31:35-36] [33]Heaven and earth will pass away, but my words will never pass away. [34]"So be careful, or your[+] hearts will be loaded down with carousing, drunkenness, and cares of this life; and that day will come on you[+] suddenly. [35]For it will come as a trap on all those who dwell on the surface of all the earth. [36]So be alert always, praying that you[+] may be counted worthy to escape all these things that will happen, and to stand before the Son of Adam."

21:29-32 In v.32, most translations have "this generation," i.e. the generation that sees the things Yeshua has just described. Liddell and Scott give the first meaning of *genea* as "persons in a family". For *genea* as "people," see God's promise to Jacob in LXX Gen. 31:3.

In "The Revelation of Peter", which was considered canonical in the second century, Yeshua says explicitly, "Do you not understand that the fig-tree is the house of Israel? ...Have you not understood that the fig-tree is the house of Israel? I faithfully say to you, when the twigs of it have sprouted forth in the last days, then shall feigned Messiahs come and awake expectation saying: 'I am the Messiah, who is now come into the world.' ...Then the twigs of the fig-tree, that is, the house of Israel, will shoot forth."

"There is no greater sign for you of redemption than this: 'And you mountains of Israel, you will send out your branches and give your fruit to My people Israel, for they are about to come.' (Ezek. 36:8)" (Tal. Sanhedrin 98a)

[37]By day Yeshua was teaching in the Temple, and by night he would go out and stay on the mountain that is called the Mount of Olives. [38]All the people came early in the morning to him in the Temple to hear him.

22 [1]Now the feast of Matzot, which is called Pesakh, drew near. [2]The chief Kohanim and the Torah scholars sought a way they might destroy him, because they feared the people. [3]The Accuser entered into Judah, the one called "the man of K'riyot," who was numbered among the twelve. [4]He went away, and talked with the chief Kohanim and captains about how he might deliver him to them. [5]They were pleased, and agreed to give him money. [6]He promised and sought an opportunity to deliver him to them in the absence of the multitude. [7]The day of Matzot came, on which the Pesakh must be sacrificed.

[8]He sent Kefa and Yoḥanan, saying, "Go and prepare Pesakh for us, so that we may eat."

[9]They said to him, "Where do you want us to prepare it?"

[10]He said to them, "Look, when you[+] have entered into the city, a man carrying a pitcher of water will meet you[+]. Follow him into the house which he enters. [11]Tell the head of the house, 'The Rabbi says to you, *Where is the guest room where I may eat Pesakh with my disciples?*' [12]He will show you[+] a large, furnished upper room. Make preparations there."

[13]They went, found things as he had told them, and they prepared Pesakh. [14]When the hour had come, he reclined with the twelve ambassadors. [15]He said to them, "I have greatly desired to eat this Pesakh with you[+] before I suffer, [16]for I tell you[+] that I will not again eat of it until it is fully realized in God's kingdom." [17]He received a cup, and when he had given thanks, he said, "Take this, and share it among yourselves, [18]for I tell you[+] that I will not drink at all again from the fruit of the vine, until God's kingdom has come."

[19]He took bread, and when he had given thanks, he broke it, and gave it to them, saying, "This is my body which is given for you[+]. Do this in remembrance of me." [20]Likewise, he took the cup after supper, saying, "This cup is the new covenant in my blood, which is poured out for you[+]. [21]But look, the hand of the one who delivers me up is with me on the table. [22]The Son of Adam indeed goes, as it has been determined, but woe to that man through whom he is delivered up!" [23]They began to argue among themselves about which of them it was who would do this thing.

[24]There arose also an argument among them about which of them was considered to be greatest. [25]He said to them, "The kings of the Gentiles dominate them, and those who have authority over them are called 'Benefactors'. [26]But you[+] are not to be like this. To the contrary, the one who is the greater among you[+], let him become as the younger, and the one who is leading, as one who serves. [27]For who is greater, the one who reclines at the table or the one who serves? Isn't it the one who reclines

---

22:7-8 Both the festival and the festival sacrifice are called by the same name, Pesakh.

22:17-18 These verses are not in the Peshitta. The Peshitta also does not contain 2Kefa, 2Yoḥanan, 3Yoḥanan, and Judah.

22:24-27 "Benefactor" was a title of honor given to one who had rendered special service to the government.

"Our Rabbis taught: Every day, the Holy One, blessed be He, weeps over these three: over the one for whom it is possible to occupy himself with Torah and does not; and over the one for whom it is not possible >>

at the table? But I am among you⁺ as one who serves. ²⁸Now you⁺ are those who have continued with me in my trials. ²⁹As my Father entrusted a kingdom to me, I entrust it to you⁺ ³⁰so that you⁺ may eat and drink at my table in my kingdom. You⁺ will sit on thrones, judging the twelve tribes of Israel."

³¹The Lord said, "Shimon, Shimon, listen, the Accuser desires to have you, to sift you as wheat, ³²but I have prayed for you, so that your faith not cease. And you, when you have returned, strengthen your brothers."

³³He said to him, "Lord, I am ready to go with you both to prison and to death!"

³⁴He said, "I tell you, Kefa, the rooster will not call out today until you deny three times that you know me.

³⁵"When I sent you⁺ out without money, sandals, or a bag for provisions, did you⁺ lack anything?" They said, "Nothing."

³⁶Then he said to them, "But now, whoever has money, let him take it, and likewise a bag for provisions. Whoever does not have a sword, let him sell his cloak and buy one. ³⁷For I tell you⁺ that this which is written must still be fulfilled in me: 'He was counted with the lawless ones.' [Is. 53:12] For the things concerning me have a purpose."

³⁸They said, "Lord look, here are two swords."

He said to them, "That's enough."

³⁹He came out and went to the Mount of Olives, as was his custom. His disciples also followed him. ⁴⁰When he was at the place, he said to them, "Pray that you⁺ do not enter into temptation."

⁴¹He drew away from them about a stone's throw. Then he knelt down and prayed, ⁴² "Father, if You are willing, remove this cup from me. Nevertheless, not my will but Yours be done."

⁴³An angel from heaven appeared to him, strengthening him. ⁴⁴Being in the agony of conflict, he prayed more earnestly. [2Mac. 3:14-22] His sweat became like large drops of blood, falling down on the ground.

⁴⁵When he rose up from his prayer, he came to the disciples, and found them sleeping because of grief. ⁴⁶He said to them, "Why do you⁺ sleep? Rise and pray that you⁺ may not enter into temptation."

⁴⁷While he was still speaking, a multitude came with one of the twelve, the one called Judah. He was leading them. He came near to Yeshua to kiss him, ⁴⁸but Yeshua said to him, "Judah, are you delivering up the Son of Adam with a kiss?" [2Sam. 20:8-10]

⁴⁹When those who were around him saw what was about to happen, they said to him, "Lord, shall

to occupy himself with Torah but he does; and over a leader who lifts himself above the community." (Tal. Chagigah 5b)

Socrates said that those who want to rule are the least fit to do so. "[T]he truth is surely this: that city in which those who are going to rule are least eager to rule is necessarily governed in the way that is best and freest from faction, while the one that gets the opposite kind of rulers is governed in the opposite way. ...The good aren't willing to rule for the sake of money or honor.... For it is likely that if a city of good men came to be, there would be a fight over not ruling, just as there is now over ruling; and there it would become manifest that a true ruler really does not naturally consider his own advantage but rather that of the one who is ruled." (Plato, The Republic, Section 520d, Section 347b-d)

we strike with the sword?" ⁵⁰A certain one of them struck the servant of the Kohen Gadol, and cut off his right ear.

⁵¹But Yeshua responded, "Let this go no farther," and he touched his ear, and healed him. ⁵²Yeshua said to the chief Kohanim, captains of the Temple, and Elders who had come against him, "Have you⁺ come out with swords and clubs as against a bandit? ⁵³When I was with you⁺ daily in the Temple, you⁺ did not stretch out your⁺ hands against me; but this is yours⁺, the hour and the power of darkness."

⁵⁴They seized him, led him away, and brought him into the house of the Kohen Gadol. But Kefa followed from a distance. ⁵⁵When they had kindled a fire in the middle of the courtyard, and had sat down together, Kefa sat among them. ⁵⁶A certain servant girl saw him as he sat in the light, and looking intently at him, said, "This man also was with him."

⁵⁷He denied Yeshua, saying, "Woman, I do not know him."

⁵⁸After a little while someone else saw him, and said, "You also are one of them!"

But Kefa answered, "Man, I am not!"

⁵⁹After about an hour passed, another confidently affirmed it, saying, "Certainly this man also was with him, for he is from the Galil."

⁶⁰But Kefa said, "Man, I do not know what you are talking about!" Immediately, while he was still speaking, a rooster called out. ⁶¹The Lord turned, and looked at Kefa. Then Kefa remembered the Lord's word, how he had said to him, "Before the rooster calls out you will completely deny me three times." ⁶²He went out and wept bitterly.

⁶³The men who held Yeshua mocked him and beat him. ⁶⁴Having blindfolded him, they struck him on the face and demanded of him, "Prophesy! Who is the one who struck you?" ⁶⁵They said many other things against him, maligning him.

⁶⁶As soon as it was day, the assembly of the Elders of the people, both chief Kohanim and Torah scholars, was gathered together. And they led him away into their Council, saying, ⁶⁷"If you are the Messiah, tell us."

But he said to them, "If I tell you⁺, you⁺ will not believe. ⁶⁸And if I ask, you⁺ will certainly not answer me or let me go. ⁶⁹From now on, the Son of Adam will be sitting at the right hand of the power of God." [Ps. 110:1]

⁷⁰They all said, "Are you then the Son of God?"

He said to them, "You⁺ say that I am."

⁷¹They said, "Why do we need any more evidence? For we ourselves have heard from his own mouth!"

23 ¹The entire group of them rose up and brought him before Pilate. ²They began to accuse him, "We found this man deceiving the nation, forbidding paying taxes to Caesar, and saying that he himself is the anointed King."

³Pilate asked him, "Are you the King of the Jews?"

He answered him, "You say so."

⁴Pilate said to the chief Kohanim and the multitudes, "I find no basis for a charge against this man."

⁵But they insisted, "He stirs up the people, teaching throughout all Judea, beginning from the Galil even to this place." ⁶But when Pilate heard the Galil mentioned, he asked if the man was from the Galil. ⁷When he found out that he was from Herod's jurisdiction, he sent him to Herod, who was also in Yerushala'im during those days.

[8]Now when Herod saw Yeshua, he was very glad, for he had wanted to see him for a long time, since he had heard many things about him. He hoped to see some miracle done by him. [9]He questioned him at length, but he gave no answers. [10]The chief Kohanim and the Torah scholars stood and accused him vehemently. [11]Herod and his soldiers humiliated and mocked him. Dressing him in luxurious clothing, they sent him back to Pilate. [12]Herod and Pilate became friends with each other that very day, for they had been hostile towards each other before that.

[13]Pilate called together the chief Kohanim, the rulers, and the people. [14]And he said to them, "You[+] brought this man to me as one who deceives the people. Yet see that I have examined him before you[+], and found no basis for a charge against this man concerning those things of which you[+] accuse him. [15]Neither has Herod, for I sent you[+] to him, and see, nothing worthy of death has been done by him. [16]I will therefore punish him and release him."

[17]Now he had to release one prisoner to them at the feast. [18]But they all cried out together, "Away with this man! Release to us Bar Abba!" [19](He was thrown into prison for a certain revolt in the city and for murder.)

[20]Then Pilate spoke to them again, wanting to release Yeshua, [21]but they shouted, "The deathstake! Hang him on the deathstake!"

[22]He said to them the third time, "Why? What evil has this man done? I have found in him no cause for death. I will therefore punish him and release him." [23]But they were insistent with loud voices, asking for him to be put to death on the stake. Their voices and the voices of the chief Kohanim prevailed. [24]Pilate decreed that what they asked for should be done. [25]He released to them the one who had been thrown into prison for revolt and murder — the one for whom they asked — but he delivered Yeshua up to their will.

[26]When they led him away, they grabbed one Shimon of Kyrene coming from the countryside, and laid the stake on him to carry it after Yeshua. [27]A large crowd of the people followed him, including women who also mourned and lamented him. [28]But turning to them, Yeshua said, "Daughters of Yerushala'im, do not weep for me, but weep for yourselves and for your[+] children. [29]For behold, the days are coming in which they will say, 'There is good for the barren, the wombs that never bore, and the breasts that never nursed.' [30]Then they will begin to tell the mountains, 'Fall on us!' and the hills, 'Cover us!' [Hos. 10:8, Is. 2:19] [31]For if they do these things in the green tree, what will be done in the dry?"

[32]There were also others, two criminals, led with him to be put to death. [33]When they came to the place that is called "The Skull," they hung him on the stake there, with the criminals one on the right and the other on the left.

[34]Yeshua said, "Forgive them Father, because they do not know what they are doing."

They cast lots, dividing his garments among them. [35]The people stood watching. The rulers with them also taunted him, "He saved others. Let him save himself, if this is the Messiah of God, His chosen one!"

[36]The soldiers also mocked him, coming to him and offering him wine vinegar [Ps. 69:22H], [37]and saying, "If you are the King of the Jews, save yourself!" [38]An inscription was also written over him in letters of Greek, Latin, and Hebrew: "THIS IS THE KING OF THE JEWS."

[39]One of the criminals who was hung mocked him, "If you are the Messiah, save yourself and us!"

[40]But the other responded and rebuked him, "Don't you even fear God, seeing you are under the

same condemnation? [41]And we indeed justly, because we are receiving the due reward for what we did, but this man has done nothing wrong." [42]He said to Yeshua, "Lord, remember me when you come into your kingdom."

[43]Yeshua said to him, "I tell you faithfully that you will be with me in the Garden today." [2Co. 12:4, Rev. 2:7]

[44]It was now about the sixth hour, and darkness came over the whole land until the ninth hour. [45]The sun was darkened, and the veil of the Temple was torn in two. [46]Crying with a loud voice, Yeshua said, "Father, into Your hands I commit my spirit!" [Ps. 31:6H] Having said this, he breathed his last.

[47]When the centurion saw what was done, he glorified God, saying, "Certainly this was a righteous man." [48]All the multitudes that came together to see this, when they saw the things that were done, returned home beating their breasts. [49]All his acquaintances, and the women who followed with him from the Galil, stood at a distance watching these things.

[50]There was a man named Yosef, who was a member of the Council, a good and just man from Ramatayim, a city of Judea. [51]He had not consented to their counsel and action. He was also waiting for God's kingdom. [52]This man went to Pilate, and asked for Yeshua's body. [53]He took it down, wrapped it in a linen cloth, and laid him in a tomb that was cut in stone, where no one had ever been laid. [54]The day was a preparation, and Shabbat was drawing near. [55]The women who had come with him out of the Galil followed after. And they saw the tomb and how his body was laid. [56]They returned, and prepared fragrances and ointments.

On Shabbat they rested in accordance with the commandment.

24 [1]But at early dawn on the first of the week, they and some others came to the tomb, bringing the fragrant ointments which they had prepared. [2]They found the stone had been rolled away from the tomb. [3]They entered in, and did not find the body of the Lord Yeshua. [4]While they were extremely perplexed about this, two men stood by them in dazzling clothing! [5]Becoming terrified, they bowed their faces down to the ground.

They said to them, "Why do you+ seek the living among the dead? [6]He is not here, but has been raised. Remember what he told you+ when he was still in the Galil, [7]saying that the Son of Adam must be delivered up into the hands of sinful men, be put to death on the tree, and rise again the third day?"

23:43 "Seven things were created before the world was created, and these are they: Torah, repentance, the Garden of Eden, Gehinnom, the throne of the Glory, the Temple and the name of Messiah." (Tal. Pes. 54a)

"In the days to come the Holy One, blessed be He, will hold a celebration for the righteous and He will sit in their midst in the Garden of Eden. And every one of them will point his finger, as it is said, 'And it will be said in that day: *Behold our God, this is the One for whom we waited, and He will save us; this is the Everpresent Lord for whom we waited, we will be glad and rejoice in His salvation.*' [Is. 25:9]" (Tal. Ta'anith 31a)

24:1 On Shabbat, "You may go to the boundary ...to attend to the dead, to bring a coffin and burial clothes for him... One may do all that is necessary for the dead, to wash and anoint him with oil..." (Tal. Shabbat 23:5,6; 151a)

[8]They remembered his words, [9]returned from the tomb, and told all these things to the eleven, and to all the rest. [10]Now they were Miryam from Magdala, Yohana, and Miryam the mother of Jacob. The other women with them told these things to the ambassadors. [11]These words seemed to them to be nonsense, and they did not believe them. [12]But Kefa got up and ran to the tomb. Stooping and looking in, he saw the lengths of linen lying by themselves, and he departed to his home, wondering what had happened.

[13]Two of them were going that very day to a village named Ammaus, which was seven miles from Yerushala'im. [14]They talked with each other about all of these things which had happened. [15]While they talked and considered these things together, Yeshua himself came near, and went with them. [16]But their eyes were kept from recognizing him. [17]He said to them, "What are you+ talking about as you+ walk in sadness?"

[18]One of them, named Halfai, answered him, "Are you a stranger staying alone in Yerushala'im and do not know the things which have happened in it in these days?"

[19]He said to them, "What things?"

They said to him, "The things concerning Yeshua of Natzrat, a man who was a prophet, mighty in word and deed before God and all the people. [20]Then the chief Kohanim and our rulers delivered him up to be condemned to death, and hung him on the stake. [21]But we were hoping that he was the one who would redeem Israel. Yet with all this, it is now the third day since these things happened. [22]Moreover, certain women of our group shocked us. They arrived early at the tomb, [23]and when they did not find his body, they came saying that they had also seen a vision of angels, who said that he was alive. [24]Some of us went to the tomb, and found it just as the women had said, but they did not see him."

[25]He said to them, "O senseless men and slow of heart to believe in all that the prophets have spoken. [26]Didn't the Messiah have to suffer these things to enter into his glory?" [27]Beginning from Moses and from all the prophets, he explained to them the things concerning himself in all the Scriptures. [28]They drew near to the village where they were going, and he acted like he would go farther.

[29]They urged him, "Stay with us, for it is almost evening, and the day is almost over." He went in to stay with them. [30]As he reclined at the table with them, he took the bread and saic a blessing. Breaking it, he gave to them. [31]Their eyes were opened, and they recognized him. Then he vanished out of their sight. [32]They said to each other, "Weren't our hearts burning within us, while he spoke to us along the way, and while he opened the Scriptures to us?" [Jer. 20: 9]

[33]They rose up that very hour, returned to Yerushala'im, and found the eleven gathered together and those who were with them. [34]They said, "The Lord has indeed been raised, and has appeared to Shimon!" [35]They related the things that happened along the way, and how he was recognized by them in the breaking of the bread.

24:25-27 The Sephardic Kaddish al Yisrael, hetzi Kaddish, et al. say, "May His kingdom reign, and may He cause His redemption to sprout, and may He bring near His Messiah." The word for "bring near," y'karave, is the word that is also generally used for sacrifices, i.e., to bring them near to God. In Ex. 28:1, Moses is commanded to bring near/hakrev Aaron and his sons to serve as kohanim/priests to the Everpresent Lord.

[36]As they said these things, Yeshua himself stood among them, and said to them, "Peace to you[+]." [37]But they were terrified and filled with fear. And they thought that they had seen a spirit.

[38]He said to them, "Why are you[+] troubled? Why do doubts arise in your[+] hearts? [39]See my hands and my feet, that it is truly me. Touch me and see, for a spirit does not have flesh and bones, as you[+] see that I have." [40]When he had said this, he showed them his hands and his feet. [41]While they still did not believe for joy, and were amazed, he said to them, "Do you[+] have anything here to eat?" [42]They gave him a piece of broiled fish. [43]He took it, and ate before them.

[44]He said to them, "This is what I told you[+] while I was still with you[+], that all things which are written in the Torah of Moses, the Prophets, and the Psalms concerning me must be fulfilled." [45]Then he opened their minds to understand the Scriptures. [46]He said to them, "This is how it is written, and why it was necessary for the Messiah to suffer and to rise from the dead the third day." [47]He also said to them that repentance and forgiveness of sins should be proclaimed in his name to all the Gentiles, beginning at Yerushala'im. [48]You[+] are witnesses of these things. [49]Listen, I send forth the promise of my Father upon you[+]. But stay in the city of Yerushala'im until you[+] are clothed with power from on high."

[50]He led them out as far as Beit Anya, and he lifted up his hands and blessed them. [51]While he blessed them, he was separated from them, and was carried up into heaven. [52]They bowed down to him, and returned to Yerushala'im with great joy. [53]They were continually in the Temple, praising and blessing God.

The Report of Yohanan

1 [1]The Word existed in the beginning, and the Word was with God [Gen. 1:1; Prov. 8:30], and God was the Word. [Wis. 7:24-26] [2]This one existed in the beginning with God. [3]All things came into existence through him. Nothing of what exists came into existence without him. [Prov. 8:22-31] [4]In him was life, and the life was the light of men. [5]The light shone in the darkness, and the darkness did not overcome it.

[6]There came a man, sent from God, whose name was Yohanan. [7]This man came as a witness so that he might testify about the light, so that all might believe through him. [8]He was not the light, but was sent so that he might bear wtiness to the light — [9]the true light that enlightens every man was coming into the world.

[10]He was in the world, and the world was made through him [Ps. 33:6], but the world did not recognize him. [11]He came to what was his own, and those who were his own did not receive him. [12]However, as many as did receive him, to them he gave the right to become children of God, to those who believe in his name. [13]These were born not of blood, nor of the will of the flesh, nor

Yohanan (like Matthias, Mark, and Luke) recounts events that took place in the first century in the land of Israel. He takes conversations that took place in Hebrew or in the Jewish Aramaic of the time, and translates them into Greek. Consequently any English translation of Yohanan's Greek text is in many places a translation of a translation. Yohanan occasionally transliterates Hebrew words into Greek, and then gives the meaning of the original words for a widespread Greek-speaking audience.

1:1 The Aramaic and Greek both have an article before "God" in "the Word was with [article] God". Neither has an article before "God" in the phrase that follows, where the word order is "God was the Word," In Aramaic, the article for the first occurrence of "God" is applied to the second occurrence as well, making the meaning the same as the word order — i.e. "God was the word." That is not the case in Greek. Most translators do not follow the word order, but put "the Word was God," because there is no article for "God" in the Greek phrase.

1:1-2 These verses are intended to bring to mind Gen. 1:1-3.

1:4-9 "R. Berekiah said: 'Israel said before the Holy One, blessed be He: Master of the Universe, because You bring light into the world, Your Name is made great in the world.' And what is the light? Redemption." (Mid. Shir haShirim I:22)

1:11 It is possible that *eis ta idia* means "to his own home" as in Yhn. 19:27; and that *hoi idioit auton* means those of his own household, his own close relatives, who did not receive him until after the resurrection. (cf. Yhn. 7:3-5; Mk. 6:1-5; 1Tim. 5:8; Acts 4:23) Lk. 4:13-30 is also interesting in this regard. But it would seem more likely that v. 11 should be understood in terms of vv. 1-10, which speak of Creation and all humanity, "which were made by him".

Rashi's comment on Gen. 49:10 is relevant. "'Until Shiloh will come' [This is] King Messiah, because the kingdom is his. And this is how Onkelos targums it." The kingdom is what is his own.

1:14 "The Word became flesh, and planted his tent among us." Compare this to 2Sam. 7:6b, "To this day, I have walked in a tent and in a tabernacle."

of the will of man, but of God. [14]The Word became flesh, and set his tent among us. [2Sam. 7:6; Is. 55:11-12] We saw his glory, a glory of the only begotten of the Father, full of grace and truth. [Ex. 34:6; Is. 16:5]

[15]Yohanan bore witness concerning him, crying out, "This is the one of whom I said, 'The one who comes after me is greater than I, because he existed before me.'" [16]We all received gracious gift upon gracious gift from his fullness [Sir. 26:15], [17]because the Torah was given through Moses; the grace and the truth came through Yeshua the Messiah. [Mi. 7:20; Ps. 25:10; 40:11; 57:4H; 85:11H; Prov. 16:6]

[18]No one has ever seen God. [Ex. 24:9-11; Yhn. 14:9] The only begotten Son, who is in the innermost being of the Father, he has made Him known. [19]This is the testimony of Yohanan when the sectarian Jews sent Kohanim and Levites from Yerushala'im to ask him, "Who are you?"

[20]He openly acknowledged and declared, "I am not the Messiah," and did not deny it.

[21]They asked him, "What then? Are you Eliyahu?" [Mal. 3:23-24H]

He said, "I am not."

"Are you the Prophet?" [Dt. 18:15-19]

He answered, "No."

[22]So they said to him, "Who are you? Give us an answer to take back to those who sent us. What do you say about yourself?"

[23]He said, "I am the voice of one crying out in the wilderness, 'Make straight the way of the Everpresent Lord,'" [Is. 40:3] as Isaiah the prophet said.

[24]The ones who had been sent were from the Perushim. [25]They asked him, "Why then do you immerse, if you're not the Messiah, nor Eliyahu, nor the Prophet?"

[26]Yohanan answered them, "I immerse in water, but among you[+] stands one whom you[+] do not know. [27]He is the one who comes after me; I am not worthy to loosen the strap of his sandal."

[28]These things were done in Beit Abara, beyond the Yarden, where Yohanan was immersing. [29]He saw Yeshua coming to him the next day, and said, "Look, the Lamb of God who takes away the sin of the world. [30]This is the one of whom I said, 'After me comes a man who is greater than I, for

---

1:16-17 Some traditional translations insert "but" into v. 17. This insertion distorts the meaning of the text into its opposite, and creates a false separation between Moses and Yeshua. The text says, "We all received gracious gift upon gracious gift". The Torah is one gracious gift — e.g. Ps. 119:29, "Remove the false way from me, and graciously grant me Your law." The grace and truth brought by Yeshua is another.

Yeshua was not aware of any opposition between himself and Moses. As he said, "If you+ were believing Moses, you would be believing me. But if you+ do not believe his writings, how will you+ believe my words?" (Yohanan 5:46-47)

"Grace upon grace, a woman who is modest and whose self-control is beyond price." (Sirach 26:15) Her first grace is modesty, and her second grace, self-control, rests upon it. Likewise, the Law is God's gracious gift to Israel through Moses. The Truth, resting upon the Law, came to Israel through Yeshua, the Messiah of whom Moses and the prophets spoke.

1:19 See "Iudaioi in Yohanan" in the ADDITIONAL NOTES.

1:28 Beit Abara, as in the Textus Receptus

he existed before me.' [31]I did not know him, but I came immersing in water so that he would be revealed to Israel." [32]Yoḥanan testified, "I have seen the Spirit descending like a dove out of heaven, and remaining upon him. [33]I did not recognize him, but the One who sent me to immerse in water said to me, 'The one on whom you will see the Spirit descending and remaining, he is the one who immerses in the Ruakh Kodesh.' [34]I have seen, and have testified that this is the Son of God."

[35]Again the next day, Yoḥanan was standing with two of his disciples. [36]Seeing Yeshua walking, he said, "Look, the Lamb of God!" [37]The two disciples heard him speak, and they followed Yeshua.

[38]Yeshua turned and saw them following, and said to them, "What are you+ seeking?"

They said to him, "Rabbi" (which is translated as 'Teacher'), "where are you staying?"

[39]He said to them, "Come and see." They came and saw where he was staying, and they stayed with him that day. It was about the tenth hour.

[40]One of the two who heard Yoḥanan and followed him was Andreas, Shimon Kefa's brother. [41]He first found his own brother, Shimon, and said to him, "We have found the Messiah," (which is translated as *christos*). [42]He brought him to Yeshua. Yeshua looked at him, and said, "You are Shimon the son of Yoḥanan. You will be called Kefa," (which is translated as *Petros*). [43]On the next day, he was determined to go out into the Galil, and he found Philip. Yeshua said to him, "Follow me." [44]Now Philip was from Beit Tzaidah, of the city of Andreas and Kefa.

[45]Philip found Nataniel, and said to him, "We have found the one of whom Moses in the Torah and the prophets wrote, Yeshua of Natzrat, the son of Yosef."

[46]Nataniel said to him, "Can any good thing come out of Natzrat?"

Philip said to him, "Come and see."

[47]Yeshua saw Nataniel coming to him, and said about him, "Behold, a real man of Israel, in whom there is no deceit."

[48]Nataniel said to him, "How do you know me?"

Yeshua answered him, "I saw you before Philip called you, when you were under the fig tree."

[49]Nataniel answered him, "Rabbi, you are the Son of God! You are the King of Israel!"

[50]Yeshua answered him, "Do you believe because I told you, 'I saw you underneath the fig tree'? You will see greater things than these." [51]He said to him, "Be assured, I tell you+, that you+ will see heaven opened, and the angels of God ascending and descending on the Son of Adam." [Gen. 28:12-16]

2 [1]On the third day, there was a marriage in Kanah of the Galil. Yeshua's mother was there, and [2]Yeshua also was invited to the marriage with his disciples. [3]When the wine ran out, the mother of Yeshua said to him, "They have no wine."

[4]Yeshua said to her, "Woman, what is that to me and you? My hour has not yet come."

[5]His mother said to the servants, "Whatever he says to you+, do it." [6]Now in accordance with the

---

1:42 "Shimon, son of Yonah" in Mt. 16:17 seems to be a reference to Shimon's sharing in the nature and calling of Yonah the prophet.

2:3-4 The response of Yeshua seems to be a comparison between the wine of the feast and his blood which will be shed when his "hour has come".

2:5 "R. Huna b. R. Nathan said: 'Whatever the master of a house tells you, do.'" (Tal. Pesachim 86b)

manner of purification of the sectarian Jews, there were six stone water jars set there; each could hold about twenty gallons. [7]Yeshua said to them, "Fill the water jars with water." They filled them up to the brim. [8]He said to them, "Now draw some out, and take it to the one in charge of the feast." So they took it.

[9]When the one in charge of the feast tasted the water which had become wine, but did not know where it came from — though the servants who had drawn the water knew — the one in charge of the feast called the bridegroom. [10]He said to him, "Everyone serves the good wine first, and then, when the guests have drunk freely, what is not as good. You have kept the good wine until now." [11]Yeshua did this first sign in Kanah of the Galil, showing his glory, and his disciples believed in him. [12]After this, he went down to Kfar Naḥum — he, his mother, his brothers, and his disciples — and they stayed there a few days.

[13]The Jewish Pesakh was near, and Yeshua went up to Yerushala'im. [14]In the Temple he found the money-changers sitting there and the sellers of oxen, sheep, and doves. [15]He made a whip of cords, and drove all out of the Temple, both the sheep and the oxen. Then he poured out the money-changers' coins, and overthrew their tables. [16]He said to those who sold the doves, "Take these things out of here! Do not make my Father's house a house of commerce!" [17]His disciples remembered that it was written, "Zeal for Your house has consumed me." [Ps. 69:10H]

[18]Therefore the Jewish authorities responded to him, "What sign do you show us, seeing that you do these things?"

[19]Yeshua answered them, "Destroy this temple, and in three days I will raise it up."

[20]So the Jewish authorities responded, "This Temple took forty-six years to build, and are you going to raise it up in three days?" [21]But he spoke of the temple of his body. [22]When he was then raised from the dead, his disciples remembered that he had said this, and they believed the scripture and the word which Yeshua had spoken.

[23]Now when he was in Yerushala'im at Pesakh, during the feast, many believed in his name, observing his miracles which he did. [24]But Yeshua did not trust himself to them, because he knew all men, [25]and because he had no need for anyone to testify about man, because he himself knew what was in man.

[1]Now there was a man of the Perushim named Nakdimon, a ruler of the Jews. [2]This man came to him by night and said to him, "Rabbi, we know that you are a teacher come from God, for no one can do these miracles that you do unless God is with him."

2:6-11 Why is changing water for purification into wine the first miracle that Yeshua performs? This simple kindness performed at a wedding seems to lack the great significance that should mark the beginning of Messiah's supernatural ministry. As Yeshua later remarks, "The works that I do in my Father's Name bear witness of me." (Yhn. 10:25) How does changing water into wine bear witness of who Yeshua is?

The significance of this sign lies in what it represents. The Word of God is often compared in the Scriptures to water that purifies. (e.g. Ps. 119:9; Eph. 5:26) Early in his presentation of who Yeshua is, Yohanan tells us that the Word became flesh. (1:14) To redeem the children of Adam, Yeshua shared in their flesh and blood. (Heb. 2:14) His blood purifies them. (Heb. 9:13-14) In other words, it seems to signify the water of the Word of God changing into human flesh and blood. "... my blood is real drink." (Yhn. 6:55)

2:19 See "Destroy this temple" in the ADDITIONAL NOTES.

³Yeshua answered him, "I assure you that unless one is born anew, he cannot see God's kingdom."

⁴Nakdimon said to him, "How can a man be born when he is old? Can he enter a second time into his mother's womb and be born?"

⁵Yeshua answered, "I assure you that unless one is born of water and ruakh, he cannot enter into God's kingdom. ⁶What is born of the flesh is flesh. What is born of the ruakh is ruakh. ⁷Do not wonder that I said to you, 'you⁺ must be born anew.' ⁸The ruakh blows where it chooses, and you hear its sound, but do not know where it comes from and where it is going. So is everyone who is born of the ruakh." [Eccl. 11:5]

⁹Nakdimon answered him, "How can these things be?"

¹⁰Yeshua answered him, "Are you a teacher of Israel and do not know these things? ¹¹I assure you that we declare what we know, and testify of what we have seen, but you⁺ don't receive our testimony. ¹²If I told you⁺ things concerning the earth and you⁺ don't believe, how will you⁺ believe if I tell you⁺ things concerning the heavens?

¹³"No one has ascended into heaven except the one who came down out of heaven, the Son of Adam. ¹⁴Even as Moses lifted up the serpent in the wilderness [Num. 21:8-9], it is necessary that the Son of Adam be lifted up in the same way, ¹⁵so that whoever believes in him may have eternal life. ¹⁶For God so loved the world that He gave His Son, the only one born as His Son, so that whoever believes in him should not be destroyed, but have eternal life. [cf. Gen. 22:2] ¹⁷For God did not send His Son into the world to pass judgment on the world, but in order that the world might be saved through him.

¹⁸"The one who believes in him is not condemned, but the one who disbelieves has been condemned already, because he has not believed in the name of God's uniquely born Son. ¹⁹This is the verdict: the light has come into the world, and men loved the darkness rather than the light, because their deeds were evil. [Gen. 1:3, Is. 2:5,5:20,9:2,49:6; Ps. 119:105, Job 24:13-16] ²⁰For everyone who is doing evil things hates the light, and does not come to the light, so that his deeds won't be exposed. ²¹But

---

3:3 "A foreigner who becomes a proselyte is like a little one newly born." (Tal.Yebamot 48b) A leper is considered as one dead. (cf. Tal. Nedarim 64b and Mid. Sh'mot Rabba 1:34, citing Num. 12:12). Therefore a leper who is cleansed would be as one born from the dead.

3:6-8,34 The Hebrew word *ruakh*, as well as the Greek *pneuma*, signifies "spirit," "wind," and "breath". The context is usually sufficient for determining which English word is most appropriate. In this chapter, the use of the English words would detract from the overall meaning of the passage, and so I have used ruakh throughout these verses.

3:8 "For the mobility of wisdom is more than any motion. By its purity, it passes and goes through all things. Because it is the breath of the power of God, and an emanation of the glory of the Almighty. Therefore no one can sneak in and defile this purity. For it is the radiance [cf. Heb. 1:3] of the everlasting light, the unspotted mirror of the actions of God, and the image of His goodness." (Wisdom 7:24-26)

3:13 No one else has gone up to heaven by his own power. God took H̲anokh (Gen. 5:24); Lucifer said, "I will ascend...," but was thrown down. (Is. 14:12-15).

3:16 "David said: 'To what extent does the son love the Father? To the extent that he delivers his soul to death for His glory.'" (Mid. Psalms 9.17)

the one who does what is true comes to the light, so that it may be revealed that his deeds have been done in God."

²²After these things, Yeshua came with his disciples into the land of Judea. He stayed there with them, and immersed. ²³Yohanan also was immersing in Einayim near Shalem, because there was abundant water there. They came and were being immersed, ²⁴because Yohanan was not yet thrown into prison. ²⁵Consequently there arose a dispute between Yohanan's disciples and a sectarian Jew about purification. ²⁶They came to Yohanan and said to him, "Rabbi, the one who was with you beyond the Yarden — to whom you bore witness — look, he immerses, and everyone is coming to him."

²⁷Yohanan answered, "A man can receive nothing unless it has been given to him from Heaven. ²⁸You⁺ yourselves testify that I said, 'I am not the Messiah, but I have been sent before him.' ²⁹He who has the bride is the bridegroom, but the friend of the bridegroom, who stands and hears him, rejoices greatly in response to the bridegroom's voice. Therefore this, my joy, is made full. ³⁰He must increase, but I must decrease. ³¹He who comes from above is above all. The one who is from the earth belongs to the earth, and speaks of the earth. The one who comes from heaven is above all. ³²He bears witness of what he has seen and heard, and no one receives his testimony. ³³Whoever has received his testimony has set his seal to this, that God is true. ³⁴For the one whom God has sent speaks the words of God, because God gives the Ruakh without measure. ³⁵The Father loves the Son, and has given all things into his hand. ³⁶The one who believes in the Son has eternal life, but the one who disbelieves the Son will not see life; to the contrary, the wrath of God remains over him."

¹So when Yeshua knew that the Perushim had heard that he was immersing and making more disciples than Yohanan — ²although Yeshua himself did not immerse, but his disciples — ³he left Judea, and departed into the Galil. ⁴He needed to pass through Shomron, ⁵so he came to a city of Shomron, called Shehem, near the parcel of ground that Jacob gave to his son Yosef. ⁶Jacob's well was there. Being tired from his journey, Yeshua then sat down by the well. It was about the sixth hour.

⁷A woman of Shomron came to draw water. Yeshua said to her, "Give me a drink," ⁸because his disciples had gone away into the city to buy food.

⁹So the woman of Shomron said to him, "How is it that you, being a Jew, ask for a drink from me, a woman of Shomron? because Jews do not use anything together with the people of Shomron."

4:3-4 "...it was absolutely necessary for those that go quickly [to Yerushala'im] to pass through that country [Samaria]; for in that road you may, in three days' time go from Galilee to Yerushala'im." (Josephus, Life 269 [52. 269])

4:9 "do not use anything together with the people of Shomron" Some passages in Talmud help us understand this. For example, we read in Tal. Megillah 28a, "May I be rewarded because I have never gone into business partnership with a Cuthean." Cuthean is a term used to designate a Samaritan.

There are opposing views in the Talmud concerning the food of Samaritans. "R. Simeon b. Eleazar was sent by R. Meir to bring some wine from the Cutheans." (Tal. Chul. 6a) "For it was taught: The matzah of a Cuthean is permitted, and one fulfils his obligation with it on Pesakh; but R. Eliezer says it is forbidden..." (Tal. Kiddushin 76a) The Soncino note (23) to Tal. Chullin 13a says, "The bread of Cutheans was forbidden to be eaten. V. Sheb. VIII, 10: He who eats the bread of a Cuthean is as one who eats the flesh of swine."

>>

[10]Yeshua answered her, "If you knew the gift of God, and who it is that says to you, 'Give me a drink,' you would have asked him, and he would have given you living water."

[11]The woman said to him, "Sir, you have nothing to draw with, and the well is deep. From where then do you have that living water? [12]Are you greater than our father Jacob, who gave us the well and drank of it himself, as did his children and his cattle?"

[13]Yeshua answered her, "Everyone who drinks of this water will thirst again. [14]But whoever drinks of the water that I will give him will surely not thirst again, since the water that I will give him will become in him a well of water springing up to eternal life."

[15]The woman said to him, "Sir, give me this water, so that I may not thirst, nor come all the way here to draw."

[16]Yeshua said to her, "Go call your husband, and come here."

[17]The woman responded, "I have no husband."

Louw and Nida, in their Greek-English Lexicon of the New Testament (34.1), note that *sugchraomai* carries the meaning of "to associate with one another, normally involving spacial proximity and/or joint activity, and usually implying some kind of reciprocal relation or involvement — 'to associate, to be in the company of, to be involved with, association.'

"...In translating terms referring to association, one may employ a number of different kinds of expressions, for example, 'to have something to do with,' 'to keep company with,' 'to go around with,' 'to join in doing things together,' or 'to become a companion of.'"

Some traditional translations put: "For Jews have no dealings with Samaritans." Such translation gives a false statement, as shown by the simple fact that Yeshua's disciples have just gone into the city to buy food from the Samaritans. (v. 8, cf. Dt. 2:6)

4:20-21 God commanded the blessing to be pronounced on Mt. Gerizim, and the curse on Mt. Ebal. (Dt. 11:29) Josephus says that a temple was built on Mt. Gerizim in the time of Alexander the Great. (cf. Antiq. 11.8.2.310,346; 12.1.1.10)

"R. Jonathan was going up to worship in Yerushala'im, when he passed the Palatanis mountain [Mt. Gerizim] and was seen by a certain Samaritan, who asked him, 'Where are you going?' He said, 'To go up to worship in Yerushala'im.' 'It would be better for you to pray at this blessed mountain than at that dunghill.'" (Mid. Gen. Rabbah 32:10; 80:3)

4:22-24 After the Babylonians exiled the Jewish inhabitants of Shomron, they brought other captive people to live there. (2K. 17:22-41) The faith of these people became a mixture of their traditional idolatry with some elements of what God had given to Israel. They imagined themselves superior to the Jews. Yeshua rebukes this conceit, and explains that true worship of God must come from His Spirit and His Truth, which He has revealed to the Jewish people. Its source is not human emotions or thoughts.

4:25 The Jewish translators of the Septuagint used *christos* to represent *mashiakh*, i.e. the Anointed One. For Greeks, the word only meant rubbed or smeared with oil or ointment; it did not refer to a person. The Greeks had no concept of God's Anointed One, and so the LXX translators used *christos* as a linguistic marker to point to *mashiakh*.

4:30-34 Mid. Exodus Rabbah 47:5 says that Moses, during the 40 days he was in the presence of God on the mountain, ate the bread of Torah and drank the water of Torah.

Yeshua said to her, "You did well to say, 'I have no husband,' ¹⁸for you have had five husbands; and the one whom you now have is not your husband. You have said this truthfully."

¹⁹The woman said to him, "Sir, I see that you are a prophet. ²⁰Our fathers worshipped in this mountain, and you⁺ say that in Yerushala'im is the place where people ought to worship."

²¹Yeshua said to her, "Woman, believe me, the hour comes when neither in this mountain nor in Yerushala'im will you⁺ worship the Father. ²²You⁺ do not know what you⁺ worship. We know what we worship, because salvation is from the Jews. ²³Yet the hour comes, and now is, when those truly submitted will worship the Father in spirit and truth, for the Father seeks such to worship Him. ²⁴God is spirit, and those who worship Him must worship in spirit and truth."

²⁵The woman said to him, "I know that Messiah comes," (he who is called *christos*). "When he has come, he will declare to us all things."

²⁶Yeshua said to her, "I am he, the one speaking to you." ²⁷At this, his disciples came, and were surprised that he was speaking with a woman. Yet no one said, "What are you seeking?" or, "Why do you speak with her?"

²⁸So the woman left her water jar, went away into the city, and said to the people, ²⁹"Come, see a man who told me everything that I have done. Can this be the Messiah?"

³⁰They went out of the city and were coming to him. ³¹In the meantime, the disciples urged him, "Rabbi, eat."

³²But he said to them, "I have food to eat that you⁺ do not know about."

³³The disciples therefore said one to another, "Has anyone brought him anything to eat?"

³⁴Yeshua said to them, "My food is to do the will of the One who sent me, and to accomplish His work. ³⁵Don't you⁺ say, 'There are still four months until the harvest comes'? I tell you⁺ to lift up your⁺ eyes and look at the fields — they are white for harvest already! ³⁶The one who reaps receives wages, and gathers fruit to eternal life, so that both the one who sows and the one who reaps may rejoice together. ³⁷For in this the saying is true, 'One is the sower, and another is the reaper.' ³⁸I sent you⁺ to reap what you⁺ have not labored on. Others have labored, and you⁺ have entered into their labor."

³⁹Many of the people of Shomron from that city believed in him because of the word of the woman, who testified, "He told me everything that I have done." ⁴⁰So when the people of Shomron came to him, they entreated him to stay with them. He stayed there two days. ⁴¹Many more believed because of what he said. ⁴²They said to the woman, "Now we believe, no longer because of what you said; because we have heard for ourselves, and know that this is indeed the Messiah, the savior of the world."

⁴³But after the two days he departed from there and went into the Galil. ⁴⁴For Yeshua himself testified that a prophet has no honor in his own country. ⁴⁵So when he came into the Galil, the Galileans received him, having seen all the things that he did in Yerushala'im at the feast, because they also went to the feast. ⁴⁶Yeshua then came again to Kanah of the Galil, where he made the water into wine.

There was a certain official of the king whose son was sick at Kfar Naḥum. ⁴⁷When he heard that Yeshua had come out of Judea into the Galil, he went to him and begged him that he would come down and heal his son, for he was at the point of death. ⁴⁸Yeshua therefore said to him, "Unless you⁺ see signs and wonders, you⁺ will surely not believe."

⁴⁹The official of the king said to him, "Sir, come down before my child dies." ⁵⁰Yeshua said to him, "Go your way, your son lives." The man believed the word that Yeshua spoke to him, and he went his

way. [51]By this time, as he was going down, his servants met him and reported, "Your child lives!" [52]So he asked them the hour when he began to get better. Then they said to him, "The fever left him at the seventh hour yesterday." [53]So the father knew that it was at that moment in which Yeshua said to him, "Your son lives." He believed, as did his whole household. [54]This is again a second sign that Yeshua did, having come out of Judea into the Galil.

5 [1]After these things, there was a Jewish feast, and Yeshua went up to Yerushala'im. [2]Now by the sheep gate in Yerushala'im, there is a pool with five porches, which is called in Hebrew, "Beit Hasda." [3]A large multitude of those who were sick, blind, lame, or paralyzed lay in these, waiting for the moving of the water. [4]

[5]There was a certain man who had been sick for thirty-eight years. [6]When Yeshua saw him lying there, and knew that he had been sick for a long time, he asked him, "Do you want to be made well?"

[7]The sick man answered him, "Sir, I have no one to put me into the pool when the water is stirred up, but while I'm coming, another steps down before me."

[8]Yeshua said to him, "Get up, take up your mat, and walk."

[9]The man was immediately healed, took up his mat, and walked. Now it was Shabbat on that day. [10]So the sectarian Jews said to the one who was healed, "It is Shabbat. It is not lawful for you to carry the mat."

[11]He answered them, "The one who made me well is the same one who said to me, 'Take up your mat and walk.'"

[12]Then they asked him, "Who is the man who said to you, 'Take up your mat and walk'?" [13]But the one who was healed did not know who it was, because there was a crowd in that place, and Yeshua had withdrawn.

[14]Afterward Yeshua found him in the Temple and said to him, "Look, you have been made well. Sin no more, so that nothing worse happens to you."

[15]The man went away, and told the sectarian Jews that it was Yeshua who had made him well. [16]Because of this, the sectarian Jews persecuted Yeshua, and sought to kill him because he did these things on Shabbat. [17]But Yeshua responded to them, "My Father is still working, and I also am working." [18]So because of this, the sectarian Jews sought all the more to kill him, because he not only broke Shabbat, but also called God his own Father, making himself equal with God.

[19]So Yeshua responded to them, "I assure you[+] that the Son can do nothing of himself, except what he sees the Father doing. For whatever things He does, the Son also does these as well. [20]For the Father loves the Son, and shows to him everything that He Himself does. He will show him greater works than these, so that you[+] may give honor. [21]For as the Father raises the dead and gives them life, even so the Son also gives life to whom he desires. [22]For the Father does not judge anyone, but He has given all judgment to the Son, [23]so that all may honor the Son even as they honor the Father. The one who does not honor the Son does not honor the Father who sent him.

5:4 is not included in the UBS. "For an angel of the Everpresent Lord went down at certain times into the pool, and stirred up the water. Whoever stepped in first after the stirring of the water was made whole of whatever disease he had."

5:20 "that you may give honor" as in LXX Lev. 19:15 and Sirach 7:29.

²⁴"I assure you⁺ that the one who hears my word and believes the One who sent me has eternal life and does not come into judgment, but has passed out of death into life. ²⁵Be assured, I tell you⁺, that the hour is coming, and now is, when the dead will hear the voice of the Son of God; and those who hear will live. ²⁶For as the Father has life in Himself, even so He gave to the Son also to have life in himself. ²⁷He also gave him authority to execute judgment, because he is a son of Adam. ²⁸Do not marvel at this, for the hour is coming in which all who are in the tombs will hear his voice. ²⁹Then they will come out: those who have done good, to the resurrection of life; and those who have done evil, to the resurrection of condemnation. [Dan. 12:1-2] ³⁰I can do nothing of myself. As I hear, I judge, and my judgment is just, because I do not seek my own will, but the will of my Father who sent me.

³¹"If I testify about myself, my testimony is not valid. ³²It is another who testifies about me. I know that the testimony which He testifies about me is true. ³³You⁺ have sent to Yohanan, and he has testified to the truth. ³⁴But the testimony which I receive is not from man. However, I say these things so that you⁺ may be saved. ³⁵He was the burning, shining lamp, and you⁺ were willing to rejoice for a while in his light. ³⁶But the testimony which I have is greater than that of Yohanan, for the works which the Father gave me to accomplish — the very works that I do — testify about me that the Father has sent me. ³⁷The Father Himself, who sent me, has testified about me. You⁺ have not heard His voice at any time, nor have you⁺ seen His form. ³⁸And you⁺ do not have His word living in you⁺, for you⁺ do not believe the one whom He sent.

³⁹"You⁺ search the Scriptures, because you⁺ understand that you⁺ have eternal life in them. And yet these are they which testify about me, ⁴⁰but you⁺ will not come to me that you⁺ may have life. ⁴¹I do not receive glory from men, ⁴²but I know you⁺, that in yourselves you⁺ do not have the love of God. ⁴³I have come in my Father's Name, and you⁺ are not receiving me. If another comes in his own name, you⁺ will receive him. ⁴⁴How can you⁺ believe? you⁺ who receive glory from one another and do not seek the glory that comes from the only God.

⁴⁵"Do not think that I will accuse you⁺ to the Father. There is one who accuses you⁺, even Moses, on whom you⁺ have set your⁺ hope. ⁴⁶For if you⁺ were believing Moses, you⁺ would be believing me, because he wrote about me. ⁴⁷But if you⁺ do not believe his writings, how will you⁺ believe my words?"

5:43 "Three were called by the Name of the Holy One, blessed be He, and these are they: the righteous, and Messiah, and Yerushala'im.... Messiah, as it is written (Jer. 23:6), 'And this is the name which he will be called, the Everpresent Lord, our righteousness.'" (Tal. Bab Bathra 75b, cf. Mid. Psalms 21:2)

5:46 Yeshua presents faith in Moses as almost a prerequisite to faith in himself. Additionally, the life of Moses foreshadows the life of Messiah in various ways. For example, Mid. Ruth 5:6 says, "The fifth interpretation speaks of King Messiah. 'Come near,' to the kingdom. 'And eat of the bread,' this is the bread of the kingdom. 'And dip your bread in the vinegar,' refers to his sufferings, as it is said, But he was wounded because of our transgressions (Is. 53:5). 'And she sat besides the reapers,' for his kingdom will be put aside for a time, as it is said, For I will gather all nations against Yerushala'im to battle; and the city will be taken (Zech. 14:2). 'And they held out to her roasted grain,' means that it will be restored to him, as it is said, And he will strike the land with the rod of his mouth (Is. 11:4). R. Berekiah said in the name of R. Levi: 'The last Redeemer ➤➤

6 [1]After these things, Yeshua went away to the other side of the lake of the Galil, which is also called the lake of Tiverya. [2]A large crowd followed him, because they saw his miracles which he performed on those who were sick. [3]Yeshua went up onto the mountain, and he sat there with his disciples.

[4]Now Pesakh, the Jewish feast, was approaching. [5]So Yeshua, lifting up his eyes and seeing that a large crowd was coming to him, said to Philip, "Where are we to buy bread so that these may eat?" [6]He said this to test him, since he himself knew what he would do. [2Ki. 4:42-44]

[7]Philip answered him, "Two hundred denarii worth of bread is not sufficient for each of them to receive a little."

[8]One of his disciples, Andreas, Shimon Kefa's brother, said to him, [9]"There is a boy here who has five barley loaves and two fish. But what are these for so many people?"

[10]Yeshua said, "Have the people sit down." Now that place was very grassy. So the men sat down, numbering about five thousand. [11]Yeshua took the loaves, and having given thanks, he distributed to the disciples, and the disciples to those who were sitting down. Then he did the same with the fish, as much as they desired. [12]When they were satisfied, he said to his disciples, "Gather up the broken pieces which are left over, so that nothing is lost." [13]So they gathered them up, and filled twelve baskets with broken pieces from the five barley loaves, pieces which were left over by those who had eaten.

[14]When therefore the people saw the miracle which Yeshua did, they said, "This is the Prophet who comes into the world." [Dt. 18:15-19] [15]Because he perceived that they were about to come and take him by force to make him king, Yeshua withdrew again to the mountain by himself.

[16]When evening came, his disciples went down to the lake, [17]and they entered into the boat and were going over the lake to Kfar Nahum. It was already dark, and Yeshua had not come to them. [18]The lake was tossed by a strong wind which was blowing. [19]So when they had rowed about three or four miles, they saw Yeshua walking on the lake and drawing near to the boat; and they were afraid. [20]But he said to them, "It is I. Don't be fearful." [21]Then they were willing to receive him into the boat. The boat was immediately at the land where they were going.

[22]On the next day, the multitude that stood on the other side of the lake saw that there was no other boat there, except the one in which his disciples had embarked, and that Yeshua had not entered into the boat with his disciples, but his disciples had gone away alone. [23]Other boats from Tiverya came near to the place where they had eaten the bread after the Lord had given thanks. [24]So when the multitude saw that Yeshua was not there, nor his disciples, they themselves got into the boats, and

[Messiah] will be like the first Redeemer [Moses]. Just as the first Redeemer revealed himself and later was hidden from them... so the last Redeemer will be revealed to them, and then be hidden from them.'"

Speaking about Is. 11:1, Mid. Psalms 21.1 says, "This is Messiah, the Son of David, who is hidden until the time of the end."

6:1 In Israel today, the lake is called "Kinneret," meaning "harp," because of its harp-like shape.

6:27 R. Hanina said, "the seal of the Holy One, blessed be He, is Truth." (Tal. Sanhedrin 64a)

6:53 (31-56) See note on "Eat my flesh, drink my blood" in the ADDITIONAL NOTES.

6:58 "your fathers," as in the Textus Receptus

came to Kfar Na<u>h</u>um, seeking Yeshua. ²⁵When they found him on the other side of the lake, they asked him, "Rabbi, when did you come here?"

²⁶Yeshua answered them, "I assure you⁺ that you⁺ do not seek me because you⁺ saw miracles, but because you⁺ ate of the loaves and were filled. ²⁷Do not work for the food which perishes, but for the food which will last to life eternal. The Son of Adam will give this to you⁺, because God the Father has set His seal upon him."

²⁸So they said to him, "What must we do in order to work the works of God?"

²⁹Yeshua answered them, "This is the work of God, that you⁺ believe in him whom He has sent."

³⁰So they said to him, "What then do you do for a sign so that we may see, and believe you? What work do you do? ³¹Our fathers ate the manna in the wilderness. As it is written, 'He gave them bread out of heaven to eat.'" [Neh. 9:15, Ps. 78:24; 105:40, Ex. 16:4,15]

³²So Yeshua said to them, "I assure you⁺ it was not Moses who gave you⁺ the bread out of heaven, but my Father gives you⁺ the true bread out of heaven. ³³For the bread of God is that which comes down out of heaven, and gives life to the world."

³⁴So they said to him, "Lord, give us this bread always."

³⁵Yeshua said to them. "I am the bread of life. The one who comes to me will not be hungry, and the one who believes in me will surely not be thirsty. ³⁶But I told you⁺ that you⁺ have seen me, and yet you⁺ do not believe. ³⁷All those whom the Father gives me will come to me. I will certainly not cast away the one who comes to me, ³⁸because I have come down from heaven not to do my own will, but the will of the One who sent me. ³⁹This is the will of my Father who sent me: that I should lose nothing of all He has given to me, but should raise it up at the last day. ⁴⁰This is the will of the One who sent me: that everyone who sees the Son and believes in him should have eternal life. And I will raise him up at the last day."

⁴¹The sectarian Jews therefore murmured concerning him, because he said, "I am the bread which came down out of heaven." ⁴²They said, "Isn't this Yeshua, the son of Yosef, whose father and mother we know? How then does he say, 'I have come down out of heaven?'"

⁴³So Yeshua responded to them, "Don't murmur among yourselves. ⁴⁴No one can come to me unless the Father who sent me draws him, and I will raise him up in the last day. ⁴⁵It is written in the Prophets, 'They will all be taught by God.' [Is. 54:13] Therefore everyone who hears from the Father, and has learned, comes to me. ⁴⁶Not that anyone has seen the Father, except the one who is from God. He has seen the Father. ⁴⁷I assure you⁺ that the one who believes has eternal life. ⁴⁸I am the bread of life. ⁴⁹Your⁺ fathers ate the manna in the wilderness, yet they died. ⁵⁰This is the bread which comes down out of heaven so that anyone may eat of it and not die. ⁵¹I am the living bread which came down out of heaven. If anyone eats of this bread, he will live forever. Yes, the bread which I will give for the life of the world is my flesh."

⁵²The sectarian Jews therefore argued with one another, saying, "How can this man give us his flesh to eat?"

⁵³So Yeshua said to them, "I assure you⁺ that unless you⁺ eat the flesh of the Son of Adam and drink his blood, you⁺ do not have life in yourselves. ⁵⁴The one who eats my flesh and drinks my blood has eternal life, and I will raise him up at the last day. ⁵⁵For my flesh is real food, and my blood is real drink. [Lev. 10:16-18; 2Sam. 23:15-17] ⁵⁶The one who eats my flesh and drinks my blood lives in me, and I in him. ⁵⁷As the living Father sent me, and I live because of the Father, so the one who feeds

on me will also live because of me. ⁵⁸This is the bread which came down out of heaven — not as our fathers ate the manna and died. The one who eats this bread will live forever." ⁵⁹He said these things as he taught in the meetingplace in Kfar Naḥum.

⁶⁰So when they heard this, many of his disciples said, "This is a difficult saying. Who can receive it?"

⁶¹But knowing in himself that his disciples murmured at this, Yeshua said to them, "Does this offend you⁺? ⁶²Then what if you⁺ were to see the Son of Adam ascending to where he was before? ⁶³It is the spirit that gives life. The flesh profits nothing. The words that I speak to you⁺ are spirit and are life, ⁶⁴but there are some of you⁺ who do not believe." For Yeshua knew from the beginning who they were who did not believe, and who it was who would deliver him up. ⁶⁵He said, "For this reason I have said to you⁺ that no one can come to me, unless it is given to him by my Father."

⁶⁶At this, many of his disciples turned away, and no longer walked with him. ⁶⁷So Yeshua said to the twelve, "Do you⁺ also want to go away?"

⁶⁸Shimon Kefa answered him, "Lord, to whom would we go? You have the words of eternal life. ⁶⁹We have come to believe and know that you are the Messiah, the Son of the living God."

⁷⁰Yeshua responded to them, "Didn't I choose you⁺ twelve, yet one of you⁺ is an enemy?" ⁷¹Now he spoke of Judah the son of Shimon, a man of K'riyot, who was one of the twelve, for he was the one who would soon deliver him over.

7 ¹After these things, Yeshua was walking in the Galil, since he did not want to walk in Judea, because the Judean authorities sought to kill him. ²Now the Jewish feast, the Feast of Sukkot, was near. ³His brothers therefore said to him, "Depart from here, and go into Judea so that your disciples also may see your deeds which you do. ⁴For no one who seeks to have himself known openly does anything in secret. If you do these things, make yourself known to the world." ⁵For even his brothers did not believe in him.

⁶Yeshua therefore said to them, "My time has not yet come, but your⁺ time is always at hand. ⁷The world cannot hate you⁺, but it hates me, because I testify about it that its deeds are evil. ⁸You⁺ go up to the feast. I am not going up to this feast yet, because my time has not yet been completed." ⁹Having said these things to them, he stayed in the Galil. ¹⁰But when his brothers had gone up to the feast, then he also went up, not publicly, but as it were in secret.

¹¹Then the Judean authorities sought him at the feast and said, "Where is that man?" ¹²There was much murmuring among the multitudes concerning him. Some said, "He is a good man." Others said, "No, to the contrary, he leads the multitude astray." ¹³Yet no one spoke openly about him for fear of the Judean authorities. ¹⁴But when it was already the middle of the feast, Yeshua went up into the Temple and taught.

¹⁵And the Judean authorities were amazed, saying, "How has this man become learned, having never been educated?"

¹⁶So Yeshua responded to them, "My teaching is not mine, but His who sent me. ¹⁷If anyone desires to do His will, he will know about the teaching, whether it is from God or if I am speaking from myself. ¹⁸The one who speaks from himself seeks his own glory. But the one who seeks the glory of the One who sent him, this one is true, and there is no wrong-doing in him. ¹⁹Didn't Moses give you⁺ the Torah, and yet none of you⁺ keeps the Torah? Why do you⁺ seek to kill me?"

²⁰The crowd answered, "You have a demon! Who seeks to kill you?"

²¹Yeshua answered them, "I did one work, and you⁺ all marvel because of it. ²²Moses has given you⁺ circumcision — not that it is from Moses, but from the fathers — and on Shabbat you⁺ circumcise a man. ²³If a man receives circumcision on Shabbat so that the Torah of Moses may not be broken, are you⁺ angry with me because I made a man completely whole on Shabbat? ²⁴Do not judge according to appearance, but judge righteous judgment."

²⁵Then some of the inhabitants of Yerushala'im said, "Isn't this the one whom they seek to kill? ²⁶Look, he speaks openly, and they say nothing to him. Can it be that the rulers actually know that this is truly the Messiah? ²⁷However, we know where this man comes from, but when the Messiah comes, no one will know where he comes from."

²⁸Yeshua therefore cried out in the Temple, teaching and saying, "You know me and know also where I am from. I have not come of myself, but the One who sent me is true, whom you⁺ do not know. ²⁹I know Him, because I am from Him, and He sent me."

³⁰Therefore they sought to take him, but no one laid a hand on him, because his hour had not yet come. ³¹Yet many in the crowd believed in him. They said, "When the Messiah comes, he won't do more miracles than those which this man has done, will he?" ³²The Perushim heard the multitude murmuring these things about him, and the chief Kohanim and the Perushim sent officers to arrest him.

³³Then Yeshua said, "I will be with you⁺ a little while longer, then I go to the One who sent me. ³⁴You⁺ will seek me, and will not find me, and where I am, you⁺ cannot come."

³⁵The Judean authorities therefore said among themselves, "Where will this man go that we will not find him? Will he go to the Diaspora among the Greeks, and teach the Greeks? ³⁶What is this statement that he said, 'You⁺ will seek me, and will not find me; and where I am, you⁺ cannot come'?"

³⁷Now on the last day, the great day of the feast, Yeshua stood and cried out, "If anyone is thirsty, let him come to me and drink. ³⁸The one who believes in me, as the Scripture has said, from within him will flow rivers of living water." [Is. 12:3] ³⁹But he said this about the Spirit, which those believing in him were to receive. For the Spirit was not yet given, because Yeshua was not yet glorified.

⁴⁰So when they heard these words, many in the crowd said, "This is truly the Prophet." [Dt. 18:15-19] ⁴¹Others said, "This is the Messiah." But some said, "What? Does the Messiah come out of the Galil? ⁴²Hasn't the Scripture said that the Messiah comes of the seed of David, and from Beit Leḥem, the village where David was?" {Mi. 5:1H} ⁴³So there arose a division in the crowd because of him.

7:22-23 "R. Eleazar ben Azariah said, 'If circumcision, which concerns one of the members of a man, overrides Shabbat, [reasoning] from light to heavy [*kal v'ḥomer*], to save a life overrides Shabbat.'" (Tal. Shabbat 132a)

"And if the [Temple] work overrides Shabbat, and a case that might involve [the saving of a] life overrides it, the Sabbath, which the [Temple] work overrides... this teaches that a case that might involve [the saving of a] life override it." (Tos. Shabbat 15:13, 15:16 in Neusner) See note to Mk. 2:27-28.

7:37-39 A lengthy discussion of the ceremony of drawing and pouring out water on Sukkot can be found beginning in Tal. Sukkah 48a. "The one who has not seen the rejoicing at the place of the water-drawing has never seen rejoicing in his life." (Tal. Sukkah 51a)

[44]Some of them would have arrested him, but no one laid hands on him. [45]So the officers came to the chief Kohanim and Perushim, who said to them, "Why didn't you[+] bring him?"

[46]The officers answered, "No one ever spoke like this man!"

[47]So the Perushim answered them, "You[+] are not also led astray, are you[+]? [48]Have any of the rulers believed in him, or any of the Perushim? [49]But this multitude that does not know the Torah is accursed."

[50]Being one of them, Nakdimon — the man who came to him by night — said to them, [51]"Does our Torah judge a man, unless it first hears from him personally and knows what he does?"

[52]They answered him, "Are you also from the Galil? Search and see that a prophet does not arise out of the Galil."

{[53]Everyone went to his own home,

8[1]but Yeshua went to the Mount of Olives. [2]Now very early in the morning, he came again into the Temple, and all the people came to him. He sat down, and taught them.

[3]The Torah scholars and the Perushim brought a woman taken in adultery. Having set her in the middle, [4]they told him, "Teacher, we found this woman in adultery, in the very act. [5]Now in our Torah, Moses commanded us to stone ones like this. [Deut. 22:22-24] What then do you say about her?" [6]They said this testing him, so that they might have a way to accuse him.

But Yeshua stooped down, and wrote on the ground with his finger. [7]However, when they continued asking him, he looked up and said to them, "Let the sinless one among you[+] throw the first stone at her." [8]Again he stooped down, and wrote on the ground with his finger.

[9]When they heard it, they went out one by one, beginning from the oldest even to the last. Yeshua was left alone, and the woman was apart. [10]Straightening up, Yeshua saw her and said, "Woman, where are they? Did no one pass sentence against you?"

[11]She said, "No one, Lord."

Yeshua said, "Neither do I pass sentence against you. Go your way. From now on, sin no more."}

[12]Again Yeshua said to them, "I am the light of the world. The one who follows me will not walk in the darkness, but will have the light of life."

[13]The Perushim therefore said to him, "You testify about yourself. Your testimony is not valid."

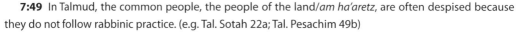

7:49 In Talmud, the common people, the people of the land/*am ha'aretz*, are often despised because they do not follow rabbinic practice. (e.g. Tal. Sotah 22a; Tal. Pesachim 49b)

7:52 Both the Textus Receptus and UBS have "a prophet". But "the prophet" is a minority reading that is consistent with 7:40, 1:21, and 1:25.

7:53-8:11 This section does not appear in many manuscripts.

8:9 In LXX, *en meso* often means "separate," e.g. Gen. 1:4,6-7.

8:12 See note to Yhn. 1:4-9. There are several places in the Midrash Rabbah that connect Messiah and light. For example, "R. Abba of Serungayya said: 'And the light dwells with him — this is the King Messiah, as it says (Is. 60:1), Arise, shine because your light has come.'" (Mid. Gen. Rabbah 1:6) "R. Hanin said [about the priests], 'By the merit of causing a lamp to continually go up [Lev. 24:2], you+ are worthy to welcome the lamp of King Messiah.'" (Mid. Lev. 31.11)

[14]Yeshua answered them, "Even if I testify about myself, my testimony is true, because I know where I've come from, and where I'm going. But you⁺ don't know where I've come from, nor where I'm going. [15]You⁺ judge according to the flesh. I judge no one. [16]Moreover even if I judge, my judgment is true, because I am not alone in it, but the Father who sent me is with me. [17]And also in the Torah — which is yours⁺ — it is written that the testimony of two people is valid. [18]I am one who testifies about myself, and the Father who sent me testifies about me."

[19]So they said to him, "Where is your Father?"

Yeshua answered, "You⁺ know neither me nor my Father. If you⁺ knew me, you⁺ would know my Father also." [20]Yeshua spoke these words in the treasury as he taught in the Temple. Yet no one arrested him, because his hour had not yet come. [21]Yeshua then said to them again, "I am going away, and you⁺ will seek me, but you⁺ will die in your⁺ sins. Where I go, you⁺ cannot come."

[22]So the Jewish authorities said, "Will he kill himself, since he says, 'Where I am going, you⁺ cannot come?' "

[23]He said to them, "You⁺ are from below. I am from above. You⁺ are from this world. I am not from this world. [24]Therefore I said to you⁺ that you⁺ will die in your⁺ sins, because unless you⁺ believe that I am he, you⁺ will die in your⁺ sins."

[25]So they said to him, "Who are you?"

Yeshua said to them, "Exactly what I have been saying to you⁺ from the beginning. [26]I have many things to say and to determine concerning you⁺, but the One who sent me is true, and the things which I heard from Him, these I say to the world."

[27]They did not understand that he spoke to them about the Father. [28]So Yeshua said to them, "When you⁺ have lifted up the Son of Adam, then you⁺ will know that I am he, and I do nothing of myself; but as my Father taught me, I say these things. [29]The One who sent me is with me. The Father has not left me alone, for I always do the things that are pleasing to Him."

[30]As he spoke these things, many believed in him. [31]Yeshua then said to those sectarian Jews who had believed him, "If you⁺ remain in my word, then you⁺ are truly my disciples. [32]You⁺ will know the truth, and the truth will make you⁺ free."

[33]They answered him, "We are Abraham's seed, and have never been in bondage to anyone. How do you say, 'You⁺ will be made free?'"

[34]Yeshua answered them, "I assure you⁺ that everyone who commits sin is the bondservant of sin. [35]A bondservant does not live in the house forever. A son remains forever. [36]If therefore the Son makes you⁺ free, you⁺ will be truly free. [37]I know that you⁺ are Abraham's seed, yet you⁺ seek to kill me, because my word finds no place in you⁺. [38]I say the things which I have seen with my Father. And you⁺ also do the things which you⁺ have heard from your father."

8:24 "R. Hanin said, 'Israel does not need the teaching of King Messiah for the time to come, for it is said (Is. 11:10), To him, the Gentiles will seek, not Israel.' If that is so, why does King Messiah come, and what does he come to do? 'To gather the exiles of Israel, and to give to them [the Gentiles] thirty commandments.'" (Mid. Genesis 98.9)

8:26 "'the authority of his lips': Whatever he [Messiah] decrees, his words are established." (Mid. on Psalms 21.3)

[39]They answered him, "Our father is Abraham."

Yeshua said to them, "If you[+] were children of Abraham, you[+] would do the deeds of Abraham. [40]But now you[+] seek to kill me, a man who has told you[+] the truth which I heard from God. Abraham did not do this. [41]You[+] do the deeds of your[+] father."

They said to him, "We were not born from sexual immorality. We have one father, God."

[42]Yeshua said to them, "If God were your[+] father, you[+] would love me, for I came forth and have come from God. For I have not come of myself, but He sent me. [43]Why do you[+] not understand what I am saying? Because you[+] cannot hear my word. [44]You are from a father — the Enemy — and you[+] want to do the desires of your[+] father. He was a murderer from the beginning, and does not stand in the truth, because there is no truth in him. When he speaks a lie, he speaks from what is his own, because he is the father of it and he is a liar. [45]But because I speak the truth, you[+] do not believe me. [46]Which of you[+] convicts me of sin? If I speak the truth, why do you[+] not believe me? [47]The one who is of God hears the words of God. That is why you[+] do not hear, because you[+] are not from God."

[48]Then the sectarian Jews answered him, "Don't we rightly say that you are a man of Shomron, and have a demon?"

[49]Yeshua answered, "I do not have a demon, but I honor my Father, and you[+] dishonor me. [50]However, I do not seek my own glory. There is One who seeks and judges. [51]I assure you[+] that if a person keeps my word, he will surely not see death."

[52]Then the sectarian Jews said to him, "Now we know that you have a demon. Abraham died, the prophets too, but you say, 'If a man keeps my word, he will surely not taste of death.' [53]Are you greater than our father Abraham, who died? The prophets died. Who do you make yourself out to be?"

[54]Yeshua answered, "If I glorify myself, my glory is nothing. It is my Father who glorifies me, of whom you[+] say that He is your[+] God. [55]You[+] have not known Him, but I know Him. If I said, 'I do not know Him,' I would be like you[+], a liar. But I know Him, and keep His word. [56]Your[+] father Abraham rejoiced to see my day. He saw it, and was glad."

[57]The sectarian Jews therefore said to him, "You are not yet fifty years old, and have you seen Abraham?"

[58]Yeshua said to them, "I assure you[+] that before Abraham came into being, I am."

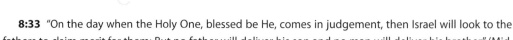

8:33 "On the day when the Holy One, blessed be He, comes in judgement, then Israel will look to the fathers to claim merit for them: But no father will deliver his son and no man will deliver his brother." (Mid. Psalms 121.1)

8:39 "So that there will no longer be the minim and the wicked of Israel saying, 'We will not go down to Gehinnom, because we are circumcised.' — What does the Holy One, blessed be He, do? He sends an angel [to such a one] and stretches his foreskin. Then they go down to Gehinnom." (Mid. Exodus 19:4)

8:44 R. Dosa b. Harkinas, of Beit Hillel, called his younger brother, who followed Beit Shammai, "the first-born of Satan." (Tal. Yebamot 16a) "R. Tarfon said, 'I was once walking on the road, and I reclined to say [the Sh'ma] in accordance with Beit Shammai and I was put in danger by robbers.' They said to him, 'You were worthy to be harmed, because you transgressed the words of Beit Hillel.'" (Tal. Berachot 1:3, cf. the discussion in 11a)

⁵⁹Therefore they took up stones to throw at him, but Yeshua was hidden, and went out of the Temple.

9 ¹As he passed by, he saw a man blind from birth. ²His disciples asked him, "Rabbi, who sinned that he was born blind, this man or his parents?"

³Yeshua answered, "Neither this man nor his parents sinned, but it is in order that the works of God might be revealed in him. ⁴While it is day, I must work the works of the One who sent me. The night is coming, when no one can work. ⁵While I am in the world, I am the light of the world."

⁶When he had said this, he spat on the ground, made mud with the saliva, and anointed the blind man's eyes with the mud. ⁷Then he said to him, "Go, wash in the pool of Shiloa̲h̲," (which means "sent"). So he went away, washed, and came back seeing. ⁸Therefore the neighbors and those who knew that he was blind before said, "Isn't this the one who sat and begged?" ⁹Others were saying, "It is he." Still others were saying, "He looks like him."

He said, "I am the one."

¹⁰So they were asking him, "How were your eyes opened?"

¹¹He answered, "A man called Yeshua made mud, anointed my eyes, and said to me, 'Go to Shiloa̲h̲, and wash.' So I went away and washed, and I received sight."

¹²Then they asked him, "Where is he?"

He said, "I don't know."

¹³They brought to the Perushim the one who had been blind. ¹⁴It was Shabbat when Yeshua made the mud and opened his eyes. ¹⁵So the Perushim also asked him again how he received his sight. He said to them, "He put mud on my eyes. I washed, and I see."

¹⁶So some of the Perushim said, "This man is not from God, because he does not keep Shabbat." Others said, "How can a man, a sinful one, do such miracles?" There was division among them. ¹⁷So they asked the blind man again, "What do you say about him, since he opened your eyes?"

He said, "He is a prophet."

¹⁸So the sectarian Jewish leaders did not believe about him that he had been blind and had received his sight, until they called the parents of the one who had received his sight. ¹⁹They asked them, "Is this your⁺ son, who you⁺ say was born blind? How then does he now see?"

²⁰His parents answered them, "We know that this is our son, and that he was born blind. ²¹But how he now sees, we do not know. Or who opened his eyes, we do not know. He is of age, ask him. He will speak for himself." ²²His parents said these things because they feared the sectarian Jewish leaders, because they had already agreed that if any man would confess him as Messiah, he would be put out of the assembly.

²³Because of this, his parents said, "He is of age, ask him."

²⁴So a second time they called the man who was blind, and said to him, "Give glory to God. We know that this man is a sinner."

²⁵He then responded, "I don't know if he is a sinner. One thing I do know, that though I was blind, now I see."

9:1 Tal. Shabbat 32b speaks of the punishments that the sins of the parents bring upon their children. In Tal. Nedarim 20a, one rabbi says that blindness comes to a child for a particular sin of its parents.

²⁶They said to him again, "What did he do to you? How did he open your eyes?"

²⁷He answered them, "I told you⁺ already, and you⁺ didn't listen. Why do you⁺ want to hear it again? You⁺ don't want to become his disciples, too, do you⁺?"

²⁸They reviled him and said, "You are his disciple, but we are disciples of Moses. ²⁹We know that God has spoken to Moses. But as for this man, we do not know where he is from."

³⁰The man answered them, "This is indeed a cause for wonder. You⁺ do not know where he is from, yet he opened my eyes. ³¹We know that God does not listen to sinners, but if anyone fears God and does His will, He listens to him. ³²Since the world began it has never been heard that anyone opened the eyes of someone born blind. ³³If this man were not from God, he could do nothing."

³⁴They answered him, "You were born completely in sins, and are you to teach us?" They threw him out.

³⁵Yeshua heard that they had thrown him out, and finding him, he said, "Do you believe in the Son of Adam?"

³⁶He answered, "Who is he, Lord, that I may believe in him?"

³⁷Yeshua said to him, "You have seen him, and it is he who also speaks with you."

³⁸He said, "Lord, I believe." and he bowed down before him.

³⁹Yeshua said, "I came into this world for judgment, so that those who do not see may see, and so that those who see may become blind."

⁴⁰Those of the Perushim who were with him heard these things, and said to him, "Are we also blind?"

⁴¹Yeshua said to them, "If you⁺ were blind, you⁺ would have no sin. But now you⁺ say, 'We see.' Therefore your⁺ sin remains.

10 ¹"I assure you⁺ that one who does not enter by the door into the sheep pen, but climbs up some other way, the same is a thief and a bandit. ²But one who enters in through the door is the shepherd of the sheep. ³The gatekeeper opens the gate for him, and the sheep listen to his voice. He calls his own sheep by name, and leads them out. ⁴Whenever he brings out his own sheep, he goes before them, and the sheep follow him, for they know his voice. ⁵They will not follow a stranger at all, but will flee from him, because they do not know the voice of strangers." ⁶Yeshua spoke this parable to them, but they did not understand what he was telling them.

⁷So Yeshua said to them again, "I assure you⁺ I am the door of the sheep. ⁸All who came before me are thieves and bandits, but the sheep did not listen to them. ⁹I am the door. If anyone enters in through me, he will be saved, and will both enter in and go out, and will find pasture. ¹⁰The thief only comes to steal, kill, and destroy. I came that they may have life, and may have it abundantly.

¹¹I am the good shepherd. The good shepherd lays down his life for the sheep. ¹²The one who is

---

9:24-25 "'You are to listen to him' (Dt. 18:15) Even if he tells you to transgress one of all the commandments that are in Torah, as with Eliyahu on Mt. Carmel." (Tal. Yebamot 90b)

9:29 "And the Everpresent Lord spoke to Moses...." is the most common phrase in the Bible, appearing more than a hundred times.

9:41 "R. Judah says, 'A blind person is not subject to [paying damages for putting someone to] shame.' In this way, R. Judah exempted him from all judgments that are in the Torah." (Tal. Baba Kama 86b-87a)

not the shepherd, but working for money — who does not own the sheep — he sees the wolf coming, leaves the sheep, and flees. The wolf snatches the sheep, and scatters them. ¹³The one working for money flees because he is working for money, and is not himself concerned about the sheep.

¹⁴I am the good shepherd. I know my own, and I'm known by my own [Ezek. 37:24-25], ¹⁵even as the Father knows me, and I know the Father. I lay down my life for the sheep. [Ezek. 34:12] ¹⁶I have other sheep which are not of this fold. I must bring them also, and they will hear my voice. They will become one flock with one shepherd. ¹⁷Therefore the Father loves me, because I lay down my life so that I may take it again. ¹⁸No one takes it away from me, but I lay it down by myself. I have power to lay it down, and I have power to take it again. I received this commandment from my Father."

¹⁹There arose again a division among the sectarian Jews because of these words. ²⁰Many of them said, "He has a demon and is insane! Why do you⁺ listen to him?"

²¹Others said, "These are not the sayings of one controlled by a demon. It is not possible for a demon to open the eyes of the blind, is it?"

²²It was the Feast of Hanukkah at Yerushala'im. ²³It was winter, and Yeshua was walking in the Temple in the porch of Shlomo. ²⁴So the Jewish authorities came around him and said to him, "How long will you keep us wondering? If you are the Messiah, tell us plainly."

²⁵Yeshua answered them, "I told you⁺, and you⁺ do not believe. The deeds that I do in my Father's Name, these testify about me. ²⁶But you⁺ do not believe, because you⁺ are not of my sheep. ²⁷My sheep hear my voice. I know them, and they follow me. ²⁸I give eternal life to them. They will surely not perish, and no one will snatch them out of my hand. ²⁹My Father, who has given them to me, is greater than all. No one is able to snatch them out of my Father's hand. ³⁰I and the Father are one."

³¹Therefore the sectarian Jews took up stones again to stone him. ³²Yeshua answered them, "I have shown you⁺ many good deeds from my Father. For which of those deeds do you⁺ stone me?"

³³The sectarian Jews answered him, "We are not stoning you for a good work, but for blasphemy, because you, being a man, make yourself God."

³⁴Yeshua answered them, "Is it not written in the Torah, 'I said, you⁺ are gods?' [Ps. 82:6] ³⁵If He called them gods to whom the word of God came — and the Scripture cannot be broken — ³⁶do you⁺ say of him whom the Father sanctified and sent into the world, 'You blaspheme,' because I said, 'I am the Son of God'? ³⁷If I do not do the works of my Father, do not believe me. ³⁸But if I do them, though

10:12-13 "A shepherd was caring for his flock, and he left the flock and entered the town: Then a wolf came and tore [a sheep], or a lion, and tore it to pieces. He is exempt [from liability]." (Tal. Baba Metzia 41a)

10:16 The Yom Kippur liturgy looks forward to the day when all peoples will "form a single band to do Your will with a whole heart." [*agudah akhat laasot ritsonkha b'lavav shalaym*]

10:25 The magnitude of this claim is immense.

10:34 "your Torah" is the majority reading. "Torah" referred to the Law, the books of Moses, and teaching in general.

10:34-37 "R. Yosi said, 'Israel accepted the Torah only so that the Angel of Death would not have dominion over them, as it is said: I said you are gods and all of you are children of the Most High; now that you have corrupted your actions, truly you will die like Adam.' [Ps. 82:6]" (Tal. Avodah Zarah 5a)

you+ do not believe me, believe the works, so that you+ may know and believe that the Father is in me, and I in the Father."

³⁹They sought again to seize him, but he escaped out of their hand. ⁴⁰He went away again beyond the Yarden into the place where Yoḥanan was immersing at first, and there he stayed. ⁴¹Many came to him. They said, "Yoḥanan indeed did no miracle, but everything that Yoḥanan said about this man is true." ⁴²Many believed in him there.

11 ¹Now a certain man was sick, Eleazar from Beit Anyah, of the village of Miryam and her sister Marta. ²And it was this Miryam who had anointed the Lord with ointment, and wiped his feet with her hair, whose brother Eleazar was sick. ³The sisters therefore sent to him, saying, "Lord, listen, the one whom you love is sick." ⁴But when Yeshua heard it, he said, "This sickness is not to death, but for the glory of God, so that the Son of God may be glorified by it." ⁵Now Yeshua loved Marta, her sister, and Eleazar. ⁶So when he heard that he was sick, he stayed two days in the place where he was. ⁷Then after this he said to the disciples, "Let's go into Judea again."

⁸The disciples told him, "Rabbi, the Judean authorities were just seeking to stone you, and are you going there again?"

⁹Yeshua answered, "Aren't there twelve hours of daylight? If a man walks in the day, he does not stumble, because he sees the light of this world. ¹⁰But if a man walks in the night, he stumbles, because the light is not in him." ¹¹He said these things, and after that he said to them, "Our friend Eleazar has fallen asleep, but I am going so that I may awaken him out of sleep."

¹²So the disciples said, "Lord, if he has fallen asleep, he will recover."

¹³Now Yeshua had spoken of his death, but they thought that he spoke of taking rest in sleep. ¹⁴So Yeshua then said to them plainly, "Eleazar is dead. ¹⁵I am glad for your+ sakes that I was not there, so that you+ may believe. Nevertheless, let's go to him."

¹⁶So Toma, who is called "the Twin," said to his fellow disciples, "Let's go also, that we may die with him."

¹⁷So when Yeshua came, he found that he had already been in the tomb four days. ¹⁸Now Beit Anyah was near Yerushala'im, about two miles away. ¹⁹Many of the Judeans had joined the women around Marta and Miryam to console them concerning their brother.

²⁰Now when Marta heard that Yeshua was coming, she went and met him, but Miryam stayed in the house. ²¹Then Marta said to Yeshua, "Lord, if you had been here, my brother would not have died. ²²Even now I know that whatever you ask of God, God will give you." ²³Yeshua said to her, "Your brother will rise again."

²⁴Marta said to him, "I know that he will rise again in the resurrection at the last day."

²⁵Yeshua said to her, "I am the resurrection and the life. He who believes in me, though he dies, yet will he live. ²⁶Whoever lives and believes in me will surely not die. Do you believe this?"

11:25 "'My portion in the land of the living!' (Ps. 142:6) This is the land whose dead will have the life of the resurrection in the days of the Messiah." (Mid. B'reshit Rabba 74:1) "Why were all the Fathers desiring burial in the land of Israel? Because the dead of the land of Israel will have the life of resurrection in the days of the Messiah and will eat in the years of the Messiah." (Mid. B'reshit Rabba 96:5)

[27]She said to him, "Yes, Lord. I have come to believe that you are the Messiah, the Son of God, the one who comes into the world."

[28]When she had said this, she went away and privately called her sister Miryam saying, "The Teacher is here, and is calling you."

[29]When she heard this, she arose quickly, and went to him. [30]Now Yeshua had not yet come into the village, but was in the place where Marta met him. [31]Then the Judeans who were with her in the house consoling her — when they saw that Miryam rose up quickly and went out — they followed her, thinking that she was going to the tomb to weep there. [32]And when Miryam came to where Yeshua was and saw him, she fell down at his feet, saying to him, "Lord, if you had been here, my brother would not have died."

[33]So when Yeshua saw her weeping and the Judeans who came with her weeping, he groaned in his spirit, and was troubled. [34]He said, "Where have you[+] laid him?"

They told him, "Lord, come and see." [35]Yeshua wept.

[36]Because of that, the Judeans said, "See how he loved him." [37]Some of them said, "Couldn't this man, who opened the eyes of the one who was blind, have also kept this man from dying?"

[38]Therefore groaning again within himself, Yeshua came to the tomb. Now it was a cave, and a stone lay against it. [39]Yeshua said, "Take away the stone."

Marta, the sister of the one who was dead, said to him, "Lord, by this time there is a stench, because he has been dead four days."

[40]Yeshua said to her, "Didn't I tell you that if you believed, you would see the glory of God?"

[41]So they took away the stone from the place where the dead man was lying. Yeshua lifted up his eyes, and said, "Father, I thank You that You have heard me. [42]I know that You always hear me, but I said this because of the crowd that stands around, so that they may believe that You sent me." [43]When he had said this, he cried out with a loud voice, "Eleazar, come out!"

[44]The one who was dead came out, bound hand and foot with wrappings, and his face was wrapped around with a cloth.

Yeshua said to them, "Release him, and let him go."

[45]Therefore many of the Judeans who came to Miryam and saw what Yeshua did, believed in him. [46]But some of them went away to the Perushim, and told them the things which Yeshua had done. [47]So the chief Kohanim and the Perushim gathered a council, and said, "What are we doing? For this man does many miracles. [48]If we leave him alone like this, everyone will believe in him, and the Romans will come and take away both our place and the nation."

[49]But a certain one of them, Kayafa, being the Kohen Gadol that year, said to them, "You[+] know nothing at all. [50]Nor do you[+] consider that it is to our benefit that one man should die for the people, and that the whole nation not perish." [51]Now he did not say this of himself, but being the Kohen Gadol that year, he prophesied that Yeshua would die for the nation, [52]and not for the nation only, but that he might also gather together into one the children of God who are scattered abroad. [53]So from

---

11:43-44 In the liturgy, the Birkat Me'en Sheva, we say, "Blessed are You, Everpresent Lord... who resurrects the dead with His utterance..."

11:48 "our place" may refer to their position or authority, or to the Temple.

that day forward they took counsel that they might put him to death. [54]So Yeshua no longer walked openly among the Judeans, but departed from there into the countryside near the wilderness, to a city called Efrayim. He stayed there with his disciples.

[55]Now the Jewish Pesakh was approaching. Many went up from the countryside to Yerushala'im before Pesakh to purify themselves.

[56]Then they were looking for Yeshua, and saying to each other as they stood in the Temple: "What do you[+] think, that he is not coming to the feast at all?" [57]Now the chief Kohanim and the Perushim had commanded that if anyone knew where he was, he should report it, so that they might arrest him.

12 [1]Then six days before Pesakh, Yeshua came to Beit Anyah, where Eleazar was, whom Yeshua had raised from the dead.

[2]So they made him a supper there. Marta served, and Eleazar was one of those who sat at the table with him. [3]Miryam then took a pound of ointment of pure nard, very precious, and anointed the feet of Yeshua, and wiped his feet with her hair. The house was filled with the fragrance of the ointment. [4]Then Judah from K'riyot, one of his disciples who was about to deliver him up, said, [5]"Why wasn't this ointment sold for three hundred denarii, and given to the poor?" [6]Now he said this not because he cared for the poor, but because he was a thief and, having the money box, used to steal what was put into it. [7]But Yeshua said, "Leave her alone. She has kept this for the day of my burial. [8]For you[+] always have the poor with you[+] [Dt. 15:11], but you[+] do not always have me."

[9]Numerous Judeans then learned that he was there, and they came, not for Yeshua's sake only, but also so that they might see Eleazar, whom he had raised from the dead. [10]However, the chief Kohanim conspired to put Eleazar to death also, [11]because on account of him many of the Judeans went away and believed in Yeshua.

[12]On the next day a large multitude had come to the feast. When they heard that Yeshua was coming to Yerushala'im, [13]they took the branches of the palm trees, went out to meet him, and cried out, "Please deliver us! Blessed is he who comes in the Name of the Everpresent Lord, the King of Israel!" [Ps. 118:26]

[14]Having found a young donkey, Yeshua sat on it. As it is written, [15]"Do not be afraid, daughter of Zion. Look, your King comes, sitting on a donkey's colt." [Zekh. 9:9] [16](His disciples did not

12:13 The waving branches and shouts of "Hoshanna!" — i.e. "Deliver us!" — are a normal part of the observance of Sukkot, which anticipates the coming of God's kingdom. It is, apparently, in that anticipation that the crowd has responded to Yeshua.

The context for "Blessed is he who comes in the Name of the Everpresent Lord," is found in Ps. 118:22-24, the verses which preced it: "The stone which the builders rejected has become the chief cornerstone. This was the doing of the Everpresent Lord; It is marvelous in our eyes. This is the day the Everpresent Lord has made. We will rejoice and be glad in it."

12:14 See not to Mt. 21:5.

12:36 The phrase "children of light" appears in the DSS Manual of Discipline.

12:40 See the ADDITIONAL NOTE on "Pharaoh's Heart".

12:41 "when" is in the Textus Receptus

understand these things at first, but when Yeshua was glorified, then they realized that these things were written about him, and that they had done these things to him.)

¹⁷So the crowd that was with him when he called Eleazar out of the tomb and raised him from the dead was testifying about it. ¹⁸Because of this a crowd also came and met him, because they heard that he had done this miracle. ¹⁹So the Perushim said to each other, "See how you⁺ accomplish nothing. Look, the world has gone after him."

²⁰Now there were certain Greeks among those who went up to worship at the feast. ²¹So these came to Philip, who was from Beit Tzaidah of the Galil, and asked him, "Sir, we want to see Yeshua." ²²Philip came and told Andreas, and Andreas in turn came with Philip, and they told Yeshua. ²³Yeshua responded to them, "The time has come for the Son of Adam to be glorified. ²⁴I assure you⁺ that unless a grain of wheat falls into the earth and dies, it remains by itself alone. But if it dies, it bears much fruit. ²⁵The one who loves his life will lose it. The one who hates his life in this world will keep it to eternal life. ²⁶If anyone serves me, let him follow me. Where I am, there my servant will be also. If anyone serves me, the Father will honor him.

²⁷"Now my soul is troubled. What shall I say, 'Father, save me from this hour'? But I came to this hour for this purpose. ²⁸Father, glorify Your Name."

Then there came a voice out of heaven, saying, "I have both glorified it, and will glorify it again."

²⁹So the crowd which stood by and heard said that it had thundered. Others said, "An angel has spoken to him."

³⁰Yeshua answered, "This voice has not come for my sake, but for your⁺ sakes. ³¹Now is the judgment of this world. Now the prince of this world will be cast out. ³²And I, if I am lifted up from the earth, will draw all people unto myself." ³³Now he said this signifying by what kind of death he would die. ³⁴The crowd responded to him, "We have heard out of the Torah that the Messiah remains forever. How do you say, 'The Son of Adam must be lifted up?' Who is this Son of Adam?"

³⁵Yeshua therefore said to them, "Yet a little while the light is with you⁺. Walk while you⁺ have the light, so that darkness does not overtake you⁺. The one who walks in the darkness does not know where he is going. ³⁶While you⁺ have the light, believe in the light, so that you⁺ may become children of light." [Gen. 1:3] Yeshua said these things, then he departed and was hidden from them.

³⁷But though he had done so many miracles before them, yet they did not believe in him, ³⁸in order that the word which Isaiah the prophet spoke might be fulfilled: "O Everpresent Lord, who has believed our report? To whom has the arm of the Everpresent Lord been revealed?" [Is. 53:1] ³⁹So they could not believe, because Isaiah said again, ⁴⁰"He has blinded their eyes and He hardened their heart. Otherwise they would see with their eyes, understand with their heart, and turn, and I would heal them." [Is. 6:10] ⁴¹Isaiah said these things when he saw his glory and spoke of him. ⁴²Although many indeed believed in him, even from among the rulers, yet because of the Perushim they did not confess it, so that they would not be put out of the assembly, ⁴³for they loved the praise of men more than the praise of God.

⁴⁴Yeshua cried out and said, "Whoever believes in me, believes not in me, but in Him who sent me. ⁴⁵The one who sees me sees Him who sent me. ⁴⁶I have come into the world as a light, so that everyone who believes in me may not remain in the darkness. ⁴⁷If anyone listens to what I say and does not believe, I do not condemn him. For I did not come to condemn the world, but to save the world. ⁴⁸The one who rejects me, and does not receive my words, has one who judges him. The word

that I spoke, the same will judge him in the last day. [49]For I did not speak from myself, but the Father who sent me, He gave me a commandment — what I should say, and what I should speak. [50]I know that His commandment is eternal life. So the things which I speak, I speak just as the Father has said to me."

13 [1]Now before the feast of Pesakh, Yeshua knew that his time had come to depart from this world to the Father. He had loved his own who were in the world, and he loved them to the end.

[2]When supper came, the Enemy had already put into the heart of Judah from K'riyot, the son of Shimon, to deliver him up. [3-4]Yeshua arose from supper, knowing that the Father had given all things into his hands and that he came forth from God and was going to God. He laid aside his outer garments, took a towel, and wrapped it around his waist.

[5]Then he poured water into the basin, and began to wash the feet of the disciples, and to wipe them with the towel that was wrapped around him.

[6]Then he came to Shimon Kefa, who said to him, "Lord, do you wash my feet?"

[7]Yeshua answered him, "You do not know what I am doing now, but you will understand later."

[8]Kefa said to him, "You will surely not wash my feet!"

Yeshua answered him, "If I do not wash you, you have no part with me."

[9]Shimon Kefa said to him, "Lord, not my feet only, but also my hands and my head."

[10]Yeshua said to him, "Someone who has bathed only needs to cleanse his feet, but is otherwise completely clean. You+ are clean, but not all of you+." [11]For he knew the one who would deliver him up. That is why he said, "You+ are not all clean." [12]So when he had washed their feet, put his outer garment back on, and sat down again, he said to them, "Do you+ know what I have done to you+? [13]You+ call me, 'Teacher' and 'Lord,' and you+ say this correctly, because I am. [14]If I, the Lord and the Teacher, have washed your+ feet, then you+ also ought to wash one another's feet. [15]For I have given you+ an example that you+ also should do as I have done to you+. [16]I assure you+ a servant is not greater than his lord, nor is one who is sent greater than the one who sent him. [17]If you+ know these things, there is good for you+ if you+ do them. [18]I do not speak concerning all of you+ — I know whom I have chosen — but that the Scripture may be fulfilled: 'He who eats my bread has lifted up his heel against me.' [Ps. 40:9LXX/41:9] [19]From now on, I tell you+ before it happens, so that when it happens, you+ may believe that I am he. [20]I assure you+ that the one who receives whomever I send, receives me. And the one who receives me, receives Him who sent me."

[21]When Yeshua had said this, he was troubled in spirit and affirmed, "I assure you+ that one of you+ will deliver me up."

[22]The disciples looked at one another, perplexed about whom he spoke. [23]One of his disciples, whom Yeshua loved, was at the table, reclining against Yeshua's chest. [24]So Shimon Kefa motioned to him, and said to him, "Tell us who it is of whom he speaks."

[25]Reclining against Yeshua's chest, he asked him, "Lord, who is it?"

[26]So Yeshua answered, "It is the one to whom I will give this piece of matzah when I have dipped

13:23-25 "Our Rabbis said, 'Even a poor man who is in Israel is not to eat [Pesakh] until he reclines.'" (Mid. Exodus Rabbah 20:18)

it." So when he had dipped the piece of matzah, he took and gave it to Judah, the son of Shimon, a man of K'riyot. ²⁷After the piece of matzah, then the Accuser entered into him.

Then Yeshua said to him, "What you do, do quickly." ²⁸Now no man at the table knew why he said this to him. ²⁹Since Judah had the money box, some thought that Yeshua told him to buy what was needed for the feast, or to give something to the poor. ³⁰Having received that piece of matzah, he then immediately went out. It was night.

³¹When he had gone out, Yeshua said, "The Son of Adam has now been glorified, and God has been glorified in him. ³²If God has been glorified in him, God will also glorify him in Himself, and He will glorify him immediately. ³³Little children, I will be with you⁺ a little while longer. You⁺ will seek me, and as I said to the Jewish authorities, so I now tell you⁺: Where I am going, you⁺ cannot come. ³⁴I give you⁺ a new commandment, so that you⁺ love one another. Just as I have loved you⁺, you⁺ also love one another. ³⁵By this everyone will know that you⁺ are my disciples, if you⁺ have love for one another."

³⁶Shimon Kefa said to him, "Lord, where are you going?"

Yeshua answered, "Where I am going, you cannot follow now, but afterwards you will follow."

³⁷Kefa said to him, "Lord, why can't I follow you now? I will lay down my life for you."

³⁸Yeshua answered him, "Will you lay down your life for me? I assure you the rooster will not call out until you have denied me three times.

14 ¹"Do not let your⁺ heart be troubled; trust in God, trust also in me. ²In my Father's house are many dwellings. [Is. 2:1-4, 56:6-8] If it were not so, I would have told you⁺, because I am going to prepare a place for you⁺. [Ex. 23:20] ³If I go and prepare a place for you⁺, I will come again and receive you⁺ to myself; so that where I am, you⁺ may be there also. [Eccl. 12:5] ⁴You⁺ know where I go, and you⁺ know the way."

⁵Toma said to him, "Lord, we do not know where you are going. How can we know the way?"

⁶Yeshua said to him, "I am the Way, the truth, and the life. No one comes to the Father, except through me. ⁷If you⁺ have known me, you⁺ will know my Father also. From now on, you⁺ know Him, and have seen Him."

⁸Philip said to him, "Lord, show us the Father, and that will be enough for us."

⁹Yeshua said to him, "Have I been with you⁺ such a long time, and you do not know me, Philip? The one who has seen me has seen the Father. How is it you say, 'Show us the Father?' ¹⁰Don't you believe that I am in the Father, and the Father in me? The words that I tell you⁺, I am not speaking from myself, but the Father who lives in me does His works. ¹¹Believe me that I am in the Father, and the Father in me; or else believe me because of the works themselves. ¹²I assure you⁺ that the one who believes in me, he also will do the works that I do. And he will do greater works than these, because

14:2-3 "…because man goes to the home of his eternity." Eccl. 12:5 "As the gazelle appears and then returns and is hidden, so the first redeemer [Moses] appeared and then was hidden…. Like the first redeemer, so will the final redeemer [Messiah] be." (Mid. Num. 11:2)

Speaking about Is. 11:1, Mid. Psalms 21.1 says, "This is Messiah, the Son of David, who is hidden until the time of the end."

14:6 A staggering claim.

I am going to my Father. ¹³Whatever you⁺ may ask in my name, that I will do, so that the Father may be glorified in the Son. ¹⁴If you⁺ ask anything in my name, I will do it. ¹⁵If you⁺ love me, you⁺ will keep my commandments.

¹⁶"I will ask the Father, and He will give you⁺ another Advocate, so that He may be with you⁺ forever — ¹⁷the Spirit of truth, whom the world cannot receive, because it neither sees him nor knows him. You⁺ know him, because he lives with you⁺, and will be in you⁺. ¹⁸I will not leave you⁺ as orphans. I will come to you⁺. ¹⁹Yet a little while, and the world will see me no more, but you⁺ will see me. Because I live, you⁺ will live also. ²⁰In that day you⁺ will know that I am in my Father, and you⁺ in me, and I in you⁺. ²¹The one who has my commandments and keeps them is the one who loves me. The one who loves me will be loved by my Father, and I will love him, and will make myself known to him."

²²Judah, not the one from K'riyot, said to him, "Lord, what has happened that you are about to make yourself known to us, and not to the world?"

²³Yeshua answered him, "If a man loves me, he will keep my word. My Father will love him, and we will come to him, and make our home with him. ²⁴The one who does not love me does not keep my words. The word which you⁺ hear is not mine, but the Father's who sent me. ²⁵I have said these things to you⁺ while still living with you⁺. ²⁶But the Advocate, the Ruakh Kodesh, whom the Father will send in my name, he will teach you⁺ all things, and will remind you⁺ of all that I said to you⁺. ²⁷Peace I leave with you⁺. My peace I give to you⁺. I do not give to you⁺ as the world gives. Do not let your⁺ heart be troubled, nor let it be fearful.

²⁸"You⁺ heard that I said to you⁺, 'I am going away, and I am coming to you⁺.' If you⁺ loved me, you⁺ would have rejoiced, because I said 'I am going to my Father,' because the Father is greater than I. ²⁹Now I have told you⁺ before it happens, so that when it happens you⁺ may believe. ³⁰I will no longer speak much with you⁺, for the ruler of this world is coming, and he has no part in me. ³¹But that the world may know that I love the Father, and as the Father commanded me, even so I do. Arise, let us go from here.

15 ¹"I am the true vine, and my Father is the vinedresser. ²He takes away every branch in me that does not bear fruit. Every branch that does bear fruit, He cleanses by pruning, so that it may bear more fruit. ³You⁺ are already clean because of the word which I have spoken to you⁺. ⁴Remain in me, even as I am in you⁺. As the branch cannot bear fruit by itself unless it remains in the vine, so neither can you⁺, unless you⁺ remain in me. ⁵I am the vine, you⁺ are the branches. The one who remains in me, and I in him, he bears much fruit, because apart from me you⁺ can do nothing. [Ps. 1:1-3] ⁶If someone does not remain in me, he is thrown out as a branch, and is dried up. Then they gather them, throw them into the fire, and they are burned. ⁷If you⁺ remain in me, and my words remain in you⁺, you⁺ will ask whatever you⁺ desire, and it will be done for you⁺.

⁸"In this is my Father glorified, that you⁺ bear much fruit and become my disciples. ⁹Even as the Father has loved me, I also have loved you⁺. Remain in my love. ¹⁰If you⁺ keep my commandments,

14:16 In modern Greek, and in modern Hebrew, *parakletos*/Advocate signifies legal counsel, i.e. a lawyer.

you⁺ will remain in my love; even as I have kept my Father's commandments and remain in His love. ¹¹I have spoken these things to you⁺ so that my joy may remain in you⁺, and that your⁺ joy may be made full.

¹²"This is my commandment, that you⁺ love one another even as I have loved you⁺. ¹³No one has greater love than this, that he lays down his life for his friends. ¹⁴You⁺ are my friends, if you⁺ do whatever I command you⁺. ¹⁵I no longer call you⁺ servants, because the servant does not know what his lord is doing. But I have called you⁺ friends, because everything that I heard from my Father, I have made known to you⁺. ¹⁶You⁺ did not choose me, but I chose you⁺. I appointed you⁺ that you⁺ should go and bear fruit, and that your⁺ fruit should remain, so that the Father might give you⁺ whatever you⁺ ask of Him in my name.

¹⁷"I am commanding you⁺ these things so that you⁺ love one another. ¹⁸If the world hates you⁺, you⁺ know that it has hated me before it hated you⁺. ¹⁹If you⁺ were from the world, the world would love those who are its own. But because you⁺ are not from the world — since I chose you⁺ out from the world — therefore the world hates you⁺. ²⁰Remember the word that I said to you⁺: 'A servant is not greater than his lord.' If they persecuted me, they will also persecute you⁺. If they kept my word, they will keep yours⁺ also.

²¹"But they will do all these things to you⁺ because of my name, for they do not know the One who sent me. ²²If I had not come and spoken to them, they would not have had sin, but now they have no excuse for their sin. ²³The one who hates me, hates my Father also. ²⁴If I had not done among them the works which no one else did, they would not have had sin. But now they have seen and also hated both me and my Father. ²⁵But this has happened so that the word may be fulfilled which was written in their Torah: 'They hated me without a cause.' [Ps. 35:19, 69:5H]

²⁶"When the Advocate has come, whom I will send to you⁺ from the Father — the Spirit of truth, who goes forth from the Father — he will bear witness to me. ²⁷You⁺ also will bear witness, because you⁺ have been with me from the beginning.

16 ¹"I have spoken these things to you⁺ so that you⁺ may not be led astray. ²They will put you⁺ out of the congregations. Yes, the hour is coming when whoever kills you⁺ will think that he offers service to God. ³They will do these things because they have not known the Father nor me. ⁴But I have told you⁺ these things, so that when the hour for them comes, you⁺ may remember that I told you⁺ about them. I did not tell you⁺ these things from the beginning, because I was with you⁺.

15:13 "R. Akiba came and taught: that your brother may live with you [Lev. 25:36]: 'your life takes precedence over the life of your fellow.'" (Tal. Baba Metzia 62a) He reasoned that your brother can only live with you if you are living.

15:14 It is perhaps in this sense that Abraham was called the beloved friend of God. (Gen. 26:5, Is. 41:8, 2Chr. 20:7)

15:25 Tal. Yoma 9b indicates that the Second Temple was destroyed because of hatred without a cause. "Torah" is sometimes used to indicate the whole of Scriptures. (e.g. Tal. Sanhedrin 91b)

16:2 The sense of the Aramaic is "offering a sacrifice to God".

⁵But now I am going to the One who sent me, and none of you⁺ asks me, 'Where are you going?' ⁶But because I have told you⁺ these things, sorrow has filled your⁺ heart. ⁷Nevertheless, I tell you⁺ the truth, it is to your⁺ benefit that I go away. For if I do not go away, the Advocate will not come to you⁺. But if I go, I will send Him to you⁺. ⁸When He has come, He will rebuke the world concerning sin, concerning righteousness, and concerning judgment. ⁹Concerning sin, because they do not believe in me; ¹⁰concerning righteousness, because I am going to my Father and you⁺ will not see me any more; ¹¹concerning judgment, because the ruler of this world has been judged.

¹²"I still have many things to tell you⁺, but you⁺ cannot bear them now. ¹³However, when He, the Spirit of truth, has come, He will guide you⁺ into all truth, because He will not speak from Himself. He will speak instead whatever He hears. He will declare to you⁺ things that are coming. ¹⁴He will glorify me, for He will take from what is mine, and will declare it to you⁺. ¹⁵Everything which the Father has is mine. Therefore I said that He takes of mine, and will declare it to you⁺. ¹⁶A little while and you⁺ will not see me. Again a little while, and you⁺ will see me."

¹⁷So some of his disciples said to one another, "What is this that he says to us, 'A little while, and you⁺ will not see me, and again a little while, and you⁺ will see me'? And, 'Because I go to the Father'?" ¹⁸So they said, "What is this that he says, 'A little while'? We don't understand what he is saying."

¹⁹Yeshua perceived that they wanted to question him, so he said to them, "Are you⁺ asking each other about this, that I said, 'A little while and you⁺ will not see me, and again a little while, and you⁺ will see me'? ²⁰I assure you⁺ that you⁺ will weep and lament, but the world will rejoice. You⁺ will be sorrowful, but your⁺ sorrow will be turned into joy. ²¹A woman, when she is giving birth, has pain, because her time has come. But when she has delivered the child, she does not remember the anguish any more, because of the joy that a person has been born into the world. ²²So you⁺ now have pain, but I will see you⁺ again, and your⁺ heart will rejoice, and no one will take your⁺ joy away from you⁺.

²³"In that day you⁺ will ask me no questions. I assure you⁺ that whatever you⁺ may ask of the Father, He will give it to you⁺ in my name. ²⁴Until now, you⁺ have asked nothing in my name. Ask, and you⁺ will receive, so that your⁺ joy may be made full. ²⁵I have spoken these things to you⁺ figuratively. But the hour is coming when I will no longer speak to you⁺ figuratively, but will tell you⁺ openly about the Father. ²⁶In that day you⁺ will ask in my name. But I am not telling you⁺ that I will pray to the Father for you⁺, ²⁷because the Father Himself loves you⁺, since you⁺ have loved me and have believed that I came forth from the Father. ²⁸I came out from the Father, and have come into the world. I leave the world again, and go to the Father."

²⁹His disciples said to him, "Now you are speaking openly, and are not speaking figuratively! ³⁰Now we know that you know all things, and do not need for anyone to question you. By this we believe that you came forth from God."

³¹Yeshua responded to them, "Do you⁺ now believe? ³²Listen, the hour is coming, yes, and has now come, that you⁺ will be scattered, everyone to his own place, and you⁺ will leave me alone. Yet I am not alone, because the Father is with me. ³³I have told you⁺ these things so that you⁺ may have peace in me. In the world you⁺ have anguish, but be encouraged, I have overcome the world."

16:8-11 There will be evidence to convict or to acquit.

17 Yeshua said these things, then lifting up his eyes to heaven, he said, "Father, the hour has come. Glorify your Son so that Your Son may also glorify You, ²even as You gave him authority over all flesh so that he gives eternal life to all whom You have given him. ³This is eternal life, that they might know You, the only real God, and Yeshua the Messiah, the one whom You have sent. ⁴I glorified You on the earth. I have accomplished the work which You have given me to do. ⁵Now Father, glorify me with Your own self with the glory which I had with You before the world existed. ⁶I revealed Your Name to the people whom You have given me out of the world. They were Yours, and You have given them to me. They have kept Your word. ⁷Now they know that everything which You have given me is from You, ⁸because I have given to them the words which You gave me. And they received them, and have truly known that I came forth from You. And they have believed that You sent me.

⁹"I pray for them. I do not pray for the world, but for those whom You have given me, because they are Yours. ¹⁰All things that are mine are Yours, and Yours are mine, and I am glorified in them. ¹¹I am no longer in the world, but these are in the world, and I am coming to You. Holy Father, keep them through Your Name which You have given me, so that they may be one, even as we are. [Ex. 23:21] ¹²While I was with them in the world, I kept them in Your Name. I have kept those whom You have given me. None of them is lost, except the son of destruction, that what is written might be fulfilled. ¹³But now I come to You, and I say these things in the world, so that they may have the fullness of my joy in themselves. ¹⁴I have given them Your word. The world hated them, because they are not of the world, even as I am not of the world. ¹⁵I do not pray that You would take them from the world, but that You would guard them from what is evil. ¹⁶They are not of the world even as I am not of the world.

¹⁷"Sanctify them in Your truth. Your word is truth. ¹⁸As You sent me into the world, even so I have sent them into the world. ¹⁹For their sakes I sanctify myself, so that they themselves also may be sanctified in truth. ²⁰I am not praying for these only, but also for those who will believe in me through their word; ²¹so that they all may be one — even as You, Father, are in me, and I in You, that they also may be in us — so that the world may believe that You sent me. ²²I have given to them the glory which You gave me, so that they may be one, even as we are one — ²³I in them, and You in me, so that they may attain full stature as one. In this way, the world may know that You sent me, and loved them, even as You loved me. ²⁴Father, what I ask is that those You have given me also be with me where I am, so that they may see my glory, which You have given me, for You loved me before the foundation of the world. ²⁵Righteous Father, the world has not known You, but I have known You. And these have known that You sent me. ²⁶I made Your Name known to them, and will make it known, so that the love with which You loved me may be in them, and I in them."

18 When Yeshua had spoken these words, he went out with his disciples over the brook Kidron. There was a garden there into which he and his disciples entered. ²Now Judah, who delivered him up, also knew the place, because Yeshua often met there with his disciples. ³Having received a detachment of troops and officers from the chief Kohanim and the Perushim, Judah then came there with lanterns, torches, and weapons. ⁴Knowing all that was coming upon him, Yeshua therefore went forth and said to them, "Whom do you⁺ seek?"

⁵They answered him, "Yeshua of Natzrat."

Yeshua said to them, "I am he." Judah, who delivered him up, was also standing with them.

[6]So when he said to them, "I am he," they drew back and fell to the ground. [7]Then he asked them again, "Whom do you[+] seek?"

They said, "Yeshua of Natzrat."

[8]Yeshua answered, "I told you[+] that I am he. So if you[+] seek me, let these go their way" — [9]that the word which he spoke might be fulfilled: "I have lost none of those whom You have given me."

[10]Then Shimon Kefa, having a sword, drew it and struck the servant of the Kohen Gadol, and cut off his right ear. The servant's name was Malluch. [11]Yeshua therefore said to Kefa, "Put the sword into its sheath. The cup which the Father has given me, shall I not drink it?"

[12]So the commanding officer, the detachment, and the officers of the Jewish authorities seized Yeshua and bound him. [13]They led him first to Ḥanan, for he was father-in-law to Kayafa, who was Kohen Gadol that year.

[14]Now it was Kayafa who had advised the Jewish authorities that it was better that one man should perish for the people. [15]Shimon Kefa followed Yeshua, as did another disciple. That disciple was known to the Kohen Gadol, and so he entered in with Yeshua into the court of the Kohen Gadol. [16]But Kefa was standing at the door outside. So the other disciple, who was known to the Kohen Gadol, went out and spoke to the woman doorkeeper, and brought in Kefa. [17]Then the servant girl who kept the door said to Kefa, "Aren't you also one of this man's disciples?"

He said, "I am not."

[18]Now the servants and the officers were standing there, having made a fire of coals because it was cold. They were warming themselves. Kefa was with them, standing and warming himself. [19]The Kohen Gadol then asked Yeshua about his disciples, and about his teaching.

[20]Yeshua answered him, "I spoke openly to the world. I always taught in meetingplaces and in the Temple, where all the Jews always meet. I said nothing in secret. [21]Why do you question me? Ask those who heard what I said to them. Look, they know what I said."

[22]When he had said this, one of the officers standing by slapped Yeshua with his hand, saying, "Do you answer the Kohen Gadol like that?"

[23]Yeshua answered him, "If I have spoken evil, testify of the evil. But if rightly, why do you hit me?"

[24]Ḥanan sent him bound to Kayafa, the Kohen Gadol. [25]Now Shimon Kefa was standing and warming himself. So they said to him, "You are not also one of his disciples, are you?"

He denied it and said, "I am not."

[26]One of the servants of the Kohen Gadol, being a relative of the one whose ear Kefa had cut off, said, "Didn't I see you in the garden with him?"

18:10 Edersheim gives the reasons for understanding the name to be Malluch. (The Life and Times of Jesus the Messiah, Vol. II, P. 544 n.1)

18:28 There are two sacrifices for Pesakh, one on the 14th and one on the 15th of Nisan. Both the lamb for the meal and the sacrifice for the festival were called by the name of the festival, i.e. Pesakh. Each hagigah, i.e. festival sacrifice, is called "the Pesakh". See the Talmudic tractates Pesachim and Hagigah.

18:31 "Forty years before the destruction of the Temple, the Sanhedrin was exiled... They did not try capital charges." (Tal. Sanhedrin 41a) The Soncino note says Jer. Tal. Sanhedrin I, 1 has, "'the right to try capital cases was taken away from them,' i.e., by the Romans."

²⁷ So Kefa denied it again, and immediately the rooster called out.

²⁸Then they led Yeshua from Kayafa into the Praetorium. It was early, and they themselves did not enter into the Praetorium, so that they would not be defiled, but might eat the Pesakh. ²⁹So Pilate went out to them, and said, "What accusation do you⁺ bring against this man?"

³⁰They answered him, "If this man were not an evildoer, we would not have delivered him up to you."

³¹Pilate therefore said to them, "Take him yourselves, and judge him according to your⁺ law."

So the Jewish authorities said to him, "It is not lawful for us to put anyone to death." ³²By this, the word which Yeshua spoke, signifying by what kind of death he would die, was fulfilled.

³³So Pilate entered again into the Praetorium. He called Yeshua, and said to him, "Are you the King of the Jews?"

³⁴Yeshua answered him, "Do you say this by yourself, or did others tell you about me?"

³⁵Pilate answered, "I am not a Jew, am I? Your own nation and the chief Kohanim delivered you to me. What have you done?"

³⁶Yeshua answered, "My kingdom is not from this world. If my kingdom were from this world, then my servants would fight, so that I would not be delivered to the Jewish authorities. But my kingdom is not now from here."

³⁷Pilate therefore said to him, "Are you a king then?"

Yeshua answered, "You say that I am a king. For this I have been born, and for this I have come into the world, so that I should testify to the truth. Everyone who is of the truth listens to my voice."

³⁸Pilate said to him, "What is truth?"

When he had said this, he went out again to the Jewish authorities and said to them, "I find no basis for a charge against him. ³⁹Moreover, you⁺ have a custom that I should release someone to you⁺ at Pesakh. So do you⁺ want me to release the King of the Jews to you⁺?"

⁴⁰Then they all shouted again, "Not this man, but Bar Abba!" Now Bar Abba was a bandit.

19 ¹So Pilate then took Yeshua and whipped him. ²The soldiers twisted thorns into a crown, put it on his head, and dressed him in a purple cloak. ³They said, "Hail, King of the Jews!" and were slapping him.

⁴And Pilate went out again and said to them, "Look, I bring him out to you⁺ so that you⁺ may know that I find no charge against him." ⁵Yeshua then came out, wearing the crown of thorns and the purple cloak. Pilate said to them, "Behold the man!"

⁶So when the chief Kohanim and the officers saw him, they shouted and said, "The deathstake! Hang him on the deathstake!"

Pilate said to them, "Take him yourselves and hang him on the stake, because I find no charge against him."

⁷The Jewish authorities answered him, "We have a law, and by our law he ought to die, because he presented himself as the Son of God."

19:1 Tal. Ketubot 37a forbids flogging a person who is to be executed.

[8]When Pilate heard this, he was more afraid. [9]He entered into the Praetorium again, and said to Yeshua, "Where are you from?" But Yeshua gave him no answer. [10]So Pilate said to him, "You're not speaking to me? Don't you know that I have power to release you, and I have power to put you to death on the stake?"

[11]Yeshua answered, "You would have no power over me at all, unless it were given to you from above. So the one who delivered me to you has greater sin."

[12]At this, Pilate was seeking to release him, but the Jewish authorities cried out, "If you release this man, you are not a friend of Caesar! Everyone who makes himself a king is speaking against Caesar!"

[13]So when Pilate heard these words, he brought Yeshua out and sat down on the judgment seat at a place called "The Pavement" — "Gabta" in Hebrew. [14]Now it was the preparation of Pesakh at about the sixth hour. He said to the Jewish authorities, "Look at your[+] king!"

[15]They cried out, "Away with him! Away with him! Put him to death on the stake!"

Pilate said to them, "Shall I put your[+] king to death on the stake?"

The chief Kohanim answered, "We have no king but Caesar!" [1Sam. 8:7]

[16]So he then delivered him to them to be put to death on the stake. Then they took Yeshua and led him away. [17]He went out, bearing his stake to the place called "The Place of a Skull," which is called "Gulgolta" in Hebrew. [18]There they nailed him on the tree, and two others with him, one on either side, and Yeshua in the middle. [19]Pilate wrote a title also, and put it on the stake. There was written, "YESHUA THE NATZRI, THE KING OF THE JEWS." [20]Therefore many of the Jews read this title, because the place where Yeshua was hung on the stake was near the city. And it was written in Hebrew, in Latin, and in Greek. [21]So the chief Kohanim of the Jews said to Pilate, "Do not write, 'The King of the Jews,' but, 'He said, *I am King of the Jews*.' "

[22]Pilate answered, "What I have written, I have written."

[23]Then when they had nailed Yeshua on the stake, the soldiers took his garments and made four portions, a portion to each soldier, and also the tunic. Now the tunic was seamless, woven from the top through the whole length. [24]Therefore they said to one another, "Let's not tear it, but cast lots for

19:10-11 People with the power of life and death over others tend to be impressed with their own power and think, therefore, that others must be afraid of them. Because Yeshua is not impressed by Pilate nor afraid of death, he remains free to do God's will. (cf. Hazon/Rev. 12:11) He tells Pilate that God, not Pilate, is in control.

19:12-13 This was a threat to bring charges to Rome against Pilate, the appointed governor. When such charges were brought in the Roman Empire, the governor was sometimes recalled. "[I]n the large majority of known cases the accused governors were convicted — or committed suicide before the trial." (Richard A. Horsley, "High Priests and the Politics of Roman Palestine," Journal for the Study of Judaism, 17, 1986, P. 28)

19:15 cf. Josephus, Ant. 14.40-47, which describes how Roman rule in Israel began when Pompey was asked to settle the dispute over who would be king.

19:19 All the things that are record as having being done to Yeshua — the secret arrest by night, the secret trial, the confiscation of property, the spitting, mocking, beating, stripping, whipping, etc., even death on the stake — the Inquisition had these things done to those they accused and convicted. With one victim, the Inquisition in Lima even placed a crown of thorns on his head, and mocked him as "King of the Jews".

it to decide whose it will be" — that the scripture might be fulfilled which says, "They parted my garments among them. They cast lots for my clothing." [Ps. 22:8] Then the soldiers did these things.

[25]His mother, his mother's sister, Miryam the wife of Halfai, and Miryam from Magdala were standing near the deathstake of Yeshua. [26]So when Yeshua saw his mother, and the disciple whom he loved standing there, he said to his mother, "Woman, behold your son." [27]Then he said to the disciple, "Behold your mother." From that hour, the disciple took her into his own household.

[28]After this, seeing that all things were now accomplished, Yeshua said, "I am thirsty" — that the Scripture might be fulfilled. [Ps. 69:22H] [29]Now a container full of sour wine had been placed there. So they put a sponge full of the sour wine on hyssop, and held it at his mouth. [30]So when Yeshua had received the sour wine, he said, "It has been fulfilled." He bowed his head, and gave up his spirit.

[31]Since it was the preparation, the Jewish authorities therefore asked Pilate that their legs might be broken, and that they might be taken away. They asked this so that the bodies would not remain on the stake on Shabbat, because that Shabbat was a highly distinguished day. [32]Therefore the soldiers came, and broke the legs of the first and of the other who had been hung on the stake along with him. [33]But when they came to Yeshua and saw that he was already dead, they did not break his legs. [34]One of the soldiers, however, pierced his side with a spear, and immediately blood and water came out.

[35]One who has seen is bearing witness, and his testimony is true. He knows that he tells the truth so that you[+] may believe. [36]For these things happened that there might be fullness to the scripture, "A bone of him will not be broken." [Ex. 12:46, Num. 9:12, Ps. 34:20] [37]Again another scripture says, "They will look on the one they pierced." [Zech. 12:10]

[38]After these things, Yosef of Ramatayim, being a disciple of Yeshua, but secretly for fear of the Jewish authorities, asked of Pilate that he might take away Yeshua's body. Pilate gave him permission. So he came and took away his body. [39]Nakdimon, who first came to Yeshua by night, also came bringing a mixture of myrrh and aloes, about a hundred pounds. [40]So they took Yeshua's body and bound it in linen cloths with spices in preparation for burial, in accordance with the Jewish custom. [41]Now in the place where he was put to death on the stake, there was a garden, and in the garden a new tomb in which no man had ever yet been laid. [42]Because of the Jewish preparation, they then laid Yeshua there, because the tomb was near at hand.

20 [1]Now on the first of the week, Miryam from Magdala went to the tomb early while it was still dark, and saw the stone taken away from the tomb. [2]So she ran and came to Shimon Kefa and to the other disciple whom Yeshua loved, and said to them, "They have taken away the Lord out of the tomb, and we do not know where they have laid him!"

[3]So Kefa and the other disciple started going toward the tomb. [4]They both ran together. The other disciple ran faster than Kefa, and came to the tomb first. [5]Stooping and looking in, he saw the linen cloths lying there, but he did not enter in. [6]Then Shimon Kefa came following him, and entered into the tomb. He saw the linen cloths lying there, [7]but the cloth that had been on his head was not lying with the linen cloths, but rolled up in a place by itself. [8]So then the other disciple who came first to the tomb also entered in, saw, and believed. [9]Though they did not yet understand the scripture that he must rise from the dead. [10]So the disciples went away again to their own homes.

[11]But Miryam was standing outside at the tomb weeping. So as she wept, she stooped and looked into the tomb. [12]She saw two angels in white where the body of Yeshua had lain, one sitting at the head, and one at the feet. [13]They said to her, "Woman, why are you weeping?"

She said to them, "Because they have taken away my Lord, and I do not know where they have laid him." ¹⁴When she had said this, she turned around and saw Yeshua standing there, but did not know that it was Yeshua.

¹⁵Yeshua said to her, "Woman, why are you weeping? Whom do you seek?"

Supposing him to be the caretaker of the garden, she said to him, "Sir, if you have carried him away, tell me where you have laid him, and I will take him away."

¹⁶Yeshua said to her, "Miryam."

She turned and said to him, "Rabboni!" which is to say, "Teacher!"

¹⁷Yeshua said to her, "Do not hold on to me, for I have not yet ascended to the Father. But go to my brothers and tell them that I am ascending to my Father and your⁺ Father, to my God and your⁺ God." ¹⁸Miryam of Magdala came and told the disciples that she had seen the Lord, and that he had said these things to her.

¹⁹Then when it was evening on that day, the first day of the week, and the doors where the disciples were assembled were locked, because of fear of the Jewish authorities, Yeshua came and stood in their midst. He said to them, "Peace to you⁺."

²⁰When he had said this, he showed them his hands and his side. So the disciples rejoiced when they saw the Lord. ²¹Yeshua then said to them again, "Peace to you⁺. As the Father has sent me, even so I send you⁺." ²²When he had said this, he breathed on them, and said to them, "Receive the Ruakh Kodesh. ²³Anyone whose sins you⁺ forgive, they are forgiven them. Anyone whose sins you⁺ retain, they have been retained."

²⁴But Toma, called "the Twin," one of the twelve, was not with them when Yeshua came. ²⁵So the other disciples told him, "We have seen the Lord!"

But he said to them, "Unless I see the print of the nails in his hands, and put my hand into his side, I will not believe."

²⁶After eight days his disciples were inside again, and Toma was with them. The doors were locked, but Yeshua came, stood in their midst, and said, "Peace to you⁺." ²⁷Then he said to Toma, "Reach your finger here, and see my hands. Reach your hand here and put it into my side. Do not be unbelieving, but believing."

²⁸Toma answered him, "My Lord and my God!"

²⁹Yeshua said to him, "Because you have seen me, you have believed. Blessed are those who have not seen, and have believed."

20:25 "He [Moses] held the Tablets, and did not believe that Israel had sinned, and saying: 'Unless my eyes see it, I will not believe it,' as it says [Ex. 32], 'And it was that, as soon as Moses came near to the camp.' He did not break them until he had seen with his eyes. Woe to them, to the children of Adam, who are witnesses to what their eyes have not seen! Was it possible that Moses did not believe the Holy One, blessed be He, when He said to him 'Because your people have corrupted [themselves]'? By this, Moses taught to Israel the right way to live: even if a person hears something from someone most faithful, it is forbidden in receiving the testimony from his mouth to do anything if one has not seen it." (Mid. Ex. Rabbah 46:1)

[30]Indeed, Yeshua did many other miracles in the presence of the disciples which are not written in this book. [31]But these are written so that you[+] may believe that Yeshua is the Messiah, the Son of God, and that, believing, you[+] may have life in his name.

21 [1]After these things, Yeshua showed himself again to the disciples at the lake of Tiverya. He showed himself this way: [2]Shimon Kefa, Toma (called "the Twin"), Nataniel of Kanah in the Galil, the sons of Zevadyah, and two others from his disciples were together. [3]Shimon Kefa said to them, "I'm going fishing."

They told him, "We also are coming with you." They went out and entered into the boat. That night they caught nothing. [4]Now when day had already come, Yeshua stood on the shore, but the disciples did not know that it was Yeshua. [5]Then Yeshua said to them, "Children, do you[+] have anything to eat?"

They answered him, "No."

[6]He said to them, "Cast the net on the right side of the boat, and you[+] will find some."

So they cast it, and then they were not able to draw it in because of the multitude of fish. [7]Then that disciple whom Yeshua loved said to Kefa, "It is the Lord!"

So when Shimon Kefa heard that it was the Lord, he wrapped his coat around himself, since he was naked, and threw himself into the lake. [8]But the other disciples came in the little boat, since they were not far from the land, but about one hundred yards away, dragging the net full of fish.

[9]So when they got out on the land, they saw a fire of coals there, and fish laid on it, and bread. [10]Yeshua said to them, "Bring some of the fish which you[+] have just caught."

[11]Shimon Kefa went up and drew the net to land, full of big fish, one hundred fifty-three. And even though there were so many, the net was not torn.

[12]Yeshua said to them, "Come and eat." None of the disciples dared ask him, "Who are you?" knowing that it was the Lord.

[13]Then Yeshua came, took the bread, and gave it to them, and the fish likewise. [14]This is now the third time that Yeshua was made known to his disciples after he had been raised from the dead. [15]So when they had eaten, Yeshua said to Shimon Kefa, "Shimon, son of Yonah, do you love me more than these?"

He said to him, "Yes, Lord. You know that I love you."

He said to him, "Feed my lambs." [16]He said to him again a second time, "Shimon, son of Yonah, do you love me?"

He said to him, "Yes, Lord. You know that I love you."

He said to him, "Tend my sheep." [17]He said to him the third time, "Shimon, son of Yonah, do you love me?"

21:15-17 "Shimon, son of Yonah" seems to be a reference to Shimon's sharing in the nature and calling of Yonah the prophet. This would be similar to Yeshua calling the brothers Yohanan and Jacob "sons of thunder". Even as Kefa had denied Yeshua three times, he is now given the opportunity to affirm his commitment to him three times as well.

Kefa was grieved because he asked him the third time, "Do you love me?" He said to him, "Lord, you know everything. You know that I love you."

Yeshua said to him, "Feed my sheep. ¹⁸I assure you that when you were young, you girded yourself, and walked where you wanted to. But when you are old, you will stretch out your hands, and another will gird you and carry you where you do not want to go." ¹⁹Now he said this, signifying by what kind of death he would glorify God. When he had said this, he said to him, "Follow me."

²⁰Then Kefa, turning around, saw a disciple following. This was the disciple whom Yeshua loved — the one who had also leaned on Yeshua's chest at the supper and asked, "Lord, who is going to deliver you up?" ²¹Seeing him, Kefa said to Yeshua, "Lord, what about this man?"

²²Yeshua said to him, "If it is my will that he remain until I come, what is that to you? You follow me." ²³So this saying went out among the brothers that this disciple would not die. Yet Yeshua did not say to him that he would not die, but, "If it is my will that he remain until I come, what is that to you?" ²⁴This is the disciple who testifies about these things, and wrote these things. We know that his testimony is true. ²⁵There are also many other things which Yeshua did, which if they were written one by one, I suppose that not even the world itself could contain the books written.

Introductory Note to Acts/
MA'ASEI haSHLI<u>H</u>IM

"Acts" was written by Luke, who also wrote a report on the life and death of Yeshua. Both books are addressed to Theophilus, who, like the governors Felix (Acts 23:26; 24:3) and Festus (Acts 26:25), bears the title, "Most Excellent." (Luke 1:3) The book contains accounts of nine trials or judicial inquiries. The location and the name of the presiding Roman official is given in all but one instance. In that instance, the magistrates had Sha'ul and Sila, who were Roman citizens, beaten without trial. For that illegal action, the magistrates could have been put to death, had their names been given.

From chapter 9 on, the focus is on Sha'ul, who is presented as an observant Jew, keeping the commandments, observing the holy days, and honoring the Temple. Sha'ul can confidently claim, "Neither against the Jewish Law, nor against the Temple, nor against Caesar, have I sinned in anything." (25:8)

In the Roman Empire, sacrifice to the emperor was required of every people as a sign of loyalty. For historical reasons, only the Jewish people were exempt. Anyone else who refused was guilty of "atheism," i.e. rejection of the state gods, which was treason. In the Temple in Yerushala'im, as part of the unique accommodation made for the Jewish people, sacrifices were offered to the God of Israel on behalf of Caesar.

If it could be demonstrated that the faith of Sha'ul (and the other disciples) was outside acceptable Jewish belief and practice, then Sha'ul (and the other disciples) would have to offer sacrifice to Caesar. If they were to then refuse, they would be guilty of the capital crime of "atheism". This is, in fact, what happened in later times.

The book of Acts closes with Sha'ul in Rome, awaiting trial before Caesar. It seems likely that Theophilus was a judicial official, perhaps the one charged with gathering the facts of a particular case — in this instance, the case of Sha'ul. The books of Luke and Acts were then written to give Theophilus those facts and, at the same time, to bear witness to the Messiahship of Yeshua and the truth of the good news. (cf. John Mauck, Paul on Trial, Thomas Nelson & Sons, Nashville, 2001)

Accordingly, Luke simply presents the conflicts which took place between Sha'ul and other Jews as an internal Jewish matter. Occasional misinterpretation of the simple definite article in the text has greatly distorted the meaning of these encounters. If we were to read that, "The Athenians rejected Socrates," or "The Athenians killed Socrates," the definite article ("the" in English and *oi/tois* in Greek) would indicate a specific group of Athenians, but not Athenians in general. Use of the definite article does not mean that all Athenians of all time were and are irreconcilable enemies of Socrates. Socrates was an Athenian himself, and so were some of his disciples. That was his culture and society. The historical context informs us that a specific group of Athenians, the contemporary civic leaders, is meant.

In the same way, Luke often uses the definite article in referring to specific groups of Jews in different cities. Traditional Church history and doctrine take the definite article when applied to the particular Jews in opposition, and generalize it to mean Jews in general, i.e. all Jews. This is not the grammatical, contextual meaning.

Additionally, the Greek definite article has a broader usage than the English. In some contexts the Greek definite article is similar to the English indefinite article "a" or "some". Fidelity to the text and >>

Acts/ *Ma'asei haShlihim*

¹ ¹I made the first account, Theophilus, about all that Yeshua began both to do and to teach, ²until the day in which he was taken up. This was after he had given commandment through the Ruakh Kodesh to the ambassadors whom he had chosen. ³After he had suffered, he also showed himself alive to them by many proofs. He appeared to them over a period of forty days, speaking about God's kingdom. ⁴Being assembled together with them, he directed them, "Don't depart from Yerushala'im, but wait for the promise of the Father, which you⁺ heard from me. ⁵For Yohanan indeed immersed in water, but you⁺ will be immersed in the Ruakh Kodesh not many days from now."

⁶So when they had come together, they asked him, "Lord, are you now restoring the kingdom to Israel?"

⁷He said to them, "It is not for you⁺ to know times or seasons which the Father has placed within His own authority. ⁸But you⁺ will receive power when the Ruakh Kodesh has come upon you⁺. You⁺ will be witnesses to me in Yerushala'im, in all Judea and Shomron, and to the end of the earth."

⁹When he had said these things, as they were watching, he was taken up, and a cloud received him out of their sight. ¹⁰While they were looking intently into heaven as he went, two men stood by them in white clothing. ¹¹And they said, "You⁺ men of the Galil, why do you⁺ stand looking into heaven? This Yeshua who was received up from you⁺ into heaven will come back in the same way as you⁺ saw him going into heaven." [Zekh. 14:1-4]

¹²Then they returned to Yerushala'im from the mountain called the Mount of Olives, which is near Yerushala'im, a Shabbat journey away. ¹³When they had come in, they went up into the upper room where they were staying. They were Kefa, Yohanan, Jacob, Andreas, Philip, Toma, Bar Talmai, Matthias, Jacob the son of Halfai, Shimon the Zealot, and Judah the son of Jacob. ¹⁴Along with the women, Miryam the mother of Yeshua, and his brothers, all of them persevered in prayer and supplication with a common purpose.

---

context requires translation that indicates when a particular group, rather than Jews in general, is intended.

Acts circulated "in two quite distinct forms, commonly called the Alexandrian and the Western. The former... has been traditionally regarded as the authentic text of Acts..." Metzger, A Textual Commentary on the Greek New Testament, P. 259

1:1 "O Theophilus" The text was most likely written for a Roman official. It is written in Greek and contains conversations and communications which took place in Greek, Hebrew, Lycaonian (14:11ff), possibly Latin (23:26-30) and other languages.

1:6-7 Yeshua had taught them about God's Kingdom. The scriptural promises of the outpouring of God's Spirit are almost all directly connected with the restoration of the kingdom. (e.g. Joel 2:25-3:2; Is. 61:1-3; Ezek. 37) The question and response concern **when** the restoration will take place.

1:12 "a Shabbat journey" is 2000 cubits/3000 feet. (cf. Tal. Eruvin 52b)

[15]In those days, Kefa stood up in the midst of the disciples — the number of names was about one hundred twenty — and said, [16]"Men, brethren, it was necessary that this scripture should be fulfilled which the Ruakh Kodesh spoke before by the mouth of David concerning Judah, who was a guide to those who seized Yeshua. [17]For he was numbered with us, and received his portion in this work. ([18]Now this man obtained a field with the reward for his wrong-doing, and, falling headlong, his body burst open and all his insides spilled out. [2Sam. 20:10] [19]It became known to everyone who lived in Yerushala'im, so that in their own language that field was called 'Ḥakal Dama,' that is, 'the field of blood.') [20]For it is written in the book of Psalms, 'Let his house become desolate. Let no one dwell in it,' [Ps. 69:25] and, 'Let another take his appointed position.' [Ps. 109:8]

[21]"So from the men who have accompanied us all the time that the Lord Yeshua went in and out among us — [22]beginning from the immersion of Yoḥanan to the day that he was received up from us — one of these must become a witness with us of his resurrection."

[23]They put forward two, Yosef called Bar Sabba (who was also called Justus), and Matthias. [24]They prayed and said, "You, O Everpresent Lord, who know the hearts of all men, show which one of these two You have chosen [25]to take part in this work and be an ambassador. Judah fell away from this so that he might go to his own place." [26]They drew lots for them, and the lot fell on Matthias, and he was counted with the eleven ambassadors.

2 [1]Now during the observance of the day of Shavuot, they were all together in one place. [2]Suddenly there came from heaven a sound like the rushing of a mighty wind, and it filled the entire house where they were staying. [3]Divided tongues like fire appeared to them, and rested upon each of them. [4]They were all filled with the Ruakh Kodesh, and began to speak with other languages, as the Spirit gave them the ability to speak.

[5]Now there were Jews staying in Yerushala'im, devout men from every nation under heaven. [6]When this sound was heard, the multitude came together and were bewildered, because everyone heard them speaking in his own language. [7]They were amazed and marveled, saying, "Look, aren't all these who speak from the Galil? [8]How are we each hearing them in our own native language? [9]Parthians, Medes, Elamites, and people from Mesopotamia, Judea, Cappadocia, Pontus, the province of Asia, [10]Phrygia, Pamphylia, Egypt, the parts of Libya around Kyrene, visitors from Rome, both Jews and proselytes, [11]from Crete and from Arabia — we hear them speaking in our languages the mighty

---

1:16 In numerous places in Acts and the various letters, I have used the old-fashioned "brethren" for "brothers" where it is not gender-specific.

2:3-4,11 The same word, *glossa*, means both "tongue" and "language".

2:6-11 "R. Yoḥanan said: 'What is meant by what is written, *The Everpresent Lord gives the word, Those who proclaim the good news are a large army* [Ps. 68:12H]? Each and every saying that went forth from the Almighty was divided into seventy languages. The school of R. Ishmael taught: 'And like a hammer that breaks the rock. [Jer. 23:29] Just as a hammer is divided into many sparks, so each and every saying that went forth from the Holy One, blessed be He, was divided into seventy languages.'" (Tal. Shabbat 88b)

Josephus says that in the time of the festivals during Nero's reign (54-68 C.E.), there were about 3 million people in Yerushala'im. (Wars 6:422-427 [6.9.3.422-27])

2:9 Mesopotamia is Aram Naharayim, e.g. Gen. 24:10.

works of God." [12]They were all amazed and perplexed. They said to each other, "What does this mean?" [13]Others mocked and said, "They are filled with new wine."

[14]But standing up with the eleven, Kefa raised his voice and spoke out to them. "You⁺ men of Judea, and all you⁺ who are residing in Yerushala'im, let this be known to you⁺, and listen to my words. [15]For these are not drunk, as you⁺ suppose, seeing it is only the third hour of the day. [16]But this is what has been spoken through the prophet Yoel: [17]*It will be in the last days*, says God, *that I will pour out My Spirit on all flesh. Your⁺ sons and your⁺ daughters will prophesy. Your⁺ young men will see visions. Your⁺ old men will dream dreams. [18]Yes, and I will pour out My Spirit on My servants and on My handmaidens in those days, and they will prophesy. [19]I will show wonders in the sky above, and signs on the earth beneath: blood, and fire, and billows of smoke. [20]The sun will be turned into darkness, and the moon into blood, before the great and glorious day of the Everpresent Lord comes. [21]It will be that whoever will call on the Name of the Everpresent Lord will be saved.'* [Joel 2:28-32]

[22]"Men of Israel, listen to these words! Yeshua the Natzri is a man commended to you⁺ by God through mighty works, wonders, and miracles which God did by him in your⁺ midst, as you⁺ yourselves also know. [23]You⁺ took him through the power of lawless men — he was delivered up by the determined purpose and foreknowledge of God — you⁺ nailed him on the stake, and put him to death. [24]God raised him up, having freed him from the agony of death, because it was not possible that he should be held by it. [25]For David says concerning him, 'I saw the Everpresent Lord always before my face, for He is on my right hand, so that I should not be shaken. [26]Therefore my heart was glad, and my tongue rejoiced. Moreover my flesh also will dwell in hope, [27]because You will not leave my soul in Sheol, nor will You allow Your Holy One to see decay. [28]You made known to me the ways of life. You will make me full of gladness with Your presence.' [Ps. 16:8-11]

[29]"Men, brothers, I may tell you⁺ freely of the patriarch David that he both died and was buried, and his tomb is with us to this day. [30]Being a prophet, he therefore knew that God had sworn with an oath to him that of the fruit of his physical body He would raise up the Messiah to sit on his throne. [Ps. 132:11, 2 Sam. 7:12] [31]Foreseeing this, he spoke about the resurrection of the Messiah, that his soul was not left in Sheol, nor did his flesh see decay. [32]And we are all witnesses that God raised up this Yeshua. [33]Therefore, having been exalted by the right hand of God, and having received from

---

2:13 In other words, They're drunk on cheap wine, wine which has not aged. This is the mockery of uninformed bystanders. The Talmud places "old wine" among those things "which are beneficial for the whole body." (Tal. Pesaḥim 42b)

2:16 "This is what has been said..." is an introduction to a midrashic, interpretive comment.

2:17 "Master of the world, I am Yours, and my dreams are Yours. I have dreamed a dream, but I don't know what it is. May it be Your will, my Everpresent Lord and God of my fathers, that all my dreams about myself and about all Israel be for good." (Birkat kohanim, Shemini Atzeret)

2:23 "lawless men" refers to Gentiles, who do not have the Torah of Moses.

"The one who says to his ambassador, 'Go out and kill a soul,' the one sent is liable [to punishment], and the one who sent him is exempt. Shammai the Elder said from what Haggai the prophet set out: 'The one who sent him is liable, for it is said, *you have slain him with the sword of the children of Ammon.* [2Sam. 12:9] ...and what does *liable* mean? He is liable by the judgment of Heaven." (Tal. Kiddushin 43a)

the Father the promise of the Ruakh Kodesh, he has poured out this which you⁺ now see and hear. ³⁴For David did not ascend into the heavens, but he himself says, 'The Everpresent Lord said to my Lord, *Sit by My right hand,* ³⁵*until I make your enemies a footstool for your feet.'* [Ps. 110:1] ³⁶So let all the house of Israel know with assurance that God has made him both Lord and Messiah, this Yeshua whom you⁺ put to death on the stake."

³⁷Now when they heard this, they were pierced in the heart and said to Kefa and the rest of the ambassadors, "Men, brothers, what should we do?"

³⁸Kefa said to them, "Change your ways, everyone of you⁺, and be immersed in the name of Yeshua the Messiah for the forgiveness of sins; and you⁺ will receive the gift of the Ruakh Kodesh. ³⁹For the promise is to you⁺ and to your⁺ children, and to all who are far off, even as many as the Everpresent Lord, our God, will call to Himself." ⁴⁰With many other words he bore witness and exhorted them, "Save yourselves from this crooked generation!"

⁴¹Then those who gladly received his word were immersed. There were added that day about three thousand souls. ⁴²They continued steadfastly in the teaching of the ambassadors, in fellowship, in the breaking of bread, and in prayer. ⁴³Fear came on every soul, and many wonders and miracles were done through the ambassadors. ⁴⁴All who believed were at the same place, and had all things common. ⁴⁵They sold their possessions and goods, and distributed them to all, according as anyone had need. ⁴⁶Day by day, continuing steadfastly with a common purpose in the Temple, and breaking bread at home, they shared their food with gladness and singleness of heart, ⁴⁷praising God, and having favor with all the people. The Lord added to them day by day those who were being saved.

3 ¹Kefa and Yoḥanan were going up into the Temple at the hour of prayer, the ninth hour. ²A certain man who was lame from his mother's womb was being carried. He was laid daily at what is called the "Beautiful Gate" of the Temple to ask charity from those who entered into the Temple. ³Seeing Kefa and Yoḥanan about to go into the Temple, he asked to receive charity. ⁴Fixing his eyes on him, Kefa, with Yoḥanan, said, "Look at us." ⁵He was attentive to them, expecting to receive something from them. ⁶But Kefa said, "I do not have silver and gold, but what I do have, this I give you. In the name of Yeshua the Natzri, the Messiah, rise up and walk!"

⁷He took him by the right hand and raised him up. Immediately his feet and his ankles received strength. ⁸Leaping up, he stood and began to walk. He entered with them into the Temple, walking, leaping, and praising God. ⁹All the people saw him walking and praising God. ¹⁰They recognized

2:34-35 Ps. 110 is applied to Messiah in Mid. Tehillim 18:29.

3:1 "R. Yose son of R. Hanina said: 'The times of prayer were established by the Fathers.' R. Joshua b. Levi says: 'The times of prayer were established as counterparts to the daily sacrifices.' ...Abraham established the morning time of prayer, as it says, *And Abraham rose up in the morning to the place where he had stood.* [Gen. 19:27] ...Isaac established the afternoon time of prayer, as it says, *And Isaac went out to meditate in the field at the beginning of the evening.* [Gen. 24:63] ...Jacob established the evening prayer, as it says, *And he lighted* [va'yiphga] *upon the place and stayed there* [Gen. 28:11], and *pegiah* means only prayer..." (Tal. Berachot 26b) In the Scriptures, God established a morning and an evening sacrifice, but no afternoon sacrifice. (Num. 28:1-8)

3:2, 10 "Beautiful," i.e. Yaffo

him, that he was the one who used to sit begging for charity at the Yaffo Gate of the Temple. They were filled with wonder and amazement at what had happened to him. ¹¹As he held on to Kefa and Yoḥanan, all the people were astonished and ran together to them in what is called Shlomo's porch.

¹²When Kefa saw it, he responded to the people, "You⁺ men of Israel, why do you⁺ marvel at this man? Why do you⁺ fix your⁺ eyes on us, as though by our own power or godliness we had made him walk? ¹³The God of Abraham, Isaac, and Jacob, the God of our fathers, has glorified His Servant Yeshua, whom you⁺ delivered up, and denied in the presence of Pilate, when he had determined to release him. ¹⁴But you⁺ denied the holy and righteous One, and asked for a murderer to be given to you⁺. ¹⁵Then you⁺ killed the prince of life, whom God raised from the dead. We are witnesses of this. ¹⁶By faith in his name, his name has strengthened this man, whom you⁺ see and know. Yes, the faith which is through him has given this man this perfect soundness in the presence of you⁺ all.

¹⁷"Now, brethren, I know that you⁺ did this in ignorance, as your⁺ rulers also did. ¹⁸But in this way, God fulfilled the things which He announced by the mouth of all His prophets, that Messiah should suffer. ¹⁹Therefore change your⁺ ways and return to God, so that your⁺ sins may be blotted out, and so that times of refreshing may come from the presence of the Everpresent Lord, ²⁰and so that He may send the Messiah, Yeshua, who was proclaimed to you⁺ before. ²¹Heaven must receive him until the times of restoration of all things, which God announced long ago by the mouth of His holy prophets. ²²For Moses certainly said to the fathers, 'The Everpresent Lord, will raise up a prophet like me for you⁺ from among your⁺ brothers. You⁺ are to listen to him in everything, whatever he says to you⁺. ²³It will be that every soul that will not listen to that prophet will be completely destroyed from among the people.' [Deut. 18:15,18] ²⁴Yes, and all the prophets from Shmuel and those who followed after, as many as have spoken, they also told of these days. ²⁵You⁺ are the children of the prophets and of the covenant which God made with our fathers, saying to Abraham, 'In your seed all the families of the earth will be blessed.' [Gen. 12:3] ²⁶Having raised up His servant Yeshua, God sent him to you⁺ first, to bless you⁺ in turning everyone of you⁺ away from your⁺ wickedness."

¹The Kohanim, the captain of the Temple, and the Tzadukim came to them as they spoke to the people. ²They were upset because they taught the people and proclaimed in Yeshua the resurrection from the dead. ³They arrested them, and put them in custody until the next day, for it was then evening. ⁴But many of those who heard the word believed, and the number of the men became about five thousand.

⁵In the morning, their rulers, elders, and Torah scholars were gathered together in Yerushala'im. ⁶Ḥanan, the Kohen Gadol, was there with Kayafa, Yoḥanan, Alexander, and as many as were from the family of the Kohen Gadol. ⁷Having placed them in the middle, they inquired, "By what power, or in what name, have you⁺ done this?"

⁸Filled with the Ruakh Kodesh, Kefa then said to them, "Rulers and elders of the people. ⁹If we are examined today concerning a good deed done to a powerless man — by what means this man has been healed — ¹⁰be it known to you⁺ all, and to all the people of Israel, that in the name of Yeshua the Natzri, the Messiah, whom you⁺ put to death on the tree, whom God raised from the dead, in him does this man stand here before you⁺ whole. ¹¹This one is 'the stone which was regarded as worthless

by you[+] the builders, which has become the head of the corner.' [Ps. 118:22] [12]There is no salvation in any other, because there is no other name under heaven that is given among men in which it is necessary for us to be saved!"

[13]Now when they saw the boldness of Kefa and Yohanan, and perceived that they were uneducated and untrained men, they were amazed. They recognized that they had been with Yeshua. [14]Seeing the man who was healed standing with them, they could say nothing against it. [15]But when they had commanded them to go aside out of the Council, they conferred among themselves. [16]They said, "What shall we do to these men? Because an obvious miracle has truly been done through them, as can be plainly seen by all who dwell in Yerushala'im. And we cannot deny it. [17]But so that this spreads no further among the people, let's severely threaten them to no longer speak to anyone in this name." [18]They called them, and ordered them not to teach in, or even utter, the name of Yeshua.

[19]But Kefa and Yohanan answered them, "Whether it is right in the sight of God to listen to you[+] rather than to God, judge for yourselves, [20]because we cannot help telling the things which we have seen and heard."

[21]When they had threatened them more, they let them go, finding no way to punish them, because of the people, since everyone was glorifying God for what had happened. [22]For the man on whom this miracle of healing was performed was more than forty years old.

[23]Being let go, they came to their own, and reported all that the chief Kohanim and the Elders had said to them. [24]When they heard it, they lifted up their voice to God with a common purpose, and said, "O Lord, You are the one who made the heaven, the earth, the sea, and all that is in them. [25]You said by the mouth of Your servant David, 'Why do the Gentiles rage, and the peoples meditate on worthless things? [26]The kings of the earth take a stand, and the rulers are gathered together against the Everpresent Lord and against His Messiah.' [Ps. 2:1]

[27]"For in accordance with this truth, in this city, against Your holy servant Yeshua whom You anointed, both Herod and Pontius Pilate, with the Gentiles and the peoples of Israel, were gathered together [28]to do as much as Your hand and Your counsel determined beforehand would happen. [29]Now, O Everpresent Lord, look at their threats, and give Your servants all boldness to speak Your word, [30]while You stretch out Your hand for healing, and for signs and wonders to be done through the name of Your holy Servant Yeshua."

[31]When they had prayed, the place was shaken where they were gathered together. They were all filled with the Ruakh Kodesh, and they spoke the word of God with boldness. [32]The multitude of those who believed were of one heart and soul. Not one of them claimed that anything of the things which he possessed was his own, but all things were shared in common among them. [33]With great

4:19 "One who disregards a king's decree because he was occupied with a commandment, even a light one, is not liable. [Whose words should be obeyed?] the words of the Master or the words of the servant? The words of the Master first. It is not necessary to speak about if a king decrees that a commandment should be disregarded. They do not listen to him." (Maimonides, Mishneh Torah, Melachim uMilchamot 3:9 [3:10 in some versions])

4:25 There is a contrast between the righteous, who meditates on God's Law (Ps. 1:2), and the wicked, who meditate on vanity (Ps. 2:1).

power, the ambassadors gave their testimony of the resurrection of the Lord Yeshua. Great grace was upon them all. ³⁴For there were not any among them who lacked, because as many as were owners of lands or houses sold them, and brought the proceeds of the things that were sold, ³⁵laying them at the feet of the ambassadors. Then distribution was made to each, according as anyone had need. ³⁶Yosef — by the ambassadors he was called Bar Nabba, which is interpreted as "Son of Exhortation" — a Levite, a man of Kyprus by birth, ³⁷had a field, sold it, brought the money and laid it at the feet of the ambassadors.

5 ¹Now a certain man named Hananyah, with Shappira his wife, sold a possession ²and kept back part of the price. His wife was also aware of it. He brought a certain part, and laid it at the feet of the ambassadors. ³But Kefa said, "Hananyah, why has the Accuser filled your heart to lie to the Ruakh Kodesh, and to keep back part of the price of the land? ⁴While you kept it, didn't it remain your own? After it was sold, wasn't it in your control? How is it that you determined this thing in your heart? You have not lied to men, but to God."

⁵Hearing these words, Hananyah fell down and died. Great fear came on all who heard these things. ⁶The young men arose and wrapped up his body. They carried him out and buried him. ⁷About three hours later, his wife came in, not knowing what had happened. ⁸Kefa began to speak to her, "Tell me whether you⁺ sold the land for 'so much.'"

She said, "Yes, for 'so much.'"

⁹Then Kefa asked her, "How is it that you⁺ have agreed together to put the Spirit of the Everpresent Lord to the test? Look, the feet of those who have buried your husband are at the door, and they will carry you out."

¹⁰She fell down immediately at his feet, and died. The young men came in and found her dead. They carried her out and buried her by her husband. ¹¹Great fear came on the whole community, and on all who heard these things.

¹²Many signs and wonders were done among the people by the hands of the ambassadors. They were all with a common purpose in Solomon's porch. ¹³None of the rest dared to join them. Nevertheless, the people honored them. ¹⁴More believers were added to the Lord, multitudes of both men and women. ¹⁵They even carried the sick out into the streets, and laid them on cots and mattresses, so that at least Kefa's shadow might overshadow some of them as he came by. ¹⁶Multitudes also came together from the cities around Yerushala'im, bringing sick people and those who were tormented by unclean spirits. And they were all healed.

¹⁷But the Kohen Gadol rose up, and all those who were with him (which is the sect of the Tzadukim), and they were filled with jealousy. ¹⁸They laid hands on the ambassadors, and put them in the public prison. ¹⁹But an angel of the Everpresent Lord opened the prison doors by night, and brought them out. He said, ²⁰"Go stand in the Temple and speak to the people all the words concerning this life." ²¹When they heard this, they entered into the Temple about daybreak, and taught.

But the Kohen Gadol and those who were with him went and called the Council together, with

4:32-36 Karl Marx' slogan was "From each according to his ability, to each according to his needs." See note to Mt. 25:15.

all the elders of the children of Israel. They then sent to the prison to have them brought. [22]But the officers who came did not find them in the prison. They returned and reported, [23]"We found the prison shut and locked securely, and the guards standing before the doors, but on opening them, we found no one!"

[24]Now when the Kohen Gadol, the captain of the Temple, and the chief Kohanim heard these words, they were very perplexed about them and what might become of this. [25]Someone came and told them, "The men whom you[+] put in prison are in the Temple, standing and teaching the people!" [26]Then the captain went with the officers, and brought them without violence, because they were afraid that the people might stone them.

[27]When they had brought them, they set them before the Council. The Kohen Gadol questioned them, [28]"Didn't we strictly order you[+] not to teach in this name? You[+] have filled Yerushala'im with your[+] teaching, and intend to bring this man's blood upon us!"

[29]But Kefa and the ambassadors answered, "We must obey God rather than men. [30]The God of our fathers raised up Yeshua, whom you[+] killed by hanging him on a tree. [31]God exalted him to His right hand to be a prince and a savior, to give Israel repentance and forgiveness of sins. [32]We are His witnesses of these things, as also is the Ruakh Kodesh, whom God has given to those who obey him."

[33]Now when they heard this, they were furious, and determined to kill them. [34]But a Parush named Gamliel, a teacher of the Torah honored by all the people, stood up in the Council and had the men put out for a little while. [35]He said to the Council, "Men of Israel, be careful what you[+] are about to do to these men. [36]For before these days Todas rose up, making himself out to be somebody. A number of men, about four hundred, joined themselves to him. He was slain, and all those who trusted him were dispersed and came to nothing. [37]After this man, Judah of the Galil rose up in the days of the census, and drew away some people after him. He also perished, and all those who trusted him were scattered abroad. [38]I tell you[+] now, stay away from these men and leave them alone, because if this plan or this work is of men, it will be overthrown. [39]But if it is of God, you[+] will not be able to overthrow it, and you[+] would even be found to be fighting against God."

[40]They were persuaded by him. Summoning the ambassadors, they beat them, ordered them not to speak in the name of Yeshua, and let them go. [41]So they departed from the presence of the Council, rejoicing that they were counted worthy to suffer dishonor for the Name.

[42]Every day, in the Temple and in the houses, they did not cease teaching and proclaiming the good news of Yeshua the Messiah.

6 [1]Now in those days, when the number of the disciples was multiplying, a complaint arose from the Hellenistic Jews against the Hebrew ones because their widows were neglected in the daily serving. [2]The twelve called the multitude of the disciples and said, "It is not appropriate for us to

---

5:36-37 Josephus mentions Todas in the time of Cuspius Fadus [Antiq. 20. 5. 1. 97] and Judah of the Galil in the time of Kyrenius. [20.5.2.102].

5:38 "R. Yoḥanan haSandlar said, 'Every assembly which is for the Name of Heaven, its end is to be raised up. And what is not for the Name of Heaven, its end is not to be raised up.'" (Tal. Avot 4:11)

6:1 The "Hellenistic" Jews had adopted much Greek, i.e. Hellenic, culture.

forsake the word of God and serve tables. ³So, brothers, select seven men of good report from among yourselves, full of the Ruakh Kodesh and of wisdom. We will appoint them over this responsibility, ⁴but we will continue steadfastly in prayer and in the serving of the word."

⁵These words pleased the whole multitude. They chose Stephen, a man full of faith and of the Ruakh Kodesh, Philip, Prochorus, Nikanor, Timon, Parmenas, and Nikolaus, a proselyte of Antioch. ⁶They set them before the ambassadors. When they had prayed, they laid their hands on them. ⁷The word of God spread, the number of the disciples in Yerushala'im greatly multiplied, and a large company of the Kohanim were obedient to the faith.

⁸Stephen, full of grace and power, performed great wonders and miracles among the people. ⁹But some of those who were of the community called "The Freedmen" — of the Kyrenians, of the Alexandrians, and of those of Kilikia and the province of Asia — rose up and argued with Stephen. ¹⁰They were not able to withstand the wisdom and the Spirit by which he spoke. ¹¹Then they privately instructed some men to say, "We have heard him speak blasphemous words against Moses and God." ¹²They stirred up the people, the elders, and the Torah scholars. They came against him, seized him, and brought him in to the Council. ¹³They set up false witnesses who said, "This man never stops speaking blasphemous words against this holy place and the Torah. ¹⁴For we have heard him say that this Yeshua the Natzri will destroy this place, and will change the customs which Moses delivered to us." ¹⁵All who sat in the Council, fastening their eyes on him, saw his face as the face of an angel.

7 ¹The Kohen Gadol was asking if these charges were true. ²He responded, "Men, brothers and fathers, listen. The God of glory appeared to our father Abraham, when he was in Aram Naharayim, before he lived in Haran. ³He said to him, 'Go out from your land and your relatives, and come into a land which I will show you.' [Gen. 12:1] ⁴Then he came out of the land of the Chaldeans, and lived in Haran. After the death of his father, God moved him from there into this land which you now inhabit. ⁵He gave him no inheritance in it, not even to plant his foot. He promised that He would give it to him for a possession, and to his seed after him, when he still had no child. [Gen. 12:7, 13:15, 15:18, 17:8] ⁶God spoke in this way, that his seed would live as strangers in a strange land, and that they would be enslaved and mistreated for four hundred years. ⁷'I will judge the nation to which they are enslaved,' [Gen. 15:13] said God, 'and after that they will come out, and serve Me in this place.' [Ex. 3:12]

⁸"He gave him the covenant of circumcision. So Abraham became the father of Isaac, and circumcised him the eighth day. Isaac became the father of Jacob, and Jacob became the father of the twelve patriarchs.

⁹"Moved with jealousy against Yosef, the patriarchs sold him into Egypt. But God was with him, ¹⁰delivered him out of all his afflictions, and gave him favor and wisdom before Pharaoh, king of Egypt. He made him governor over Egypt and over all his house.

¹¹"Now a famine and great affliction came over all the land of Egypt and Kanaan. Our fathers found no food, ¹²but when Jacob heard that there was grain in Egypt, he sent out our fathers the first time. ¹³On the second time Yosef was made known to his brothers, and Yosef's family was disclosed to Pharaoh. ¹⁴Yosef sent, and summoned his father Jacob and all his relatives, seventy-five souls. ¹⁵Jacob went down into Egypt, and he died, he and our fathers. ¹⁶And they were brought back to Shehem, and laid in the tomb that Abraham bought for a price in silver from the children of Hamor in Shehem.

[17]"But as the time of the promise approached — which God had sworn to Abraham — the people grew and multiplied in Egypt, [18]until there arose a different king, who did not know Yosef. [Ex. 1:8] [19]This one schemed against our people, mistreated our fathers, and forced them to abandon their infants so that they would not live. [Ex. 1:10] [20]At that time, Moses was born, and was pleasing to God. He was nourished three months in his father's house. [21]When he was cast out, the daughter of Pharaoh took him up [Ex. 2:5], and brought him up as her own son.

[22]"Moses was instructed in all the wisdom of the Egyptians. He was mighty in words and deeds. [23]But when he reached forty years, it arose in his heart to care for his people, the children of Israel. [24]Seeing one of them suffer wrong, he defended him. He avenged the one who was oppressed, striking the Egyptian. [25]He supposed that his people would understand that God was giving them deliverance by his hand, but they did not understand.

[26]"The next day, he again appeared to them as they fought, and urged them to be at peace, saying, 'Men, you[+] are brothers. Why do you[+] wrong one another?' [27]But the one who was wronging his neighbor repulsed him, saying, 'Who made you a ruler and a judge over us? [28]Do you want to kill me, as you killed the Egyptian yesterday?' [Ex. 2:13, 14] [29]Moses fled because of what was said, and became a stranger in the land of Midyan. [Ex. 2:15,22] There he became the father of two sons.

[30]"When forty years had passed, an angel of the Everpresent Lord appeared to him in the wilderness of Mount Sinai, in a flame of fire in a bush. [Ex. 3:1] [31]When Moses saw it, he wondered at the sight. As he came close to see, the voice of the Everpresent Lord came to him, [32]'I am the God of your fathers, the God of Abraham, the God of Isaac, and the God of Jacob.' [Ex. 3:6] Moses trembled, and did not dare to look. [33]The Everpresent Lord said to him, 'Take your sandals off your feet, because the place where you are standing is holy ground. [Ex. 3:5] [34]I have surely seen the affliction of My people who are in Egypt, and have heard their groaning. I have come down to deliver them. [Ex. 3:7] Now come, I will send you to Egypt.' [Ex. 3:10]

[35]"This Moses — whom they disowned in saying, 'Who made you a ruler and a judge?' [Ex. 2:14] — God sent him as both a ruler and a deliverer by the hand of the angel who appeared to him in the bush. [36]This man led them out, having worked signs and wonders in Egypt, in the Red Sea, and in the wilderness for forty years. [37]This is the Moses who said to the children of Israel, 'God will raise up a prophet like me for you[+] from among your[+] brothers. You[+] are to listen to him.' [Deut. 18:15,18] [38]This is the one who was in the assembly in the wilderness [Dt. 9:10; 10:4; 18:16], with the angel

---

7:14 "seventy-five" The Hebrew Masoretic text always says seventy. The LXX has seventy-five in Gen. 46:27 and Ex. 1:5. Lightfoot suggested that the larger number includes, because of Gen. 50:23, the grandchildren of Yosef who were born in Egypt. The reasoning is that, as Jacob says in Gen. 48:5, "And now your two sons, who were born to you in the land of Egypt before I came to you in Egypt, are mine..." A Commentary of the New Testament from the Talmud and Hebraica, Vol. 4, Pp. 73-75

Rashi, Num. 26:59, says that Yokheved, the mother of Moses, is included in the number of those who came into Egypt, because she was conceived outside of Egypt, but born in Egypt.

7:23,25 "his people," literally "his brothers"

7:37 "There has not again arisen in Israel a prophet like Moses or one who beholds His image." (Yigdal 7)

that spoke to him on Mount Sinai, and with our fathers. He received living words to give to us. [39]Our fathers did not want to be obedient to him, but rejected him, and turned back in their hearts to Egypt. [40]They said to Aaron, 'Make us gods which will go before us, because as for this Moses who led us out of the land of Egypt, we don't know what has become of him.' [Ex. 32:1,23] [41]They made a calf in those days, brought a sacrifice to the idol. and rejoiced in the works of their hands. [42]But God turned and gave them up to serve the forces of heaven, as it is written in the book of the prophets, 'Did you[+] offer slain animals and sacrifices to Me forty years in the wilderness, O house of Israel? [43]You[+] took up the tent of Molekh, the star of your[+] god Reifan, the images which you[+] made to bow down to. I will carry you[+] away beyond Babel.' [Am. 5:25, 26 LXX]

[44]"Our fathers had the tent of the testimony in the wilderness, even as the One who spoke to Moses commanded him to make it according to the pattern that he had seen. [Ex. 25:9] [45]That is what our fathers also received and brought in with Yeshua when they entered into the possession of the nations whom God drove out before our fathers. It was there until the days of David, [46]who found favor in the sight of God, and asked to find a dwelling for the God of Jacob.

[47]"But Solomon built him a house. [48]However, the Most High does not live in temples made with hands. As the prophet says, [49]'Heaven is My throne, and the earth a footstool for My feet. What kind of house will you[+] build Me?' says the Everpresent Lord. 'Or what is the place of My rest? [50]Did not My hand make all these things?' [Is. 66:1,2]

[51]"Stiff-necked and uncircumcised in heart and ears! [Lev. 26:41; Dt. 10:16; 30:6; Jer. 4:4] You[+] always resist the Ruakh Kodesh. You[+] are like your[+] fathers. [52]Which of the prophets did your[+] fathers not persecute? They killed those who foretold the coming of the Righteous One, of whom you[+] have now become betrayers and murderers. [53]You[+] received the Law as decrees through angels, and did not keep it." [Dt. 33:2 LXX]

[54]Now when they heard these things, their hearts were furious, and they gnashed at him with their teeth. [55]But he, being full of the Ruakh Kodesh, looked up steadfastly into heaven, and saw the glory of God with Yeshua standing on the right hand of God. [56]He said, "Look, I see the heavens opened, and the Son of Adam standing at the right hand of God."

[57]But they cried out with a loud voice, stopped their ears, and rushed at him with a common purpose. [58]They threw him out of the city, and stoned him. The witnesses put their clothes at the feet of a young man named Sha'ul. [59]They stoned Stephen as he called out, "Lord Yeshua, receive my Spirit!" [60]He knelt down, and cried with a loud voice, "Lord, do not hold this sin against them!" When he had said this, he fell asleep.

8 [1]Sha'ul was in agreement with killing him.

A great persecution arose in that day against the community which was in Yerushala'im. They were all scattered abroad throughout the regions of Judea and Shomron, except for the ambassadors. [2]Devout men buried Stephen, and lamented greatly over him. [3]But Sha'ul ravaged the community, entering house after house, and dragging both men and women off to prison.

[4]So those who were scattered abroad proclaimed the word wherever they passed through. [5]Philip went down to the city of Shomron, and proclaimed the Messiah to them. [6]When they heard, and

---

7:45 The Greek is *Iesou*, i.e. Yeshua bin Nun, commonly called "Joshua" in English.

saw the miracles which he did, the crowds listened with a common purpose to the things that were spoken by Philip, [7]because unclean spirits came out of many of those who had them. They came out crying with a loud voice. Many who had been paralyzed and lame were healed. [8]There was great joy in that city.

[9]But there was a certain man named Shimon who used to practice magic in the city, and amazed the people of Shomron, making himself out to be someone great. [10]From the least to the greatest, they all listened to him, saying, "This man is what is called the great power of God." [11]They listened to him, because he had amazed them for a long time with his feats of magic. [12]But when they believed Philip proclaiming good news about God's kingdom and the name of Yeshua the Messiah, they were immersed, both men and women. [13]Shimon himself also believed. Being immersed, he continued with Philip. Seeing signs and great miracles occuring, he was amazed.

[14]Now when the ambassadors who were at Yerushala'im heard that Shomron had received the word of God, they sent Kefa and Yoḥanan to them. [15]When they had come down, they prayed for them that they might receive the Ruakh Kodesh, [16]for the Spirit had not yet come upon any of them. They had only been immersed in the name of the Lord Yeshua. [17]Then they laid their hands on them, and they received the Ruakh Kodesh. [18]Now when Shimon saw that the Ruakh Kodesh was given through the laying on of the hands of the ambassadors, he offered them money, [19]saying, "Give me also this power, so that anyone on whom I lay my hands may receive the Ruakh Kodesh."

[20]But Kefa said to him, "May your silver perish with you, because you think you can obtain the gift of God through wealth! [21]You have neither part nor portion in this matter, because your heart is not straightforward before God. [22]Therefore turn away from this wickedness of yours, and entreat the Lord if the intent of your heart may then be forgiven you. [23]For I see you are in the gall of bitterness and in the bondage of transgression."

[24]Shimon answered, "Pray for me to the Everpresent Lord that none of the things which you[+] have spoken happen to me."

[25]When they had borne witness and spoken the word of the Everpresent Lord, they then returned towards Yerushala'im and proclaimed the good news in many villages of the people of Shomron. [26]But an angel of the Everpresent Lord spoke to Philip, saying, "Arise, and go toward the south to the way that goes down from Yerushala'im to Aza." This is a desert.

[27]He arose and went. And there was a man of Kush, a eunuch of great authority under Kandakeh, Queen of the Kushim. He was in charge of all her treasure, and had come to Yerushala'im to worship. [28]He was returning, sitting in his chariot reading Isaiah the prophet.

[29]The Spirit said to Philip, "Go near, and join yourself to this chariot."

[30]Philip ran to him, heard him reading Isaiah the prophet, and said, "Do you understand what you are reading?"

[31]He said, "How can I, unless someone explains it to me?" He urged Philip to come up and sit with him. [32]Now the passage of the Scripture which he was reading was this: "He was led as a sheep to the slaughter. As a lamb before its shearer is silent, so he does not open his mouth. [33]In his humiliation and judgment, he was taken away. Who will declare his generation? For his life is taken from the earth." [Is. 53:7,8]

[34]The eunuch responded to Philip, "Who is the prophet talking about? About himself, or about someone else?"

[35]Beginning from this scripture, Philip opened his mouth and proclaimed Yeshua to him. [36]As they went on the way, they came to some water, and the eunuch said, "Look, here is water. What prevents me from being immersed?"

[37] [38]He commanded the chariot to stand still, and they both went down into the water, both Philip and the eunuch. Then he immersed him. [39]When they came up out of the water, the Spirit of the Everpresent Lord caught Philip away, and the eunuch did not see him any more. He went on his way rejoicing. [40]But Philip was found at Ashdod. Passing through, he proclaimed the good news in all the cities until he came to Kaesarea.

[9] [1]But Sha'ul, still breathing threats and slaughter against the disciples of the Lord, went to the Kohen Gadol. [2]He asked for letters from him to the assemblies of Damascus, so that if he found any who were of the Way, whether men or women, he might bring them bound to Yerushala'im. [3]As he traveled and was approaching Damascus, a light from heaven suddenly shone around him. [4]He fell upon the ground, and heard a voice saying to him, "Sha'ul, Sha'ul, why do you persecute me?"

[5]He said, "Who are you, Lord?"

The Lord said, "I am Yeshua, whom you are persecuting. [6]But rise up, enter into the city, and you will be told what you must do."

[7]The men who traveled with him stood speechless, hearing the sound, but seeing no one. [8]Sha'ul arose from the ground, but when his eyes were opened, he saw nothing. They led him by the hand, and brought him into Damascus. [9]He was without sight for three days, and neither ate nor drank.

[10]Now there was a certain disciple at Damascus named Hananyah. The Lord said to him in a vision, "Hananyah."

He said, "Here I am, Lord."

[11]The Lord said to him, "Arise, and go to the street which is called Straight, and ask in the house of Judah for one named Sha'ul, a man of Tarsus — for he is praying, [12]and has seen in a vision a man named Hananyah coming in and laying his hands on him so that he might receive his sight."

[13]But Hananyah answered, "Lord, I have heard from many about this man, how much evil he did to those at Yerushala'im who belong to you. [14]Here he has authority from the chief Kohanim to arrest all who call on your name."

[15]But the Lord said to him, "Go, because he is my chosen vessel to carry my name before the Gentiles, kings, and the children of Israel. [16]For I will show him how much he must suffer for my name's sake."

[17]Hananyah went and entered the house. Laying his hands on him, he said, "Brother Sha'ul, the Lord, who appeared to you on the road by which you came, has sent me so that you may receive your sight, and be filled with the Ruakh Kodesh." [18]And immediately something flake-like fell from his eyes, and he received his sight. He arose and was immersed. [19]He took food and was strengthened.

8:37 is not in the UBS.

9:2 "this Way" refers to those following Yeshua. cf. Yhn. 14:6, Gen. 18:19, Is. 40:3, etc.

9:5 The Textus Receptus adds, "It is hard for you to kick against the goads," which would relate to Ps. 32:9, cf. Mid. Tehillim 32:3.

Sha'ul stayed several days with the disciples who were at Damascus. [20]Right away, he was proclaiming Yeshua in the meetingplaces — that he is the Son of God. [21]All who heard him were amazed, and said, "Isn't this the one who in Yerushala'im destroyed those who called on this name? And he came here intending to bring them bound to the chief Kohanim!"

[22]But Sha'ul was increasingly empowered, and confounded the sectarian Jews who lived at Damascus by proving that this is the Messiah. [23]When many days had passed, the sectarian Jews conspired together to kill him, [24]but their plot became known to Sha'ul. They watched the gates both day and night in order to kill him. [25]But the disciples took him by night, and let him down through the wall, lowering him in a basket.

[26]When Sha'ul had come to Yerushala'im, he tried to join himself to the disciples, but they were all afraid of him, not believing that he was a disciple. [27]Bar Nabba, however, took him, brought him to the ambassadors, and told them how he had seen the Lord on the way and that he had spoken to him. He also told them how he had spoken boldly at Damascus in the name of Yeshua.

[28]He was with them into Yerushala'im, going in and coming out, [29]speaking boldly in the name of the Lord. He spoke and argued with the Hellenistic Jews, but they were seeking to kill him. [30]When the brethren became aware of it, they brought him down to Kaesarea, and sent him off to Tarsus. [31]So the communities throughout all Judea, the Galil, and Shomron had peace, and were built up. They grew in number, walking in the fear of the Everpresent Lord and in the comfort of the Ruakh Kodesh.

[32]It happened that as Kefa went throughout all those parts, he came down also to those who lived at Lud and belonged to God. [33]There he found a certain man named Aineeas, who had been bedridden for eight years, because he was paralyzed. [34]Kefa said to him, "Aineeas, Yeshua the Messiah heals you. Get up! and put your bed in order." Immediately he arose. [35]All who lived at Lud and in Sharon saw him, and they turned to the Lord.

[36]Now at Yaffo, there was a certain disciple named Tavita, which is translated as "gazelle". This woman was full of good deeds and acts of mercy which she did. [37]But in those days she became weak and died. When they had washed her, they laid her in an upper chamber. [38]Since Lud was near Yaffo, the disciples, hearing that Kefa was there, sent two men to him, imploring him not to delay in coming to them. [39]Kefa got up and went with them. When he had come, they brought him into the upper chamber. All the widows stood by him weeping and showing the coats and garments which Tavita had made while she was with them. [40]Kefa put them all out, and knelt down and prayed. Turning to the body, he said, "Tavita, get up." She opened her eyes, and when she saw Kefa, she sat up. [41]He gave her his hand, and raised her up. Calling the widows and those who belong to God, he brought her in alive. [42]It became known throughout all Yaffo, and many believed in the Lord. [43]So he stayed many days in Yaffo with a certain Shimon, a tanner.

10 [1]Now there was a certain man in Kaesarea named Kornelius, a centurion from the military unit called "the Italian". [2]He was a devout man who feared God with all his household, generously did deeds of compassion for the people, and always prayed to God. [3]At about the ninth hour of the day, he clearly saw in a vision an angel of God coming to him, and saying to him, "Kornelius!"

[4]He looked intently at him and, being frightened, said, "What is it, lord?"

He said to him, "Your prayers and your deeds of compassion have ascended for a remembrance before God. [5]Now send men to Yaffo, and get Shimon, who is called Kefa. [6]He is staying with a certain Shimon, a tanner, whose house is by the seaside."

[7]When the angel who spoke to him had gone, Kornelius called two of his household servants and a devout soldier from those who continually waited on him. [8]Having explained everything to them, he sent them to Yaffo.

[9]Now on the next day, as they were on their journey and approaching the city, Kefa went up on the housetop to pray at about noon. [10]He became hungry and wanted to eat, but while they were preparing, he fell into a trance. [11]He saw heaven opened and a certain object descending to him, like a great sheet let down by four corners unto the earth. [12]In it there were all kinds of four-footed animals of the earth, wild animals, reptiles, and birds of the heaven. [13]A voice came to him, "Rise, Kefa, kill and eat."

[14]But Kefa said, "Not so, Lord; for I have never eaten anything that is unholy or unclean." [Lev. 10:10; Ezek. 4:14]

[15]A voice came to him again the second time, "Do not treat as unholy what God has cleansed." [16]This happened three times, and immediately the object was taken up into heaven. [17]Now while Kefa was very perplexed in himself about what the vision which he had seen might mean, the men who were sent by Kornelius, having asked for the house of Shimon, stood before the gate. [18]They called and asked whether Shimon who was called Kefa was staying there as a guest. [19]While Kefa was pondering the vision, the Spirit said to him, "Listen, three men are looking for you. [20]So stand up, get down and go with them with assurance, because I have sent them."

[21]Kefa went down to the men, and said, "Look, I am the one you[+] are seeking. Why have you[+] come?"

[22]They said, "Kornelius, a centurion, a righteous man, one who fears God, and is well spoken of by the entire Jewish nation, was directed by a holy angel to invite you to his house, and to listen to what you say." [23]So he called them in and gave them lodging.

On the next day Kefa arose and left with them, and some of the brothers from Yaffo accompanied him. [24]They entered into Kaesarea on the following day. Kornelius was waiting for them, having called together his relatives and his close friends. [25]And as Kefa was entering, Kornelius met him, fell down at his feet, and bowed down to him. [26]But Kefa raised him up, saying, "Stand up! I myself am only a man." [27]As he talked with him, he went in and found many gathered together. [28]He said to them, "You[+] yourselves know how it is unacceptable for a man who is a Jew to join himself to or come to one of an oppressing nation, but God has shown me that I should not call any man unholy or unclean. [29]So when I was sent for, I came without complaint. So I am asking, why did you[+] send for me?"

10:10-14 "There are those who say that every animal that is unclean in this age, the Holy One, blessed be He will make it clean in the time to come." (Mid. Psalms 146.4)

10:15,28; 11:9 God spoke to Aaron after the death of his sons, and said, you are "to put a difference between the holy and common/unholy/profane, and between the unclean and the clean." (Lev. 10:10) God established an important difference between what is set apart to Him and what is not. As a people, Israel was set apart to God.

10:28 In LXX, *allophulo* usually designates the Philistines or a similar people. It is not a general term for all nations. (e.g.Ex. 34:15, Judg. 3:3,, 2Sam. 1:20)

[30]Kornelius said, "From four days ago until this hour, I have been fasting. At the ninth hour, I was praying in my house. Then a man stood before me in shining clothing! [31]He said, 'Kornelius, your prayer is heard, and your deeds of compassion are remembered in the sight of God. [32]So send to Yaffo and summon Shimon, who is called Kefa. He is lodging by the seaside in the house of Shimon, a tanner.' [33]So I sent to you at once, and it was good of you to come. Now therefore we are all here present in the sight of God to hear everything that has been commanded you by God."

[34]Kefa opened his mouth and said, "I perceive that God truly does not regard outward appearance, [35]but in every nation the one who fears Him and works justice [Mic. 6:8] is acceptable to Him. [Is. 56:6-7] [36]He sent the word to the children of Israel, proclaiming the good news of peace by Yeshua the Messiah — he is Lord of all. [37]You+ yourselves know that spoken word which was proclaimed throughout all Judea, beginning from the Galil, after the immersion which Yoḥanan proclaimed. [38]You+ know how God anointed Yeshua from Natzrat with the Ruakh Kodesh and with power. And he went about doing good and healing all who were oppressed by the Enemy, because God was with him. [39]We are witnesses of everything he did, both in the Judean countryside and in Yerushala'im. They also killed him, hanging him on a tree. [40]God raised him up the third day [Hos. 6:2, Ex. 19:11], and caused him to be seen, [41]not by all the people, but by witnesses who were chosen before by God — to us, who ate and drank with him after he rose from the dead. [42]He commanded us to proclaim to the people and to testify that this is the one who is appointed by God as the Judge of the living and the dead. [43]All the prophets testify about him, that through his name everyone who believes in him will receive forgiveness of sins."

[44]While Kefa was still speaking these words, the Ruakh Kodesh fell on all those who heard the word. [45]The believers from the circumcision — all those who came with Kefa — were amazed because the gift of the Ruakh Kodesh was also poured out on the Gentiles. [46]For they heard them speaking in other languages and magnifying God.

Then Kefa responded, [47]"Can any man forbid the water for these — who have received the Ruakh Kodesh even as we did — so that they should not be immersed?" [48]He directed them to be immersed in the name of Yeshua the Messiah. Then they asked him to stay a few days.

11 [1]Now the ambassadors and the brothers who were in Judea heard that the Gentiles had also received the word of God. [2]When Kefa had come up to Yerushala'im, some who were of the circumcision argued with him, [3]saying, "You went in to uncircumcised men, and ate with them!"

[4]But Kefa began to explain to them the sequence, saying, [5]"I was in the city of Yaffo praying, and in a trance I saw a vision: a particular object, descending like a great sheet, let down from heaven by four corners. It came down right to me. [6]When I had looked intently and was wondering about it, I saw the four-footed animals of the earth, wild animals, creeping things, and birds of the heaven. [7]I also heard a voice saying to me, 'Rise Kefa, kill and eat.' [8]But I said, 'Not so, Lord, for nothing unholy

---

10:40 "on the third day" Esther told Mordecai, "Go, gather all the Jews who are present in Shushan, and fast for me; neither eat nor drink for three days, night and day. My maids and I will fast likewise. And so I will go to the king, which is against the law; and if I perish, I perish!" ...Now it happened on the third day that Esther put on her royal robes and stood in the inner court of the king's palace..." (Est. 4:16,5:1) She said, "three days, night and day," and then went on the third day.

or unclean has ever entered into my mouth.' ⁹But a voice answered me the second time out of heaven, 'What God has cleansed, you are not to treat as unholy.' ¹⁰This happened three times, and everything was drawn up again into heaven.

¹¹"At that moment, three men who had been sent to me from Kaesarea stood before the house where I was. ¹²The Spirit told me to go with them without misgivings. These six brothers also accompanied me, and we entered into the man's house. ¹³He told us how he had seen an angel standing in his house and saying to him, 'Send to Yaffo, and get Shimon who is called Kefa. ¹⁴He will speak to you words by which you will be saved, you and all your household.'

¹⁵"As I began to speak, the Ruakh Kodesh fell on them, even as on us at the beginning. ¹⁶I remembered the word of the Lord, how he said, 'Yohanan indeed immersed in water, but you⁺ will be immersed in the Ruakh Kodesh.' ¹⁷So if God gave to them the same gift as to us when we believed in the Lord Yeshua the Messiah, who was I that I could withstand God?"

¹⁸As they heard these things, they were quiet. Then they glorified God, saying, "Then God has also given to the Gentiles repentance to life!"

¹⁹Now those who were scattered abroad (by the persecution that arose after Stephen) traveled as far as Phoenikia, Kyprus, and Antioch, speaking the word to no one except to Jews only. ²⁰Now there were some of them, men of Kyprus and Kyrene, who, when they had come to Antioch, spoke to the Hellenistic Jews, proclaiming the Lord Yeshua. ²¹The hand of the Lord was with them, and a great number believed and turned back to the Lord.

11:20 *Hellenistas* appears also in 6:1 and 9:29. It seems to mean Jews who have adopted Greek ways. This is the sense given in 2Mac. 4:13.

11:26 We are told that the disciples were first called "chrestianous" in Antioch. This term also appears, in the singular, in Acts 26:28 and 1Pet. 4:16. "In all three NT passages the uncorrected Codex Alef reads 'Chrestian.' We know from many sources that this variant was widely current in the 2d century. ... On the whole it seems probable that this designation, though bestowed in error, was the original one." ("Christian," ISBE, Vol. 1, The Howard-Severance Company, Chicago, 1915, P. 622)

This name was not something which the disciples called themselves, but rather something which Gentile unbelievers called them. To Gentile unbelievers, *christos* simply meant "rubbed with an ointment." It was not a name; it was not even a noun. It was not a term that referred to a person. *Chrestos*, on the other hand, meaning "good, kind, useful," was a common slave name. The Gentile unbelievers thought that the disciples followed after someone named Chrestos.

Historical sources — Latin, Greek, and Christian — confirm this. For example, Suetonius refers to the edict of the Emperor Claudius in the year 49, saying, "Since the Jews constantly made disturbance at the instigation of Chrestus, he expelled them from Rome." In the second half of the second century, Justin, in his First Apology, refers to *christiani* as the name by which the disciples were accused.

In 1 Kefa 4:14-16, there is reference to both the incorrect name by which they were accused and also to the meaning of the word. I.e., 'They incorrectly say that we follow Chrestos [some person], but in reality we follow *chrestos* [what is good].' For more detail, see "A Little Case of Mistaken Identity" in my Copernicus and the Jews.

²²The report concerning them came to the ears of the community which was in Yerushala'im. They sent out Bar Nabba to go as far as Antioch. ²³When he had come and had seen the grace of God, he rejoiced. He exhorted them all that they should continue in the Lord with heartfelt purpose. ²⁴For he was a good man, and full of the Ruakh Kodesh and faith. And a sizable multitude were added to the Lord.

²⁵Bar Nabba went out to Tarsus to look for Sha'ul. ²⁶When he had found him, he brought him to Antioch. For a whole year they came together with the community, and taught many people. (The disciples were first called "followers of Chrestus" in Antioch.)

²⁷Now prophets came down from Yerushala'im to Antioch in these days. ²⁸One of them named Agav stood up and indicated by the Spirit that there would be a great famine all over the world, which happened in the days of Claudius. ²⁹And each of them, in accordance with how each one prospered, determined to send relief to the brethren who lived in Judea. ³⁰Then they did this, sending it to the elders by the hands of Bar Nabba and Sha'ul.

12 ¹Now about that time, Herod the king stretched out his hands to oppress some of the community. ²He killed Jacob, the brother of Yohanan, with the sword. ³When he saw that it pleased the sectarian Jews, he proceeded to arrest Kefa also. This was during the days of Unleavened Bread. ⁴When he had arrested him, he put him in prison, and delivered him to four squads of four soldiers each to guard him, intending to bring him out to the people after Pesakh. ⁵So Kefa was kept in the prison, but the community made constant prayer to God for him.

⁶The same night when Herod was about to bring him out, Kefa was sleeping between two soldiers, bound with two chains. Sentries in front of the door guarded the prison. ⁷Then an angel of the Everpresent Lord stood by him, and a light shone in the cell! He struck Kefa on the side, and woke him up, saying, "Stand up quickly." His chains fell off from his hands. ⁸The angel said to him, "Get dressed and put on your sandals." He did so. He said to him, "Put on your cloak, and follow me." ⁹Then he went out and followed him. He did not know that what was being done by the angel was real, but thought he was seeing a vision. ¹⁰When they were past the first and the second guard, they came to the iron gate that leads into the city, which opened to them by itself. They went out and went down one street, and at that moment the angel left him.

¹¹When Kefa had come to himself, he said, "Now I truly understand that the Everpresent Lord has sent out His angel and delivered me out of the hand of Herod, and from everything the people of the sectarian Jews were expecting." ¹²Pondering that, he came to the house of Miryam, the mother of Yohanan who was called Mark. Many were gathered together there and were praying. ¹³When Kefa

12:1 There is an interesting passage in Tal. Sotah 41a that refers to the Idumean ancestry of either this Herod or his son Herod Agrippa of Acts 25:13-26:32. "As it is said, 'At the end of every seven years, at the set time...' [Dt. 31:10] The assembly ḥazzan takes a Torah scroll and gives it to the head of the assembly, and the head of the assembly gives it to the Ruler. He gives it to the High Priest, and the High Priest gives it to the King. The King stands and receives it, but reads sitting. King Agrippa stood and received it and read standing, and the Sages praised him. When he came to, 'You may not put a foreigner over you' [Dt. 17:15], tears flowed from his eyes. They said to him, 'Do not fear, Agrippa, you are our brother. You are our brother.'"

knocked at the door of the gate, a servant girl named Rhoda came to answer. [14]When she recognized Kefa's voice, she was so full of joy that she did not open the gate, but ran inside and reported that Kefa was standing in front of the gate.

[15]They said to her, "You're crazy!" But she insisted that it was so. They said, "It is his angel." [16]But Kefa continued knocking. When they had opened it, they saw him, and were astonished. [17]Motioning with his hand for them to be silent, he told them how the Everpresent Lord had brought him out of the prison. He said, "Tell these things to Jacob and the brethren." Then he departed, and went to another place.

[18]Now as soon as it was day, there was more than a little commotion among the soldiers about what had become of Kefa. [19]When Herod had searched for him and did not find him, he examined the guards, and commanded that they should be put to death. He went down from Judea to Kaesarea, and stayed there.

[20]Now Herod was very angry with the people of Tzor and Tzidon. They came to him with a common purpose, and, having made Blastus, the king's administrator, their friend, they asked for peace, because their country depended on the king's country for food. [21]On an appointed day, Herod dressed himself in royal apparel, sat on the throne, and gave a speech to them. [22]The people shouted, "The voice of a god, and not of a man!" [23]At that moment, an angel of the Everpresent Lord struck him, because he did not give God the glory. Then he died, having been eaten away by worms. [2Mac. 9:1-5-12]

[24]But the word of God grew and multiplied. [25]Bar Nabba and Sha'ul returned to Yerushala'im when they had fulfilled their responsibility. They also took with them Yohanan who was called Mark.

13 [1]Now in the community that was at Antioch there were some prophets and teachers: Bar Nabba, Shimon who was called "the black," Lukius of Kyrene, Menahem who was brought up with Herod (the ruler of a fourth of the province), and Sha'ul. [2]As they served the Lord and fasted, the Ruakh Kodesh said, "Set apart both Bar Nabba and Sha'ul for me, for the work to which I have called them."

[3]When they had fasted, prayed, and laid their hands on them, they then sent them away. [4]So being sent out by the Ruakh Kodesh, they went down to Seleukia. From there they sailed to Kyprus. [5]When they were at Salamis, they proclaimed the word of God in the Jewish meetingplaces. They also had Yohanan as their helper.

[6]When they had gone through the island to Paphos, they found a certain magian, a false prophet, a Jew whose name was Bar Yeshua. [7]He was with the proconsul, Sergios Paulos, a man of understanding. This man summoned Bar Nabba and Sha'ul, and sought to hear the word of God. [8]But the magian

---

12:15 Bar Kappara said: "An angel came down in the likeness of Moses and they [men sent by Pharaoh] grabbed the angel, and left Moses to flee.'" (Mid. Song Rabbah 7:9; see also Mid. Dt. Rabbah 2:29.)

12:23 Josephus also describes this in Antiq. 19:343-50 [19.8.2.343-350]

13:6,8 *magian* as in Mt. 2:1

13:8-9 It was not uncommon for people to have more than one name which they used. Tal. Gittin 11b says "the names of most Jews who are outside the land are like the names of idolators." Tos. Git. 6:7 adds that some people used one name when in the Galilee and another name when in Judea.

Elymas— for that is the translation of his name — opposed them, seeking to turn aside the proconsul from the faith. [9]But Sha'ul, who is also called Paulos, filled with the Ruakh Kodesh, fastened his eyes on him, [10]and said, "You son of the Enemy, full of all deceit and all fraud, you enemy of all righteousness, will you not cease distorting the straight ways of the Everpresent Lord? [11]Now the hand of the Everpresent Lord is indeed upon you, and you will be blind, not seeing the sun for some time!" Immediately there fell on him a mist and darkness. He went around seeking someone to lead him by the hand. [12]When the proconsul saw what happened, then he believed, being amazed at the teaching of the Lord.

[13]Now Paulos and those with him set sail from Paphos, and came to Perga in Pamphylia. Yohanan left them and returned to Yerushala'im. [14]But passing on from Perga, they came to Antioch of Pisidia. They went into the meetingplace on the day of Shabbat, and sat down. [15]After the reading of the Torah and the Prophets, the rulers of the meetingplace sent to them saying, "Brothers, speak if you[+] have any word of exhortation for the people."

[16]Paulos stood up, motioned with his hand, and said, "Men of Israel and you[+] who fear God, listen. [17]The God of this people Israel chose our fathers, and lifted up the people when they lived as foreigners in the land of Egypt. Then He led them out of it with an outstretched arm. [18]He cared for them in the wilderness for a period of about forty years. [Dt. 1:31 LXX] [19]And when He had destroyed seven nations in the land of Kana'an, He gave them their land for an inheritance. [20]Then after these things He gave them judges about four hundred fifty years, until Shmuel the prophet. [21]Afterward they asked for a king, and for forty years God gave to them Sha'ul the son of Kish, a man of the tribe of Benjamin. [22]When He had removed him, He raised up David to be their king. He also bore witness to him, saying, 'I have found David the son of Yishai, a man after My heart, who will do all My will.' [1Sam. 13:14]

[23]"From this man's seed, in accordance with God's promise, He has brought a savior to Israel, Yeshua. [24]Before his coming, when Yohanan had first proclaimed to Israel the immersion of repentance, [25]as Yohanan was fulfilling his course, he said, 'Whom do you[+] suppose that I am? I am not the one, but indeed one comes after me, and I am not worthy to untie the sandals of his feet.'

[26]"Men, brothers, children of the family of Abraham, and those among you[+] who fear God, the word of this salvation is sent forth to us. [27]For those who dwell in Yerushala'im and their rulers — because they did not know him nor the voices of the prophets which are read every Shabbat — fulfilled the prophecies by condemning him. [28]Though they found no cause for death, they still asked Pilate to have him killed. [29]When they had finished all the things written about him, they took him down from the tree, and laid him in a tomb. [30]But God raised him from the dead, [31]and he was seen for many days by those who came up with him from the Galil to Yerushala'im. They are now his witnesses to the people. [32]We bring you[+] the good news of the promise made to the Fathers; [33]God

13:15 At that time, even as today, the practice was to read the Torah portion and then a related haftarah portion from the Writings or) Prophets.

13:33 This is the only quotation in Scripture that is designated by a chapter number, though chapter numbers were not assigned until many centuries later. The quotation is from what we have as the second >>

has fulfilled the same to us, their children, in that He raised up Yeshua. As it is also written in the first psalm, 'You are My Son. Today I have brought you forth.' [Ps. 2:7]

³⁴"Now He has spoken in this way about raising him up from the dead, no longer about to turn to decay: 'I will give you⁺ the holy and sure mercies of David.' [Is. 55:3] ³⁵Therefore He also says in another psalm, 'You will not allow Your Holy One to see decay.' [Ps. 16:10] ³⁶Indeed David, after he had served the purpose of God in his own generation, fell asleep, was gathered to his fathers, and saw decay. ³⁷But the one whom God raised up saw no decay.

³⁸"Therefore brothers, be it known to you⁺ that forgiveness of sins through this man is proclaimed to you⁺. ³⁹And by him, everyone who believes is acquitted from all things, from which you⁺ could not be acquitted by the Law of Moses. ⁴⁰Therefore beware, so that what is spoken in the prophets does not come upon you⁺: ⁴¹'Look you⁺ scoffers, wonder and perish. For I work a work in your⁺ days, a work which you⁺ will not believe at all, if one were to declare it to you⁺.'" [Hab. 1:5]

⁴²So when they were going out of the meetingplace, they insistently asked that these words might be proclaimed to them the next Shabbat. ⁴³Now when the assembly broke up, many of the Jews and many of the devout proselytes followed Paulos and Bar Nabba. Speaking to them, they urged them to continue in the grace of God.

⁴⁴The next Shabbat, almost the whole city was gathered together to hear the word of God. ⁴⁵But when some Jews saw the crowds, they were filled with zealous rivalry, and spoke against and maligned the things which were spoken by Paulos. ⁴⁶Paulos and Bar Nabba spoke out boldly and said, "It was necessary that God's word should be spoken to you⁺ first. Since indeed you⁺ push it away from yourselves, and judge yourselves unworthy of eternal life, look, we are turning to the Gentiles. ⁴⁷For this is what the Everpresent Lord has commanded us, 'I have set you for a light to the Gentiles, that you should be salvation to the uttermost parts of the earth.'" [Is. 42:6, 49:6]

⁴⁸As the Gentiles heard this, they were glad, and glorified the word of the Everpresent Lord. As many as were set for eternal life believed. ⁴⁹The word of the Lord was spread abroad throughout all the region, ⁵⁰but some Jews stirred up the devout prominent women and the chief men of the city. They stirred up a persecution against Paulos and Bar Nabba, and forced them out beyond their borders. ⁵¹But they shook off the dust of their feet against them, and came to Iconium. ⁵²The disciples were filled with joy and the Ruakh Kodesh.

14 ¹They entered together into the Jewish meetingplace in Iconium, and spoke in such a way that a great multitude both of Jews and of Greeks believed. ²But those Jews who disbelieved stirred up and embittered the souls of the Gentiles against the brothers. ³In spite of this, they stayed there

psalm. The manuscripts, however, seem to indicate that the original text of Acts said "the first psalm," i.e. the beginning of the psalms, but later scribes changed it to "the second psalm" to make it consistent with what they knew. The Talmud, however, points out that our first and second psalms were traditionally considered at that time to be one. "Note that those eighteen psalms are really nineteen. 'Happy is the man' [Ps. 1:1] and 'Why are the nations in an uproar?' [Ps. 2:1] they are one chapter." (Tal. Berachot 9b, cf. Jer. Tal. Taanit 9a) For a discussion of the rabbinic and patristic evidence, see Metzger, A Textual Commentary, Pp. 412-414.

13:47 Is. 42:6LXX and 49:6LXX also include the phrase, "to be a covenant to the family/ people".

a long time, speaking boldly in the Lord. He testified to the word of His grace, granting signs and wonders to be done by their hands. [4]But the multitude of the city was divided. Part sided with those Jews, and part with the ambassadors.

[5]When some of both the Gentiles and the Jews, with their rulers, were rushing to mistreat and stone them, [6]they became aware of it, and fled to the cities of Lykaonia, Lystra, Derbe, and the surrounding region. [7]There they proclaimed the good news.

[8]At Lystra a certain man sat without any strength in his feet, a cripple from his mother's womb, who had never walked. [9]He was listening to Paulos speaking. Paulos, having looked intently on him and seeing that he had faith to be made whole, [10]said with a loud voice, "Stand upright on your feet!" He leaped up and walked. [11]When the multitude saw what Paulos had done, they raised their voice, saying in the language of Lykaonia, "The gods have come down to us in the likeness of men!" [12]They called Bar Nabba "Zeus," and Paulos "Hermes," because he was the chief speaker.

[13]The priest of Jupiter, whose temple was in front of their city, brought oxen and garlands to the gates, and would have made a sacrifice along with the multitudes. [14]But when the ambassadors Bar Nabba and Paulos, heard of it, they tore their clothes, and sprang into the crowd, crying out, [15]"Men, why are you⁺ doing these things? We also are men of the same nature as you⁺, and bring you⁺ the good news, that you⁺ should turn from these vain things to the living God, who made the heaven and the earth and the sea, and all that is in them. [16]In the generations gone by, He let all the Gentiles walk in their own ways. [17]Yet He did not leave Himself without a witness, in that He did good and gave you⁺ rains from the heaven and fruitful seasons, filling your⁺ hearts with food and gladness." [18]Even saying these things, they barely prevented the multitudes from making a sacrifice to them.

[19]Now some Jews from Antioch and Iconium came there, and having persuaded the multitudes, they stoned Paulos, and dragged him out of the city, thinking that he was dead. [20]But as the disciples stood around him, he rose up and entered into the city. On the next day he went out with Bar Nabba to Derbe. [21]When they had proclaimed the good news to that city, and had made many disciples, they returned to Lystra, Iconium, and Antioch. [22]They strengthened the souls of the disciples, exhorting them to continue in the faith, and saying that, "We must enter into God's kingdom through many afflictions." [23]When they had chosen elders for them in every congregation, and had prayed with fasting, they commended them to the Lord, on whom they had believed.

[24]They passed through Pisidia, and came to Pamphylia. [25]When they had spoken the word in Perga, they went down to Attalia. [26]From there they sailed to Antioch, where they had been committed to the grace of God for the work which they had fulfilled. [27]When they had arrived, and had gathered the community together, they reported all the things that God had done with them, and that He had opened a door of faith to the Gentiles. [28]They stayed there with the disciples for a long time.

14:22 "The Holy One, blessed be He, gave three good gifts to Israel, and all of them were not given except through sufferings. These are they: the Torah, the Land of Israel and the age to come.'" (Tal. Berachot 5a)

15 ¹Some men came down from Judea and taught the brothers, "If you⁺ are not circumcised in accordance with the custom of Moses, you⁺ cannot be saved." [Judith 14:10] ²So when Paulos and Bar Nabba had more than a little disagreement and argument with them, they appointed Paulos, Bar Nabba, and certain other ones to go up to Yerushala'im to the ambassadors and elders concerning this question. ³Being sent on their way by the community, they passed through both Phoenikia and Shomron, reporting the turning to God of the Gentiles. They brought great joy to all the brethren. ⁴When they had come to Yerushala'im, they were received by the community and the ambassadors and the elders. Then they reported all that God had done with them. ⁵But from the sect of the Perushim, certain ones who believed rose up saying, "It is necessary to circumcise them, to command them to keep the Law of Moses."

⁶The ambassadors and the elders were gathered together to see about this matter. ⁷When there had been much discussion, Kefa rose up and said to them, "Brothers, you⁺ know that from the early days, God chose among us that by my mouth the Gentiles should hear the word of the good news and believe. ⁸God, who knows the heart, testified about them, giving them the Ruakh Kodesh, just as He did to us. ⁹He made no distinction between us and them, cleansing their hearts by faith. ¹⁰So why are you⁺ now testing God, by putting a yoke on the neck of the disciples which neither our fathers nor we were able to bear? ¹¹But by the grace of the Lord Yeshua, we believe unto salvation, in the same way that they also do."

¹²All the multitude kept silent, and they listened to Bar Nabba and Paulos reporting what miracles and wonders God had done among the Gentiles through them. ¹³After they were silent, Jacob responded, "Men, brothers, listen to me. ¹⁴Shimon has explained how God first came to receive people for His name from the Gentiles. ¹⁵This agrees with the words of the prophets. As it is written,

¹⁶'*After these things I will return. I will again build the tent of David, which has fallen. I will rebuild its ruins. I will set it up* ¹⁷*so that the rest of humanity may seek after the Everpresent Lord — all the Gentiles who are called by My Name,* says the Everpresent Lord, who does all these things.'* [Am. 9:11, 12 LXX] ¹⁸All God's works are known to Him from eternity.

¹⁹"Therefore my judgment is that we do not trouble those from among the Gentiles who turn to God, ²⁰but rather we write to them that they abstain from the defilement of idols, from sexual

15:1-2 There are many passages in Tanakh that speak of Gentiles, as Gentiles, trusting in the Everpresent Lord. Sha'ul refers to some in Rom. 15:9-12. To these could be added the promise to Abraham that he would be the father of many Gentiles, and the promise to Jacob that he would become a multitude of peoples (*ethnos* in LXX Gen. 48:4). Inasmuch as these texts refer to the Gentiles who are included as "Gentiles," it is evident that they do not become Jews.

15:16-17 "R. Nahman said to R. Isaac: 'Has anyone told you when *Bar Nafle* [son of what is fallen] will come?' 'Who is *Bar Nafle*?' he asked. 'Messiah,' he answered, 'Are you calling Messiah *Bar Nafle*?' — He said to him, 'Isn't this what is written? *In that day I will raise up the tabernacle of David ha-nofeleth* [that is fallen].'" (Tal. Sanhedrin 96b-97a)

15:19-21 "we do not trouble those from among the Gentiles who turn to God, but rather we write to them... because... Moses has those who proclaim him, being read in the meetingplaces every Shabbat." The logical connection is not explicit here, but a reasonable paraphrase seems to be: 'Because what Moses >>

immorality, from what is strangled, and from blood; [Lev. 17:110-12] ²¹because in every city from generations of old, Moses has those who proclaim him, being read in the meetingplaces every Shabbat."

²²Then it seemed good to the ambassadors and the elders, with the whole community, to choose men from among them, and send them to Antioch with Paulos and Bar Nabba — Judah (called Bar Sabba) and Sila, leading men among the brothers. ²³They wrote these things by their hand: "The ambassadors, the elders, and the brothers, to the Gentile brothers in Antioch, Syria, and Kilikia, greetings. ²⁴For we have heard that some who went out from us, without our giving them any commandment, have troubled you⁺ with words, unsettling your⁺ souls. ²⁵It seemed suitable to us, having come to a common purpose, to choose out men and send them to you⁺ with our beloved Bar Nabba and Paulos, ²⁶men who have given over their lives for the name of our Lord Yeshua the Messiah. ²⁷Therefore we have sent Judah and Sila, who themselves will also tell you⁺ the same things by word of mouth. ²⁸For it seemed appropriate to the Ruakh Kodesh and to us not to lay any great burden on you⁺, nevertheless there are these necessary things: ²⁹that you⁺ abstain from things sacrificed to idols, from blood, from things strangled, and from sexual immorality. If you⁺ keep yourselves from these, it will be well with you⁺. Farewell."

³⁰So when they were sent off, they came to Antioch. Having gathered the whole group together, they delivered the letter. ³¹When they had read it, they rejoiced over the encouragement. ³²Judah and Sila, also being prophets themselves, encouraged the brethren with many words, and strengthened them. ³³After they had spent some time there, they were sent back with greetings from the brethren to

taught is proclaimed in every city, we do not need to give the Gentile disciples extensive directives (i.e. they can learn from Moses). We do, however, need to be explicit that they refrain from some things which pervade their culture." However, if this is the correct understanding, it is somewhat odd that this is not made explicit in the letter that was sent out. vv. 23-29. However, Sha'ul, Bar Nabba, Judah, and Sila were going to bring the letter to the communities and explain it to them. (v. 27)

The distinctions which God made between Jews and Gentiles are laid out in the writings of Moses. We don't have any historical evidence that Gentile believers began frequenting the Jewish meetingplaces, something that would definitely have been noteworthy. It is, however, more than reasonable to assume that they were studying the Scriptures and learning what Moses taught. Their faith was to built upon the Scriptures.

15:29 They made no attempt to list all the universal laws that God had placed in the heart of every individual. These four categories deal with actions that were generally acceptable in the Gentile world.

Irenaeus gives "these necessary things" as: "that you⁺ abstain from meats offered to idols, and from blood, and from fornication; and whatsoever you⁺ do not wish to be done to you⁺, do not you⁺ do it to others..." (Against Heresies, XII:14)

"Our Rabbis taught: 'Seven commandments apply to the sons of Noah: societal laws, cursing the Name [of God], idolatry, sexual immorality, shedding of blood; robbery; and flesh of a living creature.' R. Hanania b. Gamaliel said, 'Not even the blood of a living creature.' R. Hidka said emasculation also. R. Simeon said sorcery also. R. Yosi said..." (Tal. Sanhedrin 56a-b cf. Dvarim Rabba I. 21) See "The Noachide Laws" and "God's Law and the New Covenant" in the ADDITIONAL NOTES.

those who had sent them. [34] [35]But Paulos and Bar Nabba stayed in Antioch, teaching and proclaiming the word of the Lord, along with many others.

[36]After a certain amount of time, Paulos said to Bar Nabba, "Let's return now and visit our brethren in every city in which we proclaimed the word of the Lord, to see how they are doing." [37]Bar Nabba planned to take Yohanan, who was called Mark, with them also. [38]But Paulos did not think it was a good idea to take someone with them who had deserted them in Pamphylia and did not go with them to do the work. [39]But the argument grew so that they separated from each other. Bar Nabba took Mark with him, and sailed away to Kyprus, [40]but Paulos chose Sila, and went out, being commended by the brethren to the grace of God. [41]He went through Syria and Kilikia, strengthening the communities.

16 [1]He came to Derbe and Lystra, and there was a certain disciple named Timothy, the son of a Jewish woman who believed, but his father was a Greek. [2]The brethren who were at Lystra and Iconium gave a good report about him. [3]Paulos wanted to have him go out with him, so he took and circumcised him, because of the Jews who were in those parts, because they all knew that his father was a Greek. [4]As they went on their way through the cities, they delivered to them the decrees to keep — those ordained by the ambassadors and elders who were at Yerushala'im. [5]So the communities were strengthened in the faith, and grew greatly in number daily.

[6]When they had gone through the region of Phrygia and Galatia, they were restrained by the Ruakh Kodesh from speaking the word in the province of Asia. [7]When they had come opposite Mysia, they tried to go into Bithynia, but the Spirit of Yeshua did not let them. [8]Passing by Mysia, they came down to Troas. [9]Paulos saw a vision in the night. There was a man of Makedonia standing, entreating him, "Come over into Makedonia and help us." [10]When he had seen the vision, we sought at once to go out to Makedonia, concluding that God had called us to proclaim the good news to them. [11]So setting sail from Troas, we made a straight course to Samothrake, and to Neapolis the following day. [12]And from there we went to Philippi, a leading city of the district of Makedonia, colonized [by Rome]. We stayed in this city a number of days.

[13]On the day of Shabbat we went forth outside the city by a riverside, where we thought there was a place of prayer. We sat down, and spoke to the women who had come together. [14]There was a certain woman named Lydia from the city of Thyatira, a seller of purple cloth, one who worshipped God. She was listening to us. The Lord opened her heart to hear the things which were spoken by Paulos. [15]When she and her household were immersed, she entreated us, "If you+ have judged me to be faithful to the Lord, come into my house and stay." So she persuaded us.

15:34 "But it seemed good to Silas to stay there."

16:13 Josephus mentions a decree which sanctioned the practice of having a *proseuche*, a place of prayer, by the water. "The Jews... may celebrate their Sabbaths, and perform their holy offices, according to the Jewish laws; may make their proseuchae at the seaside, according to the customs of their forefathers; and if anyone whether he be a magistrate or a private person, hindereth them from so doing, he shall be liable to a fine, to be applied to the uses of the city." Antiq. 14:258 (14.10.23.258)

16:16 The slave girl had a *pythona* spirit. Plutarch called ventriloquists, i.e. those who speak through another, *pythones*. (Liddell and Scott, "*python*")

¹⁶As we were going to prayer, we were met by a certain servant girl who had a spirit that spoke through her. She brought her masters an abundant livelihood by divination. ¹⁷Following Paulos and us, she cried out, "These men, who proclaim to you⁺ a way of salvation, are servants of the Most High God!" ¹⁸She was doing this for many days, but Paulos, becoming greatly annoyed, turned and said to the spirit, "I order you in the name of Yeshua the Messiah to come out of her!" It came out at that time.

¹⁹But when her masters saw that the hope of their livelihood was gone, they seized Paulos and Sila, and dragged them into the marketplace before the rulers. ²⁰When they had brought them to the magistrates, they said, "These men, being Jews, are greatly disturbing our city, ²¹and they are presenting customs which it is not lawful for us, being Romans, to accept or observe." ²²The multitude rose up together against them, and the magistrates tore their clothes off of them, and commanded them to be beaten with rods. ²³When they had beaten them with many blows, they threw them into prison, charging the jailer to securely guard them. ²⁴Having received such an order, he threw them into the inner prison, and secured their feet in the stocks.

²⁵Now about midnight, Paulos and Sila were praying and singing praises to God, and the prisoners were listening to them. ²⁶Suddenly there was a big earthquake, so that the foundations of the prison were shaken. And all the doors were instantly opened, and everyone's chains were released. ²⁷The jailer, being roused out of sleep and seeing the prison doors open, drew his sword and was about to kill himself, thinking that the prisoners had escaped. ²⁸But Paulos cried with a loud voice, "Don't harm yourself, because we are all here!"

²⁹He called for lights, rushed in, and fell down trembling before Paulos and Sila. ³⁰He brought them out and said, "Masters, what must I do to be saved?"

³¹They said, "Believe in the Lord Yeshua, the Messiah, and you will be saved, you and your household." ³²They spoke the word of the Lord to him, with all who were in his house. ³³He took them that hour of the night, and washed their wounds. And having believed in God, he and all those who were his were immersed at once. ³⁴He brought them up into his house, set food before them, and rejoiced greatly with all his household.

³⁵Now when it was day, the magistrates sent their officers to say, "Let those men go."

³⁶The jailer reported these words to Paulos, saying, "The magistrates have sent to let you⁺ go. Now therefore come out, and go in peace."

³⁷But Paulos said to them, "They have beaten us publicly without a trial, men who are Romans, and have cast us into prison! Are they now throwing us out in secret? Certainly not, but let them come themselves and bring us out!"

³⁸The officers reported these words to the magistrates, and they were afraid when they heard that they were Romans. ³⁹Then they came and begged them. When they had brought them out, they asked

16:21 Opposition to the State religion was opposition to the State. That was rebellion, and the punishment was severe. See the ADDITIONAL NOTE on "Conflict with the State and Its gods".

16:27,37-39 The jailer thought death would be better than the punishment for letting the prisoners escape. The magistrates also feared for their lives because of what they had done.

them to depart from the city. ⁴⁰They went out of the prison, and entered into Lydia's house. When they saw the brethren, they encouraged them, and departed.

17 ¹And having passed through Amphipolis and Apollonia, they came to Thessalonika, where there was a Jewish meetingplace. ²As was Paulos' custom, he went in and reasoned with them from the Scriptures, for three consecutive Shabbats. ³He explained and demonstrated that the Messiah had to suffer and rise again from the dead. "This Yeshua, whom I proclaim to you⁺, is the Messiah."

⁴Some of them were persuaded and cast their lot with Paulos and Sila, including a large multitude of the devout Greeks, and more than a few of the prominent women. ⁵However, those Jews who were not persuaded became jealous, took along some good-for-nothing men from the marketplace, gathered a crowd, and set the city in an uproar. Coming against the house of Jason, they sought to bring them out to the people. ⁶When they did not find them, they dragged Jason and certain brothers before the rulers of the city, crying out, "These who have been stirring up the world have come here also, ⁷and Jason has received them. These all act contrary to the decrees of Caesar, saying that there is another king, Yeshua!" ⁸They upset the multitude and the rulers of the city who heard these things. ⁹When they had taken security from Jason and the rest, they let them go. ¹⁰The brothers immediately sent Paulos and Sila away by night to Berea.

When they arrived, they went into the Jewish meetingplace. ¹¹Now these, being more noble than those in Thessalonika, received the word with complete eagerness, in that they examined the Scriptures daily to see whether to accept these things in this way. ¹²Therefore many of them believed, including some of the prominent Greek women, and more than a few men. ¹³But when some Jews of Thessalonika learned that the word of God was proclaimed by Paulos at Berea also, they came there likewise, agitating the multitudes. ¹⁴Then the brothers immediately sent Paulos away, to go as far as the sea, and Sila and Timothy remained there. ¹⁵Now those who escorted Paulos brought him as far as Athens. Receiving a directive for Sila and Timothy that they should come to him very quickly, they departed.

¹⁶Now Paulos waited for them in Athens. His spirit was upset within him as he observed the city to be full of idols. ¹⁷So he reasoned in the meetingplace with the Jews and the devout Gentiles, and in the marketplace every day with those who met him. ¹⁸Some of the Epicurean and Stoic philosophers also were conversing with him. Some said, "What does this babbler want to say?" Others said, "He seems to be advocating strange deities," because he proclaimed Yeshua and the resurrection.

¹⁹They took hold of him, and brought him to the Areopagus, saying, "May we know what this new teaching is which is spoken by you? ²⁰For you bring certain strange things to our ears. So we want to know what these things mean." ²¹Now all the Athenians and the foreigners living there had no other leisure activity, but to tell or to hear some new thing.

²²Paulos stood in the middle of the Areopagus, and said, "You⁺ men of Athens, in everything you⁺ observe and fear the gods. ²³For as I passed along, and observed the objects of your⁺ worship,

17:23 "But the father and maker of all this universe is past finding out; and even if we found him, to tell of him to all men would be impossible." (Plato, "Timaeus," http://www.greektexts.com/library/Plato/timaeus/eng/578.html)

I also found an altar with this inscription: 'TO AN UNKNOWN GOD.' So the one you[+] worship without knowing, this one I announce to you[+]. [24]The God who made the world and all things in it, since He possesses heaven and earth, does not live in temples made by hands. [25]Nor is He served by men's hands, as though He needed anything, seeing He Himself gives life, breath, and everything to all. [26]He made every nation of men from one blood, to live upon all the surface of the earth. He determined appointed seasons, and the boundaries of their habitations [27]so that they would seek God, if perhaps they might reach out for Him and find Him, though He is not far from each one of us. [28]'For in Him we live and move, and have our being' — as some of your[+] own poets have said: 'for we are also His offspring.' [29]Being then the offspring of God, we should not think that the nature of God is like gold, or silver, or stone, engraved by art and design of man. [30]Therefore God overlooked the times of ignorance, but He now commands that all people everywhere should change their ways, [31]because He has appointed a day in which He will judge the world in justice by the man whom He has set apart for Himself. He has given assurance of this to all men, in that He has raised him from the dead."

[32]Now when they heard of the resurrection of the dead, some mocked, but others said, "We want to hear you again concerning this."

[33]With that, Paulos went out from among them. [34]But certain men believed and joined with him, among whom were Dionysius (a member of the Areopagus), a woman named Damaris, and others with them.

18 [1]After these things Paulos left Athens, and came to Corinth. [2]He found a certain Jew named Akila, a man of Pontus by birth, who had recently come from Italy with his wife Priskilla, because Claudius had commanded all the Jews to leave Rome. He came to them, [3]and lived with them. He worked with them, because he practiced the same trade, for they were tentmakers by trade.

[4]He reasoned in the meetingplace every Shabbat, and persuaded Jews and Greeks. [5]And when both Sila and Timothy came down from Makedonia, Paulos was intensely occupied with the word, testifying to the Jews that Yeshua is the Messiah. [6]When some of them set themselves in opposition and spoke slanderously, he shook out his clothing and said to them, "Your[+] blood be on your[+] own heads. I am clean. [Ezek. 3:17-21; 33:2-9] From now on, I will go to the Gentiles."

[7]He departed from there, and went into the house of a certain man named Justus, one who worshipped God, and whose house was next door to the meetingplace. [8]Crispus, the leader of the meetingplace, believed in the Lord with all his house. Many of the Corinthians believed when they

17:28 "The first quotation is sometimes attributed to Epimenides; the second is from Aratus' Phaenomena." The Oxford Annotated Bible, ed. Herbert May & Bruce Metzger, NY, 1962, P. 1342n

17:31 "God, as the old tradition declares, holding in His hand the beginning, middle, and end of all that is, travels according to His nature in a straight line towards the accomplishment of His end. Justice always accompanies Him, and is the punisher of those who fall short of the divine law." ("LAWS," BK. IV, The Dialogues of Plato, trans. B. Jowett, Vol. 3, Oxford, Clarendon, 1892, P. 98)

17:34 The Areopagus, the oldest and most respected council of Athens, was named after the hill, mentioned in v. 19, on which it met. It was also the site of the supreme court, and is the current name of the Greek Supreme Court.

18:7-8,17 The Jewish meetingplace and assembly.

heard, and were immersed. ⁹Then through a vision in the night, the Lord said to Paulos, "Don't be afraid, but speak and do not be silent, ¹⁰because I am with you, and no one will come against you to harm you, because my people are numerous in this city."

¹¹He lived there a year and six months, teaching the word of God among them. ¹²But when Gallio was proconsul of Akhaia, some Jews rose up with a common purpose against Paulos and brought him before the judgment seat. ¹³They said, "This man persuades men to worship God contrary to the law."

¹⁴But when Paulos was about to open his mouth, Gallio said to those Jews, "If it were truly a matter of evil doing or of wicked criminal behavior, O Jews, it would be reasonable that I should bear with you⁺. ¹⁵But if there are points of disagreement about words and names and your⁺ own law, attend to it yourselves, for I do not want to be a judge of these matters." ¹⁶He drove them from the judgment seat.

¹⁷Then all the Greeks took hold of Sosthenes, the leader of the meetingplace, and beat him before the judgment seat. None of these things mattered at all to Gallio.

¹⁸Having stayed many more days after this, Paulos took his leave of the brethren, and sailed from there for Syria, together with Priskilla and Akila. He shaved his head in Kenchreae, because he had a vow. [Num. 6:5] ¹⁹They came to Ephesus, and he left them there, but he himself entered into the meetingplace and reasoned with the Jews. ²⁰When they asked him to stay with them a longer time, he declined. ²¹Saying goodbye to them instead, he said, "I will return again to you⁺ if God wills." And he went off from Ephesus.

²²When he had landed at Kaesarea, he went up, greeted the community, and went down to Antioch. ²³Having spent some time there, he left and went through the region of Galatia, and afterwards Phrygia, strengthening all the disciples.

²⁴Now a certain Jew named Apollos, an Alexandrian by birth, an eloquent man, came to Ephesus. He was powerful in the Scriptures. ²⁵This man had been instructed in the way of the Lord, although knowing only Yoḥanan's immersion. And being fiery in spirit, he spoke and taught accurately the things concerning Yeshua. ²⁶He began to speak boldly in the meetingplace. But when Priskilla and Akila heard him, they received him, but diligently explained to him the way of God.

²⁷And since he had decided to pass over into Akhaia, the brothers encouraged him, and wrote to the disciples to receive him. When he had come, he greatly helped those who had believed through [God's] grace, ²⁸for he powerfully refuted the sectarian Jews, publicly showing by the Scriptures that Yeshua is the Messiah.

19 ¹While Apollos was at Corinth, Paulos, having passed through the upper country, came to Ephesus, and found certain disciples. ²He said to them, "Did you⁺ receive the Ruakh Kodesh when you⁺ believed?"

They said to him, "No, we have not even heard that the Ruakh Kodesh is given."

³He said, "Into what then were you⁺ immersed?"

They said, "Into Yoḥanan's immersion."

⁴Paulos said, "Yoḥanan truly immersed with the immersion of repentance, telling the people that they should believe in the one who would come after him, that is, in Yeshua."

⁵When they heard this, they were immersed in the name of the Lord Yeshua. ⁶When Paulos had laid his hands on them, the Ruakh Kodesh came upon them, and they spoke with other languages and prophesied. ⁷They were about twelve men in all.

⁸He entered into the meetingplace, and spoke boldly for a period of three months, reasoning and persuading them about the things concerning God's kingdom. ⁹But when some were hardened and rejected the way, speaking evil of it before the multitude, he departed from them and separated the disciples. He reasoned daily in the school of Tyrannus. ¹⁰This continued for two years, so that all those who lived in the province of Asia heard the word of the Lord Yeshua, both Jews and Greeks.

¹¹God worked special miracles by the hands of Paulos, ¹²so that even handkerchiefs or aprons were carried away from his body to the sick. The diseases departed and the evil spirits came out from them. ¹³But some of the traveling Jewish exorcists took upon themselves to name the name of the Lord Yeshua over those who had the evil spirits. They were saying, "We put you⁺ under oath by the Yeshua whom Paulos proclaims."

¹⁴There were seven sons of a certain Skeva, a Jewish chief Kohen, who did this. ¹⁵The evil spirit answered, "Yeshua I acknowledge, and I have heard of Paulos, but who are you⁺?" ¹⁶Then the man in whom there was the evil spirit leaped on them, overpowered them each, and had his way with them, so that they fled out of that house naked and wounded. ¹⁷This became known to all, both Jews and Greeks, who lived at Ephesus. Fear fell on them all, and the name of the Lord Yeshua was greatly honored.

¹⁸Many also from those who had believed came, confessing and declaring what they had done. ¹⁹Many of those who practiced magic brought their books together and burned them before everyone. They counted the price of them, and found it to be fifty thousand pieces of silver. ²⁰So the word of the Lord was growing in might and prevailing.

²¹Now after these things had ended, Paulos determined in the spirit to go to Yerushala'im, after he had passed through Makedonia and Akhaia. He said, "After I have been there, I must also see Rome." ²²Having sent Timothy and Erastus — two of those who ministered to him — into Makedonia, he himself stayed in the province of Asia for a while.

²³About that time there arose more than a small commotion concerning the Way. ²⁴For a certain man named Demetrius, a silversmith who made silver shrines of Artemis, brought great profit to the craftsmen. ²⁵He gathered them together along with the workmen of similar occupation, and said, "Men, you⁺ know that by this business we gain our wealth. ²⁶You⁺ see and hear that not at Ephesus alone, but almost throughout all the province of Asia, this Paul has persuaded and turned away many people, saying that the things made by hands are not gods. ²⁷Not only is there danger that this trade of ours will come into disrepute, but also that the temple of the great goddess Artemis will be counted as nothing, and her majesty destroyed, she whom all the province of Asia and the world worships."

18:18,21 The Textus Receptus says, "I must by all means keep this coming feast in Yerushala'im. However..." As a faithful Jew, Sha'ul made and kept a vow and observed the holy days.

19:2 "No, we have not even heard that the Ruakh Kodesh is given." This is the reading in the Western text. The Alexandrian text has, "We have not even heard that there is a Ruah Kodesh." Sha'ul's response is appropriate for the question in the Western text, but not the one in the Alexandrian text. No one familiar with the Scriptures could have asked the question in the Alexandrian text, but it is possible that these disciples were Gentiles who were still quite ignorant of the Scriptures.

19:26 "Paul" was the Greek name by which Sha'ul was known. At the time, it was not unusual for some Jews to have both a Hebrew name and a Greek name.

[28]When they heard this they were filled with anger, and cried out, "Great is Artemis of the Ephesians!" [29]The whole city was filled with confusion, and they rushed with a common purpose into the theater, having seized Gaius and Aristarchus, men of Makedonia, Paulos' traveling companions. [30]When Paulos wanted to go in to the people, the disciples did not allow him. [31]Certain rulers of the province of Asia, being his friends, also sent to him and begged him not to take himself into the theater.

[32]Some therefore cried one thing, and some another, because the assembly was in confusion. Most of them did not know why they had come together. [33]The Jews brought Alexander out of the multitude, putting him forward. Alexander beckoned with his hand, and would have made a defense to the people, [34]but when they perceived that he was a Jew, there was one outcry from all of them. For about two hours, they cried out "Great is Artemis of the Ephesians!"

[35]When the town clerk had quieted the multitude, he said, "You[+] men of Ephesus, what man is there who does not know that the city of the Ephesians is temple-keeper of the great goddess Artemis, and of the image which fell down from heaven? [36]Seeing then that these things cannot be denied, you[+] ought to be calm and not do anything rash. [37]For you[+] have brought these men here, who are neither robbers of temples nor blasphemers of our goddess. [38]So if Demetrius and the craftsmen who are with him have a matter against anyone, the courts are open, and there are proconsuls. Let them press charges against one another. [39]But if, on the other hand, you[+] seek anything about other matters, it must be settled in the lawful assembly. [40]For we are in danger of being accused of insurrection in regard to this day. There is not one cause for which we would be able to give a reason for this commotion." [41]When he had said these things, he dismissed the assembly.

20 [1]After the uproar had ceased, Paulos sent for the disciples, encouraged them, embraced them, and departed to go into Makedonia. [2]When he had gone through those areas, and had encouraged them with extensive counsel, he came into Greece. [3]After he had spent three months there, a plot was formed against him by some Jews as he was about to set sail for Syria. So he determined to return through Makedonia. [4]He was accompanied by Sopater of Berea, Aristarchus and Sekundus of the Thessalonikans, Gaius of Derbe, Timothy, and Tychicus and Trophimus of the province of Asia. [5]But these had gone ahead, and were waiting for us at Troas. [6]We sailed away from Philippi after the days of Unleavened Bread, came to them at Troas in five days, and stayed there seven days.

[7]On the first day of the week, when the disciples were gathered together to break bread, Paulos talked to them, intending to depart on the next day. He continued his talk until midnight. [8]There were many lamps in the upper chamber where we were gathered together. [9]A certain young man named Eutychus sat in the window, sinking into deep sleep. Weighed down by his sleep, he fell down from the third story as Paulos continued to speak. He was lifted up dead. [10]Paulos went down, fell upon him, embraced him, and said, "Do not be troubled, for his life is in him." [2K. 4:17-37]

[11]When he had gone up, had broken bread and eaten, and had talked to them a long while, even until daybreak, he departed. [12]They brought the boy in alive, and were greatly encouraged.

19:34 The Ephesians perceived he was a Jew, and therefore a witness in opposition to their pantheistic beliefs. Alexander was not an associate of Sha'ul. (cf. 2Tim. 4:14)

¹³But we who went ahead to the ship set sail for Assos, intending to take Paulos aboard there, because that is what he had arranged. He himself intended to go by land. ¹⁴When he met us at Assos, we took him aboard, and came to Mitylene. ¹⁵Sailing from there, we came opposite Chios the following day. The next day we touched at Samos and stayed at Trogyllium. The following day we came to Miletus, ¹⁶for Paulos had determined to sail past Ephesus so that he might not have to spend time in the province of Asia. This was because he was hurrying, if it were possible for him, to be in Yerushala'im on the day of Shavuot.

¹⁷From Miletus he sent to Ephesus, and called to himself the elders of the community. ¹⁸When they had come to him, he said to them, "You⁺ yourselves know how I was with you⁺ all the time, from the first day that I set foot in the province of Asia. ¹⁹You know how I served the Lord with all humility, with many tears, and the trials which happened to me by the plots of some Jews. ²⁰You⁺ know how I did not shrink from declaring to you⁺ anything that was profitable, teaching you⁺ publicly and from house to house. ²¹I testified both to Jews and Greeks of repentance toward God, and faith toward our Lord Yeshua. ²²Now I indeed go bound in the Spirit to Yerushala'im, not knowing what will happen to me there, ²³except that in every city the Ruakh Kodesh affirms that chains and afflictions await me. ²⁴But so that I may finish my course and the responsibility which I received from the Lord Yeshua, to fully testify to the good news of the grace of God, I do not consider my life the greatest value.

²⁵Now I surely know that all of you⁺, among whom I went about proclaiming the kingdom, will see my face no more! ²⁶Therefore I testify to you⁺ this day that I am clean from the blood of all men [Ezek. 3:17-21; 33:2-9], ²⁷because I did not try to avoid declaring to you⁺ the whole counsel of God. ²⁸So take heed to yourselves and to all the flock in which the Ruakh Kodesh has made you⁺ overseers. Shepherd God's congregation, which He purchased with the blood of His own. ²⁹For I know that after my departure, vicious wolves will enter in among you⁺, not sparing the flock. ³⁰Men will arise from among you⁺, speaking distorted things to draw away the disciples after themselves. ³¹So be vigilant, remembering that for a period of three years I did not cease to admonish everyone night and day with tears. ³²Now brethren, I entrust you⁺ to God and to the word of His grace, which is able to build you⁺ up and give you⁺ an inheritance among all those who belong to God. ³³I coveted no one's silver, or gold, or clothing. [1Sam. 12:1-3] ³⁴You⁺ yourselves know that these hands served for my necessities, and for those who were with me. ³⁵Laboring in this way, I showed you⁺ in all things that it is necessary to help the weak and to remember the words of the Lord Yeshua which he himself said: 'It is more blessed to give than to receive.'"

³⁶When he had spoken these things, he knelt down and prayed with them all. ³⁷They all wept without restraint, and fell on Paulos' neck and kissed him. ³⁸They were sorrowful most of all because of the word which he had spoken, that they would see his face no more. Then they accompanied him to the ship.

21 ¹When we had parted from them and had set sail, we came on a straight course to Co'os, the next day to Rhodes, and from there to Patara. ²Having found a ship crossing over to Phoenikia, we went aboard, and set sail. ³When we had come in sight of Kyprus, leaving it on the left hand, we sailed to Syria, and landed at Tzor, since the ship was to unload her cargo there. ⁴Having found disciples, we stayed there seven days. These said to Paulos through the Spirit that he should not go up to Yerushala'im. ⁵When we had completed those days, we departed and went on our journey. They all, with wives and children, brought us on our way until we were out of the city. Kneeling down

on the shore, we prayed. ⁶After saying goodbye to each other, we went on board the ship, and they returned home again.

⁷When we had finished the voyage from Tzor, we arrived at Ptolemais. We greeted the brethren, and stayed with them one day. ⁸On the next day, we departed and came to Kaesarea. We entered into the house of Philip, one who proclaimed the good news, and was one of the seven. We stayed with him. ⁹Now this man had four virgin daughters who prophesied.

¹⁰As we stayed there many days, a certain prophet named Agav came down from Judea. ¹¹Coming to us, and taking Paulos' belt, he bound his own feet and hands, and said, "This is what the Ruakh Kodesh says: 'In this way, the sectarian Jews at Yerushala'im will bind the man who owns this belt, and will deliver him into the hands of the Gentiles.'"

¹²When we heard these things, both we and those who were there begged him not to go up to Yerushala'im. ¹³Then Paulos answered, "What are you⁺ doing, weeping and breaking my heart? For I am ready not only to be bound, but also to die at Yerushala'im for the name of the Lord Yeshua."

¹⁴When he would not be persuaded, we became quiet, saying, "The Lord's will be done." ¹⁵After these days we took up our baggage and went up to Yerushala'im. ¹⁶Some of the disciples from Kaesarea also went with us, bringing one Mnason of Kyprus, an elderly disciple with whom we were to stay.

¹⁷When we had come to Yerushala'im, the brothers received us gladly. ¹⁸The following day, Paulos went in with us to Jacob, and all the elders were present. ¹⁹When he had greeted them, he reported one by one the things which God had done among the Gentiles through his work. ²⁰When they heard it, they glorified God.

They said to him, "Brother, you see how many tens of thousands there are among the Jews who have believed, and they are all zealous for the Law. ²¹They have been informed about you that you teach all the Jews who are among the Gentiles to repudiate Moses, telling them not to circumcise their children or walk after the customs. ²²So what is to be done? They will certainly hear that you have come, ²³so do what we tell you. We have four men who have taken a vow. ²⁴Take them, purify yourself with them, and pay their expenses for them, so that they may shave their heads. Then all will know that there is no truth in the things that they have been informed about you, but that you yourself also walk orderly, keeping the Law. ²⁵But concerning the Gentiles who believe, we have written our decision that they should keep themselves from food offered to idols, from blood, from strangled things, and from sexual immorality."

²⁶Then Paulos took the men, purified himself the next day, and went with them into the Temple to declare the completion of the days of purification, when the offering was to be offered for every one of them. ²⁷When the seven days were almost completed, Jews from the province of Asia saw him in the Temple. Then they stirred up all the multitude and grabbed him, ²⁸crying out, "Men of Israel,

---

21:4-13 Sha'ul is warned of what will happen to him in Yerushala'im. He is determined to go, no matter what the cost. It seems that he is being tested, as, for example, Elisha was when Eliyahu told him to turn back (2K. 2:1-2), or the descendants of Rechab when Jeremiah told them to drink wine (Jer. 35).

21:20-26 In order to demonstrate that he himself observed the Law and was not teaching Jews in Diaspora to abandon it, Sha'ul, in accordance with the Law, publicly paid for the purification sacrifices to be offered for himself and the men who had taken a vow.

help! This is the man who teaches all men everywhere against the people, the Torah, and this place. Not only this, he also brought Greeks into the Temple, and has profaned this holy place!" [29]For they had seen Trophimus the Ephesian with him in the city, and they thought that Paulos had brought him into the Temple.

[30]All the city was stirred up, and the people ran together. They seized Paulos and dragged him out of the Temple. Immediately the doors were shut. [31]As they were trying to kill him, news came up to the commanding officer of the regiment that all Yerushala'im was in an uproar. [32]He immediately took soldiers and centurions, and ran down to them. When those beating Paulos saw the chief captain and the soldiers, they stopped beating him. [33]Then the commanding officer came near, arrested him, and commanded that he be bound with two chains. Then he inquired who he was and what he had done. [34]Some among the crowd shouted one thing, and some another. When he could not find out the truth because of the noise, he commanded that Paulos be brought into the barracks. [35]When he came to the stairs, he had to be carried by the soldiers because of the violence of the crowd, [36]since the multitude of the people followed, crying out, "Away with him!"

[37]As Paulos was about to be brought into the barracks, he asked the commanding officer, "Am I permitted to say something to you?"

He said, "Do you know Greek?! [38]Then you are not the Egyptian who stirred up a sedition not long ago, and led the four thousand men of the Assassins out into the wilderness?"

[39]"To the contrary," Paulos said, "I am a Jew from Tarsus in Kilikia, a citizen of no insignificant city. I ask you to allow me to speak to the people."

[40]When he had given him permission, Paulos stood on the stairs, and beckoned with his hand to the people. When there was a great silence, he spoke to them in the Hebrew language.

22 [1]"Men — brothers and fathers — listen to the defense which I now make to you[+]." [2]When they heard that he spoke to them in the Hebrew language, they were even quieter.

He said, [3]"I am a Jew, born in Tarsus of Kilikia, but brought up in this city at the feet of Gamliel, instructed according to the strict manner of the Torah of our fathers, being zealous for God, even as you[+] all are this day. [4]I persecuted this Way to the death, binding and delivering both men and women into prisons, [5]as also the Kohen Gadol and all the Council of the elders bear witness to me. And I received letters to the brothers from them. Then I traveled to Damascus to bring even those who were there to Yerushala'im in chains to be punished. [6]As I made my journey and came close to Damascus about noon, suddenly there shone from the sky a great light around me. [7]I fell to the ground, and heard a voice saying to me, 'Sha'ul, Sha'ul, why do you persecute me?' [8]I answered, 'Who are you, Lord?' He said to me, 'I am Yeshua the Natzri, whom you persecute.'

21:38 Many of the historical incidents recorded in Acts that took place in the land of Israel can be found in Josephus. (cf. Antiq. 20:169-172 [20.8.6.169-172])

21:39-40, 22:26-29 To gain the right to speak to the crowd, and to avoid an interrogation by beating, Sha'ul asserts his Roman citizenship.

22:4 See note to Acts 9:2.

22:8 "Yeshua the Natzri" It is not clear if the reference is to Yeshua's coming from Natzrat, or to his role as the Messianic Branch/*Netzer* of Is. 11:1.

⁹"Those who were with me indeed saw the light and were afraid, but they did not hear the voice of the one who spoke to me. [Dan. 10:7] ¹⁰I said, 'What shall I do, Lord?' The Lord said to me, 'Arise, and go into Damascus. There you will be told about all things which are appointed for you to do.' ¹¹Since I could not see because of the glory of that light, I was led by the hand of those who were with me, and came into Damascus. ¹²There was a certain H̱ananyah, a devout man according to the Torah, well reported of by all the Jews who lived in Damascus. ¹³He came to me, stood by me and said, 'Brother Sha'ul, see again!' In that very moment I saw again, seeing him. ¹⁴He said, 'The God of our fathers has appointed you to know His will, and to see the Righteous One, and to hear a voice from His mouth. ¹⁵For you will be a witness for Him to all men of what you have seen and heard. ¹⁶Now why do you wait? Arise, be immersed, and wash away your sins, calling on the name of the Lord.'

¹⁷"When I had returned to Yerushala'im, and while I prayed in the Temple, a vision came to me. ¹⁸I saw him saying to me, 'Hurry and get out of Yerushala'im quickly, because they will not receive you as a witness concerning me.' ¹⁹I said, 'Lord, they themselves know that in every meetingplace I was imprisoning and beating those who believed in you. ²⁰When the blood of Stephen, your witness, was shed, I also was standing by and consenting to his death, and guarding the cloaks of those who killed him.'

²¹"He said to me, 'Depart, for I will send you far off from here to the Gentiles.'"

²²They listened to him until he said that. Then they lifted up their voice and said, "Rid the earth of this fellow, for it is not right that he should live!" ²³As they cried out, they threw off their cloaks, and threw dust into the air. ²⁴The commanding officer commanded him to be brought into the barracks, ordering him to be interrogated with scourging so that he might know for what reason they shouted against him like that.

²⁵When they had tied him up with thongs, Paulos asked the centurion who stood by, "Is it lawful for you⁺, without trial or sentence, to scourge a man who is a Roman citizen?"

²⁶When the centurion heard it, he went to the commanding officer and told him, "Be careful what you are about to do, because this man is a Roman citizen!"

²⁷The commanding officer came and asked him, "Tell me, are you a Roman citizen?"

He said, "Yes."

²⁸The commanding officer answered, "I bought my citizenship for a great price."

Paulos said, "But I was born so."

²⁹Those who were about to interrogate him stepped away from him immediately, and the commanding officer also was afraid when he realized that he was a Roman, for he had tied him up. ³⁰And on the next day, desiring to know the truth about why he was accused by the sectarian Jews, he freed him from the bonds, and commanded the chief Kohanim and all the Council to come together. Then he brought Paulos down and set him before them.

23 ¹Looking steadfastly at the Council, Paulos said, "Men, brothers, I have lived as a citizen before God in all good conscience unto this day." ²H̱ananyah, the Kohen Gadol, commanded those who stood by him to hit him on the mouth.

³Then Paulos said to him, "God will strike you, you whitewashed wall! Do you sit to judge me according to the Torah, and command me to be struck contrary to the Torah?"

⁴Those who stood by said, "Do you malign God's Kohen Gadol?"

⁵Paulos said, "Brothers, I did not know that he is the Kohen Gadol. For it is written, 'You are not

to speak evil of a ruler of your people.'" [Ex. 22:28] ⁶But when Paulos perceived that the one part were Tzadukim and the other Perushim, he cried out in the Council, "Men, brothers, I am a Parush, a son of Perushim. I am being judged concerning the hope and resurrection of the dead!"

⁷When he had said this, an argument arose between the Perushim and Tzadukim, and the assembly was divided. ⁸For the Tzadukim say that there is no resurrection, and neither angel nor spirit, but the Perushim affirm both. ⁹There was a great uproar, and some of the Torah scholars of the Perushim side stood up and argued, "We find no evil in this man. Maybe a spirit or angel has spoken to him." ¹⁰When a great argument arose, fearing that they would tear Paulos in pieces, the commanding officer ordered the soldiers to go down and take him by force from among them and bring him into the barracks.

¹¹The following night, the Lord stood by him and said, "Be courageous, for as you have testified about me at Yerushala'im, so you must testify also at Rome."

¹²When it was day, some of the sectarian Jews banded together, and bound themselves with a vow, saying that they would neither eat nor drink until they had killed Paulos. ¹³There were more than forty who had made this conspiracy. ¹⁴They came to the chief Kohanim and the elders and said, "We have surely bound ourselves under a curse to taste nothing until we have killed Paulos. ¹⁵Now therefore, you⁺ with the Council inform the commanding officer that he should bring him down to you⁺ tomorrow, as though you⁺ were going to examine his case in greater detail. We are ready to kill him before he comes near."

¹⁶But the son of Paulos' sister heard of their plot, and he came and entered into the barracks and told Paulos. ¹⁷Paulos summoned one of the centurions, and said, "Bring this young man to the commanding officer, for he has something to tell him."

¹⁸So he took him, brought him to the commanding officer, and said, "Paulos the prisoner summoned me and asked me to bring this young man to you. He has something to tell you."

¹⁹The commanding officer took him by the hand and, going aside, asked him privately, "What is it that you have to tell me?"

²⁰He said, "The sectarian Jews have agreed to ask you to bring Paulos down to the Council tomorrow, as though they intended to examine him in greater detail. ²¹So do not yield to them, because more than forty men lie in wait for him. They have bound themselves with an oath neither to eat nor to drink until they have killed him. Now they are ready, waiting for the announcement from you."

23:6 The traditional liturgy is filled with references to God as the one who raises the dead. For example, in the Amidah: "...You are mighty forever, O Everpresent Lord; You bring the dead to life, and are mighty to save... Who in lovingkindness sustains the living, and with great compassion brings the dead to life... and fulfills His faithfulness to those who sleep in the dust... Who puts to death and brings to life, and causes salvation to sprout. You are faithful to bring the dead to life. Blessed are You, O Everpresent Lord, who brings the dead to life." If the Tzadukkiim had gained power over the Perushim, the liturgy would be different.

23:12 "The annulment of vows is from one expert [*mumche*], and if there is not a single expert, it is annulled by three common people." (Rashi on Num. 30:2)

²²So the commanding officer let the young man go, ordering him, "Don't tell anyone that you have explained these things to me." ²³He called to himself two of the centurions, and said, "Prepare two hundred soldiers at the third hour of the night to go as far as Kaesarea, with seventy horsemen, and two hundred men armed with spears." ²⁴He asked them to provide horses so that they might put Paulos on one, and bring him safely to Felix the governor. ²⁵He wrote a letter with this form: ²⁶"Claudius Lysias, to the Most Excellent, Governor Felix, greetings.

²⁷"This man was seized by the Jews, and was about to be killed by them, when I came with the soldiers and rescued him, having learned that he was a Roman. ²⁸Desiring to know the reason why they accused him, I brought him down to their Council. ²⁹I found him to be accused about questions of their law, but to have no accusation worthy of death or of imprisonment. ³⁰When it was made known to me that there would be a plot against the man, I sent him to you immediately, also ordering his accusers to bring their accusations against him before you."

³¹So, carrying out their orders, the soldiers took Paulos and brought him by night to Antipatris. ³²But on the next day they returned to the barracks, leaving the horsemen to go on with him. ³³When they came to Kaesarea and delivered the letter to the governor, they also presented Paulos to him. ³⁴When the governor had read it, he asked what province he was from. When he understood that he was from Kilikia, he said, ³⁵"I will hear you fully when your accusers also arrive." He commanded that he be kept in Herod's palace.

24 ¹After five days, the Kohen Gadol Hananyah came down with the elders and a particular lawyer, Tertullus. They presented a case against Paulos to the governor. ²When he was called, Tertullus began to accuse him, saying, "Most Excellent Felix, seeing that we enjoy much peace through you, and that through your foresight things are improving in this nation, ³we accept it with all gratitude both in every way and every place. ⁴But so that I do not take too much of your time, I entreat you to bear with us and hear a few words. ⁵For we have found this man to be a plague, an instigator of insurrections among all the Jews throughout the world, and a ringleader of the sect of the Natzrim. ⁶He also attempted to profane the Temple, but we arrested him and intended to judge him according to our law. ⁷However Lysias, the commanding officer, took him away out of our hands with great force, ⁸having commanded his accusers to come to you. By examining him yourself you will be able to find out all these things of which we accuse him."

⁹The sectarian Jews with him also joined in the attack, affirming that these things were so. ¹⁰When the governor had motioned to him to speak, Paulos responded. "Because I know that you have been a judge of this nation for many years, I gladly make my defense. ¹¹You can find out that it is not more than twelve days since I went up to worship at Yerushala'im. ¹²They did not find me arguing with anyone or stirring up a crowd in the Temple, the meetingplaces, or the city. ¹³Nor can they prove to you the things of which they now accuse me. ¹⁴But I confess this to you, that in accordance with the way which they call a sect, so I serve the God of our fathers, believing all things which are in accordance with the Torah, and which are written in the prophets. ¹⁵I have a hope toward God that there will soon be a resurrection, both of the just and unjust, which they themselves also look for. ¹⁶In this, I do my best to have a conscience void of offense toward God and men. ¹⁷Now after many years, I came to bring humanitarian aid to my nation and offerings; ¹⁸in which, some Jews from the province of Asia found me purified in the Temple, not with a mob or any turmoil. ¹⁹If they had anything against me, they should be here before you, so as to make accusation. ²⁰Or else let these

men themselves say what crime they found when I stood before the Council, [21]unless it is for this one thing that I cried standing among them: 'I am being judged before you[+] today concerning the resurrection of the dead!'"

[22]Knowing in greater detail the things concerning the Way, Felix put them off, saying, "When Lysias, the commanding officer, comes down, I will decide your[+] case." [23]He ordered the centurion that Paulos should be kept in custody, should have some privileges, and that none of his friends should be forbidden to visit him or help him.

[24]Now some days later, Felix came with Drusilla, his wife, who was Jewish. He then sent for Paulos, to listen to him concerning the faith in Messiah Yeshua. [25]As he reasoned about justice, self-control, and the judgment to come, Felix was fearful, and answered, "Go your way for this time, and when it is convenient for me, I will summon you." [26]At the same time, he was also hoping that money would be given to him by Paulos, so that he might release him. So he also frequently sent for him and talked with him. [27]But two years were completed, and Felix received a successor, Porcius Festus, and desiring to gain favor with the Jewish authorities, Felix left Paulos bound.

25 [1]So Festus, having come into the province, went up to Yerushala'im from Kaesarea after three days. [2]Then the Kohen Gadol and the principal men of the Jews brought charges to him against Paulos. And they entreated Festus, [3]asking a favor from him concerning Paulos, so that he would summon him to Yerushala'im. They were plotting to kill him on the way. [4]However Festus answered that Paulos should be kept in custody at Kaesarea, and that he himself was about to depart soon. [5]He said, "So let those of you[+] who are able go down with me. And if there is any fault in the man, let them accuse him."

[6]When he had stayed among them more than ten days, he went down to Kaesarea, and on the next day he sat on the judgment seat and commanded Paulos to be brought. [7]When he had come, the sectarian Jews who had come down from Yerushala'im stood around him, bringing many serious charges against him which they could not prove. [8]So Paulos said in his defense, "Neither against the Jewish Law, nor against the Temple, nor against Caesar, have I sinned in anything."

[9]But Festus, desiring to gain favor with the Jewish authorities, responded to Paulos and said, "Are you willing to go up to Yerushala'im, and be judged by me there concerning these things?"

[10]But Paulos said, "I am standing before Caesar's judgment seat, where I ought to be tried. I have done no wrong to the Jews, as you also know very well. [11]For if I have done wrong, and have committed anything worthy of death, I do not refuse to die. But if none of those things of which they accuse me is true, no one can give me up to them. I appeal to Caesar!"

[12]Then Festus, when he had conferred with the council, answered, "You have appealed to Caesar. To Caesar you will go."

[13]Now when some days had passed, Agrippas the King and Bernikeh arrived at Kaesarea and greeted Festus. [14]As they stayed there many days, Festus laid Paulos' case before the king, saying, "There is a certain man left a prisoner by Felix. [15]When I was at Yerushala'im, the chief Kohanim and the elders of the Jews informed me about him, asking for a judgment against him. [16]I answered them

24:22 See note to Acts 9:2.
25:13ff See the note to 12:3.

that it is not the custom of the Romans to give up any man before the accused has met the accusers face to face, and has had opportunity to make his defense concerning the accusation against him. [17]So when they had come together to this place, I did not delay, but sat on the judgment seat on the next day, and commanded the man to be brought. [18]When the accusers stood up, they did not bring any charge of such evil things as I expected. [19]Instead they had certain issues against him about their fear of the gods and about a certain Yeshua, who was dead, whom Paulos claimed to be alive. [20]Being perplexed how to inquire about these things, I asked whether he was willing to go to Yerushala'im and be judged there concerning these matters. [21]But when Paulos appealed to be kept for the decision of the Emperor, I commanded him to be kept until I could send him to Caesar."

[22]Agrippas said to Festus, "I also want to hear the man myself."

"Tomorrow," he said, "you will hear him."

[23]So on the next day, when Agrippas and Bernikeh had come with great ceremony, and they had entered with the commanding officers and principal men of the city into the auditorium, Paulos was brought in at the command of Festus. [24]Festus said, "King Agrippas, and all these men who are here present with us, you[+] see this man, about whom all the multitude of the Jews petitioned me, at Yerushala'im and here, crying that it's not right that he live any longer. [25]But when I found that he had committed nothing worthy of death, and as he himself appealed to the Emperor, I determined to send him. [26]I have nothing definite to write to my lord concerning him. So I have brought him forth before you[+], and especially before you, King Agrippas, so that I may have something to write after this examination. [27]For it seems to me absurd, in sending a prisoner, not to also specify the charges against him."

26 [1]Agrippas said to Paulos, "You are allowed to speak for yourself."

Then Paulos stretched out his hand and made his defense. [2]"I consider myself blessed, King Agrippas, that I am about to make my defense before you this day concerning all the things of which I am accused by the Jewish authorities, [3]especially because you are acquainted with all the customs and controversies among the Jews. Therefore I beg you to hear me patiently.

[4]"Indeed, all the Jewish authorities know my way of life from my youth up, which was from the beginning among my own nation and at Yerushala'im. [5]They have known me from before, if they are

25:27 "The first of these acts was: the 'postulatio rei,' the formal prayer of the accuser to the presiding officer of the 'quaestio' for the permission to bring an accusation against some certain person, whereupon the presiding officer investigated the facts submitted by the accuser, and according to the circumstances granted or refused the permission. If he granted the permission, there ensued the 'nominis,' and also the 'criminis delatio' whereby the accuser made a formal and definite accusation, which revealed the nature of the act, and the person of the accused. This regularly took place in the presence of the accused. Thereupon followed the 'inscriptio nominis' ('subscriptio') or 'criminis' as the formal notation of the accusation in a kind of court register, with the names of the acuser (who now formally declared himself as such) and the accused."

(A History of Continental Criminal Procedure, with special reference to France, The Continental Legal History Series, Vol. 5, Esmein Adhemar, René Garraud, Carl Joseph Anton Mittermaier, Association of American Law Schools, 1918, Pp. 21-22)

willing to testify, that I lived as a Parush after the strictest sect of our observance. ⁶Now I stand here to be judged for the hope of the promise made by God to our fathers, ⁷which our twelve tribes hope to attain, earnestly serving night and day. I am accused by the Jewish authorities concerning this hope, King Agrippas. ⁸Why is it considered unbelievable with you⁺, if God does raise the dead?

⁹"I myself truly thought that I ought to do many things contrary to the name of Yeshua the Natzri. ¹⁰I also did this in Yerushala'im. Having received authority from the chief Kohanim, I shut up in prisons many of those who belonged to God, and I also gave my vote against them when they were put to death. ¹¹Punishing them often in every meetingplace, I tried to make them blaspheme. Being enraged against them all the more, I pursued them even to foreign cities.

¹²"In doing this, I went to Damascus with the authority and commission from the chief Kohanim, ¹³On the way, O King, I saw a light at noon from the sky, brighter than the sun, shining around me and those who traveled with me. ¹⁴When we had all fallen to the earth, I heard a voice saying to me in the Hebrew language, 'Sha'ul, Sha'ul, why are you persecuting me? It is hard for you to kick against the goads.'

¹⁵"I said, 'Who are you, Lord?'

"He said, 'I am Yeshua, whom you are persecuting. ¹⁶Now get up and stand on your feet, because I have appeared to you for this purpose: to appoint you a servant and a witness both of the things which you have seen, and of the things which I will cause you to see. ¹⁷I will deliver you from the people and from the Gentiles to whom I send you. ¹⁸I send you to open their eyes so that they may turn from darkness to light, and from the power of the Accuser to God, so that they may receive forgiveness of sins and an inheritance among those who are set apart by faith in me.'

¹⁹"Therefore, King Agrippas, I was not disobedient to the heavenly vision. ²⁰On the contrary, I declared first to those of Damascus, then also Yerushala'im, throughout all the country of Judea, and also to the Gentiles, that they should change their ways and turn to God, doing deeds worthy of repentance. ²¹For this reason some sectarian Jews seized me in the Temple, and tried to kill me. ²²Having therefore obtained the help that is from God, I stand to this day testifying to both small and great, saying nothing but what the prophets and Moses said would happen — ²³how the Messiah must suffer, and how, by the resurrection of the dead, he would be first to proclaim light both to the people and to the Gentiles."

²⁴As he made his defense in this way, Festus said with a loud voice, "Paulos, you are crazy! Your great learning is driving you insane!"

²⁵But he said, "I am not crazy, Most Excellent Festus, but boldly declare words of truth and sound judgment. ²⁶Because the king, and I speak boldly to him, knows of these things. For I am persuaded that none of these things is hidden from him, because this has not been done in a corner. ²⁷King Agrippas, do you believe the prophets? I know that you believe."

²⁸Agrippas said to Paulos, "With little, you try to persuade me to become a disciple of Chrestus."

²⁹Paulos said, "I pray to God, that both with little and with much, not only you, but also all that hear me this day, might become such as I am, except for these chains."

³⁰The king rose up with the Governor, and Bernikeh, and those who sat with them. ³¹When they had withdrawn, they said one to another, "This man is doing nothing worthy of death or of

26:28 See the note to 11:26.

imprisonment." [32]Agrippas said to Festus, "This man might have been set free if he had not appealed to Caesar."

27 [1]When it was determined that we should sail for Italy, they delivered Paulos and certain other prisoners to a centurion named Julius, of the Emperor's military division. [2]Embarking in a ship of Adramyttium, which was about to sail to places on the coast of the province of Asia, we set sail. Aristarchus, a Makedonian of Thessalonika, was with us. [3]The next day, we touched at Tzidon. Julius treated Paulos kindly and gave him permission to go to his friends to receive care.

[4]Putting to sea from there, we sailed under the shelter of Kyprus, because of the headwinds. [5]When we had sailed across the sea which is off Kilikia and Pamphylia, we came to Myra, a city of Lykia. [6]The centurion found an Alexandrian ship sailing for Italy, and he put us on board. [7]When we had sailed slowly many days, and had come with difficulty opposite Knidus — the wind would not allow us to go farther — we sailed under the windbreak of Krete, opposite Salmone. [8]Sailing along it with difficulty, we came to a certain place called Fair Harbors, near the city of Lasea.

[9]When much time had passed and the voyage was now dangerous, because the Fast had already gone by, Paulos admonished them, [10]"Men, I perceive that the voyage will be with injury and much loss, not only of the cargo and the ship, but also of our lives." [11]But the centurion paid more attention to the master and to the owner of the ship than to the things which Paulos said. [12]Because the harbor was unsuitable to winter in, the majority advised leaving there, if by any means they could reach Phoenix and winter there, a port of Krete which looks southwest and northwest.

[13]When the south wind blew softly, they took up [the anchor] and sailed along Krete close to shore, thinking that they had succeeded in their objective. [14]But before long, there came a typhoon-like wind, which is called a Northeaster. [15]When the ship was caught and could not face the wind, we gave way to it, and were driven along. [16]Running under the windbreak of a small island called Kauda, we were barely able to secure the boat. [17]After they had hoisted it up, they used cables to help reinforce the ship. Fearing that they would run aground on the Syrtis sandbars, they lowered the sail, and were driven along that way. [18]Now we were extremely storm-tossed, and the next day they began to throw things overboard. [19]On the third day, they threw out the ship's tackle with their own hands. [20]Neither sun nor stars shone on us for many days. It was no small storm that beat on us. From that point, all hope that we would be saved was taken away.

[21]When they had not eaten for a long time, Paulos stood up in the middle of them, and said, "Men, you+ should have listened to me and not set sail from Krete; and not reaped this tragedy and loss. [22]Now I exhort you+ to be encouraged, because there will be no loss of life among you+, but only of the ship. [23]For this night there stood by me an angel belonging to the God whose I am and whom I serve. [24]He said, 'Do not be afraid, Paulos. You must stand before Caesar. And know that God has freely given you all those who sail with you.' [25]Therefore men, be encouraged! For I believe God that it will be exactlly as it has been spoken to me. [26]But we must run aground on a certain island."

[27]Now when the fourteenth night had come, as we were driven back and forth in the Adriatic [Sea], about midnight the sailors sensed that they were drawing near to some land. [28]They took

27:8 "Fair Harbors," i.e. *Kalos Limen*
27:9 "the Fast" refers to Yom Kippur.

soundings, and found twenty fathoms. After a little while, they took soundings again, and found fifteen fathoms. ²⁹Fearing that we would run aground on rocky ground, they cast four anchors from the stern, and longed for day to come.

³⁰The sailors were trying to escape out of the ship, and had lowered the boat into the sea, pretending that they were about to lay out anchors from the bow. ³¹Paulos said to the centurion and to the soldiers, "Unless these stay in the ship, you⁺ cannot be saved." ³²Then the soldiers cut away the ropes of the boat, and let it fall.

³³While the day was coming on, Paulos urged them all to receive some food, saying, "Today is the fourteenth day that you⁺ continue without food, having received nothing. ³⁴So I urge you⁺ to receive some food, because this is for your⁺ preservation. For not a hair from any of your⁺ heads will perish." ³⁵When he had said this and had taken bread, he gave thanks to God in the presence of all. And he broke it, and began to eat. ³⁶Then they all were encouraged, and they also took food. ³⁷In all, we were two hundred seventy-six people on the ship. ³⁸When they had eaten enough, they lightened the ship, throwing out the wheat into the sea.

³⁹When it was day, they did not recognize the land, but they noticed a certain bay with a beach, and decided to try to drive the ship onto it, if they could. ⁴⁰Casting off the anchors, they left them in the sea. At the same time, they untied the rudder ropes, hoisted up the foresail to the wind, and made for the beach. ⁴¹But coming to a place where two seas met, they ran the vessel aground. The bow struck and remained immovable, but the stern began to break up from the violence of the waves.

⁴²The soldiers' advice was to kill the prisoners so that none of them could swim out and escape. ⁴³But the centurion, desiring to save Paulos, kept them from their purpose, and commanded that those who could swim should throw themselves overboard first, to go toward the land. ⁴⁴And the rest were to follow, some on planks, and some on other things from the ship. So it happened that they all were brought safely to the land.

28 ¹And having escaped, we then learned that the island was called Malta. ²The natives showed us more than common kindness, for they kindled a fire and received us all because of the driving rain and because of the cold. ³But when Paulos had gathered a lot of sticks and put them on the fire, a poisonous snake came out because of the heat, and fastened on his hand. ⁴When the barbarians saw the animal hanging from his hand, they said to one another, "This man is surely a murderer. Though he has escaped from the sea, Justice does not permit him to live.

⁵But he shook off the animal into the fire, and was not harmed. ⁶They, however, expected him to become swollen or to suddenly fall down dead. And when they watched for a long time and saw nothing unusual happen to him, they changed their minds, and said that he was a god.

⁷Now in the neighborhood of that place were lands belonging to the chief man of the island, whose name was Publius. He received us, and hospitably lodged us as guests for three days. ⁸The father of Publius lay sick of fever and dysentery. Paulos went in to him, prayed, and, laying his hands on him, healed him. ⁹Then when this was done, the others in the island who had diseases also came, and were healed. ¹⁰And they honored us with many presents, and when we sailed, they put on board the things that we needed.

28:4 In Greek and Roman mythology, "Justice" is a goddess.

[11]After three months, we set sail in a ship of Alexandria which had wintered in the island. Its sign was "The Twin Brothers." [12]Touching at Syrakuse, we stayed there three days. [13]From there we circled around and arrived at Rhegium. After one day, a south wind sprang up, and on the second day we came to Puteoli. [14]There we found brethren and were urged to stay with them for seven days. And in this way, we went to Rome. [15]When the brethren from there heard about us, they came as far as the Market of Appius and the Three Taverns to meet us. When Paulos saw them, he thanked God, and was encouraged. [16]When we entered into Rome, the centurion delivered the prisoners to the captain of the guard, but Paulos was allowed to stay by himself with the soldier who guarded him.

[17]After three days Paulos called together the prominent Jews. When they had come together, he spoke to them. "Men and brothers, though I had done nothing against the people or the customs of the Fathers, I was delivered prisoner from Yerushala'im into the hands of the Romans. [18]When they had examined me, they desired to set me free, because there was not in me any guilt deserving death. [19]But when the Judean authorities spoke against it, I had to appeal to Caesar, not that I had anything about which to accuse my nation. [20]So for this reason, I asked to see you+ and to speak with you+, because I am bound with this chain for the hope of Israel."

[21]They said to him, "We neither received letters from Judea concerning you, nor did any of the brothers come here and report or speak any evil about you. [22]Yet we think it would be worthwhile to hear from you what you think, because, as concerning this sect, it is known to us that it is spoken against everywhere."

[23]When they had appointed a day to meet with him, many people came to him at his lodging. From morning until evening, he explained to them, bearing witness to God's kingdom, and persuading them concerning Yeshua, both from the Torah of Moses and from the Prophets. [24]Some believed the things which were spoken, and some disbelieved.

[25]When they did not agree with each other, they left after Paulos made this statement: "The Ruakh Kodesh correctly said to our fathers through Isaiah the prophet, [26]'Go to this people and say, *In hearing, you+ will hear, but will not at all understand. In seeing, you+ will see, but will not at all perceive.* [27]For the heart of this people has grown callous. Their ears are hard of hearing, they have shut their eyes. Otherwise they might see with their eyes, hear with their ears, understand with their heart, and turn again. Then I would heal them.' [Is. 6:9, 10] [28]Be it known to you+ therefore that the salvation of God is sent to the nations — they also will hear." [29]When he had said these words, the Jews departed, having a great dispute among themselves.

[30]Paulos stayed two whole years in his own rented house, and received all who were coming to him. [31]With all boldness, without hindrance, he proclaimed God's kingdom, and taught the things concerning the Lord Yeshua the Messiah.

28:11 "The Twin Brothers" would be the gods Castor and Pollux.

28:27 See the ADDITIONAL NOTES on "Pharaoh's Heart".

Jacob's Letter

1 [1]Jacob, a servant of God and of the Lord Yeshua the Messiah: greetings to the twelve tribes which are in the Diaspora. [2]Consider it all joy, my family, when you[+] encounter various testings, [3]knowing that the testing and approving of your[+] faith produces patience. [4]Let patience have its full work, so that you[+] may be complete and whole, lacking in nothing.

[5]Yet if any of you[+] lacks wisdom, let him ask of God — who gives generously to all and does not reproach — and it will be given to him. [6]But let him ask in faith, without any doubting, for the one who doubts is like a wave of the sea, driven and tossed by the wind. [7]For that man should not imagine that he will receive anything from the Lord. [8]He is a double-minded man, unstable in all his ways.

[9]Moreover, let the brother in humble circumstances glory in his high position; [10]and the rich in that he is made humble, because he will pass away like the flower in the grass. [11]For the sun arises with hear and withers the grass; its flower falls, and the beauty of its appearance perishes. [Is. 40:6-7] So also will the rich man fade away in his pursuits.

[12]There is good for the man who endures testings, because having been proven, he will receive the crown of life, which the Lord promised to those who love Him. [Gen. 22:1-19] [13]Let no man say when he is tempted, "I am tempted by God," because God cannot be tempted by evil, and He Himself tempts no one. [14]But each one is tempted when he is drawn away by his own desire and ensnared. [15]Then when the desire becomes pregnant, it gives birth to sin. And when the sin is full grown, it gives birth to death. [16]Do not be deceived, my beloved family.

[17]Every good act of giving and every perfect gift is from above, coming down from the Father of lights. With Him there is neither arbitrariness nor shifting that obscures the light. [18]He brought us forth from His own will by the word of truth, for each of us to be a first fruit of His creatures.

[19]Know this, my beloved family, and let every man be swift to hear, slow to speak, and slow to anger, [20]because the anger of man does not bring about the justice of God. [21]Therefore, putting away all impurity and increase of evil, receive the implanted word with humility, for it is able to save your[+] souls.

[22]Now be doers of the word, and not only hearers, deluding your[+] own selves. [23]For if anyone is a hearer of the word and not a doer, he is like a man beholding his likeness in a mirror. [24]For he observes himself, goes away, and immediately forgets what he is like. [25]However, the one who has

---

1:2 "my family," literally "my brothers"

1:13 "Do not say, 'It is through the Lord that I fell away,' for you should not do the things that He hates. Do not say, 'He has caused me to err,' for He has no need of the sinful man.... He has not commanded any man to do wickedly, nor has He given any man license to sin." (Sirach 15:11-12,20)

1:14-15 "R. Assi said, 'In the beginning, the evil inclination is like a thread of a spider, and in the end like a braided cartrope.'" (Tal. Sanhedrin 99b)

1:16,19, 2:1,5 "my (beloved) family," literally "my (beloved) brothers"

looked into the perfect law, the law of freedom, and has continued in it — not being a hearer who forgets, but a doer of the work — there is good for this man in what he does.

²⁶If anyone among you⁺ seems to be observant, yet does not bridle his tongue, deceiving his heart instead, this man's observance is worthless. ²⁷Pure and undefiled observance before our God and Father is this: to be concerned for the fatherless and widows in their affliction, and to keep oneself unstained by the world.

2 ¹My family, in having the faith of our Lord of glory, Yeshua the Messiah, do not judge by outward appearance. ²For if a man in fine clothing with a gold ring [Sir. 4:22] comes into your⁺ assembly, and a poor man in filthy clothing also comes in [Zekh. 3:3-4]; ³and you⁺ pay special attention to the one who wears the fine clothing, and say, "Sit here in a good place." And yet you⁺ tell the poor man, "Stand there," or "Sit by my footstool." ⁴Have you⁺ not shown partiality among yourselves, and become judges with evil opinions?

⁵Listen, my beloved family. Did not God choose those who are poor in this world to be rich in faith and heirs of the kingdom which He promised to those who love Him? ⁶But you⁺ have dishonored the poor man. Do not the rich oppress you⁺, and personally drag you⁺ before the courts? ⁷Do they not blaspheme the honorable name by which you⁺ are called?

⁸If you⁺ truly fulfill the law of the King according to the scripture, "You are to love your neighbor as yourself" [Lev. 19:18], you⁺ do well. ⁹But if you⁺ judge by outward appearance, you⁺ commit sin, being convicted by the Law as transgressors. ¹⁰For whoever keeps the whole Law and yet stumbles in one point, he has become guilty of all. ¹¹For the One who said, "Do not commit adultery," [Ex. 20:14, Dt. 5:18] also said, "Do not commit murder." [Ex. 20:13, Dt. 5:17] Now if you do not commit adultery, but do murder, you have become a transgressor of the Law. ¹²So speak, and so do, as men who are to be judged by a law of freedom. ¹³For judgment is without mercy to the one who has shown no mercy. Mercy rejoices over judgment.

¹⁴What good is it, my brethren, if a man says he has faith, but has no deeds? Such faith cannot save him. ¹⁵And if a brother or sister is naked and destitute of daily food, ¹⁶and one of you⁺ tells them, "Go

2:1 "Woe to the judge who is biased towards persons in judgment. R. Hiyya taught: 'You⁺ are not to do unrighteousness in judgment (Lev. 19:15). This teaches that the judge who perverts justice is called by five names: unrighteous, hated, detestable, robber, and an abomination. And the Holy One, blessed be He, calls him five [names]: evil, despiser, a covenant breaker, one who causes anger, and a rebel. And he causes five things in the world: he makes the land unclean, profanes the name of God, causes the Shekhinah to go up [from the earth], causes Israel to fall by the sword, and causes them to go into exile from their land. Woe to the generation which is perverted in this way!'" (Midrash Ruth I:2)

2:5 "Yes, yo[u are needy.] Do not say, 'Since I am poor, I cannot seek true knowledge.' Just apply yourself to every kind of learning and in every […] refine your heart, and your thoughts will be characterized by great insight." (DSS 4Q418 f9+9a_c:113-14)

2:5-7 "R. Yudan said: The punishment for exploiting the poor is greater than [that for] the iniquity of the generation of the flood." (Mid. Psalms 12.3)

2:14-18 This is similar to the parable Yeshua tells in Mt. 21:28-31. Obedience to God is shown by what we do, not by what we say. (cf. 3Yhn. 11)

in peace, be warmed and filled;" and yet you[+] did not give them the things the body needs, what is the benefit? [17]Even so, faith, if it has no deeds, is dead in itself. [18]Someone will say, "You have faith, and I have deeds. Show me your faith apart from your deeds, and I will show you my faith from my deeds."

[19]You believe that God is one. You do well. The demons also believe, and shudder. [20]But are you willing to acknowledge, O barren man, that faith without deeds does nothing? [21]Was not Abraham our father declared righteous from deeds, in that he offered up Isaac his son on the altar? [22]You see that faith was working with his deeds, and faith was completed by deeds. [23]Then the scripture was fulfilled which says, "Abraham believed God, and it was considered as righteousness for him." [Gen. 15:6] And he was called the friend of God. [Is. 41:8; 2Chr. 20:7] [24]You[+] see then that a man is declared righteous through deeds, and not from faith alone.

[25]In like manner was not Ra<u>h</u>av the harlot also declared righteous from deeds, in that she received the messengers and sent them out another way? [26]For just as the body without breath is dead, even so, faith without deeds is dead.

3 [1]My brethren, do not become many teachers, knowing that we will face a more demanding judgment. [2]For we all stumble in many things. If anyone does not stumble in word, that one is a perfect man, able to bridle the whole body also. [3]Now if we put bits into the horses' mouths for them to obey us, we guide their whole body also. [4]Observe that the ships also, though they are so big and are driven by strong winds, are yet guided by a very small rudder, wherever the pilot desires. [5]In the same way, the tongue is also a small part of the body, yet it boasts great things.

Consider a small fire, how large a forest it ignites! [6]And the tongue is a fire, a world of unrighteousness. The tongue is set in this way among our members, the defiler of the whole body, setting on fire the course of nature. And it is set on fire by Gehinnom.

[7]For every kind of wild animal, bird, creeping thing, and sea creature is tamed, and has been tamed by humanity. [8]But nobody can tame the tongue. It is a restless evil, full of deadly poison. [9]With it we bless our Lord and Father, and with it we curse men, who are made in the image of God. [Prov. 28:21] [10]Blessing and cursing go forth out of the same mouth. My brethren, these things ought not to be so. [11]Does a spring send out fresh water and bitter water from the same opening? [12]My brethren, can a fig tree produce olives? Or can a vine produce figs? Neither can a spring produce fresh water and salt water.

2:21 See note to Heb. 11:4-38.

3:1 "Avtalyon said, 'Teachers be warned about your words so that you are not condemned to exile, and you are exiled to a place of the evil waters; and the disciples who come after you will drink of them and will die, and it will happen that the name of Heaven is profaned." (Tal. Pirke Avot 1:11)

3:2-12 R. Simeon b. Gamliel sent his servant to "buy me good food from the market. He went and bought a tongue. Then he said to him, 'Go buy me bad food from the market.' He went and bought a tongue. ...He explained, 'From it there is good and from it there is bad." (Mid. Lev. Rabba 33.1)

3:9 "R. Yehoshua ben Levi said, 'In the hour a person walks on the road, the image of angels goes before him and proclaims and says, *Give place to the image of the Holy One, blessed be He.*'" (Mid. Tehillim 17:8)

¹³Who is wise and understanding among you⁺? Let him show by his good conduct that his deeds are done in gentleness of wisdom. ¹⁴But if you⁺ have bitter jealousy and selfish ambition in your⁺ heart, do not boast and do not lie against the truth. ¹⁵This wisdom is not what comes down from above, but is earthly, sensual, and demonic. ¹⁶For where there is jealousy and selfish ambition, there is confusion and every evil deed. ¹⁷But the wisdom that is from above is first pure, then peaceful, gentle, open to reason, full of mercy and good fruits, without partiality, and without pretension. ¹⁸Moreover, the fruit of righteousness is sown in peace for those who make peace. (Is. 32:17)

4 ¹What's the source of battles and what's the source of quarrels among you⁺? Is it not from your⁺ sensual pleasures that war in your⁺ physical bodies? ²You⁺ desire, and do not have. You⁺ covet, kill, and are unable to obtain. You⁺ fight and war, but you⁺ do not have, because you⁺ do not ask. ³You⁺ ask and do not receive, because you⁺ ask with evil intent, so that you⁺ may consume it in your⁺ sensual pleasures. ⁴You⁺ who commit adultery, do you⁺ not know that friendship with the world is hatred of God? Whoever therefore wants to be a friend of the world makes himself an enemy of God. ⁵Or do you⁺ think that the Scripture speaks without purpose? The Spirit which He caused to live in us has a strong desire. (Ex. 34:14; Dt. 4:24)

⁶Yet He gives more grace, therefore it says, "God resists the proud, but gives grace to the humble." [Ps. 138:6, Prov. 3:34] ⁷So subject yourselves to God, resist the Enemy, and he will flee from you⁺. ⁸Draw near to God, and He will draw near to you⁺. Cleanse your⁺ hands, you⁺ sinners, and purify your⁺ hearts, you⁺ double-minded. ⁹Lament, mourn, and weep. Let your⁺ laughter be turned to mourning, and your⁺ joy to gloom. ¹⁰Humble yourselves in the sight of the Everpresent Lord, and He will exalt you⁺.

¹¹Do not speak against one another, brethren. The one who speaks against a brother and judges his brother, speaks against the Law and judges the Law. But if you judge the Law, you are not a doer of the Law, but a judge. ¹²Only One is the Lawgiver. He is able to save and to destroy, but who are you to judge another?

¹³Come now, you⁺ who say, "Today or tomorrow we will go to a certain city, spend a year there, buy and sell, and make a profit" — ¹⁴you⁺ who do not know what your⁺ life will be tomorrow! It is only a vapor that appears for a little time, and then vanishes away. [2Sam. 14:14; Prov. 27:1] ¹⁵For you⁺ ought to say, "If the Everpresent Lord wills, we will live and also do this or that." ¹⁶But now you⁺ glory in your⁺ boasting. All such boasting is evil. ¹⁷To the one therefore who knows to do good and does not do it, to him it is sin.

5 ¹Come now you⁺ rich, weep and howl because of your⁺ miseries that are coming upon you⁺. ²Your⁺ riches have rotted and your⁺ garments are moth-eaten. ³Your⁺ gold and silver are corroded, and their corrosion will be a witness against you⁺, and will eat your⁺ flesh like fire. You⁺ have laid up your⁺ treasure in the last days.

⁴Know that the wages of the workers who mowed your⁺ fields, which you⁺ have kept back by fraud, cry out. And the cries of those who reaped have entered into the ears of the Commander of

3:13-18 "Everyone whose works are greater than his wisdom, his wisdom will endure. And everyone whose wisdom is greater than his works, his wisdom will not endure." (Tal. Avot 3:9)

all forces. [5]You⁺ have lived in indulgence upon the land. And you⁺ have nourished your⁺ hearts in self-gratification, as in a day of slaughter. [6]You⁺ have condemned, you⁺ have murdered the righteous; he does not resist you⁺.

[7]So be patient brethren until the coming of the Lord. See how the farmer waits for the precious fruit of the land, being patient over it, until it receives the early and late rain. [8]You⁺ also be patient. Make your⁺ hearts steadfast, for the coming of the Lord has come near.

[9]Brethren, do not grumble against one another, so that you⁺ will not be judged. Look, the Judge stands at the door. [10]Brethren, take the prophets who spoke in the Name of the Everpresent Lord for an example of suffering and of patience. [11]Notice that we call those who endured blessed. You⁺ have heard of the endurance of Job, and have seen the outcome from the Everpresent Lord — that the Everpresent Lord is full of compassion and mercy. [12]But above all things, my brethren, do not swear, either by heaven, or by the earth, or by any other oath. Instead, let your⁺ "Yes" be "Yes," and your⁺ "No," "No," so that you⁺ do not fall under judgment. [Dt. 23:21-23/22-24H, Sirach 9-11]

[13]Is any among you⁺ suffering? Let him pray. Is any cheerful? Let him sing praises. [14]Is any among you⁺ sick? Let him call for the elders of the congregation, and let them pray over him, anointing him with oil in the name of the Lord. [15]Then the prayer of faith will heal the one who is sick, and the Lord will raise him up. If he has committed sins, he will be forgiven. [16]Confess your⁺ offenses to each other, and pray for each other, that you⁺ may be healed. [Job 42:7-10]

The earnest entreaty of a righteous man is very powerful. [17]Eliyahu was a man with a nature like ours, and he prayed earnestly that it would not rain. And it did not rain on the earth for three years and six months. [18]He prayed again, and the heaven gave rain, and the earth brought forth its fruit.

[19]Brethren, if any among you⁺ wanders from the truth, and someone turns him back, [20]let him know that the one who turns back a sinner from the wandering of his way will save his soul from death, and will cover a multitude of sins.

5:5 "you have nourished your hearts in self-gratification as in a day of slaughter" seems to refer to the practice of fattening animals before they are killed to be eaten.

5:14 uses *ekklesia*, and 2:2 uses *sunagoge* as synonyms to designate the exact same thing.

5:19-20 "All who bring a single creature under the wings of the Shekhinah, they credit it to him as if he had formed him, shaped him, and brought him into the world." (Tos. Horayot 2:7)

Shimon Kefa's First Letter

1 [1]Kefa, an ambassador of Yeshua the Messiah, to those chosen who are living as strangers in the Diaspora in Pontus, Galatia, Cappadocia, the province of Asia, and Bithynia: [2]in accordance with the foreknowledge of God the Father, in holiness of the Spirit, so that you[+] may obey Yeshua the Messiah and be sprinkled in his blood. [Ex. 24:6-8; Lev. 14:1-7] Grace and increasing peace to you[+].

[3]Blessed is the God and Father of our Lord Yeshua the Messiah. He is the One who has brought us forth again to a living hope in accordance with His great mercy, through the resurrection from the dead of Yeshua the Messiah, [4]to an incorruptible and undefiled inheritance that does not fade away, kept in heaven for you[+]. [5]You[+] are being protected by the power of God through faith for a salvation ready to be revealed in the last time.

[6]You[+] greatly rejoice in this, though now, for a little while you[+] have been put to grief by various trials — if it is necessary [7]that the testing and proof of your[+] faith, which is more precious than gold that perishes, may be found to result in praise, glory, and honor at the revelation of Yeshua the Messiah, though it is tested by fire. [8]Not having seen him, you[+] love. Though you[+] do not see him now, yet believing in him, you[+] rejoice greatly with unspeakable joy that glorifies [God]. [9]You[+] are receiving the goal of your[+] faith, the salvation of your[+] souls. [10]The prophets sought and searched diligently concerning this salvation. They prophesied of the grace that would come to you[+]. [11]They were searching for what or what particular time the Spirit of Messiah which was in them was pointing to by testifying beforehand of the sufferings of Messiah and the glories that would follow them. [12]To them it was revealed that in these things, they were not serving themselves, but us. These things have now been announced to you[+] through those who proclaimed to you[+] the good news by the Ruakh Kodesh sent out from heaven. These are things into which angels desire to look.

[13]So prepare your[+] minds for action, be sober and set your[+] hope fully on the grace that will be brought to you[+] at the revelation of Yeshua the Messiah. [14]As children of obedience, do not conform yourselves to your[+] former desires, when you[+] were ignorant. [15]But just as the One who called you[+] is holy, you[+] yourselves also be holy in all of your[+] behavior, [16]because it is written, "You[+] are to be holy, because I am holy." [Lev. 11:44, 19:2, 20:7]

[17]If you[+] call on him as Father — He who judges according to each man's work, without judging according to outward appearance — pass the time of your[+] sojourning here in holy fear. [18]For you[+] know that you[+] were redeemed from the empty way of life of your[+] fathers' traditions, not by corruptible things like silver or gold, [19]but by precious blood, as of a lamb without spot, the blood

---

1:1 As an ambassador of Messiah to the Jewish people [cf.Gal. 2:7-8], Kefa writes to Jews in the Diaspora, i.e. those living outside the land of Israel.

1:18 "the empty way of life of your fathers' traditions" In parallel language in Mk. 7:8-9, Yeshua rebukes some Pharisees and teachers of the law for holding to vain traditions instead of to the commandments of God. In Gal. 1:14, Paul says that he "was extremely zealous for the traditions of my fathers."

of Messiah. [20]Indeed he was foreknown before the foundation of the world, but was revealed at the end of times for you[+]. [21]Through him, you[+] believe in God, who raised him up from the dead and gave glory to him; in order that your[+] faith and hope might be in God.

[22]Having purified your[+] souls in your[+] obedience to the truth unto genuine brotherly love, love one another fervently from the heart. [23]For you[+] have been born again, not of perishable seed, but of imperishable, through the living and abiding word of God. [24]For "All flesh is like grass, and all of its glory like the flower of the grass. The grass withers, and its flower falls, [25]but the Word of the Everpresent Lord endures forever." [Is. 40:6, 8] Now this is the word of the good news which was proclaimed to you[+].

2 [1]So putting away all evil, all deceit, pretensions, envies, and all slander, [2]long for the articulate, unadulterated milk of the Word as newborn infants, so that you[+] may grow by it unto salvation — [3]if indeed you[+] have tasted that the Lord is gracious. [4]You[+] are coming to him, a living stone rejected on the one hand by men, but chosen by God and precious. [5]As living stones also, you[+] are built up as a spiritual house, to be a holy priesthood, to offer up spiritual sacrifices, acceptable to God through Yeshua the Messiah. [6]Therefore it is contained in Scripture, "Behold, I set in Zion a chief cornerstone, chosen, precious. The one who believes in him will not be disappointed." [Is. 28:16]

[7] So to you[+] who believe, he is precious, but to those who are disobedient: "The stone which the builders rejected has become the head of the corner," [Ps. 118:22] [8]and, "a stone of stumbling, and a rock of offense." [Is. 8:14] They stumble at the Word because they disbelieve, even that to which they were appointed.

[9]But you[+] are a chosen seed, a royal priesthood, a holy nation, a people for God's own possession [Ex. 19:6; Is. 43:20], in order that you[+] may show forth the virtues of the One who called you[+] out of darkness into His marvelous light. [10]You[+] are those not a people at one time, but now God's people; who had not received mercy, but now have received mercy. [Hos. 1:10, 2:23]

[11]Beloved, I encourage you[+] as foreigners and sojourners to abstain from fleshly desires which war against the soul. [12]Have your[+] behavior among the Gentiles virtuous, so that in what they speak against you[+] as evil-doers, having observed your[+] good deeds, they may glorify God in the day of visitation. [Is. 10:3; Jer. 6:15, 10:15; Wis. 3:7; Sir. 18:20] [13]So subject yourselves to every human institution through the Lord, whether to the king as supreme, [14]or to governors as sent by him for vengeance on evil-doers and for praise to those who do well. [15]For this is the will of God, to put to

2:2 "R. Oshaia said: 'Why are the words of the Torah compared to these three liquids: to water, wine, and milk? as it is written, *'Ho, everyone who thirsts, come to the water'*; and it is written, *Come, buy and eat. Come buy wine and milk without money, and at no cost...*'" (Tal. Ta'anit 7a)

2:10 In context, the quotation from Hosea is a promise from God to restore Israel.

2:11-3:18 This section is an encouragement for those who follow Yeshua to have faith in God despite the possibility of having to suffer at the hands of people. In this, Yeshua is our primary example. Human relations, institutions, and authority structures are necessary, but like everything else in this world, they can be misused and abused. Because we have placed ourselves in subjection to God, we are willing to represent Him in this world. That may mean sharing in the sufferings of Messiah. Because we trust him, we are willing to do that.

silence the ignorance of foolish men by your[+] doing good — [16]as free, and not using your[+] freedom as a covering for evil, but as bondservants of God.

[17]Honor all men, love the brotherhood. Fear God, honor the king. [18]Household servants, be subordinate to your[+] masters with all fear — not only to the good and gentle, but also to the crooked. [19]For it is commendable if someone endures pain, suffering unjustly because of conscience toward God. [20]For what honor is there if when you[+] sin, you[+] patiently endure beating? But if, when you[+] do well, you[+] patiently endure suffering, this is commendable with God. [21]For to this you[+] were called, because Messiah also suffered for you[+], leaving you[+] an example, that you[+] should follow his steps. [22]He did not sin, "nor was deceit found in his mouth." [Is. 53:9] [23]When he was reviled, he did not return the insults. When he suffered, he did not threaten, but committed himself to the One who judges righteously. [24]He himself bore our sins in his body upon the tree, so that we, having died to sins, might live to righteousness. By his stripes you[+] were healed, [25]for you[+] were going astray like sheep [Is. 53:4-6], but are now returned to the Shepherd and Overseer of your[+] souls.

3 [1]In like manner, wives be under the authority of your[+] own husbands, so that, even if any do not obey the Word, they may be won by the behavior of their wives without a word, [2]seeing your[+] pure, reverent behavior. [3]Let your[+] beauty not be what is outward — the adorning of braiding the hair and of wearing jewels of gold, or of putting on fine clothing — [4]but in the hidden person of the heart, in the incorruptible adornment of a gentle and peaceful spirit, which is very precious in the sight of God. [5]For this is how the holy women of former times, those hoping in God, also adorned themselves, being subject to their own husbands. [6]This is how Sarah obeyed Abraham, calling him "lord". You[+] now are her children, if you[+] do what is good, and are not fearful of any unsettling thing.

[7]In like manner, husbands live with your[+] wives with understanding, giving honor to the woman as to one equipped with less strength, as being also heirs together of the grace of life, so that your[+] prayers may not be hindered.

[8]Finally, be all of one mind, compassionate, loving as brothers, tenderhearted, humble, [9]not rendering evil for evil, or insult for insult, but blessing instead, knowing that you[+] were called to this, so that you[+] might inherit a blessing. [10]For "Whoever would love life, and see good days, let him keep his tongue from evil, and his lips from speaking deceit. [11]Let him turn away from evil, and do good. Let him seek peace, and pursue it. [12]For the eyes of the Everpresent Lord are on the righteous, and His ears open to their prayer. But the face of the Everpresent Lord is against those who do evil." [Ps. 34:12-16]

[13]Now who is the one who will harm you[+] if you[+] become imitators of what is good? [14]But even if you[+] should suffer as a consequence of righteousness, there is good for you[+]. Do not fear what they fear, nor be troubled. (Is. 8:14) [15]Instead, sanctify the Messiah as Lord in your[+] hearts, and always be ready to give an answer with humility and fear to everyone who asks you[+] the reason for the hope that is in you[+]. [16]Keep a good conscience so that, whereas you[+] are maligned, those who abusively attack your[+] good manner of life in Messiah may be ashamed. [17]For it is better, if it is the will of God,

3:1-6 Abigail is an example of a godly woman who recognized her greater responsibility to God in her submission to her own husband. (1Sam. 25:2-42) See note to 1Tim. 2:9-14.

that you+ suffer for doing good rather than for doing evil, [18]since Messiah also suffered for sins once, the righteous for the unrighteous, so that he might bring you+ to God.

He was put to death in the flesh, but made alive by the spirit. [19]In this way he also went and proclaimed to the spirits in prison — [20]those who had been disobedient in the days of Noah, when God waited patiently while the ark was being built. In it, a few, that is eight souls, were saved through water. [21]This is an illustration of the immersion which now saves us, not the putting away of the filth of the flesh, but the response of a good conscience toward God through the resurrection of Yeshua the Messiah. [22]He is at the right hand of God, having gone into heaven; angels and authorities and powers having been subjected to him.

[1]Forasmuch then as Messiah suffered for us in the flesh, arm yourselves also with the same purpose. For the one who has suffered in the flesh refrains from sin, [2]no longer to live the rest of the time in the flesh for the desires of men, but for the will of God. [3]For the time that has passed was sufficient for doing the will of the Gentiles, to have walked in sensual desires, drunkenness, carousals, partying, and abominable idolatries.

[4]They think it is strange, and revile you+ for not running with them into the same excess of unthinking indulgence. [5]They will give account to the One who is ready to judge the living and the dead. [6]For this purpose, the good news was proclaimed even to the dead, so that they might be judged as men in the flesh on the one hand, but live according to God in the spirit.

[7]Now the end of all things has come near. So be of sound mind, self-controlled, and sober in prayer. [8]And above all things, be earnest in your+ love towards each other, because love covers a multitude of sins. [9]Love the foreigners among you+ without grumbling. [10]According as each has received a gift, serve each other with it as good managers of the grace of God in its various forms. [11]If any man speaks, as messages of God; if any man serves, as from the strength which God supplies — so that in all things God may be glorified through Yeshua the Messiah. To him belong the glory and the dominion forever and ever. Amen.

[12]Beloved, do not be astonished at the fiery trial which has come upon you+ to test you+, as though a strange thing were happening to you+. [13]But as you+ are partakers of the Messiah's sufferings, rejoice, so that at the revelation of his glory you+ may also rejoice and exult. [14]If you+ are insulted for the name of Messiah, there is good for you+, because the Spirit of glory and of God rests on you+.

[15]For let none of you+ suffer as a murderer, or a thief, or an evil doer, or as a meddler in other men's matters. [16]But if one suffers as a "disciple of what is good," let him not be ashamed, but let him glorify God in this name. [17]For the time has come for judgment to begin at the house of God. If it begins first with us, what will happen to those who disobey the good news of God? [18]"If it is hard for the righteous to be saved, what will happen to the ungodly and the sinner?" [Prov. 11:31] [19]Therefore those who suffer for the purpose of God, let them also entrust their souls to Him in doing good, as to a faithful Creator.

4:16 Chrestus meant "good" or "useful," and therefore was a common name. The word *chrestianon* means *"disciple of chrestus"*. It was not something which the disciples called themselves, but rather something which Gentile unbelievers called them. The Gentile unbelievers thought that the disciples went after someone named Chrestus.

>>

5 [1]As a fellow elder and a witness of the sufferings of Messiah, I exhort the elders among you[+], who will also share in the glory that will be revealed: [2]Shepherd the flock of God which is with you[+], exercising the oversight not under compulsion, but voluntarily; not from greed, but willingly; [3]not as exercising lordship over the assigned portion, but making yourselves examples to the flock. [4]When the chief Shepherd is revealed, you[+] will receive the crown of glory that does not fade away.

[5]Likewise, you[+] younger ones, be subject to those who are your[+] elders. Yes, all of you[+], gird yourselves with humility to subject yourselves to one another, because "God resists the proud, but gives grace to the humble." [Prov. 3:34] [6]Humble yourselves therefore under the mighty hand of God, so that He may exalt you[+] in due time; [7]casting all your[+] worries on Him, because He cares for you[+]. [Ps. 55:23H]

[8]Be sober and self-controlled. Be watchful. Your[+] adversary, the Enemy, walks around like a roaring lion, seeking those to devour. [9]Resist him, steadfast in the faith, knowing that your[+] brethren who are in the world are undergoing the same sufferings.

[10]Now may the God of all grace, who called you[+] by Messiah to His eternal glory — after you[+] have suffered a little while — may He restore, establish, strengthen, and place you[+] on the foundation. [11]To Him be the power forever and ever. Amen.

[12]Through Silvanus, whom I consider a faithful brother, I have written to you[+] briefly, exhorting and testifying that this is the true grace of God in which you[+] stand. [13]She who is in Babylon, chosen together with you[+], greets you[+], and so does Mark, my son. [14]Greet one another with a kiss of love. Peace be to you[+] all who are in Messiah.

The historical record shows that the believers were accused in court with the name Chrestos. For example, Justin Martyr, in his First Apology, wrote: "For we are accused of being Chrestianoi, and to hate what is chreston [good, useful] is unjust." (Iustini Martyris, Apologiae pro Christianis, ed. by Mirorslav Marcovich, Walter de Gruyter, NY, 1994, P. 12, 4:25)

To Gentile unbelievers, *christos* simply meant "rubbed with an ointment." It was not a name, nor even a noun. Kefa refers to both the incorrect name by which they were accused, and also to the meaning of the word. I.e., 'They incorrectly say that we follow Chrestos [some person], but in reality we follow *chrestos* [what is good].' Justin does the same in his Apology.

Kefa uses *onomati*, a word which, according to Liddell & Scott, means both "name" and "a false name, pretence, pretext, ...under the pretence, Thuc...." For more detail, see "A Little Case of Mistaken Identity" in my Copernicus and the Jews.

5:8 Satan "descends and deceives, then goes up and causes wrath. Authority is put upon him, and he carries off a soul." (Tal. Baba Bathra 16a)

"The authority of the Angel of Darkness embraces the governance of all wicked people, so they walk in the paths of darkness. The authority of the Angel of Darkness further extends to the corruption of all the righteous. All their sins, iniquities, shameful and rebellious deeds are at his prompting, a situation God in His mysteries allows to continue until His era dawns.... All the spirits allied with him share but a single resolve: to cause the Sons of Light to stumble. Yet the God of Israel (and the Angel of His Truth) assist all the Sons of Light." (DSS 1QS 3:20-25)

Shimon Kefa's Second Letter

1 [1]Shimon Kefa, a servant and ambassador of Yeshua the Messiah, to those who have obtained a like precious faith with us in the righteousness of our God and Savior Yeshua, the Messiah. [2]Grace to you+ and peace be multiplied in the acknowledgement of God and of Yeshua our Lord. [3]How His divine power has granted to us all things that pertain to life and godliness, through the acknowledgement of the One who called us by His own glory and virtue! [4]Through these, He has granted to us His precious and exceedingly great promises, so that through them you+ may become partakers of the divine nature, having escaped from the decay that is in the world through desire. [Gen. 3:6]

[5]Yes, and adding all diligence for this very cause, in your+ faith supply virtue. And in virtue, supply knowledge; [6]and in knowledge, self-control; and in self-control, patience; and in patience, godliness; [7]and in godliness, brotherly kindness; and in brotherly kindness, love. [8]For if these things are in you+ and abounding, they cause you+ to be neither useless nor unfruitful for the knowledge of our Lord Yeshua the Messiah. [9]For the one who lacks these things is blind, seeing only what is near, having forgotten the cleansing from his old sins. [10]Therefore brethren, be more diligent to confirm your+ being called and chosen. For if you+ do these things, you+ will never stumble. [11]For in this way, the entrance into the eternal Kingdom of our Lord and Savior, Yeshua the Messiah, will be richly supplied to you+.

[12]Therefore I will not neglect to remind you+ always of these things, though you+ know them and are established in the present truth. [13]I consider it right, as long as I am in this tent, to stir you+ up by reminding you+ — [14]knowing that the putting off of my tent is coming swiftly, even as our Lord Yeshua the Messiah made clear to me. [15]Yes, I will make every effort that you+ may always be able to remember these things even after my departure.

[16]For we did not follow cunningly devised fables when we made known to you+ the power and coming of our Lord Yeshua the Messiah, but we were eyewitnesses of his majesty. [17]For he received honor and glory from God the Father when the voice came to him from the Majestic Glory: "This

---

1:5-8 "R. Pinhas b. Jair said: 'Quickness [to obey] leads to [lit. *brings into the hands of*] cleanliness; cleanliness leads to purity; purity leads to holiness; holiness leads to humility; humility leads to the fear of sin; the fear of sin leads to godliness; godliness leads to the Holy Spirit; the Holy Spirit leads to the resurrection of the dead; the resurrection of the dead leads to Eliyahu the prophet." (Mid. Song Rabbah I:9) Eliyahu the prophet announces the coming of Messiah and the Messianic Age. See also Rom. 5:3-5. This progression is an indication of what God values in humanity.

2:5 "the righteous Noah rebuked them, urging, 'Make repentance, and if not, the Holy One, blessed be He, will bring the flood upon you, and cause your corpses to float on the water like *zikin* /gourds..." (Tal. Sanhedrin 108a) The word *zikin* is obscure; the Soncino has "gourds".

Noah was the eighth generation after Adam, but the Greek word for generation is feminine, and the form of "eighth" is masculine. It is much the same as the form of "seventh" in Jude 14. It may refer to the number of people in the ark, as in 1Kefa 3:20.

is My beloved Son, in whom I delight." [18]We heard this voice come out of heaven when we were with him on the holy mountain.

[19]We have the prophetic word confirmed. You[+] do well to take heed to it, as to a lamp shining in a dark place until the day dawns and the day star arises in your[+] hearts. [20]We know this first, that no prophecy of Scripture comes from one's own free expression [Gen. 40:8], [21]because no prophecy ever came by the will of man, but men of God spoke, being moved by the Ruakh Kodesh.

2 [1]But there were false prophets also among the people, as there will also be false teachers among you[+], who will secretly bring in destructive choices, denying even the Master who bought them, bringing on themselves swift destruction. [2]Many will follow their immoral ways, and, as a result, the way of the truth will be maligned. [3]In covetousness, they will exploit you[+] with deceptive words. Judgment long determined for them will not delay, and their destruction does not slumber.

[4]For God did not spare angels when they sinned, but cast them down to the abyss, and imprisoned them in chains of darkness to be kept for judgment. [5]And when He brought a flood on the world of the ungodly, He did not spare the ancient world, but preserved Noah, the eighth, who proclaimed righteousness. [6]And turning the cities of Sedom and Amorah into ashes, He condemned them to destruction, having made them an example to those considering living ungodly.

[7]And He delivered righteous Lot, who was oppressed by the filthy behavior of the wicked. [8]For that righteous man dwelling among them was tormented in his righteous soul day after day with seeing and hearing their unlawful deeds. [9]The Lord knows how to deliver the godly out of temptation and to keep the unrighteous for the day of judgment to be punished — [10]and especially those who despise authority and walk after the flesh in defiling desire.

Insolent, self-centered, they are not afraid to revile what is glorious, [11]whereas angels, though greater in might and power, do not revile them in judgment before the Lord. [12]But these, as unreasoning beasts, by nature born unto capture and destruction, speak evil in matters about which they are ignorant, and will surely be destroyed in their decadence, [13]suffering wrong as the payment of doing wrong. They count it pleasure to indulge themselves in the daytime. They are spots and blemishes, reveling in their deceit while they feast with you[+]. [14]Having eyes full of adultery, they cannot cease from sin — enticing unsettled souls, having a heart trained in greed — accursed children. [15]Forsaking the right way, they went astray, having followed the way of Bala'am the son of Beor, who loved the wages of wrong-doing. [16]But he was rebuked for his own disobedience; a voiceless beast of burden spoke in the voice of man and restrained the madness of the prophet.

[17]These are wells without water, clouds driven by a storm. The blackness of darkness has been reserved forever for them. [18]For uttering pompous words of vanity, through lewdness they entice in the desires of the flesh those who had barely escaped from those who turn back to error. [19]They promise them liberty, while they themselves are slaves of decadence. For by whatever a man is overcome, by the same he is also brought into bondage.

[20]For if, through the acknowledgment of the Lord and Savior Yeshua the Messiah, they have escaped the defilements of the world and they are afterwards again entangled in them and overcome, the last state has become worse with them than the first. [21]For it would be better for them not to have known the way of righteousness, than after knowing it to turn back from the holy commandment delivered to them. [22]Nevertheless, it has happened to them according to the true proverb, "The dog turns to his own vomit again, and the washed sow to wallowing in the mire."

3 [1]Beloved, this is now the second letter that I have written to you⁺. In both of them I am awakening your⁺ pure mind by reminding you⁺ [2]to remember the words which were previously spoken by the holy prophets, and the commandments spoken by us, the ambassadors of the Lord and Savior. [3]Knowing this first, that in the last days mockers will come ridiculing, walking after their own desires, [4]and saying, "Where is the promise of his coming? for since the fathers fell asleep, all things continue as they were from the beginning of Creation."

[5]For they willfully forget this, that by the word of God the heavens existed from long ago, and an earth came into existence from water and in water. [6]Through these, the world that then was, being deluged with water, perished. [7]But the present heavens and earth are kept by His word, awaiting fire, being kept unto a day of judgment and destruction of ungodly men. [8]But do not forget this one thing, beloved, that one day is as a thousand years with the Everpresent Lord, and a thousand years as one day. [Ps. 90:4]

[9]The Everpresent Lord is not slow concerning His promise, as some count slowness, but is patient with you⁺, not purposing that any should perish, but that all should come to repentance. [10]But the day of the Everpresent Lord will come as a thief in the night, in which the heavens will pass away with a great noise, and the elements will be dissolved with fervent heat, and the earth and the works that are in it will be found out. [Is. 34:4]

[11]So since all these things are going to be dissolved, what kind of people should you⁺ be? In holy living and godly service, [12]be looking for and earnestly desiring the coming of the day of God. The heavens being on fire will be dissolved, and the elements will melt with fervent heat because of it. [13]But in accord with His promise, we look for new heavens and a new earth, in which righteousness dwells.

[14]Therefore beloved, expecting these things, be diligent to be found in peace, without blemish and blameless in His sight. [15]And consider the patient endurance of our Lord as salvation, even as our beloved brother Paulos, according to the wisdom given to him, also wrote to you⁺. [16]Likewise he also speaks in all of his letters about these things. In his letters there are some things which are difficult to understand, which the ignorant and unstable twist to their own destruction, as they also do to the other Scriptures. [17]So you⁺, beloved, knowing these things beforehand, be alert. Otherwise, being carried away with the error of the lawless, you⁺ may fall from your⁺ own steadfastness. [18]Instead, grow in the grace and knowledge of our Lord and Savior, Yeshua the Messiah. To him be the glory both now and forever. Amen.

3:9 In the Amidah between Rosh haShanah and Yom Kippur, we say, "Remember us to life, O King who delights in life. And write us in the Book of Life for Your sake, O living God."

3:10 "The knowledge of the coming of three is veiled, and these are they: Messiah, something found, and a scorpion." (Tal. Sanhedrin 97a)

Yohanan's First Letter

1 ¹The Word of life is what was from the beginning. We have heard it, and we have seen it with our eyes. We examined it and our hands touched it. ²The life was revealed, and we have seen and testify and declare to you⁺ the life, the eternal life, which was with the Father, and was revealed to us. ³We declare to you⁺ what we have seen and heard, so that you⁺ also may have fellowship with us. Yes, and our fellowship is with the Father and with His Son, Yeshua the Messiah. ⁴Now we write these things so that our joy may be full.

⁵This is the message which we have heard from Him and announce to you⁺, that God is light, and in Him there is no darkness at all. ⁶If we say that we have fellowship with Him and walk in the darkness, we lie and are not doing the truth. ⁷But if we walk in the light as He is in the light, we have fellowship with one another, and the blood of Yeshua the Messiah, His Son, cleanses us from all sin.

⁸If we say that we have no sin, we deceive ourselves, and the truth is not in us. ⁹If we confess our sins, He is faithful and just to forgive us the sins, and to cleanse us from all wrong-doing. ¹⁰If we say that we have not sinned, we make Him a liar, and His word is not in us.

2 ¹My little children, I write these things to you⁺ so that you⁺ may not sin. If anyone sins, we have an advocate with the Father, Yeshua the Messiah, the just one. ²He is the atoning sacrifice for our sins, and not for ours only, but also for the whole world.

³This is how we know that we know him, if we keep his commandments. ⁴Someone who says, "I know him" and does not keep his commandments is a liar, and the truth is not in him. ⁵But whoever keeps his word, God's love has truly been made complete in him. This is how we know that we are in him. ⁶The one who says he lives in him ought himself also to walk just as he walked.

⁷Beloved, I write no new commandment to you⁺, but an old commandment which you⁺ had from the beginning. The old commandment is the word which you⁺ have heard. ⁸On the other hand, I do write a new commandment to you⁺, which is true in him and in you⁺; because the darkness is passing away, and the true light already shines. ⁹The one who says he is in the light and hates his brother is in the darkness even until now. ¹⁰The one who loves his brother remains in the light, and there is no cause of stumbling in him. ¹¹But the one who hates his brother is in the darkness, and walks in the darkness, and does not know where he is going, because the darkness has blinded his eyes.

2:1 In the Rosh haShanah liturgy: "Since there is no advocate of righteousness to plead our cause, teach Jacob, You Yourself, Your word, statute and judgment; and clear us in judgment, O King of justice."

2:2 Rashi comments on the setting apart of the Levites (Num. 8:9) and the need for all Israel to lay hands on them: "Inasmuch as the Levites were given as an atoning sacrifice instead of them [the whole congregation], they [the people] are to come and stand by their offering and lay their hands on them [the Levites]."

2:7-8 "The Torah which a person learns in this world is a passing breath before the Torah of Messiah." (Mid. Lamentations 11.7)

[12]I write to you[+] little children, because your[+] sins are forgiven through his name. [Ezek. 36:21-23] [13]I write to you[+] fathers, because you[+] know him who is from the beginning. I write to you[+] young men, because you[+] have overcome the evil one. I write to you[+] little children, because you[+] know the Father. [14]I have written to you[+] fathers, because you know the One who is from the beginning. I have written to you[+] young men, because you[+] are strong, and the word of God remains in you[+], and you[+] have overcome the evil one.

[15]Do not love the world or the things that are in the world. If anyone loves the world, the love of the Father is not in him. [Gen. 3:6] [16]For all that is in the world — the desire of the flesh, the desire of the eyes, and the boastful pride of life — is not of the Father, but is of the world. [Gen. 3:6] [17]The world is passing away with its desires, but the one who does the will of God remains forever.

[18]Little children, it is the last hour, and as you[+] heard that the Adversary of Messiah is coming, even so many adversaries of Messiah have now arisen. By this we know that it is the last hour. [19]They went out from us, but they were not of us. For if they had been of us, they would have continued with us. But they left so that they all might be revealed as not being of us.

[20]You[+] have an anointing from the Holy One, and you[+] know all things. [21]I have not written to you[+] because you[+] do not know the truth, but because you[+] do know it, and because no lie is of the truth. [22]Who is the liar but the one who denies that Yeshua is the Messiah? The one who denies the Father and the Son is the adversary of Messiah. [23]Whoever denies the Son, the same does not have the Father. The one who confesses the Son has the Father also.

[24]As for you, let what you[+] heard from the beginning remain in you[+]. If what you[+] heard from the beginning remains in you[+], you[+] also will remain in the Son, and in the Father. [25]This is the promise which He promised us, eternal life. [26]These things I have written to you[+] concerning those who would lead you[+] astray. [27]As for you[+], the anointing which you[+] received from him remains in you[+], and you[+] do not need for anyone to teach you[+]. But as his anointing teaches you[+] concerning all things, and is true and is no lie, and even as it has taught you[+], you[+] will remain in him. [28]Now, little children, remain in him, so that when he appears, we may have boldness and not be ashamed before him at his coming. [29]If you[+] know that he is just, you[+] know that all who do justice are born of him.

3 [1]Behold, how great a love the Father has bestowed on us, that we should be called children of God. [Gen. 1:26] And we are. Because of this, the world does not know us, because it did not

---

2:15-17 These basic types of temptation shed light on the temptation of Adam and Havah [Gen. 3:6], and the temptations which Yeshua faced. [Mt. 4:1-10,] From Garden to Garden, we can begin to examine and comprehend the archetype of bad decision-making as well as its cure.

3:1-2 "It is analogous to a king who brought his son out of prison and who said, 'Make a continual holiday for him, because my son has come out from darkness to light, from an iron yoke to life, from slavery to freedom, and from servitude to redemption.' In this way, the Holy One, blessed be He, brought Israel out of prison, as it says: 'He brings out the prisoners into prosperity' (Ps. 68:7). From darkness and the shadow of death, as it says: 'He brought them out of darkness and the shadow of death' (Ps. 107:14). From a yoke of iron to the yoke of Torah. From slavery to freedom, as it says: 'You are the children of the Everpresent Lord, your God' (Deut. 14:1). From servitude to redemption, as it says, 'Their Redeemer is strong, the Everpresent Commander of forces is His Name'. (Jer. 50:34)" (Mid. Ex. Rabbah 15:11)

know Him. [2]Beloved, now we are children of God, and it has not yet been revealed what we will be. But we know that when He is revealed, we will be like Him, for we will see Him just as He is. [3]Everyone who has this hope set on Him purifies himself, even as He is pure.

[4]Everyone who commits sin also acts contrary to the Law. Sin is action contrary to the Law. [5]You[+] know that He was revealed to take away sins, and there is no sin in Him. [6]Whoever stands fast in Him does not sin. Whoever sins has neither seen Him nor known Him.

[7]Little children, do not let anyone lead you[+] astray. The one who is doing what is right is righteous, even as He is righteous. [8]The one who is doing what is sin is from the Enemy, for the Enemy has been sinning from the beginning. The Son of God was revealed for this purpose, that he might undo the works of the Enemy. [9]Whoever is born of God does not continue in sin, because His seed remains in him; and he is not empowered to sin, because he is born of God. [10]The children of God and the children of the Enemy are readily apparent in this: whoever does not continue in what is right is not of God, nor is the one who does not love his brother.

[11]For this is the message which you[+] heard from the beginning so that we should love one another — [12]not as Ka'in, who was of the evil one, and killed his brother. Why did he kill him? Because his own works were evil, and those of his brother were righteous. [13]Do not be surprised, my brethren, if the world hates you[+].

[14]We know that we have passed out of death into life, because we love the brethren. The one who does not love dwells in death. [15]Whoever hates his brother is a murderer, and you[+] know that no murderer has eternal life dwelling in him. [16]We know love by this, because he laid down his life for us, and we ought to lay down our lives for the brethren.

[17]Now whoever has the world's goods and sees his brother in need, yet closes his heart of compassion against him, how is the love of God present in him? [18]My little children, we should not love in word and in tongue, but in action and in truth. [19]And by this we know that we are of the truth, and will assure our hearts before Him. [20]Since if our heart condemns us, God is greater than our heart, and knows all things. [21]Beloved, if our hearts do not condemn us, we have boldness toward God; [Sir. 14:2] [22]and whatever we ask, we receive from Him, because we keep His commandments and do the things that are pleasing in His sight. [23]This is His commandment so that we should believe in the name of His Son, Yeshua the Messiah, and love one another, even as he commanded. [24]The one who keeps His commandments dwells in Him, and He in him. By this we know that He is present in us, by the Spirit which He gave us.

[1]Beloved, do not believe every spirit, but test the spirits, whether they are of God, because many false prophets have gone out into the world. [2]You[+] know the Spirit of God by this, every spirit which confesses that Yeshua the Messiah has come in the flesh is of God. [3]But every spirit which does not confess Yeshua, this is the spirit of the Adversary of Messiah and is not of God. You[+] have heard of it, that it is coming, and it is now in the world already.

3:15 Rashi comments on Dt. 19:11, "'But if any man hates his neighbor': "Through hating him he comes to 'lie in wait for him.' Therefore they said, 'If one transgresses a light commandment, his end is to transgress a weighty commandment.' Because he transgressed against 'You shall not hate' (Lev. 19:17), his end is to shed blood."

[4]You[+] are of God, little children, and have overcome them, because the One who is in you[+] is greater than the one who is in the world. [5]They are from the world. Therefore they speak from the world, and the world hears them. [6]We are from God. The one who knows God hears us. The one who is not from God does not hear us. By this we know the spirit of truth, and the spirit of error.

[7]Beloved, let us love one another, because love is from God, and everyone who loves is born of God, and knows God. [8]The one who does not love does not know God, because God is love. [9]God's love toward us was revealed by this, that God has sent His one and only Son into the world so that we might live through him. [10]In this is love, not that we loved God, but that He loved us, and sent His Son as the atoning sacrifice for our sins. [11]Beloved, if God loved us in this way, we also ought to love one another.

[12]No one has ever beheld God. If we love one another, God abides in us, and His love has been fulfilled in us. [13]By this we know that we abide in Him and He in us, because He has given us from His Spirit.

[14]We have seen and testify that the Father has sent the Son as the savior of the world. [15]Whoever agrees that Yeshua is the Son of God, God is present in him, and he in God. [16]We know and have believed the love which God has for us. God is love, and the one who dwells in love dwells in God, and God dwells in him. [17]Love has been made complete with us in this, so that we may have boldness in the day of judgment, because as He is, even so are we in this world. [18]There is no fear in love, but love that is complete casts out fear, because fear has torment. The one who fears is not fully mature in love.

[19]We love because He first loved us. [20]If a man says, "I love God," and hates his brother, he is a liar, because the one who does not love his brother whom he has seen, cannot love God whom he has not seen. [21]We have this commandment from Him so that the one who loves God should also love his brother.

[5] [1]Whoever believes that Yeshua is the Messiah is born of God. Whoever loves the Father also loves the child who is born of Him. [2]When we love God and keep His commandments, we know by this that we love the children of God. [3]For this is the love of God, that we keep His commandments. His commandments are not burdensome, [4]because whatever is born of God overcomes the world. This is the victory that has overcome the world, our faith. [5]Since Yeshua is the Son of God, who is the one who overcomes the world, if not the one who believes?

[6]This is the one who came by water and blood, Yeshua the Messiah; not with the water only, but with the water and the blood. It is the Spirit who bears witness, because the Spirit is the truth. [7]For there are three who testify: [8]the Spirit, the water, and the blood. And the three agree as one.

4:20-21 "R. Yehoshua ben Levi said, 'In the hour a person walks on the road, the image of angels goes before him and proclaims and says, *Give place to the image of the Holy One, blessed be He.*'" (Mid. Tehillim 17:8)

5:4-5 In the liturgy, in the "Revelation of God in Nature" near the beginning of the evening Rosh haShanah service, we read, "God is in the faith by which we overcome the fear of loneliness, of helplessness, of failure and of death."

[9]If we receive the testimony of men, the testimony of God is greater, since this is God's testimony which He has testified concerning His Son. [10]The one who believes in the Son of God has the evidence in himself. The one who does not believe God has made Him a liar, because he has not believed in the testimony that God has given concerning His Son. [11]This is the testimony: that God gave eternal life to us, and this life is in His Son. [12]The one who has the Son has the life. The one who does not have the Son of God does not have the life. [13]I have written these things to you[+] who are believing in the name of the Son of God so that you[+] may know that you[+] have eternal life.

[14]This is the boldness which we have towards Him, since He hears us if we ask anything according to His will. [15]And if we know that He hears us in what we ask, we know that we have the petitions which we have asked of Him.

[16]If anyone sees his brother sinning a sin not leading to death, he should ask, and God will give him life for those who sin not leading to death. There is a sin leading to death, and I am not saying that he should make a request concerning this. [Dt. 21:22] [17]All unrighteousness is sin, but there is a sin not leading to death. [18]We know that everyone who is born of God does not sin. On the contrary, the one who has been born of God guards himself, and the evil one does not touch him. [19]We know that we are from God, and the whole world lies down with the evil one. [20]We know that the Son of God has come and given us understanding, so that we might know the One who is true. And we are in Him who is true, in His Son Yeshua the Messiah. This is the true God and eternal life.

[21]Little children, keep yourselves from idols.

5:19 "The authority of the Angel of Darkness embraces the governance of all wicked people, so they walk in the paths of darkness. The authority of the Angel of Darkness further extends to the corruption of all the righteous. All their sins, iniquities, shameful and rebellious deeds are at his prompting, a situation God in His mysteries allows to continue until His era dawns…. All the spirits allied with him share but a single resolve: to cause the Sons of Light to stumble. Yet the God of Israel (and the Angel of His Truth) assist all the Sons of Light." (DSS 1QS 3:20-25)

Yohanan's Second Letter

1 ¹The elder, to the chosen lady and her children, whom I love in truth, and not only I, but also all those who know the truth: ²for the sake of the truth which remains in us, and will be with us forever. ³Grace, mercy, and peace will be with us in truth and love from God the Father, and from Yeshua the Messiah, the Son of the Father. ⁴I rejoice greatly that I have found some of your children walking in truth, even as we have been commanded by the Father.

⁵Now I entreat you, dear lady — not as though I wrote to you a new commandment, but what we had from the beginning — that we love one another. ⁶This is love, so that we should walk according to His commandments. This is the commandment, even as you⁺ heard from the beginning, that you⁺ should walk in it.

⁷For many deceivers have gone out into the world — those who do not confess that Yeshua the Messiah came in the flesh. This is the deceiver and the adversary of Messiah. ⁸Watch yourselves so that you⁺ do not lose the things which we have accomplished, but that you⁺ may receive a full reward.

⁹Whoever does not remain in the teaching of the Messiah, and goes beyond does not have God. The one who remains in the teaching, this one has both the Father and the Son. ¹⁰If anyone comes to you⁺ and does not bring this teaching, do not receive him into your⁺ house, and do not welcome him, ¹¹because the one who welcomes him participates in his evil works.

¹²Having many things to write to you⁺, I do not want to do so with paper and ink. I hope to come to you⁺ instead and speak face to face, that our joy may be made full. ¹³The children of your chosen sister greet you.

Yohanan's Third Letter

1 ¹The elder, to Gaius the beloved, whom I love in truth. ²Beloved, I pray that you may prosper in all things and be in health, even as your soul prospers. ³For I rejoiced greatly when brothers came and testified about the truth in you, even as you walk in truth. ⁴I have no greater joy than this, to hear about my children walking in truth.

⁵Beloved, you do a faithful work in whatever you accomplish for those who are brethren and strangers. ⁶They have testified about your love before the community. You will do well to send them forward on their journey in a manner worthy of God, ⁷because they went out for the sake of the Name, taking nothing from the Gentiles. ⁸We therefore ought to receive such, that we may be fellow workers for the truth.

⁹I wrote something to the community, but Diotrephes, who loves to be first among them, does not receive us. ¹⁰So when I come, I will call attention to his deeds which he does, unjustly accusing us with wicked words. Not content with this, he himself does not receive the brethren, and he also forbids those who would, and he throws them out of the community.

¹¹Beloved, do not imitate what is evil, but what is good. The one who does good is from God. The one who does evil has not seen God. ¹²Everyone bears witness to Demetrius, as does the truth itself. And we also bear witness, and you know that our testimony is true.

¹³I had many things to write to you, but I do not want to write to you with pen and ink. ¹⁴I hope to see you soon instead, and we will speak face to face. Peace be to you. The friends greet you. Greet the friends by name.

Judah's Letter

1 ¹Judah, a servant of Yeshua the Messiah and brother of Jacob, to those who are called, beloved in God the Father, and kept for Yeshua the Messiah. ²Mercy, peace, and love be multiplied to you⁺.

³Beloved, using all diligence to write to you⁺ about the salvation we have in common, I needed to write to you⁺, exhorting you⁺ to contend earnestly for the faith which was delivered once for all time to those who belong to God. ⁴For there are certain men who have crept in secretly, even those who were long before marked out for this judgment — ungodly men, turning the grace of our God into sensuality, and denying our only Master and Lord, Yeshua the Messiah.

⁵Now I desire to remind you⁺, though you⁺ once knew this, that the Everpresent Lord, having saved a people out of the land of Egypt, afterward destroyed those who did not believe. ⁶Angels who did not keep their primary domain, but deserted their own dwelling place, He has kept in everlasting chains under darkness for the judgment of the great day. ⁷Even as Sedom, Amorah, and the cities around them, in the same way as these, having given themselves over to sexual immorality and having gone after strange flesh, are set forth as an example, suffering the punishment of eternal fire.

⁸In a similar way, these dreamers also defile the flesh, despise authority, and revile things of glory. ⁹But Mikhael, the archangel, when contending with the Enemy and arguing about the body of Moses, did not dare to bring against him an abusive condemnation, but said, "May the Everpresent Lord rebuke you!" ¹⁰These, however, revile whatever things they do not know. But as much as they know by instinct, like the unreasoning creatures, in these things they corrupt themselves.

¹¹Woe to them! For they have gone in the way of Ka'in, and rushed to the error of Bala'am for payment, and perished in the rebellion of Korah. ¹²These are hidden rocky reefs in your⁺ love feasts, eating together with you⁺ in audacity, feeding themselves. They are clouds without water, carried along by winds; autumn trees without fruit, twice dead, pulled up by the roots. ¹³They are wild waves of the sea, foaming out their own shame; wandering stars, for whom the shroud of darkness has forever been reserved.

¹⁴Hanokh, the seventh from Adam, also prophesied about these, saying, "Look, in the midst of His holy myriads, ¹⁵the Everpresent Lord came to execute judgment on all, and to punish all these ungodly ones for all their deeds of ungodliness which they have done in an ungodly way, and of all the harsh things which ungodly sinners have spoken against Him." ¹⁶These are murmurers and complainers, walking according to their own desires; and their mouths bulging with arrogant boasts, flattering people for the sake of profit.

¹⁷But you⁺, beloved, remember the words which were previously spoken by the ambassadors of our Lord Yeshua the Messiah. ¹⁸They said to you⁺ that in the end of this time there will be mockers, walking after their own ungodly desires. ¹⁹These are the ones who cause divisions, sensual, without the Spirit. ²⁰But you⁺, beloved, keep building yourselves up upon your⁺ most holy faith, praying in the Ruakh Kodesh. ²¹Keep yourselves in the love of God, looking for the mercy of our Lord Yeshua the Messiah unto eternal life. ²²Have compassion on some who are doubting, ²³but save others by

snatching them out of the fire. Have mercy with fear, hating even the clothing stained by the flesh.

[24]Now to the One who has the power to keep you[+] from stumbling and to present you[+] faultless before the presence of His glory in great joy, [25]to the only God, our Savior, through Yeshua the Messiah, our Lord, be glory and majesty, dominion and power, both now and forever. Amen.

Sha'ul/Paulos' Letter to the Romans

1 [1]Paulos, a servant of Yeshua the Messiah, called to be an ambassador, set apart for the good news of God, [2]which He promised before through His prophets in the holy Scriptures — [3]concerning His Son, who was born physically from the seed of David, [4]designated and powerfully demonstrated to be the Son of God by the Spirit of holiness, through the resurrection from the dead, Yeshua the Messiah, our Lord. [5]We received grace through him and appointment as an ambassador for obedience of faith among all the Gentiles, for his name's sake. [6]You[+] are also among them, called of Yeshua the Messiah. [7]To all who are in Rome, beloved of God, called to be holy: grace to you[+] and peace from God our Father and the Lord Yeshua, the Messiah.

[8]First, I thank my God through Yeshua the Messiah for all of you[+], that your[+] faith is proclaimed throughout the whole world. [9]For God, whom I serve in my spirit in the good news of His Son, is my witness how unceasingly I make mention of you[+] always in my prayers. [10]I am asking of Him, if by any means, I may now at last be prospered by the will of God to come to you[+]. [11]For I long to see you[+] so that I may impart to you[+] some spiritual gift in order to establish you[+]. [12]Now this is so that I may be encouraged together with you[+], each of us by the other's faith, both yours[+] and mine.

[13]Now I do not want you[+] to be unaware, brothers, that I often planned to come to you[+] so that I might have some fruit among you[+] also, even as among the rest of the Gentiles. But I have been hindered until now. [14]I am a debtor both to Greeks and to foreigners, both to the wise and to the foolish. [15]So as for me, I am eager to proclaim the good news to you[+] also who are in Rome. [16]For I am not ashamed of the good news of Messiah, since it is the power of God unto salvation for everyone who is believing, both to the Jew first and to the Greek. [17]For in it God's righteousness is revealed from faith to faith. As it is written, "But the just person is to live by faith." [Hab. 2:4]

[18]For the wrath of God is revealed from heaven against all ungodliness and unrighteousness of men who suppress the truth in unrighteousness. [19]This is because what is known about God is evident in them, since God has revealed it to them. [20]For His invisible characteristics, even His everlasting power and divine nature, are clearly seen by the creation of the world, being perceived through the things that have been made. So they are without excuse, [21]because, knowing God, they did not glorify Him as God, nor did they give thanks, but were futile in their reasoning, and their foolish heart was darkened.

[22]Professing themselves to be wise, they became fools, [23]and traded the glory of the ever-living God for the likeness of images of perishing man, birds, four-footed animals, and creeping things. [24]And therefore God gave them up to uncleanness in the desires of their hearts, to disgrace their

---

1:5-6,13 These verses indicate that the primary audience of the ambassador to the Gentiles, as in all his letters, is the Gentiles.

1:17 "Isaiah [33:15-16] came and presented them [the 613 commandments] as six.... Micah [6:8] came and presented them as three.... Isaiah [56:1] came again and presented them as two.... Amos [5:4] came and presented them as one....'Seek Me and live'... Nevertheless, Habakkuk [2:4] who came and presented them as one, as it is said, 'But the just person is to live by his faith.'" (Tal. Makkot 24a)

bodies among themselves. [25]They exchanged the truth of God for a lie, and worshipped and served the creature rather than the Creator, who is blessed forever. Amen.

[26]For this reason, God gave them up to disgraceful passions. For both their females changed the natural intimacy into what is against nature; [27]and likewise also the males, abandoning the natural intimacy of the woman, were inflamed in their appetite toward one another, males doing with males what is filthy, and receiving in themselves the due penalty of their deviant behavior. [28]Even as they chose not to retain God in their understanding, God delivered them over to a corrupt mind, to do and approve those things which are not right.

[29]They are filled with all wrong-doing, wickedness, covetousness, and maliciousness, and full of envy, murder, strife, deceit, and evil habits. They are slanderers in secret, [30]backbiters, hateful to God, insolent, haughty, boastful, inventors of evil things, disobedient to parents, [31]without understanding, disloyal, without natural affection, unforgiving, and unmerciful. [32]Knowing the ordinance of God that those who practice such things are worthy of death, they not only do these same things, but also approve of those who practice them.

2 [1]Therefore you are without excuse, every person who judges, because in that which you judge another, you condemn yourself. For you who judge practice the same things. [2]Now we know that the judgment of God is according to truth against those who practice such things. [3]O man who condemns those who practice such things and yet does the same, do you think that you will escape the judgment of God? [4]Or do you despise the riches of His goodness, restraint, and patient endurance, not recognizing that the goodness of God is what leads you to repentance?

[5]But through your hardness and unrepentant heart you are storing up treasure for yourself — wrath in the day of wrath and of revelation of the just judgment of God. [6]He "will pay back to everyone according to their deeds" [Ps. 62:12, Prov. 24:12] — [7]everlasting life to those who by endurance in good work are seeking for glory, honor, and what does not decay. [8]But to those who are self-seeking and do not obey the truth, but obey unrighteousness, there will be wrath and indignation. [9]Affliction and anguish to every soul of man who produces evil, both of the Jew first and of the Greek. [10]But glory and honor and peace to every man who does what is good, both to the Jew first and to the Greek. [11]For there is no judging by outward appearance with God.

[12]For as many as have sinned without the Law will also be destroyed without the Law. As many as have sinned in the Law will be judged by the Law. [13]For it is not the hearers of the Law who are just before God, but the doers of the Law will be declared to be just. [14]For whenever the Gentiles, who do not have the Law, naturally do the things of the Law, these, not having the Law, are a law to themselves. [15]They show the work of the Law written in their hearts, their conscience testifying with them, and their inner thoughts accusing or else defending themselves [16]in the day when God will judge the secrets of men through Yeshua the Messiah, as in my good news.

1:25 God created humanity "in His image, in the image of the likeness of His pattern." (Tal. Ketubot 8a) "In the hour that the Holy One, blessed be He, created the first Adam, the ministering angels erred and sought to say 'Holy' before him." (Mid. Genesis 8.10) I.e., the angels could not distinguish the first Adam from God.

2:4 "Because His lovingkindness has prevailed upon us..." (Ps. 117:2)

[17]But if you are named a Jew, rest in the Law and glory in God, [18]know His will and approve the things that are excellent (being instructed out of the Law), [19]and are confident that you yourself are a guide of the blind, a light to those who are in darkness, [20]a corrector of the foolish, a teacher of infants, having in the Law the form of knowledge and of the truth — [21]you therefore who teach another, do you not teach yourself? You who proclaim that a man should not steal, do you steal? [22]You who say a man should not commit adultery, do you commit adultery? You who abhor idols, do you plunder what is holy? [23]You who glory in the Law, do you dishonor God through the transgression of the Law? [24]For just as it is written, "the Name of God is blasphemed among the Gentiles because of you[+]." [Is. 52:5, Ezek. 36:20]. [25]For circumcision is indeed beneficial if you keep the Law, but if you are a transgressor of the Law, your circumcision has become uncircumcision. [Jer. 9: 26]

[26]So if the uncircumcised keeps the righteous requirements of the Law, won't his uncircumcision be considered as circumcision? [27]Won't the physically uncircumcised, if he fulfills the Law, judge you, you who are a transgressor of the Law through what is written and circumcision? [28]For being a Jew is not in the appearance, nor is circumcision what appears in the flesh. [1Sam. 16:7; Jer. 9:26; Ps. 51:6] [29]Rather it is the one who is a Jew in what is hidden — and circumcision is that of the heart [Dt. 30:6], in the spirit not in the letter — whose praise is not from people, but from God.

3 [1]Then what is the advantage of the Jew? Or what is the benefit of circumcision? [2]Much in every way! Because first of all, they were entrusted with the utterances of God. [3]So what if some were unfaithful? Will their unfaithfulness make the faithfulness of God cease? [4]Far from it! Yes, let God be found true, but every man a liar. As it is written, "That You might be justified in Your words, and might prevail in Your judgment." [Ps. 51:6H/4]

[5]But if our unrighteousness establishes the righteousness of God, what will we say? Is God unrighteous who inflicts wrath? I speak as men do. [6]Far from it! For then how will God judge the world? [7]For if through my lie the truth of God is made greater, to His glory, why am I also still judged as a sinner? [8]Why not — as we are slanderously reported and some affirm that we say — "Let us do evil, that good may come"? Those who say so are justly condemned.

[9]What then? Are we better than they? Not at all. For we previously charged both Jews and Greeks that they are all under sin. [10]As it is written, "There is no one righteous, no, not one. [11]There is no

2:19 "To justice, he who would be happy holds fast, and follows in her company with all humility and order; but he who is lifted up with pride, or elated by wealth or rank, or beauty, who is young and foolish, and has a soul hot with insolence, and thinks that he has no need of any guide or ruler, but is able himself to be the guide of others, he, I say, is left deserted of God..." ("LAWS," BK. IV, The Dialogues of Plato, trans. B. Jowett, Vol. 3, Oxford, Clarendon, 1892, P. 98)

2:26-29 The essence and purpose of being Jewish is not physical. The physical is a starting point, but the essence is the calling that God has placed within the individual Jew. For the fulfillment of this calling, praise does not come from people, but from God. Sha'ul highlights this through the hypothetical, though not possible (cf. Rom. 3:20), case of a Gentile keeping the Law. See the ADDITIONAL NOTE ON "Circumcision and the Law".

3:2 "Great is circumcision, since 13 covenants were enacted on it... It overrides Shabbat... it overrides [the laws of] leprosy..." (Tal. Nedarim 3.16 [31b])

one who understands. There is no one who seeks after God. [12]They have all turned aside. They have together become unprofitable. There is no one who does good, no, not so much as one." [Ps. 14:1-3; Ps. 53:1-3]

[13]"Their throat is an open tomb. With their tongues they have used deceit." [Ps. 5:9] "The poison of vipers is under their lips," [Ps. 140:3] [14]"whose mouth is full of cursing and bitterness." [Ps. 10:7] [15]"Their feet are swift to shed blood. [16]Destruction and misery are in their ways. [17]The way of peace, they have not known." [Is. 59:7] [18]"There is no fear of God before their eyes." [Ps. 36:1]

[19]Now we know that whatever things the Law says, it speaks to those with the Law, so that every mouth may be silenced and all the world may come under judgment before God. [20]Because no flesh will be declared righteous in His sight from the workings of the Law, because through the Law comes the knowledge of sin.

[21]But a righteousness of God separate from the Law has now been revealed, being attested by the Law and the prophets — [22]even the righteousness of God through faith in Yeshua the Messiah, to all those who believe. For there is no distinction, [23]because all have sinned and fall short of the glory of God. [2Esd. 8:35-36]

[24]We are being freely declared righteous by His grace through the redemption that is in Messiah Yeshua, [25]through faith in his blood. God set him forth to be an atoning sacrifice to demonstrate His justice, because of God's forbearance in passing over the sins that were previously committed. [26]This is to demonstrate at this present time His justice, that He might be the just One and the justifier of the one who has faith in Yeshua.

[27]Where then is the boasting? It is excluded. Through what kind of law? Of works? No, but by a law of faith, [28]because we understand that a man is justified through faith apart from the workings of the Law. [29]Or is God the God of Jews only, and not also of Gentiles? Yes, of Gentiles also [Ps. 22:27-28, Jer. 10:7], [30]since there is one God who will justify the circumcised from faith, and the uncircumcised through the faith.

[31]Do we then cause the Law to cease through faith? Far from it! No, we cause the Law to stand.

4 [1]What then shall we say that Abraham, our physical father has found? [2]For if Abraham was declared righteous from works, he has something to boast about, but not toward God. [3]For what does the Scripture say? "Abraham believed God, and it was attributed to him as righteousness." [Gen. 15:6] [4]Now to the one who works, payment is not considered to be a gracious gift, but what is owed. [5]And to the one who does not work, but believes in Him who makes the ungodly righteous, his faith is considered as righteousness for him. [6]In this way, David also speaks of the blessing on the person to whom God attributes righteousness apart from works: [7]"There is good for the ones whose actions contrary to the Law are forgiven, and whose sins are covered. [8]There is good for the person to whom the Everpresent Lord will not attribute any sin." [Ps. 32:1, 2]

[9]Is this blessing then on the circumcised, or also on the uncircumcised? For we say that faith

3:20 The Law declares what actions are sinful, and reveals that all people sin. Therefore all are condemned by it; no one, whether circumcised or uncircumcised, is declared righteous by it.

4:5 in the traditional liturgy, the Birkat haGomel says, "Blessed are You, Everpresent Lord, our God, King of the universe, who rewards good to the guilty; who rewarded me with all that is good."

was attributed to Abraham as righteousness. [Gen. 15:6] ¹⁰How then was it attributed? When he was in circumcision or in uncircumcision? Not in circumcision, but in uncircumcision. ¹¹He received the sign of circumcision — a seal of the righteousness of the faith which he had while he was in uncircumcision — so that he might be the father of all those who believe, though they be in uncircumcision, so that righteousness might be attributed to them also. ¹²It was also so that he might be the father of circumcision to those who not only are of the circumcision, but who also walk in the steps of that faith of our father Abraham, which he had in uncircumcision. ¹³For the promise to Abraham, or that to his seed, that he should be heir of the world was not through the Law, but through the righteousness of faith.

¹⁴For if those from the Law are heirs, faith has been nullified and the promise is made irrelevant. ¹⁵For the Law brings about wrath, because where there is no law, neither is there disobedience. ¹⁶For this reason it is from faith, that it may be according to grace, to the end that the promise may be sure to all the seed, not only to that which is from the Law, but also to that which is from the faith of Abraham, who is the father of us all. ¹⁷As it is written, "I have made you a father of many Gentiles." [Gen. 17:5]

God, before whom he believed, gives life to the dead, and proclaims the things that are not, as though they were. ¹⁸In hope against hope, he believed unto the end, so that he might become a father of many Gentiles, according to what had been spoken: "So will your seed be." [Gen. 15:5; 17:5] ¹⁹Without being weakened in faith, he considered his own body — already deadened since he was about a hundred years old — and the deadness of Sarah's womb. ²⁰But looking to the promise of God, he did not waver through unbelief, but grew strong through faith, giving glory to God. ²¹And he was fully assured that what He had promised, He was also able to perform. ²²Therefore it also "was attributed to him as righteousness." [Gen. 15:6]

²³Now it was not written for his sake alone that it was attributed to him, ²⁴but it was written for our sake also who believe in Him who raised Yeshua our Lord from the dead, to whom it is about to be attributed. ²⁵He was delivered up for our transgressions, and was raised for our acquittal.

5 ¹Being therefore declared righteous from faith, we have peace with God through our Lord Yeshua the Messiah. ²By faith we also have our access through him into this grace in which we stand.

And we rejoice in hope of the glory of God. ³Not only this, but we also rejoice in our sufferings, knowing that suffering produces perseverance; ⁴and perseverance, proven character; and proven character, hope. ⁵And hope does not disappoint us, because God's love has been poured out into our hearts through the Ruakh Kodesh which was given to us.

⁶For while we were still without strength, Messiah died at the right time for the ungodly. ⁷But it would be rare for someone to die for a just person, yet possibly someone would even be courageous enough to die on behalf of a good person. ⁸But God commends His own love toward us, in that while

5:3-5 This progression is an indication of what God values in humanity.

5:7-8 "R. Akiba came and taught: '*that your brother may live with you*: [Lev. 25:36] your life goes before the life of your fellowman.'" (Tal. Baba Metzia 62a) He reasoned that your life takes precedence over that of your brother because only if you are living can he live with you.

we were still sinners, Messiah died for us. [9]Much more then, being now justified by his blood, we will be saved from God's wrath through him. [10]For if while we were enemies, we were reconciled to God through the death of His Son, much more, being reconciled, will we be saved by his life.

[11]Not only so, but we also rejoice in God through our Lord Yeshua the Messiah, through whom we have now received reconciliation. [12]In this way, even as Sin entered into the world by one man, and death through Sin, so death passed to all men, because all sinned. [Wisdom 2:24] [13]For even before the Law, Sin was in the world, but sin is not charged unless law exists. [14]Death, however, reigned from Adam until Moses, even over those whose sins were not like the disobedience of Adam, who is a foreshadowing of the One who was to come.

[15]But the free gift is not like the transgression. For if the many died by the transgression of the one, much more did the grace of God, and the gift by the grace of the one man, Yeshua the Messiah, abound to the many. [16]The gift is not like what came through the one who sinned, because the judgment indeed was from one offense unto a judgment of condemnation, but the free gift is from many transgressions unto acquittal. [17]For if by the transgression of the one, death reigned through the one, so much more will those who receive the abundance of grace and of the gift of righteousness reign in life through the one, Yeshua the Messiah. [18]So then, as all men were brought to a judgment of condemnation through one transgression, even so were all men brought to acquittal unto life through one act of righteousness. [19]For as through the one man's disobedience the many were made sinners, even so, through the obedience of the one, the many will be made righteous. [20]Law entered as well, so that the transgression might abound. But where Sin abounded, grace abounded much more. [21]So that as Sin ruled by death, even so might grace rule through righteousness unto eternal life through Yeshua the Messiah our Lord.

5:12-8:3 In these verses, Sha'ul uses *hamartia*, i.e. "sin," with an article about 30 times. To try to indicate a sense of the way in which he is using the word in these places, I have capitalized "Sin". See "Sin and *Yetzer haRa*" in the ADDITIONAL NOTES.

5:13 It is simple and obvious that one can only break a law if that law exists. If no law exists, then one cannot break it. Breaking an existing law is a crime, but there is no crime without law. This is the same as the Latin *Nullum crimen sine leges*. Rom. 4:15 says the same.

5:14 "In the ninth [hour of the day he was created, Adam] was commanded to not eat from the tree. In the tenth, he stunk from sin. In the eleventh, he was judged. In the twelfth, he was driven out and went." (Tal. Sanhedrin 38b)

5:15-19 The rabbinic concept of *zakut abot*, the merits of the fathers, is similar, though it only relates to the positive effects. "The righteous are blessed. Not only is there merit for them, but they give merit to their children and their children's children to the end of all generations..." (Tal. Yoma 87a)

"Which measure abounds more? The measure of goodness or the measure of punishment? It is said, the measure of goodness is five hundred times greater than the measure of punishment." (Mid. Psalms 15.7)

5:17 Law specifies what actions will be punished as crimes, i.e. sins.

5:19 "Six things were taken away from the first Adam, and these are they: his glorious brightness, his life, his stature, the fruit of the earth, the fruit of the trees, and the lights [in heaven]." (Mid. Gen. Rabba 12:6)

6 ¹What shall we say then? Shall we continue in Sin so that grace may abound? ²Far from it! We who died to Sin, how shall we still live in it? ³Or do you⁺ not know that as many as were immersed into Messiah Yeshua were immersed into his death? ⁴Therefore we were buried with him through immersion to death, so that just as Messiah was raised from the dead through the glory of the Father, so we also might walk in newness of life. ⁵For if we have been planted with him in the likeness of his death, we will also be part of his resurrection. ⁶We know this: that our old man was put to death on the stake with him, so that the body of Sin might be made useless, so that we would no longer be in bondage to Sin. ⁷For the one who has died has been freed from Sin.

⁸But if we died with Messiah, we believe that we will also live with him, ⁹knowing that Messiah, being raised from the dead, dies no more. Death no longer has dominion over him, ¹⁰because the death that he died, he died to Sin once for all. But the life that he lives, he lives to God. ¹¹In the same way, consider yourselves also to be dead to Sin, but alive to God in Messiah Yeshua.

¹²So do not let Sin rule in your⁺ mortal body that you⁺ should listen to its desires. ¹³And do not present the members of your⁺ body to Sin as instruments of wrong-doing, but present yourselves to God as alive from the dead. And present your⁺ members to God as instruments of what is right. ¹⁴For Sin will not rule over you⁺, because you⁺ are not in subjection to law, but in subjection to grace. ¹⁵What then? Shall we sin because we are not in subjection to law but in subjection to grace? Far from it! ¹⁶To whomever you⁺ yield yourselves as bondservants to obedience, you⁺ are bondservants to him whom you⁺ obey, whether of sin unto death, or of obedience unto what is right. Do you⁺ not know this? ¹⁷But thanks be to God that though you⁺ were bondservants of Sin, you⁺ became obedient from the heart to that form of teaching to which you⁺ were handed over. ¹⁸Being made free from Sin, you⁺ became bondservants of what is right.

¹⁹I speak as men do because of the weakness of your⁺ flesh. For as you⁺ yielded your⁺ members in bondage to uncleanness and actions contrary to the Law — unto more actions contrary to the Law — even so now present your⁺ members in bondage to what is right, unto sanctification. ²⁰For when you⁺ were bondservants of Sin, you⁺ were free from what is right. ²¹What fruit did you⁺ then have at that time in the things of which you⁺ are now ashamed? For the end of those things is death. ²²But now, being made free from Sin, and having become bondservants of God, you⁺ have your⁺ fruit unto sanctification, and the outcome is eternal life. ²³For Sin pays wages in death, but the free gift of God is everlasting life in Messiah Yeshua our Lord.

7 ¹Or do you⁺ not know, brothers — for I speak to men who know the Law — that the Law has dominion over a person as long as the person lives? ²For the married woman is bound to a living husband by law. But if the husband should die, the law concerning the husband ceases to apply to her.

6:17 Sin was your master, but you have been given to a new master, the teaching of obedience to Messiah.

6:23 "The evil inclination of a person is strong against him every day and seeks to kill him." (Tal. Sukkah 52b)

7:1 "the Law has dominion over a person as long as the person lives" The Talmud also says the same. "Our Rabbis taught: 'A garment in which *kil'ayim* [the separation of materials which may not be mixed] was lost ...one may make from it a shroud for the dead.' R. Joseph said: 'This says that the commandments will >>

³So if she were joined to another man while the husband lives, then she would be called an adulteress. But if the husband were to die, she is released from the law, so that she would not be an adulteress if she became the wife of another man. ⁴So too, my brothers, you⁺ also were made dead to the Law through the body of the Messiah, for you⁺ to belong to another who was raised from the dead, so that we might bring forth fruit to God. ⁵For when we were in the flesh, the painful consequences of sins, defined by the Law, worked in the members of our body to bring forth fruit to death. ⁶But now we have ceased to work for the Law, having died to what held us. Consequently, we serve in newness of the Spirit, and not in oldness of the letter.

⁷What shall we say then? Is the Law sin? Far from it! To the contrary, I would not have known Sin, if not by the Law. For I would not have been conscious of coveting, unless the Law had said, "You are not to covet." [Ex. 20:17, Dt. 5:21] ⁸But Sin, finding an opportunity through the commandment, produced in me all kinds of coveting, for sin is dead without law. ⁹I was alive apart from law once, but when the commandment came, Sin came to life and I died. ¹⁰And the commandment, which is for life, was found to be death for me, ¹¹because Sin, finding an opportunity through the commandment, deceived me and put me to death through it. ¹²Therefore the Law indeed is holy, and the commandment holy, just, and good.

¹³Did what is good then become death to me? Far from it! But Sin, so that it might be shown to be what it is, brought forth death to me through what is good, so that Sin might become extremely sinful through the commandment. ¹⁴For we know that the Law is spiritual, but I am fleshly, sold in subjection to Sin. ¹⁵For I do not understand what I am doing. For I do not accomplish what I desire to do, but what I hate, that I do. ¹⁶But if I am doing what I do not desire, I agree with the Law as to what is right.

¹⁷So then I am no longer producing it, but the Sin which dwells in me. ¹⁸For I know that good is not dwelling in me, that is, in my flesh, because the desire to do what is right is present with me, but accomplishing it is not. ¹⁹For I do not do the good which I desire, but the evil which I do not desire, that I do. ²⁰But if I am doing what I do not desire, I am no longer producing it, but Sin which dwells in me. ²¹So I find in myself the principle that while I desire to do good, evil is present with me. ²²For I delight in the Law of God in the inner man, ²³but I see a different direction in my physical body, warring against the direction of my mind, and bringing me into captivity to the direction of Sin, which is in my members.

---

cease in the time to come.'...R. Johanan said: 'What is the meaning of what is written, *Free among the dead*? As soon as a man dies he is made free from the commandments." (Tal. Niddah 61b citing Ps. 88:5H, cf. Tal. Shabbat 151b) Of interest also is Job 3:19: "The small and great are there, and the servant is free from his master."

7:2 The death of a young woman's father frees her from his authority. (Tal. Nedarim 70b)

7:12 "though we be deprived of wealth, of cities, or of any other good strength, our Law continues immortal; nor can any Jew go so far from his own country, nor be so afraid of the harshest lord, as not to be more afraid of the Law than of him." (Josephus, Against Apion 2:277 -278 [2.39.277-8])

7:17-23 In the Midrash on Psalms 9.5, the Evil Inclination is called "King," because it rules over all the members of the body. See the ADDITIONAL NOTE on "Sin and Yetzer haRa".

[24]What a wretched man I am. Who will deliver me out of the body of this death? [25]I thank God, through Yeshua the Messiah our Lord. So then with the mind, I myself serve the direction of God, but with the flesh, the direction of Sin.

8 [1]Consequently there is now no judgment of condemnation to those in Messiah Yeshua. [2]For the direction of the Spirit of life in Messiah Yeshua delivered me from the direction of Sin and death. [3]For what the Law was unable to do, in that it lacked strength in the flesh, God did, sending his own Son in the likeness of sinful flesh and for sin. He condemned Sin in the flesh [4]in order that the righteous requirement of the Law might be fulfilled in us [Ezek. 36:26-27], who do not walk in response to the flesh, but in response to the Spirit. [5]For those who live in response to the flesh think in terms of the flesh, but those who live in response to the Spirit, think in terms of the Spirit. [6]For the fleshly mindset is death, but the mindset of the Spirit is life and peace. [7]For the fleshly mindset is hostile towards God, because it is not in subjection to the Law of God, nor indeed can it be. [Ps. 1 & 2] [8]Those whose life is in the flesh cannot please God. [9]However, your[+] life is not in the flesh but in the Spirit, if indeed the Spirit of God dwells in you[+]. But if any man does not have the Spirit of Messiah, he is not his.

[10]If Messiah is in you[+], the body is dead because of Sin, but the spirit is alive because of righteousness. [11]But if the Spirit of the One who raised up Yeshua from the dead dwells in you[+], He who raised up the Messiah from the dead will also give life to your[+] mortal bodies through the same Spirit which dwells in you[+]. [Is. 57:15] [12]So then brethren, we are debtors, but not to the flesh to live in response to the flesh. [13]For if you[+] live in response to the flesh, you[+] are about to die. But if by the Spirit you[+] put to death the deeds of the body, you[+] will live.

[14]For as many as are led by the Spirit of God, these are children of God. [15]For you[+] did not receive the spirit of bondage to be afraid again, but you[+] received the Spirit of sonship, by whom we cry, "Abba! Father!" [16]The same Spirit testifies with our spirit that we are children of God. [17]And if we

7:24-25 Sha'ul explains that it is the death of Messiah that gives victory over the Sin within.

"As for me, to evil humanity and the counsel of perverse flesh do I belong. My transgressions, evils, sins and corrupt heart belong to the counsel of wormy rot and them who walk in darkness. Surely a man's way is not his own; neither can any person firm his own step. Surely justification is of God; by His power is the way made perfect. All that shall be, He foreknows, all that is, His plans establish; apart from Him is nothing done. As for me, if I stumble, God's lovingkindness forever shall save me. If through sin of the flesh I fall, my justification will be by the righteousness of God which endures for all time." (DSS 1QS 11:9-12)

8:1-9 There is God's promise in Ezek. 36:26-27: "I will give you a new heart and put a new spirit within you; I will take the heart of stone out of your flesh and give you a heart of flesh. I will put My Spirit within you and cause you to walk in My statutes, and you will keep My judgments and do them." And the advice in Gal. 5:16: "But I say, walk in the Spirit, and you[+] will not fulfill the desire of the flesh." As was the case with Yeshua, the mind set on the Spirit will produce a life in agreement with God's Law.

8:7 "Mind and reason may be looked upon as the abode of virtue and vice; as it is in them that they seem to dwell." (Philo, "On the Creation," XXIV (73), The Works of Philo, translated by C.D. Yonge, Hendrickson Publishers, 2003)

are children, then we are heirs, heirs of God, and joint-heirs with Messiah — if indeed we suffer with him, so that we may also be glorified with him. [18]For I am convinced that the sufferings of this present time are not worthy to be compared with the glory about to be revealed toward us. [19]For the Creation waits with eager expectation for the children of God to be revealed. [20]For the Creation was subjected to futility [Eccl. 1:2], not of its own will, but because of the One who subjected it, in hope [21]that the Creation itself also will be delivered from the bondage of decay into the liberty of the glory of the children of God.

[22]For we know that the whole Creation groans and travails in pain together until now. [23]Not only so, but we also who have the first fruits of the Spirit, even we ourselves groan within ourselves, waiting for legal maturity as sons, the redemption of our body. [24]For we were saved in hope, but hope that has appeared is not hope. For who hopes for what he sees? [25]But if we hope for what we do not see, we wait for it with patience. [26]In the same way, the Spirit also helps us in our weaknesses, for we do not know how to pray as we should. But this same Spirit makes intercession with groanings which cannot be uttered. [27]The One who searches the hearts knows what the Spirit's purpose is, since the Spirit appeals to God for those who belong to God.

[28]But we know that all things work together for good to those who are loving God, to those who are called according to His purpose. [29]Because those whom He knew before [Rom. 11:2], He also appointed before to be conformed to the image of His Son, so that he might be the firstborn among many brethren. [30]Those whom He appointed before, He also called. Those whom He called, He also justified. Those whom He justified, He also glorified.

[31]What then shall we say about these things? If God is for us, who can be against us? [32]He who did not spare His own Son, but delivered him up for us all, how would He not also with him freely give us all things? [33]Who will bring an accusation against God's chosen? It is God who justifies. [34]Who is the one who condemns? Messiah is the one who died, and moreover was raised. He is at the right hand of God, and also makes intercession for us.

[35]Who will separate us from the love of the Messiah? Could affliction, or anguish, or persecution, or famine, or nakedness, or peril, or sword? [36]Even as it is written, "For Your sake we are killed all day long. We were considered sheep for the slaughter." [Ps. 44:22] [37]No, in all these things, we

---

8:21 "The Creator has made man to be as it were a charioteer and pilot over all other animals, in order that he may hold the reins and direct the course of every thing upon earth, having the superintendence of all animals and plants, as sort of viceroy of the principal and mighty King." (Philo, "On the Creation," XXIX [88])

8:29-30 "Everything is foreseen, and the authority [to choose] is given. And the world is judged in goodness, but everything in accordance with the majority of [a person's] deeds." [Tal. Avot 3:15]

8:32 Sha'ul uses the same phrase, "he did not spare," here and in Rom. 11:21. God did not spare His Son Yeshua, and God did not spare some of the natural branches of His son Israel. "

"If He did this to His own House and His own Temple — He does not respect appearance — when He comes to punish others, how much more will He do to those of others!" (Mid. Psalms 3.1)

8:36 "Concerning 'death to the son': this is about the death of the righteous, the sons of the living God, who deliver their souls to death for the unity of the Name." (Mid. Psalms 9.17)

more than overcome through the One who loved us. [38]For I am convinced that neither death, nor life, nor angels, nor principalities, nor things present, nor things to come, nor powers, [39]nor height, nor depth, nor any other created thing, will be able to separate us from the love of God which is in Messiah Yeshua our Lord.

[9] [1]I speak the truth in Messiah. I am not lying. My conscience bears witness with me in the Ruakh Kodesh, [2]because I have great grief and unceasing pain in my heart. [Jer. 9:1; 15:18] [3]For I could pray that I myself were accursed from the Messiah for my brothers, my physical kinsmen. [Ex. 32:32] [4]They are the people of Israel. The legal right as sons is theirs, and the glory, the covenants, the giving of the Law, the service, and the promises. [5]The fathers are theirs, and the Messiah is physically from them. God, who is over all, be blessed forever. Amen.

[6]Now it is not as though the word of God has come to nothing, because not all who are from Israel are Israel. [7]Neither are they all children because they are Abraham's seed. But, "In Isaac your seed will be called." [Gen. 21:12] [8]That is, it is not the children of the flesh who are children of God, but the children of the promise are counted as the seed. [9]For this is a word of promise: "At the appointed time I will come, and Sarah will have a son." [Gen. 18:10] [10-12]Not only that, but Rebekkah also had relations with only our father Isaac. When the children were not yet born, not having done anything good or bad, [12]it was said to her, "The elder will serve the younger." [Gen. 25:23] [13]Even as it is written, "Jacob I loved, but Esav I hated." [Mal. 1:2] This was in order that the purpose of God might stand in accordance with His choice, not from works, but from the One who calls.

[14]What shall we say then? There is not unrighteousness alongside God is there? Far from it! [15]For He said to Moses, "I will be merciful to whom I am merciful, and I will have compassion on whom I have compassion." [Ex. 33:19] [16]So then it is not from the one who desires, nor from the one who runs, but from God who is merciful. [17]For the Scripture says to Pharaoh, "For this very purpose I caused you to be raised up, so that I might show My power to you, and that My Name might be proclaimed in all the earth." [Ex. 9:16]

9:6-13 "'In Isaac your seed will be called' ...R. Yudan said, 'From a portion of it, but not as all of it.'" (Mid. Psalms 105.1)

Rashi comments on God's words to Jacob, "I have spoken to you" (Gen. 28:15): "what I promised to Abraham about his seed, I have promised to you and not to Esav. Because I did not say to him [Abraham], 'For Isaac will be called seed to you,' but 'in Isaac,' and not all of Isaac."

9:12-13 Gen. 29:30-31 contains the same kind of comparison. Jacob "also loved Rachel more than Leah..." "the Everpresent Lord saw that [by compasion] Leah was hated..."

9:14-23 "All is foreseen, but authority [to choose] is given." (Tal. Avot 3:15) "And R. Hanina said: 'Everything is in the hands of heaven except for the fear of heaven, as it says, *And now, Israel, what does the Everpresent Lord, your God ask of you but to fear...* (Dt. 10:12)'" (Tal. Berachot 33b) "Resh Lakish said: 'What is meant by, *To the scoffers, He scoffs, but to the lowly He gives grace*? (Prov. 3:34) If one comes to defile himself, an opening is given to him; if one comes to cleanse himself, he is helped.'" (Tal. Shabbat 104a)

9:17-18 The Hebrew words that are used in Exodus to describe what God did to Pharaoh's heart and what Pharaoh did to his own heart mean "strengthen" and "give weight to". See "Pharaoh's Heart" in the ADDITIONAL NOTES.

[18]So then, He has mercy on whom He desires, and He hardens whom He desires. [19]You will then say to me, "Why does He still find fault? For who withstands His purpose?" [20]But indeed, O man, who are you to answer back against God? Will the thing formed ask the One who formed it, "Why did You make me like this?" [Is. 29:16; 45:9] [21]Or does not the potter have a right over the clay, from the same lump to make one part an object for honor and another for dishonor? [Jer. 18:6] [22]What if God, though wanting to show His wrath and make His power known, endured with great patience objects of wrath prepared for destruction? [23]And He did so in order to make known the riches of His glory on objects of mercy which He prepared beforehand for glory — [24]even us whom He called, not only from the Jews, but also from the Gentiles.

[25]As He also says in Hoshea, "I will call them 'My people,' who were not My people, and her 'beloved' who was not beloved." [Hos. 2:23] [26]"It will be that in the place where it was said to them, 'You[+] are not My people,' there they will be called 'children of the living God.'" [Hos. 1:10] [27]Isaiah cries concerning Israel, "Though the number of the children of Israel be as the sand of the sea, it is the remnant who will be saved. [28]For the Everpresent Lord will shorten the time to fulfill the word, establishing it upon the earth." [Is. 10:22, 23, Gen. 22:17, Hos. 1:10]

[29]As Isaiah said before, "Unless the Everpresent Lord, the Commander of Forces, had left us a seed, we would have become like Sedom, and would have been made like Amorah." [Is. 1:9, Dt. 29:23, Is. 13:19, Jer. 49:18, 50:40, Amos 4:11]

[30]What shall we say then? That the Gentiles, who did not pursue righteousness, arrived at righteousness, even the righteousness which is from faith, [31]but Israel, pursuing a law of righteousness, did not arrive at [such] a law. [32]Why? Because it was not from faith, but as though from the workings of the Law. They stumbled over the stumbling stone, [33]even as it is written, "Behold, I lay in Zion a stumbling stone and a rock of offense. And the one who believes in him will not be disappointed." [Is. 28:16, 8:14]

10 [1]Brethren, the pleasure of my heart and my supplication to God for them is for salvation. [2]For I bear them witness that they have a zeal for God, but not according to knowledge. [3]For being ignorant of the righteousness of God, and seeking to establish their own righteousness, they did not subject themselves to the righteousness of God. [4]For Messiah is the goal of the Law, unto righteousness, for everyone who is believing.

[5]For Moses writes about the righteousness which is from the Law, "The man who does them will live by them." [Lev. 18:5] [6]But the righteousness which is from faith says this, "Do not say in your heart, 'Who will ascend into heaven?' (that is, to bring Messiah down). [7]Or, 'Who will descend into the abyss?' (that is, to bring Messiah up from the dead,)" [Dt. 30:12] [8]But what does it say? "The word is near you, in your mouth, and in your heart" [Dt. 30:14] — that is, the word of faith which we

---

9:29 LXX has "seed," the Hebrew has "remnant".

10:4 *telos* is translated here as "goal," according to the same usage and meaning that it holds for Sha'ul in 1Tim. 1:5: "The goal of this command is love, which comes from a pure heart and a good conscience and a sincere faith." (cf. 1Pet. 1:9) "for you are receiving the goal of your faith, the salvation of your souls." The word often carried a sense of "innate purpose".

"Law which a man learns in this age is vanity before the Law of Messiah." (Mid. Kohelet 11.7)

proclaim. [9]If then you affirm the Lord Yeshua with your mouth, and believe in your heart that God raised him from the dead, you will be saved. [10]For with the heart one believes to righteousness, and with the mouth affirmation is made to salvation.

[11]For the Scripture says, "Whoever believes in him will not be disappointed," [Is. 28:16] [12]because there is no difference for Jew and Greek, because the same Lord of all is rich to all who call on Him. [13]For "Whoever will call on the Name of the Everpresent Lord will be saved." [Joel 2:32] [14]How then will they call on Him in whom they have not believed? How will they believe in Him of whom they have not heard? How will they hear without someone proclaiming? [15]And how will they proclaim unless they are sent? As it is written: "How beautiful are the feet of those who proclaim the good news of peace, who bring glad tidings of good things." [Is. 52:7]

[16]But they did not all obey the good news, because Isaiah says, "O Everpresent Lord, who has believed our report?" [Is. 53:1] [17]So faith comes from the report, and the report through the word of Messiah. [18]But I say, did they not hear? Yes, most assuredly, "Their sound went out into all the earth, their words to the ends of the world." [Ps. 19:4] [19]But I ask, did Israel not know? First Moses says, "I will provoke you[+] to jealousy with what is no nation. With a nation void of understanding I will make you[+] angry." [Dt. 32:21] [20]Isaiah is bold and says, "I was found by those who did not seek Me. I was revealed to those who did not ask." [Is. 65:1] [21]But to Israel He says, "All day long I stretched out My hands to a disobedient and argumentative people." [Is. 65:2]

11 [1]I ask then, did God reject His people? Far from it! For I also am a son of Israel, a descendant of Abraham, of the tribe of Binyamin. [2]God did not reject His people whom He knew before. Or do you[+] not know what the Scripture says about Eliyahu? How he speaks with God concerning Israel: [3]"O Everpresent Lord, they have killed Your prophets, they have broken down Your altars. I alone am left, and they seek my life." [1 Kings 19:10,14] [4]But how does God answer him? "I have kept for myself seven thousand men who have not bowed the knee to Baal." [1 Kings 19:18] [5]So in this way there is also at this present time a remnant by His gracious choice. [6]And if by grace, then it is no longer by deeds; otherwise grace is no longer grace.

[7]What then? Israel has not obtained what it is seeking, however, those chosen obtained it, and the others were hardened. [8]Just as it has been written, "God gave them a spirit of stupor, eyes that they should not see, and ears that they should not hear, to this very day." [Dt. 29:4, Is. 29:10, 6:10] [9]David says, "Let their table be made a snare, a trap, a stumbling-block, and a retribution to them. [10]Let their eyes be darkened, that they may not see. Bow down their back always." [Ps. 69:22, 23]

[11]So I say that they did not stumble in order to fall. Far from it! But by their transgression salvation has come to the Gentiles, to bring them to jealousy. [12]Now if their transgression brings wealth to

10:15 "who proclaim the good news of peace," as in the Textus Receptus

10:19 "I will provoke them with a foolish nation." (Dt. 32:34)

"R. Hanan b. Raba said in the name of Rab: 'This is a bad wife and a large ketubah.' R. Eliezer said, 'These are the Tzadukim; for surely it says, *The fool has said in his heart: 'There is no God' etc.'* [Ps. 14:1] In a Baraitha it was taught: 'These are the people of Barbaria and the people of Mauretania who walk naked in the market; for there is nothing more despicable and abominable to the Omnipresent [*haMakom*] than the man who walks naked in the market.'" (Tal. Yebamot 63b)

the world, and their failure wealth to the Gentiles, how much more their fullness? [13]Now I speak to you[+] who are Gentiles. Inasmuch then as I am an ambassador to the Gentiles, I exalt my work, [14]if somehow I may bring to jealousy those who are my flesh, and may save some of them, [15]because if their loss brings the reconciling of the world, what will their acceptance be if not life from the dead?

[16]If the first fruit is holy, so is the lump. If the root is holy, so are the branches. [17]But if some of the branches were broken off, and you, being a wild olive, were grafted in among them and became partaker with them of the root and of the richness of the olive tree, [18]do not boast against the branches. But if you do boast against them, it is not you who support the root, but the root supports you. [19]You will say then, "Branches were broken off so that I might be grafted in." [20]True, by their unbelief they were broken off, and you stand by your faith. Don't be conceited, but fear. [21]Because if God did not spare the natural branches, neither will He spare you. [cf. Wisdom 4:5] [22]So look at the goodness and severity of God: toward those who fell, severity, but toward you, goodness, if you continue in His goodness. Otherwise you also will be cut off. [23]They also, if they do not continue in their unbelief, will be grafted in, because God is able to graft them in again. [24]Because if you were cut out of what is a wild olive tree by nature, and were grafted contrary to nature into a cultivated olive tree, how much more will these, who are the natural branches, be grafted into their own olive tree?

[25]For brethren I don't want you[+] to be ignorant of this mystery — so that you[+] don't consider yourselves wise — that a hardening has come to part of Israel until the fullness of the Gentiles has come in. [26]In the same way also, all Israel will be saved, even as it is written, "The Deliverer will come out of Zion, and he will turn away ungodliness from Jacob. [Is. 59:20] [27]This is My covenant with them, when I take away their sins." [Is. 59:21, Jer. 31:33, 34, Is. 27:9]

[28]On the one hand, they are hostile towards the good news for your[+] sake. But concerning God's choice, they are beloved for the sake of the fathers [Dt. 4:37, 7:7-8], [29]because the gifts and the calling of God are without repentance. [30]For as you[+] in time past were disobedient to God, but now have obtained mercy through their disobedience, [31]even so these also have now been disobedient, so that through the mercy shown to you[+] they also may now obtain mercy. [32]For God has enclosed all together in disobedience, that He might have mercy on all.

[33]Oh the depth of the riches both of the wisdom and the knowledge of God! How unsearchable are His judgments, and His ways past finding out! [34]"For who has known the mind of the Everpresent Lord? Or who has been His counselor?" [Is. 40:13] [35]"Or who has first given to Him, and it will be

---

11:28 The prayer about the *akedah*, the binding of Isaac, says, "Remember towards us the love of the ancients — Abraham, Isaac, and Israel, Your servants." "The righteous are blessed. Not only is there merit for them, but they give merit to their children and their children's children to the end of all generations..." (Tal. Yoma 87a)

According to Rashi, God said to Moses, "When it was necessary for you to request mercy for Israel, you reminded me of the merit of the Fathers, as though you thought that if the merit of the Fathers is completed, there is no longer hope. I will make the whole extent of My goodness pass before you on the rock — and you will be placed in a cave — and I will call out before you the Name of the Everpresent Lord, to teach you the order of requesting mercy even if the merit of the Fathers will come to an end." (Commentary on Ex. 33:19)

paid back to him?" [Job 34:7, 41:11] ³⁶For of Him, and through Him, and to Him are all things. To Him be the glory for ever! Amen.

12 ¹So, by the mercies of God, I urge you⁺ brethren to present your⁺ bodies a living sacrifice, sanctified and acceptable to God, which is your⁺ reasonable service. ²Do not be conformed to this age, but be transformed by the renewing of your⁺ mind so that you⁺ may test and demonstrate what the good and acceptable and complete purpose of God is. ³For through the grace that was given to me, I say to every man who is among you⁺ not to think of himself more highly than he ought to think. Think modestly instead, each person as God has apportioned a measure of faith.

⁴For even as we have many members in one body, and all the members do not have the same function, ⁵so we, who are many, are one body in Messiah, and individually members one of another. ⁶But we have gifts differing according to the grace that was given to us. If prophecy, let us do so according to the proportion of our faith; ⁷if service, in the serving. Or the one who teaches, in his teaching. ⁸Or the one who exhorts, in his exhortation. The one who gives, let him do it with generosity. The one who takes the lead, with diligence. The one who shows mercy, with cheerfulness.

⁹Let love be without pretension, hating what is evil, clinging to what is good. ¹⁰Love one another as family, in brotherly love preferring that others receive honor first. ¹¹Be quick, not lazy, eager in spirit, serving the Lord. ¹²Be rejoicing in hope, persevering in troubles, steadfastly continuing in prayer. ¹³Contribute to the needs of those who belong to God, and pursue kindness to the foreigner.

¹⁴Bless those who persecute you⁺ — bless, and do not curse. ¹⁵Rejoice with those who rejoice. Weep with those who weep. ¹⁶Be of the same mind one toward another; do not be conceited, but associate with the lowly. Do not be wise in your⁺ own eyes. ¹⁷Repay no one evil for evil. Respect what is honorable in the eyes of all men.

12:1 Num. 8:1-20 describes the Levites being set apart as living sacrifices.

12:15 "a person should share in the distress [of the community]" (Tal. Ta'anit 11a)

12:18 "Hillel used to say, 'Be of the disciples of Aaron, loving peace and pursuing peace; loving other created beings and bringing them near to Torah.'" (Tal. Avot 1:12)

12:20-21 The Midrash on Psalms 34:2 speaks of "your enemy" as the Yetzer haRa, and says that the way to overcome it is by responding to it with Torah, which is spiritual food and drink.

12:21-13:5 ...seems to delegitimize any revolt against authorities which God has established, regardless of how incompetent or evil they are. "R. Hanina, the sagan of the kohanim, said, 'Now pray for the peace of the government, because without fear of it, a man would swallow his neighbor alive.'"(Tal. Avot 3:2) God "put Israel under oath not to rebel against the yoke of the kingdoms, and put the kingdoms under oath that they not make their yoke heavy on Israel..." (Mid. Song of Songs 2:20)

In light of the context established by 12:21, Yeshua's disciples are to follow his example to "conquer evil with good." David's attitude and behavior towards Saul seems to be an apt illustration. In, for example, Gideon's revolt against Midian (Judg. 6:11-16), which is explicity commanded by God (6:14), we see that not all power is established by God. And in Naboth (1K. 21:3), Daniel (3:14-18,6:1-10), Kefa and Yohanan (Acts 4:18-20), et al., we see that rulers often claim authority which God has not given to them. See the ADDITIONAL NOTE on "Conflict with the State and Its gods".

[18]If possible, as much as it is up to you[+], be at peace with all men. [19]Do not seek to avenge yourselves, beloved, but give place to God's wrath. For it is written, "'Vengeance belongs to Me; I will repay,' says the Everpresent Lord." [Dt. 32:35, Ps. 94:1] [20]Therefore, "If your enemy is hungry, feed him. If he is thirsty, give him a drink. For in doing so, you will heap coals of fire on his head." [2 Kings 6:22, Prov. 25:21] [21]Don't be conquered by evil, instead conquer evil with good.

13 [1]Let every soul be in order under the authorities in place above, because no authority exists if not from God, and those which exist have been set in order by God. [2]So the one who sets himself against the authority resists what God has set in order, and those who resist will receive judgment to themselves. [3]For the princes are not a terror to good deeds, but to what is evil. [Dan. 10:13] Do you desire to have no fear of the authority? Do what is good, and you will have praise from it, [4]because it exists as a servant of God to you for what is good. But if you do what is evil, be afraid. For it does not carry the sword without purpose, since it exists as a servant of God, an avenger for wrath to the one who does evil. [5]Therefore it is a necessity to be submitted, not only because of wrath, but also because of conscience.

[6]For this reason you[+] also pay taxes, for they exist as servants of God, persevering in this very thing. [7]Therefore give back to all what is due them: taxes to whom taxes are due, tariff to whom tariff, fear to whom fear, honor to whom honor. [Mt. 22:21]

[8]Owe no one anything, except to love one another, because the one who loves his neighbor has fulfilled the Law. [9]For the commandments — "You shall not commit adultery;" "You shall not murder;" "You shall not steal;" "You shall not give false testimony;" "You shall not covet;" [Ex. 20:13-17; Dt. 5:17-21] and whatever other commandments there are — they are all summed up in this saying, namely, "You shall love your neighbor as yourself." [Lev. 19:18] [10]Love does not work evil to a neighbor. Therefore love is the fullness of the Law.

[11]And do this, knowing the time, that it is already the hour for you[+] to be roused out of sleep, for our salvation is nearer now than when we first believed. [12]The night is pressing on, and the day has drawn near. Therefore we should cast off the works of darkness, and should put on the armor of light. [13]We should walk appropriately, as in the daytime, not in carousals and drinking, not in sexual promiscuity and lustful acts, and not in strife and jealousy. [14]But put on the Lord Yeshua, the Messiah, and do not provide for the desires of the flesh.

13:1 Some manuscripts of the Western family have, "Let every authority be under the authorities in place above." This is an interesting reading, but vv. 3-4 speak to the singular "you," making it unlikely that v. 1 is addressed to authorities rather than to "every soul."

13:1-4 "One who disregards a king's decree because he was occupied with a commandment, even a light one, is not liable. [Whose words should be obeyed?] the words of the Master or the words of the servant? The words of the Master first. It is not necessary to speak about if a king decrees that a commandment should be disregarded. They do not listen to him." (Maimonides, Mishneh Torah, Melachim uMilchamot 3:9 [3:10 in some versions])

13:9 "You are not to give false testimony" is what the Textus Receptus has.

14 ¹Now receive the one who is weak in faith, not for separating over opinions. ²One has faith to eat all things. Another, being weak, eats only vegetables. ³The one who eats, let him not despise the one who does not eat. The one who does not eat, let him not judge the one who does eat, because God has received him. ⁴Who are you to judge another's servant? To his own lord he stands or falls. Yes, he will be made to stand, for the Lord has power to make him stand.

⁵One person esteems one day above another; another esteems every day. Let each be fully assured in his own mind. ⁶The one who considers the day considers it to the Lord. The one who eats, eats to the Lord, for he gives thanks to God. The one who does not eat, to the Lord he does not eat, also giving thanks to God. ⁷For none of us lives to himself, and none dies to himself. ⁸If we live, we live to the Lord, or if we die, we die to the Lord. So if we live or die, we are the Lord's, ⁹because Messiah died for this and lived again, so that he might be Lord of both the dead and the living.

¹⁰But you, why do you judge your brother? Or you again, why do you despise your brother? Because we will all stand before God's judgment seat. ¹¹For it is written, "'As I live,' says the Everpresent Lord, 'every knee will bow to Me. Every tongue will confess to God.'" [Is. 45:23] ¹²So then each one of us will give account of himself to God. ¹³Therefore let us not judge one another any more, but judge this rather, that no man put a stumbling-block in his brother's way, or an occasion for falling.

¹⁴I know and am persuaded in the Lord Yeshua that nothing is of itself impure — except that to the one who concludes something is impure, to him it is impure — ¹⁵yet if because of food your brother is grieved, you are no longer walking in love. Do not destroy with your food someone for whom Messiah died. ¹⁶So do not let your⁺ good be spoken of as evil, ¹⁷because God's kingdom is not eating and drinking, but justice, peace, and joy in the Ruakh Kodesh. [Jer. 9:23] ¹⁸Because the one who serves the Messiah in these things is acceptable to God and approved by men.

¹⁹So then, let us pursue the things of peace and the things by which we may build up one another. ²⁰Do not destroy the work of God for the sake of food. All things indeed are pure, however it is evil

14:5-6 Part of the Saturday night *Kiddush* says, " Blessed are You our Everpresent Lord, King of the universe, who distinguishes between holy and profane, between light and darkness, between Israel and the peoples, between the seventh day and the six days of work, distinguishing between the holiness of Shabbat and the holiness of a festival, and You have made the seventh day holy above the six days of work, You have distinguished and made holy Your people Israel by Your holiness. Blessed are You, O Everpresent Lord, who distinguishes between holy and holy."

14:10 "A pearl of the Rabbis of Yavneh was: 'I am [God's] creature and my fellow is [God's] creature. I work in the city and he works in the field. I rise up for my work and he rises up for his work. Just as he does not presume to limit my work, so I do not presume to limit his work. And who will say, 'I do much and he does little'? We have learned: One has a lot and one has a little; it is all one, if only he directs his heart to heaven.'" (Tal. Berachot 17a)

14:11 Part of the *Alenu* prayer is: "All the inhabitants of the earth will recognize and know that to You every knee will bow and every tongue swear. Before You, our Everpresent Lord, they will bend and fall, and give glory to Your precious Name. And they all will receive the yoke of Your Kingdom, and You will quickly reign over them forever."

for that man who creates a stumbling block by eating. [21]It is good to not eat meat, drink wine, or do anything by which your brother stumbles. [22]The faith which you have, have it to yourself before God. Happy is the one who does not condemn himself in what he approves. [23]But the one who doubts is condemned if he eats, because it is not of faith; and whatever is not of faith is sin.

[1]Now we who are strong ought to bear the weaknesses of the weak, and not please ourselves. [2]Let each one of us please his neighbor in what is good for building up. [3]For even the Messiah did not please himself, but as it is written, "The reproaches of those who reproached You fell on me." [Ps. 69:9] [4]For whatever things were written before were written for our instruction, so that we might have hope through the encouragement of the Scriptures and through endurance. [5]Now may God, who is steadfast and encouraging, cause you+ to be of the same mind one with another, in accordance with Messiah Yeshua. [6]Then with one mouth, with a common purpose, you+ may glorify the God and Father of our Lord Yeshua the Messiah. [7]So receive one another, just as the Messiah also received you+, to the glory of God.

[8]Now I say that Messiah has been made a servant of the circumcision for the truth of God, in order to confirm the promises given to the fathers, [9]and for the Gentiles to glorify God for His mercy. As it is written, "Therefore I will give praise to You among the Gentiles, and sing to Your Name." [2 Sam. 22:50, Ps. 18:49] [10]Again He says, "Rejoice, you+ Gentiles, with His people." [Dt. 32:43] [11]Again, "Praise the Everpresent Lord, all you+ Gentiles! Let all the peoples praise Him." [Ps. 117:1] [12]Again Isaiah says, "There will be the root of Jesse, he who arises to rule over the Gentiles; in him the Gentiles will hope." [Is. 11:10]

[13]Now may the God of hope fill you+ with all joy and peace in believing, so that you+ may abound in hope, in the power of the Ruakh Kodesh. [14]I myself am also persuaded about you+, my brothers, that you+ yourselves are full of good things, filled with all knowledge, able also to admonish others. [15-16]Nevertheless, because of the grace that was given to me by God that I should be a public servant of Messiah Yeshua to the Gentiles, serving the good news of God as a Kohen, I have written emphatically to you+ on some points, so as to remind you+, so that the offering up of the Gentiles may become acceptable, sanctified by the Ruakh Kodesh.

[17]Therefore I have my boasting in Messiah Yeshua in things pertaining to God. [18]For I will not dare to speak of any things except those which Messiah worked through me by word and deed for the obedience of the Gentiles, [19]in the power of signs and wonders, in the power of the Spirit of God. So that from Yerushala'im and around as far as to Illyrikum, I have fully proclaimed the good news of the Messiah. [20]And in this way, I make it my aim to proclaim the good news, where Messiah was not already named, so that I might not build on another's foundation, [21]but as it is written, "They to whom no news of him was announced will see, and those who have not heard will understand." [Is. 52:15]

[22]Therefore also I was hindered these many times from coming to you+. [23]But now, no longer having any place in these regions, and having these many years a longing to come to you+, [24]I will

---

15:9 "'Therefore I will praise You among the nations, Everpresent Lord' — with the gathering of the Diaspora. And 'I will sing praise to Your Name among the nations' — with the coming of Messiah." (Mid. Psalms 18.35)

come to you⁺ whenever I journey to Spain. For I hope to see you⁺ on my journey, and to be helped on my way there by you⁺, if I may first enjoy your⁺ company for a while.

²⁵But now, I say, I am going to Yerushala'im, serving those who belong to God. ²⁶For it has been the good pleasure of Makedonia and Akhaia to make a certain contribution for the poor among those at Yerushala'im who belong to God. ²⁷Yes, it has been their good pleasure, and they are indebted to them. For if the Gentiles have been made partakers of their spiritual things, the Gentiles also are obligated to serve them in physical needs. ²⁸So when I have accomplished this, and have sealed for them this fruit, I will go on by way of you⁺ to Spain. ²⁹I know that when I come to you⁺, I will come in the fullness of the blessing of Messiah.

³⁰Now I beg you⁺ brothers, by our Lord Yeshua the Messiah and by the love of the Spirit, that you⁺ strive together with me in your⁺ prayers to God for me. ³¹Pray so that I may be delivered from those who are disobedient in Judea, and so that my service which I have for Yerushala'im may be acceptable to those who belong to God. ³²Pray so that I may come to you⁺ in joy through the will of God, and find rest together with you⁺. ³³Now the God of peace be with you⁺ all. Amen.

16 ¹I commend to you⁺ our sister Phoebe, who is a servant of the congregation that is at Kenchrea, ²so that you⁺ receive her in the Lord in a way worthy of those who belong to God, and so that you⁺ assist her in whatever she may need from you⁺. For she herself also has been a helper of many, including me.

³Greet Priska and Akila, my fellow workers in Messiah Yeshua, ⁴who risked their own necks for my life. Not only do I give thanks to them, but so also do all the congregations of the Gentiles. ⁵Greet the congregation that is in their house. Greet Epaenetus, my beloved, who is the first fruits to Messiah of the province of Asia. ⁶Greet Miryam, who labored much for us. ⁷Greet Andronikus and Junias, my kinsmen and my fellow prisoners, who are notable among the ambassadors, who also were in Messiah before me. ⁸Greet Amplias, my beloved in the Lord. ⁹Greet Urbanus, our fellow worker in Messiah, and Stachys, my beloved. ¹⁰Greet Apelles, the approved in Messiah. Greet those who are of the household of Aristobulus. ¹¹Greet Herodion, my kinsman. Greet those of the household of Narkissus, who are in the Lord. ¹²Greet Tryphaena and Tryphosa, who labor in the Lord. Greet Persis, the beloved, who labored much in the Lord. ¹³Greet Rufus, the chosen in the Lord, and his mother and mine. ¹⁴Greet Asynkritus, Phlegon, Hermes, Patrobas, Hermas, and the brethren who are with them. ¹⁵Greet Philologus and Julia, Nereus and his sister, and Olympas, and all those who belong to God with them. ¹⁶Greet one another with a holy kiss. The Messianic communities greet you⁺.

¹⁷Now I exhort you⁺ brethren, watch out for those who cause the divisions and the snares contrary to the doctrine which you⁺ learned, and turn away from them. ¹⁸For such people do not serve our Lord Yeshua the Messiah, but their own appetite. And by their smooth and flattering speech, they deceive the hearts of the innocent. ¹⁹Since your⁺ obedience has become known to all, I rejoice therefore over

15:25-27 The Jewish believers in Yerushala'im had given sacrificially to further the work of Messiah. Because of famine and persecution, there were many poor among them. Since "salvation is from the Jews," all Gentile believers are obligated to give back materially to alleviate the physical needs of the Jewish believers. This offering is referred to in Acts 11:27-30, 1Co. 16:1-2, 2Co. 8-9, and Gal. 2:10.

you⁺. And I want you⁺ to be wise in what is good, but innocent in what is evil. [20]And the God of peace will quickly crush the Accuser under your⁺ feet. The grace of our Lord Yeshua be with you⁺.

[21]Timothy, my fellow worker, greets you⁺, as do Lukius, Jason, and Sosipater, my kinsmen. [22]I, Tertius, who wrote this letter, greet you⁺ in the Lord. [23]Gaius, my host and host of the whole community, greets you⁺. Erastus, the treasurer of the city, greets you⁺, as does Quartus, the brother. [24]

[25]Now to Him who is able to establish you⁺ according to my good news and the proclamation of Yeshua the Messiah — according to the revelation of the mystery which has been kept secret through long ages, [26]but now is revealed, and by the Scriptures of the prophets, according to the commandment of the eternal God, which is made known to all the Gentiles for obedience of faith — [27]to the only wise God, through Yeshua the Messiah, to Him be the glory forever. Amen.

16:24 — "The grace of our Lord Yeshua the Messiah be with you all. Amen." — is not in the UBS text.

Sha'ul/Paulos' First Letter to the Corinthians

1 [1]Paulos — called through the will of God to be an ambassador of Yeshua the Messiah — and our brother Sosthenes, [Acts 18:17] [2]to the community of God which is at Corinth. You+ are those who are sanctified in Messiah Yeshua, called to belong to God with everyone in every place who calls on the name of our Lord Yeshua the Messiah, theirs and ours. [3]Grace and peace to you+ from God our Father and the Lord Yeshua the Messiah.

[4]I always thank my God concerning you+ for the grace of God which was given to you+ in Messiah Yeshua — [5]that you+ were enriched in him in everything, in all speech and all knowledge. [6]In this way, what bears witness to the Messiah was confirmed in you+, [7]so that you+ are not behind in any gift, waiting for the revelation of our Lord Yeshua the Messiah. [8]He will also confirm you+ until the end, blameless in the day of our Lord Yeshua the Messiah. [9]God is faithful, through whom you+ were called into the fellowship of His Son, Yeshua the Messiah, our Lord.

[10]Now I exhort you+, brethren, through the name of our Lord Yeshua the Messiah, that you+ all communicate the same thing and that there be no divisions among you+, but that you+ be restored in the same mind and in the same purpose. [11]For concerning you+ my brethren, it has been made known to me by those who are from Chloe's household that there is strife among you+. [12]Now I mean this, that each one of you+ says, "I follow Paulos," "I follow Apollos," "I follow Kefa," and, "I follow Messiah." [13]Has the Messiah been divided? Was Paulos put to death on the stake for you+? Or were you+ immersed into the name of Paulos?

[14]I thank God that I immersed none of you+ except Krispus and Gaius, [15]so that no one should say that I immersed you+ into my own name. [16](I also immersed the household of Stefanas. Besides them, I do not know whether I immersed any other.) [17]For Messiah did not send me to immerse, but to proclaim the good news — not in wisdom of words, so that Messiah's tree of death would not be nullified.

[18]For the message of the tree of death is foolishness to those who are perishing, but it is the power of God to us, who are being saved. [19]For it is written, "I will destroy the wisdom of the wise; I will cause the discernment of their discerning men to vanish." [Is. 29:14] [20]Where is the wise man? Where is the man of letters? Where is the debater of this age? Has not God made the wisdom of this world foolish?

"First Letter to the Corinthians" is the traditional name assigned to this text, distinguishing it from the "Second Letter to the Corinthians". It is clear in the text, however, cf. 1Co. 5:9 and 7:1, that this is not the first letter, but part of an ongoing correspondence about particular issues.

1:10 "brethren," though old-fashioned, is a little more inclusive than "brothers," which is more gender specific.

1:20-21 "the Holy One, blessed be He, showed to the first Adam every generation with those in it who search and expound [*dor dor v'dorshav*], every generation with its wise men [*dor dor v'chachmav*], every generation with its leaders [*dor dor v'parnasav*]..." (Tal. Avodah Zarah 5a)

[21]For seeing that in the wisdom of God, the world through its wisdom did not know God, it was God's good pleasure — through the foolishness of the proclamation — to save those who believe. [22]For Jews are asking for a sign, Greeks are seeking after wisdom, [23]but we are proclaiming Messiah put to death on the stake — a stumbling-block to Jews, and foolishness to Gentiles. [24]But to those who are called, both Jews and Greeks, Messiah is the power of God and the wisdom of God. [25]Because the foolishness of God is wiser than men, and the weakness of God is stronger than men.

[26]For you⁺, brethren, see your⁺ calling, that not many are wise according to the flesh, not many mighty, and not many noble. [27]But God has chosen the foolish things of the world so that He might put to shame those that are wise. God has chosen the weak things of the world so that He might put to shame those that are strong. [28]And God has chosen the lowborn of the world, and the despised, and the things that are not, so that He might make useless the things that are. [29]In this way, no flesh will boast before God. [30]But you⁺ are from Him in Messiah Yeshua. To us, he was made wisdom from God, righteousness, sanctification, and redemption. [31]Indeed as it is written, "The one who boasts, let him boast in the Everpresent Lord." [Jer. 9:22-23H/23-24]

2 [1]When I came to you⁺ brethren, proclaiming to you⁺ the things that bear witness to God, I did not come with excellence of speech or of wisdom. [2]For I decided not to know anything among you⁺ other than Yeshua the Messiah, and him put to death on the stake. [3]I was with you⁺ in weakness, in fear, and in much trembling. [4]My speech and my proclamation were not in persuasive words of human wisdom, but in demonstration of the Spirit and of power, [5]so that your⁺ faith would not stand in the wisdom of men, but in the power of God.

[6]We do, however, speak wisdom among those who are fully mature, but a wisdom not of this age, nor of the rulers of this age, who are becoming useless. [7]But we speak God's wisdom in a mystery, the wisdom that has been hidden, which God foreordained before the ages to our glory. [8]None of the rulers of this age has known it, because had they known it, they would not have put the Lord of glory to death on the stake. [9]But as it is written, "For those who love Him, God has prepared, things

---

1:26-29 "Man should forever learn from the mind of the One to whom he belongs; for see that the Holy One, blessed be He, ignored all the mountains and high places and caused His Shekhinah to remain on Mount Sinai, and ignored all the beautiful trees and caused His Shekhinah to remain in a bush." (Tal. Sotah 5a)

2:6 "By the mysteries of Your insight [You] assigned all these things to make Your glory known. [But what is] the spirit of flesh that it might understand all these things and obtain insight into the council of [Your] great [wonders?]" (DSS 1QHa 5:19-20)

2:9 "All the prophets, each one, did not prophesy except to the days of the Messiah; but as for the age to come, 'no eye has seen, O God, except You, what He has prepared for him that waits for him.' [Is. 64:4] ...All the prophets did not prophesy except to those who return to God; but as for the completely righteous, 'the eye has not seen, O God, beside You, what He has prepared for him that waits for him.' ...All the prophets, each one, did not prophesy except of him who marries his daughter to a disciple of the wise, or engages in business for a scholar, or benefits a disciple of the wise with his possessions; but as for the disciples of the wise themselves — 'the eye has not seen, O God, beside You...'" (Tal. Sanhedrin 99a)

which no eye has seen, and no ear has heard, and which have not entered into the heart of man." [Is. 64:4, 65:17]

[10]But God revealed them to us through the Spirit, for the Spirit searches all things, yes, the deep things of God. [11]For who among men knows the things of a man, except the spirit of the man which is in him? Even so, no one knows the things of God except the Spirit of God. [12]Now we did not receive the spirit of the world, but the Spirit which is from God, so that we might know the things that were freely given to us by God. [13]We also do not speak these things in words which man's wisdom teaches, but which the Ruakh Kodesh teaches, comparing spiritual things with spiritual things. [14]Now the man of the soul does not receive the things of the Spirit of God, because they are foolishness to him and he cannot know them, since they are spiritually discerned. [4Mac. 1:32] [15]But the one who is spiritual discerns all things, and he himself is judged by no one. [16]"For who has known the mind of the Everpresent Lord, that he should instruct Him?" [Is. 40:13] But we have Messiah's understanding.

3 [1]Brethren, I could not speak to you+ as to spiritual men, but as to men living in response to your physical senses, as to infants in Messiah. [2]I gave you+ milk to drink, not solid food, because you+ were not yet able. But you+ are still not able, [3]because you+ are still living in response to your physical senses. Because where there is jealousy and strife among you+, are you+ not living in response to your physical senses, and walking just like other people? [4]For when one says, "I am truly of Paulos," and another, "I am of Apollos," are you+ not men? [5]What then is Apollos, and what is Paulos, but servants through whom you+ believed — and each one as the Lord gave to him? [6]I planted, Apollos watered, but God was giving the growth.

[7]So it is neither the one who plants nor the one who waters who is anything, but God who gives the growth. [8]Now the one who plants and the one who waters are one, but each will receive his own reward according to his own labor. [9]For we are God's fellow workers. You+ are God's prepared field, God's building. [10]According to the grace of God which was given to me, I laid a foundation as a wise master builder, and someone else is building on it. [2Mac. 2:29] But let each man be careful how he builds on it. [11]For no one can lay any other foundation than that which has been laid, which is Yeshua the Messiah.

[12]Now whether anyone builds on the foundation with gold, silver, costly stones, wood, hay, or stubble, [13]each man's work will be revealed, for the day will make it evident, because it is revealed in fire. And the fire itself will demonstrate what sort of work each man's work is. [14]If any man's work which he built on it remains, he will receive payment. [15]If any man's work is burned, he will suffer loss, but he himself will be saved, but as through fire.

[16]Haven't you+ understood that you+ are a dwelling of God, and that the Spirit of God lives in you+? [17]If anyone destroys the dwelling of God, God will destroy him, because the dwelling of God is holy, which you+ are. [18]Let no one deceive himself. If anyone among you+ thinks that he is wise in this age, let him become a fool, so that he may become wise. [19]For the wisdom of this world is foolishness with God. For it is written, "He has taken the wise in their craftiness." [Job 5:13] [20]And again, "The Everpresent Lord knows the reasoning of the wise, that it is worthless." [Ps. 94:11] [21]So let no one

---

2:14 "Indeed some desires are from the soul/*psuchikos*, others are from the body, and reason gives light to rule over both." (4Mac. 1:32)

boast in men. For all things are yours[+], [22]whether Paulos, or Apollos, or Kefa, or the world, or life, or death, or things present, or things that are coming. All are yours[+], [23]and you[+] are Messiah's, and Messiah is God's.

4 [1]Therefore let a man think of us as servants of Messiah, and managers of God's mysteries. [2]Moreover, it is required of managers that they be found faithful. [3]But with me it is a very small thing that I should be subjected to a judicial inquiry by you[+] or by the day of Man. Yes, I do not subject my own self to a judicial inquiry, [4]for I am conscious of nothing against myself. Yet I am not declared righteous by this, but the one who subjects me to a judicial inquiry is the Lord. [5]Therefore judge nothing before the time, until the Lord comes, who will both bring to light the hidden things of darkness, and reveal the counsels of the hearts. Then each man will have his praise from God.

[6]Now brethren, I have applied these things to myself and Apollos for your[+] sakes, so that through us you[+] might learn not to think beyond what has been written, so that none of you[+] be conceited against one another. [7]For who makes you different? And what do you have that you did not receive? But if you did receive it, why do you boast as if you had not received it?

[8]You[+] are already filled. You[+] have already become rich. You[+] have come to reign without us. Yes, and I wish that you[+] did reign, so that we also might reign with you[+]. [9]For I think that God has exhibited us, the ambassadors, last of all, like men sentenced to death. For we are made a spectacle to the world, both to angels and men. [10]We are fools for the sake of Messiah, but you[+] are wise in Messiah. We are weak, but you[+] are strong. You[+] have honor, but we have dishonor. [11]Even to this present hour, we hunger and thirst; we are naked, beaten, and homeless.

[12]We toil, working with our own hands. Being reviled, we bless. Being persecuted, we endure. [13]Being defamed, we entreat. We have become as the filth of the world, the dirt wiped off by all, even to this moment. [14]I do not write these things to shame you[+], but to admonish you[+] as my beloved children. [15]For though you[+] have ten thousand childhood guardians in Messiah, yet not many fathers. For in Messiah Yeshua, I became your[+] father through the good news. [16]I urge you[+] therefore, be imitators of me.

[17]Because of this, I have sent Timothy to you[+]. He is my beloved and faithful child in the Lord. He will remind you[+] of my ways which are in Messiah, even as I teach everywhere in every congregation. [18]Now some are puffed up, as though I were not coming to you[+]. [19]But I will come to you[+] shortly, if the Lord is willing. And I will know, not the talk of those who are conceited, but the power. [20]For the Kingdom of God is not in talk, but in power. [21]What do you[+] want? Shall I come to you[+] with a rod, or in love and a spirit of gentleness?

5 [1]It is actually reported that there is sexual immorality among you[+], and such sexual immorality as is not even mentioned among the Gentiles — that one has his father's wife. [2]You[+] are conceited, and did not mourn instead so that the one who had done this deed might be removed from among

4:3-5 "the day of Man" is used to describe the judgments of this age, in contrast to "the day of the Everpresent Lord," the time when God judges.

5:1 "There are in the Torah thirty-six [crimes punished by being cut off]: when one has intercourse with his mother, his father's wife, his daughter-in-law..." (Tal. Kerithot I:1)

you⁺. ³For most assuredly, though being absent in body but present in spirit, I have already, as though I were present, given judgment on the one who has done this thing. ⁴In the name of our Lord Yeshua the Messiah, you⁺ — being gathered together, and my spirit, with the power of our Lord Yeshua — ⁵are to deliver such a one to the Accuser for the destruction of the flesh, so that the spirit may be saved in the day of the Lord.

⁶Your⁺ boasting is not good. Don't you⁺ know that a little leaven causes the whole lump to rise? ⁷Purge out the old leaven so that you⁺ may be a new lump — just as you⁺ are unleavened, and because our Pesakh, Messiah, has been sacrificed in place of us. ⁸Therefore let us keep the feast, not with old leaven, nor with the leaven of malice and wickedness, but with the unleavened bread of sincerity and truth.

⁹I have written to you⁺ in my letter not to associate with the sexually immoral, ¹⁰yet not at all meaning with the sexually immoral of this world, or with the covetous and extortioners, or with idolaters, for then you⁺ would have to leave the world. ¹¹But now I wrote to you⁺ not to associate with anyone who is called a brother who is sexually immoral, or covetous, or an idolater, or a slanderer, or a drunkard, or one who takes the things of others for himself. Do not even eat with such a person. ¹²For what have I to do with judging those who are outside? Don't you⁺ judge those who are within? ¹³But those who are outside, God will judge. "Put away the wicked man from among yourselves." [Lam. 3:45]

6 ¹If any of you⁺ has a matter against his brother, do you⁺ have the audacity to go to law before the unrighteous, and not before those who belong to God? ²Don't you⁺ know that those who belong to God will judge the world? And if the world is judged by you⁺, are you⁺ unworthy to judge the smallest matters? ³Don't you⁺ know that we will judge angels? How much more then, things that pertain to this life?

⁴If then you⁺ have a judgment to make concerning things of this life, are you⁺ setting up as judges those who are not esteemed by the community? ⁵I say this to your⁺ shame. So is there not even one wise man among you⁺ who would be able to decide between his family? ⁶But brother goes to law with brother, and that before unbelievers! ⁷Therefore it is already a complete loss for you⁺ that you⁺ have lawsuits one with another. Why not rather be wronged? Why not rather be defrauded? ⁸No, but you⁺ yourselves do wrong and defraud, and that against your⁺ family.

5:5 There is a discussion in Tal. Sanhedrin 71 about the stubborn and rebellious son of Dt. 21:18-21. In the discussion, a mishnah states, "A stubborn and rebellious son is tried on account of his end: let him die clean and let him not die liable [to judgment]."

5:6-8 "R. Alexandri used to say as part of his prayer: 'Master of the Universe, it is open and known to You that our desire is to do Your will, yet what prevents us? The yeast in the dough [i.e. the evil inclination within us] and to have to serve [other] kingdoms.'" (Tal. Berakhot 17a)

5:9 "I have written to you..." indicates that though the traditional title of this letter is "First Corinthians," it was not the first letter Sha'ul wrote to them.

6:5,8; 8:12 "his/your⁺ family" literally "his/your⁺ brothers"

[9]Or do you[+] not know that the unrighteous will not inherit the kingdom of God? Do not be misled. Neither the sexually immoral, nor idolaters, nor adulterers, nor male prostitutes, nor homosexuals, [10]nor thieves, nor covetous people, nor drunkards, nor slanderers, nor those who seize what is another's will inherit the kingdom of God. [11]Such were some of you[+], but you[+] were washed, but you[+] were sanctified, but you[+] were justified in the name of the Lord Yeshua, and in the Spirit of our God.

[12]"All things are possible for me" — but not all things are beneficial. [Sirach 37:27-28] "All things are possible for me" — but I will not be brought under the power of anything. [13]"Foods for the belly, and the belly for foods," but God will bring both of these to nothing. And the body is not for sexual immorality, but for the Lord, and the Lord for the body. [14]Now God both raised up the Lord, and will also raise us up by His power.

[15]Don't you[+] know that your[+] bodies are members of Messiah? Shall I then take the members of the Messiah, and make them members of a prostitute? Far from it! [16]Or don't you[+] know that he who is joined to a prostitute is one body? For "The two," says He, "will become one flesh." [Gen 2:24] [17]But the one who is joined to the Lord is one spirit. [18]Flee sexual immorality! Every sin that a man does is outside the body, but the one who commits sexual immorality sins against his own body. [19]Or do you[+] not know that your[+] body is a temple of the Ruakh Kodesh, which is in you[+], which you[+] have from God? You[+] are not your[+] own, [20]because you[+] were bought with a price. Therefore glorify God in your[+] body.

7 [1]Now concerning the things about which you[+] wrote to me: it is good for a man not to touch a woman, [2]but because of sexual immoralities, let each man have his own wife, and let each woman have her own husband. [3]Let the husband give back to his wife what is due, and likewise also the wife to her husband. [4]The wife does not have authority over her own body, but the husband. Likewise also the husband does not have authority over his own body, but the wife. [5]Do not deprive one another — unless it is by consent for a season so that you[+] may have opportunity for prayer, and may be together again — so that the Accuser does not tempt you[+] because of your[+] lack of self-control. [6]But I say this by way of allowance, not by commandment.

[7]Yet I wish that all men were as I, but each man has his own gift from God, one of this kind, and another of that kind. [8]But I say to the unmarried and to widows, it is good for them if they remain even as I am. [9]But if they do not have self-control, let them marry. For it is better to marry than to burn. [10]But to the married I urge — not I, but the Lord — that the wife not be separated from her husband. [11]But if she separates, let her remain unmarried, or else be reconciled to her husband. And let the husband not leave his wife.

7:5 "Mishnah. The one who vows not to have intercourse with his wife, Beth Shammai say, 'Two weeks.' Beth Hillel say, 'One week....'" (Tal. Ketubot 5:5) In Tal. Ketubot 61b-62b, there is a discussion of how often a husband and wife should have intercourse, depending upon the occupation of the husband.

7:8 "A man has no right to live without a wife, and a woman has no right to live without a husband." (Tos. Yevamot 8:2)

7:9 Tal. Kid. 81a speaks of the "fire" of lust kindled by a man's evil inclination. Tos. Bekhorot 6:3 says that if a man is "to learn Torah and marry a wife, he learns Torah and after that he marries a wife. R. Judah said, 'If he cannot live without a wife, he marries a wife and after that he learns Torah.'"

¹²But to the rest I — not the Lord — say, if any brother has an unbelieving wife, and she is content to live with him, let him not leave her. ¹³And if a woman has an unbelieving husband, and he is content to live with her, let her not leave her husband. ¹⁴For in the wife, the unbelieving husband is set apart to God, and in the brother, the unbelieving wife is set apart to God. Otherwise your⁺ children would then be unclean, but now they are set apart to God. ¹⁵Yet if the unbeliever separates himself, let him separate himself. The brother or the sister is not under bondage in such cases, but God has called you⁺ in peace. ¹⁶For how do you know, O wife, whether you will save your husband? Or how do you know, O husband, whether you will save your wife?

¹⁷Only as the Lord has apportioned to each man, as God has called each, so let him walk. And this is what I instruct in all the communities. ¹⁸Was anyone called having been circumcised? Let him not become uncircumcised. Has anyone been called in uncircumcision? Let him not be circumcised. ¹⁹Circumcision is nothing, and uncircumcision is nothing; keeping the commandments of God is what matters. [Eccl. 12:13] ²⁰Let each man remain in that calling in which he was called.

²¹Were you called being a bondservant? Do not let that bother you. But if you get an opportunity to become free, use it. ²²For the one who was called in the Lord while a bondservant is a freedman of the Lord. Likewise the one who was called while free is a bondservant of Messiah. ²³You⁺ were bought with a price. Don't become bondservants of men. ²⁴Brethren, in whatever condition each man was called, let him remain in that condition with God.

²⁵Now concerning virgins, I have no commandment from the Lord, but I give my judgment as one who has obtained mercy from the Lord to be trustworthy. ²⁶So I think this is good — that it is good, because of the present necessity — for a man to remain as he is. ²⁷Are you bound to a wife? Do not seek to be released. Have you been released from a wife? Do not seek a wife. ²⁸But if you marry, you have not sinned. If a virgin marries, she has not sinned. Yet such will have trouble in the flesh, and I want to spare you⁺.

²⁹But I say this, brethren, the time is short, so that from now on, those who have wives may also be as though they had none. ³⁰Let those who weep be as though they did not weep; and those who rejoice as though they did not rejoice. Let those who buy be as though they did not possess; ³¹and those who have business in this world as not having it as their own. Because this worldly order is passing away, ³²and I want you⁺ to be free from anxiety.

The unmarried man is concerned for the things of the Lord — how he may please the Lord. ³³But the one who is married is concerned about the things of the world — how he may please his wife [Gen. 3:17] — ³⁴and is divided. Also the unmarried woman and the virgin are concerned about the things of the Lord in order to be holy both in body and in spirit. The married woman, however, cares about the things of the world — how she may please her husband. ³⁵I say this for your⁺ own benefit, not that I may set a snare before you⁺. I say this for what is appropriate and that you⁺ may attend to the Lord without distraction.

7:17-20 To paraphrase: 'God creates each person according to His purpose for that individual. So live in accordance with God's calling for you.' In chapter 12, Sha'ul presents the analogy of the body of Messiah, composed of different members with different functions. See the ADDITIONAL NOTE on "Circumcision and the Law".

[36]But if some man thinks he behaves inappropriately towards his virgin, if she is passing her prime, let him do what he desires. If it should be this way, he does not sin. Let them marry. [37]But he who stands steadfast in his own heart, having no necessity, but has power over his own heart to keep his own virgin, does well. [38]So then both he who gives in marriage does well, and he who does not give in marriage does better.

[39]A wife is bound by law for as long a time as her husband lives. But if the husband has died, she is free to be married to whomever she desires, only in the Lord. [40]In my judgment, however, she is happier if she remains as she is, and I think that I too have the Spirit of God.

8 [1]Now concerning things sacrificed to idols, we know that we all have knowledge. Knowledge puffs up, but love builds up. [2]If someone supposes he knows something, he doesn't yet know as he needs to know. [3]But if someone loves God, this one is known by Him. [4]So concerning the eating of things sacrificed to idols, we know that an idol in the world is nothing, and that there is no other god but one. [5]For though there are things that are called gods, whether in the heavens or on earth — just as there are many gods and many lords — [6]yet to us there is one God, the Father. All things are from Him, and we exist for Him. And there is one Lord, Yeshua the Messiah, through whom all things exist, and we exist through him.

[7]However, not all have this knowledge, but some, being accustomed to the idol, eat food even now as though it were a thing sacrificed to an idol. Then their conscience, being weak, is defiled. [8]But food does not commend us to God. For neither are we the better if we do not eat, nor are we the worse if we do eat. [9]But be careful so that this authority of yours[+] not become a stumbling-block to the weak. [10]For if a man sees you who have knowledge reclining at table in the temple of an idol, won't his conscience, if he is weak, be emboldened to eat things sacrificed to idols? [11]And through your knowledge, the one who is weak perishes, the brother for whose sake Messiah died. [12]Now in sinning like this against your[+] family and wounding their conscience when it is weak, you[+] sin against Messiah. [13]So if food causes my brother to stumble, I will certainly never eat meat, so that I may not cause my brother to stumble.

9 [1]Am I not free? Am I not an ambassador? Have I not seen Yeshua the Messiah, our Lord? Are you[+] not my work in the Lord? [2]If to others I am not an ambassador, yet at least I am to you[+], because you[+] are the seal of my being an ambassador in the Lord.

[3]This is my defense to those who examine me. [4]Have we no right to eat and to drink? [5]Have we no right to take along a wife who is a believer, even as the rest of the ambassadors, the brothers of the Lord, and Kefa? [6]Or do only Bar Nabba and I lack the right to not work? [7]What soldier ever serves at

8:5-6 "'From one source spring gods and mortal men.' (Hesiod, *Works and Days*, 107.) 'One is the race of men, one the race of gods, and from one mother [Gaia, or Earth] do we both have breath.' (Pindar, *Nemean Odes*.)" Abraham J. Heschel, The Prophets, Prince Press, Peabody, MA., 2001, II, P. 135 n. 9

9:3-18 "It is good to study Torah along with work [lit. the way of the earth], because you will come to both of them forgetting iniquity. The outcome of all Torah that is not with work is to cease and then bring iniquity" (Tal. Pirke Avot 2:2 cf. 1Sam. 12:3)

his own expense? Who plants a vineyard, and does not eat of its fruit? Or who feeds a flock, and does not drink from the milk of the flock?

⁸These things I speak are not from man, for doesn't the Torah also say the same thing? ⁹It is indeed written in the Law of Moses, "You are not to muzzle an ox while it threshes the grain." [Dt. 25:4] It is not the ox that is God's concern. ¹⁰As He surely says it because of us, it was written for our sake, because the one who plows ought to plow in hope, and the one who threshes, in hope of partaking.

¹¹If we sowed spiritual things to you⁺, is it a great thing if we reap your⁺ material things? ¹²If others partake of this right over you⁺, should not we even more? Nevertheless we did not use this right, but we endure all things so that we cause no hindrance to the good news of the Messiah. ¹³Do you⁺ not know that those who work with the priestly things eat from the Temple, and those who attend at the altar have their portion at the altar? ¹⁴Even so the Lord ordained that those who proclaim the good news should live from the good news.

¹⁵But I have used none of these things, and I do not write these things so that this may be done for me, for I would rather die than that anyone should make my boasting empty. ¹⁶For if I proclaim the good news, I have nothing to boast about, because it is a necessity for me. For woe is to me if I do not proclaim the good news. ¹⁷For if I do this voluntarily, I have a reward. But if not voluntarily, I am entrusted with a managerial responsibility.

¹⁸What then is my reward? That when I proclaim the good news, I may present the good news of Messiah without charge, so as not to abuse my authority in the good news. ¹⁹For though I am free from all, I made myself a bondservant for all, so that I might gain the more. ²⁰To the Jews I became as a Jew, so that I might gain Jews; to those who are subjected to the Law, as subjected to the Law, so that I might gain those who are subjected to the Law. ²¹To those who are without law, I became as without law — not being without law toward God, but lawful to Messiah — so that I might win those who are without law. ²²To the weak I became as weak, so that I might gain the weak. I have become all things to all these, so that I may by all means save some.

²³Now I do all for the sake of the good news, so that I may be a joint partaker of it. ²⁴Do you⁺ not know that those who run in a race all run, but one receives the prize? Run like this, so that you⁺ may win. ²⁵Every man who strives in the games exercises self-control in all things. Now they do it to receive a corruptible crown, but we an incorruptible. ²⁶I therefore run in this way: not with uncertainty. I box in this way: as not beating the air. ²⁷But I press down my body and bring it into submission, so that after I have proclaimed to others, I myself should not by any means be rejected.

9:9 "It is not the ox that is God's concern." This is comparative; i.e. "What is God's chief concern, oxen or men?" The Scriptures were written to help men live in the image and likeness of God. That, of course, includes how they treat oxen and other animals. (cf. Prov. 12:10) In Dt. 20:19-20, God establishes a prohibition against cutting down surrounding fruit trees during the siege of a city. Is God concerned about the trees or the people? Both, but He is speaking to people about how they are to live. For a clear example of this comparative sense, see Ps. 147:10-11.

9:20 as in the Textus Receptus. The UBS includes the phrase, "though not under law".

10 [1]Now brethren, I do not want you⁺ to be ignorant that our fathers were all under the cloud, and all passed through the sea. [2]And all were immersed into Moses in the cloud and in the sea. [3]All ate the same spiritual food, [4]and all drank the same spiritual drink. For they drank of a spiritual rock that followed them, and the rock was the Messiah. [5]However, God was not well pleased with most of them, for they were destroyed in the wilderness.

[6]Now these things have become examples for us, that we not also desire evil things, as they did; [7]nor be idolaters, as some of them were. As it is written, "The people sat down to eat and drink, and rose up to dance." [Ex. 32:6,19] [8]Let us also not commit sexual immorality, as some of them did, and in one day twenty-three thousand fell. [Num. 25] [9]Let us also not test the Everpresent Lord, as some of them tested Him, and were destroyed by the serpents. [Num. 21] [10]Let us also not grumble, as some of them also grumbled, and were destroyed by the Destroyer.

[11]Now these things happened to them, and they were written as examples to warn us, to whom the ends of the ages have come. [12]So let the one who thinks he stands be careful that he does not fall.

[13]No temptation has overtaken you⁺ but such as is common to man. God is faithful, who will not allow you⁺ to be tempted beyond what you⁺ are able, but will with the temptation also make a way out so that you⁺ may be able to endure it. [14]So my beloved, flee from idolatry. [15]I speak as to wise men, judge what I say.

[16]The cup of blessing which we bless, is it not fellowship in the blood of the Messiah? The bread which we break, is it not fellowship in the body of the Messiah? [17]Because we, who are many, are one loaf, one body, for we all partake of the one loaf.

[18]Concerning the physical, look at Israel: are not those who eat the sacrifices partaking together of the altar? [19]What am I saying then? That a thing sacrificed to idols is anything, or that an idol is anything? [20]To the contrary, the things which the Gentiles sacrifice, they sacrifice to demons and not to God, and I do not want you⁺ to be fellow-partakers with demons. [21]You⁺ cannot drink both the cup of the Lord and the cup of demons. You⁺ cannot partake of both the table of the Lord, and the table of demons.

[22]Or do we provoke the Lord to jealousy? Are we stronger than He? [23]All things are possible, but not all things are beneficial. [Sirach 37:27-28] All things are possible, but not all things build up. [24]Let no one seek his own, but each one his neighbor's good.

[25]Eat whatever is sold in the meat market, asking nothing for the sake of conscience, [26]because "the earth and its fullness belong to the Everpresent Lord." [Ps. 24:1; 50:12] [27]But if one of those who do not believe invites you⁺ to a meal, and you⁺ are inclined to go, eat whatever is set before you⁺, asking nothing for the sake of conscience. [28]But if anyone says to you⁺, "This was offered to idols," for the sake of the one who told you⁺, and for the sake of conscience, do not eat it. [29]Conscience I say, not your own, but the conscience of the other. For why is my liberty judged by another's conscience? [30]If I partake giving thanks, why am I reviled for the object of my giving thanks?

10:4 Rashi says of the well in Num. 21:17, that it was with them "from the beginning". Of the Rock, he says (Num. 20:10), "Because they did not recognize it, the Rock went out [from them] and lived among the rocks."

10:16-21 Having fellowship is an indication of a common bond.

[31]Whether therefore you[+] eat, or drink, or whatever you[+] do, do all to the glory of God. [32]Become without offense, both to Jews and Greeks, and to the community of God — [33]even as I also please all men in all things, not seeking my own profit, but the profit of the many so that they may be saved.

11 [1]Be imitators of me, even as I also am of Messiah. [2]Now I praise you[+] that you[+] remember me in all things, and firmly hold onto the instructions, even as I delivered them to you[+]. [3]However, I want you[+] to know that the head of every man is Messiah, and the head of the wife is the husband, and the head of Messiah is God.

[4]Every man praying or prophesying with his head covered puts his head to shame. [5]But every woman praying or prophesying with her head uncovered puts her head to shame. For it is one and the same thing as having been shaved. [6]For if a woman is not covered, let her also be shorn. But if it is shameful to a woman to be shorn or shaved, let her be covered. [7]For a man, on the one hand, is not obligated to have his head covered, being the image and glory of God, but a wife is the glory of a husband. [8]For man is not out of woman, but woman out of man. [9]Additionally, man was not created on account of the woman, but woman on account of the man. [10]For this cause the woman is obligated to have authority over her head, because of the angels.

[11]However, neither is man separate from woman, nor woman separate from man, in the Lord. [12]For as the woman is from the man, so a man is also through a woman, but all things are from God. [13]Judge for yourselves: Is it appropriate that a woman pray to God uncovered? [14]Yet Nature itself does not teach you[+] that if a man has long hair it is a dishonor to him. [15]On the other hand, if a woman has long hair, it is a glory to her, since the long hair is given to her in the place of a covering. [16]But if anyone wants to be contentious, we have no such custom, nor do the communities of God.

[17]But in giving you[+] this instruction, I do not praise you[+], since you[+] come together not for the better but for the worse. [18]For first of all, when you[+] come together in the congregation, I hear that divisions exist among you[+], and I partly believe it. [19]Because it is also necessary that there be factions among you[+], so that those who are judged to be genuine may be evident among you[+].

[20]Therefore when you[+] come together, it is not to eat the meal of the Lord. [21]For in eating, each one takes his own meal first, and one is hungry, and another is drunken. [22]Is it because you[+] do not

10:18 1Co. 9:13 leads up to this. Heb. 13:10 refers to the same.

10:33 "The property [*mammon*] of your friend is to be as valuable to you as your own." (Tal. Aboth 2:12)

11:5-6 The words used may refer to a veil, but *kalumma*, the word used in 2Co. 3:13-16 but not used here, is explicit. "And the priest shall take the barley and offer it to the woman, and shall take away from her head-dress on her head, that she may be judged with her head bare, and deprived of the symbol of modesty, which all those women are accustomed to wear who are completely blameless..." (Philo, <u>The Special Laws</u>, III.X (56) trans. by C.D. Yonge)

11:10 Tal. Sanhedrin 58b speaks of a bondwoman who is given by her master to be the wife of a slave: "When is she free again (to others)? — R. Huna said: 'When she goes bareheaded in the market.'" The Soncino note says: "Even non-Jewish married women did not walk bareheaded in the streets, and this bondwoman, though not legally married, would do likewise. If she appeared bareheaded, it was a sign that her connection with the slave to whom she had been allotted was now broken."

have houses for eating and drinking? Or do you⁺ despise the community of God, and put to shame those who do not have? What should I say to you⁺? Should I praise you⁺? I do not praise you⁺ in this.

²³For I received from the Lord that which I also delivered to you⁺: that on the night in which he was delivered up, the Lord Yeshua took bread. ²⁴When he had given thanks, he broke it, and said, "This is my body, which is broken for you⁺. Do this in remembrance of me." ²⁵In the same way he also took the cup after eating, saying, "This cup is the new covenant in my blood. [Jer. 31:31-34] As often as you⁺ drink it, do this in remembrance of me." ²⁶Because as often as you⁺ eat this bread and drink this cup, you⁺ proclaim the Lord's death [Mt. 27:37; Mk. 15:26; Lk. 23:38; Jn. 19:19] until he comes. [Zech. 14:1-4] ²⁷Therefore whoever eats this bread or drinks the Lord's cup in a manner unworthy of the Lord will be guilty of the body and the blood of the Lord. ²⁸But let a man examine himself, and so let him eat of the bread and drink of the cup. ²⁹For the one who eats and drinks in an unworthy manner eats and drinks judgment to himself, not discerning the body. ³⁰Because of this, many among you⁺ are weak and sickly, and many are fallen asleep. ³¹For if we carefully examined ourselves, we would not be judged. ³²But when we are judged, we are disciplined by the Lord, so that we should not be condemned with the world. ³³Therefore my family, when you⁺ come together to eat, wait for each other. ³⁴But if anyone is hungry, let him eat at home, so that your⁺ coming together is not unto judgment. I will set the rest in order whenever I come.

12 ¹Now concerning the things of the Spirit, my family, I do not want you⁺ to be ignorant. ²Being Gentiles, you⁺ know that you⁺ were led away to voiceless idols, in whatever way you⁺ could be led. ³So I make known to you⁺ that no man speaking by God's Spirit says, "Yeshua is accursed." No one can say, "Yeshua is Lord," but by the Ruakh Kodesh.

11:14-15 See "Nature and Long Hair" in the ADDITIONAL NOTES.

11:24 Pesakh is observed as a memorial/remembrance/*zikaron*. (e.g. Ex. 12:14) In the traditional prayer *Ya'aleh veYavo*, we say, "...the remembrance/*zikaron* of our Fathers, the remembrance of Yerushala'im Your city, and the remembrance of Messiah, Son of David Your servant..."

11:25-29 Traditionally, the cup after the Pesakh meal is *haGeulah*, the cup of redemption. Yeshua, and Sha'ul, are presenting the cup after the meal as an affirmation of God's new covenant with Israel. To drink this cup is to affirm that God will fulfill the new covenant with the redemption which it promises to all Israel.

11:26 Yeshua died for the sins of the world as the King of the Jews. He will return as the Son of David to take up his throne in Yerushala'im and restore the Davidic kingdom, extending its rule over all the earth. In eating the bread (of affliction — *ho lahmo anyo*) and drinking the cup of the new covenant, we are proclaiming the atoning death of the King of the Jews until he comes to reign over David's kingdom and all the earth.

11:33, 12:1 "my family," literally "my brothers"

12:2 In the Alenu, we say, "...for He did not assign us our portion to be like theirs, nor our lot as all their multitudes — <u>for they bow down to futility and emptiness and pray to a god that cannot help</u>. But we [bend the knee and] bow down [and give thanks] before the King over kings of kings, the Holy One, blessed be He." The Sephardic includes the underlined portion, the Ashkenazic includes the portions in brackets.

[4]Now there are various kinds of gifts, but the same Spirit. [5]There are various kinds of service, but the same Lord. [6]There are various kinds of workings, but the same God who works all things in all. [7]But to each one is given the manifestation of the Spirit for the profit of all. [8]For to one the word of wisdom is given through the Spirit, and to another the word of knowledge according to the same Spirit. [9]To another is given faith by the same Spirit, and to another gifts of healings by the one Spirit. [10]But to another, working miracles, and to another prophecy, and to another discerning of spirits. To another, different kinds of tongues, and to another the interpretation of tongues. [11]Yet the one and the same Spirit operates all of these, distributing to each one separately as he desires.

[12]For as the body is one and has many members, and all the members of the body, being many, are one body, so also is the Messiah. [13]For in one Spirit we were all immersed into one body — whether Jews or Gentiles, whether bond or free — and were all given to drink into one Spirit. [14]For the body is not one member, but many.

[15]If the foot were to say, "Because I am not the hand, I am not part of the body," is it therefore not part of the body? [16]If the ear were to say, "Because I am not the eye, I am not part of the body," is it therefore not part of the body? [17]If the whole body were an eye, where would the hearing be? If the whole were hearing, where would the smelling be? [18]But now God has set the members, each one of them, in the body just as He desired. [19]If they were all one member, where would the body be? [20]But now they are many members, but one body.

[21]The eye cannot tell the hand, "I have no need for you," or again the head to the feet, "I have no need for you[+]." [22]No, quite to the contrary, those members of the body which seem to be weaker are necessary. [23]And those parts of the body which we think to be less honorable, on those we place more abundant value. And greater decorum applies to our unpresentable parts, [24]whereas our presentable parts have no such need. God, on the other hand, joined the body together, giving greater value to that part which has need, [25]so that there should be no division in the body, but rather that the members should have the same concern for one another. [26]When one member suffers, all the members suffer with it. Or when one member is honored, all the members rejoice with it.

[27]Now you[+] are individually members of the body of Messiah. [28]God has set some in the community: first, ambassadors, second, prophets, third, teachers, then works of power, then gifts of healings, helps, administrations, and various kinds of tongues. [29]Are all ambassadors? Are all prophets? Are all teachers? Are all workers of miracles? [30]Do all have gifts of healings? Do all speak with various tongues? Do all interpret? [31]But earnestly desire the greater gifts, and yet I show you[+] an unsurpassed way.

13 [1]If I speak with the tongues of men and of angels, but do not have love, I have become an echoing gong, or a clanging cymbal. [2]If I have prophecy, and know all mysteries and all knowledge, and if I have all the faith so as to remove mountains, but do not have love, I am nothing.

12:15-20 Midrash on Psalms 39.2 contains a story of the different members of a man's body quarreling with one another.

13:1 Yoḥanan ben Zakkai is said to have studied the language of the demons and that of the ministering angels. (Tal. Baba Bathra 134a)

³If I give away all my goods to feed others, and if I deliver my body to be burned, but do not have love, it profits me nothing.

⁴Love is patient and is kind. Love does not envy. [Tobit 4:7,16] Love does not brag, does not become prideful, ⁵does not behave itself inappropriately, does not seek its own, is not provoked, takes no account of evil. ⁶Love does not rejoice in wrong-doing, but rejoices with the truth. ⁷Love covers all, believes all, hopes all, endures all. ⁸Love never fails. But where there are prophecies, their use will come to an end. Where there are various tongues, they will cease. Where there is knowledge, its use will come to an end. ⁹For we know in part, and we prophesy in part, ¹⁰but when what is complete has come, then what is partial will no longer be useful.

¹¹When I was a child, I spoke as a child, I thought as a child, I reasoned as a child. Now that I have become a man, the things of a child are not useful. ¹²For now we see an obscure image in a mirror, but then we will see face to face. [Num. 12:8, Prov. 1:6] Now I know in part, but then I will know fully, even as I also have been fully known. ¹³And now these three things remain: faith, hope, and love, but the greatest of these is love.

14 ¹Follow after love, and earnestly desire spiritual gifts, and especially that you⁺ may prophesy. ²For the one who speaks in a tongue speaks not to men, but to God, because no one understands. In the Spirit, however, he speaks mysteries. ³But the one who prophesies speaks to men for their growth, encouragement, and consolation. ⁴The one who speaks in a tongue builds himself up, but the one who prophesies builds up the congregation. ⁵Now I desire to have you⁺ all speak with tongues, even more that you⁺ would prophesy. For the one who prophesies is greater than the one who speaks with tongues, unless he interprets so that the congregation may be built up.

⁶And now brethren, if I come to you⁺ speaking with tongues, what would I profit you⁺, unless I speak to you⁺ either by way of revelation, of knowledge, of prophesying, or of teaching? ⁷Even lifeless things which produce sound, whether flute or harp, if they do not give a distinction in the sounds, how will it be known what is played on the flute or harp? ⁸And likewise, if the trumpet gives an uncertain sound, who will prepare himself for war? ⁹So also you⁺, unless you⁺ give intelligible speech with the tongue, how will it be known what is being said? For you⁺ would be speaking into the air. ¹⁰There are so many kinds of sounds in the world, and it may be that none of them is without meaning. ¹¹So if I do not know the meaning of the sound, I will be a foreigner to the one who speaks, and the one who speaks will be a foreigner to me.

¹²So also you⁺, since you⁺ are zealous for spiritual gifts, seek that you⁺ may abound to the growth of the community. ¹³Therefore let the one who speaks in a tongue pray that he may interpret. ¹⁴For if I pray in a tongue, my spirit prays, but my understanding is unfruitful. ¹⁵So what should it be? I

13:5 "love does not seek its own" advantage or agenda or rights or kind; i.e. love is not focused on, or powered by, self.

13:12 "R. Yehudah said: 'There were nine lenses through which all the [other] prophets saw [visions] ... But Moses saw [visions] through one lens...'" (Mid. Leviticus Rabbah I:14)

In Midrash on Psalms 106.2, Eccl. 8:17 — "and even if a wise man claims to know it, he will not be able to find it" — is applied to the inability of Moses to understand all that was written about Messiah.

will pray with the spirit, and I will pray with the understanding also. I will sing with the spirit, and I will sing with the understanding also. [16]Otherwise if you bless with the spirit, how will the one who occupies the place of the unlearned say the "Amen" at your giving of thanks, seeing he does not know what you say? [17]For you truly give thanks well, but the other person is not built up.

[18]I thank my God I speak with tongues more than you[+] all. [19]In the assembly, however, I choose to speak five words with my understanding, so that I might also instruct others, rather than ten thousand words in a tongue. [20]Brethren, do not be children in understanding, but in malice be little children, and in understanding be mature.

[21]In the Law it is written, "'By other tongues and by other lips I will speak to this people. Not even in this way will they hear Me,' says the Everpresent Lord." [Is. 28:11] [22]So tongues are for a sign, not to those who believe, but to the unbelieving. Prophesying, however, is for a sign, not to the unbelieving, but to those who believe. [23]If therefore the whole congregation is assembled together and all speak with tongues, and unlearned or unbelieving people come in, won't they say that you[+] are crazy? [24]If all prophesy, however, and someone unbelieving or unlearned comes in, he is examined and called to account by all. [25]The secrets of his heart are made known, and so he will fall down on his face and bow before God, declaring that God is really with you[+].

[26]What should it be then, brethren? When you[+] come together, each one has a psalm, has a teaching, has a revelation, has a tongue, has an interpretation. Let all things be done to build each other up. [27]If anyone speaks in a tongue, let it be two or at the most three, and in turn. Then let one interpret. [28]But if there is no interpreter, let him keep silent in the assembly, and let him speak to himself and to God. [29]Let the prophets speak, two or three, and let the others discern. [30]But if a revelation is made to another sitting by, let the first keep silent. [31]For you[+] all can prophesy one by one, so that all may learn, and all may be exhorted. [32]The spirits of the prophets are subject to the prophets, [33]because God is not a God of confusion, but of peace.

As in all the communities of those who belong to God, [34]let the wives keep silent in the assemblies, because they are not permitted to converse. Rather let them be compliant, as the Law also says. [Gen. 3:16] [35]If they desire to be instructed in anything, let them ask their own husbands at home, for it is shameful for wives to converse in the assembly.

[36]Or was it from you[+] that the word of God went out? Or did it come to you[+] alone? [37]If any man thinks himself to be a prophet or spiritual, let him acknowledge that what I write to you[+] is a commandment of the Lord. [38]But if anyone is ignorant, let him be ignorant.

[39]So brethren, desire earnestly to prophesy, and do not forbid speaking with tongues. [40]Let all things be done decently and in order.

15 [1]Now brethren, I remind you[+] of the good news which I proclaimed to you[+], which also you[+] received, in which also you[+] stand. [2]By this also you[+] are saved, if you[+] hold firmly the word which I proclaimed to you[+], unless you[+] believed without purpose. [3]For I delivered to you[+] first of all what I also received: that Messiah died for our sins in accordance with the Scriptures [Is. 53:5-10], [4]that he was buried and raised up on the third day in accordance with the Scriptures [Is. 53:9], [5]and

14:34-35 See note to 1Tim. 2:9-14.

that he appeared to Kefa, then to the twelve. ⁶Then he appeared to over five hundred brethren at once, most of whom still live, but some have also fallen asleep.

⁷Then he appeared to Jacob, next to all the ambassadors, ⁸and last of all, he also appeared to me, as to one born prematurely. ⁹For I am the least of the ambassadors, who is not worthy to be called an ambassador, because I persecuted the community of God. ¹⁰But by the grace of God I am what I am. His grace which was bestowed on me was not futile, but I labored more than all of them — yet not I, but the grace of God which was with me. ¹¹Whether it is I then or they, so we proclaim, and so you⁺ believed.

¹²Now if Messiah is proclaimed that he has been raised from the dead, how do some among you⁺ say that there is no resurrection of the dead? ¹³But if there is no resurrection of the dead, neither has Messiah been raised. ¹⁴If Messiah has not been raised, then our proclamation is worthless, and your⁺ faith also is pointless. ¹⁵Yes, we are found false witnesses of God, because we testified about God that He raised up the Messiah, whom He did not raise up, if it is true that the dead are not raised. ¹⁶For if the dead are not raised, neither has Messiah been raised. ¹⁷If Messiah has not been raised, your⁺ faith is an illusion — you⁺ are still in your⁺ sins. ¹⁸Then those also who are fallen asleep in Messiah have perished. ¹⁹If we have hope in Messiah in this life only, we are of all men most to be pitied.

²⁰But now Messiah has been raised from the dead. He became the first fruits of those who are asleep. ²¹For since death came by man, the resurrection of the dead also came by man. ²²For as in Adam all die, so also in the Messiah all will be made alive, ²³but each in his own order — Messiah, the first fruits, then those who are the Messiah's at his coming.

²⁴Then the end comes, when he will deliver up the Kingdom to the One who is God and Father, when He will have caused all rule and all authority and power to cease. ²⁵For he must reign until He has put all his enemies under his feet. ²⁶The last enemy that will be made of no effect is death, ²⁷for, "He put all things in subjection under his feet." [Ps. 8:6] But when He says, "All things are put in subjection," it is evident that it does not include the One who subjected all things to him. ²⁸When all things have been subjected to him, then the Son will also himself be subjected to the One who subjected all things to him, so that God may be all in all. [Zech. 14:9]

²⁹For what will those who are immersed for the dead do, if the dead are not raised at all? Why then are they immersed for the dead? [2Mac. 12:43-44]

³⁰Why do we also stand in danger every hour? ³¹By the boasting which I have in you⁺ in Messiah Yeshua our Lord, I affirm that I die daily. ³²If I fought as a man against beasts at Ephesus, what does it profit me if the dead are not raised? "Let us eat and drink, for tomorrow we die." [Is. 22:13,

---

15:8 "And if two men fight and hit a pregnant woman, and her child comes out not fully formed..." (Ex. 21:22 LXX)

15:19 In the traditional prayer on awakening, one says, "My God, the soul whichYou have put in me is pure. You have formed it in me. You breathed it into me, and You guard it within me. And in the future, You will take it from me and return it to me in the time to come...." (Tal. Berachot 60b)

15:29 In Tal. Menachot 4b, there is a discussion about when an offering for atonement can be brought for someone who has died. The primary example given is a woman who brings her burnt offering and sin offering after childbirth, but dies before the burnt offering is presented.

56:12] ³³Do not be deceived, evil company corrupts good character. ³⁴Awake to what is right and stop sinning, for some have no knowledge of God. I say this to your⁺ shame.

³⁵But someone will say, "How are the dead raised?" and, "With what kind of body do they come?" ³⁶You foolish one, what you plant is not made alive unless it dies. ³⁷What you plant — you do not plant the body that will come into being, but a bare grain, maybe of wheat or of some other kind. ³⁸But God gives it a body even as He pleased, and to each seed a body of its own.

³⁹All flesh is not the same flesh, but there is one flesh of men, another flesh of animals, another of fish, and another of birds. ⁴⁰There are also bodies in heaven and bodies on earth, but the glory of that in heaven differs from that on earth. ⁴¹There is one glory of the sun, another glory of the moon, and another glory of the stars, for one star differs from another star in glory.

⁴²The resurrection of the dead is also like this. The body is sown in decay, it is raised imperishable. ⁴³It is sown in dishonor, it is raised in glory. It is sown in weakness, it is raised in power. ⁴⁴It is sown a body from nature, it is raised a body from the spirit. There is a body from nature and there is also a body from the spirit.

⁴⁵So it is also written, "The first man, Adam, became a living soul." [Gen. 2:7] The last Adam became a life-giving spirit. ⁴⁶However, what is from the spirit is not first, but what is from nature, then what is from the spirit. ⁴⁷The first Adam is of the earth, made of dust. The second Adam is from heaven. ⁴⁸As is the one made of dust, even so are those who are made of dust. And as is the one from heaven, even so are the ones who are from heaven. ⁴⁹As we have borne the image of those made of dust, let us also bear the image of the one from heaven. [Gen. 1:26]

⁵⁰Now I say this, brethren, that flesh and blood cannot inherit the Kingdom of God. Nor does what decays inherit imperishability. ⁵¹Listen, I tell you⁺ a mystery. We will not all sleep, but we will all

15:33 "If one walks [in the counsel of the ungodly], his end is to stand [in the way of sinners]. If he stands, his end is to sit [in the seat of those who mock]; and if he sits, his end is to mock." (Mid. Psalms 1.7)

15:35-36 "*kal v'chomer* [reasoning from light to heavy]: If a grain of wheat, which is buried naked, comes forth clothed in much, how much more so the righteous, who are buried as one in their clothes." (Tal. Sanhedrin 90b, which is part of an argument that resurrection is taught in Torah. cf. Tal. Ketubot 111b)

15:40 "The beings on high and the beings below were created at the same time, yet the beings on high are empowered by the radiance of the Shekhinah, and the beings below do not eat if they do not labor.... The beings on high and the beings below were created at the same time, yet the beings on high live, and the beings below die." (Mid. Genesis Rabbah II:2)

15:44 Rashi comments on the double *yod* in *vayiytzer*/"He formed" in Gen. 2:7: "There were two formings, a forming for this age and a forming for the resurrection of the dead."

15:45 "And the Word of the Everpresent Lord created man in His likeness, in the likeness of the Everpresent Lord, the Everpresent Lord created, male and female created He them." (Targum Yonatan, Genesis 1:27)

15:45-49 "The first Adam was from one end of the world to the other... But when he stunk from sin, the Holy One, blessed be He, laid His hand upon him and made him smaller... The first Adam reached from earth to the firmament... But when he stunk from sin, the Holy One, blessed be He, laid His hand upon him and made him smaller..." (Tal. Sanhedrin 38b)

be changed, ⁵²in a moment, in the twinkling of an eye, at the last trumpet. For the trumpet will sound, the dead will be raised immortal, and we will be changed. ⁵³For this that decays must be clothed in imperishability, and this that is mortal must be clothed in immortality. [Wisdom of Sol. 9:15] ⁵⁴But when this that decays will have been clothed in imperishability, and this that is mortal will have been clothed in immortality, then what is written will take place: "Death is swallowed up in victory." [Is. 25: 8]

⁵⁵"Death, where is your victory? Death, where is your sting?" [Hos. 13:14] ⁵⁶Sin is the sting of death, and the Law is the power of sin. ⁵⁷But thanks be to God, who gives us the victory through our Lord Yeshua the Messiah. ⁵⁸Therefore my beloved family, be steadfast, immovable, always abounding in the work of the Lord, because you⁺ know that your⁺ labor in the Lord is not futile.

16 ¹Now concerning the collection for those who belong to God, as I commanded the communities of Galatia, you⁺ do likewise. ²On the first of the week, let each one of you⁺ save as he may prosper, so that no collections are made when I come. ³When I arrive, I will send whomever you⁺ approve with letters to carry your⁺ gracious gift to Yerushala'im. ⁴If it is appropriate for me to go also, they will go with me.

⁵Now I will come to you⁺ when I have passed through Makedonia, for I am going to pass through Makedonia. ⁶But it may be that I will stay with you⁺, even for the winter, so that you⁺ may send me on my journey wherever I go. ⁷For I do not wish to see you⁺ now in passing, but I hope to stay a while with you⁺ if the Lord permits. ⁸But I will stay at Ephesus until Shavuot, ⁹because a very useful door has opened to me, though there are many adversaries.

¹⁰Now if Timothy comes, see that he is with you⁺ without fear, for he does the work of the Lord, as I also do. ¹¹Therefore let no one despise him, but set him forward on his journey in peace, so that he may come to me, for I expect him with the brethren. ¹²Now concerning Apollos our brother, I greatly encouraged him to come to you⁺ with the brethren, yet it was not at all his desire to come now; but he will come when he has an opportunity.

¹³Watch. Stand firm in the faith. Be courageous. Be strong. ¹⁴Let all that you⁺ do be done in love.

¹⁵You⁺ know the household of Stefanas, that it is the first fruits of Akhaia, and that they have committed themselves to serve those who belong to God. Now I encourage you⁺ brethren ¹⁶that you⁺ also be subject to such as these, and to everyone who helps and labors.

¹⁷I rejoice at the coming of Stefanas, Fortunatus, and Achaicus, because they supplied what was lacking on your⁺ part. ¹⁸For they refreshed my spirit and yours⁺. Therefore acknowledge those who are like these.

¹⁹The communities of the province of Asia greet you⁺. Akila and Priska heartily greet you⁺ in the Lord, together with the congregation that is in their house. ²⁰All the brethren greet you⁺. Greet one another with a holy kiss.

²¹This greeting is from me, Paulos, with my own hand. ²²If any individual does not love the Lord, let him be accursed. Come, O Lord! ²³The grace of the Lord Yeshua be with you⁺. ²⁴My love is with you⁺ all in Messiah Yeshua.

15:58 "family," literally "brothers"

16:1-3 "A fund for humanitarian aid is collected by two, and distributed by three." (Tal. Baba Batra 8b)

Sha'ul/Paulos' Second Letter
to the Corinthians

1 [1]Paulos, an ambassador of Messiah Yeshua through the will of God, and Timothy our brother, to the community of God which is at Corinth, with all those who belong to God in the whole of Akhaia. [2]Grace to you[+] and peace from God our Father and the Lord Yeshua the Messiah.

[3]Blessed be the God and Father of our Lord Yeshua the Messiah, the Father of mercies and God of all comfort. [4]He encourages us in all our troubles, so that through the encouragement with which we ourselves are encouraged by God, we may be able to encourage those who are in any trouble. [5]For as the sufferings of the Messiah abound to us, even so our encouragement also abounds through Messiah.

[6]Now even if we are troubled, it is for your[+] encouragement and salvation. If we are encouraged, it is for your[+] encouragement, which works towards endurance of the same sufferings which we also suffer. [7]Our hope for you[+] is firm, knowing that since you[+] are partakers of the sufferings, so you[+] are also of the encouragement.

[8]For we don't want you[+] brethren to be uninformed about our trouble which happened to us in the province of Asia. We were excessively weighed down beyond our strength, so much so that we despaired even of life. [9]Yes, we had the sentence of death within ourselves, so that we would not trust in ourselves, but in God who raises the dead. [10]He delivered us out of such death, and will deliver us. We have set our hope on Him, that He will also still deliver us. [11]Together you[+] also are helping by prayer for us, so that thanks may be given by many on our behalf for the gift to us through many.

[12]For this is our boasting, the testimony of our conscience, that we behaved ourselves in simplicity and sincerity of God, in the world and even more so toward you[+], not in fleshly wisdom, but in the grace of God. [13]For we are writing nothing to you[+] other than what you[+] read or acknowledge, and I hope you[+] will acknowledge to the end. [14]You[+] have acknowledged us in the same way in part — that we are your[+] glory, even as you[+] also are ours in the day of the Lord Yeshua.

[15]In this confidence, I intended to come first to you[+], so that you[+] might receive a benefit a second time. [16]And I intended to pass from you[+] into Makedonia, and again from Makedonia to come to you[+], and to be sent forward by you[+] on my journey to Judea. [17]When I therefore had determined this, did I do it lightly? Or the things that I purpose, do I purpose according to the physical nature, that with me there should be "Yes, yes" and "No, no"? [18]Instead, as God is faithful, our word toward you[+] was not "Yes and no." [19]For the Son of God, Yeshua the Messiah, who was proclaimed by us among you[+] — by me, Sila, and Timothy — was not "Yes and no," but in him has been "Yes." [20]For whatever the promises of God are, the "Yes" and the "Amen" are in him, to the glory of God through us.

[21]Now God is the One who establishes us with you[+] in Messiah, and anointed us. [22]He also sealed us and gave us the down payment of the Spirit in our hearts. [23]Now I call God for a witness to my soul, that to spare you[+] I have not yet come to Corinth. [24]Not that we rule over your[+] faith, but are fellow workers with you[+] for your[+] joy, because you[+] stand firm by faith.

2 [1]But I determined this for myself, that I would not come to you⁺ again in sadness. [2]For if I make you⁺ sad, then who will make me glad, if not the one whom I make sad? [3]And I wrote this very thing to you⁺, so that when I came I would not have sadness from those who should cause me to rejoice — having confidence in all of you⁺, that my joy is that of all of you⁺.

[4]For out of much trouble and anguish of heart I wrote to you⁺ with many tears, not that you⁺ would be saddened, but that you⁺ might know the love that I have so abundantly for you⁺. [5]Now if anyone has caused sorrow, he has not caused sorrow to me — but to some — that I not burden all of you⁺. [6]This punishment given by the many is sufficient for this one. [7]So that, on the contrary, you⁺ should rather forgive him and encourage him, so that this one should not by any means be swallowed up with his excessive sorrow. [8]So I urge you⁺ to confirm your⁺ love toward him. [9]For I also wrote for this purpose, that I might know that you⁺ are proven and approved, if you⁺ are obedient in all things. [10]Now I also forgive whomever you⁺ forgive anything. For if indeed I have forgiven anything, I have forgiven that one for your⁺ sakes in the presence of Messiah, [11]so that no advantage may be gained over us by the Accuser, because we are not ignorant of his schemes.

[12]Now when I came to Troas for the good news of the Messiah, and when a door was opened to me in the Lord, [13]I had no relief for my spirit, because I did not find my brother Titus. But taking my leave of them, I went out into Makedonia. [14]Now thanks be to God, who always leads us in triumph in the Messiah, and reveals through us the aroma of the knowledge of him in every place. [15]For we are a fragrance of Messiah to God in those who are being saved, and in those who are perishing. [16]To the one, an aroma of death to death; to the other, an aroma of life to life. And who is competent for these things? [17]For we are not making merchandise of the word of God, as so many do, but we speak in Messiah from sincerity and from God, in the sight of God.

3 [1]Are we beginning again to commend ourselves? Or do we need, as some do, letters of commendation to you⁺ or from you⁺? [2]You⁺ are our letter, written on our hearts, known and read by all men. [3]It is evident that through our assistance you⁺ are a letter of Messiah, written not with ink, but with the Spirit of the living God, not on tablets of stone, but on tablets that are hearts of flesh. [4]We have such confidence through the Messiah toward God — [5]not that we are competent in ourselves to think of anything as from ourselves, but our competency is from God.

[6]He also made us competent as servants of a new covenant [Jer. 31:31-34], not by what is written, but by the Spirit. For what is written condemns to death, but the Spirit gives life. [7]What served to

---

2:15-16 *euodia*, a good smell, is the word used in passages like Ex. 29:18, "a sweet smelling fragrance, an offering by fire to the Everpresent Lord."

"R. Tanḥuma said, 'The Word of the Everpresent Lord broke through and it went forth and killed the servants of the stars who did not receive it, and gave life to Israel, for they received the Torah.'" (Mid. Ex. 5.9)

3:6-11 is somewhat similar to the discussion in Galatians where Sha'ul compares the Covenant of the Law and the New Covenant. The goal of both covenants is that Israel live in righteousness before God — "Do justice, love mercy, and walk humbly with your God." [Mic. 6:8] The Covenant of the Law shows us what is right, but it does not empower us to do what is right. The New Covenant, because of the Spirit which is given to us, does empower us to do what is right. It transforms us. (cf. Ezek. 36:26-27) God's goal for Israel and her commonwealth remains the same.

bring death came with glory in writing engraved on stones. Consequently, the children of Israel could not look steadfastly on the face of Moses because of the glory of his face. [Ex,34:29-35] But if it was like this with what was passing away, [8]will not what brings the Spirit be with much more glory? [9]For if what serves for condemnation has glory, what serves for righteousness abounds much more in glory. [10]For even in this respect, what has been made glorious has not been made glorious, because of the glory that surpasses it. [11]For if that which has a use that passes away came in glory, that which remains is much more glorious.

[12]Having such hope because of this, we use great boldness, [13]and not like Moses, who put a veil on his face so the children of Israel would not look intently unto the end of what was passing away. [14]However, their minds were dimmed, for the same veil remains at the reading of the old covenant until this very day, because it passes away in Messiah. [15]Even to this day, when Moses is read, a veil lies upon their heart. [16]But when a heart turns to the Lord, the veil is taken away. [17]Now the Lord is the Spirit and where the Spirit of the Lord is, there is freedom. [18]But beholding the glory of the Lord as in a mirror, we all with unveiled face are transformed into that same image from glory to glory, as from the Spirit of the Lord.

4 [1]Having this responsibility, for which we received mercy, we are therefore not discouraged. [2]To the contrary, we have renounced the hidden things of shame, not walking in craftiness, nor handling the word of God deceitfully. And, by revealing the truth, we are commending ourselves to every man's conscience in the sight of God.

[3]But if our good news is nevertheless veiled, it is veiled in those who are perishing. [4]The god of this age has blinded the minds of the unbelieving, so that the light of the good news of the glory of the Messiah — who is the image of God — does not dawn on them. [5]For we do not proclaim ourselves, but Messiah Yeshua as Lord, and ourselves as your[+] servants for the sake of Yeshua. [6]For it is the God who commanded light to shine out of darkness who has shined in our hearts to give the light of the knowledge of the glory of God in the presence of Yeshua the Messiah.

[7]But we have this treasure in containers of clay so that the exceeding greatness of the power may be of God, and not from ourselves. [8]We are pressed on every side, yet not crushed; perplexed, yet not to despair. [9]We are pursued, yet not forsaken; struck down, yet not destroyed. [10]We are always carrying in the body the putting to death of the Lord Yeshua, so that the life of Yeshua may also be revealed in our body. [11]For we who live are always delivered to death for the sake of Yeshua, so that the life also of Yeshua may be revealed in our mortal flesh. [12]So then death works in us, but life in you[+].

[13]But having the same spirit of faith as in what has been written — "I believed, and therefore I spoke" [Ps. 116:10] — we also believe, and therefore we also speak. [14]We know that the One who raised the Lord Yeshua will raise us also with Yeshua, and will present us with you[+]. [15]For all things are for your[+] sakes, that the grace abounding through the many may cause thanksgiving to abound to the glory of God.

3:13 "The face of Moses was as the face of the sun, the face of Joshua as the face of the moon." (Tal.Baba Bathra 75a)

[16]Therefore we are not discouraged, but though our outward being is being brought to decay, yet our inner being is being renewed day by day. [17]For our affliction, which is light and momentary, is producing for us an eternal weight of glory beyond compare. [18]We do not look at the things which are seen, but at the things which are not seen. For the things which are seen are temporary, but the things which are not seen are eternal.

5 [1]For we know that if the dwelling which is our earthly tent is destroyed, we have a building from God in the heavens, an eternal dwelling not made with hands. [2]For indeed we groan in this, longing to be clothed with our dwelling which is from heaven. [3]And surely if we have been clothed, we will not be found naked. [4]For indeed we who are in this tent do groan, being weighed down. Not that we desire to strip, but rather that we desire to be clothed, so that what is mortal may be swallowed up by life. [5]Now God is the One who made us for this very thing, who also gave to us the down payment of the Spirit.

[6]Being therefore always of good courage, and knowing that while we are at home in the body we are absent from the Lord — [7]for we walk by faith, not by appearance — [8]we are of good courage, I say, and are willing rather to be absent from the body and to be at home with the Lord. [9]So we also make it our aim, whether at home or absent, to be well pleasing to him. [10]For we must all be made known before the judgment seat of the Messiah, so that each one may receive according to the things he has done in the body, whether good or bad.

[11]Knowing therefore the fear of the Lord, we persuade men, but we are made manifest to God, and I hope that we are made manifest also in your+ consciences. [12]For we are not commending ourselves to you+ again, but are giving you+ occasion to boast about us, so that you+ may have something to answer those who boast in appearance and not in heart. [13]For if we were perplexed, it was to God. Or if we are sober-minded, it is for you+. [14]For Messiah's love compels us, having concluded this, that if one died for all, then all died.

[15]He died for all so that those who live should no longer live to themselves, but to him who died for them and was raised again. [16]Therefore, from now on, we regard no one in terms of physical nature. Even if we have known Messiah in terms of physical nature, yet now we know him so no more. [Lk. 24:15-31; Mk. 16:12; Yhn. 20:15] [17]Therefore if anyone is in Messiah, he is a new creation. The old things have passed away. Know that they have become new! [18]But all these things are from God, who reconciled us to Himself through the Messiah, and gave to us the duty of reconciliation. [19]Since God was reconciling the world to Himself in Messiah, not counting against them their transgressions, He also committed to us the word of reconciliation. [20]Therefore we are ambassadors on behalf of Messiah, as though God were entreating through us. We beg you+ on behalf of Messiah, be reconciled to God. [21]For He made him who knew no sin to be sin on our behalf, so that we might become in him the righteousness of God.

6 [1]Working together, we also exhort you+ not to receive the grace of God in vain, [2]for He says, "At an acceptable time I listened to you. In a day of salvation I helped you." [Is. 49:8] Know that now is the acceptable time. Know that now is the day of salvation.

5:17 "And a people will be created to praise the Everpresent Lord.' [Ps. 102:19H] The Holy One, blessed be He, will create them a new creation." (Mid. Leviticus 30.3)

[3]We give no occasion for offense in anything, so that what we serve is not blamed. [4]On the contrary, we are presenting ourselves in everything as servants of God — in great endurance, in afflictions, in hardships, in distresses, [5]in beatings, in imprisonments, in turmoil, in labors, in watchings, in fastings, [6]in purity, in knowledge, in patient endurance, in kindness, in the Ruakh Kodesh, in sincere love, [7]in the word of truth, in the power of God; by the armor of righteousness on the right hand and on the left, [8]by glory and dishonor, by evil report and good report; as deceivers and yet true; [9]as unknown and yet well known; as dying and look, we live; as punished and not put to death; [10]as sorrowful yet always rejoicing; as poor yet making many rich; as having nothing and yet possessing all things. [11]Our mouth is open to you+ Corinthians. Our heart is opened wide. [12]You+ are not restrained by us, but you+ are restrained by your+ own feelings. [13]Now in return, I speak as to my children, open wide your+ hearts also.

[14]Do not be unequally yoked with unbelievers [Lev. 19:19], for what partnership do justice and actions contrary to the Law have? Or what fellowship does light have with darkness? [Prov. 4:18-19] [15]What agreement does Messiah have with Beliya'al [Dt. 13:13, Jdg. 19:22, 1K. 21:13, Nah. 1:11,15]? Or what portion does a believer have with an unbeliever? [Sirach 13:17-18] [16]What agreement does a sanctuary of God have with idols? For we are a sanctuary of the living God. Even as God said, "I will dwell in them, and walk in them. And I will be their God, and they will be My people." [Ex. 19:15, Lev. 26:12, Jer. 31:1, Ezek. 37:27] [17]So "'Come out from among them, and be separated,' says the Everpresent Lord. 'Do not touch any unclean thing. I will receive you+. [Is. 52:11] [18]I will be+ a Father to you. You+ will be sons and daughters to Me,' says the Everpresent Lord, the Authority over all." [2 Sam. 7:14, 1 Chr. 17:13, Is. 43:6]

7 [1]Having these promises, beloved, let us therefore cleanse ourselves from all defilement of flesh and spirit, fulfilling holiness in the fear of God. [2]Receive us, we wronged no one. We corrupted no one, we took advantage of no one. [3]I say this not to condemn you+, for I have said before that you+ are in our hearts to die together and live together.

[4]Great is my boldness of speech toward you+. Great is my boasting for you+. I am filled with encouragement. I overflow with joy in all our affliction. [5]For even when we had come into Makedonia, our flesh had no relief, but we were afflicted on every side — conflicts on the outside, fears within. [6]Nevertheless, God — He who encourages those brought low — encouraged us by the coming of Titus; [7]and not by his coming only, but also by the encouragement with which he was encouraged concerning you+. He related to us your+ longing, sorrow, and zeal for me, so that I rejoiced even more.

[8]For though I made you+ sorrowful with my letter, I do not regret it, though I did regret it. For I see that my letter made you+ sorrowful, though just for a while. [9]I now rejoice, not that you+ were made sorrowful, but that you+ were made sorrowful to repentance. For you+ were made sorrowful in a godly way, so that you+ might not suffer loss from us in anything. [10]For godly sorrow produces

6:15 Beliya'al/Belial is one of the princes of Darkness His sons/followers are worthless and perverse. "...The first attack of the Sons of Light shall be undertaken against the forces of the Sons of Darkness, the army of Belial... a time of salvation for the People of God, and time of dominion for all the men of His forces, and eternal annihilation for all the forces of Belial." (DSS 1QM 1:1,5) "[He] made Belial for the pit, an angel of malevolence, his [dominio]n is in darkne[ss] and his counsel to condemn and convict." (DSS 1QM 13:11)

repentance to salvation, which brings no regret. But the sorrow of the world produces death. [11]Look at what diligence this very thing — that you[+] were made sorrowful in a godly way — produced in you[+]. Yes, what justification, indignation, fear, longing, zeal, and judgment! In everything you[+] demonstrated yourselves to be pure in the matter.

[12]So although I wrote to you[+], I did not write for the sake of the one who did the wrong, nor for the sake of the one who suffered the wrong, but that your[+] diligence toward us might be revealed in you[+] in the sight of God. [13]So we have been encouraged. In our encouragement we rejoiced even much more for the joy of Titus, because his spirit has been refreshed by you[+] all. [14]For if in anything I have boasted to him about you[+], I was not disappointed. But as we spoke all things to you[+] in truth, even so our boasting to Titus was found to be true. [15]His affection has increased toward you[+], while he remembers the obedience of all of you, how with fear and trembling you[+] received him. [16]I rejoice that in everything I am confident in you[+].

8 [1]Moreover we make known to you[+] brethren the grace of God which has been given in the communities of Makedonia. [2]Because in a great trial of affliction, the abundance of their joy and their deep poverty abounded to the riches of their generosity. [3]For I testify that according to their ability — yes and beyond their ability — they gave willingly, [4]fervently asking us to receive the favor and fellowship of this assistance to those who belong to God. [5]And not only as we had hoped, but they first gave themselves to the Lord and to us by the will of God.

[6]So we urged Titus that, as he had begun, so he would also complete in you[+] this kindness. [7]But as you[+] abound in everything — in faith, utterance, knowledge, all earnestness, and in your[+] love to us — see that you[+] also abound in this kindness. [8]I am not speaking a commandment, but as proving the sincerity of your[+] love through the earnestness of others. [9]For you[+] know the grace of our Lord Yeshua the Messiah, that though he was rich, yet for your[+] sakes he became poor, so that you[+], through his poverty, might become rich.

[10]I give advice in this because this is profitable for you[+]. More than a year ago, you began not only to be willing, but also to do. [11]But now complete the doing also, so that as there was the readiness to be willing, so there may also be the completion out of what you have. [12]For if the readiness is there, it is acceptable according to what one has, not according to what he does not have. [13]For this is not that others may be eased and you[+] distressed, [14]but for equality. All of your[+] abundance at this present time supplies their need, so that their abundance also may become a supply for your[+] need, in order that there may be equality. [15]As it is written, "The one who gathered much had nothing left over, and the one who gathered little had no need." [Ex. 16:18]

[16]But thanks be to God, who put the same diligence on your[+] behalf into the heart of Titus. [17]For he indeed accepted our exhortation, but being himself more diligent, he went out to you[+] of his own accord. [18]We have sent together with him the brother whose praise in the good news is known through all the communities. [19]Not only so, but he was also appointed by the communities to travel with us in this gracious work, which is administered by us to the glory of the Lord himself, and to show your[+] readiness. [20]We are being careful so that no one should find fault in us concerning this

8:1-9:15 This all refers to the relief offering for those in Yerushala'im who followed Yeshua.

abundance which is administered by us. [21]We have regard for honorable things, not only in the sight of the Lord, but also in the sight of men. [22]We have sent with them our brother, whom we have often proved to be diligent in many things, but now much more diligent, because of the great confidence which he has in you[+]. [23]As for Titus, he is my partner and fellow worker for you[+]. As for our brothers, they are the ambassadors of the communities, the glory of Messiah. [24]So show the proof of your[+] love to them before the communities, and of our boasting about you[+].

[1]It is indeed unnecessary for me to write to you[+] concerning the assistance to those who belong to God, [2]because I know your[+] readiness. I boast of it about you[+] to those of Makedonia, that Akhaia has been ready since a year ago. Your[+] zeal has stirred up very many of them. [3]But I have sent the brothers so that our boasting about you[+] in this respect may not be empty — so that, just as I said, you[+] may be prepared. [4]So that if some Makedonians come with me and somehow find you[+] unprepared, we — to say nothing of you[+] — would be ashamed of this confident boasting. [5]I thought it necessary therefore to entreat the brothers that they would go to you[+] beforehand, and arrange ahead of time the generous gift that you[+] promised earlier, that the same might be ready as a matter of generosity, and not of covetousness. [6]Knowing this: he who sows sparingly will also reap sparingly; he who sows bountifully will also reap bountifully. [7]Let each man give according as he has determined in his heart — not grudgingly or under compulsion, because God loves a cheerful giver. [Prov. 22:8LXX] [8]And God is able to make all grace abound to you[+], so that you[+], always having all sufficiency in everything, may abound to every good work. [9]As it is written, "He has scattered abroad, He has given to the poor. His righteousness remains forever." [Ps. 112:9]

[10]Now the One who supplies seed to the sower and bread for eating, may He supply and multiply your[+] sowing, and increase the fruits of your[+] righteousness. [Is. 55:10-11] [11]You[+] will be enriched in every way for every generous act, which produces thanksgiving to God through us. [12]For this assistance in giving that you[+] perform not only fills up the need among those who belong to God, but abounds also through much thanksgiving to God. [13]Through the proof given by this assistance, they will glorify God for your[+] obedience that agrees with the good news of the Messiah, and for your[+] participation in generous giving to them and to all. [14]And they themselves also, with supplication on your[+] behalf, yearn for you[+] because of the exceeding grace of God in you[+]. [15]Now thanks be to God for His unspeakable gift!

[1]Now I Paulos entreat you[+] myself by the humility and gentleness of the Messiah — I who in your[+] presence am lowly among you[+], but being absent am bold toward you[+]. [2]Yes, not being present, I beg you[+] that I may be bold with the assurance in which I intend to challenge some who consider us to be walking in response to the flesh. [3]For though we walk in the flesh, we do not wage war in response to the flesh. [4]For the weapons of our warfare are not of the flesh, but mighty before God to the throwing down of strongholds, [5]throwing down calculated plans and every high thing that exalts itself against the knowledge of God, and bringing every thought into captivity to the obedience of the Messiah. [6]We are ready to punish all disobedience, when your[+] obedience is complete.

9:7 "it is one and the same, the one who gives much and the one who gives a little, as long as he directs his heart towards his Father in heaven." (Tal Shebuot 15a)

⁷Do you⁺ look at things only as they appear? If anyone trusts in himself that he is Messiah's, let him again consider this in himself: that even as he is Messiah's, so we also are Messiah's. ⁸For even if I were to boast more about our authority — which the Lord gave for building you⁺ up, and not for tearing you⁺ down — I will not be ashamed, ⁹so that I may not seem as if I desire to terrify you⁺ by my letters. ¹⁰For they say, "His letters are weighty and strong, but his bodily presence is weak, and his speech is despicable."

¹¹Let such a person consider this, that what we are in word by letters when we are absent, we are also the same in deed when we are present. ¹²For we do not dare to number or compare ourselves with some of those who commend themselves. But they themselves, measuring themselves by themselves and comparing themselves with themselves, are without understanding. ¹³But we will not boast beyond proper limits, but within the boundary which God appointed to us, which includes even you⁺.

¹⁴For we are not overextending ourselves, as though we did not reach to you⁺. For we came as far as to you⁺ also with the good news of the Messiah. ¹⁵We are not boasting beyond proper limits in other men's labors, but having hope that as your⁺ faith grows, we, within our boundary, will be greatly enlarged by you⁺, ¹⁶so as to proclaim the good news even to the parts beyond you⁺. Not to boast within the boundary of someone else, ¹⁷but "he who boasts, let him boast in the Everpresent Lord." [Jer. 9:24] ¹⁸For it is not the one who commends himself who is approved, but the one whom the Lord commends.

11 ¹I wish that you⁺ would bear with me in a little foolishness, but indeed you⁺ do bear with me. ²For I am jealous over you⁺ with a godly jealousy, because I promised you⁺ in marriage to one husband, that I might present you⁺ as a chaste virgin to the Messiah. ³But I'm afraid that somehow, as the serpent deceived H̲avah in his craftiness, so your⁺ minds might be corrupted from the simplicity and purity that is in the Messiah. ⁴For if someone comes proclaiming another Yeshua, whom we did not proclaim, or if you⁺ receive a different spirit, which you⁺ had not received, or a different good news, which you⁺ had not accepted, you⁺ put up with that well enough.

⁵For I think that I am not in any way less than the highest ambassadors. ⁶But though I am unpolished in speech, yet I am not so in learning. No, in every way this has been made evident to you⁺ in all things. ⁷Or did I commit a sin in humbling myself that you⁺ might be exalted, because I proclaimed to you⁺ God's good news free of charge? ⁸I robbed other communities, taking wages from them that I might serve you⁺. ⁹When I was present with you⁺ and was in need, I did not burden anyone, for the brothers who came from Makedonia completely supplied my need. In everything I kept myself from being burdensome to you⁺, and I will continue to do so. ¹⁰As the truth of Messiah is in me, no one will stop me from this boasting in the regions of Akhaia. ¹¹Why? Because I do not love you⁺? God knows.

¹²But what I do, I will continue to do, so that I may cut off the opportunity from those who desire an opportunity that in their boasting they may be found to be as we are. ¹³For such men are false ambassadors, deceitful workers, masquerading as ambassadors of Messiah. ¹⁴And no wonder, for even the Accuser masquerades as an angel of light. ¹⁵It is no great thing therefore if his servants also masquerade as servants of righteousness. Their end will be according to their deeds.

¹⁶I say again, let no one think me a fool. But if so, still receive me even as a fool, that I also may boast a little. ¹⁷I do not say what I am saying as from the Lord, but as in foolishness, in this confidence

of boasting. [18]Seeing that many boast concerning the physical, I will also boast. [19]For you[+], being wise, gladly put up with fools. [20]For you[+] put up with it if someone brings you[+] into bondage, if he devours you[+], if he takes from you[+], if he exalts himself, if he hits you[+] in the face.

[21]As to dishonor, I speak as though we were weak, but wherein anyone is bold — I speak in foolishness — I am bold also. [22]Are they Hebrews? So am I. Are they sons of Israel? So am I. Are they the seed of Abraham? So am I. [23]Are they servants of Messiah? (I speak as one beside himself.) I am more so, in labors more abundant, in prisons more often, in stripes beyond measure, in deaths often. [24]Five times I received forty stripes minus one from the sectarian Jews. [25]Three times I was beaten with rods. Once I was stoned. Three times I suffered shipwreck. I have been a night and a day in the deep. [26]I have been in travels often — dangers of rivers, dangers of bandits, dangers from my countrymen, dangers from the Gentiles, dangers in the city, dangers in the wilderness, dangers in the sea, dangers among false brothers; [27]in labor and travail, in sleeplessness often, in hunger and thirst, in fastings often, and in cold and nakedness. [28]Besides those things that are external, there is that which presses on me daily, grave concern for all the communities. [29]Who is weak, and I am not weak? Who is caused to stumble, and I do not burn with indignation?

[30]If I must boast, I will boast in the things that concern my weakness. [31]The God and Father of the Lord Yeshua the Messiah, He who is blessed forevermore, knows that I do not lie.

[32]In Damascus, under Aretas the king, the governor guarded the city of the Damascenes, desiring to arrest me. [33]I was let down in a basket through a window in the wall, and escaped his hands.

12 [1]It is necessary, though not better, to boast, but I will come to visions and revelations of the Lord. [2]I know a man in Messiah, fourteen years ago — whether in the body, I do not know, or whether out of the body, I do not know, God knows — such a one was caught up into the third heaven. [3]I know such a man — whether in the body, or outside of the body, I do not know, God knows — [4]how he was caught up into the Garden, and heard unspeakable words, which it is not permitted for a man to utter. [5]On behalf of such a one I will boast, but on my own behalf I will not boast, except in my weaknesses. [6]For if I would desire to boast, I will not be a fool, for I will speak the truth. But I refrain, so that no one think more of me than what he sees in me, or hears from me.

[7]Because of the surpassing greatness of the revelations, so that I might not be exalted beyond measure, therefore a thorn in the flesh was given to me, a messenger of the Accuser, that he might assault me repeatedly, so that I would not be exalted. [8]I pleaded with the Lord three times about this, that it might depart from me. [9]And He said to me, "My grace is sufficient for you, because power is made complete in weakness." Most gladly therefore I will rather glory in my weaknesses, that the power of Messiah may rest on me. [10]Therefore I think it good to be in weaknesses, in injuries, in sufferings, in persecutions, in distresses for Messiah. For whenever I am weak, then I am powerful.

12:2-4 "Our Rabbis taught: Four men entered the Garden, and these are they: Ben 'Azzai, Ben Zoma, Aher, and R. Akiba.... Ben 'Azzai blossomed and died.... Ben Zoma blossomed and was stricken.... Aher mutilated what was planted. R. Akiba went out in peace." (Tal. Hagigah 14b) "Aher," which means "another," was R. Elisha b. Abuyah. It is generally believed that he committed apostasy, perhaps becoming a disciple of Yeshua.

¹¹I have become a fool in boasting. You⁺ compelled me, for I ought to have been commended by you⁺, because in nothing was I less than the highest ambassadors, though I am nothing. ¹²Truly the signs of an ambassador were performed among you⁺ in all perserverance, in signs and wonders and works of power. ¹³For what is there in which you⁺ were made inferior to the rest of the communities, unless it is that I myself was not a slothful burden to you⁺? Forgive me this injustice.

¹⁴Listen, this is the third time I am ready to come to you⁺, and I will not be a slothful burden to you⁺, because I do not seek what is yours⁺, but you⁺. For the children are not obligated to save up for the parents, but the parents for the children. ¹⁵I will most gladly spend and be utterly spent for your⁺ souls, loving you⁺ more abundantly, even if I am loved less. ¹⁶But if it is so, I did not burden you⁺ myself. Nevertheless, being crafty, did I take you⁺ by guile? ¹⁷Did I take advantage of you⁺ by any of those whom I have sent to you⁺? ¹⁸I urged Titus, and I sent the brother with him. Did Titus take any advantage of you⁺? Did we not walk in the same spirit? Did we not walk in the same steps?

¹⁹Have you⁺ been thinking that we are defending ourselves to you⁺? In the sight of God, we speak in Messiah; and all things, beloved, are for building you⁺ up. ²⁰For I am afraid that somehow, when I have come, I might find you⁺ not to be what I would like, and that I might be found by you⁺ what you⁺ would not like. I am afraid that somehow there might be strife, jealousy, outbursts of anger, factions, backbiting, slanderous rumors, proud thoughts, disorders. ²¹I am afraid that when I come again my God may humble me before you⁺, so that I mourn for many of those who have sinned already, and have not repented of the uncleanness, sexual immorality, and licentiousness which they have committed.

13 ¹This is the third time I am coming to you⁺. "Every word is to be established at the mouth of two or three witnesses." [Dt. 17:6, 19:15] ²I have already said, and being absent now I say beforehand — as if I were present the second time, I write to those who have previously sinned, and to all the rest. If I come again, I will not hold back, ³seeing that you⁺ seek a proof of the Messiah who speaks in me, who is not weak toward you⁺, but is powerful in you⁺. ⁴For though he was put to death on the stake from weakness, yet he lives through the power of God. For we also are weak in him, but we will live with him through the power of God toward you⁺. ⁵Examine yourselves, whether you⁺ are in the faith. Test yourselves. Or do you⁺ not yourselves know that Yeshua the Messiah is in you⁺? — unless indeed you⁺ are disapproved. ⁶But I trust that you⁺ will know that we are not disapproved.

⁷Now I pray to God that you⁺ do no evil, not that we may appear approved, but that you⁺ may do what is honorable, even if we seem to be disapproved. ⁸For we have no power against the truth, but for the truth. ⁹For we rejoice when we are weak and you⁺ are strong. And for this we also pray, that you⁺ be made whole. ¹⁰For this reason I write these things while absent, that I need not use severity when present, in accordance with the authority which the Lord gave me for building up, and not for tearing down.

¹¹Finally, brothers, rejoice. Be made whole, be encouraged. Be of the same mind, be at peace, and the God of love and peace will be with you⁺. ¹²Greet one another with a holy kiss. ¹³All those who belong to God greet you⁺. ¹⁴The grace of the Lord Yeshua the Messiah, the love of God, and the fellowship of the Ruakh Kodesh, be with you⁺ all.

Sha'ul/Paulos' Letter to the Galatians

1 [1]Paulos — an ambassador not from men, nor through man, but through Yeshua the Messiah and God the Father, who raised him from the dead — [2]and all the brethren who are with me: to the communities of Galatia. [3]Grace to you[+] and peace from God our Father and the Lord Yeshua, the Messiah. [4]He gave himself for our sins, in order to deliver us out of this present evil age, according to the will of our God and Father. [5]To Him be the glory forever and ever. Amen.

[6]I am amazed that you[+] are so quickly turning to a different good news, away from the One who called you[+] in the grace of Messiah. [7]It is not another good news, but there are some who are troubling you[+], and want to distort the good news of the Messiah. [8]But even though we or an angel from heaven were to proclaim to you[+] any good news other than that which we proclaimed to you[+], let him be accursed. [9]As we have said before, so I now say again, if any man proclaims to you[+] any good news other than what you[+] received, let him be accursed.

[10]For am I now trusting men, or God? Or am I striving to please men? For if I were still pleasing men, I would not be a bondservant of Messiah. [11]But brethren I make known to you[+] that the good news which I announced is not according to man. [12]For I did not receive it from man, nor was I taught it, but it came to me through a revelation of Yeshua the Messiah.

[13]For you[+] have heard of my former conduct in a system of Jewish observance, as to how I persecuted the community of God, and ravaged it beyond measure. [14]And I was advancing within this system of Jewish observance beyond many of my contemporaries among my people, having much more zeal for the traditions of my fathers. [15]But when God — who set me apart from my mother's womb and called me through His grace [Jer. 1:5] — was pleased [16]to reveal His Son in me so that I might proclaim him among the Gentiles, I did not immediately confer with flesh and blood. [17]Nor did I go up to Yerushala'im to those who were ambassadors before me, but I went away into Arabia. Then I returned to Damascus.

[18]Then after three years I went up to Yerushala'im to visit Kefa, and stayed with him fifteen

---

The single theme of this letter of instruction to the **Galatians** is how a person — standing before God for judgment — can be declared righteous. Or expressed with a different emphasis, what is the means of living a life that God considers righteous? Specifically, the letter deals with how God intends for Gentiles to be made righteous. Must they convert and become Jews, signified by physical circumcision, or can they be righteous and live a righteous life before God as Gentiles, without physical circumcision? Sha'ul's confrontation with Kefa in Antioch took place over this issue.

1:10 There is often a conflict between trusting/pleasing men and trusting/pleasing God. (cf. Gal. 6:12 and Y<u>h</u>n. 5:41-44)

1:15-16 From his birth, Sha'ul was set apart by God to reveal Yeshua to the Gentiles, but Sha'ul did not respond to God's call until much later.

1:18 The Greek here and in 2:9,11,14 transliterates the Aramaic Kefa. In 2:7,8, Sha'ul uses Petros, the Greek translation of Kefa. For some unstated reason, English translations traditionally transliterate the Greek translation.

days. [19]But I saw none of the other ambassadors except Jacob, the brother of the Lord. [20](Now what I write to you[+], know that before God I am not lying.) [21]Then I came to the regions of Syria and Kilikia. [22]To the communities of Judea which were in Messiah, I was still personally unknown, [23]only they were hearing, "He who once persecuted us now proclaims the faith that he once ravaged." [24]And they glorified God in me.

[2] [1]Then after a period of fourteen years I went up again to Yerushala'im with Bar Nabba, taking Titus with me also. [2]I went up concerning a revelation, and I laid before them the good news which I proclaim among the Gentiles, but privately before those who were respected, so that I might not be running, or had not run, in futility. [3]But to the contrary, not even Titus, who was with me, though a Greek, was compelled to be circumcised. [4]There were false brethren brought in secretly who came to spy out our liberty which we have in Messiah Yeshua so that they might bring us into bondage. And as for us, [5]we did not yield to them in submission, not even for a moment, so that the truth of the good news might remain continually with you[+].

[6]But from those who were considered to be important — whatever they were, it makes no difference to me, God does not accept the outward appearance of man — these who were respected gave no advice to me. [7]But to the contrary, they saw that I had been entrusted with the good news for the uncircumcision, even as Kefa with the good news for the circumcision. [8]For the One who empowered Kefa to be an ambassador to the circumcision empowered me also to the Gentiles. [9]And when they recognized the grace that was given to me, Jacob and Kefa and Yohanan — those who were considered to be pillars — they gave to me and Bar Nabba their right hands in fellowship, that we should go to the Gentiles, and they to the circumcision. [10]They only asked us to remember the poor, the very thing which I also was eager to do.

[11]But when Kefa came to Antioch, I opposed him to his face, since he stood condemned, [12]because before certain people came from Jacob, he ate with the Gentiles. But when they came, he drew back and separated himself, fearing those who were of the circumcision. [13]And the rest of the Jewish disciples joined him in his hypocrisy, so that even Bar Nabba was carried away with their hypocrisy. [14]But when I saw that they did not walk uprightly in accordance with the truth of the good news, I said to Kefa before them all, "If you, being a Jew, live as the Gentiles do, and not as the Jews do,

1:18-19 Kefa had denied Yeshua. Jacob had mocked him. [Yhn. 7:3-4] Sha'ul had persecuted Yeshua's disciples.

2:1-2 This is probably the time described in Acts 15.

2:7 Kefa was first sent to Kornelius, Acts 10.

2:8 Sha'ul was called by God to be an ambassador to the Gentiles. With that authority, he writes in this letter, and in his other letters, to Gentiles.

2:1-10 Sha'ul relates how his authority from God to teach the Gentiles was recognized by Jacob and Kefa, even as he recognized their authority from God to be His servants to the Jews.

2:10 "remember the poor" in Yerushala'im. (cf. 2Co. 8-9, Rom. 15:25-27) By giving for this purpose, the Gentiles would demonstrate that they were part of the commonwealth of Israel.

2:14 See "Kefa in Antioch" in the ADDITIONAL NOTES.

why do you compel the Gentiles to become Jews? [15]By nature we are Jews and not sinners from the Gentiles. [16]We know that a man is not declared righteous from the workings of the Law, but through faith in Yeshua the Messiah. Accordingly, we believed in Messiah Yeshua so that we might be declared righteous from faith in Messiah, and not from the workings of the Law, because no flesh will be declared righteous from the workings of the Law. [17]But if while seeking to be declared righteous in Messiah, we ourselves were also found to be sinners, is Messiah a servant of sin? Far from it! [18]For if I build up again those things which I tore down, I demonstrate that I am a transgressor. [19]For through the Law, I died to the Law so that I might live to God. [20]I have been put to death on the stake with Messiah, yet I live, and it is no longer I who live, but Messiah lives in me. That physical life which I now live, I live in faith that is in the Son of God, who loved me, and gave himself up for me. [21]I do not set aside the grace of God, because if righteousness comes through the Law, then Messiah died for nothing!"

3 [1]O foolish Galatians, who cast a spell on you[+]? Before your[+] eyes Yeshua the Messiah was previously presented to you[+] as put to death on the tree. [2]I just want to learn this from you[+], did you[+] receive the Spirit from the workings of the Law, or from hearing of faith? [3]Are you[+] so foolish? Having begun by the Spirit, are you[+] now reaching the goal by the flesh? [4]Did you[+] suffer so many things in vain, if it is indeed in vain? [5]In any case, the one who supplies the Spirit to you[+] and works miracles among you[+], is it from the workings of the Law or from the message of faith?

[6]Just as Abraham "believed God, and it was considered as righteousness for him," [Gen. 15:6] [7]recognize therefore that those who are from faith, these are children of Abraham. [8]Foreseeing that God would declare the Gentiles righteous from faith, the Scripture proclaimed the good news beforehand to Abraham, saying, "There is good for all the Gentiles in you." [Gen. 12:3] [9]So then, there is good with the faithful Abraham for those who are from faith.

[10]For as many as have their existence from the workings of the Law are subject to a curse, for it is written, "Cursed is everyone who does not continue in all things which have been written in the book of the Law, to do them." [Dt. 27:26] [11]Now that no man is declared righteous by God from the Law is evident, because "The just will live from faith." [Hab. 2:4] [12]The Law is not from faith, but "The man who does them will live by them." [Lev. 18:5]

2:16 The first appearance of the word *works* in the Scriptures is in Gen. 2:2, where God rests from all His works of Creation. No flesh will be declared righteous from the works of Creation, but that is not the intended purpose of Creation.

The usage in this verse of "no flesh" is similar to that in Jer. 12:12, Mt. 24:22, Mk. 13:20, Rom. 3:20, and 1Co. 1:29.

2:17-18 It seems that Sha'ul is referring explicitly to Kefa, who had initially acted as though the barrier had been taken down between believing Jews and believing Gentiles; but then acted as though the barrier had been rebuilt. See Eph. 2:14-16.

2:19-20 To paraphrase: By the Law I am condemned to death for my transgressions. I die that death in Messiah's death, and I now live through his life from the dead.

3:11 See note to Rom. 1:17

[13]Messiah redeemed us from the curse in the Law, having become a curse for us. For it is written, "Cursed is everyone who is hung on a tree." [Dt. 21:23] [14]This was done so that the blessing of Abraham might come on the Gentiles through Messiah Yeshua; so that we might receive the promise of the Spirit through faith.

[15]Brethren, I speak about the way of men: though it is only a man's covenant, yet when it has been ratified, no one voids it or adds to it. [16]Now the promises were spoken to Abraham and to his seed. He does not say, "to seeds," as concerning many, but as concerning one, "to your seed," which is Messiah. [17]Now I say this, the Law, which came four hundred and thirty years later [Ex. 12:40], does not annul a covenant confirmed beforehand by God, so as to make the promise inapplicable. [18]For if the inheritance is from the Law, it is no longer from a promise, but God has granted it to Abraham through a promise.

[19]Then why the Law? Because it was added in response to transgressions, until the seed should come to whom the promise has been made. It was mandated through angels in the hand of an intermediary. [20]An intermediary, however, is not just between one, but God is one.

[21]Then is the Law against the promises of God? Far from it! For if there had been a law given which had the power to bring to life, most assuredly righteousness would have been from the Law. [22]But the Scripture confines in subjection to sin all that is, so that the promise from faith in Yeshua the Messiah might be given to those who believe.

[23]However, before faith came, we were protected under the authority of the Law, enclosed for the faith which was about to be revealed. [24]By this the Law has been our childhood guardian to bring us

---

3:13 Rashi comments on Dt. 21:23, "the one who is hung is accursed": "It is an insult to the King, because humanity was made in the likeness of His image.... There is a parable of two twin brothers who looked like each other. One became king, while the other was arrested as a robber, and hanged. All who saw him said, 'The king is hung.'"

3:16 "And she called his name Seth, because 'God has appointed another seed for me.'...She hinted at the seed that would come from another place. Which is this? This is the King Messiah." (Mid. Genesis Rabbah 23:5)

Sha'ul speaks of the singular seed of Abraham, which is that of Isaac and not of Ishmael (Gen. 21:12), of Jacob and not of Esau (Gen. 25:23). This chosen seed is represented by its head, Messiah. This is explicit in 3:29.

3:17-24 The context indicates that "Law" refers here to the Covenant of the Law, which was instituted 430 years after the promise to Abraham.

3:19 "And Moses said to God: 'Behold when I (*anokhi*) come' (Ex. 3:13). ... Moses said: 'I am prepared to become the intermediary between You and them when You give them the Torah and will say, *I am (anokhi) the Everpresent Lord, your God.*'" (Mid. Ex. Rabbah 3:5)

God promised to send a prophet like Moses, because the generation in the wilderness said, "Let me not hear again the voice of the Everpresent Lord, my God..." (Dt. 18:15-16) Moses gave regulations for when Israel would want a human king, instead of having the Everpresent Lord as King. (Dt. 17:14-20) The priests also function as intermediaries between the people and God.

to Messiah, so that we might be declared righteous from faith. [25]But now that faith has come, we are no longer under a guardian.

[26]For you[+] are all children of God through faith in Messiah Yeshua. [27]For as many as were immersed into Messiah, you[+] have clothed yourselves in Messiah. [28]There is not Jew and Greek, there is not slave and free man, there is not male and female, for you[+] are all one in Messiah Yeshua. [29]If you[+] are Messiah's, then you[+] are Abraham's seed and heirs according to a promise.

4 [1]Now I am saying that so long as the heir is a child, though he is lord of all, he is not different from a bondservant [2]in that he is under childhood guardians and managers until the time pre-appointed by the father. [3]So we also, when we were children, were kept in subjection to the basic principles of the world. [4]But when the fullness of the time came, God sent out His Son, born from a woman, born subject to the Law. [5]He did this in order to redeem those who were subject to the Law, so that we might receive the right as sons. [6]And because you[+] are children, God sent out the Spirit of His Son into your[+] hearts, crying, "Abba, Father." [7]So you are no longer a bondservant, but a son, and if a son, then an heir through God.

[8]However, at that time, not knowing God, you[+] were bound by those which by nature are not gods. [9]But now that you[+] have come to know God, or rather to be known by God, why do you[+] turn back again to the powerless and destitute basic principles to which you[+] desire to be in subjection all over again? [10]You[+] observe days, months, seasons, and years.

3:23-25; 4:1-3 In a family, parents are to establish rules for their children while they are growing up. Breaking the rules brings punishment. The purpose of the rules is to protect and train the children. When the children reach adulthood, they are no longer under the authority of the parental rules, and therefore not subject to the stipulated punishments. If they have accepted the training, however, they will nevertheless choose to maturely live according to it.

"Law which a man learns in this age is vanity before the Law of Messiah." (Mid. Kohelet 11.7)

3:28 Some people have taken the verse to mean that this letter teaches that all believers are the same. That is not the case. Sha'ul is addressing the problem of divisions in the body. The verse teaches that the distinctions of gender, calling, and circumstance are transcended in the unity of Messiah. It does not teach that they cease to exist.

There are numerous places where Sha'ul speaks specifically to believers who are Jews (e.g. Rom. 2), Gentiles (e.g. Rom. 11:13-24), slaves (e.g. Eph. 6:5-8), freemen (e.g. 1Co. 7:22-23), males (e.g. Eph. 5:25-28), and females (e.g. 1Tim. 2:9-15).

Women do not cease to be women when they believe. Men do not cease to be men. The point Sha'ul is making is that women do not need to become men in order to be acceptable to God. Slaves do not need to become free. Gentiles do not need to become Jews. The predominant point of the entire letter is that Gentiles do not need to become Jews in order to be justified before God. They are supposed to be different.

The gnostic view that men and women, Jews and Gentiles, are supposed to be the same is expressed in the "Gospel of Thomas" 114: "Simon Peter said to them, 'Let Mary leave us, for women are not worthy of Life.' Jesus said, "I myself will lead her in order to make her male, so that she too may become a living spirit resembling you males. For every woman who will make herself male will enter the kingdom of heaven.'"

4:6 "your" hearts, as in the Textus Receptus

[11]I fear for you+ that I might have wasted my labor upon you+. [12]I beg you+, brethren, become as I am, for I also have become as you+ are. You+ did me no wrong, [13]but you+ know that in physical weakness I proclaimed the good news to you+ the first time. [14]You+ did not despise or treat with contempt your+ being tested by my flesh, but you+ received me as an angel of God, even as Messiah Yeshua.

[15]What was the blessing you+ enjoyed then? For I bear witness to you+ that, if possible, you+ would have plucked out your+ eyes and given them to me. [16]So then, have I become your+ enemy by speaking truthfully to you+?

[17]They are zealous after you+, but not in a good way. No, they desire to exclude you+ so that you+ become zealous after them. [18]It is, however, always good to be zealous in what is good, and not only when I am present with you+.

[19]My little children, with whom I travail again until Messiah is formed in you+ — [20]and I wanted to be present with you+ now, and change my tone, for I am perplexed about you+ — [21]tell me, you+ who desire to be under the authority of the Law, don't you+ listen to the Law? [22]For it is written that Abraham had two sons, one by the female servant, and one by the free woman. [23]The son of the female servant was born in response to the physical, but the son of the free woman was born through the promise. [24]These things contain an allegory, for these are the two covenants. One, which is Hagar, is from Mount Sinai, bringing forth into bondage. [25]For this Hagar is Mount Sinai in Arabia, and is in the same column with the Yerushala'im that exists now, and she is in bondage with her children. [26]But the Yerushala'im above, which is our mother, is free. [27]For it is written, "Rejoice, O barren, you who do not bear. Break forth and shout, you who do not travail. For more are the children of the desolate than of the one who has a husband." [Is. 54:1]

[28]Now you+, brethren, are children of promise as Isaac was. [29]But just as then the one who was born in response to the physical persecuted the one who was born by the Spirit, so it is now also. [30]However, what does the Scripture say? "Send away the female servant and her son, because the son of the female servant will not inherit with the son of the free woman." [Gen. 21:10] [31]So then brethren, we are not children of a female servant, but of the free woman. [1Mac. 2:11]

5 [1]Messiah has set us free for freedom. So stand firm and do not be entangled again in a yoke of bondage. [2]I, Paulos, tell you+ that if you+ receive circumcision, Messiah will be of no use to you+! [3]Yes, I testify again to every man who receives circumcision, that he is obligated to observe the entire Law. [4]You+ who desire to be declared righteous from the Law are deprived of what Messiah did. You+

4:21-31 Sha'ul uses the historical record of Torah to present an allegory about the Covenant of the Law and the New Covenant. He presents several other corresponding pairs — two women, two mountains, two sons — which he aligns in relationship to these two covenants. He does not always mention both parts of each pair, but, for the one familiar with Torah, they are easy to fill in. The question addressed is which covenant leads to righteousness before God.

4:26 "And now O Everpresent Lord, You are our Father. And if it so, then the Torah {is our mother], as it says, 'Do not forget the Torah of your mother.' [Prov. 1:8]" (Mid. Exodus 30:5)

5:2-6 See the ADDITIONAL NOTE on "Circumcision and the Law".

have fallen away from grace. [5]For through the Spirit, we wait for the hope of righteousness from faith. [6]For in Messiah Yeshua neither circumcision nor uncircumcision has any power, but faith working through love.

[7]You[+] were running well. Who hindered you[+] from obeying the truth? [8]This persuasion is not from the One who calls you[+]. [9]A little leaven causes the whole lump to rise. [10]I have confidence in you[+] in the Lord that you[+] will not think otherwise. But the one who is troubling you[+] will bear his judgment, whoever he is.

[11]But I, brethren, if I still proclaim circumcision, why am I still persecuted? Then the stumbling-block of the tree of death would be removed. [12]I wish that those who throw you[+] into confusion would cut themselves off. [13]For you[+] were called for liberty, brethren, only not the liberty for indulging the flesh, rather serve one another through love. [14]Because all the Law is fulfilled in this one expression: "You are to love your neighbor as yourself." [Lev. 19:18] [15]But if you[+] bite and devour one another, be careful that you[+] do not consume one another.

[16]But I say, walk in the Spirit and you[+] will not carry out the desire of the flesh. [17]For the flesh has desires contrary to the Spirit, and the Spirit contrary to the flesh. And these are antagonistic to one another, so that you[+] do not do whatever you[+] desire. [18]But if you[+] are led by the Spirit, you[+] are not in subjection to the Law. [19]Now the things the flesh produces are obvious. These are sexual immorality, uncleanness, sensuality, [20]idolatry, witchcraft and drug use, hatred, strife, jealousies, outbursts of anger, rivalries, divisions, heresies, [21]envyings, murders, drunkenness, orgies, and things like these. I forewarn you[+] about such things, even as I also said before, that those who practice such things will not inherit the Kingdom of God.

[22]But the fruit of the Spirit is love, joy, peace, patient endurance, kindness, goodness, faithfulness, [23]gentleness, and self-control. Against such things, no law exists. [24]Those who belong to Messiah have put the flesh, with its passions and desires, to death on the stake. [25]If we live by the Spirit, let us also walk by the Spirit. [26]Let us not become conceited, irritating one another, and envying one another.

6 [1]Brethren, even if a man is caught in some transgression, you[+] who are spiritual must restore such a one in a spirit of gentleness, looking to yourself so that you also are not tempted. [2]Bear one another's oppressive burdens, and in this way you[+] will give fullness to Messiah's law. [3]For if a

5:13-16 Sha'ul gives a summation of the positive point of the letter. The Spirit of God is not contrary to the Law of God. The love of God is not contrary to the Law of God. By the love of God, a person will walk in obedience to the Spirit of God and will therefore fulfill the Law of God.

5:17-23 Sha'ul shows how it is the deeds produced by the flesh — i.e. living in response to physical desires — that are opposed to the Law of God. The fruit of the Spirit is in agreement with the Law of God. This is similar to Rom. 8:4-8.

5:23 "No law exists..." Human governments often legislate against these things, but such legislation has no authority, "because there is no authority except from God." (Rom. 13:1) The midwives who disobeyed Pharaoh's command to kill every boy born to the people of Israel are a case in point. (Ex. 1:16-21) As Aquinas said, "Such decrees are not so much laws as acts of violence, because, as Augustine says, 'An unjust law does not seem to be a law at all.'" (<u>Summa Theologica</u>, Q96, Art. 4, 'Whether human laws bind a man's conscience')

man thinks himself to be something when he is nothing, he deceives himself. ⁴But let each man test his own work, and then he will have praise in himself and not in another, ⁵because each man will carry his own load.

⁶Moreover, let the one who is taught in the word share all good things with the one who teaches. ⁷Do not be led astray, God is not mocked. For whatever a man sows, that is what he will also reap. ⁸For the one who sows to his own flesh will from the flesh reap decay. But the one who sows to the Spirit will from the Spirit reap eternal life. ⁹Let us not be weary in doing good, for we will reap in due season if we do not give up. ¹⁰So then, as we have opportunity, let us do what is good toward all men, and especially toward those who are of the household of the faith. ¹¹(See with what large letters I write to you⁺ with my own hand.)

¹²As many as desire to have a good outward physical appearance, they compel you⁺ to be circumcised solely so that they will not be persecuted for the tree of death of the Messiah. ¹³For even those who receive circumcision do not keep the Law themselves, but they desire to have you⁺ circumcised, so that they may boast in your⁺ flesh. ¹⁴But far be it from me to boast, except in the tree of death of our Lord Yeshua the Messiah. Through it and upon it, the world has been put to death to me, and I to the world. ¹⁵For in Messiah Yeshua neither circumcision nor uncircumcision has any power, rather a new creation. ¹⁶As many as walk by this rule, peace and mercy be upon them, and upon the Israel of God. ¹⁷From now on, let no one cause me any trouble, for I bear the marks of the Lord Yeshua branded on my body.

¹⁸The grace of our Lord Yeshua the Messiah be with your⁺ spirit, brethren. Amen.

Sha'ul/Paulos' Letter to the Ephesians

1 [1]Paulos, an ambassador of Messiah Yeshua through the will of God: to those in Ephesus who belong to God and are faithful in Messiah Yeshua. [2]Grace and peace to you[+] from God our Father and the Lord Yeshua the Messiah.

[3]Blessed be the God and Father of our Lord Yeshua the Messiah, who has blessed us with every spiritual blessing in the heavens in Messiah. [4]In the same way, He chose us in him before the foundation of the world for us to be holy and blameless before Him. [5]So He determined before, in love, to give us the legal right as His children through Yeshua the Messiah. He did this in accordance with the good pleasure of His will, [6]to the praise of the glory of His grace. By this He made us acceptable in the Beloved. [7]We have redemption in him through his blood, the forgiveness of transgressions in accordance with the riches of His grace. [8]He made His grace abound toward us in all wisdom and understanding, [9]making the mystery of His will known to us, in accordance with His good pleasure which He set forth in him. [10]This is for governing the fullness of the times, to sum up all things in him, in Messiah, the things in the heavens and the things on the earth.

[11]In him also, we were given an inheritance, having been appointed before in accordance with the purpose of the One who works all things after the counsel of His will. [12]He did this so that we who trusted beforehand in the Messiah should be to the praise of His glory. [13]In him you[+] also, having heard the word of the truth — the good news of your[+] salvation in him — having also believed, you[+] were sealed with the Ruakh Kodesh of promise. [14]This is a down payment of our inheritance, toward the redemption of His possession, to the praise of His glory.

[15]I have heard of the faith in the Lord Yeshua which is among you[+], and the love which you[+] have toward all those who belong to God. Because of this, I also [16]do not cease to give thanks for you[+], making mention of you[+] in my prayers. [17]I pray that the God of our Lord Yeshua the Messiah, the Father of glory, may give to you[+] a spirit of wisdom and revelation in the knowledge of him.

[18]Having the eyes of your[+] heart enlightened, you[+] may know what is the hope of His calling, what are the riches of the glory of His inheritance in those who belong to God, [19]and what is the exceeding greatness of His power toward us who are believing. All is in accordance with that working of the strength of His might. [20]He brought this about in the Messiah, when He raised him from among the dead and made him to sit at His right hand in the heavens, [21]far above all principal forces, authority, power, dominion, and every name that is named, not only in this age, but also in that which is to come. [22]He put all things in subjection under his feet, and gave him to be head over all things for the community, [23]which is his body, the fullness of the one who fills all in all.

2 [1]And you[+] were dead in your transgressions and sins. [2]You[+] once walked in these, in accordance with the ruler of the powers of the air, following this worldly age. This is the spirit that now works in the children of disobedience. [3]We all also were among them, and once turned towards the desire of our flesh, carrying out the desires of the flesh and of the mind. And we were by nature children of wrath, even as the rest.

[4]But God —being rich in mercy, and because of His great love with which He loved us [5]even when we were dead in our transgressions — God made us alive together with the Messiah. You[+] have been saved by grace. [6]And He raised us up together, and seated us together in the heavens in Messiah Yeshua. [7]This is so that in the ages which are coming He might show the exceeding riches of His grace in kindness toward us in Messiah Yeshua. [8]For it is by grace you[+] have been saved through faith, and this is not from yourselves. It is the gift of God, [9]not from deeds, so that no one can boast. [10]For we are His workmanship, created in Yeshua the Messiah for good deeds, which God prepared in advance so that we would walk in them.

[11,12]Therefore remember that once you[+], the Gentiles, were at that time far from Messiah, excluded from citizenship in the commonwealth of Israel [Gen. 35:11; 48:4; 2Mac. 4:11; 8:17; 13:14], and foreigners to the covenants of the promise, having no hope and without God in the world. You[+] are called physically "uncircumcision" by those called physically "circumcision" in the flesh, made by hands. [13]But now in Messiah Yeshua, you[+] who once were far off have become near in the blood of the Messiah. [14]For he is our peace [Is. 57:19], who made both one, and took down the middle wall of the fence. [15]By his flesh, he made the hostility of commandments in ordinances of the Law cease to apply. He made peace in this way by creating the two into one new man in himself. [16]By doing this, he reconciled both in one body to God through the tree of death, which he used to put to death the hostility.

2:6-8 At the end of the evening service for Rosh haShanah, "We pray, O Lord, that by our deeds we may become worthy of Your grace, and thus be inscribed in Your Book of Life. Amen." Also in the Rosh haShanah liturgy we read: "If for Your own sake You are not forgiving unto us, O Holy One, we cannot, though we seek, find merit in our deeds." And added from the Middle Ages: "I am despoiled and naked of good works; Your righteousness alone my covering." (Yehuda haLevi in 1140) And "Your choice is better than mine, and I submit myself to Your unalterable decrees and Your supreme direction." (Bahya Ibn Pakuda in 1040, from the Machzor)

Rashi on Dt. 3:23, v'ethanan, which has the same root as *hanun*. "In every place, *hanun* speaks of a gift of grace. Even though the righteous are able to depend upon their good deeds, they do not request from the Everpresent Lord other than a gift of grace."

2:11-12 God promised Jacob, "there will be a nation and a community of nations from you." [Gen. 35:11 cf. Gen. 48:4] Sha'ul refers to this community of nations as the commonwealth/*politeia* of Israel. Gentiles who recognize the sovereignty of the King of the Jews are brought into this commonwealth. Plato uses the same word for what is usually translated as "The Republic".

Rashi, citing Mechilta, comments on "This is the statute of the Pesakh: every foreigner does not eat of it" in Ex. 12:43: "'Every foreigner' whose actions are alienated from his Father in heaven; and this implies both the Gentiles and the apostate of Israel."

2:15 The Latin Vulgate, from the 5th-6th centuries, has *novum hominem* for "new man". In ancient Rome, the phrase "new man"/*novus homo* designated someone who was the first in his family to serve in the Senate. As such, it indicated initial entry into full legal and cultural rights. The *novus homo* was often opposed by the old established noble families of Rome. This probably influenced the way the Vulgate was understood.

¹⁷He came and proclaimed peace to you⁺ who were far off and peace to those who were near. [Is. 57:19] ¹⁸For through him we both have our access in one Spirit to the Father. ¹⁹So then you⁺ are no longer foreigners and strangers, but you⁺ are fellow-citizens with the people set apart, and are of the household of God. ²⁰You⁺ are being built on the foundation of the ambassadors and prophets, Messiah Yeshua himself being the chief cornerstone. ²¹In him, the whole building, fitted together, grows into a holy temple in the Lord. ²²In him, you⁺ also are built together for a dwelling of God in the Spirit.

3 ¹For this cause I, Paulos, am the prisoner of Messiah Yeshua on behalf of you⁺, the Gentiles. ²Surely you⁺ have heard of the responsibility toward you⁺ which was given to me in the grace of God, ³how the mystery was made known to me by revelation, as I wrote briefly before. ⁴By reading that, you⁺ will be able to comprehend my understanding in the mystery of the Messiah. ⁵In other generations, this was not made known to the children of men, as it has now been revealed in the Spirit to his holy ambassadors and prophets. ⁶It is that the Gentiles might be fellow-heirs, fellow-members of the body, and fellow-partakers of His promise in Yeshua the Messiah through the good news. ⁷I was made a servant for this in accordance with the gift of the grace of God which was given to me, in accordance with the working of His power. ⁸⁻¹⁰I am less than the least of all those who belong to God. This grace was given to me to proclaim to the Gentiles the unsearchable riches of the Messiah, and to give light on what is the administration of the mystery, so that through the community the manifold wisdom of God might be made known now to the principal rulers and the powers in the heavens. This mystery has been hidden for ages in God, who created all things. ¹¹Making it known now is in accordance with the purpose of the ages which He purposed in Yeshua the Messiah our Lord. ¹²We have boldness in him, and confident access through our faith in him. ¹³Therefore I ask that you⁺ not be discouraged by my troubles for you⁺. They are your⁺ glory.

¹⁴For this cause, I bow my knees to the Father — ¹⁵from whom every family in heaven and on earth is named — ¹⁶so that He would grant you⁺ to be strengthened in the inner being with power through His Spirit, in accordance with the riches of His glory. ¹⁷I pray for the Messiah to dwell in your⁺ hearts through faith, so that you⁺, being rooted and grounded in love, ¹⁸may be strengthened to comprehend with all those who belong to God what is the breadth and length and height and depth, ¹⁹and to know the love of the Messiah which surpasses knowledge, so that you⁺ may be filled with all the fullness of God. ²⁰Now to Him who is able to do exceedingly abundantly above all that we ask or think, in accordance with the power that works in us, ²¹to Him be the glory in the community and in Messiah Yeshua to all generations forever and ever. Amen.

2:19 *Sumpolitai,* the Greek word for "fellow-citizens," is derived from *polis,* i.e. "city". In Acts 21:39, Sha'ul/Paul speaks of himself as a citizen of Tarsus. The Hebrew at that time for "citizens" was *bnay eer,* i.e. "sons of the city," (e.g. Tal. Kiddushin 49b) The city is Jerusalem.

"Our Rabbis taught: 'Let a man always live in the land of Israel, even in a town where most are idolaters, but let no one live outside the land, even in a town where most are descendants of Israel; for whoever lives in the land of Israel is like one who has a God, but whoever lives outside the land is like one who has no God. For it is said in Scripture, *To give you the land of Canaan, to be your God.* [Lev. 25:38]'" (Tal. Ketubot 110b)

4 ¹Therefore I, the prisoner of the Lord, exhort you⁺ to walk in a manner worthy of the calling with which you⁺ were called. ²Bear with one another in love with all lowliness, humility, and patient endurance, ³being eager to keep the unity of the Spirit in the bond of peace. ⁴There is one body and one Spirit, even as you⁺ also were called in one hope of your⁺ calling. ⁵There is one Lord, one faith, one immersion, ⁶one God and Father of all, who is over all, and through all, and in all. ⁷But to each one of us grace was given in accordance with the measure of the gift of the Messiah. ⁸Therefore He says, "When he ascended on high, he led captivity captive, and gave gifts to men." [Ps. 68:18] ⁹Now this, "he ascended," what does it mean but that he also descended into the lower parts of the earth? ¹⁰The one who descended is the one who also ascended far above all the heavens, that he might fill all things.

¹¹He appointed the ambassadors, the prophets, the proclaimers of the good news, and the shepherds and teachers. ¹²This is for preparing those who belong to God for the work of service, for building up the body of the Messiah. ¹³This is until we all arrive at the unity of the faith and of the knowledge of the Son of God, to a fully mature man, to the measure of the stature of the fullness of the Messiah. ¹⁴Then we will no longer be children, tossed back and forth by the waves and carried about with every wind of doctrine, by the cunning trickery of men in systematic error. ¹⁵But speaking the truth in love, we may grow up in all things into the one who is the head — Messiah. ¹⁶From him all the body is fitted and knit together through what every joint supplies. This makes the body grow up for the building up of itself in love, in accordance with the appropriate working of each individual part.

¹⁷So I say this, and bear witness in the Lord, that you⁺ no longer walk as the rest of the Gentiles also walk, in the futility of their mind. [Eccl. 1:2] ¹⁸They are darkened in their understanding and alienated from the life of God through the ignorance that is in them, because of the hardening of their hearts. ¹⁹Having lost all feeling, they gave themselves up to sensuality to crave to do everything unclean. ²⁰But you⁺ did not learn the Messiah that way. ²¹Surely you⁺ heard him and were taught in

---

4:4-6 Rashi comments on Num. 16:6, "Moses said to them, 'In the ways of the idolators, there are many customs and many priests, and they do not all gather in one house. It is not like this for us, we have only one Everpresent Lord, one ark, one Torah, one altar, and one High Priest...'"

"What is the name of King Messiah? R. Abba bar Kahana said, 'The Everpresent Lord is his name, as it says in Jeremiah 23, *And this is the name by which he will be called, "The Everpresent Lord, our righteousness."*'" (Mid. Lamentations 1.51)

4:16 Some sets of muscles, like biceps and triceps, are paired with others that have the opposite function. Together they provide smooth movement.

4:17-19 "the rest" is included in the Textus Receptus. "R. Eliezer says, 'None of the servants of the stars [i.e. idolators] has a portion in the age to come, as it is said (Ps. 9:17), *The wicked will return to the Grave, all the Gentiles who forget God.*' ...R. Joshua said to him, 'If what was written said, *The wicked will return to the Grave — all the Gentiles*, and then said nothing further, I would have said according to your words. Now that it is written, *...those who forget God*, it indicates that there also are righteous people among the servants of the stars, to whom there is a portion in the age to come.'" (Tos. Sanhedrin 13:1)

him — even as the truth is in Yeshua — [22]that you[+] put off the old man of your[+] former way of life, which is corrupt after the deceitful desires. [23]Be renewed now in the spirit of your[+] mind. [24]Put on the new man, who has been created in righteousness and holiness of the truth in accord with God.

[25]Therefore, putting away falsehood, speak truth each one with his neighbor [Zech. 8:16], because we are members one of another. [26]Be angry, yet do not sin. [Ps. 4:4] Do not let the sun set upon your[+] rage, [27]nor give opportunity to the Enemy. [28]Let the one who stole steal no more, but let him labor instead, doing with his hands what is good, so that he may have something to give to the one who has need. [29]Do not let any worthless word go forth from your[+] mouth, but only what is good and needed for building up, so that it may give grace to those who hear. [30]Do not grieve the Ruakh Kodesh of God, in whom you[+] were sealed for the day of redemption. [31]Let all bitterness, indignation, anger, commotion, and slander be put away from you[+], along with all malice. [32]And become kind to one another, tenderhearted, forgiving each other, just as God also forgave you[+] in Messiah.

5 [1]So be imitators of God as beloved children. [2]Walk in love, even as the Messiah also loved us and gave himself up for us, an offering and a sacrifice to God for a sweet-smelling fragrance. [3]But as is appropriate for those who belong to God, let these not even be mentioned among you[+]: sexual immorality and all uncleanness, or covetousness, [4]filthiness, foolish talking, or coarse jesting, which are not appropriate, but rather giving of thanks.

[5]Know this for sure, that no sexually immoral or unclean or covetous person — who is an idolater — has any inheritance in the Kingdom of the Messiah and God. [6]Let no one deceive you[+] with empty words, for because of these things the wrath of God comes upon the children of disobedience. [7]Therefore do not be partakers with them.

[8]For you[+] once were darkness, but now are light in the Lord. Walk as children of light, [Prov. 4:18-19, Eccl. 2:14] [9]because the fruit of the light is in all goodness and righteousness and truth, [10]demonstrating what is well-pleasing to the Lord. [11]Have no fellowship with the unfruitful works of the darkness, but rather rebuke them instead. [12]For it is a shame even to speak of the things which are done by them in secret. [13]But all things that are rebuked are revealed by the light, because light is what reveals everything. [14]Therefore He says, "Awake, you who sleep. Arise from the dead, and the Messiah will shine on you." [Is. 52:1; 60:1]

[15]So watch carefully how you[+] walk, not as unwise, but as wise. [16]Buy time, because the days are evil. [17]So do not be foolish, but understand what the will of the Lord is. [18]Do not be drunken with wine, which is a waste of life, but be filled with the Spirit, [19]speaking to one another in psalms, songs of praise, and songs of the Spirit, singing and making melody in your[+] heart to the Lord. [20]Give thanks to God the Father always for all things in the name of our Lord Yeshua, the Messiah.

4:26 "It is the way of flesh and blood that one who is angry is not [at the same time] favorable; and when he is favorable, he is not angry. But the Holy One, blessed be He, when He is angry, in the midst of His anger, He is favorable." (Mid. Psalms 2.17)

5:8 "children of light" The phrase appears throughout the DSS Manual of Discipline, e.g. 1QS 1:9-10, 4Q177 f12_13i:7,11, 4Q548 f1ii_2:9-16.

²¹Subject yourselves one to another in the fear of Messiah. ²²Wives, submit yourselves to your⁺ own husbands, as to the Lord. ²³For the husband is the head of the wife, and the Messiah also is the head of the community, being himself the savior of the body. ²⁴But as the community is submitted to the Messiah, so let the wives also be to their own husbands in everything.

²⁵Husbands, love your⁺ wives, even as the Messiah also loved the community and gave himself up for it ²⁶so that he might sanctify it. He cleansed it by the washing of water with the word, ²⁷so that he might present a glorious community to himself, not having spot, wrinkle or any such thing, but that it might be holy and blameless.

²⁸Husbands ought also to love their own wives in this way, as their own bodies. The one who loves his own wife loves himself. ²⁹For no man ever hated his own flesh, but nourishes and cherishes it. This is what the Lord also does for the community, ³⁰because we are members of his body, of his flesh and bones. [2 Sam. 19:12] ³¹"For this reason, a man will leave his father and mother, and will be joined to his wife. The two will become one flesh." [Gen. 2:24] ³²This mystery is great, but I am speaking about Messiah and the community. ³³Nevertheless, each of you⁺ must also love his own wife even as himself, and let the wife see that she respects her husband.

6 ¹Children, listen in the Lord to your⁺ parents, because this is right. ²"Honor your father and mother" — which is the first commandment with a promise — ³"so that it may be well with you, and you may live long on the earth." [Ex. 20:12, Dt. 5:16] ⁴You⁺ fathers, do not provoke your⁺ children to anger, but nurture them in the discipline and instruction of the Lord.

⁵Servants, in the sincerity of your⁺ heart, be obedient with fear and trembling to those who are your⁺ physical masters, as to the Messiah. ⁶Do not do it just when they are looking, as men-pleasers, but as servants of the Messiah, doing the will of God from your⁺ inner being. ⁷Serve with good will as unto the Lord, and not unto men, ⁸knowing that whatever good thing each one does, whether he is bound or free, he will receive the same again from the Lord.

⁹Masters, do the same things to them, and refrain from threatening, knowing that the One who is both their Master and yours⁺ is in heaven, and there is no judging by outward appearance with Him.

¹⁰Finally, be empowered in the Lord and in the strength of His might. ¹¹Put on the whole armor of God, so that you⁺ may be able to stand against the deceitful schemes of the Enemy. ¹²For our struggle is not against flesh and blood, but against the principalities, against the powers, against the world-rulers of the darkness of this age, and against the spiritual powers of wickedness in the heavenly places. ¹³Therefore put on the whole armor of God, so that you⁺ may be able to resist in the evil day, and, having done all, to stand. ¹⁴Stand therefore, having stengthened yourself with truth [Is. 11:5], having put on the breastplate of justice [Is. 59:17], ¹⁵and having fitted your⁺ feet with the preparation of the good news of peace. [Is. 52:7] ¹⁶Above all, take up the shield of faith, with which you⁺ will be able to quench all the fiery darts of the evil one. ¹⁷And receive the helmet of salvation [Is. 59:17; cf. Wis. 5:17-19], and the sword of the Spirit, which is the word of God. ¹⁸With all prayer and supplication, pray in the Spirit at all times, and stay alert for this very thing, in all perseverance

6:12 This should be understood in light of 1:21-22 and 3:10 [found in 3:8-10 in this version].
6:12-18 See the ADDITIONAL NOTE on "War in Heaven".

and supplication for all those who belong to God. [19]And pray on my behalf that a word may be given to me in opening my mouth with boldness to make known the mystery of the good news. [20]I am an ambassador in chains for this. Pray that I may speak boldly in it, as I ought to speak.

[21]Now so that you[+] also may know my affairs, what I am accomplishing, Tychicus, the beloved brother and faithful servant in the Lord, will make all things known to you[+]. [22]I have sent him to you[+] for this very purpose, so that you[+] may know our affairs, and that he may encourage your[+] hearts.

[23]Peace be to the brethren, and love with faith from God the Father and the Lord Yeshua the Messiah. [24]Grace be with all those who genuinely love our Lord Yeshua the Messiah.

Sha'ul/Paulos' Letter to the Philippians

1 ¹Paulos and Timothy, servants of Yeshua the Messiah: to all those at Philippi who belong to God in Messiah Yeshua, including the overseers and those who serve. ²Grace and peace to you⁺ from God our Father and the Lord Yeshua the Messiah. ³,⁵In every remembrance of you⁺, I thank my God for your⁺ fellowship in furtherance of the good news from the first day until now. ⁴In every request of mine on behalf of all of you⁺, I always make my requests with joy. ⁶I am confident of this very thing, that the One who began a good work in you⁺ will continue to complete it up to the day of Yeshua the Messiah. ⁷So it is right for me to think this way about all of you⁺, because I have you⁺ in my heart, inasmuch as both in my bonds and in the defense and confirmation of the good news, you⁺ all are partakers with me of grace. ⁸For God is my witness how I long after all of you⁺ in the tender mercies of Messiah Yeshua.

⁹Now I pray this so that your⁺ love may yet abound more and more in knowledge and all discernment. ¹⁰Then you⁺ may demonstrate the things that are excellent, so that you⁺ may be sincere and without offense until the day of Messiah, ¹¹being filled with the fruits of righteousness, which are through Yeshua the Messiah, to the glory and praise of God.

¹²Now I want you⁺ brethren to know that the things which happened to me have turned out to the further advancement of the good news. ¹³Consequently it became evident to the whole Praetorian guard, and to all the rest, that my chains are in Messiah. ¹⁴And most of the brethren, trusting in the Lord in greater measure because of my chains, are bold to speak the word of God without fear. ¹⁵Now some indeed proclaim the Messiah out of envy and strife, but others proclaim through good will. ¹⁶The former insincerely proclaim the Messiah from selfish ambition, thinking that they add affliction to my chains. ¹⁷The latter, however, do it out of love, knowing that I am appointed for the defense of the good news.

¹⁸What then? In every way, regardless of whether in pretense or in truth, Messiah is proclaimed. I rejoice in this, yes, and I will rejoice. ¹⁹For I know that this will turn out to my salvation through your⁺ supplication and the provision of the Spirit of Yeshua the Messiah. ²⁰As it is my earnest expectation and hope that I will not be put to shame in anything, but with all boldness Messiah will be magnified in my body, now also as always, whether by life or by death. ²¹For to me to live is Messiah, and to die is gain.

²²But if [I am] to live physically, this will bring me fruit from my labor. Yet I don't reveal what I will choose. ²³Now I am hard pressed between the two, having the desire to depart and be with Messiah, which is far better, ²⁴but to remain in the flesh is more necessary for your⁺ sake. ²⁵And being persuaded of this, I know that I will remain, and continue with all of you⁺, for your⁺ advancement and joy in the faith. ²⁶Then your⁺ rejoicing for me may abound in Messiah Yeshua through my presence with you⁺ again.

²⁷Live only in a manner worthy of the good news of the Messiah, as citizens, so that, whether I come and see you⁺ or am absent, I may hear the things concerning you⁺ — that you⁺ stand firm

1:13 The Praetorian guard were special personal bodyguards for the Roman emperors.

in one spirit, with one soul striving for the faith of the good news. [28]Also don't be frightened by the adversaries in anything. This is a demonstration of destruction for them, but to you[+] of salvation, and that from God. [29]Since it has been granted to you[+] on behalf of Messiah, not only to believe in him, but also to suffer on his behalf, [30]having the same conflict which you[+] saw in me, and now hear is in me.

[1]So if there is any encouragement in Messiah, if any consolation of love, if any fellowship of the Spirit, if any tender mercies and compassion, [2]make my joy full by being like-minded, having the same love, being of one soul, of one mind. [3]Do nothing through factional strife or through conceit, but in humility esteem each other above one's own self — [4]each of you[+] not just considering your[+] own interests, but also the interests of others.

[5]For let this mind be in you[+] which was also in Messiah Yeshua. [6]Existing in the form of God, he did not think of equality with God as a prize to be grasped. [7]He emptied himself instead [Is. 53:12], taking the form of a bondservant, being made in the likeness of men. [8]And being found in human form, he humbled himself, becoming obedient to death, yes, the death of the stake. [9]Therefore God also highly exalted him, and gave to him the name which is above every name, [10]so that at the name of Yeshua every knee should bow [Is. 45:23], of those in heaven, those on earth, and those under the earth; [11]and that every tongue should confess that Yeshua the Messiah is Lord, to the glory of God the Father.

[12]So then my beloved, even as you[+] have always obeyed — not only in my presence, but now much more in my absence — work out your[+] own salvation with fear and trembling. [13]For it is God who works in you[+] both to desire and to accomplish His good pleasure. [14]Do all things without murmurings and disputes, [15]so that you[+] may become blameless and harmless children of God, without blemish in the midst of a crooked and perverse generation. You[+] are seen among them as lights in the world. [16]Give close attention to the word of life, giving me praise in the day of Messiah, since I did not run in vain nor labor in vain. [17]Yes, and if I am poured out upon the sacrifice and service of your[+] faith, I rejoice, and share in rejoicing with you[+] all. [18]In the same way, you[+] also rejoice, and share in rejoicing with me.

[19]But I hope in the Lord Yeshua to send Timothy to you[+] soon so that I also may be encouraged when I know how you[+] are doing. [20]For I have no one else like-minded, who will truly care about you[+], [21]because they all seek their own, not the things of Yeshua the Messiah. [22]But you[+] know his trustworthiness, that as a child serves a father, so he served with me in the good news. [23]Therefore I hope to send him at once, as soon as I see how it goes with me, [24]but I trust in the Lord that I myself also will come shortly. [25]Yet I considered it necessary to send my brother Epaphroditus to you[+] — my fellow worker, and fellow soldier, your[+] representative and servant to my need. [26]For he longed for

2:4 "Let your friend's property be as precious to you as your own…" (Tal. Pirke Avot 2:17)

2:5-8 "R. Joseph said: 'Man should always learn from the mind of his Creator; for see that the Holy One, blessed be He, ignored all the mountains and high places and caused His Shekhinah to remain on Mount Sinai, and ignored all the beautiful trees and caused His Shekhinah to remain in a bush." (Tal. Sotah 5a)

2:7 In Is. 53:12, we read that Messiah literally "emptied his soul to death".

you⁺ all, and was very troubled, because you⁺ had heard that he was sick. ²⁷For indeed he was sick, nearly to death, but God had mercy on him — and not on him only, but also on me, that I might not have sorrow on sorrow. ²⁸Therefore I have sent him the more eagerly so that you⁺ may rejoice when you⁺ see him again, and that I may be the less sorrowful. ²⁹Receive him therefore in the Lord with all joy. And hold people like this in honor, ³⁰because he came near to death for the work of Messiah, risking his life to supply what was lacking in your⁺ service toward me.

3 ¹Finally, my family, rejoice in the Lord. To write the same things to you⁺ is truly not tiresome to me, and it is a safeguard for you⁺. ²Beware of the dogs, beware of those who work evil, beware of those who mutilate. ³For we are the circumcision who are serving God by the Spirit, rejoicing in Messiah Yeshua, and not trusting in the flesh. [Jer. 17:5] ⁴Though If any other man thinks that he has confidence in the flesh, I could more: ⁵circumcision on the eighth day, of the people of Israel, of the tribe of Benjamin, a Hebrew of Hebrews; concerning the Law, a Parush; ⁶concerning zeal, persecuting the community; concerning the justice which is in the Law, becoming blameless.

⁷However, what things were gain to me, these I have counted loss because of the Messiah. ⁸Yes, most assuredly, and I count all things to be loss for the excellency of the knowledge of Messiah Yeshua, my Lord. I have suffered the loss of all things for him, and count them as worthless that I may gain Messiah ⁹and be found in him. I do not have a righteousness of my own — that which is from the Law — but rather that which is through faith in Messiah, the righteousness which is from God by faith. ¹⁰By knowing him, the power of his resurrection, and the fellowship of his sufferings, I am becoming conformed to his death, ¹¹if somehow I may attain to the resurrection from the dead. ¹²Not that I have already received, or am already made complete, but I am in pursuit, if also I may take hold of that for which Messiah Yeshua has also taken hold of me.

¹³My famiy, I do not regard myself as yet having taken hold, but one thing I do: forgetting the things which are behind, and stretching forward to the things which are ahead, ¹⁴I am in pursuit of the goal of the prize of the high calling of God in Messiah Yeshua. ¹⁵Therefore, let as many of us as are mature think this way. If in anything you⁺ think otherwise, God will also reveal that to you⁺.

¹⁶Nevertheless, to the extent that we have already attained, let us walk orderly by the same rule. ¹⁸For many walk — of whom I told you⁺ often, and now tell you⁺ even weeping — as the enemies

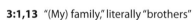

3:1,13 "(My) family," literally "brothers"

3:3 See the ADDITIONAL NOTE on "Circumcision and the Law".

3:5 The Aramaic has "a Hebrew, son of Hebrews".

3:20 According to Liddell and Scott, Aristotle used *politeuma* to signify "government". Sometimes the word is translated as "citizenship". It is the framework that governs our lives. (cf. Phil. 1:27 Sha'ul is comparing two types of people, those who are governed by their physical desires (vv. 18-19) and those who are governed by God's order (vv. 17,20).

For those who follow Messiah, citizenship is in the commonwealth of Israel. (Eph. 2:11-19) "There is no end of the increase of His government and peace; upon the throne of David and over His kingdom, to order it and establish it in judgment and justice from that time forward and forever. The zeal of the Commander of forces will do this." (Is. 9:6H)

of Messiah's tree of death. [19]Thinking about the things of earth, their end is destruction, their god is the stomach, and their glory is in their shame. [17]Brethren, together follow my example and observe closely those who walk the same way, even as you[+] have us for a pattern, [20]because our governing realm has its beginning in the heavens, from which we are awaiting a savior also, the Lord Yeshua the Messiah. [21]He will transform our lowly body so that it is conformed to his glorious body, according to the working of his power to subject all things to himself.

[1]Therefore my beloved brethren — beloved and longed for, my joy and crown — stand firm in this way in the Lord. [2]I exhort Euodia and I exhort Syntyche to be of the same mind in the Lord. [3]Yes, I entreat you also, true partner in the yoke. Help these women who labored together with me in the good news, with Clement also, and the rest of my fellow workers, whose names are in the book of life. [4]Rejoice in the Lord always. Again I will say, rejoice! [5]Let your[+] gentleness be known to all men. The Lord is near. [6]Be anxious in nothing, but in everything, let your[+] requests be made known to God by prayer and petition with thanksgiving. [7]The peace of God, which surpasses all understanding, will guard your[+] hearts and your[+] minds in Messiah Yeshua.

[8]Finally, brethren, whatever things are true, whatever things are honorable, whatever things are just, whatever things are pure, whatever things are kind, whatever things are of good report, if something of virtue and if something of praise, think about these things. [9]The things which you[+] learned, received, heard, and saw in me — do these things, and the God of peace will be with you[+].

[10]But I rejoice in the Lord greatly that now at length you[+] have revived your[+] concern for me. You[+] were indeed concerned at the time, but you[+] lacked opportunity. [11]Not that I speak in regard to need, for I have learned to be content in whatever circumstances I am in. [12]I know how to be humbled, and I know also how to abound. In everything and in all things I have learned the secret both to be filled and to be hungry, both to abound and to be in need. [13]I have strength for all things through Messiah, who empowers me. [14]You[+] did well, however, that you[+] joined with me in my affliction. [15]You Philippians also know that in the beginning of the good news, when I departed from Makedonia, no congregation communicated with me in the matter of giving and receiving but you[+] only. [16]For even in Thessalonika you[+] sent once and again to my need. [17]Not that I seek for the gift, but I seek for the fruit that increases to your[+] account. [18]But I have all things, and abound. I am filled, having received from Epaphroditus the things that came from you[+], a sweet-smelling fragrance, an acceptable and well-pleasing sacrifice to God. [19]My God will supply every need of yours[+] according to His riches in glory in Messiah Yeshua. [20]Now to our God and Father be the glory forever and ever. Amen.

[21]Greet all who belong to God in Messiah Yeshua. The brethren who are with me greet you[+]. [22]All those who belong to God greet you[+], especially those from Caesar's household. [23]The grace of the Lord Yeshua the Messiah be with your[+] spirit.

Sha'ul/Paulos' Letter to the Colossians

1 [1]Paulos, an ambassador of Messiah Yeshua through the will of God, and Timothy our brother: [2]to those who belong to God and are faithful brethren in Messiah at Colossae. Grace to you⁺ and peace from God our Father.

[3-5]Having heard of your⁺ faith in Messiah Yeshua and of the love which you⁺ have toward all those who belong to God, through the hope which is laid up for you⁺ in the heavens, we give thanks to God, the Father of our Lord Yeshua the Messiah, praying always for you⁺. You⁺ heard this before in the word of the truth of the good news. [6]This has come to you⁺, even as it is in all the world. It is bearing fruit and growing, as it does in you⁺ also, since the day you⁺ heard and knew the grace of God in truth. [7]This is what you⁺ learned from Epaphras our beloved fellow servant, who is a faithful servant of the Messiah on our behalf. [8]He also declared to us your⁺ love in the Spirit.

[9]For this cause, since the day we heard it, we also do not cease praying and asking for you⁺ that you⁺ would be filled with the knowledge of His will in all spiritual wisdom and understanding. [10]We pray for you⁺ to walk worthily of the Lord, to please Him in all respects, bearing fruit in every good work, and increasing in the knowledge of God. [11]We pray for you⁺ to be strengthened with all power according to the might of His glory, for all endurance and perseverance with joy. [12]We are giving thanks to the Father, who made us fit to be partakers of the portion in the light assigned to those who belong to God. [13]He delivered us out of the power of darkness, and removed us into the Kingdom of the Son of His love.

[14-15]In him who is the image of the invisible God, the firstborn of all creation, we have our redemption, the forgiveness of our sins. [16]For all things in the heavens and on the earth were created by him, the visible and the invisible, whether thrones or dominions or principalities or powers. All things have been created through him, and for him. [17]He is before all things, and in him all things are held together. [18]He is the head of the body, the community. He is the beginning, the firstborn from the dead, so that he might have the preeminence in all things. [19]For all the fullness was pleased to dwell in him, [20]and to reconcile all things to Himself through him, whether things on the earth, or things in the heavens, having made peace by him, through the blood of his tree of death.

[21]You⁺ once were excluded by evil deeds, and were enemies in your⁺ mind. [22]Yet now he has reconciled you⁺ in the body of his flesh through death, to present you⁺ holy, without blemish, and blameless before him — [23]if indeed you⁺ continue in the faith, grounded and steadfast, and not moved away from the hope of the good news which you⁺ heard. This good news is being proclaimed in all Creation under heaven. I, Paulos, have become a servant of it.

1:15 "The Holy One, blessed be He, said to Moses, 'In the same way that I made Jacob a firstborn' — as it is said (Ex. 4:22) *Israel is My son, My firstborn* — so I will make Messiah the King firstborn' — as it is said (Ps. 89:28) *I will also give him to be firstborn.*" (Mid. Exodus 19.7)

[24]Now I rejoice in my sufferings for you[+], and fill up in my flesh what is lacking of the afflictions of Messiah for his body, which is the community. [25]I was made a servant of the community with responsibility in God's household, which was given to me concerning you[+], to fulfill the word of God — [26]the mystery which has been hidden from the ages and from the generations. But now it has been revealed to those who belong to Him. [27]God was pleased to make known to them what are the riches of the glory of this mystery among the Gentiles, which is Messiah in you[+], the hope of glory. [28]We proclaim him, admonishing every man and teaching every man in all wisdom, so that we may present every man wholly mature in Messiah Yeshua. [29]For this I also toil, striving according to his working in me in power.

2 [1]For I want you[+] to know how greatly I strive for you[+], for those at Laodikea, and for as many as have not seen me in person. [2]I do this so their hearts may be encouraged, being knit together in love, and so they will have all riches of the full assurance of understanding. I do this for them to know Messiah, the mystery of God. [3]All the treasures of wisdom and knowledge are hidden in him. [4]Now I say this so that no one may delude you[+] with persuasiveness of speech. [5]For though I am physically absent, yet I am with you[+] in the spirit, rejoicing and seeing your[+] orderliness and the steadfastness of your[+] faith in Messiah. [6]So as you[+] received Messiah Yeshua the Lord, walk in him, [7]rooted and built up in him, and established in the faith — even as you[+] were taught — abounding in it in thanksgiving.

[8]Take heed so that no one makes you[+] a prey through philosophy and empty deceit, following the tradition of men, following the system of the world, and not following Messiah. [9]For all the fullness of the nature of God dwells bodily in him. [10]And you[+] are made complete in him, who is the head of all principality and authority. [11]In him you[+] were also circumcised with a circumcision not made with hands, in the putting off of the body of the sins of the flesh, in the circumcision of the Messiah. [12]You[+] have been buried with him in immersion, in which you[+] were also raised with him through faith in the action of God, who raised him from the dead.

[13]When you[+] were dead in your[+] transgressions and the uncircumcision of your[+] flesh, He made you[+] alive together with him, having forgiven us all our transgressions, [14]wiping out the handwriting in the ordinances which were set in opposition to us. He has also taken it out of our midst, nailing it to the tree of death. [15]Having disarmed the principalities and the powers, He made a show of them openly, triumphing over them in it.

[16]Therefore do not let anyone judge you[+] in food, or in drink, or with respect to a feast day or a new moon or sabbatical days. [17]These are a shadow of the coming things, and the body is Messiah's.

2:13 As Messiah's ambassador to the Gentiles, Sha'ul is writing to Gentiles, "being dead in your sins and the uncircumcision of your flesh ..." What he wrote must therefore be understood in terms of the audience to whom he wrote.

2:16-19 Sha'ul mentions some things — meat, drink, feast days, new moons, and sabbaths — by which some people were judging others. Sha'ul does not tell the Gentile believers to observe these things, nor does he tell them not to observe these things. He simply tells them that, whether they observe them or not, they should not let anyone judge them by these things. (This is complementary to his exhortation in Rom. >>

[18]Don't let anyone cheat you[+], desiring humility of mind and worship of the angels, intruding into things which he has not seen, vainly conceited by his fleshly mind, [19]and not holding firmly to the Head [2Ch. 13:1], from whom all the body, being supplied and knit together through the joints and ligaments, grows with increase from God.

[20-22]So if you[+] died with Messiah by the system of the world, why, while living in the world, do you[+] subject yourselves to edicts according to the commandments and teachings of men? "Do not handle, do not taste, do not touch" — all of which things perish with use. [23]These things indeed have the sound of wisdom in self-imposed observance, humility, and neglect of the body, but are not of any value against the indulgence of the flesh.

3 [1]So if you[+] were raised together with the Messiah, seek the things above where the Messiah is, seated at the right hand of God. [2]Set your[+] mind on the things above, not on the things on the earth, [3]because you[+] have died, and your[+] life has been hidden with the Messiah in God. [4]When the Messiah, your[+] life, is revealed, then you[+] also will be revealed with him in glory. [5]Therefore, let the members of your[+] body, which are on the earth, be deadened to sexual immorality, uncleanness, depraved passion, evil desire, and covetousness, which is idolatry. [6]On account of these things, the wrath of God comes on the children of disobedience.

[7]You[+] also once walked among them when you[+] lived in these things. [8]But now put off all these things: anger, wrath, malice, slander, and foul language out of your[+] mouth. [9]Do not lie to one another, seeing that you[+] have put off the old man with his deeds, [10]and have put on the new, which is being renewed unto knowledge after the image of the One who created him — [11]where there is not Greek and Jew, circumcision and uncircumcision, barbarian, Scythian, bondservant, freeman; but Messiah is all things and in all.

[12]Therefore, as those chosen by God, holy and beloved, put on a heart of compassion, kindness, humility, gentleness, and patient endurance. [13]Bear with one another, and forgive each other. If anyone should have a complaint against any, even as the Lord forgave you[+], so you[+] do the same.

14:1-13: do not judge one another.) These things, projected as a shadow by the light shining on Messiah, are an image only. It is Messiah who is to be sought. The ones who are judging others are "vainly puffed up," though they think that they speak in humility.

"The shadow of God is his word, which he used like an instrument when he was making the world. And this shadow, and, as it were, model, is the archetype of other things." (Philo, "Allegorical Interpretation, III," XXXI (95), The Works of Philo, trans. C.D. Yonge)

2:20-23 Sha'ul speaks of "commandments and teachings of men." He is not speaking of the commandments of God. Some people, most likely gnostics, were prohibiting the touching, tasting, and handling of certain things. Gnostics believed that the physical world was evil, and consequently they believed in the saving power of esoteric, mystical knowledge. In contrast, Sha'ul speaks of the revealed mystery of Messiah.

3:10-11 Sha'ul explains that though there are many different kinds of disciples, Messiah is only one. The unity of Messiah transcends the distinctions. See the note to Gal. 3:28. Josephus says the Scythians were descended from Magog. (Antiquities 1:123 [1. 6. 1. 123])

[14]And above all these things is love, which is the bond of full maturity. [15]And let the peace of God rule in your+ hearts, to which also you+ were called in one body; and be thankful. [16]Let the word of the Messiah dwell in you+ richly — teaching and admonishing one another in all wisdom with psalms, songs of praise, and songs of the Spirit, singing with grace in your+ heart to God. [17]Whatever you+ do in word or in deed, do all in the name of the Lord Yeshua, giving thanks to God the Father through him.

[18]Wives, submit yourselves to your+ husbands as is appropriate in the Lord. [19]Husbands, love your+ wives, and do not be bitter against them. [20]Children, listen to your+ parents in all things, for this is well-pleasing to the Lord. [21]Fathers, do not provoke your+ children, so that they will not be discouraged.

[22]Bondservants, listen in all things to those who, concerning the physical, are your+ masters, not just as men-pleasers when they are looking, but in simplicity of heart, fearing God. [23]And whatever you+ do, work heartily as for the Lord, and not for men, [Eccl. 9:10] [24]knowing that you+ will receive from the Lord the reward of the inheritance, because you+ serve Messiah the Lord. [25]But the one who does wrong will receive what he did wrong, and there is no judging according to outward appearance. [Is. 11:2-4]

4 [1]Masters, give to your+ servants what is just and equitable, knowing that you+ also have a Master in the heavens.

[2]Continue steadfastly in prayer, watching in it with thanksgiving, [3]praying together for us also, that God may open to us a door for the word, to speak the mystery of the Messiah — for which I also have been bound — [4]so that I may reveal it as I ought to speak. [5]Walk in wisdom toward those who are outside, buying the time. [6]Let your+ speech always be with grace, seasoned with salt, that you+ may know how you+ ought to answer each one.

[7]My affairs will all be made known to you+ by Tychicus, the beloved brother, faithful servant, and fellow bondservant in the Lord. [8]I am sending him to you+ for this very purpose, so that you+ may know our circumstances and that he may encourage your+ hearts. [9]I am sending him together with Onesimus, the faithful and beloved brother, who is one of you+. They will make known to you+ everything here.

[10-11]Aristarchus, my fellow prisoner, greets you+, and Mark, the cousin of Bar Nabba, and Yeshua who is called Justus. These are of the circumcision. You+ received commandments about Mark: receive him if he comes to you+. These are my only fellow workers for the Kingdom of God, men who have been a comfort to me.

[12]Epaphras, who is from you+, a servant of Messiah, greets you+, always striving for you+ in his prayers, so that you+ may stand fully mature and complete in all the will of God. [13]For I testify about him that he has much labor for you+, for those in Laodikea, and for those in Hierapolis. [14]Luke, the beloved physician, and Demas greet you+. [15]Greet the brethren who are in Laodikea, Nymphas and the congregation that is in his house. [16]When this letter has been read among you+, have it read also in the community of the Laodikeans, and you+ also read the letter from Laodikea. [17]Tell Archippus, "Take heed to the responsibility which you have received in the Lord, so that you fulfill it."

[18]The salutation of Paulos, by my own hand. Remember my chains. Grace be with you+.

4:5 See note to Eph. 4:17-19

Sha'ul/Paulos' First Letter
to the Thessalonikans

1 ¹Paulos, Sila, and Timothy, to the community of the Thessalonikans, in God the Father and the Lord Yeshua the Messiah. Grace to you⁺ and peace.

²We always give thanks to God for all of you⁺, mentioning you⁺ in our prayers before our God and Father. ³We remember without ceasing your⁺ work of faith, labor of love, and patience of hope in our Lord Yeshua the Messiah. ⁴Brethren, we know that you⁺ are chosen, loved by God. ⁵We know that our good news came to you⁺ not in word only, but also in power, in the Ruakh Kodesh, and with much assurance. You⁺ know what kind of men we showed ourselves to be among you⁺ for your⁺ sake.

⁶You⁺ became imitators of us and of the Lord, having received the word in much affliction, with the joy of the Ruakh Kodesh. ⁷By this you⁺ became an example to all in Makedonia and in Akhaia who believe. ⁸For the word of the Lord has sounded forth from you⁺, not only in Makedonia and Akhaia, but your⁺ faith toward God has also gone forth in every place. So there is no need for us to say anything. ⁹For they themselves report about us what kind of a reception we had from you⁺; and how you⁺ turned to God from idols, to serve a living and true God, ¹⁰and to wait for His Son from heaven. He raised him from the dead — Yeshua, who delivers us from the wrath that is coming.

2 ¹For you⁺ yourselves know, brethren, our visit to you⁺ was not in vain. ²But, as you⁺ know, having suffered before and having been shamefully treated at Philippi in much conflict, we grew bold in our God to tell you⁺ the good news of God. ³For our exhortation was not from error, nor from uncleanness, nor in deception. ⁴But even as we have been approved by God to be entrusted with the good news, so we speak — not as pleasing men, but God, who tests our hearts.

⁵For as you⁺ know, we never used a word of flattery nor a pretense for covetousness. God is a witness. ⁶Nor were we seeking glory from men, neither from you⁺ nor from others, when we might have claimed authority as ambassadors of Messiah. ⁷But we were gentle among you⁺, as when a nursing mother takes care of her own children. ⁸Even so, affectionately longing for you⁺, we were well pleased to impart to you⁺ not only the good news of God, but also our own souls, because you⁺ had become very dear to us.

⁹For you⁺ brethren remember our labor and travail. Working night and day so that we might not burden any of you⁺, we proclaimed to you⁺ the good news of God. ¹⁰You⁺ are witnesses with God how we blamelessly behaved ourselves in holiness and righteousness toward you⁺ who believe. ¹¹As you⁺ know, we exhorted, comforted, and implored every one of you⁺ as a father does his own children, ¹²to the end that you⁺ should walk in a worthy manner for God, who calls you⁺ into His own kingdom and glory.

¹³For this cause we also unceasingly thank God that when you⁺ received from us the message you⁺ heard, you⁺ accepted it not as the word of men, but as the word of God, which it is in truth. It also works in you⁺ who believe. ¹⁴For you⁺ brethren became imitators of the communities of God in Messiah Yeshua which are in Judea. For you⁺ also suffered the same things from your⁺

own countrymen, even as they did from the Judeans, [15]those who killed both the Lord Yeshua and the prophets, and drove us out. They did not please God, and are contrary to all men. [16]They forbid us to speak to the Gentiles for their salvation. So they continue to fill up their sins, but the fullness of wrath has come upon them.

[17]But we, brethren, being separated from you[+] for a short time — in presence, not in heart — tried even harder with great desire to see your[+] face, [18]because we wanted to come to you[+]. Indeed I, Paulos, tried once and again, but the Accuser hindered us. [19]For what is our hope, or joy, or crown of rejoicing? Isn't it even you[+] before our Lord Yeshua at his coming? [20]For you[+] are our glory and our joy.

3 [1]Therefore, when we could not stand it any longer, we thought it good to be left behind at Athens alone. [2]Then we sent our brother Timothy, God's servant in the good news of the Messiah, to establish you[+] and to comfort you[+] concerning your[+] faith. [3]Let no one be intimidated by these afflictions, because you[+] know that we are appointed to this task. [4]For also when we were with you[+], we told you[+] beforehand that we were about to suffer affliction, even as it happened, and as you[+] know. [5]For this cause I also, when I could not stand it any longer, sent that I might know your[+] faith, for fear that the Tempter had tempted you[+] in some way, and our labor would be in vain.

[6]But now Timothy has come to us from you[+], and has brought to us good news of your[+] faith and love — that you[+] always have good memories of us, longing to see us, even as we also long to see you[+]. [7]Because of this, brethren, in all our distress and affliction, we were comforted over you[+] through your[+] faith. [8]For now we live, if you[+] stand fast in the Lord. [9]For what thanksgiving can we render again to God for you[+], for all the joy with which we rejoice because of you[+] before our God? [10]Night and day we pray intently that we might see your[+] face, and might restore what is lacking in your[+] faith. [11]Now may our God and Father Himself, and our Lord Yeshua the Messiah, direct our way to you[+]. [12]And may the Lord make you[+] to increase and abound in love one toward another, and toward all men, even as we also do toward you[+]. [13]This is so that he may establish your[+] hearts blameless in holiness before our God and Father, at the coming of our Lord Yeshua with all those who belong to him.

4 [1]Finally then brethren, we beg and exhort you[+] in the Lord Yeshua that you[+] abound more and more, inasmuch as you[+] received from us how you[+] ought to walk and please God. [2]For you[+] know what commandments we gave you[+] through the Lord Yeshua. [3]For this is the will of God, your[+] sanctification: for you[+] to abstain from sexual immorality, [4]for each one of you[+] to know how to possess his own physical being in sanctification and honor, [5]not in the passion of desire like the Gentiles who do not know God. [6]No one should cheat and take advantage of his brother in this matter, because the Lord is an avenger in all these things, as we also forewarned you[+] and testified. [7]For God did not call us for uncleanness, but in sanctification. [8]So the one who rejects this is not rejecting man, but God, who has also given His Ruakh Kodesh to you[+].

[9]But concerning brotherly love, you[+] have no need that one write to you[+], because you[+] yourselves are taught by God to love one another. [10]For indeed you[+] do it toward all the brethren who are in all Makedonia. But we exhort you[+] brethren that you[+] abound more and more, [11]and that you[+] make it your[+] ambition to lead a quiet life, and to do your[+] own business, and to work with your[+] own hands, even as we commanded you[+]; [12]so that you[+] may walk honorably toward those who are outside, and may not be in need of anything.

[13]But we do not want you[+] to be ignorant, brethren, concerning those who fall asleep, so that you[+] do not grieve like the rest of men, who have no hope. [14]For if we believe that Yeshua died and rose again, even so God will bring with him those who have fallen asleep in Yeshua. [15]For we tell you[+] this by the word of the Lord, that we who are alive, who are left to the coming of the Lord, will certainly not go before those who have fallen asleep. [16]For the Lord himself will descend from heaven with a shout, with the voice of the chief angel, and with the trumpet of God. The dead in Messiah will rise first, [17]then we who are alive, who are left, will be caught up together with them in the clouds, to meet the Lord in the air. So we will be with the Lord forever. [18]Therefore encourage one another with these words.

5 [1]But concerning the times and the seasons, you[+] brethren have no need that anything be written to you[+]. [2]For you[+] yourselves know explicitly that the day of the Lord comes like a thief in the night. [3]For when they are saying, "Peace and safety," then sudden destruction will come upon them like birth pains upon a pregnant woman, and they will not escape. [Is. 13:6-13] [4]But you[+] brethren are not in darkness that the day should overtake you[+] like a thief.

[5]You[+] are all children of light, and children of the day. We do not belong to the night, nor to darkness. [6]So then let us not sleep, as the rest do, but let us watch and be sober. [7]For those who sleep, sleep in the night, and those who are drunken are drunken in the night. [8]But since we belong to the day, let us be sober, putting on the breastplate of faith and love, and the hope of salvation for a helmet. [9]For God did not appoint us to wrath, but to the obtaining of salvation through our Lord Yeshua, the Messiah. [10]He died for us so that, whether we wake or sleep, we may live together with him. [11]So exhort one another, and build each other up, even as you[+] also do. [12]But we beg you[+] brethren to recognize those who labor among you[+] and lead you[+] in the Lord and admonish you[+], [13]and to respect and honor them in love for the sake of their work.

Be at peace among yourselves. [14]We exhort you[+] brethren, admonish the disorderly, encourage the fainthearted, support the weak, be patient toward all. [15]See that no one returns evil for evil to anyone, but always follow after what is good for one another and for all.

[16]Rejoice always. [17]Pray without ceasing. [18]Give thanks in everything, because this is God's will in Messiah Yeshua for you[+]. [19]Do not quench the Spirit. [20]Do not despise prophecies, [21]but demonstrate and prove all things, and hold firmly what is good. [22]Abstain from every form of evil.

5:2 "The knowledge of the coming of three is veiled, and these are they: Messiah, something found, and a scorpion." (Tal. Sanhedrin 97a)

5:3 It will be like the wife of Doctor Bernard Rieux as she was going on vacation: "'Je me sens très bien,' disait-elle." Then the plague came. Albert Camus, La Peste, Gallimard, 1947, P. 16

5:5-8 The phrase "children of light" appears throughout the DSS in the Manual of Discipline (Community Rule), War Scroll, and some lesser fragments.

5:17 "When you pray, pray in the the meetinghouse that is in your city. And if you are not able to pray in the meetinghouse, pray in the midst of your field. And if you are not able to pray in the midst of your field, pray within your house. And if you are not able to pray within your house, pray upon your bed. And if you are not able to pray in your bed, commune in your heart." (Mid. Psalms 4.9)

[23]May the God of peace Himself sanctify you[+] completely. May your[+] whole spirit, soul, and body be preserved blameless at the coming of our Lord Yeshua the Messiah. [24]Faithful is He who calls you[+], who will also do it. [25]Brethren, pray for us. [26]Greet all the brethren with a holy kiss. [27]I solemnly charge you[+] by the Lord that this letter be read to all the brethren.

[28]The grace of our Lord Yeshua the Messiah be with you[+].

Sha'ul/Paulos' Second Letter
to the Thessalonikans

1 [1]Paulos, Sila, and Timothy, to the community of the Thessalonikans in God our Father, and the Lord Yeshua the Messiah. [2]Grace to you[+] and peace from God our Father and the Lord Yeshua the Messiah.

[3]We are obligated to always give thanks to God for you[+] brethren, because it is appropriate since your[+] faith grows exceedingly, and the love of each and every one of you[+] towards one another abounds. [4]So we ourselves give you[+] praise in the communities of God for your[+] patience and faith in all your[+] persecutions and in the afflictions which you[+] endure.

[5]This is a demonstration of the righteous judgment of God, for you[+] to be counted worthy of the Kingdom of God, for which you[+] also suffer. [6]This is because it is a righteous thing with God to repay affliction to those who afflict you[+], [7]and to give relief to you[+] who are afflicted with us, when the Lord Yeshua is revealed from heaven with his mighty angels in flaming fire. [8]He will take vengeance on those who do not know God and on those who do not listen to the good news of our Lord Yeshua. [9]They will suffer the penalty, eternal destruction from the presence of the Lord and from the glory of his might. [10]It will happen in that day when he comes to be glorified in those who belong to him, and to be the object of awe among all those who have believed — because our testimony to you[+] was believed.

[11]To this end we also pray always for you[+] that our God may count you[+] worthy of the calling, and may fulfill every desire of goodness and work of faith, with power. [12]In this way, the name of our Lord Yeshua may be glorified in you[+], and you[+] in him, according to the grace of our God and the Lord Yeshua the Messiah.

2 [1]Now brethren, concerning the coming of our Lord Yeshua the Messiah and our gathering together to him, we ask you[+] [2]not to be quickly shaken in your[+] mind or troubled, either by spirit or by word or by a letter that seems to be from us saying that the day of the Lord has come. [3]Do not let anyone deceive you[+] in any way, because it will not happen unless there is first the falling away and the Man who opposes the Law is revealed, the son of destruction. [4]He is the one

2:3 "Disaster will be to the bones of those who calculate the end, because they will say, 'Since the end [of the time] has already come, and he [Messiah] has not come,' and 'Therefore he will not come.'" (Tal. Sanhedrin 97b)

2:3,8 The enemy of Messiah is "the Lawless one," "the Man of Lawlessness," i.e the Outlaw. He is the one who lives in disregard of God's Law. The Lord will destroy him.

2:9-12 "the Man of the Lie, who had rejected the Law in the presence of their entire [company.]" (DSS 1QpHab 5:11-12) "Now from the day the Beloved Teacher passed away to the destruction of all the warriors who went back to the Man of the Lie will be about 40 years." (DSS CD 20:13-15)

2:11 "the lie" If this is referring to a specific lie, rather than to all that is false, then it may be a reference to Gen. 3:4-5, where the Serpent tells Havah/Eve that God is lying and that humanity can know [and determine] good and evil without God.

who opposes and exalts himself against all that is called god, or that is worshipped, in that he sits in the Temple of God, setting himself up as god. [5]Do you[+] not remember that I told you[+] these things when I was still with you[+]?

[6]Now you[+] know what is restraining him, so that he is revealed in his own time. [7]For the mystery of opposition to the Law is already working, only there is one who restrains now, until he is taken out of the way. [8]Then the Lawless one will be revealed. The Lord will destroy him with the breath of his mouth, and make him powerless with the brightness of his coming. [9]He is the one whose coming is according to the working of the Accuser with all power and signs and lying wonders. [10]His coming is with all deception of wickedness for those who are being lost, because they did not receive the love of the truth that they might be saved. [11]Because of this, God will send to them a powerful deception, for them to believe the lie, [12]so that they all might be judged who did not believe the truth, but had pleasure in wrong-doing.

[13]But we are bound to always give thanks to God for you[+] brethren who are loved by the Lord, because God chose you[+] as firstfruits for salvation through sanctification of the Spirit and belief in the truth. [14]He called you[+] to that through our good news, so that you[+] might obtain the glory of our Lord Yeshua the Messiah. [15]So then brethren, stand firm and hold firmly the instructions which you[+] were taught by us, whether by word, or by letter.

[16]Now our Lord Yeshua the Messiah himself, and God our Father, who loved us and gave us eternal comfort and good hope through grace, [17]comfort your[+] hearts and establish you[+] in every good work and word.

3 [1]Finally brethren, pray for us, that the word of the Lord may spread rapidly and be glorified, even as with you[+] also. [2]And pray that we may be delivered from unnatural and evil men, because not all have faith. [3]But the Lord is faithful, who will establish you[+] and guard you[+] from the evil. [4]We have confidence in the Lord concerning you[+], that you[+] both do and will do the things we communicate. [5]May the Lord direct your[+] hearts into the love of God, and into the endurance of Messiah.

[6]Now in the name of our Lord Yeshua the Messiah, we command you[+] brethren that you[+] withdraw yourselves from every brother who is walking disorderly and not after the instruction which they received from us. [7]For you[+] know how you[+] ought to imitate us. For we did not behave disorderly among you[+], [8]nor did we eat bread from anyone's hand without paying for it. But in labor and travail we worked night and day, that we might not burden any of you[+]. [9]This was not because we do not have the right, but to make ourselves an example to you[+], so that you[+] would imitate us. [10]For even when we were with you[+], we charged you[+] this: "If anyone does not want to work, let him not eat either." [11]For we hear that some among you[+] are walking disorderly, not working at all, but are busybodies. [12]Now those who are that way, we charge and exhort in the Lord Yeshua the Messiah that they work with quietness so that they may eat their own bread.

[13]But you[+], brethren, do not be weary in doing what is good. [14]If anyone does not listen to our word in this letter, mark that one and do not associate with him, so that he may be ashamed. [15]Do not count him as an enemy, but admonish him as a brother.

[16]Now may the Lord of peace himself give you[+] peace at all times in every way. The Lord be with you[+] all.

[17]The greeting by my own hand, Paulos, which is a sign in every letter I write like this. [18]The grace of our Lord Yeshua the Messiah be with you[+] all.

The Letter to the Hebrews

1 ¹At many times and in various ways, God spoke long ago to the fathers through the prophets. ²At the end time of these days, He has spoken to us by a Son whom He appointed heir of all things, and also through whom He made the worlds. ³He is the radiance of glory, the very image of His nature [Wisdom 7:24-26; Gen. 1:26-27]; upholding all things by the word of His power. [Gen. 1:3]

When he had made purification for sins, he sat down on the right hand of the Majesty on high, ⁴having surpassed the angels to the same degree that he has inherited a name superior to theirs. ⁵For to which of the angels did He ever say, "You are My Son, today I have become your Father"? [Ps. 2:7] and again, "I will be a Father to him, and he will be a Son to Me"? [2Sam. 7:14]

⁶Again, when He brings the firstborn into the world He says, "Let all the angels of God bow down to him." [Dt. 32:43 LXX; Ps. 97:7, 88:26-27] ⁷On the one hand, He says of the angels, "Who makes His angels winds, and His servants a flame of fire." [Ps. 103:4LXX/104:4H; Lk. 2:13-14] ⁸But of the Son, He says, "Your throne, O God, is forever and ever. The scepter of uprightness is the scepter of Your kingdom. ⁹You have loved justice, and hated actions contrary to the Law. Therefore God, your God, has anointed you with the oil of gladness beyond your companions." [Ps. 45:7-8H/44:7-8LXX]

¹⁰And, "In the beginning, O Everpresent Lord, You laid the foundation of the earth, and the heavens are the works of Your hands. ¹¹They will perish, but You continue. They all will grow old as a garment does. ¹²You will roll them up as a cloak, and they will be changed, but You are the same. Your years will not fail." [Ps. 102:26-28H]

¹³But to which of the angels has He ever said, "Sit at My right hand, until I make your enemies

---

In "The Letter to the Hebrews," as in most of the Messianic Writings, the quotations from Tanakh tend to be from the Septuagint. The Septuagint was used because: 1. Almost all of the Messianic Writings were written in Jewish Greek, so a Jewish-Greek text of Tanakh was helpful for quotations. 2. At the time of Yeshua, most Jews were living in the Greek world, and therefore the Septuagint was the text used by many Jews, if not by most. It is important to keep in mind that at that time, there was no standardized Hebrew text. The Masoretic text developed over the following centuries. (There were also variations of the Greek text.) In this letter there are two particular textual differences from the Masoretic text that are noted below, 8:8-12 and 10:5-10. See the "Introduction to the Messianic Writings".

1:3 "It [Wisdom] is the radiance of the everlasting light, the unspotted mirror of the actions of God, and the image of His goodness." (Wisdom 7:24-26)

1:6 Their bowing down is a recognition of his sovereignty. "The Holy One, blessed be He, said to Moses, 'In the same way I made Jacob a firstborn... so I will make Messiah the King a firstborn...'" (Mid. Ex. 19.7)

1:8 The throne of David is "the throne of the kingdom of the Everpresent Lord." (1Chr. 28:5) It is "the throne of the Everpresent Lord." (cf. 1Chr. 29:23, 2Chr. 9:8)

1:9 "God has anointed you" indicates that he is God's Anointed, i.e. Messiah.

the footstool of your feet"? [Ps. 110:1] ¹⁴Aren't they all ministering spirits, sent out for service on behalf of those who are about to inherit salvation?

2 ¹Because of this, it is necessary for us to pay all the more attention to the things that were heard, so that we do not drift away. ²For if the word spoken through angels was confirmed, and every transgression and act of disobedience received what it deserved, ³how will we escape if we neglect so great a salvation? Having been spoken through the Lord first, it was confirmed to us by those who heard. ⁴God bore witness with them, both by signs and wonders, and by various works of power and the Ruakh Kodesh in accordance with His will.

⁵For He did not subject to angels the world to come, of which we speak. ⁶But He bears witness in a particular place, saying, "What is man, that You remember him? or a son of Adam, that You watch over him? ⁷You made him a little lower than the angels. You crowned him with glory and honor. ⁸You have put all things in subjection under his feet, and set him over the works of Your hands." [Ps. 8:4-6]

For in subjecting all things to him, He left nothing that is not subject to him. But now we do not yet see all things subjected to him. ⁹However, we do see Yeshua, who has been made a little lower than the angels. He was crowned with glory and honor through the suffering of death, that by the grace of God he might taste death for everyone.

¹⁰Because it was fitting for the One by whom and for whom all things exist, in bringing many children to glory, to bring the author of their salvation to fulfillment through sufferings. ¹¹For both the one who sanctifies and those who are sanctified are all from One. Because of this, he is not ashamed to call them brothers, ¹²saying, "I will declare Your Name to my brothers. In the midst of the congregation I will sing Your praise." [Ps. 22:22]

¹³And again, "I will put my trust in Him." [Is. 8:17, Ps. 11:1, 25:20] And again, "Behold, here I am and the children whom God has given me." [Is. 8:18] ¹⁴Inasmuch then as the children have flesh and blood in common, he likewise also partook of the same, so that through death he might end the work of the one who has the power of death, that is the Enemy, ¹⁵and might deliver whoever was guilty and in slavery by fear of death through all of life — ¹⁶for it certainly does not take hold of angels, but takes hold of the seed of Abraham. ¹⁷Therefore he was obligated to be made like his brothers in all things, so that he might become a merciful and faithful Kohen Gadol towards God, in order to make atonement for the sins of the people. ¹⁸Since he was tempted in what he suffered, he has the power to help those who are tempted.

3 ¹Therefore, holy brethren, partakers of a calling from Heaven, consider Yeshua the Messiah, the ambassador and Kohen Gadol of what we all acknowledge. ²He was faithful to the One who appointed him, just as Moses also was in His whole house. [Num. 12:7] ³For he has been counted worthy of more glory than Moses, inasmuch as the one who built the house has much more honor than the house. ⁴For every house is built by someone, but God is the One who built all things. ⁵As a servant, Moses was truly faithful in all His house, which is supporting evidence for those things which were going to be spoken. ⁶But as a Son, Messiah is over his own house. We are his house, if indeed we hold fast the boldness and the glory of our hope firm unto the end.

2:15 "fear of death" See note to Mt. 10:28.

[7]Therefore just as the Ruakh Kodesh says, "If you+ will hear His voice today, [8]do not harden your+ hearts, as in the rebellion, as in the day of testing in the wilderness, [9]where your+ fathers tested Me, tried Me, and saw My deeds for forty years. [10]Therefore I was angry with that generation, and said, 'They always go astray in their heart, and they have not known My ways.' [11]As I swore in My wrath, 'They will not enter into My rest.'" [Ps. 95:7-11]

[12]Pay attention, brethren, so that there will not be in any one of you+ an evil heart of unbelief, to fall away from the living God. [13]Instead, encourage each other every day, as long as it is called "today," so that none of you+ is hardened by the deceitfulness of sin. [14]For we have become partakers of the Messiah, if we hold the beginning of our confidence firm to the end [15]in what is said — "If you+ will hear His voice today, do not harden your+ hearts, as in the rebellion." [Ps. 95:7]

[16]For some who came out of Egypt by Moses, but not all, heard and rebelled. [17]Now with whom was He displeased forty years? Was it not with those who sinned, whose bodies fell in the wilderness? [18]To whom did He swear that they would not enter into His rest, if not those who were disobedient? [19]We see that they were not able to enter in because of disbelief.

4 [1]Therefore we should fear, so that none of you+ might seem to come short of the promise that remains of entering into His rest, [2]because we have had the good news proclaimed to us, even as they did. But the word they heard did not profit them, because it was not joined with faith by those who heard. [3]For those who have believed do enter into that rest, even as He has said, "As I swore in My wrath, they will not enter into My rest," [Ps. 95:11] although the works have been finished since the foundation of the world. [4]For somewhere He has said this about the seventh day, "God rested on the seventh day from all His works." [Gen. 2:2, Ex. 20:11, 31:17] [5]And once more in this place, "They will not enter into My rest." [Ps. 95:11]

[6]Since therefore it is left to some to enter it, and those to whom the good news was proclaimed before did not enter in because of disobedience, [7]He again designates a certain day "today," saying through David such a long time afterward — just as has been said — "If you+ will hear His voice today, do not harden your+ hearts." [Ps. 95:7]

[8]For if Yeshua son of Nun had given them rest, He would not have spoken afterward of another day. [9]Therefore there remains a Shabbat rest for the people of God. [10]For the one who has entered into His rest has himself also rested from his works, as God did from His. [11]Let us therefore be diligent to enter into that rest, so that no one falls in the same pattern of disobedience.

[12]For the Word of God is living and active, and sharper than any two-edged sword. It penetrates even to the dividing of soul and spirit, and of joints and marrow, and discerns the thoughts and intentions of the heart. [13]There is no creature that is hidden from His sight, but all things are naked and exposed before the eyes of Him for whom the word concerns us.

4:5 "in this place" refers to the reference to Ps. 95 in Heb. 3:15.

4:8 "son of Nun" is in the Aramaic, but not in the Greek. This is the person commonly called "Joshua" in English bibles.

4:10 "On Shabbat they used to say, 'A psalm, a song for the day of Shabbat.' A psalm, a song for the time to come, for the day that will be all Shabbat and peaceful rest for everlasting life." (Tal. Tamid 7:4, 33b — the last mishnah, referring to Ps. 92.)

[14]Having then a great Kohen Gadol who has passed through the heavens, Yeshua the Son of God, let us hold tightly to our commitment. [15]For we do not have a Kohen Gadol who cannot sympathize with our weaknesses, but one who has likewise been tempted in all things, yet without sin. [16]Let us therefore approach the throne of grace with boldness, so that we may receive mercy, and may find grace for timely help.

5 [1]For every Kohen Gadol taken from men is appointed for men in things toward God, so that he may offer both gifts and sacrifices for sins. [2]He is able to have compassion on those who are ignorant and going astray, because he himself is also surrounded with weakness. [3]Because of this, just as he brings sin offerings for the people, so he is obligated to do for himself.

[4]No one takes this honor on his own, but he is called by God, just as Aaron was. [5]In the same way, the Messiah did not glorify himself to become a Kohen Gadol, but rather the One who said to him, "You are my Son, today I have become your father." [Ps. 2:7] [6]Just as He also says in another place, "You are a Kohen forever, after the order of Malki-Tzedek." [Ps. 110:4/109:4LXX]

[7-8]In the days of his flesh, with strong cries and tears, he brought prayers and entreaties to the One who had the power to save him from death, and he was heard. Though he was a Son, he learned obedience by the things he suffered, because of fear. [9]His purpose being fulfilled, he became the source of eternal salvation to all those who obey him, [10]being designated by God as a Kohen Gadol after the order of Malki-Tzedek.

[11]The Word has much about him that is hard to explain, since you+ have become slow of hearing. [12]For though you+ are obligated to be teachers because of the time, you+ again need to have someone teach you+ the basics of the beginning of the revealed words of God. You+ have come to need milk, and not solid food. [13]For everyone who lives on milk is unskilled in the word of righteousness, for he is an infant. [14]But solid food is for those who are mature, who have trained their senses through use to discern both good and evil.

6 [1]So, leaving the beginning discussion of Messiah, let us press on to full maturity, not laying again a foundation of repentance from dead works, of faith toward God, [2]of the teaching about immersions, laying on of hands, resurrection of the dead, and eternal judgment. [3]We will do this, if God permits.

[4]For concerning those who were once given light, have tasted of the heavenly gift, have become partakers of the Ruakh Kodesh, [5]have tasted the good Word of God and the powers of the age to come, [6]and have then fallen away, it is impossible to renew them again to repentance, since they again put the Son of God on the deathstake for themselves, and put him to public shame. [7]For land that drinks the rain that often comes upon it, and bears plants suitable for those who cultivate it, shares in the blessing from God. [8]But that which produces thorns and thistles is rejected and is close to a curse, and its end is to be burned.

[9]But even though we speak like this, beloved, we are persuaded of better things about you+, things that accompany salvation. [10]For God is not unjust to forget your+ work and the love which you+

4:13 The word translated as "exposed" refers to a neck bent back and unprotected from a blow.

4:15 "The Merciful One, He will send to us His Messiah who walks blamelessly..." (Brit Milah liturgy)

5:7-8 "because of fear" is placed as in the Aramaic text.

showed toward His Name in having served, and in continuing to serve, those who belong to Him. [11]Now we desire that each one of you[+] show the same pursuit toward the full assurance of hope until the end, [12]so that you[+] do not become unresponsive, but imitators of those who inherit the promises through faith and patient endurance.

[13]For when God made a promise to Abraham, He swore by Himself, since He could swear by none greater. [14]He said, "Surely in blessing, I will bless you, and in multiplying I will multiply you." [Gen. 22:17] [15]Having patiently endured, he obtained the promise in this way. [16]For men swear by what is greater, and the oath is the conclusion to all their controversies. [17]God confirmed it in this way with an oath, being determined to abundantly demonstrate the unchangeable nature of His will to the heirs of the promise. [18]So by two unchangeable actions in which it is impossible for God to lie, those who have fled for refuge may have strong encouragement to take hold of the hope set before them.

[19]We have this hope as an anchor of the soul, which is both sure and steadfast, and yet enters into the place within the veil. [20]Yeshua entered there for us as a forerunner, having become a Kohen Gadol forever after the order of Malki-Tzedek.

7 [1]For this Malki-Tzedek, king of Shalem, Kohen of God Most High, met Abraham returning from the victory over the kings, and blessed him. [2]Abraham also divided to him a tenth part of everything. He is first, by translation, King of Righteousness; and then also King of Shalem, which is "king of peace". [3]Without father, without mother, without genealogy, having neither beginning of days nor end of life — made like the Son of God — he remains a Kohen forevermore.

[4]Now consider how great this man was. Even Abraham, the patriarch, gave a tenth out of the best spoils to him. [5]On the one hand, those of the sons of Levi who receive the office of Kohen have a commandment to take one-tenth from the people according to the Law — that is, from their relatives, though these have come out of the loins of Abraham. [6]On the other hand, he who is not descended from them has taken one-tenth from Abraham, and has blessed the one who has the promises. [7]And beyond all dispute, the lesser is blessed by the greater. [8]In the one case, people who die receive the tenths, but in the other, it is one of whom it is testified that he lives. [9]We might say that even Levi, who receives the tenth, has paid the tenth through Abraham, [10]because he was still in the loins of his father when Malki-Tzedek met him.

[11-12]Now if there were fulfillment of the purpose through the Levitical priesthood, what further need was there for another Kohen to arise after the order of Malki-Tzedek, and not be called after the order of Aaron? With the priesthood being changed, it is a necessity for a change of law to take place also, since the people were given law concerning it. [13]For the one about whom these things are said belongs to another tribe, from which no one has attended at the altar. [14]For it is quite evident that our Lord has arisen out of Judah, a tribe about which Moses said nothing concerning a priesthood.

[15]And it is much more evident if another Kohen arises according to the likeness of Malki-Tzedek, [16]who has been made such, not according to a law of a commandment concerning the flesh, but after the power of an endless life. [17]For this testimony is given: "You are a Kohen forever, in accordance with the order of Malki-Tzedek." [Ps. 110:4] [18]For there is a setting aside of a previous commandment

---

6:13-18 Philo discusses this issue in "Allegorical Interpretation, III," LXXII-LXXIII. The Everpresent Lord confirms His calling for Israel as a holy nation with both a covenant and a curse in Dt. 29:10-15.

because of its weakness and lack of accomplishment. [19]Because the Law did not bring anything to completion — in contrast to the bringing in of a better hope, through which we draw near to God. [Heb. 5:9]

[20,22]Inasmuch as Yeshua was not made a Kohen without an oath, by so much more has he become the guarantee of a better covenant. [21]For they indeed have been made Kohanim without an oath, but he with an oath by the One who says of him, "The Everpresent Lord swore and will not change His mind, 'You are a Kohen forever, in accordance with the order of Malki-Tzedek.'" [Ps. 110:4]

[23]In the one case, those who become Kohanim are many, because they are prevented by death from continuing. [24]But he, because he lives forever, has his priesthood which is not passed on to another. [25]Therefore he is also able to save completely those who draw near to God through him, since he is always alive to make intercession for them.

[26]For such a Kohen Gadol — holy, guiltless, undefiled, separated from sinners, and made higher than the heavens — was appropriate for us. [27]He does not need, like those Kohanim Gedolim, to offer up sacrifices daily, first for his own sins, and then for the sins of the people. For he did this once for all, when he offered up himself. [28]For the Law appoints as Kohanim Gedolim men who have weakness; but the word of the oath, which came after the Law, consecrates a Son forever. [Lev. 4:5; 21:10]

8 [1]Now the main point of the things we are saying is this: we have such a Kohen Gadol, who is seated at the right hand of the throne of the Majesty in the heavens. [2]He is a servant of the holy things and the true place of God's presence which the Everpresent Lord set up, not man. [3]For every Kohen Gadol is appointed to offer both gifts and sacrifices. Consequently, it is necessary that this one also have something to offer. [4]For if he were on earth, he would not be a Kohen at all, seeing there are Kohanim who offer the gifts according to the Law. [5]They serve in the representation and shadow of the things in heaven. Accordingly, Moses was warned by God when he was about to make the place of God's presence, since He said, "See that you make everything according to the pattern that was shown to you on the mountain." [Ex. 25:40]

[6]But now he has obtained a public duty, which has been made law on better promises, that is superior to the same degree that he is also the mediator of a better covenant. [7]Because if that first had been faultless, then a place would never have been sought for a second. [8]For He said to them, finding fault, "'Behold, the days come,' says the Everpresent Lord, 'when I will make a new covenant with the house of Israel and with the house of Judah, [9]not like the covenant which I made with their fathers in

---

7:28 Lev. 4:5 and 21:10 in the Septuagint show that *teteleiomenon* should sometimes be translated as "consecrated," i.e. set apart for a purpose.

8:2ff The Hebrew *"Mishkan,"* often translated as "Tabernacle," literally means "the place of the dwelling".

8:8-12 quotes Jer. 31:31-34 from the Septuagint.

8:8-9 Rashi comments, in Lev. 26:9, on "And I will establish My covenant with you," which is there promised in consequence of Israel's disobedience to God's Law: "A new covenant, not like the first covenant which you have broken, but a new covenant which will not be broken, as it says (Jer. 31:31ff)." He cites the midrash Sifra.

the day that I took them by the hand to lead them out of the land of Egypt. For they did not continue in My covenant, and I did not take care of them,' says the Everpresent Lord. [10]'For this is the covenant that I will make with the house of Israel after those days,' says the Everpresent Lord: 'I will put My laws into their mind. I will also write them on their heart. I will be their God, and they will be My people. [11]They will not teach every man his fellow-citizen, and every man his brother, saying, 'Know the Everpresent Lord,' for all will know Me, from the least of them to the greatest of them. [12]For I will be merciful concerning their unrighteousness, and I will no longer remember their sins and lawless deeds.'" [Jer. 31:31-34/38:31-34LXX]

[13]By saying "a new covenant," He has made the first old. Now what is becoming old and grows aged is close to disappearing.

9 [1-2]Now indeed the first covenant had regulations for public service, because a place of God's presence was prepared, a place which was both holy and in the world. In the first part, which is called the Holy Place, were the menorah, the table, and the consecrated bread. [3]Past the second veil was the covered place which is called the Holy of Holies. [4]It had a golden incense altar, and the ark of the covenant overlaid on all sides with gold, in which were a golden pot holding the manna, Aaron's rod that budded, and the tablets of the covenant. [5]Above it were cherubim of glory overshadowing the place of atonement. We cannot now speak in detail of these things.

[6]But these things having been prepared in this way, the Kohanim continually go into the first covered place, completing the services. [7]However, only the Kohen Gadol goes into the second, once

---

8:9 The Septuagint for Jer. 31:32 (38:32LXX) has, "because they did not continue in My covenant, and I did not esteem them." The Masoretic has "they broke My covenant, though I was a husband to them."

The difference comes from one Hebrew word, actually one Hebrew letter. The Masoretic has *ba'alti*. The Septuagint translates as though the Hebrew word were *ba<u>h</u>alti*. Does the Septuagint give the original, or is it a midrashic comment? We cannot tell. In terms of what God says throughout Jeremiah, either term would be consistent. (E.g. 9:13-16, 12:7-9, 16:11-13 on the one hand, or 3:1,8,14,20 on the other. In Jer. 12:7-8, the Hebrew text says that God hated His dearly beloved.) The New JPS translation of Jer. 31:32, like the quotation in Heb. 8:9, follows the Septuagint. It has, "a covenant which they broke, so that I rejected them — declares the LORD." Their explanatory note says, "Taking *ba'alti* as equivalent to *ba<u>h</u>alti*; cf. 3:14."

8:10-11 "This is the covenant..." What follows is the actual text of God's New Covenant with Israel. First and foremost is that God puts His Law within us and writes it on our hearts. As Yeshua said, he came to bring the fullness of the Law/Torah. Next is the affirmation of the relationship between the God of Israel and the people of Israel.

8:11 "fellow-citizen" The Masoretic text has *re'a*, which is usually translated as "neighbor". The Septuagint has *politen*, which is usually translated as "citizen". This is also the case for Prov. 11:9, 24:28, and Zech. 13:7.

9:4 In Tal. Yoma 51b-52a, Mishnah 5:1, there is a disagreement over the exact location of the incense altar. Some say there were two curtains, one cubit apart, between the Holy of Holies and the Holy place, and that the incense altar was located between the two curtains. "R. Nathan said: 'The Sages did not determine whether the holiness of the separating cubit was that of inside [the Holy of Holies] or of outside [in the Holy Place].'" Others say there was only one curtain.

in the year; not without blood, which he offers for himself and for the unintentional sins of the people. [8]The Ruakh Kodesh is indicating by this that the way into the Holy Place was not yet revealed while the first place of God's presence was still standing. [9]This is a symbol of the present age, where gifts and sacrifices are offered that are incapable of making the one who serves clean in conscience — [10]only in foods, drinks, and various washings — physical requirements put in place until a time of restoration.

[11]Now as a Kohen Gadol of the coming good things, Messiah came through the greater and perfect place of God's presence, not made with hands; that is to say, not of this creation. [12]And not through the blood of goats and calves, but through his own blood, he entered in once for all into the Holy of Holies, having obtained eternal redemption. [13]For if the blood of goats and bulls, and the ashes of a heifer sprinkling those who have been profaned, sanctify for the cleansing of the flesh, [14]how much more will the blood of the Messiah, who offered himself without blemish to God through the eternal Spirit, cleanse your[+] conscience from dead works to serve the living God?

[15]And by this means, he is the mediator of a new covenant. In this manner, a death has occurred for release from the transgressions under the first covenant, so that those who have been called might receive the promise of the eternal inheritance. [16]For where there is a covenant, the death of what confirms the covenant must be presented, [17]because a covenant is confirmed over dead bodies. For it is never in force while what confirms the covenant lives.

9:15 Joshua and Caleb are promised an "eternal inheritance" in the land. (Josh. 14:9) This seems to be the sense in which the term is used in Tanakh. (cf. 1Chr. 28:8, Ezra 9:12, Ps. 37:18)

In LXX Esther 14:5, Mordechai prayed, "I have heard from my birth in the tribe of my family that You, O Everpresent Lord, took Israel from all the nations and our fathers from all their ancestors for an eternal inheritance and have done what You said to them." The phrase should also be understood in terms of Heb. 1:14 and 6:12,17.

9:15 A midrashic comment explains nehilot in Ps. 5:1 (cf. Dt. 32:8-9) as the plural of nahalah, therefore meaning "two inheritances": "the inheritance when you[+] inherit Him [God], and the inheritance when He inherits you[+]." (Mid. Psalms 5.1)

9:15-18 The "testament" that appears in most translations is from the mistranslation that appeared in the Latin Vulgate. In Jer. 31:31-34H/38:31-34LXX the Latin Vulgate translators correctly translated brit/diatheke as "covenant". In Hebrews 8:8-12, which is quoted verbatim from the Septuagint version of Jeremiah, they made the error of putting testamentum. This significantly distorts the meaning of the original text. 1) "Testament" is unrelated to the text, the context, and the rest of the Scriptures. 2) The erroneous term "Old Testament" was then applied to the first 39 books of the Bible, and "New Testament" was then erroneously applied to the last 27 books. Consequently, people thought that the last 27 books replaced the first 39 books, leading to a multitude of doctrinal errors and massive confusion.

In Jewish Greek, diatheke always means "covenant," never "testament." See "There are No Testaments in the Bible" in the ADDITIONAL NOTES.

9:17 The sacrficial death of the animals inaugurates the covenant, their blood seals it.

[18]Therefore even the first covenant was not dedicated without blood. [19]For when every commandment had been spoken by Moses to all the people according to the Law, he took the blood of the calves with water, scarlet wool, and hyssop, and sprinkled both the scroll itself and all the people, [20]saying, "This is the blood of the covenant which God has commanded for you+." [Ex. 24:8]

[21]Moreover, in the same way, he sprinkled the place of God's presence and all the objects of service with the blood. [22]According to the Law, in general, everything is cleansed with blood and apart from shedding of blood there is no forgiveness. [Lev. 17:11] [23]Therefore it was necessary that the representations of the things in the heavens should be cleansed with these, but the heavenly things themselves with better sacrifices than these.

[24]Indeed, Messiah has not entered into holy places made by hands, which are copies of the actual ones, but into heaven itself, to appear in the presence of God for us now. [25]He does not need to offer himself often, as the Kohen Gadol enters into the Holy of Holies year by year with the blood of another. [26]Otherwise he would have had to suffer often since the foundation of the world. But now once, at the consummation of the ages, he has been revealed to put away sin by the sacrifice of himself. [27]Inasmuch as to die once is stored up and awaiting men, and judgment after this [2Esd. 14:35], [28]in the same way, the Messiah also, having been offered once to bear the sins of many, will appear a second time, separated from sin, to those who are eagerly waiting for him for salvation.

10 [1]Since the Law has a shadow of the good things to come, not the very image of these things, it can never completely cleanse those who draw near with the same yearly sacrifices which they offer continually. [2]Otherwise would they not have ceased to be offered, because those who serve, having once been cleansed, would have had no more consciousness of sins? [3]But in those sacrifices there is a yearly reminder of sins, [4]because it is impossible for the blood of bulls and goats to take away sins.

[5]So when he comes into the world, he says, "Sacrifice and offering You did not desire, but a body You prepared for me. [6]In burnt offerings and sacrifices for sin You had no pleasure. [7]Then I said,

---

9:19 According to Metzger, "the text without *kai ton tragon* [and the goats] is supported by an impressive combination of witnesses..." (A Textual Commentary on the New Testament, P. 668)

9:24 In Ps. 18:6, David said, "He heard my voice from His Temple." Since the First Temple was not built until the reign of Solomon, we know that David was referring to the Temple in Heaven.

9:27 See note to Mt. 10:28.

10:1-4 We are reminded of a very important difference between the Covenant of the Law and the New Covenant. The Covenant of the Law provided for ongoing sacrifices for ongoing sins. Each sin required another sacrifice. There was no end to the sacrifices because there was no end to the sins. Additionally, atonement could only be made for sins that had already been committed, not for sins that would be committed in the future.

One of the stipulations of the New Covenant is, "I will remember their sins and iniquities no more." (Jer. 31:34/Heb. 10:17) That is what God promised to do for those who enter into the New Covenant. Therefore, the sacrifice which establishes the New Covenant must bring forgiveness for all sins and iniquities, whether committed before or after that sacrifice is offered. No other sacrifices are necessary to bring forgiveness.

'Behold, I have come — in the scroll of the book it is written of me — to accomplish Your purpose, O God.'" [Ps. 39:7-9LXX/40:7-9H]

⁸Saying initially, "Sacrifices and offerings, burnt offerings and sacrifices for sin, You did not desire nor did You have pleasure in them" [Ps. 40:7H] — these are offered according to the Law — ⁹then he has said, "Behold, I have come to accomplish Your purpose." [Ps. 40:9H] He takes away the first, that he may establish the second.

¹⁰We have been sanctified by this purpose through the offering of the body of Yeshua the Messiah, once for all time. ¹¹On the one hand, every Kohen stands serving daily and repeatedly offering the same sacrifices which can never take away sins. ¹²On the other hand, this Kohen, when he had offered one sacrifice for sins forever, sat down on the right hand of God; ¹³waiting from that time until his enemies are made the footstool of his feet. [Ps. 110:1] ¹⁴For by one offering he has fully cleansed forever those who are being sanctified.

¹⁵The Ruakh Kodesh also testifies to us, in that He says: ¹⁶"'This is the covenant that I will make with them after those days,' says the Everpresent Lord, 'I will put My laws on their heart, I will also write them on their mind.'" [Jer. 31:33] After saying this, He then says, ¹⁷"I will no longer remember their sins and their actions contrary to the Law." [Jer. 31:34] ¹⁸Now where there is forgiveness of these, there is no longer an offering for sin.

¹⁹Brethren, we therefore have boldness to enter into the Holy of Holies by the blood of Yeshua, ²⁰by a new and living way which he consecrated for us through the veil, which is his flesh. ²¹And having a Kohen Gadol over the house of God, ²²let us draw near with a true heart in full assurance of faith, having our hearts sprinkled from an evil conscience, and having our body washed with pure water. ²³Let us hold fast the confession of hope without wavering, because the One who promised is faithful.

²⁴Let us consider how to encourage one another to love and good deeds, ²⁵not forsaking our own assembling together, as the habit of some is, but encouraging one another, and so much the more as

10:5-7 The quotation is from Ps. 39:7-9LXX, which corresponds to Ps. 40:7-9H. For the first of these verses, the Masoretic has, "Sacrifice and offering You did not desire, my ears You have opened for me." The Septuagint has the same. The Messianic Writings have, "Sacrifice and offering You did not desire, but a body You prepared for me." We do not currently have an older text of the psalm with those words. That is not unusual for a time when there was no standardized text. Likewise the Talmud, in Sanhedrin 93b, says, "it is written of David, 'He prospered in everything to which he turned.'" The Soncino note simply says about this that, "There is no such verse in the Bible." Today we have a text that has been standardized, but that was not done until the second century C.E.

"...the rabbinic literature itself, in quotations from the Bible, exhibits more frequently than is generally realized readings that differ from those preserved in our so-called 'masoretic' texts, readings that are not due to faulty memory and that crop up in Hebrew manuscripts and/or biblical quotations in Mechilta, Sifra, Sifre, the Gemara, the grammatical works of ibn Janah, etc."[31] Harry Orlinsky, "The Masoretic Text: A Critical Evaluation," in <u>The Canon and Masorah of the Hebrew Bible</u>, ed. Sid Z. Leiman, Ktav Publishing House, NY, 1974, P. 852 See the ADDITIONAL NOTE on "The Septuagint".

<u>Midrash on Psalms</u> 40.4 relates the passage to what is required of Israel's kings in Dt. 17:18-19.

10:11-14 See note to 10:1-4.

you[+] see the Day approaching. [26]For if we sin willfully after we have received the knowledge of the truth, there no longer remains a sacrifice for sins, [27]but a certain fearful expectation of judgment, and a fiery zeal which is going to consume the enemies. [Is. 26:11]

[28]A man who disregards the Law of Moses dies without compassion on the testimony of two or three witnesses. [29]The one who has trodden under foot the Son of God, and has considered unholy the blood of the covenant with which he was sanctified, and has insulted the Spirit of grace — how much worse punishment do you[+] think he will deserve? [30]For we know Him who said, "'Vengeance is Mine,' says the Everpresent Lord, 'I will repay.'" [Dt. 32:35] Again, "The Everpresent Lord will judge His people." [Dt. 32:36] [31]It is a fearful thing to fall into the hands of the living God. [1Sam. 24:10-14]

[32]But remember the former days in which you[+] were given light and endured a great struggle with sufferings. [33]On the one hand you[+] were made a spectacle in both reproaches and oppressions. And on the other hand you were becoming companions of those who were so treated. [34]For you[+] had compassion on the prisoners, and also accepted the seizure of your[+] possessions with joy, knowing that you[+] have for yourselves a better possession and an enduring one. [35]So do not throw away your[+] boldness, which has a great reward.

[36]For you[+] need endurance so that, having done the will of God, you[+] may receive the promise. [37]"In a very little while, the One who is coming will come, and will not delay. [38]But My righteous one will live from faith. If he turns back, My soul has no pleasure in him." [Hab. 2:3,4] [39]But we are not of those who turn back into destruction, but of those who are faithful to the preservation of the soul.

11 [1]Now faith is the foundation of things hoped for, the certainty of things not seen. [2]For those of older times obtained a good report by this. [3]By faith, we understand that the ages were established by the spoken word of God, so that what is seen has not been made out of things which are visible. [2Mac. 7:28]

[4]In faith, Hevel offered to God a better sacrifice than Ka'in, through which he obtained confirmation that he was righteous — God testifying about his gifts. [Gen. 4:4] And through it, though having died, he still speaks. [5]By faith, Hanokh was taken away, so that he would not see death. And he was not found, because God took him away, for it was testified of him before he was taken away that he pleased God. [Gen. 5:24; Sir. 44:16; Wis. 4:10-11] [6]But apart from faith, it is impossible to please Him, for it is necessary that the one who comes to God believes that He exists and that He is a rewarder of those who seek Him.

[7]In faith, Noah, being warned about things not yet seen, feared God and prepared an ark for the salvation of his house. By this he condemned the world, and became heir of the righteousness which is from faith.

[8]In faith, Abraham obeyed when he was called to go out to the place which he would receive for an inheritance. He went out, not knowing where he was going. [9]In faith, he lived as a stranger in the promised land, as though foreign, dwelling in tents with Isaac and Jacob, the fellow-heirs of the same

---

10:38 See note to Rom. 1:17.

11:1ff The Hebrew *emunah* can be translated as either "faith" or "faithfulness". Ex. 17:12 illustrates some of its range of meaning: "And the hands of Moses became heavy... and Aaron and Hur supported his hands.... And his hands were *emunah*/steady until the going down of the sun."

promise. [Gen. 28:4] ¹⁰For he was awaiting the city which has foundations whose builder and framer is God. [1Mac. 2:52-61, Is. 28:16]

¹¹By faith, when Sarah herself was barren and past the time of life, he received power to father a child, since he considered faithful the One who had promised. ¹²Therefore also from one man, and him as good as dead, were born as many as the stars of the heaven in multitude, and as innumerable as the sand which is by the shore of the sea. [Gen. 15:5, 22:17, 32:12]

¹³These all died in faith, not having received the promises, but having seen and embraced them from a distance, and having confessed that they were foreigners and sojourners upon the land. ¹⁴For those who say such things make it clear that they are seeking their own homeland. [Ezek. 37:25] ¹⁵If they had truly been remembering the one from which they went out, they would have had opportunity to return. ¹⁶However, as it is, they are reaching for a better one, that is, one from heaven.

11:4-38 "When the time drew near for Mattathias to die, he said to his sons, '...Be zealous for the Law, and give your lives for the covenant of our Fathers. And remember the deeds of the Fathers which they did in their generations, and receive great glory and an everlasting name. Was not Abraham found faithful when he was tested, and it was considered as righteousness for him? Joseph in his time of distress kept the commandment and became lord of Egypt. Pinchas our father for being truly zealous received the covenant of an everlasting priesthood. Joshua [Yeshua], by fulfilling the word, became a judge in Israel. Caleb, by bearing witness in the congregation, received an inheritance of land. David, by his mercy, inherited a royal throne forever. Eliyahu, by being truly zealous for the Law, was taken up into heaven. Hananiah, Azariah, and Mishael were faithful and were saved from the flame. Daniel, by his integriity, was delivered from the mouth of lions....' (1Mac. 2:49-60)

11:11 Some apply the verse to Sarah, which is in the nominative case, and translate "she received power to establish a seed". If Sarah is taken as the subject of the verse, it brings to mind Gen. 3:15, where God promises to establish hostility between the seed of the Serpent and the seed of the woman. Tal. Niddah 31a and Tal. Berachot 60a speak of a woman also providing seed in the formation of a child. Though the vocabulary of standard English translation is biologically inadequate, the original recognizes that both the mother and the father contribute to the genetic makeup of the child.

In this text, however, Abraham is the subject of verses 8-10. He is also the subject of v. 12 — "from one [masc.]... as good as dead [masc.]" — which repeats the promise which God made to Abraham of seed as numerous "as the stars of the heavens..." Given that Abraham is the father of all who believe, it seems likely that he is still the subject in v. 11.

11:13-14 Abraham, Isaac, and Jacob lived as strangers in the land that God had promised to them. (v. 9)

11:16 "I will also gather all nations, and bring them down to the Valley of Jehoshaphat. Then I will enter into judgment with them there on account of My people, My heritage Israel, whom they have scattered among the nations. They have also divided up My land." (Joel 3:2) God calls the people of Israel "My heritage," and the land of Israel "My land". (cf. Lev. 25:23, Is. 14:23, Ezek. 36:5, 1K. 8:36) The manna in the wilderness was "bread from heaven" which God provided on the earth. (Yhn. 6:41-51,58; Ps. 105:40, 78:24) God's Spirit descended from heaven (Yhn. 1:32) upon Yeshua, who came down from heaven (Yhn. 3:13) to live on the earth.

why?
forerunner
to Jesus

Therefore God is not ashamed of them, to be called their God, because He has prepared a city for them.

[17]Being tested, Abraham offered up Isaac by faith — he who had received the promises was offering up his only son. [18]Since it was said about him, "In Isaac your seed will be called," [Gen. 21:12] [19]he considered that God was able to raise him up, even from the dead. From there, figuratively speaking, he also received him back.

[20]In faith, Isaac blessed Jacob and Esav concerning things to come. [21]In faith, Jacob, when he was dying, blessed each of the sons of Yosef, and bowed down upon the top of his staff. [22]In faith, Yosef, when his end was near, made mention of the exodus of the children of Israel, and gave instructions concerning his bones.

[23]When Moses was born, he was hidden for three months by his parents in faith, because they saw the child was good [Gen. 1:4,10,12,18,21,25], and they were not afraid of the king's command. [24]When Moses had grown up, in faith he refused to be called the son of Pharaoh's daughter, [25]choosing to suffer affliction with God's people rather than to have the temporary enjoyment of sin. [26]He considered the disgrace of the Messiah to be greater riches than the treasures of Egypt, because he looked to the reward. [27]In faith, he left Egypt, not fearing the anger of the king, because he persevered while seeing the invisible. [Ex. 2]

[28]In faith, he kept the Pesakh and the sprinkling of the blood, so that the destroyer of the firstborn could not touch them. [29]By faith, they passed through the Red Sea as on dry land. When the Egyptians tried to do so, they were swallowed up.

[30]By faith, the walls of Yeriho fell down, after they had been encircled for seven days. [31]By faith, Rahav the harlot, having received the spies in peace, did not perish with those who were disobedient.

[32]What more shall I say? For the time would fail me if I spoke about Gideon, Barak, Shimshon, Yiftah, David, Shmuel, and the prophets. [33]Through faith they conquered kingdoms, did works of righteousness, attained promises, stopped the mouths of lions, [34]extinguished the power of fire, escaped the edge of the sword, were made strong from weakness, became mighty in war, and routed foreign armies. [35]Women received their dead raised to life. Yet others were tortured, not receiving their deliverance, so that they might obtain a better resurrection. [36]Still others underwent testing by mocking and whipping, and by chains and imprisonment beyond that. [37]They were stoned. They were sawn apart. They were tempted. They were slaughtered with the sword. They went around in sheepskins, in goatskins, being destitute, afflicted, mistreated. [38]They wandered in deserts, mountains, caves, and the holes of the earth. The world was not worthy of them.

[39]But all these, their faith testifying of them, did not receive the promise, [40]God having foreseen something better for us, so that they should not receive fulfillment apart from us.

11:19 In the Yom Kippur liturgy, appeal is made to God for the forgiveness of our sins because of "the ashes of Isaac," as though Isaac had been presented as a burnt offering.

11:26 Moses and Messiah, in seeking the redemption of Israel, shared a common disgrace.

11:37 "They were tested/*epristhesan*." Wisdom 11:9 says "They were tested/*epeirasthesan*."

12 [1]Therefore, since we are surrounded by so great a cloud of witnesses [Is. 43:10, Dt. 31:28], let us also lay aside every weight and the abundant sin around us. And let us run with patience the race that is set before us, [2]looking to Yeshua, the author and finisher of the faith. He endured the stake because of the joy that was set before him, despising the shame, and has sat down at the right hand of the throne of God. [3]Indeed, think again about the one who has endured such rejection by sinners against himself, so that you+ do not grow weary, fainting in your+ souls. [Wis. of Sol. 2:18-20] [4]In striving against sin, you+ have not yet resisted unto blood, [5]and you+ have forgotten the exhortation which reasons with you+ as children: "My child, do not take lightly the chastening of the Everpresent Lord, nor faint under His reproof [Job 5:17], [6]because the Everpresent Lord trains those He loves, and disciplines every child whom He receives." [Prov. 3:11,12; Judith 8:27, Ps. 94:12-13]

[7]If you+ endure training, God brings you+ near as children, because what child is there whom his father does not train? [Dt. 8:5-6] [8]But if you+ are without training, of which all have been made partakers, then you+ are illegitimate, and not children. [9]On the one hand then, we have had our physical fathers to train us, and we paid them respect. Shall we not much rather be subject to the Father of spirits, and live? [10]For they indeed trained us for a few days as seemed good to them, but He for our benefit, that we may be partakers of His holiness.

[11]But no training truly seems to come with joy, but with pain. Yet afterward it yields the peaceful fruit of righteousness to those who have been trained by it. [12]Therefore lift up the hands that hang down, and restore the weakened knees. [13]Make straight paths for your+ feet, so that what is lame will not be twisted, but be healed instead.

[14]Pursue peace with all and the sanctification without which no one will see the Lord. [15]Look after each other so that there is no one who falls short of the grace of God; so that no root of bitterness springing up cause trouble for you+ and many become defiled through it; [16]so that there not be any sexually immoral person, or profane person like Esav, who gave up his birthright for one meal. [17]For you+ know that when he afterward desired to inherit the blessing, he was rejected, because, though he sought it diligently with tears, he found no place for repentance. [Gen. 27:38]

[18]For you+ have not come to a mountain that can be touched and that is burning with fire, and to blackness, darkness, and storm. [19]Those who heard the blast of a shofar and the sound of words [Dt. 4:12] begged that nothing more be spoken to them, [20]since they could not endure what was

12:3 "May my soul be silent to those who insult me. May my soul be as the dust to all." (Meditation after the Amidah)

12:4-8 "Chastisements are good because by them three good gifts were given to Israel... And these are they: the Torah, the age to come, and the land of Israel." (Mid. Psalms 94.2)

12:5-7 Literally "sons... son," but given here as "children... child" in the same way that "the sons of Israel" usually refers to the entire people, regardless of gender.

12:7 as in the Textus Receptus

12:20 "The Torah which the Holy One, blessed be He, gave was the light of white fire, and its writing was in dark fire... (Dt. 33:2)" (Mid. Shir HaShirim 5:15)

commanded: "If even a wild animal touches the mountain, it is to be stoned." [Ex. 19:12] [21]And the appearance was so terrifying that Moses said, "I am full of fear and trembling." [Dt. 9:19]

[22]But you[+] have come to Mount Zion, and to the city of the living God, heavenly Yerushala'im, and to tens of thousands of angels gathered in celebration, [23]to the community of the firstborn written down in heaven. You[+] have come to God, the Judge of all, to the spirits of just men who have been made whole, [24]to Yeshua, the mediator of a new covenant, and to the blood of sprinkling that speaks better than that of Hevel. [Gen. 4:9-11]

[25]See that you[+] do not refuse the One who speaks. For if they did not escape when they refused the one who warned on the earth, how much more will we not escape who turn away from the One who warns from heaven. [26]His voice shook the earth then, but now He has promised, saying, "Yet once more I will shake not only the earth, but also the heavens." [Hag. 2:6] [27]This phrase, "Yet once more," indicates the removing of those things that are shaken, which have been made, so that those things which are not shaken remain. [28]Having received an unshakeable kingdom, let us therefore have grace, through which we serve God acceptably with reverence and fear, [29]because our God is a consuming fire. [Ex. 24:17, Dt. 4:24,9:3]

13 [1]Continue in brotherly love. [2]Do not forget to love the foreigners, for in doing so some have shown hospitality to angels without knowing it. [Gen. 18 & 19] [3]Remember those who are imprisoned, as if imprisoned with them, and those who are mistreated, because you[+] also are in the body. [4]Since marriage is completely honorable and the bed is to be undefiled, God will judge adulterers and the sexually immoral.

[5]Do not be covetous. Be content with the things you[+] do have, since He has said, "I will never leave you, nor will I ever forsake you." [Dt. 31:6] [6]Consequently we have courage to say, "The Everpresent Lord is my helper, I will not fear. What can man do to me?" [Ps. 118:6]

[7]Remember your[+] leaders, men who spoke the word of God to you[+], and carefully observe the end result of their way of life. Imitate their faith. [8]Yeshua, the Messiah, is the same yesterday, today, and forever.

[9]Do not be carried away by intricate and strange teachings. For it is good that the heart be established by grace, not by foods which did not benefit those involved. [10]We have an altar from which those who serve in the place of God's presence have no authority to eat. [11]For the animals whose blood is brought by the Kohen Gadol into the holy place as an offering for sin — their bodies are burned outside the camp. [12]Therefore, in order to sanctify the people through his own blood, Yeshua also suffered outside the gate. [13]Let us therefore go out to him, bearing his reproach outside the camp.

[14]For we do not have here an enduring city, but we are seeking the one that is coming. [15]Let us therefore continually offer up through him a sacrifice of praise to God — this is the fruit of lips praising His name. [16]But do not forget to be doing good and sharing, for God is pleased with such sacrifices.

[17]Trust and give way to your[+] leaders, because they watch over your[+] souls as those who must give an account. In this way, they may do it with joy, and not with groaning, for that would be unprofitable for you[+].

[18]Pray for us, for we trust that we have a good conscience, desiring to conduct ourselves well in all things. [19]And I urge you[+] even more to do this so that I may be restored to you[+] sooner.

²⁰Now may the God of peace — who raised from the dead our Lord Yeshua, the great shepherd of the sheep, with the blood of an eternal covenant — ²¹may He uphold you⁺ in every good thing to do His will. May He work in us what is pleasing in His sight, through Yeshua the Messiah, to whom be the glory forever and ever. Amen.

²²Now I encourage you⁺ brethren, bear the word of exhortation, for I have written briefly to you⁺. ²³Be aware that our brother Timothy has been set free. If he comes soon, I will see you⁺ with him. ²⁴Greet all of your⁺ leaders and all those who belong to God. Those from Italy greet you⁺. ²⁵Grace be with you⁺ all.

Sha'ul/Paulos' First Letter to Timothy

1 [1]Paulos, an ambassador of Messiah Yeshua by the command of God our Savior and Messiah Yeshua our hope: [2]to Timothy, my genuine child in faith. Grace, mercy, and peace from God our Father and Yeshua the Messiah our Lord.

[3]As I asked of you when I was going into Makedonia, stay in Ephesus so that you might admonish certain men not to teach a different doctrine [4]nor pay attention to myths and countless genealogies, which bring disputes rather than serving God's household in faith. [5]The goal of the commandment, however, is love out of a pure heart, a good conscience, and genuine faith. [6]Some, having missed the mark, have turned aside from these things to empty talking. [7]They desire to be teachers of the Law, though they understand neither what they say, nor what they insist upon.

[8]Now we know that the Law is good, if a man uses it lawfully. [9]We know this, that law is not enacted for a righteous man, but for the lawless and disobedient, for the ungodly and sinners, for the unholy and profane, for murderers of fathers and murderers of mothers, for all murderers, [10]for the sexually immoral, for homosexuals, for kidnappers, for liars, for perjurers, and for anything else opposed to sound teaching, [11]which is in accord with the good news of the glory of the blessed God, with which I was entrusted.

[12]And I thank Yeshua the Messiah our Lord, the one who has empowered me, because he counted me faithful, appointing me to service, [13]although I was previously a blasphemer, and a violent persecutor. But because I did it in unbelief and ignorance, I obtained mercy. [14]The grace of our Lord abounded exceedingly with faith and love which is in Yeshua the Messiah. [15]The saying is faithful and worthy of all acceptance that Yeshua the Messiah came into the world to save sinners, of whom I am foremost. [16]However, I obtained mercy for this so that Yeshua the Messiah might display all his patient endurance in me first, as a pattern to those who were about to believe in him unto eternal life. [17]Now to the King of the ages, immortal, invisible, to God alone, be honor and glory forever and ever. Amen.

[18]I set this instruction before you, my child Timothy, according to the prophecies previously made concerning you, so that by them you may fight the good fight. [19]Have faith and a good conscience, which some have thrust away and have been shipwrecked concerning the faith. [20]Among these are Hymenaeus and Alexander, whom I delivered to the Accuser so that they might be taught not to slander.

1:2 "Everyone who teaches Torah to the son of his fellowman, Scripture lifts him up as though he had fathered him." (Rashi, commenting on Num. 3:1)

2:1-2 "R. Hanina, the *sagan* of the priests, said, 'Now pray for the peace of the government, because without fear of it, a man would swallow his neighbor alive.'" (Tal. Avot 3:2)

2:9 This is not a strict prohibition of certain types of adornment, but a comparison. I.e., where will you put your effort to make yourself attractive to others — good deeds? or hairstyle, jewelry, and expensive clothes?

2 [1]So I urge first of all that petitions, prayers, intercessions, and giving of thanks be made for all men, [2]for kings and all who are in high position, that we may lead a tranquil and quiet life in all godliness and holiness. [Jer. 29:7] [3]For this is good and acceptable in the sight of God our Savior, [4]who desires all people to be saved and to come to full knowledge of the truth. [5]For there is one God, and one mediator between God and men, the man Messiah Yeshua, [6]who gave himself as a ransom for all — the evidence being given in its own times. [7]And I was appointed a public messenger and an ambassador for it, a teacher of the Gentiles in faith and truth. I am telling the truth, I am not lying.

[8]I desire therefore that the men in every place pray, lifting up holy hands without anger and argument. [9]In the same way, let the women also adorn themselves in modest clothing, with discretion and propriety — not with braided hair, gold, pearls, or expensive clothing, [10]but with good deeds, which is appropriate for women professing godliness.

[11]Let a woman learn peaceably with all compliance. [12]And I do not entrust to a wife either to teach or exercise authority over a husband, but to be peaceable. [13]For Adam was first formed, then Havah. [14]Adam was not deceived, but the woman, being deceived, fell into transgression. [Sir. 25:24] [15]Yet she will be delivered through her child-bearing, if they continue in faith, love, and holiness with self-control. [Gen. 3: 16]

2:9-14 The Greek word *gune* can mean either "woman" or "wife," depending upon context. Likewise, the word *aner* can mean either "man" or "husband," depending upon context. The same is true of the Hebrew *ishah* and *ish*. In translation, it is necessary to choose in terms of context.

Since Sha'ul illustrates his point with the example of Adam and Havah/Eve, and childbearing, "wife" and "husband" seem most appropriate. Even as in 1Co. 7:4, "The *gune* does not have authority over her own body, but the *aner*. Likewise also the *aner* does not have authority over his own body, but the *gune*." Mistranslation would communicate something quite different from what Sha'ul intended.

In a related passage in 1Kefa 3:1, Kefa advises wives to live in such a way that their husbands may be won by their behavior alone, without speaking a word. Likewise, in 1Co. 14:33-35, Sha'ul instructs the married women to ask their husbands at home if they don't understand something, rather than speaking out in the assembly.

Additionally, we know that God does use women to instruct men. For example, "He [Apollos] began to speak boldly in the meetingplace. But when Priskilla and Akila heard him, they took him aside, and explained to him the way of God more accurately." (Acts 18:26) Philippos had 4 daughters who were prophets, i.e. they gave messages from God to the people. (Acts 21:9) This was not considered unusual, as shown by 1Co. 11:5.

Huldah was a female prophet (2K. 22:14), as was Deborah. (Judg. 4:4-9) Deborah was also a judge, authoritatively deciding cases on the basis of Torah, and commanding Barak to go into battle against Sisera.

2:13 "The beginning of Sin is by a woman, and because of her we must all die." (Sirach 25:24)

2:15 "For three sins, women die in childbirth: because they are not observant of menstrual purity, giving the first of their dough, and kindling the [Shabbat] lights." (Tal. Shabbat II.6)

R. Yehudah bar Zevina said that the birth of Moses was painless, because "What was written about Havah [Eve] does not apply to righteous women." (Tal. Sotah 12a)

3 ¹This is a faithful saying: if a man aspires to have oversight, he desires a good work. ²The overseer therefore must be without reproach, the husband of one wife, temperate, sensible, modest, hospitable, able to teach. ³He should not be given to wine, not a violent person but gentle, not quarrelsome, not loving money. ⁴He must be one who leads his own house well, having children in obedience with all propriety. ⁵But if a man has not known how to lead his own house, how will he take care of the community of God? ⁶He must not be one just beginning to grow, otherwise, being puffed up, he may fall into the condemnation of the Enemy. ⁷Moreover he must have a good reputation with those who are outside, to avoid falling into reproach and the snare of the Enemy.

⁸For the same reason, those who serve must be respectful, not speaking one thing and doing another, not addicted to much wine, not greedy for money; ⁹holding the mystery of the faith in a pure conscience. ¹⁰Let them also first be tested, then, if they are blameless, let them serve. ¹¹In the same way, their wives must be respectful, not slanderers, self-controlled, faithful in all things. ¹²Let those who serve be husbands of one wife, leading their children and their own houses well. ¹³For those who have served well obtain a good step forward for themselves, and great boldness in the faith which is in Messiah Yeshua.

¹⁴I write these things to you, hoping to come to you shortly — ¹⁵but in case I am delayed — so that you may know how men ought to behave themselves in the household of God, which is the community of the living God, the pillar and ground of the truth. ¹⁶Without controversy, the mystery of godliness is great: He who was revealed in the flesh was justified in the spirit, seen by angels, proclaimed among the Gentiles, believed on in the world, and received up in glory.

4 ¹But the Spirit says explicitly that in later times some will fall away from the faith, paying attention to seducing spirits and teachings of demons. ²In the hypocrisy of those who speak lies, they are scorched in their own conscience. ³They forbid marriage and command to abstain from foods which God created to be received with thanksgiving by those who are faithful and know the truth. ⁴For all

4:1-5 Sha'ul speaks of false teaching that will arise in later times from deceiving spirits. This false teaching will prohibit marriage and the eating of certain foods.

God gave the Torah to Israel and prohibited specific types of marriage, i.e. the marriage of certain close relatives. We do not know of any one at the time when Paul wrote to Timothy who was teaching that incest was now permissible. That was not the issue. Sha'ul speaks about some who were teaching, or would in the future teach, that marriages which God had permitted were now prohibited.

In like manner, some were teaching the same thing about food. God had specified what things were "foods" to be received with thanksgiving and what things were not. Blood is not a food, though some people eat it. Human beings are not food, though some people eat human flesh.

There were those who were teaching, or would teach, that it was wrong to eat certain foods which God had permitted. They were prohibiting what God had permitted. Sha'ul is not talking about prohibitions which came from God. He is very explicit that he is talking about teaching that was demonically inspired, forbidding marriage which God has permitted, and forbidding foods which God has permitted. The second century Christian sect of the Encratites, and others, forbid marriage and the eating of any meat.

that God created is good, and nothing is to be rejected, if it is received with thanksgiving, ⁵because it is sanctified through the word of God and prayer.

⁶If you instruct the brethren in these things, you will be a good servant of Messiah Yeshua, nourished in the words of the faith and the good teaching which you have followed. ⁷But refuse old wives' tales and what defiles. Instead, exercise yourself to godliness, ⁸for bodily exercise has some value, but godliness has value for all things. It has the promise of the life which is now, and of that which is to come. ⁹This saying is faithful and worthy of all acceptance. ¹⁰For to this end we both labor and contend, because we have set our trust in the living God, who is the Savior of all men, especially of those who believe. ¹¹Command and teach these things.

¹²Let no man despise your youth, but be an example to those who believe — in word, in your way of life, in love, in faith, and in purity. ¹³Until I come, pay attention to the reading, to exhortation, and to teaching. ¹⁴Do not neglect the gift that is in you, which was given to you by prophecy, with the laying on of the hands of the elders. ¹⁵Be diligent in these things. Give yourself wholly to them so that your progress may be revealed to all. ¹⁶Give careful attention to yourself and to your teaching. Continue in these things, because in doing this you will save both yourself and those who hear you.

5 ¹Do not rebuke an older man, but exhort him as a father, the younger men as brothers, ²the elder women as mothers, the younger as sisters in all purity. ³Honor widows who are truly widows. ⁴But if any widow has children or grandchildren, let them learn first to be godly towards their own family, and to repay their parents, for this is acceptable in the sight of God. ⁵Now the one who is truly a widow and left alone has her hope set on God, and continues in petitions and prayers night and day. ⁶But the one who gives herself to pleasure is dead while she lives. ⁷Command these things also, so that they may be without reproach. ⁸But if anyone does not provide for his own, and especially his own household, he has denied the faith, and is worse than an unbeliever.

⁹Let a widow be enrolled who is not less than sixty years old, having been the wife of one man, ¹⁰being approved by good deeds — if she has brought up children, if she has been hospitable to strangers, if she has washed the feet of those who belong to God, if she has given relief to the afflicted, and if she has diligently attended to every good work.

¹¹But refuse younger widows, because when they live indulgently, contrary to the Messiah, they desire to marry — ¹²incurring condemnation, because they have cast off their primary faith. ¹³Besides, they also learn to be idle, going about from house to house — not only idle, but also gossips and busybodies, saying things which they should not. ¹⁴I counsel therefore that the younger widows marry, bear children, rule their household, and give no occasion to the Accuser for reproach. ¹⁵For already some have turned aside after the Accuser. ¹⁶If any believer has widows, let that one provide relief for them, and do not let the community be burdened, so that it might provide relief to those who are truly widows.

¹⁷Let the elders who lead well be counted worthy of double honor, especially those who labor in the word and in teaching. ¹⁸For the Scripture says, "You are not to muzzle the ox when it treads out the grain." [Dt. 25:4] And, "The laborer is worthy of his wages." [Lev. 19:13]

5:9-16 The discussion is about which widows the community should commit itself to financially support, and what is then expected of these widows.

[19]Do not receive an accusation against an elder, except at the word of two or three witnesses. [20]Those who sin, rebuke in the sight of all, so that the rest also may fear. [21]I charge you in the sight of God, Messiah Yeshua, and the chosen angels, that you observe these things without prejudice, doing nothing in partiality. [22]Lay hands hastily on no one; do not be a participant in other men's sins. Keep yourself pure. [23]No longer drink water only, but use a little wine for the sake of your stomach and your frequent infirmities.

[24]Some men's sins are evident, preceding them to judgment, and some also follow after. [25]In the same way also there are good deeds that are obvious, and those that are otherwise cannot be hidden.

[1]Let as many as are servants under the yoke consider their own masters worthy of all honor, so that the Name of God and the teaching not be blasphemed. [2]Those who have believing masters, let them not disdain them because they are brothers, but let them serve them all the more, because those who are being helped by the good work are beloved believers. Teach and exhort these things.

[3]If anyone teaches a different doctrine, and does not yield to sound words — those of our Lord Yeshua the Messiah — and godly teaching, [4]he is conceited, knowing nothing, but obsessed with controversies, disputes, and trivial arguments. From these come envy, strife, slander, evil suspicions, and [5]constant attacks of men corrupted in mind and destitute of the truth, who suppose that godliness is a means of gain.

[6]But godliness with contentment is of great profit, [7]because we brought nothing into the world, and it is obvious that we are not able to carry anything out either. [8]But having food and clothing, we will be content with that. [9]But those who are determined to be rich fall into temptation, a snare, and many foolish and harmful desires, which sink men in ruin and destruction. [10]For the love of money is a root of every evil. Striving after it, some have been led astray from the faith in their greed, and have pierced themselves through with many sorrows.

[11]But you, man of God, flee these things, and pursue justice, godliness, faith, love, patience, and gentleness. [Is. 1:17; Dt. 16:20; 27:19] [12]Fight the good fight of faith. Lay hold of the eternal life to which you were called, and to which you testified in the sight of many witnesses by acknowledgment of what is good. [13]I charge you before God, who gives life to all things, and before Messiah Yeshua, who testified before Pontius Pilate by acknowledgment of what is good, [14]that you keep the commandment without spot, blameless, until the appearing of our Lord Yeshua the Messiah; which, [15]in its own times, will show who is the blessed and only Ruler, the King of those who reign as kings, and Lord of those who rule as lords. [16]He alone has immortality, dwelling in unapproachable light. No man has seen nor can see Him. To Him be honor and eternal power. Amen.

5:24 "Everyone who does one good deed in this age, it goes before him and walks in front of him in the age to come, as it is said, 'Your righteousness will go before you, and the glory of the Everpresent Lord will be your rearguard.' [Is. 58:8] And everyone who transgresses one transgression, it takes hold of him and leads him to the Day of Judgment, as it is said, 'They take hold of him in the paths of their way.' [Job 6:18] " (Tal. Avodah Zara 5a)

6:15 In the traditional Alenu prayer, we say, "we bow the knee and worship and give thanks before the King who reigns over kings, the Holy One, blessed be He."

[17]Charge those who are rich in this present world that they neither be haughty nor have their hope set on the uncertainty of riches, but on God, who richly gives us all things to enjoy. [18]Exhort them to do good, that they be rich in good deeds, ready to distribute, willing to share; [19]laying up in store for themselves a good foundation for the future, so that they may lay hold of what is truly life.

[20]Timothy, guard what was committed to you, turning away from the empty chatter and oppositions of what is falsely called knowledge. [21]Professing this, some have erred concerning the faith. Grace be with you[+].

Sha'ul/Paulos' Second Letter to Timothy

1 [1]Paulos, an ambassador of Yeshua the Messiah through the will of God, according to the promise of the life which is in Messiah Yeshua: [2]to Timothy, my beloved child. Grace, mercy, and peace from God the Father and Yeshua the Messiah, our Lord.

[3]I am thankful to God as I unceasingly remember you in my petitions night and day. I serve Him as my fathers did, with a pure conscience. [4]I long to see you, remembering your tears, that I may be filled with joy. [5]I am reminded of the unpretentious faith that is in you, which lived first in your grandmother Lois, then your mother Eunice, and, I am persuaded, in you also.

[6]For this cause, I remind you to kindle the gift of God which is in you through the laying on of my hands. [7]For God did not give us a spirit of fear, but of power, love, and a disciplined mind. [Prov. 25:28] [8]Therefore do not be ashamed of the testimony of our Lord, nor of me his prisoner, but endure hardship for the good news by the power of God. [9]He saved us and called us with a holy calling, not according to our deeds, but according to His own purpose and grace. This was given to us in Messiah Yeshua before the beginning of the age, [10]but has now been revealed by the appearing of our Savior, Yeshua the Messiah. He nullified the power of death, and brought life and immortality to light through the good news.

[11]I was appointed for this as a public messenger, an ambassador, and a teacher of the Gentiles. [12]For this cause I also suffer these things, but I am not ashamed, because I know the one whom I have believed, and I am persuaded that he is able to guard what I have committed to him for that day.

[13]In faith and love which is in Yeshua the Messiah, hold to the pattern of sound words which you have heard from me. [14]Through the Ruakh Kodesh who dwells in us, guard that good thing which was committed to you.

[15]You know this, that all who are in the province of Asia, Phygelus and Hermogenes among them, turned away from me. [16]May the Lord grant mercy to the house of Onesiphorus, for he often refreshed me, and was not ashamed of my chains. [17]On the contrary, when he was in Rome, he sought me very diligently, and found me. [18]May the Lord grant to him to find mercy from the Lord in that day. And you know very well in how many things he served at Ephesus.

2 [1]So you my child, be strengthened in the grace that is in Messiah Yeshua. [2]The things which you have heard from me among many witnesses, present them to faithful men who are competent and able to teach others. [3]Endure hardship with me as a good soldier of Yeshua the Messiah. [4]In order to please the one who enrolled him as a soldier, no one serving as a soldier entangles himself in the affairs of life. [5]Likewise, if anyone competes in athletics, he is not crowned unless he has competed by the rules. [6]The farmers who labor must be the first to get a share of the crops. [7]Consider what I say, and may the Lord give you understanding in all things.

[8]Remember Yeshua the Messiah, risen from the dead, of the seed of David, in accordance with my good news. [9]I suffer hardship in it to the point of chains as a criminal — but God's word is not chained. [10]Therefore I endure all things for the sake of those chosen, so that they also may obtain the salvation which is in Messiah Yeshua with eternal glory. [11]This saying is faithful, for if we died with him, we will also live with him. [12]If we endure, we will also reign with him. If we deny him,

he also will deny us. ¹³If we are faithless, he remains faithful, because he cannot deny himself.

¹⁴Remind them of these things, charging them in the sight of God not to argue about words, to the subverting of those who hear, but to no profit. ¹⁵Give diligence to present yourself approved by God, a worker who does not need to be ashamed, using the Word of Truth correctly. ¹⁶But stay away from those who profanely babble, because they will proceed further in ungodliness, ¹⁷and their word will consume like gangrene. Such are Hymenaeus and Philetus, ¹⁸men who have erred concerning the truth. They say that the resurrection is already past, and overthrow the faith of some. ¹⁹Nevertheless, God's firm foundation stands, having this seal: "The Everpresent Lord knows those who are His." And, "Let every one who names the Name of the Everpresent Lord depart from wrong-doing."

²⁰Now in a great house there are not only objects of gold and of silver, but also of wood and of clay. Some are for honor, and some for dishonor. ²¹So if anyone cleanses himself from these things, he will be an object for honor, sanctified, and suitable for the master's use, prepared for every good work.

²²Flee from youthful desires [Gen. 39:10-13], but pursue justice, faith, love, and peace with those who call on the Lord out of a pure heart. [Dt. 16:20] ²³But refuse foolish and ignorant disputes, knowing that they generate strife. ²⁴The Lord's servant must not quarrel, but be gentle towards all, able to teach, patient, ²⁵correcting in gentleness those who oppose him. Perhaps God may give them repentance leading to a full knowledge of the truth, ²⁶and they may recover themselves out of the snare of the Enemy, having been taken captive by him for his will.

3 ¹But know this, that dangerous times will come in the last days. ²For men will be lovers of self, lovers of money, boastful, arrogant, blasphemers, disobedient to parents, ungrateful, unholy. ³They will be without natural affection, unforgiving, slanderers, without self-control. They will be savage, opposed to what is good, ⁴traitors, obstinate, conceited, lovers of pleasure rather than lovers of God; ⁵holding a form of godliness, but having denied the power of it.

Turn away from these. ⁶For from these are those who creep into houses and make captives of gullible women loaded down with sins, led away by various desires, ⁷always learning and never able to come to the knowledge of the truth. ⁸Even as Jannes and Jambres opposed Moses, so these also oppose the truth — men corrupted in mind, reprobate concerning the faith. ⁹But they will not advance further, for their folly will be evident to all men, as that of these [Jannes and Jambres] also came to be.

¹⁰But you have closely followed my teaching, conduct, purpose, faith, patient endurance, love, steadfastness, ¹¹the persecutions and the sufferings — such as what happened to me at Antioch, Iconium, and Lystra. I endured those persecutions, and the Lord delivered me out of them all. ¹²Yes, and all who desire to live godly in Messiah Yeshua will suffer persecution. ¹³But evil men and impostors will grow worse and worse, deceiving and being deceived.

¹⁴But you, remain in the things which you have learned and of which you have been assured, knowing from whom you have learned them. ¹⁵From infancy, you have known the holy writings

2:24 "That they should not say, 'How hard the teacher is, and the disciple is obstinate [and arrogant].'" (Tal. Sotah 13b) In his commentary on Dt. 3:26, Rashi adds "and arrogant".

3:8 Pharaoh's magicians are known by these names in some Jewish literature and Greek texts. cf. The Jewish Encyclopedia article, "Jannes and Jambres". In Tal. Menachot 85a, they are called "Yoḥana and Mamre".

which are able to make you wise for salvation through faith, which is in Messiah Yeshua. [16]Every scripture is inspired by God and profitable for teaching, reproof, correction, and the discipline which is in righteousness, [17]so that the person who belongs to God may be complete, thoroughly equipped for every good work.

[1]Before God and Yeshua the Messiah, who will judge the living and the dead when he appears with his kingdom [Is. 11:1-4], I earnestly entreat you to [2]proclaim the word, be ready in season and out of season. Reprove, rebuke, and exhort with all patient endurance and teaching. [3]For there will be a time when they will not listen to sound teaching, but, having itching ears, they will heap up for themselves teachers after their own desires, [4]and will turn their ears away from the truth, and turn aside to fables. [5]But you, be sober in all things, endure hardship, do the work of a messenger of the good news, and fulfill your responsibility.

[6]For I am already being offered, and the time of my release has come. [7]I have fought the good fight. I have finished the course. I have kept the faith. [8]From now on, there is stored up for me the crown of righteousness which the Lord, the righteous judge, will give to me in that day; and not to me only, but also to all those who have loved his appearing.

[9]Be diligent to come to me soon, [10]because Demas, having loved this present age, has forsaken me and gone to Thessalonika, Crescens to Galatia, and Titus to Dalmatia. [11]Only Luke is with me. Take Mark, and bring him with you, for he is useful to me for service. [12]Now I sent Tychicus to Ephesus. [13]When you come, bring the cloak that I left at Troas with Karpus and the books, especially the parchments. [14]Alexander the coppersmith did much evil to me. The Lord will repay him according to his deeds. [15]You must also beware of him, because he greatly opposed our words.

[16]At my first defense, no one came to help me, but all left me. May it not be held against them. [17]But the Lord stood by me and strengthened me, so that the message might be fully proclaimed through me, and that all the Gentiles might hear. And I was delivered out of the mouth of the lion. [18]The Lord will deliver me from every evil work, and will preserve me for his heavenly kingdom. To him be the glory forever and ever. Amen.

[19]Greet Priska and Akila, and the house of Onesiphorus. [20]Erastus remained at Corinth, but I left Trophimus sick at Miletus. [21]Be diligent to come before winter. Eubulus salutes you, as do Pudens, Linus, Claudia, and all the brethren. [22]The Lord be with your spirit. Grace be with you[+].

3:14-17 "An intelligent man will trust in the Law; and the Law is faithful to him, making questions clear." (Sirach 33:3) "R. Simeon b. Azzai says, 'Scripture comes only to admonish and teach you how strong you must be in the commandments.'" (Rashi, Dt. 12:23)

Spinoza claimed that there is no god or wisdom beyond Man. "Thus to suppose that knowledge of natural and spiritual phenomena can be gained from the prophetic books, is an utter mistake..." <u>A Theologico-Political Treatise</u>, Part I, Ch. 2:6, trans. by R.H.M. Elwes, P. 27.

4:3 "Why do you tickle my ears? Why do you entertain me?" (Seneca, <u>Epistulae Morales</u> 75)

4:13 "parchments" refers to vellum, which is made from prepared animal skins.

Sha'ul/Paulos' Letter to Titus

1 [1]Paulos, a servant of God and an ambassador of Yeshua the Messiah. In accordance with the faith of God's chosen and the knowledge of the truth, which is according to godliness. [2]In hope of eternal life, which God, who cannot lie, promised before the ages of time. [3]Yet He revealed His word in its own time in the message with which I was entrusted by the command of God our Savior. [4]To Titus, my genuine child according to a common faith. Grace and peace from God the Father and the Lord Yeshua the Messiah, our Savior.

[5]I left you in Crete for this reason, that you would set in order the things that were lacking, and appoint elders in every city as I directed you: [6]if anyone is blameless, the husband of one wife, having children who believe and are not accused of loose or unruly behavior. [7]For the overseer must be blameless as God's manager, not self-willed, not easily angered, not given to wine, not violent nor greedy for dishonest gain. [8]He must be given instead to hospitality, a lover of what is good, discrete, just, holy, and capable. [9]He must hold to the faithful message of the teaching, so that he may be able both to encourage with sound teaching, and to rebuke those who contradict.

[10]For there are many who are unruly, vain talkers and deceivers, especially some from the circumcision. [11]Their mouths should be silenced: men who overthrow whole houses, teaching things which they should not, for the sake of dishonest gain. [12]One of them, a prophet of their own, said, "Cretans are always liars, evil beasts, and lazy gluttons."

[13]This evidence is true. For this cause, reprove them sharply, so that they may be sound in the faith, [14]not paying attention to Jewish fables and commandments of men, turning away from the truth. [15]All things are pure to those who are pure. To those who are defiled and unbelieving, however, nothing is pure, but both their mind and their conscience are defiled. [16]By words they claim to know God, but by their deeds they deny him, being abominable, disobedient, and unfit for any good work.

2 [1]But you, speak the things which are suitable to sound teaching: [2]that older men should be self-controlled, sensible, sober-minded, sound in faith, love, and patience. [3]Older women likewise should act appropriately in holy behavior, not slanderers nor enslaved to much wine, teachers of what is good. [4]This is so that they may train the young women to love their husbands and their children, [5]to be sober-minded, undefiled, building a home, kind, being in submission to their own husbands, so that God's word is not blasphemed.

[6]Exhort the younger men likewise to be self-controlled. [7]Present yourself in all things as a pattern of good deeds. In your teaching show integrity, seriousness, [8]and soundness of speech that cannot be condemned, so that the one who opposes you may be ashamed, having no evil thing to say about you. [9]Exhort servants to be in submission to their own masters, and to be well-pleasing in all things: not talking back, [10]not stealing, but showing all good faithfulness, so that they may be well-behaved in all things of the teaching of God our Savior.

1:13 "This testimony is true" is simply an affirmation that one of the vain deceivers did say this about Cretans.

[11]For the grace of God which brings salvation has appeared to all men, [12]instructing us that, having denied ungodliness and worldly desires, we should live soberly, righteously, and godly in this present age; [13]looking for the blessed hope and appearing of the glory of the great God and of our Savior, Yeshua the Messiah. [14]He gave himself for us that he might redeem us from all actions contrary to the Law, and purify for himself a people for his own possession, zealous for good deeds. [15]Speak these things, exhort, and reprove with all authority. Let no man despise you.

3 [1]Remind them to be subject to rulers and authorities, to be obedient, to be ready for every good work, [2]to malign no one, to be uncontentious, to be gentle, showing all humility toward all men. [3]For we also were once foolish, disobedient, deceived, serving various desires and pleasures, living in malice and envy, hateful, and hating one another. [4]But when the kindness of God our Savior and His love toward humanity appeared, [5]He saved us, not by works which we did in righteousness, but according to His mercy, through the washing of regeneration and renewing by the Ruakh Kodesh. [6]He poured the Spirit out upon us richly, through Yeshua the Messiah our Savior, [7]so that, having been declared righteous by His grace, we might be made heirs according to the hope of eternal life.

[8]This saying is faithful, and I desire that you strongly affirm these things so that those who have believed God may be conscientious to be eager for good deeds. These things are good and profitable to men. [9]But stay away from foolish inquiries, genealogies, conflicts and disputes about law, because they are unprofitable and vain. [10]Avoid a divisive man after a first and second warning, [11]knowing that such a one distorts and sins, being self-condemned.

[12]When I send Artemas to you, or Tychicus, be diligent to come to me to Nicopolis, for I have determined to winter there. [13]Send Zenas the lawyer and Apollos on their journey speedily, so that nothing may be lacking for them. [14]Let our people also learn to be eager for good deeds for pressing needs, so that they are not unfruitful.

[15]All who are with me greet you. Greet those who love us in faith. Grace be with you[+] all.

3:5 n *Avinu Malkenu* in the Yom Kippur liturgy we pray, "Our Father, our King, be gracious to us and answer us. because we have no deeds."

Sha'ul/Paulos' Letter to Philemon

1 [1]Paulos, a prisoner of Messiah Yeshua, and Timothy our brother: to Philemon, our beloved fellow worker, [2]to the beloved Apphia, to Archippus, our fellow soldier, and to the community in your house. [3]Grace to you[+] and peace from God our Father and the Lord Yeshua the Messiah.

[4]I thank my God always, making mention of you in my prayers. [5]I hear of your love and faith which you have toward the Lord Yeshua, and toward all those who belong to God. [6]I pray that the fellowship of your faith may become active in the knowledge of every good thing which is in you in Messiah Yeshua. [7]For we have much joy and comfort in your love, because the hearts of those who belong to God have been refreshed through you, brother.

[8]Therefore, though I have much boldness in Messiah to order you to do what is appropriate, [9]yet for love's sake I rather appeal, being such a one as Paulos the aged, and now also a prisoner of Yeshua the Messiah. [10]I entreat you for my child Onesimus, whose father I have become in my chains. [11]He once was useless to you, but now is useful to you and to me. [12]I am sending him back to you — he that is my own heart. [13]I desired to keep him with me in your place, so that he might serve me in my chains for the good news, [14]but I did not wish to do anything without your consent, in order that your goodness would not be as of necessity, but of your willingness. [15]For perhaps he was therefore separated from you for a while so that you might possess him forever, [16]no longer as a slave, but more than a slave, a beloved brother, especially to me, but how much more rather to you, both in the flesh and in the Lord.

[17]If then you consider me a companion, receive him as you would receive me. [18]Yet if he has wronged you at all, or owes you anything, put this to my account. [19]I, Paulos, have written this

From prison, Paul sent Onesimus back to his master, **Philemon**, as a beloved son and brother, rather than as a slave. Through contact with Paul, Onesimus had put his faith in the Lord. Perhaps Onesimus had previously given bad service (v. 11) to Philemon or had stolen something from him (v. 18). In any case, he voluntarily chooses to return, despite whatever punishment it may bring. Paul exhorts Philemon to receive him as a brother, and show him the love due to one who is Paul's son (vv. 9-10). Paul asks this on the basis of Onesimus' transformation (vv. 11,13), and on the basis of Philemon's regard for and debt to Paul (vv. 17-20). Paul is confident that Philemon will do even more than he asks of him.

Messiah comes to set the captive free, whether in life or in death. (Is. 61:1/Lk. 4:18) Even if a person is enslaved in this age, that will change. In his agony, Job spoke of the deliverance of the grave. "Captives also enjoy their ease; they no longer hear the slave driver's shout. The small and the great are there, and the slave is freed from his master." (Job 3:18-19)

The goal is freedom, but there are lessons to learn from slavery. "For the one who was called in the Lord while a bondservant is a freedman of the Lord. Likewise the one who was called while free is a bondservant of Messiah." (1Co. 7:22) Sha'ul himself was a prisoner at the time he wrote this letter (cf. v. 23) — physically a prisoner, but always free in the Lord. On slavery, see "Regulating the Actions of Hard Hearts" in the ADDITIONAL NOTES.

with my own hand. I will repay it, not to mention to you that you owe to me even your own self besides. [20]Yes brother, let me have joy from you in the Lord. Refresh my heart in the Lord. [21]I write to you having confidence in your obedience, knowing that you will do even beyond what I say.

[22]Also, prepare a guest room for me, for I hope that through your[+] prayers I will be restored to you[+].

[23]Epaphras, my fellow prisoner in Messiah Yeshua, greets you, [24]as do Mark, Aristarchus, Demas, and Luke, my fellow workers. [25]The grace of the Lord Yeshua the Messiah be with your[+] spirit.

Hazon, the Revelation to Yohanan

1 [1]The revelation of Yeshua the Messiah, which God gave him to show to his servants the things which must happen soon. He sent and made it known by his angel to his servant Yohanan, [2]who is bearing witness to the Word of God, the testimony of Yeshua the Messiah, and everything he saw. [3]There is good for the one who reads and those who hear the words of the prophecy and observe the things that are written in it, for the time is near.

[4]Yohanan, to the seven communities that are in the province of Asia. Grace to you[+] and peace from the One who is and who was and who is to come; and from the seven Spirits [Is. 11:2] who are before His throne; [5]and from Yeshua the Messiah, the faithful witness, the firstborn from the dead, and the ruler of the kings of the earth. To him who loves us and freed us from our sins by his blood — [6]and he made us to be a kingdom, priests to his God and Father — to him be the glory and the dominion forever and ever. Amen.

[7]Look, he is coming with the clouds [Dan. 7:13], and every eye will see him, including those who pierced him. All the tribes of the land will mourn over him. [Zech. 12:10] Even so, amen. [8]"I am the Alef and the Tav," says God, the Everpresent, "who is and who was, and who is to come, the Sovereign over all."

[9]I, Yohanan — both your[+] brother and companion in the affliction, kingdom, and perseverance of Messiah Yeshua — I was on the island that is called Patmos for the sake of the Word of God and the testimony of Yeshua the Messiah. [10]In the Spirit, I was in the day of the Everpresent Lord, and I heard behind me a loud voice like a shofar. [11]It said, "What you see, write in a scroll and send

---

For those who live in a world of freedom of thought and speech, it is difficult to imagine what it is like to live in a repressive society where neither is permitted. In such societies, those who choose not to submit to the totality of enslavement by the State communicate illegally with each other. They secretly publish and distribute their thoughts, their hope, and their faith. They learn to communicate indirectly by allusion and by reading between the lines.

Yohanan lived under the oppression of the Roman Empire. He had been exiled to Patmos because he had been consistently expressing his faith and living according to it. There Yeshua gave to him visions of the destruction of all the ungodly kingdoms of this world, as well as visions of the restoration of Yerushala'im and the establishment of the Kingdom of God upon the earth. That was an encouraging message for the disciples, but a very dangerous message to carry throughout the Roman Empire.

We would prefer that this Hazon were easier to understand. By design, it is not. Nevertheless, the destruction, judgment, and restoration presented in it are quite clear, even if the details are not.

1:8 Yohanan recorded all this to send to the seven believing communities in Asia, which were Greek speaking. The Greek text, has "the Alpha and the Omega," which are the first and last letters of the Greek alphabet. The Aramaic has Alef and Tav, which are the first and last letters of the Hebrew alphabet. Also in 22:13. It seems likely that Yeshua would have spoken to Yohanan in Hebrew (or Jewish Aramaic), their native language.

1:9 These three go together: the affliction, the perseverance, and the kingdom.

to the seven communities — to Ephesus, Smyrna, Pergamum, Thyatira, Sardis, Philadelphia, and to Laodikea."

[12]I turned to see the voice that spoke with me. Having turned, I saw seven golden menorot. [13]And among the menorot was one like a son of Adam, clothed with a robe reaching down to his feet, and with a golden sash around his chest. [14]His head and his hair were white as white wool, like snow. His eyes were like a flame of fire. [15]His feet were like fine bronze, as if it had been refined in a furnace. His voice was like the voice of many waters. [16]He had seven stars in his right hand. Out of his mouth proceeded a sharp two-edged sword. [Is. 49:2] His face was like the sun shining at its brightest. [17]When I saw him, I fell at his feet like a dead man.

He laid his right hand on me, saying, "Do not be afraid. I am the first and the last [Dan. 10:5-10], [18]and the living one. I was dead, and yet see, I am alive forevermore. I have the keys of Death and of Sheol. [19]Write therefore the things which you have seen, and the things which are, and the things which will happen hereafter. [20]This is the mystery of the seven stars which you saw in my right hand and the seven golden menorot: the seven stars are the angels of the seven communities. The seven menorot are the seven communities.

2 [1]"Write to the angel of the community in Ephesus. The one who holds the seven stars in his right hand, who walks in the midst of the seven golden menorot, says these things: [2]I know your deeds, your labor, and your perseverance. I know that you cannot tolerate evil men, and have tested those who call themselves ambassadors yet they are not, and have found them false. [3]You have perseverance and have endured for the sake of my name, and have not grown weary. [4]But I have this against you, that you have left your first love. [5]Remember therefore from where you have fallen. Change your ways, and do the first deeds. But if you do not, I am coming to you swiftly, and will remove your menorah out of its place, unless you change your ways. [6]Nevertheless you have this: that you hate the deeds of the Nikolaitans, which I also hate. [7]The one who has an ear, let him hear what the Spirit says to the communities. To the one who overcomes I will give to eat of the tree of life, which is in the middle of the Garden of my God.'

[8]"Write to the angel of the community in Smyrna. The first and the last, who was dead and has come to life, says these things: [9]I know your affliction, and poverty, but you are rich. And I know the blasphemy of those who declare themselves to be Jews yet they are not, but they are an assembly of the Accuser. [10]Do not fear any of the things which you are about to suffer. Be aware that the Enemy is about to throw some of you[+] into prison so that you[+] may be tested, and you[+] will be afflicted for ten days. Be faithful unto death, and I will give you the crown of life. [11]The one who has an ear, let

---

1:12 *menorot* is the plural of menorah

1:18 "There are three keys in the hands of the Holy One, blessed be He, that He did not deliver into the hands of an ambassador. And these are they: the key of rain, the key of having life, and the key of the resurrection of the dead." (Tal. Ta'anit 2a) Sheol is the realm of the dead.

2:2,9,20 Yeshua addresses the pretension of "those who call themselves ambassadors but are not," (2:2) "those who declare themselves to be Jews, but they are not," (2:9, 3:9) and the woman "who calls herself a prophetess," but is not. (2:20)

2:11 "'Let Reuben live' in this age, 'and not die' in the age to come.'" (Rashi on Dt. 33:6)

him hear what the Spirit says to the communities. The one who overcomes will not be harmed by the second death.'

[12]"Write to the angel of the community in Pergamum. He who has the sharp two-edged sword says these things: [13]'I know your deeds and where you dwell — where the Accuser's throne is. You hold firmly to my name, and did not deny my faith in the days of Antipas my witness, my faithful one, who was killed among you[+], where the Accuser dwells. [14]But I have a few things against you, because you have some there who hold the teaching of Bala'am, who taught Balak to throw a stumbling-block before the children of Israel: to eat things sacrificed to idols, and to commit sexual immorality. [15]So you also have some who likewise hold to the teaching of the Nikolaitans. [16]Repent therefore, or else I am coming to you quickly, and I will make war against them with the sword of my mouth. [17]The one who has an ear, let him hear what the Spirit says to the communities. To the one who overcomes, I will give to him of the hidden manna, and I will give him a small white stone, and a new name written on the small stone, which no one knows but the one who receives it.'

[18]"Write to the angel of the community in Thyatira. The Son of God, who has his eyes like a flame of fire, and his feet are like fine bronze, says these things: [19]'I know your deeds, your love, faith, service, patient endurance, and that your last deeds are more than the first. [20]But I have this against you, that you tolerate the woman Izevel, who declares herself a prophetess. She teaches and seduces my servants to commit sexual immorality, and to eat things sacrificed to idols. [21]I gave her time to change her ways, but she refuses to change her ways of sexual immorality. [22]Watch, I will throw her into a bed, and those who commit adultery with her into great trouble, unless they turn away from her deeds. [23]I will kill her children with Death, and all the communities will know that I am the one who searches hearts and motives. I will give to each one of you[+] according to your[+] deeds. [24]But I say to you[+], to the rest who are in Thyatira, as many as do not have this teaching, who do not know what some call 'the deep things of the Accuser,' to you[+] I say, I am not putting any other burden on you[+]. [25]Nevertheless, hold firmly what you[+] have, until I come. [26-27]The one who overcomes, and the one who keeps my works to the end, I will give to him authority over the nations, as I also have received of my Father. He will rule them with a rod of iron, shattering them like clay pots. [Ps. 2:8] [28]And I will give him the morning star. [29]The one who has an ear, let him hear what the Spirit says to the communities.'

3 [1]"And write to the angel of the community in Sardis. He who has the seven Spirits of God [Is. 11:2] and the seven stars says these things: 'I know your deeds, that you have a reputation of being alive, but you are dead. [2]Be vigilant and strengthen the things that remain, which are about to die, for I have not found your deeds complete before my God. [3]Remember therefore how you have received and heard. Be on guard, and change your ways. So if you will not watch, I will come upon you as a thief, and you will not know what hour I will come upon you. [4]Nevertheless you have a few names in Sardis who did not defile their garments. They will walk with me in white, for they are worthy. [5]The one who overcomes will be arrayed in this way, in white garments. I will never blot his

---

3:5 Yeshua speaks of those whose names will not be blotted out of the Scroll of Life, implying that there are those whose names will be blotted out.

name out of the Scroll of Life, and I will confess his name before my Father, and before His angels. [6]The one who has an ear, let him hear what the Spirit says to the communities.'

[7]"Write to the angel of the community in Philadelphia. He who is holy, he who is true, he who has the key of David [Is. 22:22], he who opens and no one can shut, and who shuts and no one opens, says these things: [8]'I know your deeds. Look, I have set before you an opened door which no one can shut, because you have a little power, and have kept my word, and did not deny my name. [9]Look, I will make those of the assembly of the Accuser — those who say they are Jews yet they are not, but they lie — watch, I will make them to come and bow down before your feet and recognize that I have loved you. [Is. 49:23; Jer. 31:3] [10]Because you have kept my command to endure, I also will keep you out of the hour of testing, which is to come on the whole world, to test those who dwell on the earth. [11]I am coming quickly! Hold firmly what you have, so that no one takes your crown. [12]The one who overcomes, I will make him a pillar in the Temple of my God, and he will never again depart. I will write on him the Name of my God, and the name of the city of my God — the new Yerushala'im, which comes down out of heaven from my God — and my own new name. [13]The one who has an ear, let him hear what the Spirit says to the communities.'

[14]"Write to the angel of the community in Laodikea: the Amen, the Faithful and True Witness, the origin of God's creation, says these things: [15]'I know your deeds, that you are neither cold nor hot. I wish you were cold or hot. [16]So because you are lukewarm, and neither hot nor cold, I am about to spit you out of my mouth. [17]You say, "I am rich, and have gotten riches, and have need of nothing." And you do not know that you are one who is wretched, miserable, poor, blind, and naked. Because of this, [18]I counsel you to buy from me gold refined by fire so that you may become rich, and white garments so that you may clothe yourself and the shame of your nakedness may not be revealed, and eye salve to anoint your eyes so that you may see. [19]As many as I love, I rebuke and discipline. Be zealous therefore, and change your ways. [20]Look, I stand at the door and knock. If anyone hears my voice and opens the door, then I will come in to him, and will feast with him, and he with me. [21]The one who overcomes, I will give to him to sit down with me on my throne, as I also overcame and sat down with my Father on His throne. [22]The one who has an ear, let him hear what the Spirit says to the communities.'"

4 [1]After these things I looked and saw a door opened in heaven. And the first voice which I heard, like a shofar, was speaking with me, saying, "Come up here, and I will show you the things which must happen after this."

[2]Immediately I was in the Spirit. There was a throne set in heaven, and one sitting on the throne! [3]And the appearance of the one sitting was like a jasper stone and a sardius. There was a rainbow around the throne, like an emerald in appearance. [4]Around the throne were twenty-four thrones. On the thrones twenty-four elders were sitting, dressed in white garments, and they had golden crowns on their heads. [5]And from the throne go forth flashes of lightning, thunderings, and sounds. There

3:9 Yeshua repeats God's promise made to Israel in Is. 49:23 and Jer. 31:3. See note to 2:2,9,20.

3:12 "Rabbah said in the name of R. Yoḥanan: 'The righteous will in time to come be called by the Name of the Holy One, blessed be He, because it is said: *Every one who is called by My Name, and I created him for My glory. I have formed him, yes, I have made him.'* [Is. 43:7]" (Tal. Baba Bathra 75b)

were seven lamps of fire burning before his throne, which are the seven Spirits of God. [6]In front of the throne was something like a sea of glass, similar to crystal.

To the side of the throne and around the throne were four living creatures full of eyes in front and in back. [7]The first creature was like a lion, and the second creature like a calf. The third creature had a face like a man, and the fourth was like a flying eagle. [8]The four living creatures, each one of them having six wings, are full of eyes around and within. Day and night, they do not cease to say, "Holy, holy, holy is God, the Everpresent, the Sovereign over all, who was and who is and who is to come!" [Is. 6:1-4]

[9]When the living creatures give glory, honor, and thanks to Him who sits on the throne, to Him who lives forever and ever, [10]the twenty-four elders will fall down before Him who sits on the throne, and will bow down to Him who lives forever and ever. And they will throw their crowns before the throne, saying, [11]"You are worthy, our Lord and God, the Holy One, to receive the glory, the honor, and the power, for You created all things, and through Your will they were created and exist!"

[5][1]In the right hand of the One who sat on the throne, I saw a scroll written inside and on the back, sealed shut with seven seals. [2]I saw a mighty angel proclaiming with a loud voice, "Who is worthy to open the scroll, and to undo its seals?" [3]No one in heaven above, nor on the earth, nor under the earth, was able to open the scroll or look in it. [4]And I continued to weep, because no one was found worthy to open the scroll or look in it. [5]One of the elders said to me, "Do not weep. Look, the Lion which is from the tribe of Judah, the Root of David, has overcome so as to open the scroll and its seven seals."

[6]And I saw in the midst of the throne and of the four living creatures, and in the midst of the elders, a Lamb situated as though it had been slaughtered. It had seven horns and seven eyes, which are the seven Spirits of God, sent out into all the earth. [7]Then he came, and he took it out of the right hand of the One who sat on the throne. [8]Now when he had taken the scroll, the four living creatures and the twenty-four elders fell down before the Lamb, each one having a harp, and golden bowls full of incense, which are the prayers of those who belong to God. [9]They sang a new song, saying, "You are worthy to take the scroll, and to open its seals, because you were slaughtered, and with your blood you purchased people for God out of every tribe, language, people, and nation. [10]And you made them a kingdom and priests to our God, and they will reign upon the earth."

[11]I looked, and I heard something like the sound of many angels around the throne, the living creatures, and the elders. And the number of them was ten thousands of ten thousands, and thousands of thousands. [12]With a loud voice, they were saying, "The Lamb who has been slaughtered is worthy to receive the power, and riches, wisdom and strength, honor and glory, and blessing!"

5:1-5 The traditional practice with a deed of redemption was to have both a sealed copy and an open copy. If a dispute arose about some provision of ownership, and the accuracy of the open copy were challenged, then the sealed copy would be opened and recognized as authoritative. (cf. Jer. 32:7-14)

5:9-10 "This is King Messiah who in the future will guide all the peoples of the world in repentance." (Mid. Song of Songs 7:11)

5:10 The redeemed will reign upon the earth in both the millennial age and the time of the new heavens and new earth. "The heavens, the heavens, belong to the EverpresentLord; but He has given the earth to the children of Adam." (Ps. 115:16)

¹³I heard every created thing which is in heaven, on the earth, beneath the earth, on the sea, and everything in them, saying, "To the One who sits on the throne, and to the Lamb be the blessing, the honor, the glory, and the dominion, forever and ever! Amen!"

¹⁴The four living creatures said, "Amen!" The elders fell down and worshipped.

6 ¹I saw that the Lamb opened one of the seven seals, and I heard one of the four living creatures saying with a voice like thunder, "Come!" ²Then I saw a white horse, and the one who sat on it had an archer's bow. A crown was given to him, and he came out to conquer, and it was evident that he was conquering.

³When he opened the second seal, I heard the second living creature saying, "Come!" ⁴And another horse, fiery red, went out. Power was given to the one who sat on it to take peace from the earth, that they would kill one another. There was given to him a great sword.

⁵And when he opened the third seal, I heard the third living creature say, "Come!" There was a black horse, and the one who sat on it had a balance in his hand! ⁶I heard a voice in the midst of the four living creatures saying, "A quart of wheat for a denarius, and three quarts of barley for a denarius! Do not damage the oil and the wine!"

⁷And when he opened the fourth seal, I heard the voice of the fourth living creature say, "Come!" ⁸Then I looked, and there was a pale horse, and the one who sat on it, his name was Death. And Sheol followed with him. And authority was given to them over one fourth of the earth, to kill with the sword, with famine, with death, and by the wild animals of the earth.

⁹And when he opened the fifth seal, I saw underneath the altar the souls of those who had been slain for the sake of the Word of God and the testimony which they maintained. ¹⁰And they cried out with a loud voice, saying, "How long, O Holy and True Master, until You judge and avenge our blood on those who dwell on the earth?" ¹¹A white robe was given to each of them. And they were told that they were to rest for a short time more, until it is completed — that their fellow servants and their brethren were also about to be slain, even as they had been.

¹²Then I looked when he opened the sixth seal, and there was a great earthquake. The sun became black as sackcloth made of hair, and the moon became as blood. ¹³The fiery objects of the heaven fell to the earth, like a fig tree dropping its unripe figs when it is shaken by a great wind. ¹⁴And heaven departed like a scroll being rolled up. Every mountain and island were moved out of their places. ¹⁵The kings of the earth, the great, the rich, the commanding officers, the powerful, and every slave and free person hid themselves in the caves and in the rocks of the mountains. ¹⁶And they were saying to the mountains and the rocks, "Fall on us, and hide us from the face of the One who sits on

---

6:6 A denarius was equal to the daily wage of a laborer. (cf. Mt. 20:2) "In the footsteps of Messiah, harshness will be strong, and the noble will be rare. The vine will give its fruit, but the wine will be expensive." (Tal. Sota 9:15 [49b])

6:9 "R. Eliezer said, 'The souls of the righteous are hidden under the throne of glory... but those of the wicked go on being shut up..." (Tal. Shabbat 152b)

6:12 " If its face is red as blood, the sword is coming to the world; if it is like sackcloth, the arrows of famine are coming to the world; if it is like both, the sword and the arrows of famine are coming to the world." (Tal. Sukkah 29a) The Tosephta to this (1:7) has "pestilence and famine".

the throne, and from the wrath of the Lamb, ¹⁷for the great day of their wrath has come; and who is able to stand?" [Is. 2:19-21, 3:10-21, 13:6-13]

7 After these things, I saw four angels standing at the four corners of the earth, holding the four winds of the earth so that no wind would blow on the earth, or on the sea, or on any tree. ²I saw another angel that had ascended from the rising of the sun, having the seal of the living God. He cried with a loud voice to the four angels to whom it was given to harm the earth and the sea. ³He said, "Do not harm the earth, nor the sea, nor the trees, until we have sealed the bondservants of our God on their foreheads!" ⁴I heard the number of those who were sealed, one hundred forty-four thousand, sealed out of every tribe of the children of Israel.

⁵Of the tribe of Judah were sealed twelve thousand,

Of the tribe of Reuven twelve thousand,

Of the tribe of Gad twelve thousand,

⁶Of the tribe of Asher twelve thousand,

Of the tribe of Naftali twelve thousand,

Of the tribe of Menasheh twelve thousand,

⁷Of the tribe of Shimon twelve thousand,

Of the tribe of Levi twelve thousand,

Of the tribe of Yisashḥar twelve thousand,

⁸Of the tribe of Zevulun twelve thousand,

Of the tribe of Yosef twelve thousand,

Of the tribe of Benjamin were sealed twelve thousand.

⁹After these things I saw a great multitude which no one could number, out of all nations, tribes, peoples, and languages! They were standing before the throne and before the Lamb, clothed in white robes, with palm branches in their hands. ¹⁰They cried with a loud voice, saying, "Salvation to the One who sits on the throne of our God, and to the Lamb!"

¹¹All the angels were standing around the throne, and the elders and the four living creatures. And they fell on their faces before His throne, and bowed down to God, ¹²saying, "Amen! Blessing, glory, wisdom, thanksgiving, honor, power, and might, be to our God forever and ever! Amen."

¹³One of the elders responded, saying to me, "These who are clothed in white robes, who are they, and from where did they come?"

¹⁴I told him, "My lord, you know."

He said to me, "These are those who came out of the great affliction [Jer. 30:5-7], and they have washed their robes, and made their robes white in the blood of the Lamb. ¹⁵Therefore they are before the throne of God. They serve Him day and night in His Temple. The One who sits on the throne will be as a tent over them. [Is. 4:5] ¹⁶They will not hunger any more, nor will they thirst any more. Nor will the sun or any heat beat upon them any more, ¹⁷because the Lamb which is in the midst of the throne will shepherd them, and will lead them to fountains of living waters. And God will wipe away every tear from their eyes." [Is. 25:8]

8 ¹When he opened the seventh seal, there was silence in heaven for about half an hour. ²I saw the seven angels who stand before God, and seven trumpets were given to them. ³Another angel came and stood over the altar, having a golden censer. He was given abundant incense for him to add it to the prayers of all those who belong to God, upon the golden altar which was before the

throne. ⁴The smoke of the incense, with the prayers of those who belong to God, went up before God from the angel's hand. ⁵The angel took the censer, and he filled it with the fire of the altar, and threw it upon the earth. There followed crashing thunders, flashes of lightning, and an earthquake. [LXX Esth. 1:1c]

⁶The seven angels who had the seven trumpets prepared themselves to sound. ⁷The first sounded, and there followed hail and fire mixed with blood, and they were thrown to the earth. [Ex. 9:23-26] One third of the earth was burned up, and one third of the trees were burned up, and all green grass was burned up.

⁸The second angel sounded, and something like a great mountain burning with fire was thrown into the sea. One third of the sea became blood, ⁹and one third of the living creatures that were in the sea died. One third of the ships were destroyed.

¹⁰The third angel sounded, and a great fiery object fell from the sky, burning like a torch. It fell on one third of the rivers, and on the springs of the waters. ¹¹The name of the fiery object is called "Wormwood". [Dt. 29:18, Jer. 9:15,23:15, Am. 5:7,6:12] One third of the waters became wormwood. Many people died from the waters, because they were made bitter.

¹²The fourth angel sounded, and a third of the sun was struck, and a third of the moon, and a third of the stars — so that a third of them would be darkened, and a third of the daylight would not appear, and the night likewise. ¹³I saw and heard an eagle flying in mid-heaven, saying with a loud voice [Jel 2:30-31], "Woe! Woe! Woe for those who dwell on the earth, because of the other voices of the trumpets of the three angels who are about to sound!"

9 ¹The fifth angel sounded, and I saw a fiery object from heaven which had fallen to the earth. The key to the pit of the abyss was given to him. ²He opened the pit of the abyss, and smoke went up out of the pit, like the smoke from a huge furnace. The sun and the air were darkened because of the smoke from the pit. ³Then out of the smoke came forth locusts on the earth [Ex. 10:12-15, Joel 2:1-11, Nah. 3:15-17], and power was given to them, as the scorpions of the earth have power. ⁴They were told that they should not hurt the grass of the earth, nor any green thing, nor any tree, but only the people who do not have the seal of God on their foreheads. ⁵They were not given power to kill them, but to torment them for five months. Their torment was like the torment from a scorpion when it stings a person. ⁶In those days people will seek death, and will not find it. They will desire to die, and death will flee from them.

⁷The locusts were shaped like horses prepared for war. On their heads were crowns like gold, and their faces were like the faces of men. ⁸They had hair like the hair of women, and their teeth were like those of lions. ⁹They had breastplates like breastplates of iron. The sound of their wings was like

---

8:7 "the hail will descend tomorrow... 'there had been nothing like it before in Egypt', [Ex. 9:18] which is to tell you there had been nothing like it in the world nor in Egypt. ...but there will be in the Time to Come... in the days of Gog and Magog, as it is says: 'Which I have reserved to the time of trouble, to the coming day of war' (Job 38:22-23), and likewise, 'An overflowing rain, and great hailstones...' (Ezek. 38:22)." (Mid. Exodus Rabba 12:2)

9:13-15 "'In the sixth [year] there will be sounds of thunder, in the seventh wars, at the departure of the seventh the son of David comes.' — War is also the beginning of redemption." (Tal. Megila 17b)

the sound of chariots with many horses running to war. ¹⁰They have tails like those of scorpions, and stings. In their tails they have power to injure men for five months. ¹¹They have a king over them, the angel of the abyss. His name in Hebrew is "Avaddon," but in Greek, he has the name "Apollyon." ¹²The first woe is past. Watch, there are still two woes coming after this.

¹³The sixth angel sounded. I heard a voice from the horns of the golden altar which is before God. ¹⁴It said to the sixth angel who had one trumpet, "Release the four angels who are bound at the great river Euphrates!"

¹⁵The four angels who had been prepared for that hour and day and month and year were released, so that they might kill one third of mankind. ¹⁶The number of the armies of the horsemen was two hundred million. I heard the number of them. ¹⁷I saw the horses in the vision like this: the heads of the horses were like heads of lions. Out of their mouths proceed fire, smoke, and brimstone. And those who sat on them had breastplates of fiery red, hyacinth blue, and brimstone yellow. ¹⁸One third of mankind was killed by these three plagues — by the fire, the smoke, and the brimstone, which proceeded out of their mouths. ¹⁹For the power of the horses is in their mouths and in their tails, because their tails are like serpents, and have heads. And with them they cause pain.

²⁰The rest of mankind, who were not killed by these plagues, did not turn away from the deeds of their hands; to not worship demons, and the idols of gold, and of silver, and of bronze, and of stone, and of wood — idols which can neither see, nor hear, nor walk. [Ps. 115:2-8] ²¹They did not change their ways of murders, nor of witchcraft and drug use, nor of sexual immorality, nor of thefts.

10 ¹I saw a mighty angel coming down out of the sky, clothed with a cloud. A rainbow was upon his head. His face was like the sun, and his feet like pillars of fire. ²He had in his hand a little open scroll. He set his right foot on the sea, and his left on the land. ³He cried out with a loud voice as a lion roars. When he cried out, the seven thunders uttered their voices. ⁴When the seven thunders sounded, I was about to write, but I heard a voice from heaven saying, "Seal up the things which the seven thunders said, and do not write them."

⁵The angel whom I saw standing on the sea and on the land lifted up his right hand to heaven, ⁶and swore by the One who lives forever and ever, the One who created heaven and the things that are in it, the earth and the things that are in it, and the sea and the things that are in it. [Ps. 24:1-2, Ex. 20:11] He swore that there will be delay no longer. ⁷Instead, in the days of the voice of the seventh angel, when he is about to sound, then the mystery of God, which He declared to His servants the prophets, is completed. ⁸The voice which I heard from heaven spoke with me again, saying, "Go, take the scroll which is open in the hand of the angel who stands on the sea and on the land."

⁹I went to the angel, telling him to give me the little scroll. He said to me, "Take it and eat it. It will make your stomach bitter, but it will be as sweet as honey in your mouth."

¹⁰I took the little scroll out of the angel's hand and ate it. It was as sweet as honey in my mouth. When I had eaten it, my stomach became bitter. [Ezek. 2:8-3:3] ¹¹Then he said to me, "You must prophesy again over many peoples, nations, languages, and kings."

11 ¹A reed like a rod was given to me, and I was told, "Rise and measure the Temple of God, the altar, and those who worship in it. ²Leave out the court which is outside of the Temple, and do not measure it, since it has been given to the Gentiles. They will tread the holy city under foot for forty-two months. ³I will give power to my two witnesses, and they will prophesy one thousand two hundred sixty days, clothed in sackcloth." ⁴These are the two olive trees and the two menorot,

standing before the Lord of the earth. [Zech. 4] ⁵If anyone desires to harm them, fire proceeds out of their mouth and devours their enemies. If anyone desires to harm them, he must be killed in this way. ⁶These have the power to shut up the sky, so that no rain falls during the days of their prophecy. [1Kings 17:1] They have power over the waters, to turn them into blood, and to strike the earth with every plague, as often as they desire. [Ex. 4:9]

⁷When they have finished their testimony, the wild beast that comes up out of the abyss will make war with them, overcome them, and kill them. ⁸Their dead bodies will be in the open place of the great city, which by the Spirit is called Sedom and Egypt [Is. 1:9-10, 3:9, Jer. 23:14]; there also their Lord was put to death on the stake. ⁹Those among the peoples, tribes, languages, and nations will look at their dead bodies for three and a half days, and will not allow their dead bodies to be laid in a tomb. ¹⁰Those who live on the earth will rejoice over them, and they will be glad. They will give gifts to one another, because these two prophets tormented those who live on the earth.

¹¹After the three and a half days, the breath of life from God entered into them, and they stood on their feet. Great fear fell on those who saw them. ¹²I heard a loud voice from heaven saying to them, "Come up here!" They went up into heaven in the cloud, and their enemies saw them. ¹³In that day there was a great earthquake, and a tenth of the city fell. Seven thousand people were killed in the earthquake, and the rest were terrified, and gave glory to the God of heaven. ¹⁴The second woe is past. Watch, the third woe comes quickly.

¹⁵The seventh angel sounded, and great voices in heaven followed, saying, "The kingdom of the world has become the Kingdom of our Lord and of His Messiah. He will reign forever and ever!"

¹⁶The twenty-four elders, who sit on their thrones before the throne of God, fell on their faces and bowed down to God. ¹⁷They said, "We give you thanks, O God, the Everpresent Lord, the Sovereign over all, the One who is and who was, because You have taken Your great power, and are reigning. ¹⁸The nations were angry, and Your wrath came [Ps. 2:1-5], as did the time for the dead to be judged, and to give reward to Your bondservants the prophets, as well as those who belong to God, and those who fear Your name, the small and the great; and to destroy those who destroy the earth."

¹⁹And the Temple of God that was in heaven was opened, and the ark of His covenant was seen in His Temple. And there were flashes of lightning, noises, thunders, an earthquake, and great hail.

12 ¹A great sign was seen in heaven: a woman clothed with the sun, and the moon under her feet, and a crown of twelve stars on her head. ²She was pregnant, and cried out in pain, laboring to give birth. (Mic. 4:10-13) ³Another sign was seen in heaven: a great red Dragon having seven heads

---

11:3-12 "He [God] added: 'Moses, by your life, as you gave your soul to them in this world, so too in the age to come when I bring Eliyahu the prophet to them, the two of you will come as one.'" (Mid. D'varim Rabbah 3:17) The Havdalah hymn, Eliyahu haNavi, speaks of Eliyahu as "the man who did not taste death or burial."

11:7-11 At the time this was written, it was inconceivable that a world-wide audience could view these dead bodies, their being raised back to life, and their being taken up into heaven.

11:19 In Ps. 18:6, David said, "He heard my voice from His Temple." Since the First Temple was not built until the reign of Solomon, we know that David was referring to the Temple in Heaven. The same would be true of Ps. 11:4: "The Everpresent Lord is in His holy Temple; the throne of the Everpresent Lord is in Heaven."

and ten horns, and seven crowns on his heads! [4]His tail swept one third of the stars of the heaven, and threw them to the earth. The Dragon stood before the woman who was about to give birth, so that when she gave birth he might devour her child. [5]She gave birth to a son, a male child who is soon to shepherd all the Gentiles with a rod of iron. [Ps. 2:8-9] Her child was caught up to God and to His throne. [6]The woman fled into the wilderness, where she has a place prepared by God, so that they may feed her there one thousand two hundred sixty days.

[7]Then there was war in heaven. Mikhael and his angels warred against the Dragon. The Dragon and his angels fought, [8]but they did not prevail. [Dan. 12:1] There was no longer a place found for them in heaven. [9]The great Dragon was thrown down, the ancient Serpent, the one who is called the Enemy and the Accuser, the deceiver of the whole world. [Is. 27:1] He was thrown down to the earth, and his angels were thrown down with him. [Is. 14:12-15, Exek. 28:16,17]

[10]I heard a loud voice in heaven, saying, "The salvation, the power, and the Kingdom of our God, and the authority of His Messiah have now come, because the Accuser of our brethren has been thrown down, who accuses them before our God day and night. [11]They conquered him through the blood of the Lamb, through the word of their testimony, and they did not love their life, even to death. [1Mac. 9:10] [12]Because of this, let the heavens and those who have planted their tent in them rejoice. Woe to the earth and to the sea, because the Enemy has gone down to you[+] having great wrath, knowing that he has but a short time."

[13]When the Dragon saw that he was thrown down to the earth, he persecuted the woman who gave birth to the male child. [14]Two wings of the great eagle were given to the woman, so that she might fly into the wilderness to her place away from the face of the Serpent, so that she might be fed for a time, and times, and half a time. [15]The Serpent spewed water out of his mouth like a river after the woman so that he might cause her to be carried away by the river. [16]The earth helped the woman, and the earth opened its mouth and swallowed up the river which the Dragon spewed out of his mouth. [17]The Dragon grew angry with the woman, and went away to war against the rest of her seed, who keep the commandments of God and have the testimony of Yeshua.

12:7-9 "because it is he [Mikhael, Dan. 12:1] who presents Israel's needs and speaks for them, as it says: Then the angel of the Everpresent Lord responded and said: 'O Everpresent Commander of all, how long will You not have compassion on Yerushala'im' (Zech. 1:12), and he said: 'And there is no one being strong with me, except Mikhael your prince' (Dan. 10:21). R. Yose said: 'What are Mikhael and Samael like? ["Samael" is a name used by the rabbis to designate 'Satan' or 'the Angel of Death'] To a defender and a prosecutor standing in a court: each one speaks, and when each has finished, the defender knows that he has been victorious, and he begins to praise the judge that his verdict will go forth... Satan prosecutes, while Mikhael teaches the merits of Israel...'" (Mid. Exodus Rabba 18:5)

12:9 The Accuser "descends and deceives, then goes up and causes wrath. Authority is put upon him, and he carries off a soul." (Tal. Baba Bathra 16a)

"Raba said in the name of R. Yohanan, 'In the age to come, the Holy One, blessed be He, will make a sukkah for the righteous from the skin of Leviathan [the Dragon Serpent].'" (Tal. Baba Bathra 75a)

12:10-12 See the ADDITIONAL NOTE on "War in Heaven".

13 ¹Then I saw a wild beast coming up out of the sea. It stood on the sand of the sea, having ten horns and seven heads. On his horns were ten crowns, and on his heads, blasphemous names. ²The wild beast which I saw was like a leopard. His feet were like those of a bear, and his mouth like the mouth of a lion. The Dragon gave him his power, his throne, and great authority. ³One of his heads was as if fatally wounded, but his fatal wound was healed, and the whole earth was amazed at the wild beast. ⁴They bowed down to the Dragon, because he gave his authority to the wild beast, and they bowed down to the wild beast, saying, "Who is like the wild beast? Who is able to make war with him?"

⁵A mouth speaking great things and blasphemy was given to him. Authority to make war for forty-two months was given to him. ⁶He opened his mouth for blasphemy against God, to blaspheme His Name, His tent, and those who set their tents in heaven. ⁷It was given to him to make war with those who belong to God, and to overcome them. Authority over every tribe, people, language, and nation was given to him. ⁸All who dwell on the earth will bow down to him — everyone whose name has not been written from the foundation of the world in the Scroll of Life of the Lamb who has been slain. ⁹If anyone has an ear, let him hear. ¹⁰If anyone is for captivity, he goes away into captivity. If anyone kills with the sword, he is to be killed with the sword. Here is the endurance and the faith of those who belong to God.

¹¹I saw another wild beast coming up out of the earth. He had two horns like a lamb, and he spoke like a dragon. ¹²He exercises all the authority of the first wild beast in his presence. He makes the earth and those who dwell in it to bow down to the first wild beast, whose fatal wound was healed. ¹³He performs great signs, even making fire come down out of heaven to the earth in front of men. ¹⁴He deceives those who dwell on the earth through the signs which it was given to him to perform before the wild beast. He tells those who dwell on the earth that they should make an image to the wild beast who had the wound of the sword and lived. ¹⁵It was given to him to give breath to the image of the wild beast, and that the image of the wild beast should speak; and to cause as many as would not bow down to the image of the wild beast to be killed. [Ex. 20:4-5; Dan. 3] ¹⁶He causes all — the small and the great [20:12], the rich and the poor, the free and the slave — to be given a mark on their right hand or on their forehead, ¹⁷so that no one would be able to buy or to sell, unless he has that mark, the name of the wild beast, or the number of his name. ¹⁸Here is wisdom: the one who has understanding should figure out the number of the wild beast, for it is the number of a man. His number is six hundred sixty-six.

14 ¹I looked, and the Lamb was standing on Mount Zion, and with him one hundred forty-four thousand, having his name and the Name of his Father written on their foreheads! ²I heard a sound from heaven, like the sound of many waters, and like the sound of great thunder. The sound which I heard was like that of harpists playing on their harps. ³They sing a new song before the throne, and before the four living creatures and the elders. No one could learn the song except the one hundred forty-four thousand, those who had been redeemed from the earth. ⁴These are those who were not defiled with women, because they are virgins. They follow the Lamb wherever he goes.

13:8 "from the foundation of the world" is correctly placed as in Rev. 17:8.

[Ps. 44:15LXX/45:14] These were redeemed from among men, the first fruits to God and to the Lamb. ⁵No lie was found in their mouth. They are blameless.

⁶I saw another angel flying in the midst of heaven, having the everlasting good news to proclaim to those who dwell on the earth and to every nation, tribe, language, and people. ⁷He said with a loud voice, "Fear the Everpresent Lord, and give Him glory, because the hour of His judgment has come. Bow down to the One who made the heaven, the earth, the sea, and the springs of waters!" [Ps. 24:1-2]

⁸Another angel followed, saying, "It has fallen. Babel, the great city, has fallen, because she made all the nations drink of the wine of the fury of her sexual immorality." [Jer. 50-51]

⁹And a third angel followed, saying with a great voice, "If anyone bows down to the wild beast and his image, and receives a mark on his forehead or on his hand, ¹⁰he also will drink of the wine of the wrath of God, which is prepared full strength in the cup of His anger. (Ps. 75:8) He will be tormented with fire and brimstone in the presence of the holy angels, and in the presence of the Lamb. ¹¹The smoke of their torment goes up forever and ever. They have no rest day and night, those who bow down to the wild beast and his image, and whoever receives the mark of his name. ¹²Here is the endurance of those who belong to God, those who keep the commandments of God and the faith of Yeshua."

¹³I heard the voice from heaven saying, "Write, 'There is good for the dead who die in the Lord from now on.'"

"Yes," says the Spirit, "that they may rest from their labors, for their deeds follow with them."

¹⁴I looked, and behold, a white cloud, and one sitting on the cloud, like a son of Adam, having a golden crown on his head, and a sharp sickle in his hand. ¹⁵Another angel came out from the Temple, crying with a loud voice to the one who sat on the cloud, "Send forth your sickle and reap, for your hour to reap has come, because the harvest of the earth is dried up!" ¹⁶The one who sat on the cloud thrust his sickle upon the earth, and the earth was reaped.

¹⁷Another angel came out from the Temple which is in heaven. He also had a sharp sickle. ¹⁸And another angel came out from the altar, the one who has power over fire. And he called with a powerful voice to the one who had the sharp sickle, saying, "Send forth your sharp sickle, and gather the clusters of the vine of the earth, for the earth's grapes are fully ripe!" ¹⁹The angel thrust his sickle into the earth, and gathered the vintage of the earth, and threw it into the great winepress of the wrath of God. ²⁰The winepress was trodden outside of the city, and blood came out from the winepress, up to the bridles of the horses, to a distance of two hundred miles. [2Mac. 12:16]

14:1-5 "I have kept seven thousand as a remnant in Israel, all the knees which have not bowed to Baal, and every mouth that has not kissed him." (1Kings 19:18)

The Greek word translated as "defiled/polluted" also appears in LXX Zech. 14:2 to describe the women defiled by an invading army.

14:20 Speaking of the destruction brought by the Romans in ending the Bar Kokhba Revolt, Mid. Lamentations Rabbah 2:4 says: "They killed some of them until the horses waded in blood up to the nostrils, and the blood rolled stones of forty *se'ah* and went into the sea for four miles."

15 [1]I saw another great and marvelous sign in heaven, seven angels having the seven last plagues, because the wrath of God is completed in them. [2]I saw something like a sea of glass mixed with fire, and those who overcame the wild beast, his image, and the number of his name, standing on the sea of glass, having lyres of God. [3]They sang the song of Moses [Dt. 32], the servant of God, and the song of the Lamb, saying, "Great and marvelous are Your deeds, O God, the Everpresent Lord, the Sovereign over all. Righteous and true are Your ways, You King of the nations. [4]Who will not fear You, O Everpresent Lord, and glorify Your Name, because only You are holy! For all the nations will come and bow down before You [Jer. 10:7], because Your just actions have been revealed."

[5]After these things I looked, and the Temple of the tent of meeting in heaven was opened. [6]The seven angels who had the seven plagues came out, clothed with pure, bright linen, and wearing golden sashes around their chests.

[7]One of the four living creatures gave to the seven angels seven golden bowls full of the wrath of God, who lives forever and ever. [8]The Temple was filled with smoke from the glory of God, and from His power. No one was able to enter into the Temple until the seven plagues of the seven angels were finished.

16 [1]I heard a loud voice out of the Temple saying to the seven angels, "Go and pour out the seven bowls of the wrath of God upon the earth!"

[2]The first went and poured out his bowl over the earth, and it became a harmful and evil sore on the people who had the mark of the wild beast and who bowed down to his image. [3]The second angel poured out his bowl into the sea, and it became as the blood of a dead man. Every living thing in the sea died.

[4]The third poured out his bowl on the rivers and springs of water, and it became blood. [5]I heard the angel of the waters saying, "You are righteous, O Everpresent Lord, who is and who was, the Holy One, because You have judged these things. [6]For they poured out the blood of the prophets and those who belong to God, and You have given them blood to drink, because they deserve it." [Ex. 7:19-21] [7]I heard the altar saying, "Yes, O God, the Everpresent Lord, the Sovereign over all, true and just are Your judgments."

[8]The fourth poured out his bowl over the sun, and it was given to him to scorch men with fire. [9]People were scorched with great heat, and people blasphemed the Name of God who has the power over these plagues. They did not change their ways and give Him glory.

[10]The fifth poured out his bowl on the throne of the wild beast, and his kingdom was darkened. They gnawed their tongues because of the pain, [11]and they blasphemed the God of heaven because of their pains and their sores. They did not turn away from their deeds.

[12]The sixth poured out his bowl on the great river, the Euphrates. Its water was dried up, so that the way might be made ready for the kings who come from the rising of the sun. [13]I saw three unclean spirits, something like frogs, coming out of the mouth of the Dragon, and out of the mouth of the wild beast, and out of the mouth of the false prophet. [14]Indeed they are spirits of demons, performing signs, which go forth to the kings of the whole inhabited earth, to gather them together for the war of that great day of God, the Sovereign over all.

15:5-16:1; 16:19 See note to 11:19.

[15]"Know that I come like a thief. There is good for the one who watches, and keeps his clothes, so that he does not walk naked, and they see his shame." [16]He gathered them together into the place which is called in Hebrew, "Har Megiddo". [Joel 4:1-17H/3:1-17,2Chr. 35:22]

[17]The seventh poured out his bowl into the air. A loud voice came forth out of the Temple of heaven, from the throne, saying, "It is done!" [18]There were lightnings, noises, and thunders. And there was a great earthquake, so great an earthquake, so mighty, such as had not been since humanity was upon the earth. [19]The great city was divided into three parts [Zech. 14:4-5], and the cities of the nations fell. Babel the great was remembered in the sight of God, to give to her the cup of the wine of the fierceness of His wrath. [20]Every island fled away, and the mountains were not found. [21]Great hailstones, weighing about one hundred pounds, came down out of the sky upon people. People blasphemed God because of the plague of the hail, for this plague is exceedingly severe.

17 [Jer. 50-51] [1]One of the seven angels who had the seven bowls came and spoke with me, saying, "Come here. I will show you the judgment of the great harlot who sits upon many waters. [2]The kings of the earth committed sexual immorality with her, and those who inhabit the earth have gotten drunk with the wine of her sexual immorality." [3]He carried me away in the Spirit into a wilderness.

I saw a woman sitting on a scarlet-colored wild beast, full of blasphemous names, having seven heads and ten horns. [4]The woman was clothed in purple and scarlet, and covered with gold and precious stones and pearls. She had in her hand a golden cup full of abominations and the impurities of her sexual immorality. [5]And on her forehead a name was written, "MYSTERY, BABEL THE GREAT, THE MOTHER OF THE HARLOTS AND ABOMINATIONS OF THE EARTH." [6]I saw the woman drunken with the blood of those who belong to God, and with the blood of the witnesses of Yeshua. When I saw her, I wondered with great astonishment.

[7]The angel said to me, "Why do you wonder? I will tell you the mystery of the woman, and of the wild beast that carries her, which has the seven heads and the ten horns. [8]The wild beast that you saw was, and is not, and is about to come up out of the abyss and to go into destruction. Those who dwell on the earth, and whose names have not been written in the Scroll of Life from the foundation of the world, will be amazed when they see that the beast was, and is not, and yet is.

[9]"Here is the mind that has wisdom. The seven heads are seven mountains, on which the woman sits. [10]There are also seven kings. Five have fallen, the one is, the other has not yet come. When he comes, he must remain a little while. [11]The wild beast that was and is not is himself also an eighth, and is of the seven; and he goes to destruction. [12]The ten horns that you saw are ten kings who have received no kingdom as yet, but they receive authority for one hour as kings with the wild beast. [13]These have one mind, and they give their power and authority to the wild beast. [14]These will war against the Lamb, but the Lamb will conquer them, since he is Lord of lords, and King of kings. And they who are with him are called, and chosen, and faithful."

[15]He said to me, "The waters which you saw, where the harlot sits, are peoples, multitudes, nations, and languages. [16]The ten horns which you saw, and the wild beast, these will hate the harlot, and will make her desolate. They will make her naked, and will eat her flesh, and will burn her with fire. [17]For God has put in their hearts to do His purpose with one mind, and to give their kingdom to the wild beast, until the words of God have been fulfilled. [18]The woman whom you saw is the great city which reigns over the kings of the earth."

18

¹After these things, I saw another angel coming down out of heaven, having great authority. The earth was illuminated with his glory. ²He shouted with a mighty voice, saying, "Fallen, fallen is Babel the great, and she has become a habitation of demons, a prison of every unclean spirit, and a prison of every unclean and hateful bird! ³For all the nations have drunk of the wine of the rage of her sexual immorality. The kings of the earth committed sexual immorality with her, and the merchants of the earth grew rich from the power of her rich living."

⁴I heard another voice from heaven, saying, "Come out of her, My people, so that you⁺ do not share in her sins, so that you⁺ do not receive of her plagues. ⁵For her sins have reached to heaven, and God has remembered her iniquities. ⁶Give back to her just as she has given to you⁺, and repay her double according to her deeds. In the cup which she mixed, pour out to her double. [Ps. 75:9H] ⁷As much as she glorified herself and lived in unrestrained indulgence, give to her that much torment and mourning. For she says in her heart, 'I am enthroned a queen, and am not a widow, and will never see mourning.' ⁸Therefore her plagues will come in one day — death, mourning, and famine — and she will be completely burned with fire, because the Everpresent Lord who has judged her is strong.

⁹"The kings of the earth, who committed sexual immorality and lived in unrestrained indulgence with her, will weep and wail over her when they look at the smoke of her burning. ¹⁰They will stand far away because of fear of her torment, saying, 'Woe, woe, the great city, Babel, the strong city! For your judgment has come in one hour.' ¹¹The merchants of the earth weep and mourn over her, for no one buys their merchandise any more — ¹²merchandise of gold, silver, precious stones, pearls, fine linen, purple, silk, scarlet, every fragrant wood, every object of ivory, every object made of the most expensive wood, of bronze, iron, and marble; ¹³and cinnamon, incense, perfume, frankincense, wine, olive oil, fine flour, wheat, sheep, horses, chariots, and the bodies and souls of men. ¹⁴The ripe fruits of the desire of your soul have departed from you, and all the richness and the brightness have departed from you, and you will never find them again.

¹⁵"The merchants of these things, whom she made rich, will stand far away for fear of her torment, weeping and mourning. ¹⁶They will say, 'Woe, woe, the great city, she who was clothed in fine linen, purple, and scarlet, and covered with gold and precious stones and pearls! ¹⁷For such great riches are made desolate in an hour.' Every shipmaster, all who sail anywhere, sailors, and as many as gain their living by the sea, stood far away. ¹⁸And they cried out as they looked at the smoke of her burning, saying, 'What compares to the great city?' ¹⁹They cast dust on their heads and cried, weeping and mourning, saying, 'Woe, woe, the great city, in which all who had their ships in the sea were made rich by reason of her great wealth!' For she is made desolate in one hour.

18:15-19 Ezek. 28:2-19 describes the fall of God's "anointed cherub". "By your great wisdom in trade you have increased your riches, and your heart is lifted up because of your riches.... By the abundance of your trading you became filled with violence within, and you sinned." (Ezek. 28:5,16)

18:21-23 The phrase "never more" appears here six times.

18:23 God's judgment on Yerushala'im (Jer. 7:34, 16:9, 25:10) also included causing the voice of the bride and the voice of the bridegroom to cease. But He also promised to restore these to Yerushala'im. (Jer. 33:10-11)

[20]"Rejoice over her, O heaven, and you+ holy ambassadors and prophets, for God has avenged you+ against her." [21]A mighty angel took up a stone like a great millstone and threw it into the sea, saying, "In this way, Babel, the great city, will be thrown down with violence, and will never more be found. [22]The voice of harpists, musicians, flute players, and trumpeters will never more be heard in you. No craftsman of any craft will ever more be found in you. The sound of a mill will never more be heard in you. [23]The light of a lamp will never more shine in you. The voice of the bridegroom and of the bride will never more be heard in you. [Jer. 33:10-11] For your merchants were the princes of the earth; for all the nations were deceived with your witchcraft and drug use. [24]In her was found the blood of prophets and of those who belong to God, and of all who have been slain on the earth."

19 [1]After these things I heard a loud voice of a great multitude in heaven saying, "Praise the Everpresent Lord! Salvation, power, and glory belong to our God, [2]because His judgments are true and righteous. [Ps. 19:9] For He has judged the great harlot who corrupted the earth with her sexual immorality, and He has avenged the blood of His servants [Dt. 32:43, 2 Kings 9:7] shed by her hand."

[3]A second said, "Praise the Everpresent Lord! Her smoke goes up forever and ever." [Is. 34:10] [4]The twenty-four elders and the four living creatures fell down and bowed down to God who sits on the throne, saying, "Amen! Praise the Everpresent Lord!"

[5]A voice came forth from the throne, saying, "Give praise to our God, all you+ His servants, you+ who fear Him, the small and the great!"

[6]I heard a sound like a great multitude, like many waters [Ezek. 43:2], and like mighty thundering saying, "Praise the Everpresent Lord! Because our God, the Everpresent Lord, the Sovereign over all, reigns! [7]Let us rejoice and be exceedingly glad, and let us give the glory to Him. For the marriage of the Lamb has come, and his wife has made herself ready." [8]It was given to her to be clothed in fine linen, pure and bright, for the fine linen is the righteous deeds of those who belong to God.

[9]He said to me, "Write, 'There is good for those who are called to the marriage supper of the Lamb.'" He said to me, "These are the true words of God."

[10]I fell down before his feet to bow down to him. He said to me, "See that you don't! I'm a fellow bondservant with you and with your brethren who have the testimony of Yeshua. Bow down to God, because the testimony of Yeshua is the spirit of prophecy."

[11]I saw heaven opened, and there was a white horse. And the one who sat on it is called Faithful and True! In righteousness he judges and makes war. [12]His eyes are like a flame of fire, and on his head are many crowns. He has a name written which no one but he himself knows. [Ex. 6:3] [13]He is clothed in a garment dipped in blood. His name is called "The Word of God." [14]The armies which are in heaven followed him on white horses, clothed in fine linen, white and pure. [15]Out of his mouth goes forth a sharp sword, so that he might strike the nations with it. He will rule them with a rod of iron. [Ps. 2:8] He treads the winepress of the fierceness of the wrath of God, the Sovereign over all. [16]He has a name written on his garment and on his thigh, "KING OF KINGS, AND LORD OF LORDS."

[17]I saw an angel standing in the sun. He cried with a loud voice, saying to all the birds that fly in the sky, "Come! Be gathered together to the great supper of God, [18]so that you+ may eat the flesh of kings, the flesh of captains, the flesh of mighty men, and the flesh of horses and of those who sit on them, and the flesh of all men, both free and slave, small and great." [19]I saw the wild beast, the kings

of the earth, and their armies gathered together to make war against the one who sat on the horse, and against his army. [Zekh. 14:1-5] [20]The wild beast was taken, and with him the false prophet who worked the signs before him, with which he deceived those who had received the mark of the wild beast and those who bowed down to his image. These two were thrown alive into the lake of fire that burns with brimstone. [21]The rest were killed with the sword which came forth out of the mouth of the one who sat on the horse. All the birds were filled with their flesh.

20 [1]I saw an angel coming down out of heaven, having the key of the abyss and a great chain in his hand. [2]He seized the Dragon, the old serpent, which is the Enemy and the Accuser who deceives the whole inhabited earth. He bound him for a thousand years, [3]threw him into the abyss, shut it, and sealed it over him, so that he would no longer lead the nations astray — until the thousand years were finished. After this, it is necessary that he be released for a short time.

[4]I saw thrones, and they sat on them, and judgment was given to them. I saw the souls of those who had been beheaded for the testimony of Yeshua and for the word of God — even those who did not bow down to the wild beast or his image, and did not receive the mark on their forehead or on their hand. They lived and reigned with Messiah for the thousand years. [5]The rest of the dead did not live until the thousand years were finished. This is the first resurrection. [6]Blessed and holy is the one who has a part in the first resurrection. The second death has no power over these, but they will be priests of God and of the Messiah, and will reign with him one thousand years.

[7]And after the thousand years, the Accuser will be released from his prison. [8]Then he will come out to deceive the nations which are in the four corners of the earth, Gog and Magog, to gather them together unto war. The number of them is as the sand of the sea. [9]They went up over the breadth of the earth, and surrounded the beloved city and the camp of those who belong to God. Fire came down out of heaven and devoured them. [10]The Enemy who deceived them was thrown into the lake of fire and brimstone, where the wild beast and the false prophet are also. They will be tormented day and night forever and ever.

20:1-3,10 "Again the Everpresent Lord said to Raphael, 'Bind Azazyel hand and foot; cast him into darkness; and opening the desert which is in Dudael, cast him in there. Throw upon him hurled and pointed stones, covering him with darkness. There shall he remain for ever; cover his face, that he may not see the light. And in the great day of judgment let him be cast into the fire.'" (1Enoch 10:6-9)

20:4 Daniel 7:9 says, "I watched the vision until thrones were put in place, and the Ancient of Days was seated..." In an argument in Tal. Sanhedrin 38b, we read, "'One was for Himself and one for David.' This is R. Akiba's view."

20:4-6 "Tanna debe Eliyahu said, 'The existence of the age is six thousand years; two thousand without form, two thousand of Torah, two thousand the days of Messiah.'" (Tal. Avodah Zarah 9a)

20:6 "R. Hanina said, 'There is no death in the Age to Come except for idolators only.'" (Mid. Genesis 26:2) "Blessed are You, Everpresent Lord, the One who restores souls to dead bodies." (Tal. Berachot 60b)

Rashi says that when Jacob went down to Egypt and saw Joseph, Jacob said, "I thought that it was given to me to die two deaths, in this age and in the age to come... now that you still live, I will only die one time." (Rashi on Gen.46:30)

[11]I saw a great white throne and the One who sat on it. The earth and the heaven fled away from His face; no place was found for them. [12]I saw the dead, the great and the small, standing before the throne, and scrolls were opened. Then another scroll was opened, that of Life. The dead were judged out of the things which were written in the scrolls, according to their deeds. [13]The sea gave up the dead who were in it. Death and Sheol gave up the dead who were in them. They were judged, each one according to his deeds. [14]Death and Sheol were thrown into the lake of fire. This is the second death, the lake of fire. [15]If anyone was not found written in the Scroll of Life, he was cast into the lake of fire.

21 [1]I saw a new heaven and a new earth, because the first heaven and the first earth have passed away, and the sea is no more. [2]I saw the holy city, new Yerushala'im, coming down out of heaven from God, made ready like a bride adorned for her husband. [3]I heard a loud voice from the throne saying, "Look, the tent of God is with men, and He will set His tent with them, and they will be His peoples, and God Himself will be with them. [4]He will wipe away every tear from their eyes. Death will be no more; nor will there be mourning, crying, or pain any more. The first things have passed away."

[5]The One who sits on the throne said, "Watch, I make all things new." He said, "Write, for these

20:11-13 "For from the beginning the Son of Man was hidden, and the Most High preserved him in the presence of His might, and revealed him to those chosen. And the congregation of the chosen and holy will be sown, and all the chosen will stand before him on that day. And all the kings and the mighty and the exalted and those who rule the earth will fall down before him on their faces, and worship and set their hope upon that Son of Man, and petition him and plead for mercy at his hands." (1Enoch 62:7-9)

20:12 In the liturgy, in *Avinu Malkenu*, we pray, "...Our Father, our King, inscribe us in the book of good life.... in the Book of the righteous and pious.... in the Book of the upright and whole.... in the Book of provision and good means of sustenance.... in the Book of forgiveness, pardon, and atonement.... in the Book of redemption and salvation."

At the end of the evening service for Rosh haShanah, "We pray, O Lord, that by our deeds we may become worthy of Your grace, and thus be inscribed in Your Book of Life. Amen."

"Rabbi Kruspedai said, 'Rabbi Yohanan said, *Three books will be opened on Rosh haShana, one for the completely wicked, one for the completely righteous, and one for those who are between them. The completely righteous will be immediately written and sealed to life. The completely wicked will be immediately written and sealed to death. Those who are between them stand suspended from Rosh haShanah until Yom Kippur. If they merit it, they are written to life; if they do not merit it, they are written to death.'" (Tal. Rosh haShana 16b)

"Be smart about three things and you will not come into the power of transgression: know what is above you, an eye that sees and an ear that hears, and all your deeds are written in a book." (Tal. Pirke Avot 2:1)

21:2 "R. Yohanan said, 'The Holy One, blessed be He, said I will not come into Yerushala'im above until I come into Yerushala'im below.'" (Mid. Psalms 122:4)

21:3 In the traditional liturgy, we ask God to "Spread over us the tent/*sukkah* of Your peace."

21:4ff Mid. Exodus Rabbah 15:21 comments on Is. 42:9 — "Behold, the former things are come to pass, and I declare new things" — and speaks of ten things that will be renewed in the Age to Come, connecting each with appropriate Scripture.

>>

words are faithful and true." ⁶He said to me, "It is done! I am the Alef and the Tav, the Beginning and the End. I will give freely from the spring of the water of life to the one who is thirsty. ⁷The one who overcomes will inherit all things. I will be his God, and he will be My child. ⁸But for the cowardly and those who disbelieve, the abominable and murderers, the sexually immoral and those who practiced witchcraft and drug use, the idolaters and all liars, their part is in the lake that burns with fire and brimstone, which is the second death."

⁹One of the seven angels who had the seven bowls full of the seven last plagues came and spoke with me, saying, "Come here. I will show you the bride, the wife of the Lamb." ¹⁰He carried me away in the Spirit to a great and high mountain, and showed me the holy city, Yerushala'im, coming down out of heaven from God, ¹¹having the glory of God. Her radiance was like a most precious stone, as a jasper stone, clear as crystal. ¹²It had a great and high wall, twelve gates and inscribed names, which are the names of the twelve tribes of the sons of Israel. [Ex. 28:21; 39:14; Ezek. 48:31-34] And there were twelve angels at the gates. ¹³On the east there were three gates, and on the north three gates. There were also three gates on the south, and three gates on the west. ¹⁴The wall of the city had twelve foundation stones, and in them twelve names of the twelve ambassadors of the Lamb. [Ex. 24:4]

¹⁵The one who spoke with me had a golden reed so that he might measure the city, its gates, and its walls. ¹⁶The city has four sides, and its length is as great as its breadth. He measured the city with the reed — twelve thousand stadia. Its length, breadth, and height are equal. ¹⁷And he measured its wall, one hundred forty-four cubits, by the measure of a man [Dt. 3:11], which the angel had.

¹⁸Its wall was constructed of jasper. The city was pure gold, like clear glass. ¹⁹The foundations of

"The first is that He will give light to the world, for it says: 'The sun will no more be your light by day... but the Everpresent Lord will be an everlasting light unto you' (Is. 60:19)... The second thing is that He will bring out living water from Yerushala'im and heal with it all those who have a disease... The third is that He will make trees give their fruit in every month, and when a man eats of them he will be healed... The fourth is that they will rebuild all the desolate cities... The fifth is that He will build Yerushala'im with sapphire stones... The sixth is that 'The cow and bear will feed' ... The seventh is that He will bring all the animals, birds and creeping things and make a covenant with them and with all Israel... The eighth is that there will no longer be weeping or wailing in the world.... The ninth is that there will no longer be death in the world... The tenth is that there will no longer be any sighing, wailing or anguish, but all will rejoice, for it says: 'And the ransomed of the Everpresent Lord will return, and come to Zion with singing.' (Is. 35:10)."

21:6 The Greek text, has "the Alpha and the Omega," which are the first and last letters of the Greek alphabet. The Aramaic has Alef and Tav, which are the first and last letters of the Hebrew alphabet. Also in 1:8.

21:7 The Greek *huios* is generally translated as "son," but in LXX Gen. 36:2 it is used to translate the Hebrew *bat*, i.e. daughter, in "Anah the daughter of Zibeon the Hivite". So I have used the generic "child" here, even as "*bnei*/sons of Israel" is usually translated as "children of Israel".

21:9-14 The Scriptures use a variety of metaphors. Here the bride of the Lamb is also the new Yerushala'im, a city. In 19:7-8, she is presented more like what appears in Eph. 5:25-27. 1Kefa 2:5 says that Yeshua's disciples are "living stones" being built into a house for him.

the wall of the city were adorned with all kinds of precious stones. The first foundation was jasper, the second sapphire, the third chalcedony, the fourth emerald, [20]the fifth sardonyx, the sixth sardius, the seventh chrysolite, the eighth beryl, the ninth topaz, the tenth chrysoprases, the eleventh jacinth, and the twelfth amethyst. [Tobit 13:16-17] [21]The twelve gates were twelve pearls. Each one of the gates was made of one pearl.

The broad open space of the city was pure gold, like transparent glass. [22]I saw no temple in it, because God — the Everpresent Lord, the Sovereign over all — and the Lamb, are its temple. [23]The city has no need of the sun, nor of the moon, to shine in it, for the glory of God gives light to it, and its lamp is the Lamb. [Is. 24:23] [24]The Gentiles will walk in its light. The kings of the earth bring their glory and honor into it. [25]Its gates will never be shut by day, because there will be no night there. [26]And they will bring the glory and the honor of the Gentiles into it. [27]There will never enter into it anything that defiles, nor one who causes an abomination or a lie, but only those who are written in the Lamb's Book of Life.

22

[1]He showed me the river of living water, bright as crystal, going forth from the throne of God and of the Lamb. [Jer. 2:13; Zech. 14:8] [2]In the midst of its broad open space, and on both sides of the river, was the tree of life, bearing twelve kinds of fruit, yielding its fruit every month. The leaves of the tree were for the healing of the Gentiles. [3]And there will no longer be any curse. The throne of God and of the Lamb will be in it, and His servants will serve Him. [4]They will see His face, and His name will be upon their foreheads. [5]There will be no night, and they need no lamp nor light from the sun, because God, the Everpresent Lord, will shine upon them. [Num. 6:24-27, Is. 60:3,19-20] They will reign forever and ever.

21:16 Twelve thousand stadia is about 1500 miles. "Now Egypt is one sixtieth of Kush, Kush one sixtieth of the world, the world one sixtieth of the Garden, the Garden one sixtieth of Eden, Eden one sixtieth of Gehenna: we find that all the entire world is like the cover of a pot to Gehenna." (Tal. Pesahim 94a)

In Ezekiel 40, there is a description of a new Yerushala'im. The Dead Sea Scrolls also speak of the dimensions of the New Yerushala'im. cf. Florentino García Martínez, ed., The Dead Sea Scrolls Translated: The Qumran Texts in English, trans. Wilfred G. E. Watson, 2nd ed., Brill, Leiden, 1996, Pp. 129-135

21:17 One hundred forty-four cubits is two hundred sixteen feet.

21:21 In Midrash on Psalms 87.2, commenting on Is. 54:11-12, it is said that the pearls for the gates of the new Yerushala'im will be so big that the entrance through each one will be 15 feet wide by 30 feet long.

21:23-24 "The light which was created in the six days of the Beginning, is not able to enlighten the day, because it would eclipse the light of the sun. Nor can it by night, for was it not created only to enlighten by day?' Then where is it? In a storehouse [genizah], it is established for the righteous in the Age to Come, as it says, 'And the light of the moon will be as the light of the sun, and the light of the sun will be seven times [as bright], as the light of the seven days.' (Is. 30:26)." (Mid. Genesis Rabbah 3:6)

21:24-26 "In the Age to Come, all the peoples will come to bring gifts to King Messiah." (Mid. Ex. Rabba 35:5)

21:27 "Rabbah said in the name of R. Yohanan: 'Yerushala'im of the age to come is not like Yerushala'im of this age. Everyone who wants to go up to Yerushala'im of this age goes up, but to that of the age to come only those who are invited will go up to her.'" (Tal. Baba Bathra 75b) Contrast this with Zech. 14:16-19

[6]He said to me, "These words are faithful and true. The Everpresent Lord, the God of the spirits of the prophets, sent His angel to show to His bondservants the things which must happen soon."

[7]"Watch, I am coming quickly. There is good for the one who keeps the words of the prophecy of this scroll."

[8]Now I, Yohanan, am the one who heard and saw these things. When I heard and saw, I fell down to bow down before the feet of the angel who had shown me these things. [9]He said to me, "See that you don't! I am a fellow bondservant with you, and with your brethren the prophets, and with those who keep the words of this book. Bow down before God." [10]He said to me, "Do not seal up the words of the prophecy of this book, for the time is near. [11]The one who acts unjustly, let him continue to act unjustly. The one who is filthy, let him continue to be filthy. The one who is righteous, let him continue to do what is right. The one who is consecrated, let him continue to be consecrated."

[12]"Watch, I am coming quickly. My reward is with me to repay to each one according to his work. [13]I am the Alef and the Tav, the First and the Last, the Beginning and the End. [14]Blessed are those who do His commandments, so that they may have the right to the tree of life, and may enter in by the gates into the city. [15]Outside are the dogs, those who practiced witchcraft and drug use, the sexually immoral, the murderers, the idolaters, and everyone who loves and practices falsehood. [16]I, Yeshua, have sent my angel to bear witness to you[+] concerning these things for the communities. I am the root and the offspring of David, the Bright and Morning Star."

[17]The Spirit and the bride say, "Come!" The one who hears, let him say, "Come!" The one who is thirsty, let him come. The one who is willing, let him take the living water freely. [18]I testify to everyone who hears the words of the prophecy of this book, if anyone adds to them, may God add to him the plagues which are written in this book. [19]If anyone takes away the things which are written in this book from the words of the book of this prophecy, God will take away his part from the tree of life and out of the holy city. [20]The one who bears witness to these things says, "Yes, I am coming quickly."

Amen! Yes, come, Lord Yeshua. [21]The grace of the Lord Yeshua be with all. Amen!

22:13 See note to 21:16.

22:16 Yeshua identifies himself in terms of his return: "I am the root and offspring of David" — he is coming to Yerushala'im to rule from David's throne; "the Bright and Morning Star" — which appears when night is darkest, signalling the coming of the dawn. "King Messiah, if he is from the living, David is his name. If he is from the dead, David is his name." (Mid. Lam. 1.51)

22:18 "Whoever adds..." Mid. BaMidbar Rabbah 14:4 says, "The Holy One, blessed be He, says: 'I have written twenty-four books for you. Be careful, and do not add to them.' Why? 'Of making many books there is no end.' [Eccl. 12:12] Everyone who reads a verse that is not from the twenty-four books, it is as if he read from the books [of the heretics] which were put outside. This is the reason for the warning, 'Be careful of making many books,' for whosoever does so has no portion in the Age to Come."

22:20 After Ya'aleh veYavo, we pray, "May our eyes witness Your return to Zion with compassion. Blessed are You, O Everpresent Lord, who returns His Divine Presence to Zion."

22:20-21 "'Blessed be the Everpresent Lord forever. Amen and amen.' [Ps. 89:52] ...'Amen' in this world, and 'Amen' in the age to come." (Mid. Psalms 89.4 and 106.9)

ADDITIONAL NOTES

These are brief comments on complex issues.

THE SEPTUAGINT

By 332 B.C.E., Alexander the Great had established Greek rule over Israel and the rest of the Middle East. Though his rule was short, its impact lasted for centuries. Jews living in Diaspora began to speak and read Greek and not Hebrew, becoming separated from the Scriptures. Even in the land of Israel, the use of Greek was widespread. "Thus it came about that, although the common people spoke Aramaic, Greek was also known at least to the learned, so that Palestine [sic] was bilingual. Greek terms were used to designate such essentially Jewish institutions as the Sanhedrin, and it has been claimed that more than 1100 Greek terms are used in the Talmud."[1]

We are told that the Septuagint translation of the Torah from Hebrew into Greek was begun in Alexandria sometime in the third century B.C.E., under King Ptolemy. The modern name of the translation comes from the traditional story of its seventy (*septuaginta* in Latin) translators. The rest of Tanakh and the Apocrypha were then translated in the following hundred years. The story of the beginning of the Septuagint is presented in "The Letter of Aristeas," which was written in the second century B.C.E.[2]

There is general agreement on the indispensability of the Septuagint for understanding the text of the Messianic Writings. There is general disagreement on the accuracy of the Septuagint for knowing the original Hebrew text of Tanakh. Some have claimed it to be superior to the Masoretic text. Others have claimed it to be completely unreliable and irrelevant. A correct assessment lies, most likely, between these two extremes.

Philo, echoing "The Letter of Aristeas," said of the translators, "they, like men inspired, prophesied, not one saying one thing and another another, but every one of them employed the self-same nouns and verbs, as if some unseen prompter had suggested all their language to them. …these translators [were] not mere interpreters but hierophants and prophets to whom it had been granted to their honest and guileless minds to go along with the most pure spirit of Moses."[3]

Josephus (Antiq. 12:86-12:118 [12.2.11.86-12.2.15.118]) and Tal. Megila 9a also echo the praise found in the Letter of Aristeas. To the contrary, however, Megillat Ta'anit says that, on the day the Septuagint Torah translation was completed, darkness descended upon the world for three days. The Talmud both praises and condemns the translation.

"The two conflicting opinions expressed in the Talmud regarding the attitude of the sages toward the Septuagint, one of which was favorable and the other derogatory, were due to the chronological historical development of Judaism and Christianity. During the Second Commonwealth the Septuagint was highly regarded by the Jews. In fact, Philo said that the men who translated the Pentateuch into Greek were inspired prophets. The sages of the Talmud also spoke very highly of the Septuagint. The seventy-two men who translated the five books of Moses were regarded by the sages as having divine inspiration. They were called *Zekenim*, a title which was given only to scholars. Only when the Christians made use of the Septuagint for the purpose of furthering Christianity and hence interpolated Christological passages, did a change of attitude towards it come over the rabbis. According to the rabbis of the later period, the day when the Pentateuch was translated into Greek was as bad a day for Israel as the day when the golden calf was melted."[4]

It may also be that there was a positive attitude toward the initial translation of the Torah, but a negative attitude toward the subsequent translation of the rest of Tanakh. "R. Yehuda said, 'When

our Rabbis allowed Greek, they did not allow it except for a Torah scroll, and this is because of what King Ptolemy did ...who gathered seventy-two elders..." (Tal. Megila 9a)

Since we do not have the original text of Tanakh, we can only judge the accuracy of the LXX, or any other translation, by secondary standards. To a lesser extent, the same is true of the Masoretic text, which is not a translation. There is evidence that the Masoretic texts do not always follow what had previously been recognized as the traditional text. Standardization of the Hebrew text began in the second century C.E.

Harry Orlinsky pointed out that, "the rabbinic literature itself, in quotations from the Bible, exhibits more frequently than is generally realized readings that differ from those preserved in our so-called 'masoretic' texts, readings that are not due to faulty memory and that crop up in Hebrew manuscripts and/or biblical quotations in Mechilta, Sifra, Sifre, the Gemara, the grammatical works of ibn Janah, etc."[5]

Sometimes the Septuagint is more in agreement with the older traditional text than the Masoretic is. "The Haggadah text begins with the text *Avadim Havinu* and includes the phrase *uvizroa netuya* (Deut. 6:21) which is not Masoretic but accords with the Septuagint. Likewise the wise son asks (in all texts up to the 13th century) *Ma haeduth* (Deut. 6:20) and includes the word *othanu* in accordance with the Septuagint in opposition to M.T. *ethchem*."[6]

In Orlinsky's view, "the Septuagint of Samuel... not only fails to coincide with our preserved, so-called masoretic text, but is often clearly superior to it."[7] But, again, since we do not have the original Hebrew manuscripts, there is a measure of subjectivity in all such judgments.

> *Since we do not have the original text of Tanakh, we can only judge the accuracy of the LXX, or any other translation, by secondary standards.*

This does not mean in any way that the LXX as a whole is a better text than the Masoretic; far from it. It simply means that the Masoretic text must be understood to be a close approximation of the originals. Occasionally, the LXX, like the Dead Sea Scrolls, can be helpful in trying to determine what the original text of Tanakh most likely was.

Almost always, however, the LXX is very helpful in understanding the compiled texts of the Messianic Writings.

FOOTNOTES

1. W.D. Davies, Paul and Rabbinic Judaism: Some Rabbinic Elements in Pauline Theology, London, SPCK, 1948, P. 5

2. R.H. Charles, ed., "The Letter Of Aristeas," The Apocrypha and Pseudopigrapha of the Old Testament, Vol. 2, The Clarendon Press, Oxford, 1963

3. "De Vita Mosis II," 7:37-38, The Works of Philo: Complete and Unabridged, trans. C.D. Yonge, Hendrickson Publishers, Peabody, Mass.,1993, P. This claim of supernatural inspiration leads to one of the criticisms of the LXX: the original Hebrew text contains subtleties and intentional ambiguities which no one translation can accurately reproduce.

4. Solomon Zeitlin, in Aristeas to Philocrates; Letter of Aristeas, Moses Hadas, Harper, NY, 1951, P. 81 n.110 Masekhet Soferim 1:6-7 calls that day as great a tragedy as the day of the Golden Calf.

5. Harry Orlinsky, "The Masoretic Text: A Critical Evaluation," in The Canon and Masorah of the Hebrew Bible, ed. Sid Z. Leiman, Ktav Publishing House, NY, 1974, Pp. 833-877 The quoted portion is on P. 852.

"There are in the Mishnah sixteen variations... In the Talmud, 105 such variations occur..." Alfred Edersheim, The Life and Times of Jesus the Messiah, Vol. 2, Longmans, Green, and Co., London, 1903, P.691

6. Herbert Basser, "The Development of the Pharisaic Idea of Law as a Sacred Cosmos," Journal for the Study of Judaism, Vol. XVI, 6/85, no.1, P.110 n.17

7. Orlinsky, "The Masoretic Text: A Critical Evaluation," op. cit., P. 854

"The Virgin will be Pregnant"

Some people claim that Matthias's citation of Isaiah 7:14 is inaccurate and inappropriate for three reasons: 1) *Almah*, the Hebrew word that Isaiah uses, does not mean "virgin," but rather "young woman" or "young maiden." 2) If Isaiah had wanted to say "virgin," he would have used *betulah*. 3) The context has nothing to do with the Messiah, since the prophecy is fulfilled in the birth of Isaiah's second son. In brief, however, all three claims are false.

1) Matthias quotes from the LXX, the most widely used Jewish Greek text of the first century. The LXX was translated in the 2d and 3d centuries before the Common Era. Since three-fourths of the Jewish population lived in Diaspora in the first century, the LXX was probably the most widely used Jewish text of the Scriptures. The Jewish translators of the LXX chose to translate *almah* into Greek as *parthenos*, i.e. "virgin".

The root meaning of almah *and its usage in cognate languages means "to hide, to conceal."[2] The Talmud affirms this meaning in Sotah 12b.*

Almah is never used in Tanakh to describe a woman who is not a virgin. (Likewise, the original English "maiden" or "maid" referred to a woman who is a virgin.) Other Jewish translations translate *almah* as "virgin". As Cyrus Gordon, the renowned Jewish scholar and archaeologist, observed: "The commonly held view that 'virgin' is Christian, whereas 'young woman' is Jewish is not quite true. The fact is that the Septuagint, which is the Jewish translation made in pre-Christian Alexandria, takes *almah* to mean 'virgin' here. Accordingly, the New Testament follows Jewish interpretation in Isaiah 7:14.

"Therefore, the New Testament rendering of *almah* as 'virgin' for Isaiah 7:14 rests on the older Jewish interpretation..."[1] There is a long, long history of *almah* meaning "virgin".

The root meaning of *almah* and its usage in cognate languages means "to hide, to conceal."[2] The Talmud affirms this meaning in Sotah 12b. Given the sexual meaning of the Biblical phrase "to uncover the nakedness," the root meaning of *almah* would indicate a woman who has not been uncovered, i.e. one who has not had sexual relations.

In Yigdal, God is described as *ne'alam*, i.e. unknowable.

If Isaiah had only wanted to indicate "a young woman," He would have used *na'arah*.

2) As for *betulah* being the clear, unequivocal word for "virgin," that also is simply not the case. "R. Nahman b. Isaac explained: 'It is the opinion of the following Tanna, because it was taught: A *betulah*, the only meaning of *betulah* is young woman (*na'arah*); and so it is said in Scripture, And the young woman (*na'arah*) was fair to look upon, a *betulah*.'" (Tal. Yebamoth 61b)

The verse R. Nahman b. Isaac referred to is Gen. 24:16: "The girl [Rebekah] was very beautiful, a *betulah*; and no man had ever lain with her." We are told both that Rebekah was a *betulah*, and also that "no man had ever lain with her."

Each young woman in Jabesh Gilead was described in the book of Judges in a similar way. "They found among the people living in Jabesh Gilead four hundred young women [*na'arot*], *betulot*, who had not known a man by lying with a male, and they took them to the camp at Shiloh in Canaan." (Judg. 21:12)

In both these cases in Scripture, the information that the woman was physically a virgin is additional to the fact that she was a *betulah*. By itself, the word *betulah* was not considered sufficient to indicate virginity. The Rabbis considered it to be an indication of a legal status.

"Who is regarded as *betulah*? Any woman, even though she is married, who has never yet observed a flow....Our Rabbis taught: [If a virgin] married and observed a discharge of blood that was due to the marriage, or if when she bore a child she observed a discharge of blood that was due to the birth, she is still called a *betulah*, because the virgin of whom the Rabbis spoke is one that is so in regards to menstrual blood but not one who is so in regard to the blood of virginity." (Niddah, I,2; 8b; cf 11b) The Tosefta for Niddah I. 4 says, "Who is a *betulah*? Any girl who has never seen a drop of blood in her life, and even if she is married and has had children, I call her a *betulah* until she will see the first drop of menstrual blood."

In this Talmudic passage, the married girl is still considered a *betulah*, even if she has had sexual intercourse, naturally conceived, and given birth to a child. Elsewhere the Talmud asks the question: "May a high priest marry a *betulah* who has become pregnant?" (Tal. Chagigah 14b-15a)

In Jer. 31:3H, God promises to rebuild as a *betulah* an Israel whom He had destroyed and sent into exile for her harlotry.

3) The immediate context of Isaiah 7:14 is chapters 7 through 12. These chapters form a unit. Some parts of this prophetic portion were fulfilled within three years following the imminent invasion of Judah. Some were fulfilled later, and some have not yet been fulfilled.

Isaiah said, "Here I am, and the children the Everpresent Lord has given me. We are for signs and wonders in Israel from the Everpresent Lord, Commander of Forces, who dwells on Mount Zion." (Is. 8:18) The prophecies connected to the name of *She'ar Yashuv* — "a remnant will return" — Isaiah's first son, have not yet been completely fulfilled. (cf. Is. 10:20-22) Nor have the prophecies connected to Isaiah's name — "the Everpresent Lord is salvation". Nor have all the prophecies connected to the name of Isaiah's second son. (cf. Is. 8:7-10)

If Isaiah's wife-to-be, the prophetess, is the *almah* of 7:14, then she also is a sign to Israel. In that case, Isaiah should have said, "Here am I, the children the Everpresent Lord has given me, and my second wife. We are for signs and wonders in Israel from the Everpresent Lord Almighty, who dwells on Mount Zion."

The *almah* of 7:14 is for a sign in Israel. Isaiah does not mention the prophetess, or any wife he ever had, as being a sign to Israel. If she were the fulfillment of the almah of 7:14, he would have mentioned her even as he mentioned his children.

The prophecies connected to "Emmanuel," the prophesied son of the *almah*, have not been fulfilled. The ancient rabbis found at least 16 Messianic prophecies in Isaiah 7 to 12. Some of these are transparently Messianic, others are embedded in the context. All of these rabbinically acknowledged

Messianic references are part of the scriptural context for Is. 7:14. In fact, the only portion in all of Scripture in which the ancient Rabbis found more Messianic prophecies is Isaiah chapters 49 to 54.

Is. 9:5-6H says: "For to us a child is born, to us a son is given, and the government will be on his shoulders. And he will be called Wonderful Counselor, Mighty God, Everlasting Father, Prince of Peace. Of the increase of his government and peace there will be no end. He will reign on David's throne and over his kingdom, establishing and upholding it with justice and righteousness from that time on and forever. The zeal of the Almighty Everpresent Lord will accomplish this." This is a unique child, the Messiah of Israel. The prophecy does not speak at all of the sons of Isaiah.

The entire eleventh chapter of Isaiah was recognized as referring to Messiah and his kingdom. For example: "A shoot will come up from the stump of Jesse; from his roots a Branch will bear fruit. The Spirit of the Everpresent Lord will rest on him – the Spirit of wisdom and of understanding, the Spirit of counsel and of power, the Spirit of knowledge and of the fear of the Everpresent Lord – and he will delight in the fear of the Everpresent Lord. He will not judge by what he sees with his eyes, or decide by what he hears with his ears; but with righteousness he will judge the needy, with justice he will give decisions for the poor of the earth. He will strike the earth with the rod of his mouth; with the breath of his lips he will slay the wicked. Righteousness will be his belt and faithfulness the sash around his waist....

"In that day the Root of Jesse will stand as a banner for the peoples; the goyim/Gentiles will rally to him, and his place of rest will be glorious. In that day the Lord will reach out his hand a second time to reclaim the remnant that is left of his people from Assyria..." (Is. 11:1-5,10-11) This unique child is the Messiah. No one ever connects the prophecy with Isaiah's sons.

The sign/*ot* that God is promising in Is. 7:14 is deep as Sheol and as high as Heaven. What qualifies as such a tremendous sign? Exactly that which the prophet prophesies: a virgin conceiving and giving birth to a child who is "God with us".

The prophecy of the supernaturally conceived son in Is. 7:14 is related to the prophecy of the supernatural son in Is. 9:6-7, and to the prophecy of the supernatural son in Is. 11. They all point to the Messiah.

The three claims that Matthias's citation of Isaiah 7:14 is inaccurate and inappropriate are not true. The claims are in opposition to both the scriptural and historical record, including the Talmud. (I deal with this issue more extensively in my booklet, "God, the Rabbis, and the Virgin Birth".)

FOOTNOTES

1. Gordon, Cyrus H., "Almah in Isaiah 7:14," The Journal of Bible & Religion, Vol. 21 (April 1953), P. 106
2. The Complete Hebrew-English Dictionary, Reuben Alcalay, Massadah Publishing Co., Tel Aviv, 1965, P. 1907

"Your Children Saw Your Kingdom"

In the traditional liturgy (often after *Mi Khamokha*), we read: "Your children saw Your Kingdom as You parted the sea before Moses. They responded, 'This is my God,' and they said, 'The Everpresent Lord will reign forever and ever.'" [*malkhutekha ra'u vanekha bokaa yam lifney Moshe zeh eli anu v'amru adonai yimlokh l'olam vaed*]

God's Kingdom was not then established at the Red Sea, and no one physically saw it, but the people expressed confidence that "the Everpresent Lord will reign forever and ever." So the phrase, "Your children saw Your Kingdom," was used at the time of the liturgy to mean something other than the fullness of the Kingdom upon the earth. We want to understand what the phrase meant then, in its historical context. Apparently the phrase meant that by seeing God's power and glory, the people saw and recognized the nature of His Kingdom. They did not see its fullness, but they saw what it is.

> ...the phrase, "Your children saw Your Kingdom," was used at the time of the liturgy to mean something other than the fullness of the Kingdom upon the earth. We want to understand what the phrase meant then, in its historical context. Apparently the phrase meant that by seeing God's power and glory, the people saw and recognized the nature of His Kingdom. They did not see its fullness, but they saw what it is.

It seems that when Yeshua spoke about his disciples seeing his kingdom, he was using the phrase in the same contemporary sense. It is similar to his response to the question brought by the disciples of Yohanan — "Are you the One who is coming, or should we look for another?" [Mt. 11:2-5] "Yeshua answered them, "Go and tell Yohanan the things which you⁺ hear and see: the blind receive their sight, the lame walk, the lepers are cleansed, the deaf hear, the dead are raised up, and the poor have the good news proclaimed to them." I.e., 'The answer to your question is in what you see, if you are able to understand it.'

It is also similar to his response to the authorities in the Temple when they asked him to state clearly whether or not he claimed to be the Messiah: "I told you⁺, and you⁺ do not believe. The deeds that I do in my Father's Name, these testify about me." [Yhn. 10:25] That is to say, 'If you have seen God's power in healing, deliverance, etc., then you know who I am. My actions have told you.' Many people physically saw the miracles, but did not "hear" them proclaiming Yeshua to be the Messiah. But that is how he "told" them. There was no physical voice to hear, but the visible deeds were a clear answer to the question about his nature and identity.

It is why he responded to Filipos, "The one who has seen me has seen the Father." Yoh. 14:9b Something other than natural eyesight is implied. 'If you "see" me, then you "see" the Father.'

Those who have eyes to see can see. Those who have ears to hear can hear. "The heavens declare the glory of God, and the expanse tells of the work of His hands. Day to day, speech pours forth, and night to night reveals knowledge. There is no speech and there is no language where their voice is not heard." Ps. 19:2-4H

"The Seat of Moses"

Throughout Matthias 23, Yeshua denounced the Torah scholars and Perushim for their actions and their teachings. He condemned their teaching on the exaltation of leaders (vv. 6-12), on oaths (v. 16-23), on purity (vv. 25-28.), on self-righteousness (v. 27-33). He says it is not likely that they will escape the condemnation of Gehinnom, and that anyone who is convinced to follow them becomes "twice as much a son of Gehinnom as" they are. (v. 15)

Earlier, Yeshua had explicitly warned his disciples to "'Take heed and beware of the leaven of the Perushim and Tzadukim'... they understood that he did not tell them to beware of the leaven of bread, but of the teaching of the Perushim and Tzadukim." (Mt. 16:6,12) Yeshua told a group of Perushim, "you⁺ disobey the commandment of God for the sake of your⁺ tradition." (Mt. 15:3)

They, on the other hand, saw some of his actions, like healing a man on Shabbat, as contrary to the Torah. Ultimately, in keeping with their understanding of Torah, they decided that anyone who recognized Yeshua as the Messiah should be thrown out of the synagogue, and that Yeshua himself should be killed.

Yeshua presented himself as the authoritative interpreter of Torah, the Word of God clothed in flesh. For example, "You have heard, but I say to you..." [Mt. 5:21,27,33,38,43] There were some Perushim, such as Nakdimon, who believed in him, but in general, the Perushim and the leadership are presented in the text as Yeshua's main antagonists. The cause of that antagonism was twofold: 1) He did not acknowledge their authority; and 2) They did not acknowledge his authority.

All of this makes the passage that we have in the Greek text of Mt. 23:2-3 seem very strange: "The Torah scholars and the Perushim have been sitting on the seat of Moses. 3So do and observe all things that they tell you⁺, but do not do according to their works, because they say, and do not do."

What did Yeshua mean by "the seat of Moses"? It is a phrase that he uses only this once, and he is the only one who uses it. It does not appear anywhere else in the Bible, or in Talmud, Midrash, or the Apocryphal writings. To what was Yeshua referring?

So the things that the Torah scholars and Perushim were doing which should not be imitated were things they told others to do, but did not do themselves. Yet because they sat in "the seat of Moses," they had the right to tell people to do certain things. Yeshua affirmed their practice of tithing, but condemned them for neglecting justice, mercy, and faith.

"Observe and do all things that they tell you⁺" should be "Do and observe all things that they tell you⁺. (Mt. 15:6) He called them "blind guides" (Mt. 23:24), "...blind leaders of the blind. And if the blind leads the blind, both will fall into a ditch." (Mt. 15:14)

And he explicitly told his disciples to beware of the teaching of the Torah scholars and Perushim, so that they themselves would not become children of Gehinnom. We have ample evidence that Yeshua himself did not advocate the invalidation of Torah.

Contextually, obeying the Perushim and Torah scholars is connected to their sitting on the seat of Moses. The admonition to not do what they do is connected to their own failure to follow Torah.

What did Yeshua mean by "the seat of Moses"? It is a phrase that he uses only this once, and he is the only one who uses it. It does not appear anywhere else in the Bible, or in Talmud, Midrash, or the Apocryphal writings. To what was Yeshua referring?

An actual stone chair in the synagogue?

Some say there was a stone chair in the synagogues called "the seat of Moses," from which the Torah was taught. In the ruins of seven synagogues, archaeologists have found a stone chair. These chairs differ significantly one from another, and scholars disagree on their purpose. The vast majority of synagogue ruins do not contain any stone chair.

"The actual term 'Cathedra of Moses,' however, has never been found on any archaeological artifact... it is more probably that the cathedra was merely a piece of furniture on which an important person sat, as was the case elsewhere in the ancient world."[1]

Let's put this in perspective. In the ruins of many synagogues throughout the world, archaeologists have found a mikveh, the bath for ritual immersion. Abundant references to the mikveh appear throughout Talmud and Tosefta, as well as in the Midrashim. Rashi, Rambam, the Shulhan Arukh, the Maharal, the Zohar, et al. speak about it. The Rabbis regulated everything about the mikveh, and it is a normal part of traditional Jewish observance throughout history and remains so today.

Let's compare that to the stone chairs. Only seven have been found. These seven stone chairs vary greatly one from another, and some may not even have been for sitting.[2] The Rabbis do not regulate them in any way; they do not even mention them. There are no stone chairs found in modern synagogues.

There is absolutely no record of anyone calling such a stone chair "the seat of Moses". Torah does not speak of it, nor do the Rabbis or later commentators. It is never mentioned in the synagogue liturgy. It is totally absent from Jewish practice — ancient, medieval, and modern.

Additionally, the Rabbis did not teach that the person reading or teaching from Torah should sit. In at least some situations, they prescribed that the person reading or teaching from Torah was to stand, not sit. (e.g. Meg. 21a; III:1) So there is no evidence to support the claim that the stone chair was "the seat of Moses," or that it was the place from which Torah was taught. There is only unsupported conjecture.

A metaphor for authoritative Torah teaching?

Others say that the phrase does not refer to an actual chair, but is a metaphor that symbolizes the authority to interpret and teach Torah. If it was such a metaphor, then it would have been extremely important, since, as in political theory, there is no authority higher than that which decrees what the Law is.[3] It would have been infinitely more important to the Rabbis than the mikveh, because all the rabbinic prescriptions for the mikveh (and for everything else) depended upon the establishment of rabbinic authority.

The Rabbis wrote extensively about the importance of recognizing their authority. They connected themselves to every scripture they could. So there is every reason to believe that they would have retained anything that might have furthered their claims. But no Pharisaic or rabbinic literature even mentions "the Seat of Moses" as a symbol of their authority. The actual phrase itself appears only once, in the 5th or 6th century Pesikta deRav Kahana.[4] Neither the Perushim nor the Rabbis used "the Seat of Moses" as a metaphor for authoritative Torah teaching.

Is it conceivable that Yeshua would have told his disciples and the crowds that they should follow the teaching of the Perushim, and therefore reject his own? For example, their teaching nullified his on basic issues concerning Gentiles, faith, salvation, and Messiah.

Consider their teaching on Yeshua's authority to forgive sins (Lk. 5:21) or their teaching about healing on Shabbat (Lk. 6:7,11). The Scriptures say they rejected the purpose of God for themselves. (Lk. 7:30) They also rejected the commandments of God, choosing to replace them with their own commandments. (Mk. 7:9) They took away the key of knowledge and hindered those who wanted to enter into God's kingdom. (Lk. 11:52) Yeshua said, "Beware of the Torah scholars… they will receive greater condemnation." (Lk. 20:46) It is therefore not possible that Yeshua told his talmidim to follow the teaching of the Torah scholars and Perushim, and the historical evidence shows that, in fact, they did not.

A metaphor for the authority to decide civil cases?

It may not be possible to know with certainty what Yeshua meant by "the seat of Moses," but it is possible to suggest a meaning that is consistent with all that he says elsewhere, is consistent with Tanakh, is consistent with how his disciples lived, and is also consistent with rabbinic literature.

There are three passages in the Scriptures where we read that Moses sat. The first is where "Moses fled from before Pharaoh and lived in the land of Midian; and he sat down by a well." (Ex. 2:15b) This act led to Moses meeting and marrying Zipporah. That could provide many metaphors, but it's difficult to imagine how the Torah scholars and Perushim could have gained any authority by sitting in this seat.

The second passage refers to the battle against Amalek. "And the hands of Moses were heavy, and they took a stone and put it under him, and he sat on it." (Ex. 17:12a) This incident also could provide many metaphors, but it was a one time occurrence, a miraculous incident, without any prescribed imitation for Israel. Neither the Rabbis nor anyone else make much of it. It does not seem likely that this would provide the content for what Yeshua had in mind.

The third passage, however, may speak directly to the point. "And so it was, on the next day, that Moses sat to judge the people; and the people stood before Moses from morning until evening…. 'When they have a difficulty, they come to me, and I judge between one and another; and I make known the statutes of God and His laws.'" (Ex. 18:13-16)

Moses sat to judge disputes between people, explaining his decisions according to the statutes and laws of God. Torah, after all, was given as national law for the civil society of Israel. It includes a judicial function. These cases that came before Moses appear to be what we would call civil cases, rather than criminal cases, since they involve disputes between two parties.

The Talmud does speak about such court cases: "at the time of the completion of the case all agree that the judges sit and the litigants stand, for it is written: 'And Moses sat to judge the people; and the people stood.'" (Tal. Shevuot 30b) This refers to cases where two people "have some dispute with each other." The Talmud presents the actions of Moses as a precedent in deciding the same kind of cases, cases where the judges sit as Moses did, i.e., in his place.

The father-in-law of Moses counselled him to delegate to others the authority to sit and judge, and to focus instead on teaching the people what God had commanded. And Moses did that. (Ex. 18:20-26)

Before Moses died, he made provision for the continuance of civil order, for others who would sit and judge in his place. "You are to appoint judges and officers in all your gates, which the Everpresent your God gives you, according to your tribes, and they are to judge the people with just judgment."

(Dt. 16:18) Such judges were acting in the place of Moses. When they sat to judge, they were "sitting in his seat," exercising the authority that God had given to him.

The responsibility to teach Torah, the laws of purity, etc. was also delegated, but it was delegated to the priests. (cf. Dt. 24:8; Mal. 2:6-9; Hag. 2:11) So if Yeshua had been telling Israel to obey the Torah scholars and Perushim rather than the priests in such matters, then he would have been teaching (and sinning) against the Law of God. The priests also exercised the judicial function sometimes, but they were not the only ones who did. (e.g. Dt. 17:9-10)

It seems likely that Yeshua was telling Israel to obey the Torah scholars and Perushim who were acting as judges in these kind of civil cases. In that case, he would have been calling his disciples and the crowds to recognize the authority which the Torah gave to the judge. He would have been upholding Torah, rather than rejecting it.

At the time of Yeshua, did the Torah scholars and the Perushim function as judges in disputes between people? Those kind of disputes were settled "in the gates" of the different towns and communities. 1Maccabees presents the Torah scholars as having authority to establish justice. (1Mac. 5:42; 7:12) The Talmud claims that the Rabbis had this authority.[5] (e.g. Tal. Sanhedrin 6b)

Certainly the Torah scholars and the Perushim (and the Rabbis) claimed more authority than this; they claimed to be the authorized interpreters and teachers of Torah.[6] But Yeshua never recognized them as that. If he had, then he would have been declaring himself to be a blasphemer and imposter. To the contrary, he presented his own teaching as authoritative. All the people noticed that Yeshua "taught them as one having authority, and not as the Torah scholars." (Mt. 7:28-29) And the Torah scholars challenged that authority. (Mk. 1:27-28) But at that time, Yeshua did not function as a judge, especially not in civil disputes. (cf. Luke 12:13-14)

There is no reason to believe that Yeshua spoke of sitting "on the seat of Moses" as the equivalent of having the authority to interpret or decree Torah. If he had, he would certainly have applied it to himself. His interaction with the Torah scholars and Perushim, as well as his repeated warnings about their teachings, amply shows that he did not recognize their having such authority. Yeshua's disciples also never recognized the Torah scholars and Perushim as having such authority.

There is, however, reason to believe that Yeshua spoke of sitting "on the seat of Moses" as the equivalent of having authority to decide case law, according to Torah, between different disputants. In this sense, it could be said that the Torah scholars and Perushim "sat on the seat of Moses".

It is something that Yeshua could have meant by "the seat of Moses," because it is consistent with the rest of what he taught, and it is consistent with the Scriptures. The lives of his disciples demonstrate faithfulness to this principle.[7] In light of this, Lk. 22:29-30 — "You⁺ will sit on thrones, judging the twelve tribes of Israel" — would likely indicate that, in the Messianic Kingdom, those whom Yeshua chooses will exercise this same function.

FOOTNOTES

1. Levine, Lee I., The Ancient Synagogue: The First Thousand Years, Yale U. Press, New Haven, 2000, Pp. 350,351. See the entire discussion, Pp. 347-351.

2. "Roth and, more recently, Rahmani interpret the cathedra as the place where the Torah scroll was placed after it was read." (Levine, The Ancient Synagogue, P. 350)

3. "In the seventeenth century Locke's *Of Civil Government* stated in chapter thirteen that, 'there can be but one supreme power, which is the legislative, to which all the rest are and must be subordinate.' Thomas Hobbes' *Leviathan* stated in chapter twenty-six that 'the legislator... is... the sovereign.'" A. London Fell, <u>Origins of Legislative Sovereignty and the Legislative State, Vol. 1, Corasius and the Rennaissance, Systematization of Roman Law</u>, Oelgeschlager, Gunn & Hain, Publishers, Inc., Cambridge, MA, 1983, P. 1

4. Pesikta deRav Kahana, Perek Aleph, Siman Yod. See also Levine, <u>The Ancient Synagogue</u>, op.cit., P. 347 n. 167

5. The equivalent of "the seat of Moses" appears in a letter written in 1191, in Judeo-Arabic, by the Exilarch Samuel of Mosul. For the Sephardic Jewish community at the time, the Exilarch was "the King on earth," and the Gaon was the chief judge. There was a conflict between the two over finances and power. Jacob Mann, <u>Texts and Studies in Jewish History and Literature, Vol. 1</u>, Ktav Publishing House, NY, 1972, Pp. 228-248

    In terms of finances, the conflict concerned the right to receive the half-shekel tax that was stipulated in Torah for support of the Tabernacle and Temple. (cf. Ex. 30:13-16) In terms of power, the conflict concerned the right of lawful ordination and the right to exercise the judicial function.

    Samuel writes on behalf of a school, whose head he had appointed. The school "is portrayed as the throne of the Torah in direct succession from Moses. He who opposes the authority of the school is opposing God and Moses his messenger." Ibid., P. 237

    The designation was not connected to interpretation of Torah, but to the right to decide civil cases. "The Exilarch upon the request of Netanel [Hallevi] confirms his appointment as head of the school. At an assembly of elders and other people in Bagdad he bestowed this title upon Netanel and now he lets it be known that Netanel is president of the supreme Jewish court in Egypt, having the right to establish law courts in every district and to command obedience to his behest." Ibid., P. 231

    About the same time, Maimonides wrote about the qualifications for the leader of the Great Sanhedrin. He said, "The one who is greater in wisdom than all the others is appointed head over them. He is the head of the yeshiva and is called *Nasi* by the sages in every place. He is the one who stands in the place of Moses our Teacher." (<u>Mishneh Torah</u>, Sanhedrin 1.3) In a later portion, Maimonides speaks of the Great Sanhedrin as a whole as functioning in the place of Moses. (Ibid., Sanhedrin 5.1) I.e., it is in the exercise of judicial responsibility that one can occupy the place of Moses.

6. In modern legal philosophy, there is ongoing disagreement over the role of judges. Some view judges as servants of the Law; others view them as creators of the Law. Some see the responsibility of the judge as being the strict application of the Law; others see it as being to make the Law responsive to society. The Biblical view is that the judges are under the Law, not over it.

7. 1Co. 6:1-8, written to Gentile disciples of Yeshua living outside the land, encourages them not to bring suit against each other in the regular courts, but to find members of their own body of believers who can adjudicate.

    (This note is an abridgement of the chapter on "The Seat of Moses" in my forthcoming book on Biblical Law.)

The Death of Messiah

In addition to the Messianic Writings, other ancient Jewish texts speak of Messiah dying. The Talmud says that Zech. 12:9-14 speaks of the death of Messiah: "It is good for the one who says it is about the killing of Messiah the son of Joseph, according to what is written: 'And they shall look upon me because they have thrust him through, and they will mourn for him as one mourns for his only son.'"[1] (According to some scholars, one of the parchment fragments of the Dead Sea Scrolls, also speaks of Messiah being pierced and killed, but much of the text is missing.[2])

It is not clear why the Rabbis spoke here of Messiah as "the Son of Joseph," but they apparently wanted to distinguish between the suffering Messiah and the conquering Messiah. It seems to refer to Joseph who was sold into slavery in Egypt. Israel, Joseph's father, believed his son had died. It is worth noting that during the time Joseph was exiled from the land and people of Israel, he was brought up from the pit and exalted as ruler over the land. There he became the savior of Israel and of the nations.

In Tal. Sanhedrin 98b, "The Rabbis said: 'His [Messiah's] name is 'the leper scholar,' as it is written, Surely he hath borne our griefs, and carried our sorrows: yet we did esteem him a leper, smitten of God, and afflicted.'"[3] This text that the Rabbis applied to Messiah is from Isaiah 53:4.

The text in Isaiah continues: "But he was pierced for our transgressions, he was crushed for our iniquities; the chastening that brought us peace was upon him, and in his stripes there is healing for us. ...He was oppressed and afflicted, ...he was brought as a lamb to the slaughter... By oppression and judgment he was taken away. And who can speak of his descendants? For he was cut off from the land of the living...

"He was given a grave with the wicked, and with the rich in his death, though he had done no violence, nor was any deceit in his mouth. Yet the Everpresent Lord desired to crush him and cause him to be weak. and though the Everpresent Lord makes his life a guilt offering, he will see his offspring and prolong his days, and the desire of the Everpresent Lord will prosper in his hand.

"... Therefore I will give him a portion among the great, and he will divide the spoils with the strong, because he emptied his soul unto death, and was numbered with the transgressors. For he bore the sin of many, and interceded for the transgressors."[4]

It is not clear why the Rabbis spoke here of Messiah as "the Son of Joseph," but they apparently wanted to distinguish between the suffering Messiah and the conquering Messiah. It seems to refer to Joseph who was sold into slavery, in Egypt.

The eighteenth of the Psalms of Solomon, written around the middle of the first century B.C.E., contains the following prayer: "May God cleanse Israel in the day of mercy and blessing, in the day of election when He brings back His Messiah."[5] This presents Messiah coming once, departing this earth through death or some supernatural means, and then coming again to bring cleansing, mercy, and blessing to Israel.

In 4 Ezra, a first century document sometimes called the Apocalypse of Ezra, God says, "For My son the Messiah will be revealed with those who are with him, and those who remain will rejoice 400 years. And after these years My son the Messiah will die, and all who draw human breath."[6]

2 Baruch, written during the second half of the first century C.E., is believed to have Pharisaic-Rabbinic roots. It says, "And it will come to pass after these things, when the time of the coming

of the Messiah is fulfilled, that He will return in glory. Then all who have fallen asleep in hope of him will rise again."[7] Messiah is presented as having come and gone, but his return will bring the resurrection of the dead.

FOOTNOTES

1. Tal. Sukkah 52a
2. 4Q285
3. Soncino translation
4. Is. 53:5-12
5. Psalms of Solomon, cited in James H. Charlesworth, "The Concept of the Messiah in the Pseudepigrapha," Aufstieg und Niedergang Der Romischen Welt, II, Religion, de Gruyter, Berlin, 1979, P.199
6. 4 Ezra 7:28-29, ibid., P.202
7. 2 Baruch 30:1-2, ibid, P.200

Atonement through the Death of Another

In Tanakh, God prescribes the sacrifice of specific animals as a means of providing atonement for human sins. It is not clear why God accepts the death of the animals in the place of the death of the sinner, but it is clear that He does. In the Messianic Writings, God accepts the death of Yeshua in the place of the death of the sinner. There are also rabbinic passages which indicate that the death of one person can bring forgiveness to others.

God explicitly forbids human sacrifice, but He commanded Abraham to offer Isaac. In response to Abraham's obedience, God then commanded him not to offer Isaac, providing instead a ram. In the Yom Kippur liturgy, appeal is made to God for the forgiveness of our sins because of "the ashes of Isaac," as though he had been presented as a burnt offering.

In the extended Kedushah for the Yom Kippur Musaf service, we read: "Let there be an advocate for the ancient people... Our righteous Messiah is turned away from us; we shudder in horror, and there is no one to justify us. He carries the load of our iniquities and the yoke of our transgressions. And he is wounded because of our transgressions. He bears the heaviness of our sins on his shoulder, that he may find forgiveness for our iniquities. There is healing for us in his wound." (The Hebrew text can be found in The Complete Artscroll Machzor, Yom Kippur, Mesorah Publications, 1986, Pp. 827-828)

Much of this text is derived from Is. 53:5-12: "But he was wounded for our transgressions, bruised for our iniquities. The chastisement for our peace was upon him, and by his stripes we are healed. All we like sheep have gone astray; we have turned, every one, to his own way; and the Everpresent Lord has laid on him the iniquity of us all....

"He was taken away in humiliation and judgment, and who in his generation considered that he was cut off from the land of the living for the transgressions of My people; it was their plague. And they made his grave with the wicked, but with a rich man at his death; because he had done no violence, and no deceit in his mouth. Yet the Everpresent Lord desired to bruise him, to put him to grief.

"When You make his soul a guilt offering, he will see his seed, he will lenthen his days, and the desire of the Everpresent Lord will prosper in his hand. He will see the labor of his soul, and be satisfied. By his knowledge My righteous Servant will make many righteous, because he will carry their iniquities. Therefore I will give him a portion with the many, and he will divide the plunder with the strong because he emptied his soul unto death, and he was numbered with the transgressors, and he carried the sin of many, and interceded for the transgressors."

In this passage, which Tal. Sanhedrin 98b and the Targum also refer to Messiah, it is evident that the Everpresent Lord puts Messiah to death as a guilt offering for the sins and iniquity of the people. There are other passages in Tanakh which the Rabbis understood to indicate that the death of the righteous brings atonement for others.

God told Israel to set apart cities of refuge to which someone who accidentally killed another was to flee to escape vengeance. (Num. 35:6-34) When the high priest died, anyone who had committed manslaughter was free to return home from the cities of refuge. In some way, the death of the high priest put an end to the guilt of the one who had accidentally killed another.

In Tal. Makkot 11b, the question is raised as to whether atonement comes from the exile of the one who committed manslaughter or from the death of the high priest. R. Abaye says, "Do you think it is exile which atones? It is the death of the [high] priest which atones."

In Moed Katan 28a, "R. Ammi said, 'Why is Miriam's death [Num. 20:1] connected with the Torah portion about the red heifer? [Num. 19] This is to tell you that even as the red heifer atones, even so the death of the righteous atones.

"R. Eleazar said, 'Why is Aaron's death [Num. 20:26,28] connected with the priestly clothing? Even as the priestly clothing atones [Lev. 16:4,24,32,33], so the death of the righteous atones.'" (cf. Tal. Zevachim 88b)

"R. Hiyya b. Abba said, 'The sons of Aaron died on the first of Nisan. Then why is their death remembered on Day of Atonement? This is to teach that as the Day of Atonement brings atonement, in the same way the death of the righteous brings atonement.... And from where do we know that the death of the righteous brings atonement? Because it is written, *And they buried the bones of Saul [and Jonathan his son]* (II Sam. 21:14), and it is then written, *After that God was entreated for the land.*'" (Mid. Leviticus Rabbah 20:12)

The Talmud speaks about the plague that came when King David numbered the people, connecting its end with the death of someone righteous. (Num. 24) R. Eleazar said that the plague ended because of the death of Abishai. "R. Eleazar said, 'The Holy One, blessed be He, said to the [destroying] Angel: Take for Me a great man among them, that in him many debts can be paid for them.' ...Samuel said, 'He saw the ashes of Isaac [as though he had been sacrificed]'" (Tal. Berachot 62b)

There is also a case where the death of the wicked brings atonement. God commends Pinchas for putting to death Zimri and the Midianite woman he brought into his tent. Pinchas executed God's judgment and "made atonement for the children of Israel". (Num. 25:13, cf. Tal.Sanhedrin 82b)

Rashi commented on the setting apart of the Levites (Num. 8:9) and the need for all Israel to lay hands on them: "Inasmuch as the Levites were given as an atoning sacrifice instead of them [the whole congregation], they [the people] are to come and stand by their offering and lay their hands on them [the Levites]."

King David committed adultery with Bathsheba, and then had her husband Uriah killed in battle.

(2Sam. 11 &12) When David confessed his sin and turned away from it, God forgave him and did not put him to death. But, as judgment on David's sin, God put to death the innocent son of David, to whom Bathsheba had given birth.

"Destroy this temple"

"Some stood up and gave false testimony against him, saying, 'We heard him say, I will destroy this Temple that is made with hands, and in three days I will build another made without hands.'" (Mk. 14:57-58)

Why is this false testimony? Yeshua had said that the Temple would be destroyed [cf. Mt. 24:2], and he had said, "'Destroy this temple, and in three days I will raise it up.' So the Jewish authorities responded, 'This Temple took forty-six years to build, and are you going to raise it up in three days?' But he spoke of the temple of his body." [Y<u>h</u>n. 2:19-21]

The false witnesses were accusing Yeshua of saying that he would 1) destroy the Temple and 2) replace it with another. He had never said that he would destroy it. Nor had he ever said that he would replace it. That is why their testimony was false.

Some have taught that God destroyed the Temple, thus rejecting the Jews, in order to raise up the new Temple of Yeshua's body, choosing "the Church" in replacement of the Jews. The Scriptures do speak of believers together as "the temple of the Ruakh Kodesh". [1Co. 6:19] And they do say that in the Age of the New Heavens and New Earth, there will be no Temple building in Yerushala'im, because "God — the Everpresent, the Sovereign over all — and the Lamb, are its temple." [<u>H</u>azon 21:22]

But both those things are the result of God fulfilling to the Jewish people His promises to them: "I will dwell in your midst. ...You will be My people, I will be your God." [E.g. Ezek. 36:28, 43:7] Neither of them is presented as rejection or replacement. The Scriptures never mention "the Church"; the *ekklesia* in the Septuagint text is explicitly the *kahal Yisrael*. (cf. Dt. 23 LXX)

There are many things in this age (and in the age to come) that both are what they are and yet also represent something that is coming. Marriage is one of those things. Yeshua said that "in the resurrection they neither marry, nor are given in marriage." [Mt. 22:30] But it would be a serious error to teach that God has done away with marriage now. [cf. 1Tim. 4:3] Even the life which we have in this age is a shadow and representation of life in the Age to Come.

We are to seek and pray now for the coming of the Messianic Kingdom (with its Temple). It is evident that God has a continuing purpose for the Temple. [cf. Ezek. 40-48] Yeshua weeps because of the coming destruction of Yerushala'im, her children, and the Temple. (Mt. 23:37-39, Lk. 19:41)

The teaching of those today who say that Yeshua has destroyed and replaced the Temple is remarkably close to the false testimony that the false witnesses gave against him long ago. The Scriptures characterize Yeshua's work as fulfillment, not replacement.

"Cleansing the Food"

Concerning Mk. 7:18-19, "Many modern scholars, following the interpretation suggested by Origen and Chrysostom, regard *katharizon* [to cleanse] as connected grammatically with *legei* [said] in ver. 18, and take it as the evangelist's comment on the implications of Jesus' words concerning Jewish dietary laws." (A Textual Commentary on the New Testament, P. 95n.) This is not, however, the result of scholarship, but rather the result of theological bias. It is asserted in opposition to the text.

Origen and Chrysostom were antagonistic towards God's Law and God's people, the Jews. So they suggested that "cleansing all the food" should be re-interpreted as a declaration by Yeshua that "All foods are clean." The phrase does not appear in Mt. 15:16-17. Their "suggestion" cannot be sustained from the text, and cannot be reconciled with 1) Yeshua saying "I did not come to abolish the Law, but to bring it to fullness." Nor can it be reconciled with 2) the fact that years later none of the talmidim believed that Yeshua had said anything that made unclean animals clean. In Acts 10, for example, Kefa still declares, "I have never eaten anything that is unholy or unclean."

Nor can it be reconciled with 3) the historical record, which shows that all the ambassadors continued to live in accordance with God's Law. Irenaeus condemned as heretics those who maintained that the Law had passed away. "For all those who are of a perverse mind, having been set against the Mosaic legislation judging it to be dissimilar and contrary to the doctrine of the gospel, have not applied themselves to investigate the causes of the differences of each covenant. Since, therefore, they have been deserted by the paternal love, and puffed up by Satan, being brought over to the doctrine of Simon Magus, they have apostatized in their opinions from Him who is God, and imagined that they have themselves discovered more than the ambassadors, by finding out another God; and [have imagined] that the ambassadors proclaimed the good news still somewhat under the influence of Jewish opinions, but that they themselves are purer and more intelligent than the ambassadors." (Ante-Nicene Christian Library, Vol. 5/1, trans. by A. Roberts and J. Donaldson, T & T Clark, Edinburgh, 1867, P. 309)

Whatever Origen's and Chrysostom's problems may have been — and they both had major problems — they did not produce their own translations. And so they did not insert their theology into the text itself. Not even the Latin Vulgate did that in this passage.

Tal. Berachot 60b gives a roughly contemporaneous view, speaking of the importance of the bodily openings that God has created in man. These bodily openings are a way in which He "heals all flesh". Commenting on this section and speaking about "the belly and the bowels," Rashi says that in this way, through the elimination of waste, "all the body is kept healthy." That is the function of the kidneys and liver. The prayer Asher Yatzar, to be said every time the body excretes, says, "If one of them [the orifices of the body] is closed up, it is impossible to endure for even a short time."

Whatever Origen's and Chrysostom's problems may have been — and they both had major problems — they did not produce their own translations. And so they did not insert their theology into the text itself. Not even the Latin Vulgate did that in this passage. [It reads *quia non introit in cor eius sed in ventrem et in secessum exit purgans omnes escas*. I.e. "because it does not go into his heart but goes into his belly and goes out into the latrine, purging all food."]

Some modern translators do insert their theology into the text, significantly changing its meaning. Yeshua is not commenting on God's distinction between clean and unclean animals. He is commenting on the ritual washing of hands.

Iudaioi in Yo<u>h</u>anan

One distinction of Yo<u>h</u>anan's book is that he uses the Greek word *Iudaioi* more than 50 times. In contrast, the word appears only 12 times in Matthias, Mark, and Luke combined. If we subtract their use of the title "King of the Jews," then *Ioudaioi* appears only 4 times in the three put together. The usages in Yo<u>h</u>anan are significant not only numerically, but also historically. For centuries, they have been used in the Church to legitimize anti-Jewish feeling, doctrine, policy, and behavior.

Consistent with this anti-Judaic purpose, *Ioudaioi* was always translated as "the Jews," that is, all Jews. That is bad translation, because Yo<u>h</u>anan uses the term with three different meanings, depending upon the context.

1. The primary meaning of the word is "the inhabitants of Judea," as distinct from the inhabitants of Galilee". I.e., it means "the Judeans." "
2. A general term for the descendants of Abraham, Isaac, and Jacob, i.e. "the Jews."
3. "The Jewish authorities" as a whole, or specifically the leaders of the Pharisees, i.e. "the sectarian Jews."

The third meaning is the one overwhelmingly used by Yo<u>h</u>anan, distinguishing the authorities, who were appointed Roman officials, from the common Jewish people. (cf. Word Studies in the New Testament, M.R. Vincent, AP&A, Wilmington, DE, 1972, P. 398, and The Expositor's Greek Testament, Vol.I, Pp. 692,709,763) Yo<u>h</u>anan's first use of *Iudaioi*, in 1:19, illustrates this: "The *Iudaioi* sent Kohanim and Levites..." These *Iudaioi* are specifically identified in 1:24 as being "the Perushim". In this translation of the Messianic Writings, the word is translated according to its meaning in context. For greater detail, see the chapter "The Use of *Iudaioi* in Yo<u>h</u>anan" in my book Copernicus and the Jews.

"Eat my flesh, drink my blood"

This is a difficult passage today, as it was when Yeshua said these things. It is an understatement to say that eating human flesh and drinking any kind of blood was absolutely forbidden by God. But Yeshua begins by comparing himself to the manna in the wilderness which God provided from Heaven. What does he want those who hear him to understand?

Yeshua is the Word of God which came down from Heaven. "The rain and the snow come down from heaven and do not return there, but water the earth and make it bring forth and bud, so that it may give seed to the sower and bread to the eater. In the same way, so will My word be that goes forth from My mouth. It will not return to Me void, but it will accomplish what I please, and it will prosper in the thing for which I sent it." (Is. 55:10-11) The Word of God is said to give seed to the sower and bread to the eater. Likewise, "Man is not to live by bread alone, but by every Word which goes forth from the mouth of God." (Dt. 8:3; Mt. 4:4; Lk. 4:4) As Jeremiah said, "Your words were found, and I did eat them..." (Jer. 15:16) Ordinary bread sustains us for daily life. God's Word sustains us for everlasting life. In that sense, we must eat of Yeshua.

Anyone who presented a peace offering to God was to eat of the flesh of that sacrifice. (Lev. 7:11-20) So if we present Yeshua to God as our peace offering — in accordance with Isaiah 53:5 and Ephesians 2:14 — we are required to eat of his flesh.

Additionally, Yeshua is the offering for our sins. The priests are required to eat the sin offering. (cf. Ex. 29:33) As Moses said to Aaron after the death of Nadab and Abihu, "Why have you not eaten the sin offering in a holy place, since it is most holy, and God has given it to you to bear the guilt of the congregation, to make atonement for them before the LORD?" (Lev. 10:17; cf. Lev. 6:16-29) Here, the eating is connected with the atonement.

God called Israel to be "a kingdom of priests" (Ex. 19:6), and this is to be realized in the New Covenant. (e.g. 1Kefa 2:5) Consequently, all those who function as priests would be required to eat of the sin offering, which is what Yeshua is.

[There is a discussion in Tal. Sanhedrin 98b about Messiah and his coming. R. Hillel claims that Messiah has already come, a claim which is opposed by others. Literally, he says, "...there will be no Messiah for Israel, since they have already eaten/consumed him during the reign of Hezekiah."]

> As Jeremiah said, "Your words were found, and I did eat them..." (Jer. 15:16) Ordinary bread sustains us for daily life. God's Word sustains us for everlasting life. In that sense, we must eat of Yeshua.

These metaphors are clear, but the passage becomes more difficult when Yeshua says explicitly that we must not only eat his flesh, but also drink his blood in order to have eternal life. How should we understand this? The very thought of drinking blood is repulsive, yet Yeshua said that we need to drink his blood. That is very difficult to understand, but the Scriptures do provide us with a context.

Concerning animals which are to be eaten, Israel is commanded, "You are not to eat the blood; you are to pour it on the ground like water." (Dt. 12:16) Since the life of the flesh is in the blood (Lev. 17:10-12), this is equivalent to pouring out the life first.

When the Philistines controlled Bethlehem, David expressed his longing for the water of his home town. "So the three mighty men broke through the camp of the Philistines, drew water from the well

of Bethlehem that was by the gate, took it, and brought it to David. Nevertheless he would not drink it, but poured it out to the Everpresent Lord. Then he said, 'Far be it from me, O Everpresent Lord, that I should do this! Is this not the blood of the men who went in jeopardy of their lives?' Therefore he would not drink it." (2Sam. 23:16-17)

The Scriptures use this metaphor of water and blood to present the transient nature of our lives. As the wise woman of Tekoa told King David: "For we will surely die, and are like water spilled on the ground which cannot be gathered up again...." (2Sam. 14:14)

The daily sacrifices in the Temple were to be offered with a drink offering, as were some other sacrifices. (Num. 28:2-15) The drink offering represented the life that was poured out to God. Sha'ul the ambassador spoke of his own life in this way. "For I am already being poured out as a drink offering, and the time of my departure is at hand." (2Tim. 4:6) In the Talmud, a connection is made between pouring out blood, pouring out water, and pouring out a drink offering. (Tal. Pesachim 22a)

In Ps. 22:15H, Messiah, the Son of David, prophetically says, "I am poured out like water, and all My bones are out of joint. My heart is like wax; it has melted within Me." We know that after Yeshua died, a soldier pierced his side with a spear and out came water and blood. (Yhn. 19:34)

The poured out blood of Yeshua's sacrifice is as the drink offering that accompanies his death. His disciples need to drink his cup to be connected to this sacrifice which establishes the New Covenant. (cf.Mt. 20:22-23) "For this is my blood of the new covenant, which is poured out for many for the forgiveness of sins." (Mt. 26:28) See the note above for Yhn. 2:6-11.

The Noachide Laws and the Council in Yerushala'im

The concept of the Noachide Laws is presented in the Talmud as the basic laws that are binding upon non-Jews. Some think there is a correlation between the stipulations listed by the council of believers in Yerushala'im and the Noachide Laws of the Rabbis. There is a similarity in that both speak of the obligations that God has placed upon non-Jews, but the differences between the concept of the Noachide Laws and the concept of the council in Yerushala'im are immense.

The Midrash does place the giving of these laws back in the Garden of Eden, long before the time of Noah, assigning a metaphorical meaning to each word in Gen. 2:16. "'And the Everpresent Lord gave commandment to humanity, saying, You may surely eat from every tree of the garden. [Gen. 2:16]. R. Levi said: 'He commanded concerning six commandments: And He commanded is about idolatry... The Everpresent Lord is about blessing the Name [This is a rabbinic euphemism for blasphemy.]... God: these are the judges [referring to government]... To humanity: this is the shedding of blood... Saying, this is the revealing of nakedness... [As the Soncino note points out, this would include incest, adultery, pederasty, and bestiality.] Of every tree of the garden you may surely eat: commands him against theft...'" (Mid. Gen. Rabbah 16:6)

The problem is not primarily one of content, but of concept. Having Law from God is good, but it is not sufficient. The Gentiles have the same problem with the Law God has given them as Israel does with the Law in the covenant God made with Israel in the wilderness. The Law is holy, righteous, spiritual, and good, but the people are not. People break God's Law. Unless they have a means of atonement, the Law condemns them to death. (cf. Rom. 1:32)

In the Messianic Writings, those Gentiles who recognize the King of the Jews as Lord are grafted into Israel's olive tree to enter into the New Covenant God has made with Israel. They remain wild branches, but they become fellow-citizens, fellow-heirs, fellow-members, and fellow-partakers. Yeshua's atonement is available to them. They are not only children of Noa<u>h</u>; they have been adopted as children of Abraham.

The Rabbinic construct does not provide Gentiles with any atonement, grace, promise, or covenant. In effect, the Noachide Laws function as a means of keeping the Gentiles separated from Israel. In contrast, in Acts 15, and throughout the Messianic Writings, we are presented with the inclusion of the believing Gentiles in the commonwealth of Israel, having legal standing as children of Abraham. We are told that if Gentiles are not brought into the commonwealth of Israel, they remain "without hope and without God". (Eph. 2:11-12)

All of these things are evident in Tanakh. For example, the necessity of sacrifice and God's grace is shown in Gen. 3:21 and Gen. 4:3-5. In Gen. 17:4, Abraham is called to be "the father of many Gentiles." And in Gen. 28:3 and 48:4, Jacob receives the promise to become a community of peoples.

It is also important to keep in mind that there was no rabbinic system at the time of the council in Jerusalem presented in Acts 15. There was no body of rabbinic teaching and no rabbinic authority. Those things developed over the centuries following the destruction of the Second Temple in 70 C.E. There were Pharisaic traditions, but those of Beit Shammai prevailed at this time. They were later replaced by those of Beit Hillel and those instituted by R. Akiba. (For details, see my book, <u>Rabbi Akiba's Messiah: The Origins of Rabbinic Authority</u>.)

See the ADDITIONAL NOTE on "God's Law and the New Covenant," and the ADDITIONAL NOTE on "Biblical Law for Gentile Children of Abraham".

God's Law and the New Covenant

The New Covenant is made between God and Israel. The primary characteristic of those who enter into it is: "I will put My law in their inner being, and will write it on their hearts. And I will be their God, and they will be My people." (Jer. 31:33/Heb. 8:10). In the New Covenant, Israel will be God's people in every respect, having His law in our inner being and written upon our hearts. God promised Israel, "I will put My Spirit within you+ and cause you+ to walk in My statutes, and you+ will keep and do My judgments." (Ezek. 36:27)

Regarding the commandments of the Law, Moses told Israel, "Therefore keep and do them, because this is your+ wisdom and your+ understanding in the sight of the peoples who will hear all these statutes, and say, 'Surely this great nation is a wise and understanding people.'" (Deut. 4:6)

That is why all Israel was given an additional requirement: "And these words which I command you today are to be on your heart, and you are to teach them diligently to your children..." (Deut. 6:6-7) All Israel is to think and meditate on what God has commanded, and understand it well enough to teach future generations.

Meditating on God's Law enables us to see what God is seeking. Here's a simple example. "When you build a new house, then you are to make a railing for your roof, that you may not bring guilt of bloodshed on your household if anyone falls from it." (Deut. 22:8)

Beyond the specifics about a house and a roof, this statute lays out a principle of personal liability. It is a practical example of what love of one's neighbor entails. So far as your own property is concerned, you must act to insure your neighbor's safety. Other statutes lay out the principle of compensation if you are negligent in that responsibility. (e.g. Ex. 21:19,22,36)

Murder is wrong because humanity was made in the image and likeness of God. (Gen. 9:6) If you meditate on that, you will be able to see what value the commandment is protecting. Every action that destroys that image and likeness of God in another is wrong.

Yeshua illustrated the fullness of that law, what it means when that law is written on the heart: "... Everyone who is angry with his brother without a cause will be guilty in the judgment. And whoever calls his brother, 'Brainless!' will be in danger of the Council. And whoever says, 'Stupid fool!' will be in danger of the fire of Gehinnom." (Mt. 5:22)

The connection between the purpose of a particular commandment or statute and the values it is protecting is not always obvious. For example, Yeshua went on to say, "Again you⁺ have heard that it was said to those of long ago, 'You are not to make false vows, but are to perform your vows to the Everpresent Lord.' But I tell you⁺, do not swear at all, not by heaven, for it is the throne of God; nor by the earth, for it is the footstool of His feet, nor by Yerushala'im, for it is the city of the great King. Nor should you swear by your head, for you cannot make one hair white or black. " (Mt. 5:33-36)

What is the relationship between "you cannot make one hair white or black" and "you are not to swear falsely"? If you make an oath to the Lord, you must do what you have vowed, but you do not control many things about yourself or about the world. You do not have the power to declare something and make it happen. So in order not to swear falsely, you had best "not swear at all".

If you take to heart the commandment given at Sinai, you will become aware of your own limitations. When you are truly aware of your own limitations, you will be content to let your "Yes" be "Yes," and your "No" be "No." You are not in control, God is.

For all those whose ancestors were brought out of Egypt by the Everpresent Lord, the role of God's Law in the New Covenant is quite clear, even if the details require some meditation. The Law which God gave us at Sinai — "These words which I command you today are to be upon your heart." (Dt. 6:6]

Biblical Law for Gentile Children of Abraham

Long before God gave Israel His Law at Mt. Sinai, He confirmed certain promises to Isaac, "because Abraham obeyed My voice and kept My charge, My commandments, My statutes, and My laws." (Gen. 26:5) Abraham could not have kept God's commandments, statutes, and laws unless there were some that already existed and were applicable to him, as they were to all the nations, i.e. Gentiles, at that time.

God was not speaking of the covenant which He would make with Israel centuries later. He was speaking of His requirements for all humanity. The Judge of all the earth will judge every person according to His Law. Every person will be found guilty of having broken God's Law, because that is what sin is, the breaking of God's Law. (cf. 1Yhn. 3:4b)

There is a Latin legal saying, *Nullum crimen sine leges*. I.e., there is no crime without law. It is simple and obvious that one can only commit a crime, i.e. break a law, if that law exists. If no law exists, then one cannot break it. Sha'ul says the same thing. "...Sin is not charged unless law exists.... For the Law brings about wrath, because where there is no law, neither is there disobedience." (Rom. 5:13, 4:15) The Law defines Sin, telling us what actions are prohibited and what actions are commanded. (cf. Rom. 7:7)

"What is known about God is evident in them, since God has revealed it to them.... Knowing the ordinance of God that those who practice such things are worthy of death, they not only do these same things, but also approve of those who practice them.... They show the work of the Law written in their hearts, their conscience testifying with them, and their inner thoughts accusing or else defending themselves in the day when God will judge the secrets of men through Yeshua the Messiah, as in my good news." (Rom. 1:19,32, 2:15-16)

God did not give written Law to the other nations, or to the people who existed before the nations were created at the Tower of Babel. But He nevertheless gave them law. If He had not given them law, then He could not have charged them with sin. It would have been impossible for them to have sinned unless certain actions had been either forbidden or commanded.

The law that the people of those generations violated, and that their descendants continue to violate, did not come from Moses, since God brought judgment on certain actions long before Moses was born, long before Israel was created. The law that they violated had been implanted in the very nature of humanity. It is a law to which all people are subject.

God's Law did not begin at Sinai, and it is not for Jews only. There were no Jews in the time of Abraham. God's Law begins with God. The difference between good and evil, right and wrong, permitted and prohibited, comes from who God is, and from humanity having been created in His image and likeness. God wrote His values, as well as His authority to command, in the human constitution.

That is why, long before Sinai, it was wrong for Ka'in to murder Hevel. Hevel was made in the image of God; and Ka'in, who was also made in the image of God, knew that. When Ka'in killed his brother, it was an act of violence against the image of God, and therefore an act of violence against God. After the flood, God told Noah, "Whoever sheds the blood of humanity, by humanity his blood is to be shed, because He made humanity in the image of God." (Gen. 9:6)

In the time of Abraham, God did not explain to Abimelekh that adultery was sin. He did not

reason with him. God simply informed him that he was under sentence of death for his crime. (Gen. 20) Abimelekh already knew that adultery was sin, as his responses to God and Abraham show.

Yeshua explained that divorce is wrong because of the created nature of humanity, since the two, male and female, are designed to be joined together as one. (cf. Mt. 19:4-6) For the same reason, adultery is a transgression of the created nature of humanity. The law against adultery had been given long before Sinai. It was given in Creation.

"The men of Sedom were exceedingly wicked and sinful against the Everpresent Lord." (Gen. 13:13) God executed judgment on their sins, i.e. their crimes. It should be noted that their sins were not solely of a sexual nature. "See that this was the iniquity of your sister Sedom: she and her daughter had pride, abundance of food and quiet prosperity. But she did not strengthen the hand of the poor and needy." (Ezek. 16:49) In negecting the needs of the poor, the people of Sedom had sinned against the shared nature of humanity. They had, like Ka'in, abandoned the responsibility to care for the well-being of their brother(s and sisters).

The Scriptural record shows what actions God judged; it shows that non-Jews can and do sin. The Scriptures give us a fairly stable way of determining the content of the legal order that God established for humanity. Unlike God's covenantal Law with Israel, this universal law is not compiled in one particular place, but evidence of it appears throughout the text.

It is Biblical case law that reveals the common law. By showing God's judgments on various human actions — both approval and disapproval — the Bible illustrates the nature and general content of this universal law. The content of that Law can be determined in a way similar to the method of interpretation used to determine common law in the Anglo-American legal tradition. A case by case decision making process produces a corpus of legally binding decisions which collectively reveal what was commonly known and accepted. The judge does not legislate the law, he recognizes it.

In the Scriptures, God both legislates the Law and judges those who break it. His laws do not need to be commonly accepted before they are applied. They simply need to have been given, as they were in Creation, and therefore internally known or knowable.

By examining as case law the different judgments that God brings upon non-Jews, it is possible to determine the content of the universal law that God gave to humanity when He created us in His image and likeness.

When Messiah rules over all the earth, "Many people will come and say, 'Come, and let us go up to the mountain of the Everpresent Lord, to the house of the God of Jacob. He will teach us His ways, and we will walk in His paths,' because the Law will go forth out of Zion, and the word of the LORD from Yerushala'im." (Is. 2:3)

Since all the earth is to be brought under Messiah's rule and be judged by him, there will still be universal Law that is applicable to all peoples and nations.

With God's Law, as with any legal system, there are some laws that are applicable to all, and some that are applicable to a particular person, like the high priest, or to a particular group of people, like the Levites. Some laws are applicable to women but not to men, and vice versa. Some laws are applicable to Jews and not to Gentiles. Sin and obedience are defined by the laws that are applicable to a particular person.

(See the ADDITIONAL NOTE on "The Noachide Laws".)

Circumcision and the Law

God called Abraham "so that he would command his children and his household after him, that they keep the way of the Everpresent Lord, to do righteousness and justice, so that the Everpresent Lord will bring to Abraham what He has spoken to him." (Gen. 18:19) To confirm His calling, God made a covenant with Abraham, the covenant of circumcision. (Gen. 17) It was a physical mark to signify that Abraham, Abraham's seed, and their physical desires were submitted to God's purposes.

The value of the mark was not intrinsic; it lay in what the mark signified. It signified that Abraham's physical descendants (through Isaac and Jacob) are to be a holy people, a distinct people who are God's representatives in the earth.

In order to fulfill God's purpose, it was, and is, necessary that Abraham's descendants be like their father. Centuries before God made a covenant with Israel at Sinai, he commended Abraham, who "obeyed My voice and kept My mandate, My commandments, My statutes, and My laws." (Gen.26:5) From the beginning, God had given Law to all of humanity; Abraham lived in accordance with it. (See the ADDITIONAL NOTE on "Biblical Law for Gentile Chidren of Abraham")

At Sinai, God gave Israel national Law. It contained the universal Law which Abraham had obeyed, but it also contained specific commandments, statutes, and laws to enable Israel to fulfill its distinct calling. Moses told all Israel: "Keep therefore and do them; for this is your wisdom and your understanding in the sight of the peoples, which will hear of all these statutes, and say, 'Surely this great nation is a wise and understanding people' — because what great nation has God so near to it, as the Everpresent Lord our God is in all that we call upon Him? And what great nation has statutes and judgments as righteous as all this Torah which I set before you today?" (Deut. 4:6-8)

Circumcision signifies that Israel is a distinct people with a distinct calling from God, but it doesn't guarantee that Israel will live up to that calling. Moses spoke of his own "uncircumcised lips" as the reason for his inability to faithfully communicate God's message. (Ex. 6:12, 30) Stephen spoke of "uncircumcised ears" which kept people from hearing what God was saying. (Acts/Ma'asei 7:51)

But the part of a man which is most in need of circumcision is his heart. That is why Moses said, "Therefore circumcise the foreskin of your+ hearts, and do not stiffen your+ necks any more." (Dt. 10:16) It is why Jeremiah spoke of Israel as being "uncircumcised in heart". (Jer. 9:25H, 4:4)

But it is God who opens the ears of people so that they can hear His voice. It is God who opens the lips of people so that they can declare His message and His praise. And it is God who promises to circumcise the hearts of Israel. (cf. Dt. 30:6) "...When their uncircumcised hearts are humbled, and when they accept their iniquity — then I will remember My covenant with Jacob, and I will also remember My covenant with Isaac and My covenant with Abraham; and I will remember the land." (Lev. 26:41-42)

Circumcision is the sign that sets apart the people of Israel for God's Kingdom. But it is only a sign, signifying what God truly desires.

Conflict with the State and Its gods

In the century before Yeshua was born, Cicero had admonished the State to "let no one have private gods — neither new gods nor strange gods, unless publicly acknowledged, are to be worshiped privately — let the temples which the fathers have constructed in the cities, be upheld — let the sacred chapels and consecrated groves in country places be protected — let the customs of the fathers be preserved in the families — let the gods who have always been accounted celestial be worshipped, and those gods likewise who have merited celestial honours by their illustrious actions, as Hercules, Bacchus, Æsculapius, Castor, Pollux and Quirinus."[1]

A generation before Yeshua, "Maecenas counselled Augustus: 'Honor the gods according to the custom of our ancestors, and compel others to worship them. Hate and punish those who bring in strange gods.'"[2]

In the Roman Empire, as under many governments then and since, the State was seen as the only source of authority. It legitimized all other authorities. Accordingly, it authorized worship of those gods which were amenable to its purposes. Such gods were only authorized insofar as they were of use to the State.[3] As long as the gods supported the State, they were legal.

Opposition to, or departure from, the worship of the gods approved by the State was opposition to the State itself. It was rebellion, and the punishment was severe. Julius Paulus, a second century jurist, recorded the following decree: "Of those people who introduce new religions with unknown customs or methods by which the minds of men could be disturbed, those of the upper classes shall be deported, those of the lower classes shall be put to death."[4]

Of all Rome's subject people, only the Jews found it impossible to obey these laws. Concerning other gods, the God of Israel had commanded: "You are not to bow down to them or worship them; for I, the Everpresent Lord, your God, am a jealous God: to those who hate Me, visiting the iniquity of the fathers on the descendants to the third and fourth generation; but to those who love Me and keep My commandments, showing love to a thousand generations." (Ex. 20:5-6)

The God of Israel claims to be the ultimate authority, the delegating source of all lesser authorities. Accordingly, He is the One who authorizes or delegitimizes the State, not vice versa.

On numerous occasions, Jews had chosen to resist or let themselves be slaughtered rather than bow down to the gods of those who ruled over them. The Romans found this incomprehensible, but were for the most part willing to make an accomodation.[5] In general, so long as loyalty to the Emperor could be assured, it was counterproductive to provoke such zeal.

Part of the Roman accomodation was a special tax on the Jews, to be paid by each individual in place of sacrifice to the emperor. (cf. Mt. 17:24-27, 22:17-21) "He [Caesar] also laid a tribute upon the Jews wheresoever they were and enjoined every one of them to bring two drachmae every year into the Capitol, as they used to pay the same to the Temple at Jerusalem. And this was the state of the Jewish affairs at this time."[6]

"Thus, after Augustus, when the worship of the Roman emperors became an imperial religion and was cultivated with obsequious zeal in the provinces, the Jews, and they alone, were not required to manifest their loyalty in any of the usual forms of adoration such as burning incense before the image of the emperor, or to take oath by the emperors. In strictness this exemption would have extended only to peregrine Jews, not to such as acquired the status of Roman citizens, and particularly not

to freedmen, who in law were bound to worship the sacra of their former masters. But here also an exception was made in their favor, and various other privileges were accorded to them."[7]

From a Roman perspective, these were privileges, but from a Jewish perspective, these were impositions. Some emperors were more zealous than others in collecting the tax.

"Domitian's [emperor from 81-96 C.E.] energetic collection of the special poll-tax on Jews, the *fiscus Judaicus*, which was exacted from those who without openly professing their adhesion to Judaism lived like Jews, as well as from born Jews who concealed their race, gave occupation to the informers whom he encouraged; and their denunciations probably included some more highly placed in society than the mass of Roman Jewry."[8] He also tortured witnesses to provide the evidence he needed.[9]

The Roman tax collectors worked hand-in-hand with the ever-increasing number of informers. The torture of witnesses aided the practice of extortion. In general, the Romans were not interested in theological disputes; they were interested in control.

(For additional information, see "The Roman Trials," in my Rabbi Akiba's Messiah: The Origins of Rabbinic Authority.)

The Scriptures say that God has all authority, some of which He delegates. He delegates certain authority within the family and within the community. He delegates other authority to employers, teachers, and to the civil government. He defines each sphere of authority.

The power to enforce a command is not the same as the authority to issue that command. Authority is the right to be obeyed. The Scriptures teach that God is the only One who can give that right. But people with power often claim authority which they do not have. They often use their power to compel obedience to their commands, commands which may extend beyond their authority or which may be contrary to God's commands.

FOOTNOTES

1. The Political Works of Marcus Tullius Cicero: Comprising his Treatise on the Commonwealth; and his Treatise on the Laws, Vol. 2 (.19), trans. by Francis Barham, Edmund Spettigue, London, 1841-42, P. 50

2. Philip Schaff, History of the Christian Church, Vol. 2, Scribner, New York, 1883, P.42

3. As Eberhard Arnold points out, "The Roman Empire, as the clearest and most typical example of a State, shows that a unified State religion, however broad and tolerant the concept, will of necessity appear indispensable to the very existence of such a State. Therefore any religion that excludes or opposes the religious State-concept or the recognized State religions is an extremely dangerous attack on the State at its very core. The Roman emperor-cult was but the sum total, the visible culmination, of the State religion which pervaded all of Roman civilization. Consequently, on this point there could be no tolerance on the part of Rome until later a new religious concept of the State placed the institutional Church at the service of the State." Eberhard Arnold, The Early Christians after the Death of the Apostles, Plough Publishing House, Rifton, NY, 1972, P. 335

4. Legal decree according to the second-century jurist Julius Paulus. Five books of Collected Sentences, Book V.21.2

5. From time to time, some emperors were not willing to make accomodation. According to Suetonius, "Tiberius suppressed foreign cults and Egyptian and Jewish religious rites and forced those who were enslaved by this kind of superstition to burn their religious vestments and all the paraphernalia of their cults. He dispersed Jewish youths to provinces with a more rugged climate, ostensibly to do military service. Others belonging to

this people, or persons holding similar beliefs, he removed from the city on pain of slavery for life if they did not want to obey." Suetonius, on Tiberius, who ruled A.D. 14-37, ch.36, cited in Arnold, P. 61

6. Josephus, The Jewish War, 7.6.6.218 (7:218)
7. G.F. Moore, Judaism in the First Centuries of the Christian Era, Harvard U. Press, Cambridge, 1927-40, P.350
8. Ibid., Pp. 350-351
9. cf. Suetonius, The Twelve Caesars, "Titus Flavius Domitianus," Ch. XII, Trans. by Robert Graves, Penguin Books, NY, !980, P. 264

Sin and Yetzer haRa

The Rabbinic concept of *yetzer hara*, i.e. "the evil inclination," is similar to that of "Sin" in the Messianic Writings. It is something that lives in all people and inclines them to do what is wrong.

In commenting on Gen. 2:25, Rashi says that, "There was not given to him [Adam] an evil inclination until he ate from the tree." But his view is very problematic. If Adam had no evil inclination before he ate from the tree, then why did he eat from the tree? He knew it was wrong.

However, the rabbinic view is also expressed that, following that first sin, humanity is subject to Sin, and the Yetzer haRa, from the time when the process of birth begins.. "Antoninus also enquired of Rabbi, 'From what time does the Evil Inclination rule in man, from the formation, or from going out? 'From the formation,' he replied. 'If so,' he objected, 'it would rebel in its mother's womb and go out. But it is from when it goes out.' Rabbi said: 'Antoninus taught me this thing, and Scripture supports him, for it is said, 'At the door [of birth] sin lies in wait. (Gen. 4:7)'" (Tal. Sanhedrin 91b) Rashi says the same. (Gen. 8:21)

There is a related view presented in Tal. Baba Metzia 107a, in commentary on Dt. 28:6, "You will be blessed in your coming in, you will be blessed in your going out." The commentary says, "That your going out from the world will be as your coming into the world: as your coming into the world was without sin, even so may your going out from the world be without sin."

In general, the Rabbis speak of the Yetzer haRa as being the hidden cause for the imagination of humanity being evil and unclean, and for their hearts being hard and unclean. The Rabbis speak of it as being our enemy and the thing that causes us to stumble. In short, the Rabbis speak of the Yetzer haRa in much the same way that the Messianic Writings speak of Sin.

There is an interesting passage in Tal. Sukkah 52a that connects the death of Messiah and the death of the *yetzer hara*. "'And the land will mourn, every family apart; the family of the house of David apart, and their wives apart.' (Zech. 12:12) Is it not, they said, an *a fortiori* argument? If in the future when they will be engaged in mourning and the Evil Inclination will have no power over them, the Torah nevertheless says men separately and women separately, how much more so now when they are engaged in rejoicing and the Evil Inclination has sway over them.

"What is the cause of the mourning? R. Dosa and the Rabbis differ on the point. One explained, 'The cause is the slaying of Messiah the son of Joseph,' and the other explained, 'The cause is the slaying of the Evil Inclination.'

"It is well according to him who explains that the cause is the slaying of Messiah the son of Joseph, since that well agrees with the Scriptural verse, 'And they will look upon me because they have thrust

him through, and they will mourn for him as one mourns for his only son.' (Zech. 12:12)

"But according to him who explains the cause to be the slaying of the Evil Inclination, is this an occasion for mourning? Is it not rather an occasion for rejoicing? Why then should they weep? As R. Judah expounded: 'In the time to come the Holy One, blessed be He, will bring the Evil Inclination and slay it in the presence of the righteous and the wicked. To the righteous it will have the appearance of a towering hill, and to the wicked it will have the appearance of a hair thread. Both the former and the latter will weep; the righteous will weep saying, *How were we able to overcome such a towering hill!* The wicked also will weep saying, *How is it that we were unable to conquer this hair thread!...*

"R. Avira or, as some say, R. Joshua b. Levi, made the following exposition: The Evil Inclination has seven names. The Holy One, blessed be He, called it 'Evil,' as it is said, 'For the imagination of man's heart is evil from his youth.' Moses called it 'the Uncircumcised,' as it is said, 'Circumcise therefore the foreskin of your heart.' David called it 'Unclean,' as it is said, 'Create in me a clean heart, O Lord,' which implies that there is an unclean one. Solomon called it 'the Enemy,' as it is said, 'If your enemy is hungry, give him bread to eat and if he is thirsty give him water to drink. For you will heap coals of fire upon his head, and the Everpresent Lord will reward you.' Do not read 'will reward you' but 'will cause it to be at peace with you.' Isaiah called it 'the Stumbling-Block,' as it is said, 'Throw away, throw away, clear the way, take up the stumbling-block out of the way of My people.' Ezekiel called it 'Stone,' as it is said, 'And I will take away the heart of stone out of your flesh and I will give you a heart of flesh.' Joel called it 'the Hidden One,' as it is said, 'But I will remove far off from you the hidden one.'"

"The Holy One, blessed be He, created the *yetzer hara*, but He created the Torah to swallow it up." (Tal. Baba Batra 16a)

There is also the view that the Yetzer haRa is necessary for this age: "'And God saw every thing that He had made, and behold, it was very good' (Gen.1:31), This is the Evil Inclination. And therefore the Evil Inclination is called good. This is to teach that if it were not for the Evil Inclination, a man would not take a wife, and would not father children from her, and the world would not be established." (Mid. Psalms 9.1)

Pharaoh's Heart

The two main Hebrew words that are used in Exodus to describe what God did to Pharaoh's heart and what Pharaoh did to his own heart mean "strengthen" (*hazakh*) and "give weight to" (*kaved*). By extension, *kaved* also means "to glorify or honor," because of the weight, i.e. importance, given to someone or something.

When the Scriptures speak about Pharaoh, translators usually present these two words as "to harden". Probably the translators do that because the Greek word that is used in both the Septuagint and the Messianic Writings, *skleruno*, commonly means "to make hard". It appears, for example, in the modern word "arteriosclerosis," which means "a hardening of the arteries". To the modern mind, therefore, this hardening means taking away the possibility of choice.

Skleruno, however, also means "to make stubborn, to be obstinate". The translators of the Septuagint chose this word to illustrate that Pharaoh's heart — his determined purpose — was not going to weaken and cause him to back down from what he wanted to do. God did not put anything into Pharaoh's heart that was not already there. He merely made it strong so that Pharaoh would proceed with what was already in his heart.

Whether by his own choice or by the action of the Everpresent Lord, Pharaoh made his own desires weighty. He glorified them; he glorified his own heart. In a literary example of this meaning, Pearl Buck wrote of a particular General preparing for battle. "Day and night he had such thoughts as this and he strengthened himself with his anger, and he told himself that he and his men could vanquish any attack from the enemy, for had he not fought this same enemy at home and now?" The Promise, Chapter XXI

1 Maccabees 1:1-4 speaks of Alexander the Great. He started and won many wars, killing many people. He plundered many nations and made them his tributaries. He was exalted and his heart was lifted up. then he became sick and died..

With Pharaoh, it is as though God said to him, "Do what's in your heart." (cf. Rev. 22:11) God purposed to use the evil that was in Pharaoh's heart to bring about redemption for Israel.

He did the same with Judah from K'riyot. Though he was a thief and would soon betray Yeshua, Yeshua made him the treasurer of the group. When Judah was ready to betray him, Yeshua said, "What you do, do quickly." (Yhn. 13:27b) God used the evil in Judah's heart to bring salvation to the world.

Since Yeshua is "gentle and humble in heart" (Mt. 11:29), those who follow him and learn from him will be the same. A humble heart is the opposite of one that is lifted up. (cf. Dt. 8:14, 2Ch. 26:6, Ezek. 28:2, 5, 17)

God looks on the heart; He sees, measures, and judges it. Hatred in the heart is as murder, and lust is as adultery. That is why we are commanded, "Guard your heart, because the issues of life come out of it." (Prov. 4:23)

Nature and Long Hair

"Yet Nature itself does not teach you+ that if a man has long hair it is a dishonor to him. On the other hand, if a woman has long hair, it is a glory to her, since the long hair is given to her in the place of a covering." This is a literal translation of the text of 1Co. 11:14.

Traditional translations make the verse a rhetorical question which states that nature itself teaches that long hair is a dishonor to a man. That would not seem to be either 1) true, or 2) consistent with the rest of Scriptures.

1) At the time that Paul wrote this letter to the believers in Corinth, people in the Greek world did not consider long hair to be a dishonor to a man. As Liddell and Scott note: "In early times the Greeks wore their hair long... At Sparta the fashion continued. At Athens it was so worn by youths up to the 18th year, when they offered their long locks to some deity; and to wear long hair was considered as a sign of aristocratic habits." Corinth is between Athens and Sparta, about 50 miles from Athens, and about 100 miles from Sparta.

Men in China, Japan, and India wore their hair long; likewise the tribes of Europe and the Americas. In modern Europe, aristocrats, judges, et al. have worn long hair wigs as a sign of status. In general, it is not naturally evident that long hair is a dishonor to man.

2) Throughout the Scriptures, there is no indication that nature teaches that long hair is a dishonor to a man. To the contrary, we read that Absalom, with his long hair, was the most handsome man in Israel. "Now in all Israel there was no one who was praised as much as Absalom for his good looks. From the sole of his foot to the crown of his head there was no blemish in him. And when he cut the hair of his head — at the end of every year he cut it because it was heavy on him — when he cut it, he weighed the hair of his head at two hundred shekels according to the king's standard." [2Sam. 14:25-26]

Furthermore, God commanded the Nazirite to be holy. The long hair of the Nazirite, far from indicating dishonor, signified this holiness and separation to the Everpresent Lord. "All the days of the vow of his separation no razor is to come upon his head; until the days are fulfilled for which he separated himself to the Everpresent Lord, he is to be holy. He is to let the locks of the hair of his head grow." [Num. 6:5]

God commanded that Samson, as a Nazirite from birth, was not to cut his hair at all. It signified the separation **to** God of one who was chosen to deliver Israel from the Philistines. [Judg. 13:5] Consistent with that, the cutting of his hair signified his being separated **from** God and His power. (In Acts 18:18, Sha'ul, who was not a Nazirite, had his hair cut as part of a vow,)

In general, there is no evidence in the Scriptures that God considers long hair dishonorable for a man. Additionally, there are specific cases in the Scriptures where a man is supposed to cover his head. A king wears a crown on his head. (e.g. Zech. 6:11) God prescribed that the Kohen Gadol wear a turban on his head. (Ex. 28:36-38) In mourning, the Kohen Gadol, "on whose head the anointing oil was poured and who is consecrated to wear the garments, is not to uncover his head or tear his clothes;" (Lev. 21:10) The words used in this chapter of Sha'ul's First Letter to the Corinthians seem to specifically refer to a veil.

Shimon Kefa in Antioch

In Gal. 2:14, Sha'ul says that Kefa was living as a Gentile. What did Sha'ul mean? Both Sha'ul and Kefa describe the Gentiles as living immorally. (cf. 1 Thes. 4:5; 1 Kefa 4:3) Was Kefa living immorally like the Gentiles? Sha'ul does not mention that. It is not the issue that he addresses.

Both Sha'ul and Kefa describe the Gentiles as worshipping idols. (cf. 1Co. 12:2; 1Kefa 4:3) Was Kefa worshipping idols as the Gentiles did? No, that also was not the case, nor the issue that Sha'ul addresses. Kefa was faithful to the God of Israel.

To what then was Sha'ul referring when he said that Kefa was living as a Gentile? Was Kefa eating the meat of animals which God had forbidden to Jews as food? No, that was not the case, nor the issue that Sha'ul addresses. Sha'ul never mentions what Kefa ate.

We know historically that Kefa and all the ambassadors lived as Jews in accordance with the Law of Moses. As Irenaeus points out, "And the *apostolos* [i.e., ambassadors] who were with Jacob allowed the Gentiles to act freely, yelding us up to the Spirit of God. But they themselves, while knowing the same God, continued in the ancient observances.... Thus did the *apostolos*... scrupulously act according to the dispensation of the Law of Moses..." Against Heresies Ante-Nicene Christian Library, Vol. 5/1, trans. by A. Roberts and J. Donaldson, T & T Clark, Edinburgh, 1867, Pp. 313-314

The issue was not what Kefa ate, but rather with whom he ate. Kefa was eating with the Gentiles. "You went in to uncircumcised men, and ate with them!" (Acts 11:3)

Eating at the same table was important, because it signified acceptance and equality. Before Joseph made himself known to his brothers, seeming to be an Egyptian, he ate separately from them. (Gen. 43:32) Table fellowship did not take place with those who were not regarded as having equal status.

The somewhat contemporary view expressed in the Talmud is that Jews who ate with uncircumcised Gentiles were as Gentiles themselves. (cf. Avodah Zarah 35b; Chullin 13a) Even though they were not eating the food of the Gentiles, by eating with them they were identifying themselves with the Gentiles. This is what Kefa had done.

This view is reflected in Luke 5:30: "Their Torah scholars and the Perushim murmured against his talmidim, saying, 'Why do you⁺ eat and drink with the tax collectors and sinners?'" Nothing is said about what they ate. The issue was with whom they ate. Eating and drinking with the tax collectors and sinners indicated acceptance of them. Also, see 1Co. 5:9-11, "Do not even eat with such a person."

At first, Kefa had eaten with the Gentile believers, signifying that they were fully members of the body of Messiah, though uncircumcised. By eating with them, he indicated that the wall was broken down which divided Jews from believing Gentiles (Eph. 2:14-16). That demonstrated his belief that the Gentiles were made righteous by their faith in Messiah, and were thereby brought into the commonwealth of Israel. The statutes which commanded Israel to be separated from the Gentiles did not apply to these who were grafted in.

By withdrawing from table fellowship with them, Kefa was visibly reversing his position, signifying that uncircumcised Gentiles had never been, and could not be, acceptable to God. In so doing, he condemned himself for having earlier entered into table fellowship with them. He condemned himself by indicating that the wall which divided Jews from Gentiles needed to be rebuilt, whether or not the Gentiles had turned in faith to the God of Israel. (cf. Eph. 2:14-16)

Regulating the Actions of Hard Hearts

"**W**hen you go out to war against your enemies, and the Everpresent, your God, gives them into your hands, and you take them into captivity; and you see a woman of beautiful physique among the captives, and you desire her to take her to yourself as a wife; then you are to bring her into the midst of your house. And she is to trim her nails, and put away from her the clothes of her captivity; and is to live in your house and weep a month of days for her father and her mother. And after that you may go in to her and be her husband, and she is to be a wife to you. And if it is that you do not delight in her, then you are to send her out according to what is in her soul. But you are not to sell her for money; you are not to use her as a slave, because you have humbled her." (Dt. 21:10-14)

Commenting on the phrase "and you desire to take her to yourself as a wife" (v. 11), Rashi says,"The Torah is only speaking in opposition to the evil inclination, because if the Holy One, blessed be He, does not permit her, the man will marry her though forbidden. But if he marries her, his end will be to hate her... and he will father from her a stubborn and rebellious son." (Rashi connects the text to what follows in Dt. 21:18-21 about "a stubborn and rebellious son.")

In Rashi's understanding, in a righteous world, the man should not be permitted to marry the woman, but because that prohibition will have disastrous consequences for others — the woman and her future son — God makes allowance in His Law for such marriages. The marriage is a bad thing, but it is to be preferred to the rape and enslavement that armies commonly practiced. The conditions that God establishes are for the purpose of controlling Man's evil inclination.

For a whole month, the woman will live in the midst of the man's home, mourning her parents, day after day. She is to shave her head, making her less attractive. The man is not to touch her during this time. If the man still desires the captive woman after a month of this living situation, then he may marry her. The conditions prohibit an immediate response to lust, and discourage unfeeling exploitation. The closing admonition serves to turn the thoughts of the man away from a moment of sexual pleasure to the responsibilities of an entire married life. And there is the suggestion of the possibility that such a life, begun with a forced marriage, may turn out to be less than pleasant.

In a sense, this seems a little strange. In this case, God's Law does not prohibit what is evil, it regulates it. But all law is designed to regulate human behavior. People do not always naturally do what is right; they do not always naturally do what the Law requires. Adam and Havah are our first example. If they did, there would be no need for the Law. "Knowing this, that law is not made for a righteous man, but for the lawless and unruly, for the ungodly and sinners, for the unholy and profane, for murderers of fathers and murderers of mothers, for manslayers..." (1 Tim. 1:9)

We are presented with a similar situation in regard to divorce. God hates divorce, but He permits and regulates it because of the hardness of human hearts. Compared to the evils that would otherwise result, divorce can be the lesser evil. Yeshua said, "Moses, because of the hardness of your hearts, permitted you to divorce your wives, but from the beginning it was not so." (Mt. 19:8)

Apparently the same is true of slavery as well. Slavery is an evil. Yet Sha'ul does not speak directly against slavery in his letter to Philemon, though he clearly understands that freedom is better than slavery. "Were you called being a bondservant? Do not let that bother you. But if you get an opportunity to become free, use it." (1 Co. 7:21)

Slavery was, and is, instituted by humanity. In the Scriptures, God makes accomodation for slavery — He regulates it, but does not command its abolition. At the same time, He is presented as the Liberator, the one who will put an end to all slavery.

In God's Law, He commanded Israel, "If a slave has taken refuge with you, do not hand him over to his master. Let him live among you wherever he likes and in whatever town he chooses. Do not oppress him." (Dt. 23:15-16) Those who fought against slavery in the times since then often drew their motivation and direction from the Scriptures. The "Underground Railroad" acted on this particular principle, in defiance of the American pre-Civil War "Fugitive Slave Law," which required anyone finding a lost slave to return him to his master.

There are No Testaments in the Bible

There is no such thing in the Bible as an "Old Testament" or a "New Testament." The terms come from an English transliteration of a Latin mistranslation of a Greek quotation of a Hebrew text.

The Latin Vulgate translation was begun by Jerome in 382 C.E. to replace the Old Latin versions, which were poorly translated from the Septuagint. To be more accurate, Jerome translated Tanakh from the Hebrew text. He also translated the "gospels". Other people translated Acts, the letters, and Hazon/Revelation.

The Vulgate text also has various poorly translated passages, and, consequently, some serious problems. Primary among these problems is its use in Heb. 8:8-9 of the Latin *testamentum* to translate the Greek *diatheke*, which was used to translate the Hebrew *brit*.

In the time of Jeremiah, God promised that He would "cut a new covenant [*brit* in the Masoretic, diatheke in the Septuagint] with the house of Israel and with the house of Judah, not like the covenant/brit/diatheke which I cut with their fathers..." (Jer. 31:31-32/38:31-32LXX) In Hebrews 8:8-9, these verses are quoted verbatim from the Septuagint.

In Jer. 31:31-32, the Latin Vulgate accurately translates either the Hebrew or the Greek of the Septuagint as *foedus novum non secundum pactum*, meaning "a new alliance not in accordance with the covenant..." It is a little strange that in the first part of the verse it translates *brit/diatheke* as *foedus*, i.e. alliance, and four words later it translates *brit/diatheke* as *pactum*, i.e. covenant, but the difference is insignificant. The text is clearly using the same word in the same context in an obvious comparison. Either Latin word would have been correct to translate the one Hebrew word that appears twice.

In Hebrews 8:8-9, the exact same Greek words are quoted from the Septuagint. Translated by someone other than Jerome, the Latin Vulgate significantly distorts the text. It speaks of God making "a new testament not in accordance with the testament I made with their fathers" — *testamentum novum non secundum testamentum quod feci patribus eorum*. For some reason, the translators of the Vulgate abandoned the two correct Latin words used by Jerome in Jeremiah 31:31-32, *foedus* and *pactum*, and switched to an incorrect word, *testamentum*, to translate the exact same Greek words.

The Hebrew word *brit* appears about 300 times in Tanakh. It always refers to a covenant, never to a testament, and never to a set of books. The same is true of the more than 300 times that *diatheke* appears in the Septuagint. Jerome translated *brit/diatheke* correctly throughout Tanakh, with the

exception of 12 passages. It is difficult to know why he used *testamentum* in these 12 passages, since they all refer to a covenant, but the passages are nevertheless clear.

In the Apocrypha and the Messianic Writings, the Vulgate translators systematically switched to *testamentum*, though in these passages, *diatheke* also always refers to a covenant, never to a testament. In Latin, as well as in English, a testament is a last will, a solitary declaration of how to dispose of one's property after one's death. A covenant, on the other hand, is a commitment made between those who are alive as to how they will treat each other while they live. In classical or *koine* Greek, *diatheke* generally means "testament," but it never carries that meaning in the Jewish Greek of the Scriptures.

Almost every current translation, in every language, adopts the Latin distortion in its text, its title, or both. So we have English (or Spanish, or French, or Russian, or pick a language) translations that reproduce the incorrect Latin translation of a Greek translation of a Hebrew original. Even when the translators reject the incorrect "testament" in the text, they still retain these grossly incorrect designations for the two parts of the Bible.

The traditional mistranslation affects more than a word, a verse, or a chapter. It leads to errors that feed and support some very bad theology. And since people act in response to what they actually believe, this bad theology has produced some very painful history.

The use of "testament" in the titles of the two parts of the Bible — "New Testament" and "Old Testament" — communicates an imaginary conflict between the two parts, whereas the text of the New Covenant is actually given in Tanakh in Jeremiah. The false terminology fuels the illusion that Tanakh, the foundational part of the Scriptures, has passed away. It creates the false image of the "new" Scriptures superceding the "old" Scriptures. To the contrary, however, the Scriptures do not get old. God explicitly denies that possibility. (cf. Is. 40:8)

> *The traditional mistranslation affects more than a word, a verse, or a chapter It leads to errors that feed and support some very bad theology And since people act in response to what they actually believe, this bad theology has produced some very painful history .*

When the Messianic Writings refer to "the Old Covenant," "the first Covenant," or "the former Covenant," the reference is not to the first 39 books of the Bible, but to the covenant God made with Israel in the wilderness after redeeming Israel from Egypt. The "New Covenant," or "the second Covenant," is the agreement God promised Israel in Jeremiah 31:31-34. It is not the last 27 books of the Bible.

For these reasons, the commonly used Hebrew designation for the Messianic Writings — *brit chadashah*, i.e. "New Covenant" — is just as incorrect. Franz Delitsch uses *brit* for *diatheke* in every place except Heb. 9:16-17. In these two verses, he transliterates *diatiki*, and then accordingly distorts the rest of the text. Zalkinson and the MHNT use *tzva'a*, i.e. "testament," and likewise distort the text.

Diatheke appears about 30 times in the Messianic Writings, also always referring to a covenant, never to a set of books or writings. It is used to refer to God's covenants with Abraham, the Covenant of the Law, and the New Covenant.

In 2Cor. 3:14-15, Paul uses two expressions: "when the old covenant is read," and "when Moses is read." He is referring to the common Jewish practice of reading through the five books of Moses in the course of every year. In the course of reading the books of Moses, we read the text of the

Covenant of the Law. That covenant — not the scriptures — becomes the "old covenant" when the new covenant of Jeremiah 31 is introduced.

Various systems of interpretation are built on the false assumption. Because the Law of God is contained within the Covenant of the Law, people are told that the Law of God has passed away, and that only the laws of men need to be obeyed. They are told that Yeshua annulled the Law and the Prophets, though he himself explicitly denied that he came to do that, and warned people not to think it. (cf.Mt. 5:17-19) People are told that the good news is incompatible with the Law, the Writings, and the Prophets, even though Yeshua's ambassadors proclaimed the good news from the Law, the Writings, and the Prophets. And whereas the new covenant is an affirmation of God's faithfulness to Israel despite Israel's unfaithfulness to God, the "New Testament" becomes for many a declaration that God has rejected Israel.

The Context

The error in the Vulgate, and in all translations which follow it, seems to stem from a misunderstanding of Hebrews 9:15-18. The context of this passage is a comparison between God's two major covenants with Israel.

Heb. 6:20-8:6 presents a discussion of the superiority of the priesthood of Melchizedek, the priesthood in which Yeshua serves as the New Covenant High Priest, to that of Aaron, the priesthood of the Old Covenant.

Heb. 8:6-12 explains that Yeshua is the mediator of the New Covenant between God and Israel; and presents the text of that New Covenant, which God promised in Jer. 31:31-34.

Heb. 8:13-9:8 compares the covenants in terms of the sanctuary and access to it.

Heb. 9:9-14 compares the sacrifices of the Old Covenant — goats, bulls, and heifers — to the one sacrifice of the New Covenant — the voluntary death of Yeshua.

Heb. 9:19-10:22 continues this comparison of the sacrifices, focusing on the blood of the sacrifice that inaugurates each covenant, and what it has the power to accomplish.

Heb. 10:23-39 is an exhortation to stand firm in the faith, because the punishment for breaking the New Covenant will be greater than the punishment for breaking the Old Covenant.

This entire section, from Heb. 6:20 to 10:39, is a comparison between the Covenant of the Law and the New Covenant. There is no discussion of a testament. There is no "first testament" mentioned; there is no second, or new, testament mentioned. A "testament" is completely unrelated to the cleansing and purification brought by the sacrifices in the different covenants. A testament does not require a sacrifice.

To inaugurate the Covenant of the Law, Moses sacrificed animals. He then sprinkled their blood on the people of Israel, saying, "This is the blood of the covenant..." (Ex. 24:8) In Exodus 24:8, Jerome translated correctly, but in Hebrews 9:20, which quotes the very same words, the other Vulgate translators changed the text to "This is the blood of the testament..." The text is quite clear that Moses spoke about a covenant, not a testament.

The second problem with the translation concerns the phrase "the first testament," which appears in verses 15 and 18. Again, no such thing exists. To what does it refer?

Heb. 9:18 refers to the inauguration of the Covenant of the Law, explaining that "the first covenant ՝s not dedicated without blood." The covenant which God made at Sinai with Israel did not contain

anyone's last will and testament. Animals were put to death to establish the covenant. They did not leave a last will and testament. The covenant at Sinai, made between God and Israel, was put into effect as a defining aspect of God's living relationship with Israel. It is not the testament of anyone.

Next, there is no such thing as "the mediator of a new testament". A mediator is one who serves to bring agreement or reconciliation between different parties. A testament, on the other hand, is the declaration of one individual.

The same Greek words which appear in Heb. 9:15, *diathekes mesites*, are usually correctly translated in Heb. 8:6 as "the mediator of a covenant". The same words in Heb. 12:24 speak of "Yeshua, the mediator of a new covenant." Paul uses the same word word for mediator, *mesites*, when he tells Timothy, "For there is one God and one mediator between God and men, the man Yeshua the Messiah." (1 Tim. 2:5)

Speaking of the Covenant of the Law, Paul explained in Gal. 3:20 that "A mediator, however, does not represent just one party; but God is one." Yeshua is the mediator of the new covenant between God and those with whom it is made, i.e. the house of Israel and the house of Judah.

In these verses in Hebrews, some translations correctly use "covenant," but have other problems because the translators did not understand the use of a related word, *diathemenou*. They translate it as "the one who makes the covenant," which is a logical and contextual impossibility. There must be at least two who make a covenant. If there were only one, then there could not be a covenant and there could not be a "mediator," which is what Messiah is called in verse 15.

With this mistake, Heb. 9:16-17 become: "For where a covenant is, there must of necessity be the death of the one who made it. For a covenant is valid only when men are dead, for it is never in force while the one who made it lives." [NASB] These are both false statements. Neither is true, for example, concerning God's covenant with Noah. Neither God nor Noah died to establish the covenant. Neither statement is true for God's covenant with Abraham, nor His covenant with David, nor His covenants with Israel. Neither is true for any covenant.

A covenant establishes a relationship between the living. It is only in force while those whom the covenant binds are living. In verse 17, *epi nekrois*, which literally means "over dead bodies," is incorrectly translated as "when men are dead". In the context, *diathemenou* (in vv. 16-17) is logically connected to the sacrificed Messiah (*christou* in vv. 14-15), the dead bodies (*nekroisin* v. 17), and the sacrificed calves (*moschonin* v. 19). These all speak of the death that confirms a covenant.

Verses 16-17 provide the reason for what is stated in v. 18: "This is why even the first was not put into effect without blood." "The first," according to vv. 19-20, clearly refers to the covenant that involved Moses. In this passage, we are given a very simple statement: because a *diatheke* only goes into effect "over dead bodies"/*epi nekrois*, the calves were put to death to affirm the *diatheke* at Sinai. That *diatheke* is clearly a covenant, the first covenant, not a testament.

In his literal translation of the Scriptures, Robert Young, compiler of the Analytical Concordance that bears his name, translated *diathemenou* as "covenant victim." This gives the same consistent sense as that which is presented in the Messianic Writings.

Furthermore, since there must be at least two parties involved to make a covenant, which "one" of the parties needs to die? Or do all the parties to a covenant have to die for it to be in effect? To the contrary, however, the death of the parties would not put the covenant into effect; it would make the present and future fulfillment of the covenant impossible.

Since Heb. 9:15 speaks of Messiah as the mediator of the new covenant, he mediates between the parties making the covenant. Messiah is the mediator, not a maker of the covenant. The parties to the New Covenant, as presented in Jer. 31:31-34/Heb. 8:8-12, are God and the house of Israel. The death of Messiah, therefore, would only be the death of the mediator, not "the death of the one who made it."

The Messianic Writings do speak of an "inheritance" for those who are faithful to God, but they always use a word, *kleronomia*, which is unrelated to *diatheke*. Forms of the word appear 46 times in the Messianic Writings. (e.g. Mt. 19:29; Lk. 12:13; Eph. 3:6) They appear 8 times in Hebrews, including Heb. 9:15.

Kleronomia is also the word that is used in the Septuagint, from which the writer of Hebrews quotes. (e.g. Num. 18:23; 2Chr. 31:1) So if the writer of Hebrews wanted to say "testament" rather than "covenant" in Heb. 9:16-17, he would have used *klerodotema*, not *diatheke*. If the writer of Hebrews wanted to say "testator" in Heb. 9:16-17, i.e. the one who makes a testament, he would have used *klerodotes*, not *diathemenou*.

The entire argument in Hebrews is based on what is readily apparent concerning the covenant of the Law. It must, therefore, make sense in terms of both the covenant of the Law and the New Covenant. Otherwise, it would prove nothing, and would be pointless.

[This note is an abridgement of "Dr. Frankenstein's Neighborhood Bible Club" in my <u>Copernicus and the Jews</u>.]

War in Heaven

Hazon/Revelation 12:7-10 speaks of an important war in heaven. Actually, it is the final battle of a war that has been going on for a long time. A few passages in the Scriptures give us glimpses of related events.

An angel showed Zeḥaryah the prophet "Yeshua, the Kohen Gadol standing before the angel of the Everpresent Lord, and the Adversary standing at his right hand to accuse him. And the Everpresent Lord said to the Adversary, 'The Everpresent Lord rebuke you, Adversary! Indeed, the Everpresent Lord who has chosen Yerushala'im rebuke you! Is this not a firebrand plucked from the fire?' Now Yeshua was clothed with filthy garments and standing before the angel." (Zech. 3:1-2)

In the vision, this Yeshua, who was Kohen Gadol in the time of Zeḥaryah, represents his people and symbolizes the Messiah. (cf. Zech. 3:8) As high priest, he stands before God to intercede for Yerushala'im and her children. He is clothed in filthy garments because he represents a people who are guilty and unclean. The Adversary is seeking to accuse, and thereby destroy, Yerushala'im and the Jewish people.

Daniel the prophet knew that the 70 years of desolation for Yerushala'im which Jeremiah had prophesied were completed. So he fasted and prayed, confessing Israel's sins, and trusting in God's mercy and faithfulness. In response to Daniel's prayer, the archangel Gavriel came to give him wisdom and understanding. (cf. Dan. 9)

Daniel continued to pray and fast for the restoration of Yerushala'im, Israel, and the Jewish people. response to that ongoing prayer, someone else came from heaven. The description of this man is

much the same as the description Yoḥanan gives of Yeshua. (Compare Dan. 10:5-6,8 with Hazon/ Rev. 1:13-17.)

This man from heaven told Daniel that he had come in response to Daniel's prayer, but for 21 days a demonic power had prevented him from getting through. As Daniel continued to pray, Mikhael, the archangel who stands guard over Israel, came and fought against this demonic power, enabling the man from heaven to get through.

He told Daniel that at the time of the end, "Mikhael, the great prince who stands over the sons of your people, will arise. And there will be a time of trouble which has not been since there was a nation until that time; and at that time your people, all who are found written in the book, will escape." (Dan. 12:1)

That is why Mikhael is the one who leads this war in heaven against the Accuser. This time, however, he does not fight alone. Yoḥanan saw "**Mikhael and his angels** waging war with the Dragon." Something had happened so that Mikhael received reinforcements.

All the forces of Evil — the Accuser and his angels — are fighting this battle against the restoration of Israel. They know that when they lose this battle, they lose everything. The Accuser and his angels will forever be cast out of heaven. The salvation, power, and kingdom of God and the authority of His Messiah will come. The resurrection of the dead follows it.

Daniel was only one man, but his faithful, ongoing prayer had affected the war in heaven. At the time of the end, apparently, others have been doing as Daniel did. Their prayers also affect what happens in heaven. What happens in heaven determines what will happen on the earth.

The God of Israel tells us who these others are: "On your walls, O Yerushala'im, I have appointed guardians. All day and night they will never keep silent. You — those who remind the Everpresent Lord — take no rest for yourselves, and give Him no rest until He establishes and makes Yerushala'im a praise in the earth." (Is. 62:6-7)